WILLIAMSON ON KNOWLEDGE

Williamson on Knowledge

Edited by
PATRICK GREENOUGH
and
DUNCAN PRITCHARD

With replies by
TIMOTHY WILLIAMSON

OXFORD
UNIVERSITY PRESS

OXFORD
UNIVERSITY PRESS

Great Clarendon Street, Oxford OX2 6DP

Oxford University Press is a department of the University of Oxford.
It furthers the University's objective of excellence in research, scholarship,
and education by publishing worldwide in

Oxford New York

Auckland Cape Town Dar es Salaam Hong Kong Karachi
Kuala Lumpur Madrid Melbourne Mexico City Nairobi
New Delhi Shanghai Taipei Toronto

With offices in

Argentina Austria Brazil Chile Czech Republic France Greece
Guatemala Hungary Italy Japan Poland Portugal Singapore
South Korea Switzerland Thailand Turkey Ukraine Vietnam

Oxford is a registered trade mark of Oxford University Press
in the UK and in certain other countries

Published in the United States
by Oxford University Press Inc., New York

British Library Cataloguing in Publication Data

Data available

Library of Congress Cataloging in Publication Data

Williamson on knowledge / edited by Patrick Greenough and Duncan Pritchard ; with replies by Timothy Williamson.
p. cm.
Includes bibliographical references and index.
ISBN 978-0-19-928752-9 (pbk) —ISBN 978-0-19-928751-2 (hbk) 1. Williamson, Timothy. Knowledge and
its limits. 2. Knowledge, Theory of. I. Greenough, Patrick. II. Pritchard, Duncan. III. Williamson, Timothy.
BD201.W545 2009
121—dc22   2009014878

Typeset by Laserwords Private Limited, Chennai, India
Printed in Great Britain
on acid-free paper by
CPI Antony Rowe, Chippenham, Wiltshire

ISBN 978-0-19-928751-2 (Hbk)
ISBN 978-0-19-928752-9 (Pbk)

1 3 5 7 9 10 8 6 4 2

Acknowledgements

There are a number of people that we would like to thank for their help in the production of this volume. First and foremost, we would like to thank Tim himself for his willingness to collaborate on this project in the first place—clearly, there could have been no volume of this sort without his help. Even in the midst of an incredibly busy schedule he has somehow found the time to engage with all of these papers in his usual energetic style. In so doing, he has demonstrated an intellectual generosity that will come as no surprise to those who know him.

Thanks also go to Peter Momtchiloff at Oxford University Press for his encouragement—and quite considerable patience—throughout this project, and to all those at Oxford University Press who were involved in putting this volume together.

Thanks also go, of course, to the contributors who stuck with the project over some considerable period of time.

Patrick Greenough and Duncan Pritchard

St Andrews and Edinburgh
July 2008

Contents

Contents

Contributors

Anthony Brueckner (University of California, Santa Barbara)

Quassim Cassam (University of Warwick)

Elizabeth Fricker (Oxford University)

Sanford C. Goldberg (Northwestern University)

Alvin Goldman (Rutgers University)

Patrick Greenough (University of St Andrews)

John Hawthorne (Oxford University)

Frank Jackson (La Trobe University/Princeton)

Mark Kaplan (University of Indiana)

Jonathan Kvanvig (Baylor University)

Maria Lasonen-Aarnio (Oxford University)

Ram Neta (University of North Carolina at Chapel Hill)

Duncan Pritchard (University of Edinburgh)

Stephen Schiffer (New York University)

Ernest Sosa (Rutgers University)

Matthias Steup (St Cloud State University)

Neil Tennant (Ohio State University)

Charles Travis (Kings College London)

Timothy Williamson (Oxford University)

Introduction

Patrick Greenough and Duncan Pritchard

Even by conservative estimates, Timothy Williamson's book *Knowledge and its Limits* (*KAIL*) is one of the most important works of philosophy published in the last twenty-five years. It has now been a number of years since *KAIL* first came out, and it is thus a good time to reflect and take stock of the tremendous impact that this work has had on contemporary philosophy, and on contemporary epistemology in particular. This is precisely what this volume offers: a snapshot of the first wave of critical reaction to *KAIL* from some of the leading lights—both established and up-and-coming—of the profession.

The big idea that underlies *KAIL* is that of 'knowledge-first epistemology'. In essence, what Williamson tried to do in *KAIL* was to reverse the trajectory of much if not all recent thinking in epistemology. Rather than treat other key epistemic notions—typically, belief and justification—as basic and then attempt to analyse knowledge in terms of them, he instead treats knowledge as primary and elucidates other notions relevant to epistemology in terms of their relationship to knowledge. With respect to belief, for example, Williamson holds the following array of claims: the telos of belief is knowledge such that belief is that state which aims at knowing, (mere) belief is a kind of botched attempt at knowing, to believe that *p* is to treat *p* as if one knows that *p*. Thus knowledge is central to our understanding of belief.

Given the seemingly intractable problems facing the project of giving a reductive analysis of knowledge that have surfaced in the post-Gettier literature, the knowledge-first thesis has prima facie plausibility. If that were all there were to this thesis, however, then the idea might warrant little more than an exploratory paper. What is significant about this proposal, however, is the number of surprising theses that follow from and lend support to the knowledge-first thesis. Several of the key ideas of knowledge-first epistemology were present in Williamson's writings before *KAIL*, of course. Indeed, one can, with hindsight, see many of these themes informing the epistemic account of vagueness that he put forward in a number of his earlier works. Still, it is only with *KAIL* that we are able to see the view fully expressed.

One can distinguish five key and interrelated themes in knowledge-first epistemology, as Williamson develops the view. Taking them in roughly the order in which they appear in *KAIL*, we begin with the thesis that knowledge is a state of mind. According to standard accounts of knowledge, knowledge cannot be a state of mind for the simple reason that it is, in part at least, a composite of a mental state—belief—plus something non-mental—the truth believed (at least where the truth in question concerns a fact about the external world). Accordingly, or so the thought ran, knowledge, unlike belief, cannot be a mental state. Drawing upon recent developments in the philosophy of mind, Williamson argues against this conventional wisdom; indeed, he suggests that the internalist conception of mental states that is presupposed in the traditional conception is unsustainable.

Next, Williamson offers us a thesis concerning the relationship between causal explanations of action and knowledge. On the standard conception of this relationship, attributions of knowledge in causal explanations of action can always be replaced in favour of the corresponding belief ascriptions without loss. This sort of view essentially buys into the idea that knowledge is not a mental state, however, for it supposes that it is merely the mental state component of knowledge as traditionally conceived (that is, belief) that is able to carry the explanatory burden in this regard. If knowledge is a mental state, however, as Williamson alleges, then it ought to be able to bear some of this explanatory burden. Williamson offers a strong case for thinking that this is indeed so.

Thirdly, we have Williamson's famous cognitive-homelessness thesis. Although it is now common in the literature for philosophers to reject the so-called Cartesian picture of the mind that lies at the heart of both internalist philosophy of mind and internalist epistemology, Williamson persuasively argues that a remnant of this picture still has an illicit grip on the contemporary philosophical imagination. The idea in question is that of *luminosity*—namely, that there exist at least some mental states that are (non-trivially) luminous in the sense that whenever one is in such a state one is thereby in a position to know that this is the case. Candidate luminous states might be the state of feeling cold, or the state of being in pain, or indeed, more generally, the state of it appearing to be the case that p. However, knowledge, as Williamson argues, requires a margin for error such that one is in a position to know that a condition C obtains only if C obtains in all relevantly similar cases. Such a principle follows from the idea that knowledge requires safety (which is roughly the idea that, if one is in a position to know that C obtains, then it is not an easy possibility that one forms the false belief that C obtains), plus the idea that our powers of discrimination are limited. The principle of luminosity together with a margin for error principle generates a contradiction in a straightforward way. The upshot of this, according to Williamson, is that one should abandon the Cartesian idea of a 'cognitive home'—that is, a theatre of thought and experience within which our core mental states obtain and to which we bear some kind of special epistemic access. One special case of Williamson's anti-luminosity argument is targeted against the KK principle, the principle that says that, if a subject knows that *p*, then that subject is in a position to know that they know that *p*. Thus a certain form of access-internalism for knowledge is also undermined by the fact that knowledge requires a margin for error.

Fourthly, we have the knowledge account of evidence. If one adopts the traditional conception of knowledge that analyses knowledge into other epistemic terms, including evidence, then one is unable, on pain of circularity, to analyse these other epistemic notions in terms of knowledge. According to knowledge-first epistemology, however, there is no such restriction on this score. Indeed, Williamson forcefully argues that one's knowledge just is one's evidence. This is perhaps the most initially striking thesis of the book. One casualty of this account is what Williamson calls 'the phenomenal conception of evidence', the view that, if two subjects are in the same phenomenal state, then those subjects are in the same evidential state. According to such a view, a subject who is a bodiless brain in a vat who is fed the non-veridical phenomenal experience *e* and another subject who has the phenomenal experience *e*, only veridically so, have identical evidence for any mundane occurrent belief about the external world acquired on the basis of *e*. But, on such a conception, since the former subject lacks knowledge about the external world (because his or her beliefs are false), so must the latter subject, since his or her evidence is identical. Thus, with the phenomenological conception of evidence out of the way, Williamson gains a foothold against certain forms of scepticism.

Finally, we have the knowledge account of assertion. Typically, it is simply taken as given that either truth or justification is the norm of assertion. On the justificationist account, this norm runs: assert *p* only if one justifiably believes that *p*. On the alethic account, this norm runs: assert *p* only if it is true that *p*. In contrast, Williamson forcefully argues for a fundamental rule of assertion that makes knowledge the central notion: assert *p* only if one knows that *p*. Part of the motivation for some weaker rule is clearly the thought that to demand anything more epistemically robust would be to make the rule unduly hard to follow. As Williamson argues, however, we should not confuse breaches of the rule that are blameless with cases in which the rule has not been breached. Thus, it is perfectly open to Williamson to concede that, if I reasonably believe that *p*, but do not know that *p*, and assert that *p* on this basis, my conduct on this score may well be blameless. Still, I will, by Williamson's lights, have broken the fundamental rule of assertion. Equally, with the KK principle out of the picture, one can satisfy the norm of assertion in asserting some proposition *p* without knowing that one knows that *p*.

More generally, Williamson argues that there are strong considerations in favour of the knowledge account of assertion, such as cases—for example, lottery cases—in which we have clear intuitions that a certain assertion would be improper even though the agent concerned, while lacking knowledge of the target proposition, has excellent grounds for believing that p. If the fundamental rule of assertion demands an epistemic standing that falls short of knowledge, however, then it is hard to see how one could possibly accommodate such intuitions. Further evidence for the knowledge rule comes from the so-called *challenge data*: a legitimate way to query an assertion is with the retort 'How do you know?'—but such a query presupposes that the subject knows the content asserted. Equally, one can query the very legitimacy of an assertion with the more aggressive challenge 'Do you know?' The very aggressive nature of this challenge strongly suggests that knowledge is the norm of assertion. Finally, Williamson argues that the knowledge account best explains all the so-called Moorean data, and in particular the conversational infelicity of the assertion 'p but I do not know that p'.

Although the distinction between the core themes of knowledge-first epistemology and the applications of knowledge-first epistemology is not crystalline, one can regard the other key claims of *KAIL* as falling into the latter category. Most strikingly, Williamson offers a novel response to the problem of scepticism, one that demonstrates how the non-luminosity of our evidence ensures that we are able to have the widespread knowledge of the external world that the sceptic claims is impossible. In addition, Williamson offers new insights into Fitch's paradox of knowability, the surprise examination paradox, evidential probability, the nature of reliability, and much else besides.

We have foregone the temptation to summarise Tim's replies to each contribution on the grounds that much of their philosophical flavour would be lost in the process. Likewise, we have chosen not to burden the reader with any attempt to summarize the contributions themselves. The contributions can speak for themselves and need no help (or hindrance) from the editors.

1

E = K and Perceptual Knowledge

Anthony Brueckner

According to Timothy Williamson (2000: ch. 9), all evidence is knowledge, and all knowledge is evidence: E = K. He argues for the following theses:

(1) All evidence is propositional.
(2) All propositional evidence is knowledge.
(3) All knowledge is evidence.

(1)–(3) entail E = K. In an earlier paper I argued that Williamson's views on knowledge, justification, and evidence commit him to an implausible view about *perceptual* knowledge and justification.[1] Williamson (2005b) has responded to my criticism, and in this chapter I wish to reconsider the issues.

1. THE PROBLEM

Evidence justifies belief and always comes in the form of propositions, on Williamson's view. A bloody knife is not evidence. Neither are perceptual experiences. These are not evidence because they are not propositions. The most that Williamson (2000: 197) is willing to grant regarding the epistemic role of experience is that, in some cases, it may be that "the evidence for an hypothesis h consists of propositions e1,..., en which count as evidence for one only because one is undergoing a perceptual experience." Williamson, though, does not endorse this view. He just says that it is "consistent with E = K" (Williamson 2000: 197).

When evidence e serves to justify S's belief that P in a given case, S must, according to Williamson, grasp the proposition e. But he initially says nothing about whether S must, further, *believe* e. It seems fairly clear that e can function as S's justifying evidence for P *only if* S also believes e. If e is merely a proposition that S grasps but does not believe, or perhaps disbelieves, then why would e count as evidence that justifies S's belief of P? Williamson eventually does bring

---

[1] See Brueckner (2005).

belief into the picture. It is "granted" by him that knowledge entails belief (Williamson 2000: 202). Since he maintains that E = K, his overall position has the consequence, which he notes, that S believes e: since e is evidence, e is known, and knowledge entails belief.

Williamson considers a pair of cases involving perceptual experience: S sees a mountain in normal, favorable circumstances and correctly believes that it is a certain shape, and S sees another mountain in unfavorable circumstances and is under the illusion that it is that same shape he perceived in the favorable case (but it is some other shape).[2] What is S's evidence in each case? The evidence will consist in believed propositions, as we have just seen. In the favorable case, S's evidence is the true proposition expressed by his utterance of "It is that shape." Williamson specifies this as the proposition that *the mountain is that shape*. Call this proposition *M*. But M cannot be S's evidence in the unfavorable case, since M is *false* in that case. Since E = K, and knowledge is factive, the false M cannot constitute S's evidence in the unfavorable case. Williamson (2000: 198) says: "If perceptual evidence in the case of illusions consists of true propositions [since E = K and knowledge is factive], what are they? The obvious answer is: the proposition that things appear to be that way." Thus, S's evidence in the unfavorable case, according to Williamson, is the proposition that *the mountain appears to be that shape*, not M.

This parallels the situations in Williamson's "good case" of ordinary perceptual knowledge and his "bad case" of being a brain in a vat. The skeptic maintains that I have the same evidence in both the good case and the bad case, and he exploits this "Sameness of Evidence Lemma" in his skeptical argument.[3] If my evidence is the same in both cases, then it fails to discriminate between them and hence underdetermines a justified verdict as to which case I am in, even when I am in the *good* case. But, according to Williamson, the alleged "lemma" is false: in the good case, my evidence consists of true propositions like M, while, in the bad case, my evidence consists of *different* true propositions about how things appear. Thus the skeptic is stymied, since his needed "lemma" is false.

My criticism of Williamson on perceptual knowledge in the earlier paper concerned a case like the favorable mountain case. Consider my belief of the proposition that my cup is red (call this proposition *C*). Suppose that this is an instance of perceptual knowledge. So my belief of C is justified. There will thus be evidence e, which serves to justify my belief of C, and e will be a true proposition which I believe. Which proposition? Since we are in a favorable case, e will not be a proposition about how things appear. Such propositions are reserved for their role in unfavorable cases of illusion and hallucination. Further,

---

[2] I have added some detail to Williamson's example in order to make it exactly parallel to Williamson's "good case" of normal perceptual knowledge involving veridical experience and his "bad case" of brain-in-a-vat error involving exactly similar unveridical perceptual experience.

[3] For a discussion of this, see Brueckner (2005).

my perceptual experiences of the cup do not constitute the evidence e in question, since these experiences are not propositions and so cannot be justifiers. Taking our lead from the favorable mountain case, we are forced to conclude that e is some proposition like M, the proposition that *the mountain is that shape.* Which proposition, though? Well, presumably the proposition that the cup is red.[4] This proposition is C itself. My belief of C is justified in virtue of, or justified by, my belief of the evidential proposition e. Since e = C, my belief of C is justified *in virtue of,* or is justified *by*, my belief of C! This is clearly an unacceptable view of the structure of perceptual justification and knowledge.

2. WILLIAMSON REPLIES

Let us turn to Williamson's reply. He asks: "Why does . . . [Brueckner] take my account of perceptual knowledge to imply any such thing . . . [as that my belief of C is justified in virtue of my belief of C]? He does not clearly explain, but his account offers some clues" (Williamson 2005b: 468). The clues to the mystery were precisely those given in the previous paragraph, which replicates the discussion in the earlier paper. In our search for the evidential, propositional justifier e, which serves to justify my belief of C, we were led inexorably, following Williamson's own lead, to the proposition C itself. In his reply, he points to no other evidential proposition as an alternative candidate.

Here is Williamson's picture of how my belief of C is justified:

> When one's total evidence is ε, the justified level of confidence (credence) in a hypothesis h is measured by the conditional probability of h on ε . . . In the present simple case, the proposition that his cup is red is part of Brueckner's total evidence, and therefore has conditional probability 1 on his evidence. His knowledge that his cup is red justifies his belief that his cup is red. If we want to use the somewhat obscure expression 'in virtue of' (Brueckner's, not mine), we can say: his belief that his cup is red is justified in virtue of his knowledge that his cup is red. (Williamson 2005b: 468–9)

Williamson goes on to consider, in his reply, the inference from

(K) My belief that my cup is red is justified in virtue of (or *because of*, as Williamson prefers) my knowledge that my cup is red.[5]

to

(J) My belief that my cup is red is justified in virtue of (or because of) my belief that my cup is red.

---

[4] Williamson (2005b) alludes to propositions that I know concerning the shape of the cup and its location. But I do not see how the proposition that the cup is round, or the proposition that the cup is on the table, could play the role of e, the justifier for the proposition that the cup is *red*.

[5] For Williamson, the 'because of' is explanatory rather than causal.

He affirms (K), agrees that (J) is unacceptable, but holds that (K) does not entail (J). He reconstructs several bad arguments from (K) to (J). After disposing of a final bad argument, Williamson (2005b: 469) says: "Perhaps Brueckner had a very different argument in mind. If so, I have no idea what it was."

I do think that Williamson's overall position commits him to (J), but it had never occurred to me to try to argue from (K) (which I did not consider in the paper) to (J). The reasons given above for thinking that Williamson is stuck with (J) are quite different. At the risk of beating a dead horse, let us rehearse these reasons. Start by considering a case that is different from the cup case. Suppose that I am justified in believing that Miles is sad and that my evidence is that he is crying in a characteristic way. Then I am justified in believing that Miles is sad in virtue of, or because of, my belief of my evidential justifier—namely, the proposition that Miles is crying in a characteristic way. Similarly, suppose that I am justified in believing that my cup is red and that my evidence is e. Then I am justified in believing that my cup is red in virtue of, or because of, my belief of my evidential justifier—namely, e. If e = C (the proposition that my cup is red), then I am justified in believing that my cup is red in virtue of, or because of, my belief that my cup is red. *That* is the problem for Williamson's overall view.

3. FURTHER CONSIDERATION OF WILLIAMSON'S REPLY

Let us return to Williamson's (K): I am justified in believing that my cup is red in virtue of, or because of, *my knowledge that my cup is red*. How exactly is this supposed to work? Suppose that I have not yet looked at my cup. So I do not yet know C (the proposition that my cup is red). So C is not yet a part of my total evidence and so cannot be used to justify any beliefs. I need to gain some evidence that will serve to justify a belief of C on my part if I am to come to *know* C and thus enable C to become part of my total evidence. I look at the cup and come to believe C. If I am to be justified in now believing C and thus be in a position to know C, I must have some evidence that serves to justify the belief. Williamson says that it is in virtue of, or because of, *my knowledge of C* that I am justified in believing C. But what is the evidence that generated my knowledge of C, enabling that knowledge to serve as the evidential justifier for my belief of C? We seem to be missing a step. To put the question another way, how did the proposition C come to enter into my total evidence and hence attain the status of knowledge? C must have gotten into my total evidence as a result of my coming justifiably to believe it on the basis of some evidence. But *what* evidence? Now it looks as if we are back to saying that my evidence for believing C is C itself: so I am justified in believing C in virtue of, or because of, my belief of C.

Williamson could bite the bullet and hold that my belief of C is *self-justifying*: (J) above is true—my belief of C justifies my belief of C. Williamson shows no inclination to accept this view of perceptual justification, and it seems to be very unattractive. On the face of it, the view would seem to imply that every true belief about one's immediate environment is justified since justified by itself.[6] A proponent of this unattractive view could try to block this result by holding that only those true beliefs about one's surroundings that are *properly experientially based* are self-justifying. But, in that case, the experiences, not the allegedly self-justifying belief, are really doing the justificatory work.

We must distinguish the foregoing unattractive view from a related view that follows from Williamson's conception of evidence. Williamson notes a curious consequence of that conception. If e is part of S's total evidence, then e is evidence for itself. This is because, on Williamson's conception of evidence, e is evidence for a hypothesis h if and only if S's total evidence includes e, and the conditional probability of h given e is greater than the probability of h. The second requirement will be met for h = e if e's probability is less than 1, since Prob(e/e) = 1. Williamson (2000: 187) notes: "Certainly [the consequence that e is evidence for itself] . . . does not make it trivially easy to have evidence for e, for e is evidence for itself only if S's evidence includes e. By E = K, that requires S to know e, which may not be easy." Returning to our discussion of (K), we cannot use the consequence under consideration to answer the foregoing questions about how my belief of C becomes justified and how C then is able to enter into my body of total evidence. C becomes evidence for itself only when C becomes known by me. The question I put to Williamson was: how does C come to be evidentially justified and known? This question cannot be answered by pointing out that once C becomes known, it trivially becomes evidence for itself. That point applies to *all* propositions that I come to know, including principles of string theory. So the point does not illuminate the issues about the nature of perceptual justification and knowledge.

Williamson could give up the view that perceptual knowledge is evidentially based. But this would be a major change in his overall view. For example, he raises the question "is all justified belief justified by evidence?" He answers as follows: "It is far from obvious that any belief is justified in the truth-directed sense [relevant to knowledge] without being justified by evidence. . . E = K supports the plausible equation of truth-directed justification with justification by evidence" (Williamson 2000: 207–8). However, suppose that Williamson accepts the suggested move: perceptual justification and knowledge are not evidentially based. What then is the source of perceptual justification? Perhaps Williamson could maintain that *my experience of the red cup* (i) justifies my belief of C, and (ii) thus enables that belief to amount to knowledge. But this would be a case of justification and knowledge that does not involve reasons

---

[6] Tyler Burge (2003a) has recently maintained that beliefs of elementary logical truths are self-justifying in that they provide rational support for themselves. Even if Burge is right, the perceptual case seems to be quite different.

Anthony Brueckner

for belief, since such reasons are always propositional. Williamson (2000: 197) writes: "The threatening alternative [to my view of perceptual knowledge] is that [experience] ε can itself be evidence for h, without the mediation of any such [evidential propositions] e1, . . . , en." Even so, Williamson might stretch to this "threatening alternative" and agree with those who hold that perceptual experiences have propositional content, in that they represent the world as being a certain way. Then experiential justifiers, though not themselves *propositions*, would be sufficiently *like* propositions for the purpose of playing a reason-giving role in perceptual justification.[7]

This suggested move would give rise to a problem for Williamson. His case against skepticism depends upon his denial of the "Sameness of Evidence Lemma." But, if he accepts the view that contentful experiences serve as justifiers for perceptual beliefs, then he must retract his denial of the "lemma." This is because I *do* have the same experiential justifier (standing in for a believed evidential proposition) in both the good case and the bad case. In each case, I have experience that, say, represents me to have two hands. In the good case, this experience is veridical. In the bad case, my experience is unveridical, since in this case I am a handless brain in a vat. Thus the skeptic can resuscitate and revamp his argument, now holding that my putative experiential "justifier" in the good case is no good, because it does not enable me to discriminate the good case from the bad case. The putative experiential justifier underdetermines a justified verdict as to which case I am in, even when I am in the good case. So embracing the "threatening alternative" would ruin Williamson's case against skepticism.

Williamson is a *disjunctivist* regarding the propositional evidence one possesses in the favorable and unfavorable mountain cases: the proposition M—that the mountain is that shape—is one's evidence in the favorable case, whereas a different proposition about how things appear is one's evidence in the unfavorable case. We now see that it is problematic to hold that, in the favorable case, M is one's justifying evidence for believing that the mountain is that shape. This is just the same difficulty we found in the red cup case. But, if Williamson were to grasp the "threatening alternative," he could do this in a similarly disjunctivist way. He could hold that I have experiences of *different types* in the good case and in the bad case. He could hold that, at the level of experience, there is "no common factor" in the two cases. In this way, he could once again deny the skeptic's claim that I have the same experiential justifier in both the good and the bad cases. Williamson's case against skepticism would be back on track.

I think that this version of the "threatening alternative" is problematic. Fitting this alternative into Williamson's scheme of things requires that we conceive of experiences as having propositional content, so that they can mimic reason-giving beliefs of evidential propositions, whose contents are accessible to the believer.

---

[7] See, e.g., Brewer (1999), Pryor (2000), and Huemer (2001).

Disjunctivism about the experiential justifiers seems to require that the propositional contents of the veridical experiences be *singular* propositions, with cups and snowy mountains as constituents in the good cases. Though it is unclear what the disjunctivist will say about experiential content in the bad cases (no content? a non-singular content?), he will at any rate say that the bad cases do not share the singular content of the good cases. But if one develops the "threatening alternative" in the foregoing disjunctivist manner, it becomes rather unclear whether the experiencer has access to the reason-giving contents of his experiences. How can he tell whether he has an experience with a reason-giving singular content (the good case) or, instead, an experience with no singular content (the bad case)? How can he tell whether or not he is *under the illusion of entertaining a singular perceptual content*, in John McDowell's phrase?[8]

So there is pressure towards eschewing a disjunctivist version of the "threatening alternative." If experiential content, then, is the same in both the good and the bad case, there we are back to a variant of the skeptic's "Sameness of Evidence Lemma": in both the good and the bad case, my putative experiential justifier is an experience whose non-singular content represents me to have two hands. Since my putative justifier does not discriminate between the good and the bad cases, the putative justifier does not warrant a verdict that I am in the good case even when I am in the good case.

If Williamson rejects the suggested move just considered, then what are his remaining options? One is to hold that *nothing* justifies my perceptual beliefs—not experience, not believed evidential propositions. Another is to hold that my perceptual beliefs are justified in some coherentist way. Williamson shows no sign of embracing either of these unattractive options. I conclude that his overall position has a serious problem regarding perceptual justification and knowledge.

---

[8] See McDowell (1986).

2

Can the Concept of Knowledge be Analysed?

Quassim Cassam

1. OVERVIEW

In *Knowledge and its Limits* Timothy Williamson (2000) argues for what I am going to call the Unanalysability Hypothesis (UH), the hypothesis that "the concept *knows* cannot be analysed into more basic concepts" (p. 33).[1] Williamson's defence of UH constitutes the negative phase of his discussion. The positive phase consists in an attempt to give a modest positive account of the concept of knowledge that is not an analysis in the traditional sense. There is room for such an account because, as Williamson emphasizes, it does not follow from the fact that a concept cannot be analysed into more basic concepts that no reflective understanding of it is possible.

Williamson puts forward a range of arguments in support of UH. The first is what I am going to call the Distinct Concepts Argument (DCA). This argument assumes that every standard analysis of the concept *knows* equates it with some conjunctive concept like *justified true belief*. With this assumption in place, the aim of DCA is to show that every standard analysis of *knows* is "incorrect as a claim of concept identity, for the analysing concept is distinct from the concept to be analysed" (p. 30). Another argument in support of UH is the Inductive Argument, according to which "experience confirms inductively . . . that no analysis of the concept *knows* of the standard kind is correct" (p. 30). A third argument is the False Expectations Argument, according to which one should not expect the concept *knows* to have a non-trivial analysis in more basic terms. Few concepts have such analyses, and there is no special reason to expect *knows* to be one of them.

In the positive phase of his discussion, Williamson argues that "knowing is the most general factive stative attitude, that which one has to a proposition if one has any factive stative attitude to it at all" (p. 34). This leads to the suggestion that, "if one knows that A, then there is a specific way in which one

---

[1] All references in this form are to Williamson (2000).

knows; one can see or remember or . . . that A" (p. 34). 'See' and 'remember' are examples of *factive mental states operators* (FMSOs). An FMSO is the realization in natural language of a factive stative attitude. In these terms, one principle to which Williamson subscribes is that 'know' is an FMSO. Another is that, if Φ is an FMSO, then from 'S Φs that p' one may infer 'S knows that p'. According to Williamson, these two principles "characterize the concept of knowing uniquely, up to logical equivalence, in terms of the concept of an FMSO" (p. 39).

My discussion will be divided into three parts. In the first part I will concentrate on DCA. I will also comment briefly on the other arguments for UH, but my main aim will be to show that DCA does not work. In the second part I will argue that Williamson's positive account of the concept of knowledge amounts to a kind of analysis. Traditional conceptual analysis is 'reductive', whereas Williamson's account is largely non-reductive. Nevertheless, it has some reductive elements, and I will attempt to bring these out. Finally, I will discuss the principle that, if one knows that A, then there is a specific way in which one knows. I will distinguish between different 'ways of knowing' and suggest that the sense in which seeing that A is a way of knowing that A is very different from the sense in which remembering that A is a way of knowing that A. What distinguishes seeing that A from some other 'ways of knowing' is that it is potentially a way of *coming* to know that A. The notion of a way of coming to know that A is significant because, as I will argue in conclusion, it holds the key to understanding *how* one knows that A and *what it is* for one to know that A.

2. THE DISTINCT CONCEPTS ARGUMENT

The Distinct Concepts Argument relies on the notion of a *mental concept*, so let us start by briefly considering this notion. Although Williamson himself does not attempt a formal definition of it, he does argue at one point that the concept *true* is not mental because "it makes no reference to a subject" (p. 30). So a concept will not count as mental unless it refers to a subject. This is obviously a long way from constituting a definition of the notion of a mental concept, but Williamson's idea is presumably that we have an intuitive grasp of what mental concepts are, and that this is enough for the purposes of DCA. Now consider the case of a concept C that is the conjunction of the concepts $C_1, \ldots, C_n$. Williamson's proposal is that "C is mental if and only if each C_i is mental" (p. 29). On this account, *believes truly* is not a mental concept of a state, since *true* is not a mental concept. By the same token, *has a justified true belief* is not a mental concept. These concepts are not mental because they have "irredundant non-mental constituents, in particular the concept *true*" (p. 30).

Having accepted that *believes truly* and *has a justified true belief* are not mental concepts, let us also accept, at least for the sake of argument, that *knows* is a mental concept. What follows from this? What follows straightforwardly is that the concept *knows* cannot be the same concept as the concept *believes truly* or the concept *has a justified true belief.* The point is that, if C is a mental concept and D is not a mental concept, then they cannot be the same concept. But, as Williamson sees things, every standard analysis of the concept of knowledge takes it that this concept *is* the very same concept as some conjunctive concept like *has a justified true belief.* So every standard analysis of the concept *knows* is incorrect.

Crucially, it does not matter for the purposes of this argument which particular conjunctive concept the concept of knowledge is equated with, as long as it has the concept *true* as a constituent. For example, suppose that, instead of equating the concept of knowledge with the concept *has a justified true belief,* one equates it with the concept *has a reliably caused true belief.* Williamson's argument would still go through, since "it applies to any of the concepts with which the concept *knows* is equated by conjunctive analyses of the standard kind" (p. 30). As long as the analysing concept is not mental, it cannot be the same as the concept being analysed, and this is the crux of DCA.

Here, then, is a breakdown of the main components of the Distinct Concepts Argument:

(*a*) Every standard analysis of the concept *knows* equates it with some conjunctive concept that has the concept *true* as a non-redundant constituent.
(*b*) The concept *true* is not a mental concept.
(*c*) Any concept with a non-redundant non-mental constituent is not a mental concept.
(*d*) So the conjunctive concepts with which the concept *knows* is equated by analyses of the standard kind are not mental concepts.
(*e*) The concept *knows* is a mental concept.
(*f*) A mental concept cannot be the very same concept as a non-mental concept.
(*g*) So the mental concept *knows* cannot be the same concept as any of the conjunctive concepts with which it is equated by standard analyses.
(*h*) So every standard analysis of the concept *knows* is incorrect.

The question is whether this argument works, and I have already indicated that I do not think that it does. It is now time to explain why not.

To begin to get a sense of what might be wrong with DCA, consider the following parallel line of reasoning: let us say that a *marital status concept* is one that, when applied to an individual, says something about that individual's marital status. So, for example, *married, single, bachelor, separated,* and *divorced* all count as marital status concepts. Furthermore, where C is the conjunction of the concepts $C_1, \ldots, C_n$, let us stipulate that C is a marital status concept if and only if each C_i is a marital status concept. On this account, *unmarried man* is not a marital status concept, since *man* is not a marital status concept. But *bachelor* is a marital status concept. So *bachelor* and *unmarried man* cannot be the same concept.

Something has clearly gone wrong here, because *bachelor* and *unmarried man* are identical if any concepts are. But, if we are not prepared to conclude on the basis of the argument that I have just given that *bachelor* and *unmarried man* are not the same concept, why should we conclude, on the basis of a parallel argument, that *knows* and *has a justified true belief* are not the same concept? Perhaps the reason is this: the sense in which *unmarried man* is not a marital status concept is that it is not what might be called a *pure* marital status concept. It is not a pure marital status concept because one of its constituents, the concept *man*, is not a marital status concept. To put it another way, to describe someone as an unmarried man is to say something about his sex as well as his marital status. But if this is why unmarried man is not a marital status concept, then *bachelor* is not going to count as a marital status concept either; to describe someone as a bachelor is, after all, also to say something about his sex as well as his marital status. So there is no longer any basis for the claim that *bachelor* and *unmarried man* cannot be the same concept.

On the face of it this is where the parallel with DCA breaks down. Williamson's point is that *knows* and *has a justified true belief* cannot be the same concept because *knows* is a *purely* mental concept whereas concepts like *has a justified true belief* are not "purely mental" (p. 30). On this reading of DCA, both (*d*) and (*e*) need to be slightly modified. Premiss (*d*) should be read as claiming that the conjunctive concepts with which *knows* is equated by standard analyses are not purely mental because they have at least one non-mental constituent. In contrast, (*e*) now needs to be read as the claim that the concept *knows* is purely mental. The argument still goes through but is only as compelling as the case for accepting this version of (e). So what is now needed is an argument for the view that the concept *knows* is purely mental that does not presuppose the non-identity of the concept *knows* and conjunctive concepts like *has a justified true belief.*

What is Williamson's argument for (*e*)? It is important to note at this point that the primary concern of chapter 1 of *Knowledge and its Limits* is not to defend the thesis that the *concept* of knowledge is mental or purely mental. The primary concern of this chapter is to defend the thesis that *knowing* is a state of mind. This is a metaphysical rather than a conceptual thesis. Furthermore, Williamson does not argue for the metaphysical thesis from first principles. He maintains that "our initial presumption should be that knowing is a mental state" (p. 22), and then tries to disarm a range of arguments against this presumption. He also points out that it does not follow directly from the fact that knowing is a mental state that the concept *knows* is mental in his sense, but he nevertheless argues that someone who concedes that knowing is a mental state should also concede that the concept *knows* is mental—that is, purely mental.

It might be helpful to divide this argument for (*e*) into two parts. First there is the presumption that knowing is mental state. Let us call this Williamson's Presumption (WP). Then there is the move from WP to (*e*). Assuming that the move from WP to (*e*) is defensible, the interesting question is whether WP is correct. The problem is that WP is not just the presumption that knowing is a state of mind. It is the presumption that it is "merely a state of mind" (p. 21). That is to say, it is the presumption that "there is a mental state being in which is necessary *and sufficient* for knowing p". Presumably, it is only because *knowing* is 'merely' a state of mind that the *concept* of knowing can plausibly be regarded as 'purely' mental. So everything depends on whether we should accept the existence of an initial presumption to the effect that knowing is merely mental.

In defence of his presumption, Williamson claims that "prior to philosophical theory-building, we learn the concept of the mental by examples" (p. 22). Our paradigms include not just mental states such as pleasure and pain but also non-factive propositional attitudes such as believing and desiring—that is, attitudes that one can have to falsehoods. In contrast, knowing is factive, since one can know that p only if p is true. So how is it that factive attitudes also come out as mental given that they are different from non-factive attitudes and also from mental states that are not attitudes at all? Williamson's answer to this question is that "factive attitudes have so many similarities to non-factive attitudes that we should expect them to constitute mental states too" (p. 22). Indeed, he suggests that there are *no* pre-theoretical grounds for omitting factive propositional attitudes from the list of paradigmatic mental states. The idea that the mental includes knowing and other factive attitudes "is built into the natural understanding of the procedure by which the concept of the mental is acquired" (p. 22).

What are the similarities between factive attitudes and non-factive attitudes? Trivially, factive and non-factive attitudes are attitudes, and attitudes are states of mind. So this is one respect in which factive and non-factive attitudes are similar to one another. But this is not enough for Williamson's purposes. What he needs to establish is that knowing is sufficiently similar to believing to sustain the presumption that knowing is, like believing, *merely* a state of mind. This is the point at which the idea that knowing is factive might appear to be in conflict with the idea that it is merely a state of mind. As Williamson's own discussion illustrates, it takes a good deal of sophisticated argument to weaken the prejudice that a factive attitude cannot be merely a state of mind, and this is difficult to reconcile with the suggestion that we have a pre-theoretical commitment to the idea that knowing is merely mental.

There is also a question about the suggestion that WP is built into the procedure by which the concept of the mental is acquired. The procedure that Williamson has in mind is that of learning the concept of the mental by examples, but one might wonder whether this procedure is sufficiently well defined to sustain the suggestion that WP is built into it. Prior to philosophical theory-building, what we acquire by example are concepts of particular types of mental state rather than the concept of the mental as such. It is arguable that the procedures by means of which we acquire the concept of the mental leave it open whether knowing is mental in the bland sense that there is a mental state being in which is merely necessary for knowing or in the "unexpected" (p. 21) sense that there is a mental state being in which is necessary and sufficient for knowing. To acquire the concept of the mental as such is to abstract from the differences between different types of mental state, and this already involves taking on theoretical commitments that might be described as 'philosophical'. If this is right, then it is perhaps doubtful whether we have any conception of the mental as such, prior to some philosophical theory-building.

This is not an argument for the view that knowing is not merely a state of mind or, for that matter, for the view that the concept of knowing is not purely mental. What is at issue here is Williamson's overall strategy for defending these claims rather than their truth or falsity. He thinks that the default position in the metaphysics of knowing is that knowing is merely a state of mind, and that the burden of proof is therefore on those who reject this position to show what is wrong with it. On this account, defending WP is largely a matter of eliminating putative differences between knowing and non-factive attitudes that have mistakenly been thought to count against the idea that knowing is merely mental. What I have been suggesting, in contrast, is that the idea that the merely mental includes knowing is not as clearly and deeply entrenched in our ordinary thinking about the mental as Williamson implies, and that this undermines any attempt to represent WP as the default position in this area. While this is not a knockdown argument against (*e*), or against DCA, it does raise a question about Williamson's argumentative strategy.

Another potentially problematic aspect of DCA is premiss (*a*). On the face of it, this premiss misrepresents what analytic epistemologists are after when they analyse the concept of knowledge. Their aim is to uncover non-circular "necessary and sufficient conditions for someone's knowing a given proposition" (Gettier 1963: 121). Such analyses are given in the form 'S knows that p if and only if . . .', and there is no suggestion that what is on the right-hand side of such biconditionals is equivalent in meaning to what is on the left-hand side.[2] But, if their two sides are not equivalent in meaning, then it is hard to see how they can reasonably be regarded as expressing one and the same concept. At any rate, it is hard to see how they can reasonably be regarded as expressing one and the same concept if we take it that concepts are meanings.[3] So it seems that the first

---

[2] e.g. Goldman (1992a: 82) says that he is "not interested in giving the *meaning* of 'S knows p'; only its *truth conditions*".

[3] See Fodor (1998b) for the idea that concepts are word meanings.

step of DCA is mistaken. Standard analyses of the concept of knowledge do not equate this concept with the conjunctive concepts that appear on the right-hand side of their biconditionals.

In fact, matters are a bit more complicated than this suggests. It is one thing to point out that standard analyses of *knows* do not explicitly endorse the first step of DCA, but it might nevertheless be the case that they are committed to (*a*), whether they realize it or not. To see why this might be so compare the following biconditionals:

(B) S is a bachelor if and only if S is an unmarried man.

(G) O is made of gold if and only if O is made of the element with the atomic number 79.

Both (B) and (G) are correct, but there are two important differences between them. First, the concept expressed by the right-hand side of (B) is, on most views of concept identity, the same as the concept expressed by its left-hand side. This is not true of (G), since *made of gold* and *made of the element with the atomic number 79* are clearly distinct concepts. Secondly, the truth of (B) but not of (G) can be established solely by means of conceptual analysis. It looks as though all one needs to do in order to establish the truth of (B) is to analyse the concept *bachelor*, whereas one cannot establish the truth of (G) just by analysing the concept *gold*.

These differences might lead one to suppose that it is only because the concepts expressed by the two sides of (B) are identical that its truth can be established solely by means of conceptual analysis. If this supposition is plausible, then the first step of DCA begins to look a bit more plausible. For analytic epistemologists are not just interested in identifying necessary and sufficient conditions for S to know that p. They are interested in identifying necessary and sufficient conditions that can be uncovered solely by analysing the concept of knowledge. Perhaps this means that its biconditionals will have to be like (B) rather than like (G). The suggestion, in other words, is that, if we want to establish the correctness of biconditionals of the form 'S knows that p if and only if. . .' just by analysing the concept of knowledge, it had better be the case that the concepts expressed by their two sides are identical. This is exactly what one would expect if one is serious about the analogy between analysing the concept *knows* and analysing the concept *bachelor*. Just as *bachelor* and *unmarried man* are the same concept, so one would expect *knows* and any suitable conjunctive analysing concept to be the same concept.

But is it true that it would be possible for conceptual analysis to establish the relevant biconditionals only if the concepts expressed by their two sides are identical? Consider Grice's account of conceptual analysis in his paper 'Postwar Oxford Philosophy'. The basic claim of this paper is that "to be looking for a conceptual analysis of a given expression E is to be in a position to apply and withhold E in particular cases, but to be looking for a general characterization of the types of cases in which one would apply E rather than withhold it" (Grice 1989: 174). Grice's assumption here is that analysing expressions is the best way of analysing the concepts that those expressions express. At the same time, he emphasizes that conceptual analysis is not the same as lexicography. To see why not consider this pair:

(1) father ←—→ male parent
(2) awe ←—→ mixture of fear and admiration

Although both (1) and (2) give necessary and sufficient conditions for the correct application of an expression, or of the concept expressed by it, Grice thinks that only (2) is a genuine piece of conceptual analysis. Someone who knows the meaning of 'male parent' but who does not assent at once to (1) shows that he does not know the meaning of 'father'. In contrast, someone who does not assent at once to (2) does not thereby show that he does not know what 'awe' means. Such a person might be able correctly to apply and withhold this expression in particular cases and yet not be convinced without further argument and examples that (2) is an accurate general characterization of the correct use of the expression.

The next issue is whether *awe* and *mixture of fear and admiration* are the same concept. This is a tricky issue, since it raises questions about the nature of concept identity that neither Grice nor Williamson addresses. Nevertheless, it is easy to see why one might think that *awe* and *mixture of fear and admiration* cannot be the same concept. For the fact that someone can know the meaning of 'awe' without immediately assenting to (2) suggests that (2) is potentially informative, in a way that (1) is not. But (2) would not be as informative as it is if *awe* and *mixture of fear and admiration* were the same concept, so *awe* and *mixture of fear and admiration* are not the same concept. Yet the correctness of (2) can be established by conceptual analysis. So it is false that conceptual analysis, at least as Grice conceives of it, can establish necessary and sufficient conditions for the application of a particular concept only by finding a conjunctive concept that is identical to the concept being analysed.

This argument is not decisive, since one might have doubts about the suggestion that concepts are individuated in the way that it implies.[4] Nevertheless, it remains difficult to avoid the suspicion that the issue of concept identity that figures so prominently in Williamson's discussion is something of a red herring. We have so far found no clear evidence either that analytic epistemologists who rely on conceptual analysis to establish necessary and sufficient conditions for propositional knowledge actually think that concepts like *knows* and *has a justified*

---

[4] There are some trenchant criticisms of the informativeness test for concept identity in Fodor (1998b).

true belief are identical or that they are committed to thinking this. Why, then, does Williamson make so much of the issue of concept identity in DCA? The reason is that he regards the programme of analysis as one that has its origins "in great philosophical visions" (p. 31). Russell's logical atomist conception of thought and language is one such vision, and Williamson implies that providing an analysis in Russell's sense of the concept of knowledge really would be a matter of finding a conjunctive concept with which this concept is identical. So if something like Russell's vision is needed to motivate the programme of analysis, then it cannot be wrong to represent conceptual analysis in the way that DCA represents it. At the same time, this reading makes the pursuit of analyses look even more like a "degenerating research programme" (p. 31), given that "the philosophical visions which gave it a point are no longer serious options" (p. 32).

Although this line of thinking goes some way towards explaining and justifying the opening premiss of DCA, it still falls short of vindicating it. What seems plausible is that a commitment to Russell's vision, or something like it, would be *one* way of motivating the programme of analysis. What is much less plausible is that some such vision is *necessary* to motivate the project of analysing the concept of knowledge. As far as most standard analyses of the concept of knowledge are concerned, the central question is: what is knowledge? They think that the best way of answering this question—call it (W)—is to analyse the concept of knowledge, and that is why they proceed as they do. There is no suggestion here of some further overarching philosophical vision in which the project of analysis is grounded. In particular, the assumption that analysing the concept of knowledge is the best way of answering (W) seems independent of any commitment to Russell's programme. On a Gricean conception of analysis, it is also independent of any commitment to the idea that the analysing concept must be the same as the concept being analysed. Yet the project of analysing the concept of knowledge still has a point: the point is to help us understand what knowledge is.

But is it plausible that we can explain what knowledge is by analysing the *concept* of knowledge? We do not think that we can explain what water is just by analysing the concept of water, so why should we treat knowledge any differently?[5] The obvious answer to this question is that knowledge, unlike water, is not a natural kind.[6] So what kind of kind is it? Williamson claims that knowing is a state of mind and compares it with the property of being coloured. Anything that is coloured has a more specific colour property, so "being coloured is being red or green or . . . if the list is understood as open-ended, and the concept *is coloured* isn't identified with the disjunctive concept" (p. 34). In the same way,

---

[5] Some epistemologists argue that we should not treat knowledge differently and that "the subject matter of epistemology is knowledge itself, not our concept of knowledge" (Kornblith 2002: 1).

[6] For a contrary view see Kornblith (2002).

"knowing that A is seeing or remembering or . . . that A if the list is understood as open-ended, and the concept *knows* isn't identified with the disjunctive concept" (p. 34). On this account, the fundamental problem with traditional attempts to analyse the concept of knowledge is not that they try to answer (W) by focusing on the concept of knowledge. The real problem is that what they try to do with this concept is to analyse it in terms of necessary and sufficient conditions. Just as it does not make sense to explain what it is for something to be coloured by giving necessary and sufficient conditions for something to be coloured, so it does not make sense to explain what knowledge is by giving necessary and sufficient conditions.

At this point, however, concept identity is no longer the main issue. Since it is no longer being suggested that the pursuit of analyses is pointless without Russell's vision in the background, it is irrelevant whether conceptual analysis in Russell's sense is committed to identifying the analysing concept with the concept being analysed. Most current analyses of the concept of knowledge are Gricean rather than Russellian, and the present objection is not that Gricean analyses are unmotivated or that they cannot achieve what they set out to achieve without equating *knows* with conjunctive concepts like *justified true belief.* Instead, the objection is that finding necessary and sufficient conditions for someone's knowing a given proposition is, in principle, a bad way of trying to achieve what many analytic epistemologists are trying to achieve—that is, a bad way of trying to explaining what knowledge is. Given that this worry has nothing to do with the somewhat intractable questions about concept identity that are at the heart of DCA, it probably makes sense to abandon this argument. Whereas DCA looks like an attempt to knock out a version of analytic epistemology with a single blow, the point that Williamson should be emphasizing is simply that he has a better way of doing things.

Before moving on to the positive phase of Williamson's discussion we should have a brief look at the other arguments for UH. The Inductive Argument assumes that "no currently available analysis in terms of belief is adequate" (p. 4). Although this assumption is not uncontroversial, we can let it pass for present purposes. The question is whether it is reasonable to conclude on the basis of four decades of failure that no analysis of the concept *knows* of the standard kind is correct. On the one hand, there is the worry that four decades is not a long enough period of time in the history of philosophy to warrant such pessimism. On the other hand, time is not the only relevant factor here. Given that attempts to analyse the concept of knowledge have succumbed to a "pattern of counterexamples and epicycles" (p. 31), it is not unreasonable to conclude that all such attempts suffer from a common underlying defect. So, while a successful analysis might be around the corner, there is no reason to believe that this is the case. It seems, therefore, that the Inductive Argument carries considerable weight unless it is wrong to assume that no currently available analysis is correct.[7]

The False Expectations Argument says that there is no special reason to expect an analysis of *knows*. Assuming that truth and belief are necessary for knowledge, "we might expect to reach a necessary and sufficient condition by adding whatever knowing has which believing truly may lack" (p. 32). But that expectation is based on a fallacy, Williamson claims. For example, "although being coloured is a necessary and sufficient condition for being red, we cannot state a necessary and sufficient condition for being red by conjoining being coloured with other properties specified without reference to red. Neither the equation 'Red = coloured + X' nor the equation 'Knowledge = true belief + X' need have a non-circular solution" (p. 3).

One question about this argument is whether the analogy with *red* is appropriate. Since Locke introduced the distinction between simple and complex ideas and insisted that simple ideas cannot be broken down, those who have gone in for conceptual analysis have been careful to argue that only complex concepts are analysable. From this perspective, *red* is the paradigm of a simple concept. Its unanalysability should therefore come as no surprise, but it does not follow that the concept of knowledge cannot be analysed. More cautiously, it does not follow that the concept of knowledge cannot be analysed if this concept is complex rather than simple. If *knows* is simple, or if there is not a viable simple/complex distinction, then the False Expectations Argument goes through. The fact is, however, that Williamson does not establish the simplicity of *knows* or the unsustainability of the distinction between simple and complex concepts. As things stand, therefore, the False Expectations Argument is inconclusive.

3. WILLIAMSON'S PROPOSAL

Let us now consider the positive phase of Williamson's discussion. His main positive proposal is that knowing is merely a state of mind. Specifically, knowing is "the most general factive stative attitude, that which one has to a proposition if one has any stative attitude to it at all" (p. 34). A factive attitude is one that one can have only to truths, and we have already seen that the linguistic expression of a factive stative attitude is a factive stative mental state operator (FMSO). If Φ is an FMSO, it "typically takes as subject a term for something animate and as object a term consisting of 'that' followed by a sentence" (p. 34), the inference

---

[7] As I read it, the Inductive Argument is Williamson's best argument for UH. This is not made explicit in the text, and the fact that so little time is spent on this argument might easily mislead one into thinking that it is less important in Williamson's eyes than, say, DCA.

from 'S Φs that p' to 'p' is deductively valid, and 'S Φs that p' entails that 'S grasps the proposition that p'. In addition, if Φ is an FMSO, it is semantically unanalysable.

It is against this background that Williamson identifies the two principles that he represents as characterizing the concept of knowing uniquely, 'up to logical equivalence', in terms of the concept of an FMSO. There is the principle that 'know' is an FMSO and the principle that, if Φ is an FMSO, then from 'S Φs that p' one may infer 'S knows that p'. In these terms, both 'sees that' and 'remembers that' are examples of FMSOs. As Williamson puts it, "if you see that it is raining, then you know that it is raining. If you remember that it was raining, then you know that it was raining" (p. 37). 'Know' is therefore "the most general FMSO, one which applies if any FMSO applies" (p. 39).

How, then, does this account of the concept of knowledge differ from analysis in the traditional sense? Analysis in this sense is both *decompositional* and *reductive*; it proceeds by dismantling the concept of knowledge, and represents the concepts into which it analyses the concept of knowledge as more basic than this concept. Williamson's account is "explicitly not a decomposition of the concept *knows*" (p. 40). He is not claiming that this concept 'contains' or 'embeds' the concept of an FMSO in anything like the sense in which, on the traditional conception, the concept *knows* contains the concepts of truth or belief or justification. But does this mean that his account is not in any sense a reductive account? Since he characterizes the concept of knowledge in terms of the concept of an FMSO, the question is whether the concept of an FMSO is more basic than the concept of knowledge. If so, then we would have to conclude that Williamson's account is reductive even if it is not decompositional.

What would it be for the concept of an FMSO to be more basic than the concept *knows*? One form of basicness is what might be called *explanatory basicness*. A concept C is more explanatorily basic than another concept D if and only if C can be explained without using D but D cannot be explained without using C. So if it turns out that we can explain the concept of an FMSO without employing the concept of knowledge, but that we cannot explain the concept of knowledge without employing the concept of an FMSO, then we will be forced to conclude that the concept of an FMSO is more basic than the concept of knowledge. Although explanatory basicness is not the only form of basicness, the distinguishing feature of reductive approaches to the concept of knowledge is precisely that they attempt to analyse this concept in terms of concepts that are more basic in the explanatory sense.

Is it true that the concept of an FMSO is explanatorily more basic than the concept of knowledge? We have already seen that Williamson explains the concept of knowledge in terms of the concept of an FMSO, but he explicitly denies that the concept of an FMSO has to be explained in terms of the concept of knowledge. In an important passage, he claims that the notion of an FMSO "has been explained without essential reference to the notion of knowing, although 'know' is an example of an FMSO" (p. 37). This suggests that the concept of an FMSO is explanatorily more basic than the concept of knowledge. And, if this is right, then what Williamson is proposing is a non-decompositional but nevertheless reductive account of the concept of knowledge.

It is helpful to compare this approach to giving a positive account of the concept of knowledge with Strawson's approach in *Analysis and Metaphysics*. In his discussion, Strawson is concerned to distinguish between two forms of conceptual analysis, reductive and non-reductive.[8] The former tries to explain concepts like *knowledge* by breaking them down into explanatorily more basic concepts. In contrast, non-reductive conceptual analysis tries to explain such concepts by relating them to concepts at the same level—that is, concepts that are no more basic. From the perspective of reductive conceptual analysis, circularity is a major issue. If one analyses one concept C in terms of another concept D, it must not turn out that D cannot be explained without reference to C. In contrast, non-reductive conceptual analysis is much more relaxed about circularity. Its aim is not so much to analyse concepts as to elucidate them, and the concepts that one uses to elucidate a given concept need not be any more basic. As far as non-reductive analysis is concerned, circularity need not be a vice.

In these terms, Strawson is a practitioner of non-reductive conceptual analysis. The same does not appear to be true of Williamson. For a start, he is not relaxed about circularity. Thus, in the first few pages of *Knowledge and its Limits*, he considers the proposal that Gettier-type counter-examples to the traditional tripartite definition of knowledge can be circumvented by strengthening the justification condition, but he rejects this proposal on the grounds that the required standard of justification is unlikely to be "independent of knowledge itself" (p. 4). In contrast, Williamson's own account of the concept of knowledge in terms of the concept of an FMSO will not be circular in this way if, as he claims, the concept of an FMSO can be explained without essential reference to the concept of knowing.

How seriously should we take the suggestion that the concept of an FMSO is explanatorily more basic than the concept of knowledge? Perhaps Williamson's thought is that the concept of an FMSO can be characterized by reference to the various marks listed above and that none of these marks makes any reference to knowledge. So this is the sense in which the concept of an FMSO can be explained without essential reference to the concept of knowing. On the other hand, the two principles that Williamson uses to characterize the concept of knowing 'up to logical equivalence' tell a different story. The second of these principles states that, if Φ is an FMSO, then from 'S Φs that p' one may infer 'S knows that p'. This does not look like a principle that does not involve the

---

[8] See Strawson (1992: ch. 2) for an account of this distinction.

concept of knowledge or that is independent of knowledge itself. What it suggests is rather that we will not have understood the notion of an FMSO unless we regard factive mental states as states of *knowledge*. But it is difficult to see how this can be reconciled with the suggestion that the concept of an FMSO can be explained without essential reference to the concept of knowing.

It seems, then, that Williamson's modest positive account of the concept of knowledge contains both reductive and non-reductive elements. The reductive line of thinking is the one that uses the concept of an FMSO to characterize the concept of knowledge while insisting that the notion of an FMSO can itself be explained without essential reference to the concept of knowledge. The non-reductive line of thinking is the one that uses the concept of an FMSO to characterize the concept of knowledge while insisting that the notion of an FMSO cannot be explained without essential reference to the concept of knowledge. If we emphasize the non-reductive dimension of Williamson's thinking, then we will see him as elucidating the concept of knowledge in something like Strawson's sense. If, on the other hand, we emphasize the reductive dimension of Williamson's thinking, then we will not be able to see him as doing non-reductive conceptual analysis. Either way, it appears that what Williamson is doing can legitimately be described as a form of conceptual analysis.[9]

4. WHAT IS KNOWLEDGE?

The final issue concerns the suggestion that, if one knows that A, then there is a specific way in which one knows. What is right about this is that, if a subject S is said to know that A, then one question that can always legitimately be asked is: *how* does S know?[10] It might seem that it is in connection with this question—call it (H)—that Williamson's 'ways of knowing' come into our picture of knowledge. For once we have identified a specific way in which S knows that A, it would appear we have answered (H). What we are reluctant to accept is that it can be a brute fact that S knows that A without there being a specific way in which he knows it; it cannot be that A 'just knows'. On the present reading, this is the sense in which, if one knows that A, there is a specific way in which one knows it.

---

[9] Not if conceptual analysis must be decompositional and reductive, but Strawson's discussion suggests that this characterization of conceptual analysis is too narrow.

[10] As Austin (1979: 77) remarks, "when we make an assertion such as 'There is a goldfinch in the garden' or 'He is angry', there is a sense in which we imply that we are sure of it or know it . . . On making such an assertion, therefore, we are directly exposed to the questions (1) 'Do you *know* there is?' 'Do you *know* he is?' and (2) '*How* do you know?' If in answer to the first question we reply 'Yes', we may then be asked the second question, and even the first question is commonly taken as an invitation to state not merely *whether* but also *how* we know." Austin goes on to make several very useful points about (2).

At this point, however, we run into the following difficulty: a satisfactory answer to (H), as this question is usually understood, will need to explain how S *came to know* that A—that is, how S *acquired* this piece of knowledge. For example, we can say that S came to know that A by seeing that A. Seeing that A is a way of coming to know that A, and we can explain how S knows that A by reference to a specific way of coming to know. But are ways of coming to know that A the same as Williamson's 'ways of knowing'? The problem is that, for Williamson, remembering that A is a way of knowing that A, yet it is hard to see how it can be a way of coming to know that A. Remembering that A is a way of retaining the knowledge that A, not a way of acquiring it. This suggests that Williamson's ways of knowing need not be ways of coming to know.

So what does it mean to say that seeing that A and remembering that A are both ways of knowing that A, even though they are not both ways of coming to know that A? All it can mean is that certain entailments hold, specifically, the entailment from 'S sees that A' to 'S knows that A' and from 'S remembers that A' to 'S knows that A'. The problem, however, is that there are many such entailments that have no bearing on (H). For example, 'regret' and 'realize' are both FMSOs, which means that one can infer 'S knows that A' from 'S regrets that A' as well as from 'S realizes that A'. Yet regretting or realizing that A are not ways of coming to know that A. Indeed, it is not even clear that they are ways of knowing that A; it sounds distinctly odd to say that realizing that it is raining is a way of knowing that it is raining or that regretting that one never learned to play the piano is a way of knowing that one never learned to play the piano. This suggests that a problem with the notion of an FMSO is that it is far too undiscriminating. There are important differences between 'see', 'remember', and 'realize' that the description of all of them as FMSOs overlooks, and this is one of the limitations of Williamson's framework.

Suppose, then, that we insist on distinguishing between different kinds of FMSO and focus on those that can be used to answer (H). I have suggested that seeing that A is one such FMSO. Because seeing that it is raining is potentially a way of coming to know that it is raining, I can explain how I know that it is raining by reference to the fact that I can see that it is raining. But seeing that it is raining is obviously not the only way of coming to know that it is raining. I can also come to know this by hearing the rain lashing against the windows of my apartment, by listening to a weather report on the radio, and so on. With this in mind, we also find ourselves in a position to explain what it is to know that it is raining. Instead of trying to explain this by specifying non-circular necessary and sufficient conditions for knowing that it is raining, we now have another possibility. The alternative is to identify some of the many different ways of coming to know that it is raining and thereby to explain what it is to know that it is raining. More generally, the suggestion is that we can explain what this kind of knowledge is, or what it consists in, by identifying acceptable answers to the question 'how do you know?'

In fact, this can be only part of the story. As well as being acquired, knowledge can also be retained and transmitted. A more complete account of what knowledge is will therefore also say something about the different ways of retaining and transmitting it. For example, it will point out that keeping a written record of what one knows about a particular subject can be a way of retaining one's knowledge as well as a way of transmitting it to others. Nevertheless, acquisition remains at the centre of this conception of knowledge. If one has no conception of the different ways in which knowledge can in principle be acquired, one does not fully understand what knowledge is. Yet there is no suggestion that particular ways of coming to know that A are necessary conditions for knowing that A. Although I can acquire the knowledge that it is raining by seeing that it is raining, seeing that it is raining is not a necessary condition for knowing that it is raining. It is a sufficient condition, but this still does not mean that knowledge is being explained by reference to conditions for knowing as distinct from ways of coming to know.

Suppose that ways of coming to know that A are described as *means of knowing* that A. Then what we now have is what might be called a Means Response to (H) and to (W). This response does not treat knowledge as a natural kind or as something that is to be studied by analysing the concept of knowledge into more basic concepts. Instead, the Means Response explains how one knows that A by identifying the means by which one actually came to know it, and it explains what it is to know that A by identifying different possible means of knowing it, including the means by which one actually came to know it. Since there may be countless different means of coming to know that A, the Means Response does not try to come up with a complete list. To understand what it is to know that A, all one needs is an open-ended list of means of knowing that A, perhaps together with some indication of whether some means of knowing that A are more basic than others. In drawing up its list of means, the Means Response relies on armchair reflection rather than empirical science. It can still be described as 'analysing' the concept of knowledge, but it is not engaged in the kind of reductive conceptual analysis that Williamson criticizes.

One worry about the Means Response is that it puts the cart before the horse. The worry is that the question 'what is knowledge?' is prior to the question 'what are the different means by which it is possible to come to know?', and that (W) must therefore be answered before (H) can be answered. Intuitively, one cannot figure out how something is acquired unless one already knows what it is, and this implies that the Means Response is wrong to try to answer (W) on the basis of its response to (H)—that is, by helping itself to the notion of a means of knowing. On reflection, however, it is clear that this objection fails. Consider the question 'what is cricket?' A good way of answering this question would be to explain how cricket is played, and it would be bizarre to object that this kind of explanation fails, because it is not possible to explain how cricket is played unless one already knows what cricket is. The position is rather than one explains what cricket is by describing how it is played. The 'what' question is not prior to the 'how' question, and the same goes for (W) and (H).[11] Describing how knowledge is acquired, retained, and transmitted is as good a way of explaining what knowledge is as describing how cricket is played is of explaining what cricket is. In both cases, the focus is on means—means of playing cricket in the one case and means of acquiring, retaining, and transmitting knowledge in the other.

The Means Response to (W) is not ultimately very different from Williamson's response to this question. There is barely any difference between Williamson's proposal that 'knowing that A is seeing or remembering or . . . that A if the list is understood as open-ended, and the concept knows isn't identified with the disjunctive concept' (p. 34) and the suggestion that (W) can be answered by producing an open-ended list of means of knowing. The one difference is that means of knowing are, in the first instance, means of coming to know and so will exclude many of Williamson's 'ways of knowing'. Nevertheless, the Means Response has the same basic structure as Williamson's account. The interesting final question that needs to be considered, therefore, is whether the Means Response is the end of the story or whether a philosophically satisfying response to (H) and to (W) needs to go beyond the identification of means.

The most straightforward reason for thinking that a Means Response to (H) and (W) is insufficient is this: suppose that a person S is said to know that it is raining by seeing that it is raining, and that this is how S's knowledge that it is raining is explained. This explanation is no good if it is not possible for S to see that it is raining—that is, if there is some obstacle that prevents S from seeing that it is raining. Some obstacles are comparatively superficial. For example, it might be too dark for S to see or his eyesight might not be good enough. On the other hand, it is sometimes suggested that there are deep epistemological obstacles that stand in the way of anyone being able to see that it is raining, and that that is why the proposed explanation of S's knowledge does not work. For example, sceptics argue that S cannot see and thereby know that it is raining unless he can eliminate the possibility that he is dreaming that it is raining, and that this is not a possibility that S can possibly eliminate.[12]

If there are obstacles to seeing that it is raining that take the form of epistemological requirements that cannot be met, then it will not do just to say that S knows that it is raining because he can see that it is raining. It also needs to be shown that the obstacle-generating requirements are not genuine and that

---

[11] The analogy is not perfect. There are lots of different ways of acquiring knowledge, but it is not true in the same sense that there are lots of different ways of playing cricket. In addition, describing how cricket is played will not tell someone what cricket is if it is not understood that cricket is a game.

[12] Stroud is someone who emphasizes the importance of dealing with obstacles to knowing. See, e.g., Stroud (2000).

there is therefore nothing that prevents S from seeing that it is raining.[13] This would be what might be called an *obstacle-dissipating* response to (H) and to (W). For example, one way of dissipating the alleged obstacle would be to insist on a distinction between what is necessary for seeing that it is raining and what is necessary for knowing that one sees that it is raining. With this distinction in place, we can argue that being able to eliminate the possibility that one is dreaming is only necessary for knowing that one sees that it is raining rather than for seeing that it is raining. This is an obstacle-dissipating supplement to the Means Response, and the present suggestion is that this response will not be philosophically satisfying unless it is supplemented in this way.

This is still not the end of the line. In addition to showing that there is nothing that prevents S from seeing that it is raining, a philosophically satisfying account of S's knowledge might also need to include an account of what *makes it possible* for S to see that it is raining and thereby to know that it is raining. For example, it is arguable that S could not see that it is raining without a capacity for spatial perception or grasp of the concept *rain* and other related concepts.[14] These are what might be described as *enabling conditions* for seeing that it is raining.[15] They enable or make it possible for S to see that it is raining and thereby also enable or make it possible for him to know that it is raining by seeing that it is raining. So the proposed explanation of S's knowledge that it is raining is a multi-levels explanation, one that operates at the level of means, the level of obstacle-dissipation, and the level of enabling conditions.

In these terms, Williamson's modest positive account of the concept *knows* operates largely at the level of means. This is a reflection of his somewhat minimalist conception of what it would be to answer (W) and (H). By Williamson's lights, it is not that it is not possible to go beyond the identification of means

---

[13] Another possibility would be to show that the epistemological requirements can be met. For example, McDowell (1998: 238) argues that it *is* possible to know that one is not dreaming: "one's knowledge that one is not dreaming, in the relevant sort of situation, owes its credentials as knowledge to the fact that one's senses are yielding one knowledge of the environment—something that does not happen when one is dreaming." As McDowell (1998: 238–9) goes on to admit, however, this line of thinking does not meet the obstacle-generating requirement on its own terms; it does not show that one is not dreaming "*independently* of the epistemic status of whatever putative perceptual knowledge is in question".

[14] A capacity for spatial perception is the capacity to perceive spatial properties such as location. It is not possible to see that it is raining without seeing that it is raining somewhere, and the perception of location is a form of spatial perception. See Kant (1932) for a defence of the idea that the perception of space is required for the perception of any objective state of affairs. What Kant says is much less plausible for auditory than for visual perception.

[15] For more on the notion of an enabling condition, see Dretske (1969: 82–3). The enabling conditions that Dretske is interested in can be established only empirically, but not all enabling conditions are like that. There are also a priori enabling conditions for seeing that it is raining, ones that can be established non-empirically. For example, we can know just by armchair reflection that it would not be possible to see that it is raining if one lacked the concept *rain*. It does not follow, of course, that one cannot see rain without the concept *rain*. See Williamson (2000: 38) for an explanation and defence of this distinction.

or 'ways of knowing' but that it is not necessary to do so. What is necessary is that we are prepared to tackle obstacles to knowing as and when we encounter them. This does not mean that we are under any obligation in epistemology to anticipate and rebut every potential obstacle or to provide a substantive account of what makes it possible to see that A or to know that A by seeing that A. This is the sense in which Williamson's positive account amounts to a form of explanatory minimalism. It is content to represent knowing as the determinable of which seeing, remembering, realizing, and so on are determinates without attempting to explain what makes these attitudes ways of knowing or of coming to know.

For all its attractions, explanatory minimalism is too austere to be the source of much philosophical satisfaction. What we seek in epistemology is, as Stroud (2000: 4) puts it, "some kind of *explanation* of our knowledge—some account of how it is possible". Different epistemologists have different conceptions of what a good explanation should look like, but it is hard not to think that explanatory minimalism takes too much for granted. Once we agree that 'S sees that A' entails 'S knows that A', it is all too easy to 'explain' S's knowledge that A by pointing out that he sees that A. The problem is that S's ability to see that A is itself something that we should be trying to understand and explain.[16] Perhaps it is only in the context of philosophy that this needs explaining, but philosophy is, after all, what we are doing. What needs explaining is how there can be such a thing as seeing that A, and this means that the philosophy of knowledge must be prepared to think in general terms about potential obstacles to seeing that A as well as the enabling conditions for this kind of seeing. Viewed in this light, Williamson's ingenious account of knowing is the beginning rather than the end of the story in epistemology.[17]

[16] Perhaps the entailment from 'S sees that A' to 'S knows that A' also calls for some kind of explanation. There is a very interesting attempt to explain it in chapter 3 of Drestske (1969), though Dretske's explanation relies on a reductive analysis of the concept of knowledge in terms of the concept of a conclusive reason. See, e.g., Dretske (1969: 124).

[17] I thank Tim Williamson and other members of David Charles's discussion group for useful comments. Thanks also to Ciara Fairley for helpful discussions and comments.

3

Is Knowing a State of Mind? The Case Against

Elizabeth Fricker

1. WILLIAMSON'S SURPRISING THESIS

In *Knowledge and its Limits* (*KAIL*), chapters 1 and 2, Timothy Williamson argues for what he rightly advertises as a surprising thesis: that knowing is a mental state (henceforth KMS).[1] His billing of his thesis as not merely 'banal', but 'unexpected' (*KAIL* 21), gives a key clue as to how it is to be understood. Knowing, Williamson tells us, is a 'central case of a mental state'; it is 'a mental state in every reasonable sense of that term' (*KAIL* 22, 28). Knowing is not merely mental in a relaxed sense which counts as such states which are comprised of a more purely mental component together with a non-mental one—which are, as Williamson puts it, 'metaphysically hybrid' (*KAIL* 50).[2] Williamson sets out to persuade us of a thesis that is surprising and metaphysically radical: the state of knowing, despite its factiveness—entailment of a fact external to the knower's mind[3]—is not a conjunction of a mental with an extra-mental component, but is a simple general mental state: 'What matters is . . . rejection of a conjunctive account of knowing' (*KAIL* 48).[4]

---

[1] These chapters of *KAIL* are largely based on Williamson's earlier article 'Is Knowing a State of Mind?' (Williamson 1995). The present discussion is an updated version of a critique I wrote in 1997 of the arguments in that piece. Though not previously published, this critique had some circulation, and is the work of mine cited by Williamson in *KAIL*, ch. 2 (p. 57). I gave a talk based on this material at a one-day conference on Williamson's work at Senate House, University of London, in March 2001. Williamson's argument is about propositional knowledge, cases of knowing that P, for some proposition P.

[2] 'there is no more restrictive but still reasonable sense of "mental" in which knowing can be factored, like believing truly, into a combination of mental states with non-mental conditions' (*KAIL*, p. 28).

[3] Namely, the fact known about. This is not part of the knower's mental states, putting aside the special case where the object of her knowledge is some aspect of her own mind.

[4] In his dialectic Williamson contrasts the view that knowing is a simple (not a 'hybrid') state with the view that it is a *conjunction* of a mental with an extra-mental component, arguing for the former and against the latter. This dialectic is flawed by its neglect of the very real possibility that states of knowing consist in a mental state, say of belief, with some causal or nomological relation to a non-mental state—not a mere conjunction, but two components and a crucial relation

The case made for KMS in *KAIL* is not offered as a simple knock-down argument. Rather, Williamson develops a persuasive overall package of related theses, including KMS. His strategy against resistance to KMS is one of attrition: he tackles in turn various apparent obstacles to KMS, seeking to undermine each purported ground for resistance. By the end, he maintains, the opponent of KMS is left clinging to an unmotivated dogmatic prejudice.[5]

In this discussion I aim to show, first, that Williamson's case for KMS is not proven: while he removes some obstacles to accepting knowing as a fully mental state, he has no argument that compels KMS. Secondly, I argue that, despite this removal of some obstacles, others remain: there are still strong grounds to resist KMS, which are not merely an expression of inertial prejudice in our thinking about the mental, and about knowing.

In his earlier discussion 'Is Knowing a State of Mind?' (Williamson 1995) Williamson acknowledged that one convinced of a general Internalism[6] about the mental is committed to denying KMS, since knowing is a factive state. There his main concern was to argue for what I will call the *Weaker Thesis: for one who accepts externalism about mental content, there is no good ground not to take the further step of accepting factive mental states as fully mental.*[7] In *KAIL*, chapter 3, the development of the account of prime conditions is intended to undermine some of the kind of thinking that motivates Internalism—part of Williamson's campaign of attrition against Internalism about the mind. In this discussion I will not directly address this large issue. Rather, I will focus on the Weaker Thesis, arguing (see Section 4 below) that it is false: even for one who accepts externalism about content, there remain strong grounds to resist Williamson's proposed extension of it to allow factive attitudes, including knowing as fully mental states. Thus, *pace* Williamson, the combination of accepting externalism about content, while regarding factive attitudes as at most weakly mental, is an argumentatively stable position.

---

between them. Call such accounts *three-component hybrid accounts* of either 'knows' or knowing. This neglect vitiates Williamson's case both at the metaphysical level, and in his arguments against the analysability of 'knows'. Re the latter, while addressing the classic analysis of knowledge as justified true belief, it leaves out of the reckoning reliabilist and causal accounts of 'knows'. The present discussion focuses on other parts of Williamson's case, and I largely omit mention of this further complicating factor in what follows. Its existence further strengthens my overall case that Williamson's arguments against the analysability of 'knows', and in favour of his account of knowing as a simple state, are inconclusive and on balance unpersuasive, even to an externalist about content.

  [5] Cf. *KAIL* 58: 'If taking the externalist attitude of rational belief to a given content can contribute to one's mental state, why cannot taking the externalist attitude of knowledge to that content also contribute to one's mental state? [Once content-externalism is admitted] . . . the denial that knowing is a mental state [is] ill-motivated.' In this discussion I develop a substantial answer to Williamson's rhetorical challenge.

  [6] See definition in Mark 3 of the mental below.

  [7] In Williamson's own words: 'the case for externalism about mental attitudes is as good as the case for externalism about mental contents' (*KAIL* 51).

As part of his package of views, Williamson maintains that 'knows' has no analysis 'of the standard kind'—this being one that factors knowing into a conjunction of mental and non-mental components, notably the mental state of (rational) belief plus truth and some other factors. Call this thesis NASK. If NASK were false, 'knows' having an a priori necessary and sufficient condition in terms of belief plus some other (non-factive) mental and non-mental components, this would establish the falsity of KMS: knowing would be revealed a priori to be a conjunctive 'metaphysically hybrid' state.[8] For purposes of this discussion I will assume that NASK holds—and, further, that there is no three-component hybrid analysis of the kind overlooked by Williamson (see n. 3 above): existence of such a three-component hybrid analysis would equally suffice to refute KMS.[9] I will argue that, even so, the case for KMS versus other non-metaphysically radical accounts of knowing remains wide open (Sections 3 and 4 below).

In short: if either NASK is false, or general internalism about the mental is true, the falsity of KMS is entailed. For dialectical purposes in this discussion I will assume that NASK is true, and that externalism about content is also true. I will argue that, even on these concessive assumptions, Williamson's case for KMS as developed in *KAIL* falls seriously short of establishing its intended conclusion.

2. CLARIFYING KMS: MARKS OF THE MENTAL

Before we can assess Williamson's case for his thesis that knowing is a factive mental state, we need to get clear about exactly what it means. To say that knowing is factive is to say that the inference from 'A knows that P' to P is an entailment. This is clear and uncontroversial.[10] *KAIL*, §1.4, proposes that knowing that P is the generic state of which a number of more specific factive mental states are various species: remembering that P; seeing that P; knowing through the sense of touch that P—as in 'she could feel that the bone was broken'. A complementary characterisation of 'knows' is given, as 'the most general factive mental state operator' (see Section 3 below). Thus, it is proposed, knowing that P stands to seeing that P much as being coloured stands to being red; and this is portrayed in the syntax and semantics of the natural language expressions for these states (*KAIL* 34).

To say that knowing is a factive *state* contrasts it with a process or event. This is surely right. Williamson clinches the point by citing the deviance of

---

[8] Here I follow Williamson in ruling out the possibility of an error theory—that our concept 'knows' could be complex, while it in fact denotes a simple state. It is doubtful whether this is even coherent, and it can surely be discounted.

[9] This assumption is for dialectical purposes only. My object is to show that, even if Williamson were right about NASK, this is very far from establishing KMS. In fact, the dialectical relation between NASK and KMS is subtle and bi-directional—see n. 41 below.

[10] *KAIL* 35 convincingly sees off the suggestion that it is only a conversational implicature, not an entailment.

continuous-tense sentences such as: 'She was knowing for 20 minutes' (*KAIL* 35). There are hard questions about the nature of states to which we return below.

Before this we first clarify what it really means to say that a state is a *mental* state. Williamson wisely declines to give a definition of 'mental' (*KAIL* 27), and suggests that 'we learn the concept of the mental by examples'. These examples include, he claims, both non-factive and factive propositional attitudes, including knowing. Thus, he claims, our pre-theoretical conception of the mental includes knowing, though, he admits, theoretical reasons to change the everyday classification might emerge (*KAIL* 22). I am not convinced by this contention, since I am not convinced that there is a firm non-philosophers' usage of 'mental' or associated generic classification together of certain states of persons at all. If this is right, then Williamson's contention must be reinterpreted as the claim that our various characteristic practices involving the concepts of both non-factive and factive attitudes are so similar that they hang together. But then this point transforms into a second claim, actually a little argument, that Williamson makes regarding the prima facie mentalness of knowing: a state is justly counted as 'mental' just if it sufficiently resembles paradigm instances; non-factive propositional attitudes such as believing and hoping are amongst the paradigms; and the factive attitudes including knowing resemble these in key respects, so that they are properly classed as mental also (*KAIL* 21–2).

The further substantive discussion in *KAIL*, chapters 1 and 2, licenses interpreting this last view into the following account, which we can endorse, of what it takes for a state to be mental:

MM The mental (i.e. mental states of persons) is characterised by various distinctive marks. Hence if a state—e.g. knowing—can be shown to have all of these marks of the mental, then there is no ground to deny that it is a mental state, and compelling grounds to accept that it is one.

Williamson in effect endorses this proposed sufficient condition for mentalness of a state in his discussion; and his subsequent argumentation concerning knowing addresses it. He prosecutes his case for the mentalness of knowing by setting out to demonstrate that various entrenched marks of the mental are satisfied by knowing,[11] and that other putative marks of it that knowing does not satisfy either have already been, or if not should be, abandoned on independent grounds.[12] Having endorsed MM, we can agree that this is the standard for

[11] Cf. *KAIL* 22: '[*KAIL* 1 and 2] eliminate some putative differences between knowing and non-factive attitudes that might be thought to disqualify knowing as a mental state . . . the differences dissolve on inspection.'

[12] MM proposes a sufficient condition for a state's being mental. Is there a set of marks that it is necessary for a state to satisfy, to count as mental? Or is the position rather this: there are various typical marks of the mental, and the more of them a state satisfies, the better a case of a mental state it is? The discussion below suggests this model. Another typical mark is intentionality; but it is debatable whether all mental states satisfy it. One might suggest that special access (M1) is the

success of his project: to establish that knowing is a factive mental state, it is sufficient that Williamson show it to satisfy all the marks of the mental. If it satisfies only some of them, then it will be revealed as at most a second-class mental state.

The most deeply entrenched and crucial marks of the mental are these:

> *Mark 1: Special Access.* We have psychologically immediate and epistemically basic non-inferential knowledge of our own mental states. Thus there is an epistemic asymmetry between first-person and third-person mental knowledge: I have a special way of knowing about my own mental states, not based on evidence, which others lack.[13]

> *Mark 2: Causal–Explanatory Role in Relation to Action.* Mental predicates are apt to feature in causal explanations of action and other behaviour. They do so within an everyday theory of the mind, 'folk psychology', of whose principles we all have a tacit grasp. Typical folk psychological explanations rationalise the action explained.

Williamson prosecutes his case for KMS by arguing that knowing fulfils both of these marks. He discusses Mark 1 (M1) (*KAIL*, §1.2), and concludes that: 'Any genuine requirement of privileged access on mental states is met by the state of knowing p' (*KAIL* 25). On the way he points out that a stronger conception of first-person special access, as 'transparency'—that is, that one is infallible and potentially all-knowing about one's own mental states—which knowing does not satisfy, has now been generally abandoned. In a substantial and persuasive discussion, Williamson also argues that the factive state of knowing pulls its own proper explanatory weight in the explanation of action, satisfying Mark 2 (M2) (*KAIL*, §2.4).

There is much to be said on both these large issues. However, these topics are not my focus in this discussion. In this context, I will simply concede that Williamson makes a persuasive case that knowing satisfies both of these marks—special access, and explanatory role within folk psychology in relation to action. This being so, knowing does indeed pass the test to be considered a *Weakly mental* state—this notion being defined as a state that satisfies both M1 and M2 (see below). A state that does so indeed hangs together, in our self-ascriptive and

---

crucial and indispensable feature. This certainly picks out all and only the conscious mental states. But the relaxed sense of 'mental' arguably extends to include states that do not fully satisfy it: with Freudian psychology, we have learnt to extend our conception of the mental to include beliefs and desires blocked from self-acknowledgement—yet still mental, in that they clearly drive behaviour, featuring in the explanation of non-verbal action. However, it may plausibly be claimed that these states count as mental only because, first, there is a special explanation of why they are blocked from the usual kind of self-access and, second, therapy can remove this block to enable access. It would be a further, dubious step to count as 'mental' subpersonal processing to which conscious attention has no access routes at all. (Although for some purposes and perspectives in cognitive psychology the personal/subpersonal and access/no-access distinction is unimportant.)

[13] Fricker (1998) discusses alternative explanations of this epistemic asymmetry.

explanatory practices, with a bunch of state types we call 'mental'—sensations and other conscious experiences, and non-factive propositional attitudes.

We have quickly conceded to Williamson that knowing qualifies as a Weakly mental state. But, as I understand it, and wish to contest it, Williamson's claim in KMS amounts to more than this. To explain what more, we introduce two further marks of the mental. These marks allow us to distinguish, within the category of Weakly mental states, an inner core that are also *Purely mental*.

> *Mark 3: Internality or 'narrowness'*. An internalist about the mental holds that a genuine mental state can have no constitutive dependence on any feature of the person's environment—cannot be 'world-involving': all truly mental states must be 'narrow', not 'broad'. (Given a mild physicalism, this internalism can be expressed as the thesis that a person's mental states supervene on the physical state of her own body—her environment plays no role in fixing them.)[14]

As observed above, an 'internalist' about the mental—a subscriber to Mark 3 (M3)—cannot allow any factive state to be (fully) mental. In this discussion I have bracketed the large issue of Internalism, to focus on the project of showing Williamson's Weaker Thesis to be false. However, we should note that Williamson's argumentative strategy in relation to M3 is part of his broader one of persuasion. He develops a package of complementary theses incompatible with M3. His idea is to undermine the motivation and rationale for M3 by, as it were, progressively isolating it. Regarding knowing specifically, Williamson seeks to show that this factive state satisfies all the other, well-motivated marks of the mental; so that refusing knowing the status of a fully mental state on the grounds that it is not internal looks less and less attractive, the proponent of Internalism increasingly dogmatic and ungrounded.

There is a fourth idea, M4, about the 'truly' mental. It is connected with M3, Internalism, but is not the same as it. The boldest and ultimate objective of Williamson's arguments in *KAIL*, chapters 1 and 2—the 'surprising' thesis he seeks to persuade us of—is that knowing, despite its factiveness, satisfies M4. I will first state this fourth mark, and then explain it.

> *Mark 4*: A state is mental in the fullest sense just if it is *Purely mental*.

The notion of being Purely mental is introduced by this stipulation: Say a type of state is a *Weakly mental* type just if it exhibits M1 and M2—Special Access and Role in Action Explanation. Now, a state-type *ms1* is a *Purely mental* state-type just if *ms1* is Weakly mental and it is not the case that: a person's being in *ms1* consists, in each instance, in her being in some component mental

---

[14] The idea of internalism, contrasted with its denial, starts with Putnam (1975). A classic statement of one argument for it is given in Fodor (1981). See *KAIL*, §2.1, for a more rigorous definition.

state *ms2* distinct from *ms1*, plus some non-mental condition obtaining.[15] If a state is Weakly mental, but is not Purely mental, I will call it *Impurely mental*. Following Williamson, and following McDowell (1982), I will also talk of such Impurely mental states being 'metaphysically hybrid'.[16]

We can get the feel of Pure and Impure mentalness with an example. Someone might accept that *seeing that P* is a (factive) Weakly mental state, but insist that it is only Impurely mental: each instance of a person's seeing that P consists in her being in some component Purely mental state, plus a certain non-mental condition (plausibly including a condition on causation of the component Purely mental state) about her environment obtaining. Such Impure Weakly mental predicates, she agrees, provide a useful classification, since—the usual environment usually being there—we can, for everyday convenience, combine the Purely mental with the environmental components in a person's situation, and get some notational economy, maybe even increased explanatory power, by doing so.[17] But—she continues—seeing that P is Impure, a metaphysically hybrid state, each instance of it being realized, constituted, by a Purely mental state, plus an environmental condition. 'Disjunctivism' about perception as propounded by McDowell and others[18] opposes this view, denying the metaphysical hybridness of seeing. Williamson's most ambitious argumentative goal in *KAIL*, chapters 1 and 2, the one I am here contesting, is the extension of this denial that a factive mental state is and can be at most Impurely mental, metaphysically hybrid, to factive propositional attitudes generally, and especially to knowing.

I said that M3 and M4 are connected. The main way in which they are is this. What we might call a *moderate Internalist's* position regarding the mental will allow that some broad states hang together with paradigm narrow mental states in some important respects—satisfying M1 and M2—and are Weakly mental. (These may include factive attitudes, but also some non-factive intentional states, such as beliefs, and perceptual experiences, whose contents are, it is supposed, constitutively dependent on the environment.) The nub of her (moderate) Internalism is her insistence that these broad states are at most Impurely mental. Thus the moderate Internalist rejects disjunctivism about perception in the manner sketched above. Similarly we have seen, in the debate over whether mental content is constitutively dependent on the environment, the development of 'two component' theories of content. Such theories admit that

---

[15] And, we should clarify in light of the point in n. 4: the non-mental condition may be that the mental state is caused in a certain manner by a non-mental state of affairs or fact.

[16] If, as the Internalist avers, being narrow (M3) were included in the marks of the mental, so that to qualify as Weakly mental a state must be narrow, it would be immediate that all Weakly mental states were Purely mental—a narrow state cannot have a non-mental condition as a component.

[17] This is, in my view, the reason why a Weakly mental factive state can indeed, as Williamson maintains, pull its proper weight in action explanation. This fact is no evidence at all that such a state is Purely mental. See Section 4.

[18] See Hinton (1973), Snowdon (1980), and McDowell (1982).

the truth-conditions of beliefs and desires, as attributed in ordinary language, are 'broad'; but insist that there is a more fully mental core component of content that is individuated narrowly—perhaps by a narrow functional role, or maybe by its phenomenal character. (The former is most plausible for attitude content, the latter for the content of conscious experience.)[19]

In short, M3 and M4 are linked thus: for the moderate Internalist (a position with some currency and plausibility) a state satisfies M4 only if it satisfies M3: only narrow states are Purely mental. 'Broad' states may be Weakly mental, but are only Impurely so; each instance of any broad mental state has a narrow mental fillet, its core Purely mental component.

In contrast, true *Externalism* about the mind denies that broad states can be at most Impurely mental. The whole point of true externalism is to deny that, where an ordinary-language mental state type is world involving, it follows that it must be metaphysically hybrid, factoring into an internal component together with a non-mental condition. True Externalism holds that there are mental states whose 'essence involves the world', as Williamson puts it,[20] but that are not compound states—that is, that *there are states that satisfy M4, though not M3*. Throughout this discussion, 'Externalism' denotes this strong form of externalism.

A moderate Internalist is committed to insisting that a factive state can be at most Impurely mental. In arguing against the view that the factive state of knowing is only Impurely mental, Williamson takes as his target such an internalist stance. Nonetheless, and crucially for our discussion below, there is room for a view that regards factive attitudes as Impurely mental, *although the envisaged Purely mental core component of such a metaphysically hybrid factive state is not a narrow state, but is itself broad*. This is the view I shall advocate below regarding states of knowing, in opposition to Williamson's contention.[21]

The last key observation we need to make in relation to M3 and M4, for present purposes, is that the moderate Internalist, or anyone insisting that some class of Weakly mental states is only Impurely so, faces a task: to identify, or at least make plausible the claim of the existence of, a typology of states that constitute the Purely mental core of the allegedly Impure Weakly mental states.

In what follows I will argue that Williamson has not shown that states of knowing are Purely, as opposed to Impurely, mental, and that there are good grounds to resist this metaphysically radical claim. But to make good this opposition to Williamson, I must—in line with the observation just

---

[19] See Woodfield (1982) and Pettit and McDowell (1986).   [20] Williamson (1995: 563).

[21] It is also possible for an Impurely mental state to have a core component that is itself only Impurely mental, in turn having a further mental component. This might be the view of a moderate internalist, about factive attitudes: the factive state of knowing that P, say, would be Impurely mental, having as a component the belief that P; but this belief would in turn be Impurely mental, having as a component a narrow mental 'fillet'—say a narrow functional role. This in not the view argued for in what follows. As one previously convinced by the arguments for Externalism about mental content, my concern is to argue against the Weaker Thesis, and against Williamson's proposed extension of Externalism to include factive states amongst the Purely mental.

made—make a plausible case that there exists a Purely mental component to the state of knowing, or at least to each instance of it. (Similarly, the moderate Internalist who proposes a 'two-component' theory of mental content must be able to give an account of what the narrow fillets of broad contents are, and to show these to be genuinely mental states.)

We have conceded that knowing is a Weakly mental state. But Williamson's main claim regarding the state of knowing amounts to more than this. Williamson claims that 'knowing is a mental state in every reasonable sense of that term' (*KAIL* 28). In particular, he denies that knowing is metaphysically compound: 'there is no more restrictive . . . sense of mental in which knowing can be factored . . . into a combination of mental states with non-mental conditions' (*KAIL* 28). Thus: 'To know is not merely to believe while various other conditions are met; it is to be in a new kind of state, a factive one. What matters is . . . rejection of a conjunctive account of knowing' (*KAIL* 47–8). His denial that the state of knowing is 'conjunctive' (is not a 'metaphysical hybrid'—part mental, part non-mental (*KAIL* 51)) leaves no room for doubt that KMS is to be understood as asserting more than the modest thesis, already conceded, that knowing is a Weakly mental state.[22] This is so, since knowing being Weakly mental is consistent with it having a 'hybrid general essence'—indeed sits quite happily with it (see start of Section 4).[23]

However Williamson's discussion leaves it uncertain exactly how much stronger than the modest thesis his claim about knowing is, in a key respect. Williamson's claim that knowing is not 'conjunctive' is made about the 'general state' of knowing. But this thesis is consistent with knowing being Impurely mental, as defined above. This is so, since Pure mentalness is defined in terms of each realizing instance of the state in question not being constituted by a conjunction of a mental with a non-mental condition. Every realizing instance of a factive Weakly mental state could be made up of a Purely mental and a non-mental condition, though there is no 'general essence' of the state qua type. (The point is entirely general.) Thus, each instance of knowing could be a metaphysical hybrid, despite there being no compound general condition CC (the conjunction of a mental with a non-mental condition) such that: it is metaphysically necessary that knowing is instantiated just when CC is instantiated.[24]

---

[22] Williamson's thesis is that states of knowing are not compound at the mental level. He does not deny that a person's mental state may supervene on her total physical state, together with that of her environment, and that this determining base consists of separable internal and external components (*KAIL* 52).

[23] Cf. also *KAIL* 6: 'What is at stake is much more than whether we apply the word "mental" to knowing. If we could isolate a core of states which constituted "pure mind" by being mental in some more thoroughgoing way than knowing is, then the term "mental" might be extended to knowing as a mere courtesy title. On the conception defended here, there is no such core of mental states exclusive of knowing.'

[24] I hear it objected: 'But if each instance is hybrid, then each hybrid realizing instance is a sufficient condition, and when all these are disjoined the result is a condition which is sufficient and

If the state of knowing were only Impurely mental, then this thesis would hold:

> *CI (Compound Instances)*: Every instance of someone's knowing that P consists in her being in some mental condition short of knowing, plus some non-mental condition obtaining.

If CI were true, then a supervenience thesis would hold, and there would be a whole lot of minimal sufficient conditions for knowing:

> *Supervenience of Knowing*: In every situation Si in which someone NN knows that P, there is a weakest[25] compound (mental and non-mental) condition CC(Si) that holds of NN, specifiable without predicating 'knows' of NN, such that any other situation in which CC(Si) obtained would be one in which she knows that P.[26]

This supervenience thesis is not just the relatively uncontroversial thesis that whether someone knows supervenes on a complete physical description of her and her environment.[27] The 'internal' component of each minimally sufficient condition specifies critical aspects of the person's mental state short of knowing that P—her belief that P, perhaps plus some mental rationality condition.

In what follows, I will argue against the thesis that knowing is Purely mental—that is, I will argue against the denial of CI and the Supervenience of Knowing. Specifically, I will argue that no convincing case is made by the considerations adduced in *KAIL*, chapters 1 and 2, to show that knowing is Purely, rather than only Impurely, mental. If Williamson did not intend to establish that knowing is Purely mental, but only that there is no *general* metaphysically necessary and sufficient compound condition for knowing, then he does not claim what I deny. The rhetoric of *KAIL*, which advertises a bold and metaphysically surprising thesis, suggests the assertion that knowing is Purely mental. Whatever Williamson had in mind, it is surely important

---

necessary.' This would be true if the possible instances were finite, and specifiable in advance. But this may not be so—the general situation where one has supervenience without reduction.

[25] CC(Si) is a weakest (minimal) sufficient condition for knowing that P just if: In Si CC(Si) holds of NN, and NN knows that P; and in any other situation in which CC(Si) holds of NN, NN knows that P; and for all conditions CC(Si)-minus, which include some but not all components of CC(Si), there are possible situations in which CC(Si)-minus holds of NN, but NN fails to know that P.

[26] An exception to this principle is when P is a second-level proposition, that NN knows that Q, for some Q. The many minimally sufficient conditions for knowledge posited in this principle need not be discoverable a priori, nor need they be simple or perspicuous. However, each will contain any a priori necessary conditions for knowledge; thus it is plausible that the core of the mental part of each minimally sufficient condition will be NN's confident belief that P. Since environmental and contextual facts can feature in such a minimally sufficient condition, this principle is consistent with various kinds of contextualism regarding knowledge (though not with the view that knowledge-ascriptions are relative to interests or other features of the ascriber).

[27] As already noted, Williamson himself acknowledges this may well be so.

to assess this issue. If Williamson is happy to agree that knowing is only Impurely mental, then he has asserted nothing that a moderate Internalist could not agree with. If the Purely mental components of instances of knowing are internal, then the moderate Internalist picture of the mind—its true essence being internal phenomenal properties directly available to introspective gaze, with some other relational properties correlated with this by context—is intact.

Someone who rejects CI may do so because she holds its contrary—that instances of knowing are not compound at the mental level. Alternatively, she may reject talk of realizing and constitution of instances altogether. Although he says little about them, Williamson commits himself to this idea of realizing instances and what constitutes them making sense, at various points.[28] Myself, I do not see how one can do without some notion of an instance of a general state, and of what constitutes its realization—these are familiar general ideas, with uncontroversial examples.

We are done with the clarifications. In the last two sections of this discussion I move on to the arguments—my account of Williamson's case for KMS, as explicated above, and my critique of it.

In the next section I discuss the relation between NASK and KMS. As I see it, KMS, and the associated account of 'knows', is offered by Williamson as the best explanation of the supposed datum of NASK. But, I observe, it is not the only candidate explanation; nor is it the best one—there are other possible accounts of 'knows' and knowing on which the latter is only Impurely mental that are prima facie plausible. Moreover, these other candidates do better than Williamson's at explaining the existence of various a priori necessary conditions for knowing. The position at the end of the next section is, therefore, that—even granted the essential permitting supposition of NASK—KMS is not proven, and the balance of evidence is still against it.

In my final section I reinforce the case against KMS, by arguing against Williamson's Weaker Thesis (WT). This is the thesis that, once externalism about attitude content has been accepted, no ground remains to resist accepting externalism about factive attitudes. I argue that WT is false—there are good grounds for an externalist about content yet to find counter-intuitive and unacceptable the extension of it to count factive attitudes as Purely mental. The final tally, accordingly, is that, while Williamson makes a persuasive case that

---

[28] Vide *KAIL* 63: 'Different people can share the state of knowing that there was a diamond in the house . . . no doubt the particular circumstances that in some sense realize the state in a given case can be described in many different ways.' My contention in this discussion is that Williamson fails to refute, or even to provide a persuasive case against, the view that knowing is realized in each instance by belief satisfying various further conditions. *KAIL* 40 makes the disclaimer that: 'No claim is made about the essences of . . . tokens [of the state of knowing].' But, if so, then Williamson's thesis is not after all so 'unexpected': it is not metaphysically radical.

knowing is a weakly mental state, he gives no arguments that compel or even afford strong evidence for the view that it is Purely mental; and there remain strong grounds to resist this extension of externalism to factive attitudes.

3. NASK AND KMS: NOT PROVEN

In this section I examine the relationship between KMS and NASK, in particular considering to what extent the supposed truth of NASK is evidence for KMS. First we pause to clarify just how NASK—Williamson's thesis that 'knows' has 'no analysis of the standard kind' should be understood. Williamson explicitly has in mind the traditional analysis of 'knows' as justified true belief, and more sophisticated recent variants of this classic proposal. His 'standard kind' is one that reveals knowing as metaphysically compound, a conjunction of the mental component of belief with extra-mental conditions.

Articles have been written about what exactly an analysis of a concept is. Here, I will simply take NASK to be the *denial that 'knows' has an a priori necessary and sufficient condition revealing it as a conjunction of belief and some further conditions.* This weak version of NASK (it is the weakest version that retains the idea that the relation between analysans and analysandum is knowable a priori) is apt for our current enquiry, since it is already strong enough to entail the falsity of KMS. (Thus it would not help Williamson's cause that some stronger analysability claim were false, if this weak claim were true—that would already be enough to sink KMS.)[29]

As already observed, KMS entails NASK, and accordingly the latter's falsity would decisively refute KMS: if knowledge is revealed a priori to be a metaphysical hybrid (remember we have dismissed an error theory of our concept 'knows'), then the case against Williamson's core claim of KMS, that a 'conjunctive account of knowing' is to be rejected, is settled.[30]

But does NASK entail KMS? It does not. For someone who disbelieved in any a posteriori metaphysical necessities, the lack of an a priori hybrid general essence of knowing would show knowing to lack any hybrid general essence. But Williamson allows that: 'A simple concept might be defined by ostension of complex exemplars' (*KAIL* 50)—he allows it to be coherent to suppose there to be a hybrid general essence of knowing that can be known of only a posteriori,

---

[29] Our weak version of NASK does not insist that the concepts in the analysans—plausibly including belief, and justifiedness or rationality—be conceptually prior to 'knows'. Again, even if these concepts were interdependent with 'knows', so long as a compound condition necessary and sufficient for knowing in terms of them exists, that suffices to falsify KMS—KMS being a metaphysical, not a conceptual thesis.

[30] Recall too the point from n. 3: a three-component hybrid analysis of 'knows', e.g. of knowledge as belief caused by the fact believed in, would equally refute KMS, though this possibility does not feature in Williamson's dialectic.

though KMS explicitly repudiates this.[31] So there is no entailment from no-a priori-hybrid-essence to no-hybrid-essence—from NASK to KMS. A fortiori, if we construe KMS in the strongest sense identified earlier, as denying also that instances of knowing are metaphysically hybrid, the entailment fails.

Williamson in *KAIL*, chapters 1 and 2, offers us a metaphysical thesis about the state of knowing, together with a complementary account of the concept 'knows'. As I see it, NASK features in his argumentation as a datum, an explanandum—the supposedly now well-demonstrated historical failure of attempts to devise analyses of 'knows' of the standard, hybrid, kind. Williamson offers his complementary accounts of knowing, and 'knows', as the best and correct explanation of this supposed datum.

I said that Williamson's accounts of 'knows' and knowing are complementary. Strictly, given Williamson's admission that a simple concept could be introduced by means of complex examplars, his account of 'knows' as an 'FMSO' (more below) does not entail his view of knowing, but is consistent with it having a hybrid general essence, and certainly with its instances being compound. Neither Williamson nor I holds a kind of idealism according to which the structure of the world can simply be read off the semantic structure (or lack of it) in our concepts. So metaphysical accounts of the state of knowing, and accounts of 'knows', are to some extent independent—namely, as already observed, no inference can validly be made from lack of complexity in the concept, to lack of complexity in the state; though the converse inference is more valid.

Notwithstanding this, there may be affinity between a certain account of the concept, and one of the state. This is the position with Williamson's account of 'knows' as a 'factive mental state operator' (FMSO), and his view of knowing.

The account of 'knows' as an FMSO is quite thin. It characterises 'knows' in terms of its semantic unanalysability, and two distinctive patterns of inference: the factiveness inference from 'A knows that P' to P; and a set of inferences from various more specific FMSOs—seeing, hearing, remembering that P—to knowing that P. 'Knows', Williamson tells us, is 'the most general FMSO, the one that applies if any FMSO at all applies' (*KAIL* 39).[32]

Williamson's thin FMSO account posits that 'knows' exhibits no semantic complexity apart from the two distinctive inferences.[33] As such, it sits well with KMS—the view of knowing as a simple factive mental state. Williamson asserts

---

[31] Thus 'Internalists [or others] who regard knowing itself as complex do not thereby commit themselves to the same view of the concept "knows"' (*KAIL* 50).

[32] As Williamson notes, his account fits within the general model for account of concepts in terms of 'possession conditions' suggested in Peacocke (1992): grasp of these two patterns of inference proper to 'knows' is part of what it is to possess the concept it expresses.

[33] The entailment from various other FMSOs to 'knows' is, on Williamson's account, a reflection of relations between states—knowing that P being the generic state of which various more specific factive states are species. Indeed, there is almost a non-hybrid analysis in these terms to be had (to know that P is to see that P, or remember that P, or . . .); it is lacking only because there is no definite finite list of the specific states of which knowing is the genus.

that 'knows' does not admit of analysis, and that instead its semantic role is simply to denote an attitude.[34] His insinuation, albeit only that, is that 'knows' is just as one would expect it to be, if it is introduced into the language by training on samples of the simple factive state of knowing. Thus his metaphysical thesis KMS, and his account of the concept 'knows', hang together, and are mutually supportive. In short: a pair of complementary conjectures are offered to us by Williamson—KMS, and the thin FMSO account of 'knows'. Moreover, this pair is together offered, in the persuasive case developed in *KAIL*, chapters 1 and 2, as the best and correct explanation of the alleged datum of NASK. The failure of attempts to find a hybrid analysis of 'knows' is just what one would expect, if the true situation is as Williamson suggests: knowing is a simple factive mental state 'whose essence involves the world', and 'knows' is introduced by training on samples of this state.[35]

But even if it is accepted that 'knows' has no hybrid analysis, Williamson's thin FMSO account of 'knows' is not the only game left in town. There are other candidate accounts of 'knows', bringing with them their own, different, and competing explanation of why it does not admit of a standard analysis. Williamson's FMSO account being thin, these alternatives could well incorporate the short list of relatively uncontroversial semantic features of 'knows' in the FMSO account, but differ from it in saying more. Crucially for our current concern, they may also differ in suggesting a different accompanying metaphysic. Two such NASK-compatible accounts of 'knows' I will now mention sit naturally with the view that instances of knowing are hybrid.

First, a plausible account of 'knows' entailing NASK, and explaining it, is that it is a 'family resemblance' concept. That is to say, it has implicit semantic complexity, in the sense that its users' skill in recognizing instances is mediated by sensitivity to critical features, which are, with enough reflection, articulable by the user herself—and might be cited to justify her application of the concept. But the critical features to which users are, constitutively, sensitive in particular cases cannot be set out in an exceptionless necessary and sufficient condition, recognizable a priori as correct, because this semantic complexity tacitly grasped by them is open-ended, perhaps also potentially inconsistent, in a way that resists such neat capture. This family-resemblance-concept (FRC) hypothesis about 'knows' entails NASK, but fits with treating particular states of knowing

---

[34] *KAIL* 36 asserts that 'knows' is 'semantically unanalysable', thereby contrasting with 'a semantically analysable expression [that] has a more complex role than that of simply denoting an attitude'—by implication, this last is a correct characterization of 'knows' and other FMSOs.

[35] Cf. *KAIL* 50–1: 'We may assume that all attempts so far to carry out the reductionist programme for knowledge have failed. That suggests that it is misconceived . . . A conception of knowing that is thoroughly externalist . . . will dispense with the programme. On such a conception . . . knowing is not a metaphysical hybrid, because it cannot be broken down into such elements.'

as 'metaphysically hybrid'. This is so since, on the FRC view of 'knows', in each case in which 'knows' is rightly applied, this will be in recognition of knowledge-making features of that situation; though there is no general set of such features whose presence is necessary and sufficient for all cases of knowing.

Secondly, 'knows' would exhibit supervenience on knowing-making features in each instance, while resisting a general reduction, if it were primarily an evaluative concept—supervenience without reduction being a typical and symptomatic feature of evaluative concepts. Again, this would be an account of 'knows' that entails NASK, and is entirely compatible with the view that instances of knowing are hybrid: constituted by belief that meets certain further conditions rendering it worthy of the accolade 'knowledge'. Moreover, that 'knows' is primarily evaluative is a view with considerable plausibility: to describe someone as knowing something is to give an epistemic thumbs-up to her belief, allowing that she indeed has the right to be sure of it; first-person claims to know very clearly do this.[36]

It is beyond the scope of this discussion fully to develop and defend either of these two suggestions about 'knows' and knowing. Their dialectical purpose in this discussion is served by citing their existence, and the fact that each has some prima facie plausibility.[37] This being so, Williamson's offered package of KMS and the FMSO account of 'knows' is not the only candidate explanation for NASK; there are at least these two other possible accounts of 'knows', which go with the view that instances of knowing are a hybrid complex, not a simple factive state. If, as I have claimed, at least one of these non-metaphysically radical alternative packages has significant prima facie plausibility, then not only does NASK not entail KMS; it is not even significant evidence in favour of it.[38]

Thus far, then, in our reconstruction of the case for KMS, Williamson's KMS-plus-FMSO package is just one of several possible explanatory packages for the supposed datum of NASK. Is it nonetheless the best package? My final claim in this section is that it is not so, since it does badly with regard to an important desideratum concerning which the FRC and evaluative-concept conjectures about 'knows' both do well: ability to explain the existence of various necessary conditions for knowing.

---

[36] A sufficient reason why no simple reductive account in these terms can be given—knowledge as belief of which one is properly sure—is that it does not incorporate the factive aspect of knowing. It is beyond the scope of this discussion to develop and defend an alternative account of 'knows'; however, I observe that one central difficulty with 'knows', as with other Weakly mental concepts, is to give an account that adequately covers both the first- and the third-person usage of it. Perhaps pinpointing this source of the difficulty is the clue to finding a correct account.

[37] To refute KMS would require demonstrating some non-metaphysically radical account of 'knows' and knowing to be correct; here I am content with the more modest goal of showing KMS not proven, and, with serious obstacles to its acceptance, the balance of the case remaining against it.

[38] The FRC and evaluative accounts of 'knows' are not sharply distinct: various necessary conditions for knowing will be part of the FRC account; these can be seen as entrenched theory about what is needed for a belief to be worthy of the title 'knowledge'. Thus these two accounts are not mutually exclusive.

   Williamson acknowledges that there are various necessary conditions for knowing. These are a priori-ish: if not strictly a priori, then at least very well entrenched (for convenience, I will refer to them as a priori, without the qualification.) Amongst these Williamson himself admits (and invokes in his arguments in *KAIL*, §2.4, for the superior explanatory power of knowing over states falling short of it!) all these: if one knows that P, then one believes that P (*KAIL*, §1.5); one's belief is true (*KAIL*, §1.4; p. 60); it is justified (*KAIL* 57); it is not based on other false beliefs (*KAIL* 62; there are no misleading defeaters (*KAIL* 63). Williamson tells us that the fact that a concept has a priori necessary conditions does not guarantee that these can be supplemented to yield a condition that is necessary and sufficient, and cites as an example where this fails: being coloured/being red (*KAIL* 32). But this example does not provide any insight into why, in the rather different case of knowing, these a priori necessary conditions exist, if not because of implicit semantic complexity in 'knows'. Williamson further suggests that one condition may be a priori necessary for another, not because appreciation of this is involved in grasp of either of those concepts; rather, it may be that two concepts are such that, though learned independently of any linkage between them, once mastered 'the area demarcated by one concept might be so safely within the area demarcated by the other that one could know by a priori reflection that the former is sufficient for the latter' (*KAIL* 44).[39] This bold new assertion of the possibility of synthetic a priori truth is intriguing, but without further exploration it remains the case that the existence of various a priori necessary conditions for knowing strongly suggests that 'knows' either is analysable, or has some other kind of semantic complexity. The default hypothesis is that these conditions are knowable by us to be necessary for knowing just through reflection, because our tacit grasp of them mediates our everyday applications of the concept—either as elements in a family resemblance concept, or as deeply entrenched folk theory about what is necessary for the 'right to be sure'.

   Williamson acknowledges the need to explain why justification and reliability are so important for knowing (*KAIL* 41). He gestures at the possibility of doing so in terms of the metaphysics of states, suggesting that it may be essential to a state of knowing that it be entered in a certain way (*KAIL* 41). I am sceptical that there is a genuinely different explanation to be had here, in place of my preferred one in terms of implicit semantic complexity. Why should it be that a state of knowing must have a certain history, if not because our concept includes in it that, say, justification is required for knowledge? I do not believe there is

---

[39] Actually—see my concluding section—Williamson is sailing dangerously close to the wind here. If it is true that the concepts of belief, and of knowing, are learned separately, but—as Williamson suggests (*KAIL* 44)—it is then just obvious that belief is necessary for knowing, the explanation is surely because it is just obvious that belief is the principal mental component of knowing—as Williamson's own suggestions about belief—that (confident) belief is indiscriminable 'from the inside' from, and psycho-functionally very similar to, knowing, suggest (*KAIL* 46, 47).

a coherent account of the source of these supposed essential features of states other than explaining them as conceptual in origin. Recasting epistemology in terms of the metaphysics of mental states either is just a notational variant on the traditional analytic method, or is deeply misconceived.

Williamson's claim that our everyday concept 'knows' does not admit of an analysis that reveals states of knowing as hybrid would be disputed by many. While supposing NASK true, I have highlighted the gap between this supposed datum, and the stronger thesis that 'knows' has no implicit semantic complexity beyond the two characteristic inferences posited in Williamson's thin FMSO account. In maintaining that 'knows' is exhaustively described by the thin FMSO account, and that its role is simply to denote the simple factive attitude of knowing, Williamson has a good deal of explaining away to do. He must explain away the many a priori necessary conditions for knowing.[40] And there is a further phenomenon he must explain away: the undeniable illumination that the near-misses (if so they be) in the recent attempts at analysing knowledge have provided. If the concept is really semantically so simple, how is it that explications of 'knows' in terms of justifiedness, or alternatively reliability, have hit on something that resonates as correct with ordinary language-users, as bringing out something they implicitly grasp as involved in knowledge? These data about tacitly grasped necessary conditions support the family-resemblance or evaluative-concept hypothesis about 'knows', over against Williamson's proposed thin FMSO account.

KMS entails NASK: the production of a clearly correct 'hybrid' necessary and sufficient condition for knowing would refute both Williamson's conceptual thesis about 'knows' and his metaphysical thesis about knowing. But the converse implication fails. NASK does not entail KMS; rather, KMS-plus-the-thin-FMSO-account (KMS/FMSO) is offered by Williamson as the best and correct explanation of NASK. However, in this section we have seen that KMS/FMSO is only one of several alternative competing explanatory packages—accounts of 'knows' and knowing—each of which, if correct, would explain NASK. We saw that there are other prima facie plausible explanatory packages that are metaphysically non-radical; that is to say, there are other prima facie plausible accounts of 'knows' that go with the view that instances of knowing are a hybrid complex. They fit with the thesis of Compound Instances, which, in the previous section, we identified as something Williamson must deny, if KMS is indeed the metaphysical surprise he advertises it to be. We saw also that these metaphysically

---

[40] As remarked, Williamson appeals to a number of the generally accepted necessary conditions for knowing—no misleading defeaters, etc.—in his argument in *KAIL*, §2.4, for the explanatory superiority of knowing over believing, or even believing justifiedly. In other chapters of *KAIL* the necessity of reliability for knowing is a central plank in various arguments. There is surely a tension between this method, and his main claim KMS. Are all these conditions really 'manifestly included' in knowing, despite not being built into our concept of it—and despite the supposed simplicity of the state of knowing?

non-radical conjectures about 'knows' and knowing are better explainers of the data about 'knows' than KMS/FMSO, since they explain better the various acknowledged a priori necessary conditions for knowing.

All this being so, we may conclude that the supposed truth of NASK is in itself no evidence at all for the truth of KMS/FMSO. However, if Williamson provides strong independent arguments for the truth of KMS, unconnected with the supposed datum of NASK, this would provide reason to accept both NASK, and KMS/FMSO, as the correct explanation of NASK, rather than some non-metaphysically radical account of 'knows' and knowing.

So Williamson cannot use the supposed fact of NASK to argue for KMS. A convincing positive case for KMS from other considerations needs to be made.[41] We earlier determined that a state is mental in the fullest sense just if it satisfies all the marks of the mental; and is mental in a weaker sense if it satisfies some of them. Having identified privileged access (M1), and causal-explanatory role as part of folk psychology in relation to action (M2) as undoubted marks of the mental, we conceded to Williamson that knowing satisfies these, and so qualifies as Weakly mental. Whether it counts as fully—that is, Purely rather than Impurely—mental turns on whether it also satisfies M4. If Internalism (M3) is maintained, then no factive state can do so. We remarked earlier that Williamson's aim is to make M3 look less and less attractive, as a necessary condition for full mentalness, by mounting a persuasive cumulative case that various states—including knowing and other factive attitudes—satisfy all other marks of the mental; thus, as he avers, continuing to insist on M3 is revealed as an unmotivated dogma that should be dropped.[42]

In this discussion I have deliberately set aside Internalism (M3) as a mark of the mental. The issue of the Weaker Thesis I seek to address is effectively this: if M3 has been abandoned, are there then any good reasons left to deny that knowing satisfies M4? In particular, since we have accepted that knowing satisfies M1 and M2, and thereby qualifies as Weakly mental, we have a Key Question: *is there ever any good reason to hold that a Weakly mental state is*

---

[41] In this discussion I have accepted for dialectical purposes that NASK holds. Taking back that temporary assumption, we can describe the overall evidential/dialectic relation between NASK and KMS thus: as just noted, if there were a strong independent case for KMS, this would establish NASK. Equally, if NASK were independently established, this would be weak evidence in favour of NASK. Thus any evidence for either can be part of a persuasive overall package establishing both. However, what must be guarded against in this situation of mutual reinforcement is double-counting. In his original article (Williamson 1995) the structure of the overall case is not made very clear; and there is a danger the reader may be bamboozled—it is illegitimately circular simultaneously to cite NASK as establishing KMS, and KMS as establishing NASK; but the perceived strength of Williamson's case for his package diminishes as one removes all such double-counting from the evidence.

[42] Vide quotes in nn. 5 and 11 above.

nonetheless only Impurely mental? To say a state is Impurely mental is to say that: it is available to non-inferential first-person ascription, and it explains action within folk psychology; yet its instances are compound—a combination of a Purely mental state with an environmental condition. The nub of Williamson's case for KMS, as I understand it, is to answer 'No' to this Key Question—if M3 has been already abandoned, there is no good reason left to insist, despite its satisfying M1 and M2, that knowing is only Impurely mental, having compound instances.

It is consistent with a state being Weakly mental that it have a hybrid general essence. If NASK were false, knowing having a hybrid a priori necessary and sufficient condition, then, despite satisfying M1 and M2, it would be revealed to be hybrid, as such only Impurely mental. On the other side, as Williamson points out, if NASK holds, then those who insist that, despite satisfying M1 and M2, knowing is hybrid, have a task: to display, or at least make a good case for the existence of, the Purely mental components of each instance of knowing.[43]

We have seen that NASK is not in itself evidence for KMS, so that an independent case must be made for KMS. Williamson's offered case, as I understand *KAIL*, chapters 1 and 2, is:

1. knowing satisfies M1 and M2, and so is Weakly mental;
2. (Weaker Thesis) M3 having been abandoned, there is no good reason to insist that a state, even a factive one, which is thus Weakly mental is nonetheless Impurely mental;

and, moreover, Williamson claims,

3. the attempt by the opponent of KMS to produce the needed mental fillets of (each instance of)[44] the supposedly Impurely mental state of knowing is a failure.

If 1–3 were all true, Williamson would indeed have made a strong case for KMS. In my last section I will contest both 2 and 3. In addition, I will start by arguing that the fact that knowing satisfies M1 and M2—is Weakly mental—is no evidence at all for its being Purely mental, this being a further, independent matter.

---

[43] Similarly, the Internalist about the mental, conceding that content ascriptions in natural language are broad, perforce 'insists that they fail to reflect the structure of the underlying facts. On this view, such ascriptions characterize the subject by reference to a mixture of genuinely mental states and conditions on the external environment. The challenge . . . is to make good this claim by isolating a level of description of contentful attitudes that is both narrow and genuinely mental . . .' (*KAIL* 54).

[44] The opponent of KMS who has conceded NASK might either seek to show that knowing has an a posteriori general essence, or, more weakly, that each instance is a hybrid complex. I think the first is implausible—'knows' does not seem to be a natural kind concept—and do not pursue this in what follows.

4. EXTERNALISM ABOUT CONTENT WITH HYBRIDISM ABOUT FACTIVE ATTITUDES: A STABLE INTERMEDIATE POSITION

I have observed that Williamson seeks to make a cumulative persuasive case for KMS—that is, the claim that knowing is a Purely mental state. But is there such a case to be made? As I understand it, the implicit argument of IKASOM runs thus: 'Since "knows" is semantically unanalysable, and knowing exhibits M1 and M2, there is no good reason not to take ordinary language at face value, and accept knowing as a factive Purely mental state, satisfying M4 also; no good reason to go on insisting that knowing is and must be metaphysically hybrid.' Thus, the way that discussion of M1 and M2 features in Williamson's case for KMS is this: by arguing that knowing satisfies M1 and M2, Williamson seeks to mount a persuasive case that M3 should be dropped, and to undermine prejudices about the mental that generate the idea that knowing must be metaphysically hybrid. This opens the way to accepting that knowing satisfies M4, and knowing is a mental state in the fullest sense—it is Purely mental. So, although M4 is logically independent of M1 and M2, it is dialectically dependent on them, in Williamson's argumentation.

But is it true, as this persuasive case requires, that the fact that a type of state satisfies M1 and M2 is evidence that it also satisfies M4 (is Purely mental, not having hybrid instances)? I do not see that it is. First, there is no necessitation from a state's satisfying M1 and M2, to its being Purely mental. It would take too much space to explore fully the link between privileged access, and Pure/Impure mentalness, but, given that the privileged access requirement posited in M1 is not perfect transparency,[45] but a weaker non-inferential access property, there is no evident reason why a hybrid state could not exhibit it—if broadness is not a barrier to M1, why should hybridness be one?

Equally, there is no necessitation from M2 to M4. Williamson (*KAIL*, §§3.4–6) develops a precise account of what it is for a state-type S1 to pull its explanatory weight, in terms of the correlation coefficient between it, and the outcome S2 to be explained—the higher the correlation coefficient (or, more or less equivalently, the conditional probability of S2 on S1), the better an explainer of S2 is S1. It is in these terms that he convincingly argues that a person's

---

[45] This weakening—which I accept—is an essential part of Williamson's argument that a broad state can satisfy M1. In an earlier draft I suggested that M1 presents a problem for KMS. I no longer want to press this point; not because I think there are no differences regarding special access between factive versus non-factive attitudes; but because special access seems more generally to come in degrees for different, non-controversially mental states (cf. n. 12 above), and as such is not the main difficulty for KMS.

knowledge of a fact is sometimes a better explainer of his or her action than his or her mere belief, true belief, or even justified true belief (*KAIL*, §2.4).

So: what does the fact that knowing is a good explainer of action in its own right tell us about M4? Not much, actually. There is absolutely no tension between knowing's being a good explanatory state, and each instance of knowing being a conjunctive, hybrid phenomenon. Consider, for instance, this conjunctive property: being-suicidally-depressed-AND-having-to-hand-a-bottle-of-tablets-such-that-an-overdose-would-kill-one. This predicate may be a good explainer of suicide attempts by overdose, and a far better explainer of such suicide attempts than either conjunct taken on its own. (It will be, if someone who is suicidally depressed lacks the initiative to search for tablets.) Whether or not this example is empirically plausible, the general point is clear: a conjunctive phenomenon may be nearly sufficient for the occurrence of a certain type of event, while neither conjunct is anywhere near to being sufficient for it. Given this, and if the conjunctive phenomenon occurs frequently, we may gain some economy of notation by having a single predicate picking out this conjunctive phenomenon, and used to give such explanations. Thus, if someone's being in a certain mental state, together with her environment's being a certain way, is nearly sufficient for her to do a certain action, and if her environment is usually that way; then a 'wide' predicate applying just if both the mental and the environmental condition hold will be a useful explainer. But the 'general state' pleonastically associated with this predicate is at most Impurely mental. (No one would be tempted to say that the hybrid condition in my example is a Purely mental state!)[46]

So a state's satisfying M1 and M2 is consistent with it being hybrid, either a general hybrid essence, or hybrid instances. Is satisfying M1 and M2 nonetheless evidence for satisfying M4—does it persuade for M4, though not entailing it? Suppose one is trying to tell whether someone has a certain illness, where this requires detecting the presence of a certain virus. There are various typical and distinctive symptoms, effects caused by the virus. Then if a patient exhibits some of the distinctive symptoms, this is evidence that she has the virus, and so will also have the other symptoms. But the various marks of the mental are not symptoms of a single underlying phenomenon. That a state satisfies M1 and M2

---

[46] It might be objected against this example that my phenomenon has a hybrid general essence, which knowing does not. Actually, the brilliant discussion of 'prime' conditions in *KAIL*, ch. 3 amounts to a demonstration of how easily it can come about that a state whose instances are all hybrid can nonetheless fail to have a conjunctive hybrid essence (although it should also be noted that adding a third component, a causal (say) relation between internal and external might do the trick). This being so, *KAIL*, chs. 1–3, in fact provides a good case for the thesis—in itself substantial, interesting, and novel—that there are Impurely mental predicates, of which 'knows' is one, which are indeed genuinely mental in a 'relaxed' but significant sense (satisfying M1 and M2), but whose realizing instances are hybrid: there is in each instance a component mental state, which constitutes the broad Impure state in virtue of a certain extra-mental condition holding. But Williamson wants more than this: see *KAIL* 6, quoted above, n. 23.

is not evidence of some underlying nature that makes it probable that it also satisfies M4.

On the contrary, our previous discussion has made it look plausible that, amongst mental states, there are some Purely mental ones—the core of mentality; and others that qualify as Weakly mental, but are Impurely so—those whose instances are hybrid, but are reliably available to non-inferential access, and have a proper explanatory role regarding action *in the context of the type of environment that their subject usually inhabits.*[47] If this is right, then satisfying M1 and M2 but being Impurely mental describes a class of mental state types, and there is no evidential link from a state's satisfying M1 and M2, to its being Purely mental (M4). I conclude that, insofar as Williamson's case for knowing being Purely mental trades on this supposed evidential link, it is fallacious.

Though this suggestion is a part of Williamson's case, it is by no means all of it, however. Satisfying M1 and M2 makes knowing Weakly mental. We have just seen that this fact is neutral regarding M4—so far as being Weakly mental goes, this is equally consistent with being either Purely or Impurely mental. The rest of Williamson's case, as I understand it, involves two claims. First, we have the Weaker Thesis—that if externalism about content has been accepted, there is then no good reason left to resist extending externalism to accept also Purely mental factive attitudes.[48] WT (plus the rejection of internalism) opens the way to accepting that the Weakly mental state of knowing is also Purely mental. Secondly, Williamson claims that ordinary language favours the view that knowing (along with other more specific factive attitudes such as perceiving that P) is Purely mental—since, he claims, 'knows' is correctly described by his thin FMSO account, so that to take it at face value is to take it to denote the simple factive state of knowing. Knowing, he urges, is, as our language presents it, a simple factive mental state whose 'essence involves the world'; the insistence that, despite this linguistic cloak of simplicity, it is and must be hybrid, and the consequent (unsuccessful) search for the presumed components of the hybrid state of knowing, or at least of each instance of it, is an unmotivated metaphysical prejudice.

In the rest of this discussion I will first examine WT, and argue that it is a substantial thesis. Then, to see whether WT is nonetheless true, I will first consider and reject Williamson's claim that ordinary language unambiguously favours the view that knowing is simple. Finally, I will discuss whether the required Purely

---

[47] Why is this remark not an argument for Internalism about the Purely mental? Because—as will appear shortly—cooperation in some fundamental respects from one's environment is required for a potentially minded creature to have a mind, that is to enjoy states with objective content, at all. Slice off too much of the usual environment, and you slice off the content with it. But, as I maintain below, this is not true if one slices off the fact from a factive attitude. Hence one can analyse factive attitudes as having hybrid instances that have a still *recognizably mental* Pure component.

[48] WT amounts to a conditional: if externalism about content should be accepted, then factive attitudes as Purely mental should be accepted. Williamson's stronger thesis, which summarizes his whole case for KMS, is WT plus assertion of its antecedent.

mental fillets of knowing, or at least of each instance of knowing, can be found. My overall conclusion is that, *pace* Williamson, externalism about content combined with hybridism about factive attitudes is a dialectically stable position; and remains the best motivated one notwithstanding all Williamson's arguments.

Regarding the Weaker Thesis, we first observe that it is not trivially true.[49] Certainly, an externalist about content cannot consistently hold that the 'broadness' of knowing and other factive states *ipso facto* shows them not to be Purely mental—that would be to assert internalism (M3), which is precisely what she has already relinquished. But this fact does not entail the Weaker Thesis (WT). Far from being trivial, I propose that: *WT will hold just if all the various arguments against internalism (and for externalism) regarding contents have equally sound analogues regarding factive attitudes.*[50] This latter is a substantial proposition. To see whether it is correct we need to look back at what the arguments are, which (in my own view) force the acceptance of externalism about content, to check whether they indeed have analogues that go through for factive attitudes. I will argue that they do not, and WT is false. First, to confirm its non-triviality, I briefly state and reject a shorter argument for WT.

Williamson's suggestion seems to be that, once one has taken one dose of externalism, as it were, one can have no grounds for qualms about accepting another. Here is one argument that has this consequence:

> The crucial proposition accepted by an externalist about content is that 'mental states have constitutive dependence on the environment'. Once this proposition has been accepted, it has been so across the board, for all forms of such dependence. So someone who accepts externalism about content cannot consistently find the proposal that there are Purely mental factive attitudes counterintuitive.

This argument is unsound, because it misidentifies the proposition crucially involved in accepting externalism about content. One is impelled to accepting externalism about content through accepting a specific proposition: that the content of a mental state is typically fixed by certain of its causal-cum-contextual relations to what it is about.[51] (This means there is no content independently

---

[49] WT appears simply to be asserted in *KAIL*, rather than announced as the conclusion of an argument. However, it may be that Williamson's intention is to assert WT in the light of his examination of various respects in which, as he has argued, arguments for externalism about content can be run also for factive attitudes—he does give such arguments, as we have seen, regarding explanation of action, and regarding support from ordinary language. If this is his dialectical intention, it conforms with the test for WT proposed here. (Though I disagree over the result of applying this test!)

[50] Cf. Williamson's suggestion that: '[in response to [the internalist] challenge] . . . one overall argumentative strategy is to show that objections to the involvement of factive attitudes in genuine mental states are sound only if corresponding objections to the involvement of wide contents in genuine mental states are also sound' (*KAIL* 51). Showing this is showing that WT holds.

[51] The less specific proposition is covertly existential: 'There is some manner in which some mental states depend constitutively on the environment.' Thus of course the externalist about

of such relations; which is why, as will be discussed shortly, there are no narrow mental fillets of broad contents.) There are positive reasons to think that mental content is fixed in part by crucial relations between a person and the referents of some of her content-bearing states—by a broad 'conceptual role' that extends into the thinker's environment.[52] But the fact that content is fixed partly by certain causal-cum-contextual relations, so that mental content is 'broad', does not entail, nor even suggest, that there are other ways in which mental states are environmentally dependent. That is a new and independent proposition. WT is not a trivial truth. This being so, an externalist about content is perfectly entitled to find KMS and its like counter-intuitive, and to seek to resist it.

Is WT nonetheless true? Do all the sound arguments that favour or force externalism about mental content have equally sound analogues regarding factive attitudes? One argument, which is a key part of Williamson's case, is the claim already mentioned, that ordinary language favours the view that knowing is Purely mental. (I will not review the position on this matter regarding content, except to say that it is widely accepted that ordinary language truth-conditions of many propositional attitudes are broad.[53]) Is this so? In Section 3 we saw that, if, contra NASK, 'knows' had an a priori necessary and sufficient condition, then it would be a datum that knowing is hybrid. In the absence of such, there is no unambiguous datum: both the correct semantic account of 'knows', and of the nature of states of knowing, is game for philosophical theorizing and argument. Williamson offers his thin FMSO account of 'knows', and claims that ordinary language favours his thesis that states of knowing are simple, not hybrid. It is true that, with no hybrid necessary and sufficient condition for knowing to hand, the thesis that states of knowing are nonetheless hybrid (either a general hybrid essence, or at least each instance is hybrid) has the status of a philosophical theory or conjecture, not a fact. To be confirmed, this conjecture must be made good by producing, or anyway providing a convincing argument for the existence of, the needed hybrid general essence; or, if it is conceded to Williamson that there is no hybrid general essence, then an argument that each instance of knowing is hybrid. (We return to this point in a moment.) Notwithstanding this, ordinary language does not unambiguously favour Williamson's claim that states of knowing are simple, because, as we saw in Section 3, it is by no means a datum that his thin FMSO account of 'knows' is correct. On the contrary, the uncontroversial fact that there are several a priori necessary conditions for knowing counts against his thin account of 'knows', and in favour of accounts of its semantics that favour the view that instances of knowing are hybrid. I

content accepts it also, since it is entailed by the more specific one. She is not thereby committed to believing in other forms of constitutive dependence on the environment.

[52] This is not the place to sketch a theory of content. Recent landmarks in the vast literature on this subject include Peacocke (1992) and Fodor (1998b).

[53] Classic statements include Putnam (1975) and Burge (1979, 1986). See also Woodfield (1982) and Pettit and McDowell (1986).

conclude that, on the matter of whether ordinary language supports externalism, there is not a clearly sound argument supporting externalism about knowing and other factive states—what the correct account of 'knows' is is not a datum, but is up for theoretical kidnapping, like almost all the key questions in this vexed topic.[54] More strongly, I repeat the conclusion from Section 3 that ordinary language, if anything, supports the view that states of knowing are hybrid, since accounts of 'knows' that favour this view of the metaphysics of knowing do better than the thin FMSO account at explaining why there are various a priori necessary conditions for knowing.

Notwithstanding this, Williamson is entirely right that, given that knowing is agreed to be Weakly mental, then, without a correct necessary and sufficient condition for knowing to hand, the burden of proof is on the proponents of hybridness to argue for the existence of the mental fillets of knowing that must exist—as a general essence of knowing, or at least for each complex instance—if their denial of KMS is correct. It is to this last, crucial matter for our target question of whether or not knowing satisfies M4, and is 'mental in every reasonable sense of the term' as Williamson would have us accept—that we finally turn.

I think that externalism about the mental is counter-intuitive, and that we should buy into it no further than we are forced to. Externalism about mental content is counter-intuitive, because we think of a person's mental states as states of her; thus discovering a covert relationality in the fixation of their content is surprising. Externalism about factive attitudes would be even more so—since when someone knows (or remembers, or perceives) a fact, what is known, and the mental representation of it involved in the knowing, seem to non-philosophically primed common sense clearly to be distinct existences.[55]

In the case of externalism about mental content, we are (in my view) forced to accept the counter-intuitive thesis, because there is a compelling argument for it. (Here is the disanalogy with the case for externalism about factive attitudes, which renders WT false.) We observed that ordinary language individuates many contents broadly. This being so, the proponent of internalism about content has a task: to display the narrow fillets of mental content that must exist, if her internalism is to be vindicated, despite this broadness of OL contents. In my view internalism about content founders on this requirement.

---

[54] At the risk of being a bore, I recapitulate the point that, even if Williamson's thin FMSO account of 'knows' were correct, this would not settle the question whether states of knowing are simple in favour of Williamson, since 'a simple concept may be introduced by means of complex exemplars'.

[55] One implication of the present discussion is that the final judgement on KMS will turn, inter alia, on the stance taken on large general issues in metaphysics about the nature of properties and states. It would extend an already long discussion too far, to probe more deeply the question of why externalism is counter-intuitive, as it surely is.

Its proponents postulate narrow conceptual roles, or intrinsic phenomenology, as these components. But, despite their efforts, narrow components of mental contents *which are themselves recognisably mental* have not been produced.[56] Content involves carrying information, and information depends on place in a functioning system. One result is that there is a covert relationality in the fixation of mental content: intrinsic phenomenology is not sufficient for it; a creature must be embedded in an environment by the right kind of causal and nomological links. Thus externalism about content is not in the end so surprising and counter-intuitive: without some degree of cooperation from her usual environment, a creature cannot enjoy states with objective content at all.

Since—as just suggested—broad mental contents lack Purely mental narrow fillets, these broad states are nonetheless Purely mental. Knowing would be equally so, if states of knowing lacked a Purely mental non-factive fillet. This is the surprising claim that Williamson seeks to persuade us of. We have agreed with Williamson that, assuming NASK correct, the burden of proof is on the denier of KMS to show that such non-factive mental fillets of knowing exist. Unlike the situation regarding narrow fillets of content, I believe this can be done. (Thus WT is false: the argument that forces acceptance of externalism about content lacks a sound analogue for externalism about factive attitudes including knowing.)

It is consistent with NASK that there exists a mental condition that is necessary for knowing, and that is sufficient on the mental side for knowing—that is such that 'knowing adds nothing mental to it' (*KAIL* 56). Displaying a clearly correct such condition would show that each instance of knowing has a Purely mental component, and refute KMS. (Such a condition sufficient on the mental side for knowing might exist, consistently with NASK, if just the non-mental constituents in knowing resist advance general statement. This would be so, for instance, if 'knows' were evaluative, but it was clear in advance—a piece of platitudinous theory about knowing—that justified belief is the sole mental ingredient of the right to be sure.)

So to refute KMS it suffices to show that there is mental condition Mk such that, for every possible situation S(Mk − K) in which Mk holds which is not a case of knowing, there is a possible situation S(Mk + K) in which Mk holds and which is a case of knowing, such that the difference between S(Mk − K) and S(Mk + K) consists exclusively in non-mental factors.[57]

[56] That is to say, the proposed states do not satisfy M1 or M2. For reasons of space I just state my own view here, without defence. If I were wrong, this would not favour KMS; nor would it mean that WT holds, if this is read as saying that there are arguments for externalism that work, in each case. The literature on this large issue is huge. See in particular the editors' introduction to Pettit and McDowell (1986).

[57] This condition sufficient on the mental side for knowing would be, in each case of knowing, the mental component of that instance. Instances of knowing could be hybrid, even if no such *general* condition sufficient on the mental side for knowing can be stated. But the insistence that instances of knowing are hybrid would, as Williamson claims, begin to look strained and dogmatic, if no such general condition can be formulated.

Whether such a general condition exhausting the mental component in knowing can be formulated is thus an absolutely crucial question in the case for KMS. It is discussed in *KAIL*, §2.3, but the issue is misleadingly billed as an issue for the Internalist. (The Internalist is, of course, committed to the existence of a Purely mental fillet of each instance of knowing; but so, equally, is the Externalist about content who nonetheless wants to resist KMS. However the general Internalist is committed to this fillet being a 'narrow' state; the content-Externalist resister of KMS can allow the mental constituent of knowing to be a broad, but non-factive, Purely mental state.) We can quickly agree with Williamson that an irrationally held belief could not be knowledge, whatever the environment, and the candidate mental component of knowing is: believing rationally or justifiedly (*KAIL* 57).[58] If justified belief is the mental component of knowing, then this condition holds:

(J) For any possible situation S(JB − K) of justified belief which is not an instance of knowing, there is a possible situation S(JB + K) which is an instance of knowing, where S(JB − K) and S(JB + K) differ only in non-mental factors.

Apart from two special cases (*KAIL* 56)—belief in a necessarily false proposition, and belief about some aspect of one's own mental state—where (J) fails, but which we surely need not worry about, since they are clearly special, Williamson's case against justified belief being the mental component of knowing for which (J) holds is confined to the claim that there are 'notorious difficulties in stating a correct justification condition on knowledge' (*KAIL* 57). But this is surely not enough to win over opponents, on this crunch issue for KMS. Moreover, the fact, acknowledged by Williamson, that belief and justification are a priori necessary conditions for knowing tells in favour of (J), and against KMS. The case made for KMS in *KAIL* from direct, potentially conclusive arguments against states of knowing being hybrid is not proven.

The fact that belief and justification are a priori necessary conditions for knowing, and that there are no other mental a priori necessary conditions for knowing, indeed makes it look very much as if these two together encapsulate all that is needed on the mental side for knowing. Williamson (*KAIL*, §1.5) concludes, after some discussion, that belief is very likely a necessary condition for knowing, and spends some time on explaining how this is so, consistently with KMS. However, there seems to me to be tension between some things he says here, and KMS. Williamson would be on safe ground in his claim that

---

[58] My own view is that justified belief is the mental fillet of knowing, but, while Purely mental, it is not a narrow mental state: being justified is itself a 'broad' (but not factive) Purely mental condition, not one that supervenes on one's physical state. That is another story, not told here. Crucially, I do not accept Williamson's own view that what it is for a belief to be justified itself has to be explained in terms of knowledge—belief is justified, according to Williamson, when it is supported by what one knows. I think one can give an independent, mentalistic (though not narrow) account of justifiedness of belief.

belief is necessary for knowing, yet is not in any interesting sense a component of knowing—is not the key mental part of hybrid instances of knowing—if he espoused a disjunctive account of believing. That is to say, if he maintained that 'believes' does not pick out a real mental kind, but has as its reference a disjunctive state, whose disjuncts are the state of knowing (a real kind), and that of mere opining—this latter covering all and only cases of believing without knowing, and also a real kind. But in a convincing discussion Williamson rejects this view, on the ground that believing-without-knowing is neither a positively specifiable concept, nor one that picks out a real kind. Instead, Williamson offers materials that allow one to give a unified description of the state of believing. He suggests, convincingly, that 'believing P is, roughly, treating P as if one knew P'.[59] If, as seems plausible, one can spell out what it is to do the latter, this will provide an account of belief in terms of its psychological role, which reveals it as a unified functional state. Williamson himself provides one aspect of this role—namely that to treat P as if one knows it is to rely on it in practical reasoning—one might add that it is confidently to tell others that P, vouching to them for its truth; and to regard whether P as settled, not seeking further evidence on the matter.

But if 'believes' is a real unified mental state, and is a priori necessary for knowing, and moreover picks out the psychological role that is what is involved, on the mental side, in knowing—how one 'treats' propositions one takes oneself to know—then we seem to have arrived pretty much at what it is for believing to be the principal mental component of knowing: the main mental component of each instance of knowing, and very plausibly—if (J) above can be vindicated—the main part of a condition sufficient on the mental side for knowing. What I mean by this is that: in each case in which someone knows that P, this fact about her is constituted by her believing that P, and some other conditions also being satisfied, in virtue of which her belief qualifies as knowledge. As we saw in 2, instances of knowing can be thus compound, consistently with 'knows' having no hybrid necessary and sufficient condition. Despite a battery of arguments that are so novel, ingenious, densely argued, and rigorous that they amount to a dazzling display of philosophical brilliance, Williamson in chapters 1 and 2 of *KAIL* provides no conclusive or even very persuasive case against this common-sense view of the metaphysics of knowing and believing.

I conclude that WT is false: the argument that compels Externalism about content lacks a sound analogue extending Externalism to the factive attitude

---

[59] This proposal is convincing as a characterization of certain belief. One flaw throughout Williamson's discussion is that he ignores the fact that our ordinary concept of belief includes both states indiscriminable from the inside from knowing—i.e. fully confident belief, where one takes oneself to know—and also belief that is less certain or confident than knowledge. This is one further reason to doubt that the whole psychological phenomenon of belief can be fully explained, as Williamson suggests, as a 'botched attempt at knowledge'; instead it is a real, independent psychological phenomenon.

of knowing. *Pace* Williamson, a view that combines Externalism about content with the thesis that knowing is an Impurely mental state is a stable, defensible, and, as things currently stand, the best-evidenced view of knowing.[60]

[60] My thanks to Robert Audi, John Hawthorne, Christopher Peacocke, and Stephen Schiffer for detailed comments on earlier drafts; and to commentators from audiences in Senate House, London, in March 2001, and on various occasions in Oxford.

4

The Knowledge Account of Assertion and the Nature of Testimonial Knowledge

Sanford C. Goldberg

1. IN DEFENCE OF A THIRD-PERSON ORIENTATION ON THE NORM OF ASSERTION

Under what conditions is it appropriate to assert that *p*? In his (1996), and more recently in his (2000), Timothy Williamson defends what he calls the knowledge rule of assertion:

(KR) One must: assert *p* only if one knows *p*. (2000: 243)

This account has been roundly criticized by many. Most see it as too demanding, and urge that it be replaced with, for example, one of the following:

(JR) One must: assert *p* only if one is justified in believing that *p*. (Kvanvig 2003, Chapter 9, this volume)

(BKR) One must: assert *p* only if one believes that one knows that *p*. (cf. Adler 1996: 108)

(JKR) One must: assert *p* only if one is justified in believing that one knows that *p*.[1]

In this chapter I will not be revisiting the standard arguments for and against (KR). Rather, I want to examine the utility of (KR) in connection with the role that an account of assertion might play in an attempt to specify the conditions on testimonial knowledge. In particular, I want to examine whether (KR) can be combined with other plausible claims to yield a natural and simple account of these conditions.

There are three reasons why I want to examine this issue.

---

[1] Interestingly, Kvanvig (Chapter 9, this volume) appears to think that (JR), together with internalist conception of justification, implies (JKR).

My first and most general reason is this. Most discussions of the norm of assertion are from within the speaker's point of view: proposals are evaluated in terms of how they bear on a speaker's attempt to conform to the postulated norm. This strikes me as an overly narrow orientation, since the norm of assertion bears not just on speakers, but also on hearers. In particular, hearers take an interest in the propriety of assertions because hearers are the potential consumers of (others') assertions. On this topic we can ask what implications a proposed norm would have, both for the hearer's task of assessing whether a given assertion conforms to the norm, and also for the upshot of a hearer's verdict that an assertion does so conform. This is particularly important with respect to (KR), as our answer to these questions might suggest that (KR) is the basis of a simple and natural account of testimonial knowledge—one on which a hearer's assessment of the propriety of a speaker's assertion plays the major role.

This brings me to a second reason for examining the norm of assertion from the perspective of the link between assertion and testimonial knowledge. Suppose it turns out that (KR) is the basis of a simple and natural account of the conditions on testimonial knowledge. If no other account of these conditions—that is, no account *not* involving (KR)—is as simple and natural, then this might count as offering some independent support for (KR). So an examination of (KR)'s connection to the conditions on testimonial knowledge is an examination of a possible basis of independent support for (KR) itself.

There is a third reason for taking a testimonial-knowledge orientation to evaluating (KR), having to do with the lessons we might learn even if it turns out that (KR) does not yield a simple and natural account of testimonial knowledge. Such a negative result has the potential to tell us something interesting about (KR) specifically, assertion more generally, or even the nature of and conditions on testimonial knowledge. Precisely what lessons we should draw from a negative verdict is something that will have to be established by argument, and I will examine these topics below. My present point is that such topics are naturally generated by taking a third-person approach to assertion's norm(s).

2. (KR) AND THE POSSIBILITY OF A SIMPLE ACCOUNT OF TESTIMONIAL KNOWLEDGE

Consider, then, how it might be thought that (KR) can be combined with other plausible claims to yield a simple and natural account of testimonial knowledge. I should say at the outset, though, that, in developing what I am calling the (KR) account of testimonial knowledge, I am going beyond anything that Williamson himself has said in defence of (KR). Indeed, it may well be that Williamson himself would reject the proposed account. But my purpose is not the exegesis of Williamson, so much as it is exploring the potential uses of (KR)—whether Williamson himself would endorse them or not.

Suppose that (KR) is true. And suppose, too, that hearers can reliably distinguish cases of assertion that conform to (KR) from cases of assertion that do not. Then it would seem that we have a simple account of how hearers' reliance on this discriminatory capacity is used to acquire (testimonial) knowledge through others' assertions. The account might go as follows. Assertions conforming to (KR) are assertions that manifest the speaker's knowledge that p, and hence are (both true and) safe. Consider then a hearer, A, who can reliably distinguish assertions that do conform to (KR) from those who do not. Since assertions conforming to (KR) are (both true and) safe, A's capacity to distinguish assertions conforming to (KR) is *ipso facto* a capacity to distinguish assertions that are (true and) safe. To see how this affects the epistemic status of beliefs formed through the employment of this discriminatory capacity, suppose then that A's discriminatory abilities here are perfect: an assertion observed by A is (true and) safe if and only if A (employing her relevant discriminatory ability) regards it as conforming to (KR). In such a situation, if A regards an assertion as conforming to (KR), then not easily would the assertion have been made under conditions in which it was false. The result is that A's capacity to distinguish assertions that conform to (KR) is itself the basis of a reliable (safe) belief-forming procedure,[2] one that operates as if it embodied the principle to believe all and only those assertions that A regards as conforming to (KR). Of course, to the extent that A's discriminatory capacity is not perfect but rather merely reliable—as in: if A (employing her relevant discriminatory ability) regards an observed assertion as conforming to (KR), then it is very probable (though not guaranteed) that the assertion she observed was (both true and) safe—there will be a corresponding diminution in the safety of the testimonial beliefs she forms through this procedure. For in that case beliefs formed through a reliable (though not infallible) procedure of this sort will have an epistemic status reflecting the following modal property: it is very probable that it could not easily have happened that the observed assertion was made under conditions in which it was false. A's testimonial beliefs would then be reliable (or safe) to the degree that A was reliable in her discriminations of those assertions that conform to (KR).[3] On such an account, testimonial knowledge reflects (i) the *de facto* reliability of our capacity to distinguish normatively acceptable assertions (here conceived as assertions conforming to (KR)), and (ii) our disposition to accept assertions (and to form beliefs in what they assert) only in those cases in which we regard the assertion as normatively acceptable.

Several things are noteworthy about this account.

---

[2] I will be speaking of reliability rather than safety, the species of reliability figuring in Williamson (2000). But all of my claims can be reformulated in terms of the latter notion.

[3] This point suggests that Williamson ought to regard testimonial knowledge as a kind of (interpersonally) iterated knowledge (as in: I know that p in virtue of knowing that your assertion that p was itself knowledgeable). Variants on such a view are developed in Adler (1996) and defended in Sutton (2007). For a discussion of the virtues and drawbacks of such a view, see Goldberg (2007).

First, the proposed account need not assume that the discriminatory capacity in question, or the belief-forming procedure of which it is a part, is one whose workings can be dredged to conscious thought and articulated in the form of explicit reasons. When it comes to our assessment of the relevant properties of assertion, maybe we operate in the same way that the naive chicken-sexer operates regarding the sex of chicks. Or maybe our reliance on this (assertion-directed) discriminatory capacity in the fixation of testimonial belief is analogous to our reliance on perceptual experience in the fixation of perceptual belief: in the latter case, belief is the natural and automatic output of the process, and is interrupted only in those cases in which we take ourselves to have a positive reason to refrain from belief. Admittedly, disputes arise regarding whether such subpersonal reliability in a belief-forming process suffices for knowledge. But we can disregard such disputes here. The present point is only that the foregoing account of testimonial knowledge can be endorsed whether one's background ideology in epistemology is externalist or internalist.[4] (If one is internalist one will add a positive-reasons condition to conditions (i) and (ii) above.)

Secondly, the account in question is both simple and natural. It is simple, in that it traces our capacity for the acquisition of testimonial knowledge to our reliance in belief-fixation on our reliable capacity to discriminate appropriate assertion. And it is natural, in that, at least at first blush, mature hearers do appear to rely on something like this kind of discriminatory capacity. Here the point can be made that hearers typically engage in some rudimentary sort of monitoring for the trustworthiness of observed speech, prior to accepting the say-so in question. Admittedly, this monitoring may be subcognitive, and in any case its implications for the epistemology of testimony may be less clear than many have thought.[5] But the point remains that, prima facie, a case can be made for thinking that hearers do possess (and, for the purposes of testimonial belief-fixation, can be characterized as relying on) something like the discriminatory capacity postulated by the proposed (KR) account.[6]

---

[4] For my purposes here, I will regard an account of knowledge internalist if it regards internalist justification as a necessary condition on knowledge.

[5] For example, Fricker (1994) has argued that the need to monitor for trustworthiness strongly favours reductionist accounts of testimonial justification over their anti-reductionist rivals. (Reductionism is the view, roughly, that one is not justified in accepting the say-so of another unless one has positive reasons to trust that say-so—reasons that themselves do not ultimately rest on other testimony. And anti-reductionism holds, roughly, that one is justified in accepting the say-so of another in the absence of any relevant defeaters.) But it is by no means clear that the appeal to the need to monitor for trustworthiness favours reductionism over anti-reductionism; see Goldberg and Henderson (2006).

[6] This issue is actually significantly more vexed than I am suggesting. What evidence would distinguish the hypothesis that hearers possess the discriminatory capacity postulated by the (KR) account, as against the hypothesis that hearers possess the discriminatory capacity postulated by some non-(KR) account? I will delve into this in Section 3 below, but these issues in the psychology of trust deserve more sustained attention than I will be able to give them here.

Thirdly, it is by no means obvious that there is as simple and natural an account of testimonial knowledge once one surrenders (KR). I will bring the point out in connection with (JR), but the point will be easily generalizable to any other non-(KR) account of assertion. Suppose that (JR) is true. In that case, a hearer's reliable ability to discriminate appropriate from non-appropriate assertions is tantamount to the ability to discriminate reliably those testimony cases involving expressions of justified belief from those that do not involve expressions of justified belief. Arguably, such a capacity would help in the hearer's pursuit of justified belief.[7] But, if the hearer aims at knowledge, it is clear that the capacity to discriminate assertions in conformity with (JR), even in conjunction with a belief-forming process that follows a policy to form belief only in those assertions that are regarded as appropriate, will not yield what is desired. To see this, suppose (with what we might call the (JR)-account) that justified belief is what results from our reliance (in belief-fixation) on our reliable capacity to discriminate appropriate assertion. Even so, since justified belief is not knowledge, the (JR) account will have to postulate something over and above this reliance on our capacity to discriminate appropriate assertion, in order to account for a hearer's acquisition of testimonial knowledge.

Our point is perfectly general. Let *e* be any non-knowledge-entailing epistemic status. On the assumption that *e* is the proper epistemic norm of assertion, the result will be that a hearer's reliance on her capacity to discriminate appropriate assertion will (in the best case) yield belief that has *e*. But then, since a belief's having *e* does not render the belief knowledge (even if the belief is true), the account will have to be supplemented, to make clear the conditions under which a belief that has *e* manages to amount to knowledge. At a minimum, the resulting account of testimonial knowledge will be less simple than the account yielded by (KR) itself.

In sum. What we might call the (KR) account of testimonial knowledge—developed by supplementing (KR) itself with several plausible claims about the belief-forming process implicated in testimony cases—appears to be simpler and more natural than any account that would be generated without (KR). This might be thought to be some independent support for (KR), at least insofar as we consider candidate norms of assertion from the perspective of hearers' consumption (rather than speakers' production) of assertion. In particular, (KR) appears to yield a simple and natural account of *the upshot* of successful consumption.

---

[7] The matter is potentially vexed by the need for an account of how the hearer's determination, that the speaker has expressed what *for the speaker* is a justified belief, bears on the justification of *the hearer's* belief formed through trusting acceptance of the attestation. On some (internalist) views of justification, this will be a vexed matter. In particular, if the justification of a belief is a matter of its rationality within the subject's belief corpus, then the issue is urgent: how does my determining that your belief is rational within your belief corpus affect the rationality within my belief corpus of the belief I form in trusting you (when you give verbal expression to that belief)? Of course, on other, more externalist views of justification, the matter is not as vexed. For a discussion, see Goldberg (2007).

3. TO WHAT FEATURE(S) OF ASSERTION ARE HEARERS SENSITIVE?

The crux of the foregoing (KR) account lies in the claim that hearers reliably discriminate assertions that satisfy (KR) from those that do not. But we might ask: what sort of evidence would confirm the hypothesis that hearers possess this discriminatory capacity, as against the hypothesis that hearers possess the discriminatory capacity postulated by some non-(KR) account?

If we ask this question from the perspective of Williamson's strongly externalist approach to epistemology, one proposal is a non-starter. (For what it is worth, I would say it is a non-starter *regardless* of whether one is externalist or internalist; but I will not pursue this here.) This proposal would pursue this matter by querying *subjects themselves* about how they go about deciding whether to accept an observed assertion. For one thing, it is objectionable to assume that subjects 'decide' such matters. But, even if we waive this first point, a subject's own self-reports are of dubious value in the present context. Given Williamson's safety-based epistemology, the question is whether hearers' testimonial beliefs are safely formed and sustained. The (KR) account of testimonial knowledge proposes to analyse testimonial belief-formation in terms of the hearer's capacity to discriminate testimonies satisfying (KR) from those that do not. What I identified above as the crux of the account concerns a particular discriminative capacity. What matters is how *in point of fact* this capacity functions: to what conditions is it sensitive? Whether the hearer herself knows much about the relevant sensitivities is entirely irrelevant. And, for what it is worth, it would appear that hearers themselves are largely in the dark about the processing involved in their 'decision' to accept or reject observed testimony. This is a point that is accepted even by those who favour a more *internalist* approach to the epistemology of testimony (see, e.g., Fricker 1987: 149–50; 1994: 154). In sum, we should not address the issue, regarding our capacity to discriminate normatively acceptable assertion, by querying hearers themselves.

Rather, it seems best to address the issue by assembling the relevant empirical data. To get data to bear on our issue, we begin with a simplifying assumption. We assume that a hearer *A*'s discriminatory capacities regarding the propriety of assertions are manifested in her actual reactions (as opposed to the way she *thinks* she reacts) to observed assertions. More specifically, the content of our assumption here is this: *A* accepts an assertion if and only if she (implicitly) regards the assertion as meeting the standard or norm for assertion.[8] Then we can

---

[8] I should acknowledge that my assumption here—that we can get at hearers' sensitivity to the propriety of assertions in this way—is a substantive one. To see this we need only note that the present way of enquiring into hearers' sensitivity to the propriety of assertions might well yield a different characterization than what would be yielded by querying them directly. Again, it

get a handle on *A*'s discriminatory capacities regarding the norm of assertion by examining *A*'s consumption patterns, as follows. First, we separate the assertions she observes into those she accepts, those she rejects, and those regarding which she remains neutral.[9] Then we construct the simplest account that would predict her actual consumption pattern. We then regard an empirically adequate account as a proto-theory regarding the feature(s) of assertion to which she is duly sensitive. We need not suppose that *A* herself is aware that she is so sensitive, or that on reflection she would endorse the proposed account of her sensitivity (let alone articulate the same account herself). Rather, we will regard an account as adequate so long as it is empirically adequate.

To illustrate how this might work, suppose that we have collected a good deal of data regarding *A*'s assertion consumption patterns, and that we have placed all of the assertions she has observed into three categories, which we label Acceptance ($S+$), Rejection ($S-$), and Neutral ($S0$). Putting the members of $S0$ to the side for the time being, we have confirming evidence for (KR) to the degree that *being knowledgeable* both correlates positively with membership in $S+$, and correlates negatively with membership in $S-$. Consider then how (KR) might be assessed vis-à-vis its competitors including (JR) and (JKR). For this we might want a comparative judgement: what property of assertion is such that its presence best predicts membership in $S+$, and its absence best predicts membership in $S-$: *being knowledgeable, being justifiably believed by the speaker to be knowledgeable,* or *being (internalistically) justified*?[10] (KR) is to be favoured on this score if and only if the property in question is *being knowledgeable*.

It is worth making clear how the various proposals might claim a relative advantage over their rivals on the present score. To this end, I offer Table 4.1. (Again, I restrict myself to $S+$ and $S-$.)

The relative advantage that any particular account would enjoy would be a matter of its ability to handle the cases that are handled by the other account(s), without running into the difficulties of (cases that cannot be handled by) the other account(s). To get a very rough index on this, we might say that each account can be evaluated by the ratio of the C ('Confirming') cases to the

is to be borne in mind that the present discussion is taking place in the context of a proposed account of the sort of knowledge—testimonial knowledge—one acquires through accepting others' assertions. So long as we are conceiving of knowledge in the externalist way Williamson does, the proposed account will then have to advert to, e.g., the safety of the relevant belief-forming process. Since the workings of that process, and in particular the way in which it distinguishes proper from improper assertions, may well be inaccessible to even sustained reflection, hearers' *opinions* about their sensitivity to the propriety observed assertions are not to the point. (Indeed, I regard it as a virtue of taking a third-person orientation on the norm of assertion that it indicates how we might investigate the relevant norm(s) without having to rely on speaker intuitions alone.)

⁹ This tripartite categorization system is itself a simplification: no doubt her reactions to assertion will be more graded than this acknowledges. Further complication to the theory could be added to handle this, but I will keep things simple here.

¹⁰ Of course, to apply this method we need an independent way to determine which category (being knowledgeable, etc.) fits arbitrary assertion. I will assume that we have such a way.

Table 4.1.

The account	Confirming cases	Disconfirming cases
The (KR) account	[C1]: assertions in $S+$ that are knowledgeable; [C2]: assertions in $S-$ that are not knowledgeable.	[D1]: assertions in $S+$ that are not knowledgeable; [D2]: assertions in $S-$ that are knowledgeable.
The (JR) account	[C3]: assertions in $S+$ that are cases of justified belief; [C4]: assertions in $S-$ that are not cases of justified belief.	[D3]: assertions in $S+$ that are not cases of justified belief; [D4]: assertions in $S-$ that are cases of justified belief.
The (JKR) account	[C5]: assertions in $S+$ that are cases in which the speaker is justified in believing that she knows whereof she speaks; [C6]: assertions in $S-$ that are cases in which the speaker is not justified in believing that she knows whereof she speaks.	[D5]: assertions in $S+$ that are cases in which the speaker is unjustified in believing that she knows whereof she speaks; [D6]: assertions in $S-$ that are cases in which the speaker is justified in believing that she knows whereof she speaks.

total cases (the confirming ones and the D ('Disconfirming') ones). When $n(Cm)$ = the number of cases in (Cm), the index of the (KR) account will be given by $[n(C1) + n(C2)]/[n(C1) + n(C2) + n(D1) + n(D2)]$ — this figure records the percentage of correct predictions that are made by the (KR) account. (*Mutatis mutandis* for the other accounts.)

If we are going to compare accounts by comparing the percentage of correct predictions each makes, it is clear that we will need to have data regarding the members of $S+$ and $S-$. Short of a detailed description of hearers' patterns of consumption of others' say-so, we cannot begin to determine which factors best predict these patterns. However, in advance of collecting such data,[11] I want to offer some initial grounds for doubt regarding whether (KR) will emerge as the victor on this comparison.

To begin, let us generate some speculations regarding what factors are most likely to predict hearers' reactions to proffered assertion.[12] (Our speculations will have to be borne out by the evidence; I am merely offering what I take to be a not unreasonable initial hypothesis.) When it comes to speech, the factors relevant to hearers' consumption patterns regarding observed assertions can be grouped into three main categories. There are factors pertaining to (i) the hearer's estimate (prior to her having observed the testimony) of the plausibility of the

[11] See, e.g., Gilbert et al. (1990), Gilbert (1991, 1992), Gilbert et al. (1993) for some discussion about the conditions that elicit hearers' trust in an observed assertion. (I thank Peter Graham for pointing me to this literature.)

[12] Here I focus on assertion in speech; a full account would have to generalize to cover consumption of the written word as well.

attested proposition, (ii) the hearer's estimate of the reliability and authority of the speaker, both in general and on the particular subject matter at hand; and (iii) the specific features of the assertion that the hearer judges to be indications of, for example, the *sincerity* of the speaker and the *confidence* with which the assertion is made. Meaningful generalizations over a wide range of hearers may be beyond the question, given wide divergence among distinct hearers in factors of type (i) and (ii). (That Golda asserts with confidence might predict that you—who do not know her track record of unreliability—will accept her initial assertions, but it will not predict that I will, given that I already know that she is unreliable. Similarly, if you know all about nuclear physics but I do not, presumably this will show up in how the two of us will respond to assertions regarding that subject matter.) But this will not prevent us from trying to generalize in those cases in which audiences are equally impoverished with respect to factors of type (i) and (ii). These will be cases in which testimony is given by an unknown speaker regarding a subject matter about which hearers are equally ignorant, where the ignorance in question amounts to the hearers not having any significant prior probability regarding the attested proposition.[13] (Call such cases stranger-testimony.) With regard to stranger-testimony it is plausible to think that consumption patterns will best be predicted by sincerity- and confidence-indicating factors exhibited in the assertoric speech act itself. This enquiry will thus give us some indication of the relative effects of factors of type (iii) on our consumption patterns; and, assuming that stranger-testimony is not uncommon, we will be able to formulate some relatively robust generalizations regarding our responses to observed assertion.

To pursue the rough index for each of the accounts in cases involving stranger-testimony, it is worthwhile comparing the accounts along the following four dimensions: cases of acceptance that are easily accounted for [= (C1), (C3), and (C5)]; cases of rejection that are easily accounted for [= (C2), (C4), and (C6)]; cases of acceptance that are not accounted for [= (D1), (D3), and (D5)]; and cases of rejection that are not accounted for [= (D2), (D4), and (D6)]. To the extent that, for example, instances of (C1) are more common than instances of (C3) and than instances of (C5), (KR) scores highest along the first dimension, since this would show that it has more confirming instances along this dimension than the other two accounts have (and *mutatis mutandis* for the

---

[13] There may be no cases in which one has no prior probability. But I am imagining cases in which the subject matter is such that there is a wide range of propositions, incompatible with each other, regarding which the speaker's prior probability would not meaningfully discriminate. Such cases can easily be imagined. Consider such matters as: the proverbial price of tea in China (I may have no basis for discrimination beyond thinking it is probably not less than x or more than y, for some x and y); the whereabouts of a particular low-ranking politician on a given evening (I may suppose that she is somewhere in the southern part of the USA, without having any basis for further discrimination); the score of an obscure sporting event (say, the outcome of an American baseball game to a European unfamiliar with baseball, or the outcome of a cricket match to an American unfamiliar with cricket); and so forth.

second dimension); to the extent that instances of (D1) are more common than instances of (D3) and than instances of (D5), (KR) scores lowest along the third dimension, since this would show that it has more disconfirming instances along this dimension than the other two accounts have (and *mutatis mutandis* for the fourth dimension).

Consider then the first dimension. Here our question is this: given the members of $S+$, which property is most instantiated by those members, that of *being knowledgeable, being an expression of a justified belief,* or *being an expression regarding which the speaker is justified in taking herself to know whereof she speaks*? (Let us designate these as the K-property, the J-property, and the JBK-property, respectively.) If we are restricting our enquiry to cases involving stranger-testimony, then it would appear that there will be more cases of (C3) and (C5) than there will be of (C1).[14] In such cases, whether the hearer accepts the testimony typically turns on whether she regards the assertion as sincere and made with sufficient confidence. But note that whether a speaker appears, for example, confident is a function of the speaker's own (perhaps subcognitive) self-assessment: speakers who take themselves to know whereof they speak, or who take themselves to be justified in making their assertion, will assert with confidence; whereas speakers who do not, will typically not assert with confidence.[15] But then if, for example, apparent confidence is something to which hearers are sensitive in their consumption patterns, it stands to reason that in stranger-testimony cases $S+$ will contain a good deal of assertions made under conditions in which the speaker took herself to know, or to be justified (as these will be the more 'confident' assertions). The result would then be that, unless assertions made under conditions in which the speaker took herself to know, or to be justified, correlate perfectly with assertions that are actually knowledge-expressing, the (JKR) or (JR) account will better predict membership in $S+$ than will the (KR) account. (KR) stands to be inferior to the other two along the first dimension.

Let us then move to the second dimension, involving rejection cases that are accounted for. Which account best predicts membership in $S-$? Here the matter is slightly murkier, but, to the extent that we can say anything reasonable on the matter, (KR) appears to be in an intermediate position relative to its rivals. Here our question is this: given the members of $S-$, which property is most instantiated by those members, that of *not having the K-property, not having the J-property,* or *not having the JBK-property*? In cases of stranger-testimony, a not unreasonable initial supposition is that assertions are rejected when they fail to

---

[14] I repeat: these speculations will have to be borne out by the evidence; I am merely offering what I take to be a not unreasonable initial hypothesis, meant to spur further interest in the matter rather than settle anything decisively.

[15] This point appears implicit in an assumption that, Adler contends, is part of 'our acceptance of ordinary testimony'—the assumption being that 'if X didn't *believe* he knew that p, he would not assert to me that p' (Adler 1996: 108; emphasis added).

appear sincere, or when they appear to be made with less than full confidence. The question, then, is how these three properties correlate with these appearances.

Sticking with just the (KR) and the (JKR) accounts—most of what I say in connection with the (JKR) account will apply, *mutatis mutandis*, to the (JR) account—we can ask: Which is more likely in cases in which a hearer rejects an observed assertion, that the speaker she observed was not justified in taking herself to know whereof she spoke, or that the speaker did not speak knowledgeably? Again, a not unreasonable first guess is that the former will tend to be favoured in cases in which the decisive factors are those of type (iii), for reasons already given in connection with the first dimension. There are four cases to consider: (*a*) knowledgeable assertion with the JBK-property, (*b*) knowledgeable assertion without JBK, (*c*) knowledge-less assertion with JBK, and (*d*) knowledge-less assertion without JBK. As neither (*a*) nor (*d*) gives us a reason to prefer the (KR) over the (JKR) account or vice versa—(*a*) disconfirms both, whereas (*d*) confirms both[16]—I focus on (*b*) and (*c*). The paradigm case of (*b*), knowledgeable assertion lacking the JBK property, would be the naive chicken-sexer case: on an externalist account of knowledge, the naive chicken-sexer knows the sex of the chicks, even though she is not internalistically justified in believing that she knows. The result is that, while she might make assertions—the feeling of confidence she has in her opinions is enough to inspire her to assert—nevertheless her assertions will typically be less than fully confident, since her lack of internally accessible reasons is salient even to her largely unreflective mind.[17] Next, consider (*c*), knowledge-less assertion with the JBK property. Given the introspective accessibility of the justification, it is likely that she will assert with confidence[18]—in which case, given that this is a stranger-testimony case, it is likely that her testimony will be consumed, hence not in $S-$ to begin with, hence not in (C2). Our question,

---

[16] Although a serious treatment of the (JR) account would require examining these cases, at least where the J-property and the JBK-property are not co-instantiated.

[17] I do not here address the propriety of making an assertion under such conditions; I am examining only our capacity to discriminate appropriate assertion, as this capacity is employed in cases of observed assertion.

[18] The issue is more vexed than this, of course. In order to accommodate the link between justification and truth, most internalist accounts of justification have distinguished between having internalistically sanctioned grounds, being aware of those internalistically sanctioned grounds, being aware that those internalistically sanctioned grounds justify one's target belief, and being justified in believing that those internalistically sanctioned grounds justify one's target belief (where the analysis could repeat indefinitely for justification at the metalevel). To the extent that internalist justification requires only internalistically sanctioned grounds, the speaker's epistemic self-assessment in cases of assertions meeting this standard may not differ that much from her epistemic self-assessment in cases of assertions meeting the knowledge standard. But then assertions from these two classes may well have similar trappings of confidence, and so may elicit similar consumption patterns in the hearer—contrary to my claim above. In reply I grant the point but contend that, even so, there will be some cases in which the two accounts make different predictions: presumably these will be the cases in which the speaker's assertion conforms to some more robust internalist accessibility requirement.

then, is which is likely to be more common among the cases in which the hearer rejects the assertion: naive chicken-sexer cases (= cases in which the assertion is knowledgeable in a brutely externalist way), or cases in which the speaker does not know but has justification for supposing she does? My (hopefully not unreasonable) guess is that there will be more of the former case. My reasons here are the same as above: internalist justification of this sort typically correlates with speaker-confidence, which, in cases of stranger-testimony, correlates in turn with a hearer's acceptance, not rejection, of the assertion. If so, (C6) will have more instances than (C2). In sum, it is not unreasonable to anticipate a negative verdict for the (KR) account on the second dimension: it does not fare as well as the (JKR) account.

I believe, but will not argue, that we get results in connection with the third and fourth dimension that parallel those we got in connection with the first and second: the (KR) account does not do as well against its two competitors. If I am correct about this, then the empirical data will favour, for example, the (JKR) account over the (KR) account when it comes to empirical adequacy in respect of the patterns of consumption exhibited in hearers' reactions to observed assertion. In one respect, this result is no more surprising than is the following claim: in cases of stranger-testimony, we accept assertions in which the speaker speaks *as if* she were knowledgeable. Our hope, of course, is that speaking as if one is knowledgeable correlates well with actually being knowledgeable; but we recognize the fallibility of the inference, and the theorist can resign herself to the idea that this is the most relevant sort of evidence one can have as a hearer in a stranger-testimony case.

Still, one who seeks to defend the superiority of the (KR) account on the present score might query whether the restriction to stranger-testimony cases is even-handed. It might be alleged, for example, that this restriction prejudices matters against the (KR) account. Once we allow in cases in which the hearer (the hearer's probability function) assigns a substantive prior probability (or improbability) to the attested proposition, and where in addition the hearer has knowledge of the general reliability of the speaker and of her authority with respect to the present subject matter, will not (KR) fare better than it did in cases of stranger-testimony? To the extent that a hearer is relevantly knowledgeable—she has knowledge of factors of type (i) and (ii), and little false beliefs regarding such factors—the answer may well be affirmative. But the difficulty is that hearers' consumption patterns are informed, not only by what they know of such factors, but also by what they *merely believe* about such factors; and, for hearers with a good deal of relevant false belief, this will affect their consumption patterns, and will yield different results regarding $S+$ and $S-$. This is the reason that I think we get the clearest picture of hearers' consumption patterns by focusing on cases involving stranger-testimony, where a hearer's background belief corpus, though relevant, will play a less significant role in predicting the consumption patterns themselves.

I have gone on long enough, given that the foregoing few pages are speculations in front of the empirical evidence. But there is a point to such speculation. At the very least it suggests that we ought not to be confident that the (KR) account will outperform its rivals on the matter of predicting the consumption patterns of observed assertion. If not, then a case can be made for thinking that one of its competitor accounts, rather than the (KR) account itself, is to be preferred as an account of our (largely subcognitive) sensitivity to observed assertion. To be sure, even such an account would be something of an idealization; but it will involve less idealization, and in any case less ad hoc idealization, than the (KR) account would appear to involve. The ultimate upshot, of course, would be that it is no longer clear whether the simplicity of the (KR) account of testimonial knowledge gives us a reason to favour that account over its rivals. In which case the apparent virtue of the (KR) account, which I originally aimed to bring out in connection with a third-person approach to the norms of assertion, is merely apparent.

4. CONCLUSION

Our conclusion is a mixed verdict. (KR) affords the simplest account of the conditions on testimonial knowledge. (I myself am very attracted to this account.) But there are questions whether this account is empirically adequate: we have some reason to suppose that its knowledge-based account of hearer sensitivity to observed assertion will idealize quite a bit from the sensitivity actual hearers exhibit. Admittedly, these reasons are speculative; and a final verdict will have to await a detailed investigation into the psychology of trust. But I offer the foregoing argument in the spirit of suggesting that we cannot yet not regard the simplicity of the (KR) account of testimonial knowledge as a virtue, as this simplicity is purchased at the cost of what (in advance of the empirical evidence) appears to be empirical inadequacy—more empirical inadequacy, in any case, than its competitor accounts. For my own part, hoping as I am that we will be able to accept the simplest account of testimonial knowledge, I would hope that subsequent empirical work will vindicate the (KR) account—the foregoing scepticism I have expressed notwithstanding. But I am convinced that we are not in a position to accept this account until such time as we have the relevant empirical results in hand.

5

Williamson on Knowledge and Evidence

Alvin Goldman

1. METHODOLOGICAL QUESTIONS

Timothy Williamson's project in *Knowledge and its Limits* (Williamson, 2000)[1] includes proposals for substantial revisions in the received approach to epistemology. One received view is that knowledge is conceptualized in terms of a conjunction of factors that are individually necessary and jointly sufficient for knowing. A central aim of epistemology is to state such necessary and sufficient conditions. Against this received view, Williamson argues that

> a necessary but insufficient condition need not be a conjunct of a non-circular necessary and sufficient condition. Although being coloured is a necessary but insufficient condition for being red, we cannot state a necessary and sufficient condition for being red by conjoining being coloured with other properties specified without reference to red. Neither the equation 'Red = coloured + X' nor the equation 'Knowledge = true belief + X' need have a non-circular solution.   (p. 3)

Williamson further argues that we have inductive reasons for thinking that no analysis of the concept *knows* of the standard kind is correct. The inductive reasons are simply the history of failed attempts at such "factorizing" or "decompositional" analyses. Williamson not only rejects the prospect of explaining knowledge in terms of belief, justification, and evidence, but he proposes to reverse the order of explanation. "That order of explanation has been reversed in this book. The concept *knows* is fundamental, the primary implement of epistemological inquiry" (p. 185).

It is not altogether easy, however, to reconcile this radical program with other things Williamson says in the book. In particular, the book contains two rather unrelated *accounts* of knowing, and one of these accounts appeals to some of the same ingredients that traditional (or semi-traditional) analysts have used in the past. The first account, which appears in chapter 1, says that knowing is

---

[1] All page numbers refer to this work.

the most general factive stative propositional attitude. The account is presented in terms of three conditions:

(1) If Φ is an FMSO [factive mental state operator], from 'S Φs that A' one may infer 'A'.
(2) 'Know' is an FMSO.
(3) If Φ is an FMSO, from 'S Φs that A' one may infer 'S knows that A'. (p. 39)

The latter two principles, says Williamson, "characterize the concept of knowing uniquely, up to logical equivalence, in terms of the concept of an FMSO" (p. 39). Williamson adds that this account is not a decomposition of the knowledge *concept*; it would be implausible to claim that everyone who thinks that John knows that it is raining thereby thinks that John has the most general factive stative propositional attitude to the proposition that it is raining. This remark is intended, no doubt, to distinguish this characterization of knowledge from traditional *analyses*.

But the second type of account Williamson offers seems closer to traditional analyses. He acknowledges that knowing seems to be "highly sensitive" to such factors as justification, causation, and reliability, over wide ranges of cases. "Any adequate *account* of knowing should enable one to understand these connections" (p. 41; emphasis added). He clearly indicates that he regards truth, belief, and reliability (more precisely, safety) as necessary conditions for knowing. "No reason has emerged to doubt the intuitive claim that reliability is necessary for knowledge" (p. 100), and "A reliability condition on knowledge was implicit in the argument of section 5.1 and explicit in sections 4.3 and 4.4" (p. 123). So Williamson does not abandon the prospect of giving an *account*, if not an *analysis*, of knowing, along something approaching traditional lines. Such an enterprise is sprinkled through the middle chapters of the book. Although his account never formulates sufficient conditions for knowing, and therefore departs from the enterprise of traditional analysts, it does go some distance in a fairly orthodox direction. It is therefore a bit difficult to piece together the different strands of his methodological thinking.

I wish to examine the 'second' account of knowledge Williamson offers. In light of his rejection of traditional analyses, however, it is unclear how to proceed. What criteria of adequacy should be imposed on an account of the sort Williamson offers? What standards should be used in judging this attempt? Williamson himself, of course, denies that an account is required to provide a sufficient and non-circular condition for knowing, and he does not attempt to provide one. But what if we are not yet persuaded that knowing has no non-circular sufficient condition (of the traditional kind)? How should we rate the success of Williamson's account compared to rival accounts that do offer sufficient (and non-circular) conditions?

To illustrate the puzzle, return to an epistemological "yesterday," when Gettier (1963) first propounded his counterexamples to the justified true belief (JTB) analysis of knowing. Suppose that supporters of the JTB analysis had responded: "Professor Gettier, your two examples are extremely interesting. But what they purport to show is that JTB is not sufficient for knowing. We do not claim, however, that JTB is a sufficient condition; we do not believe that the knowledge concept admits of any non-circular sufficient condition. So the JTB account is completely in order. It is wholly adequate, and not open to criticism you have advanced by means of your examples."

Few epistemologists would be impressed by this response, either then or now; nor should they be impressed. Whether or not Williamson is right about the "unanalyzability" of *knows*, the JTB analysis obviously misses some important facts or elements, as post-Gettier investigations have demonstrated. To rest content with the JTB account would be a laugher today. It is obviously incomplete, and we have some fairly good ideas about how to repair it, or at least to improve upon it. This is not to say there is unanimity among epistemologists. Nevertheless, some sort of additional conditions in an "anti-luck" vein are widely agreed to be necessary for a satisfactory account of knowing. Thus, testing a set of conditions for sufficiency, as Gettier did, is a salutary epistemological exercise.

Let me turn this example into a general proposal for an adequacy condition on accounts of knowing (or other philosophically interesting concepts). An adequate set of conditions, I propose, should be both *correct* and *complete*. Completeness, however, can be interpreted in two different ways, depending on whether the target of the account is or is not susceptible of (non-circular) sufficient conditions. If sufficient conditions exist, then a complete account should provide *all necessary and sufficient conditions* (that are philosophically significant). If no (non-circular) sufficient conditions exist, as in the case of *red*, then a complete account should provide *all necessary conditions* (that are philosophically significant). Under this proposal, even someone like Williamson who is dubious about "factorizing" analyses could agree that Gettier proved something important—namely, that the JTB account *omits* some necessary conditions for knowing, and hence is inadequate.

The moral I would extract from this discussion is the following. It always pays to subject any proposed account of a concept to sufficiency tests. If an account fails a sufficiency test, this proves or suggests one of two things. It suggests that either there is some *sufficient* condition that has not yet been identified or that one or more *necessary* (but insufficient) conditions have been *omitted*. In either case, the use of sufficiency tests should prove instructive in going beyond the proffered account. This is the moral I shall pursue in making a critical examination of Williamson's account of knowing.

Let me clarify what my critique will not be aimed at. Although I shall question the adequacy of Williamson's account, I will not challenge the *implications* Williamson draws from this account. A major part of Williamson's aim is to derive certain theoretical conclusions from a safety account of knowing,

such conclusions as anti-luminosity and the denial of the KK principle. These
conclusions are drawn from the *necessity* of the conditions he proposes. I will not
take issue with any of these conclusions.[2] I suspect that any changes in the account
of knowing that my worries might motivate would leave these implications intact.
Nonetheless, epistemologists are interested in getting as adequate an account
of knowing as possible. My objections (insofar as they are directed at knowing
rather than evidence) are devoted to this end.

2. THE NON-SUFFICIENCY OF SAFETY

The account of knowing Williamson develops in chapters 4–7 belongs to the
reliability family. Williamson locates his preferred form of reliability in the
"safety" category, but there remain questions about the account's adequacy and
its alleged superiority to other theories in the reliability family.

Williamson's first pass at the kind of reliability he regards as relevant to
knowledge occurs in the following passage:

For present purposes we are interested in a notion of reliability on which, in given
circumstances, something happens reliably if and only if it is not in danger of not
happening. That is, it happens reliably in a case α if and only if it happens (reliably or
not) in every case similar enough to α. In particular, one avoids false belief reliably in α if
and only if one avoids false belief in every case similar enough to α.   (p. 124)

Elsewhere he refers to this reliability notion as "safety from error," and presents a
principle for knowledge that invokes the safety-from-error notion. "Now assume
a connection between knowledge and safety from error . . . For all cases α and
β, if β is close to α and in α one knows that C obtains, then in β one does not
falsely believe that C obtains" (p. 128).

Here we have, in kernel form, Williamson's safety account of knowing. There
are two straightforward questions to ask about it. Is safety necessary for knowing,
and is it sufficient? (Of course, Williamson does not claim that safety is sufficient.
But, since he offers no further condition, we have to ask whether the condition he
has offered is "complete.") The sufficiency question is addressed in this section
and Section 5, and the necessity question is addressed in Sections 3 and 4.

Sherrilyn Roush (2005: 122–3) presents a counterexample to the sufficiency
of the safety account—not Williamson's version of safety, exactly, but near
enough. S has a fairy godmother whose special mode of operation is to make
true anything that S believes. So, for any p, when S actually believes p, it is true.
Moreover, in close counterfactual situations, the fairy godmother would still
make p true if S believed it. So the safety condition is fulfilled. But fulfillment
of this condition does not guarantee that S's belief in p intuitively counts as

---

[2] Thanks to Dennis Whitcomb for emphasizing the need to be clear on this point.

knowing. To flesh out an appropriate example, suppose S comes to believe *p* by applying a fallacious mode of reasoning to some false and unjustified prior beliefs q and r. Or, suppose S comes to believe *p* by idle wishful thinking. S lacks even a wisp of evidence, or what she takes to be evidence, for *p*. Still she believes it, and the fairy godmother secures its truth. Does S's belief in *p* qualify as knowledge? Intuitively, no, though the safety condition is satisfied.

Is the safety requirement really satisfied, one might wonder? Is there not a close situation in which the fairy godmother takes a break from her duties, or simply does not exist? In such a situation, *p* might easily be false though S still believes it.[3] However, we can stipulate facts about the actual case that make the absence or dereliction of the fairy godmother in a counterfactual case extremely remote, hence not a threat to safety. Suppose the actual world is one in which certain human agents, including S, have a fairy godmother as a matter of nomological necessity. Then the non-existence of such a godmother does not obtain in any close world.

A different objection to this example is that, if S has a fairy godmother who always ensures the truth of S's beliefs, at least for future-oriented beliefs, then S will accumulate excellent inductive evidence that her future-oriented beliefs always turn out true. If so, will not S *know* each future-oriented proposition she believes?[4] Here we need to be careful about the time of the belief. Until S has time to reflect on the fact of her believing, say, *p*, she does not yet have inductive evidence for that particular proposition. Only after the belief in *p* is formed can S identify it as one of her beliefs and infer from her believing it that it will somehow come true. Until this further inference is made, her belief does not qualify as knowledge. But the belief is safe even before the inferential step is taken, which shows that safety does not suffice for knowing.

There are other kinds of cases that can also serve as counterexamples to the sufficiency of safety. Suppose S is looking at an orange harvest moon perched over the horizon (Goldman 1976). S correctly believes that it is the moon, and, in possible cases in which the moon has slightly different properties, he would still believe it is the moon. For example, if it were slightly larger or smaller, if its rocky face had slightly different peaks or valleys, and so on, S would still correctly believe it is the moon. In short, S avoids false belief in every case similar enough to the actual one; or so it initially seems.

Now consider a counterfactual scenario, one in which what is perched over the horizon is not the moon but a large orange hot-air balloon, which looks from S's perspective just as the moon looks to him in the actual scenario. If this case transpired, S would mistake the hot-air balloon for the moon—that is, would mistakenly believe that the perceived object is the moon. Of course, the large orange balloon is vastly closer to S than the moon is, and in physical terms—size, composition, and so on—bears little resemblance to the moon. But it would

---

[3] Thanks here to Karson Kovakovich.   [4] Igal Kvart offered this argument.

present a very similar appearance to S as the moon presents in the actual scenario. Finally, assume that orange hot-air balloons are moderately common in S's part of the world. Then I am inclined to say that S does not know, in the actual situation, that what he sees is the moon.

Does Williamson's safety condition handle this case correctly? Does S's moon belief pass Williamson's safety test and thereby qualify for knowledge? If so, the safety condition is not sufficient for knowing. So let us ask whether the moon belief passes the safety test.

Williamson says that his notions of reliability, stability, safety, and robustness concern what could easily have happened. They depend on what happens under "small variations in initial conditions" (p. 123). When illustrating these ideas, Williamson invariably chooses examples featuring small variations in the physical features of the objects in question—for example, small variations in the height of a tree. If we take this to be a prototype of his notion of 'closeness,' it appears that the case in which the moon is present in S's visual field and the case in which a hot-air balloon is present in S's visual field are extremely distant from one another. The moon is vastly larger than a hot-air balloon, has vastly greater mass, is composed of very different material, and is much farther from S than is the hot-air balloon. So the balloon case would not seem to qualify as 'close' to the moon case. Hence, it should not matter under the safety requirement that S makes a mistake in the balloon case. So S's belief in the moon case appears to be safe, and therefore should be an item of knowledge according to the safety account. But, intuitively, the balloon alternative keeps S from knowing. Thus, passing the safety condition is not sufficient for knowing.

Perhaps Williamson's criterion of closeness should be interpreted differently. Maybe his notion of closeness is intended to incorporate a relativization to a cognizer's *evidence* in the actual state of affairs. Applying this idea to the present case, the moon/balloon scenarios would be close to one another *relative to S's perceptual experience*. Williamson, however, never incorporates any such relativization to experience into his account of closeness; this is entirely my own suggestion. His illustrations all involve unrelativized properties of the objects in question. So the moon/balloon example seems to stand as a counterexample to the sufficiency of his safety condition. This suggests either that safety needs to be characterized somewhat differently, or that additional conditions are needed, or both.

3. SAFETY AS NECESSARY FOR KNOWING

Is safety (as Williamson characterizes it) necessary for knowing? Neta and Rohrbaugh (2004: 399–400) offer two counterexamples to its necessity. Here is their presentation of the examples:

(A) I am drinking a glass of water which I have just poured from the bottle. Standing next to me is a happy person who has just won the lottery. Had this person lost the lottery, she would have maliciously polluted my water with a tasteless, odorless, colorless toxin. But since she won the lottery, she does no such thing. Nonetheless, she *almost* lost the lottery. Now, I drink the pure, unadulterated water and judge, truly and knowingly, that I am drinking pure, unadulterated water. But the toxin would not have flavored the water, and so had the toxin gone in, I would still have believed falsely that I was drinking pure, unadulterated water. . . Despite the falsity of my belief in the nearby possibility, it seems that, in the actual case, I know that I am drinking pure, unadulterated water.

(B) I am participating in a psychological experiment, in which I am to report the number of flashes I recall being shown. Before being shown the stimuli, I consume a glass of liquid at the request of the experimenter. Unbeknownst to either of us, I have been randomly assigned to the control group, and the glass contains ordinary orange juice. Other experimental groups receive juice mixed with one of a variety of chemicals which hinder the functioning of memory without a detectable phenomenological difference. I am shown seven flashes and judge, truly and knowingly, that I have been shown seven flashes. Had I been a member of one of the experimental groups to which I was almost assigned, I would have been shown only six flashes but still believed that I had been shown seven flashes due to the effects of the drug. It seems that in the actual case I know that the number of flashes is seven despite the envisaged possibility of my being wrong. And yet these possibilities are as similar in other respects as they would have to be for the experiment to be well designed and properly executed.

Neta and Rohrbaugh's examples strike me, intuitively, as correct. However, they rightly consider the possible objection that their examples should not be considered cases of knowledge because of their similarity to the fake-barns example (Goldman 1976, although the example is originally due to Carl Ginet[5]). Most people agree that in the fake-barns example Henry does not know he is seeing a barn (though he is), apparently because of the close possibility that what he is seeing is a mere façade. Neta and Rohrbaugh argue that their examples (A) and (B) are not analogous to the fake-barn case because Henry's *actual* circumstances are unfavorable in a way in which the actual circumstances of the agents of (A) and (B) are not. There really are fake barns in Henry's neighborhood. By contrast, the threats to knowledge in (A) and (B) remain purely counterfactual. Although things *could* have gone epistemically less well, and almost did so, in each case the threat was avoided and the actual case remains epistemically unproblematic. This response is plausible but not wholly compelling. After all, one might say in the fake-barns case that the threat of a fake barn being before *Henry* remains counterfactual, so the

---

[5] Most regrettably, Ginet was not credited in the original publication (Goldman 1976). I belatedly tried to set the record straight by adding an endnote with the credit in a subsequent reprinting of "Discrimination of Perceptual Knowledge" (Goldman 1992b). Few people, however, seem to have noticed that endnote. Others, meanwhile, have quite properly called attention to the fact that credit for the example should go to Ginet.

threat to Henry's knowledge, if Neta and Rohrbaugh are right, ought to be avoided.

However, the problem should not be laid at Neta and Rohrbaugh's doorstep. There is an important question that should be directed to Williamson—namely, how his theory intends to interpret "closeness"? The question can be divided into two. First, which "qualitative" features of objects in a pair of cases α and β are relevant to determining their degree of closeness? Secondly, which kinds of world transformations count as staying relatively close to actuality versus straying farther afield? I would expect Williamson to respond by saying that all these matters are simply *vague* (see p. 100). I do not necessarily disagree with Williamson about the appropriateness of this response. But it does raise a question of whether his theory constitutes any advance over an earlier theory in the reliabilist tradition—namely, the *relevant-alternatives* theory. If we interpret a 'relevant' alternative as a 'close' alternative, then the relevant-alternatives theory also says that a true belief fails to be knowledge if there is a close alternative in which the agent does not avoid having a false belief. I shall return to a comparison of Williamson's theory and relevant-alternatives theory in the next section.

Let us further probe the necessity of the safety condition and the interpretation of closeness by looking at the dachshund-wolf example (Goldman 1976). Depending on how closeness is interpreted, this threatens to be a counterexample to the safety condition. I look at a nearby dachshund and truly believe that what I see is a dog. Had I not been seeing a dachshund, I would have been seeing a wolf, and would have falsely believed myself to be seeing a dog. Clearly, this is a case of knowing. At any rate, the fact that what I would see if the dachshund were not there is a wolf, and I would mistake the wolf for a dog, does not disqualify this as an instance of knowing. Intuitively, this is because the wolf would not look anything like the dachshund. However, my belief in the actual case that what I am seeing is a dog may not be safe, because the wolf case may be close enough to the dachshund case. Why would it be close? First, the wolf case is close to the dachshund case because the world-transformation, as we stipulated, is a minor one. Secondly, the wolf physically resembles the dachshund to a moderate degree. They are both furry quadrapedal mammals belonging to the canine family. If Williamson chose to weight the dimension of world-transformation over the dimension of physical similarity, this case could well be one in which there is knowledge but the safety condition is violated.

Williamson discusses the dachshund-wolf example in his critique of Nozick's sensitivity theory (1981), but he is silent about how his own theory would handle the example. He might proceed by appealing to the fact that the *basis* for belief in the wolf case is different from the basis for belief in the dachshund case. While discussing Nozick, who invokes sameness of 'method' in his sensitivity theory, Williamson indicates that he favors an improvement in his own safety theory that introduces a sameness-of-basis qualification. Recall that his earlier formulation of safety was: "For all cases α and β, if β is close to α and in α one knows that C obtains, then in β one does not falsely believe that C obtains." He now writes:

In a more careful version of [the foregoing], we might qualify both 'know' and 'believe' by 'on a basis B'. Knowledge on one basis (for example, seeing an event) is quite consistent with false belief in a close case on a very different basis (for example, hearing about the event). (p. 128)

With the addition of a sameness-of-basis qualification, Williamson might argue that knowledge in the dachshund case is not disqualified because belief in the wolf case does not have the same basis as belief in the dachshund case.

Whether this argument succeeds depends on how 'bases' are construed. One possibility is to construe bases, at least in perceptual examples, as perceptual appearances. Since the wolf appearance is quite different from the dachshund appearance, the sameness-of-basis requirement would not be fulfilled. Hence the safety condition is not violated, yielding the verdict that the agent knows in the dachshund case, in conformity with intuition. However, it is most unlikely that Williamson would avail himself of this approach, because appearances are likely to be individuated *internally*, and internal individuation of bases is something Williamson staunchly opposes. In discussing Nozick's theory, Williamson cites Nozick's endorsement of an internal criterion of method individuation, and expresses opposition to that criterion.

Another possibility is to construe 'bases' as very general methods for arriving at belief. In the passage quoted above, the examples of 'bases' are seeing and hearing. The general-methods interpretation of 'bases,' however, will not help with the dachshund-wolf case, because the agent uses vision in both the dachshund and the wolf case. So under this interpretation the sameness-of-basis test is passed, which implies that safety is violated in the dachshund case. Yet, intuitively, the agent knows.

A third possible construal of 'bases' would include specific external objects involved in the method of belief acquisition. The basis of belief in the dachshund case might be *seeing the dachshund*, and the basis of belief in the wolf case might be *seeing the wolf*. This kind of external individuation would suit Williamson's favored approach quite nicely. And it would have the desired result in the dachshund-wolf example, because the two cases would then have different bases. Safety would not be violated, and knowledge would be preserved.

However, this approach does not work in the moon-balloon example. Seeing the moon in the actual case and seeing the balloon in the counterfactual case would be different bases. Hence safety would not be violated, and the agent would know it is the moon. But our intuitive verdict about the moon case is that the person does not know. Similarly, in an identical-twin case, one should not be said to know that it is Judy when one would mistake her twin Trudy for Judy. But the belief that it is Judy in both cases would have different bases under the present 'externalist' construal of 'basis,' because in the one case the basis is seeing Judy and in the other it is seeing Trudy. Difference of basis implies that safety is not violated and knowledge is (wrongly) sustained. So under this kind of external individuation of basis, the safety theory does not get things right.[6]

4. SAFETY VERSUS RELEVANT ALTERNATIVES

We noted in the previous section that Williamson's safety theory bears a close resemblance to the relevant-alternatives (RA) theory, and we wondered whether the safety theory constitutes an advance over RA theory. Let us now pursue that question further.

My own version of RA theory (Goldman 1976) added an element not featured in the basic formulation of safety theory. That RA theory (which was restricted to *perceptual* knowledge) said that S's true belief of object O that it has property F gets disqualified from being knowledge if there is a relevant *perceptually equivalent* situation in which the perceptual object lacks F (so that S's belief of the perceptual object that it has F would be false). Perceptual equivalence was intended to be understood in an internalist fashion. More precisely, although perceptual equivalence applies to external objects or situations, it does so in virtue of producing a mental condition that supervenes on the physical state of the agent's brain (that is, the 'percept' experienced by the cognizer). Presumably, Williamson would not endorse this conception of perceptual equivalence as a condition on knowledge. However, Williamson does add a sameness-of-basis qualification to his safety theory, as we have seen. This addition may have been motivated by a desire to handle such examples as the dachshund-wolf example. But we were unable to identify a satisfactory interpretation of 'basis' that suits Williamson's externalist approach and handles pertinent cases properly. So there is reason to prefer the RA theory to his safety theory. At a minimum, there is no reason to regard safety theory as superior to RA theory.

In discussing versions of reliability theory different from his own, especially Nozick's sensitivity theory, Williamson offers an argument against a theory that uses internal criteria of method- or basis-individuation. Let us examine this argument.

If methods are individuated internally, so that whether one is using method M supervenes on the physical state of one's brain, then (3) will indeed have some skeptical consequences. [Formula (3) reads: "Necessarily, if S knows *p* via method M then if *p* were false, S would not believe *p* via M."] But why should one accept (3) on those terms? The internal individuation of methods appears gerrymandered precisely to make trouble for our claims

---

[6] A somewhat similar argument appears in Whitcomb (2005).

to knowledge of the external world. Moreover, (3) is implausible in some examples when methods are individuated internally. My knowing by sight in the ordinary way that a mountain stands here seems compatible with the assumption that if no mountain had stood here, a bizarre chain of circumstances would have occurred as a result of which I would have hallucinated a mountain of just this appearance. That type of hallucination occurs only in worlds very unlike the actual world, we may suppose, and the mechanism that produces it is absent from the actual world. I actually satisfy (3) for knowing by sight many other things about my present environment, including that there is any *icy* mountain here; my eyesight is actually working perfectly and I have every ordinary reason to believe that it is. To block the unwarranted consequence of (3) that I do not know that a mountain stands here, one must individuate methods externally rather than internally.   (p. 156)

This argument against internal individuation of methods, however, is less than compelling. The argument adduces trouble for internal individuation only when internal individuation is paired with a sensitivity condition, which allows a very remote possibility to disqualify knowledge. But the prime culprit in producing this inappropriate verdict seems to be the sensitivity approach, not the internal individuation of methods. Williamson pins the blame on internal individuation, but this choice is inadequately motivated. So why not opt for (my version of) RA theory with its internal individuation of bases, rather than Williamson's safety theory?

5. PROCESS RELIABILITY

Having argued that Williamson's brand of safety offers no advance over RA theory, and may even be inferior to it, I now want to compare Williamson's safety theory to another variant of reliabilism. One component of many reliability theories that apparently has little attraction for Williamson is process reliability. The idea is that the global reliability (truth ratio) of the process or method by which a belief is formed (or sustained) is critical to its knowledge status. Both the safety theory and RA theory highlight conditions that mainly concern the modal neighborhood of the target belief. They do not straightforwardly address the global reliability of the psychological process(es) that is (are) causally responsible for the belief. But any theory that ignores the mode-of-causation issue will not successfully capture all relevant conditions on knowing.[7]

Does Williamson's attention to the 'basis' of belief reflect an interest in process reliability? That is far from clear. Although Williamson requires that the belief basis be the *same* if a counterfactual case is to be relevant to safety, he does not say that the basis of the actual belief must be globally reliable. Nor is it clear that

---

[7] I emphasize the relevance to knowledge of both global reliability and local (modal) reliability in Goldman (1986).

what he means by a 'basis' is the sort of thing that *could* have a global reliability property. Let us distinguish between two ontological types that could bear causal relations to (resultant) beliefs. The first ontological type is a *ground* for belief, where prime examples of grounds are mental *states* such as perceptual experiences or (other) beliefs. The second ontological type is a cognitive or computational *process* or *operation*, which might take one or more grounds as inputs and produce a belief as an output. It is the second ontological type that has global reliability properties, because the same process or operation is presumably applied to many sets of inputs and generates many belief outputs. Some of these outputs would be true and others false; so the generating process or operation will have a statistical property of generating truths a certain proportion of the time. Instances of the first ontological type—grounds—are not the sorts of things that have global reliability properties. The term 'basis' is most naturally applied to grounds, not to processes or operations. So it seems unlikely that Williamson's appeal to 'bases' in his safety theory is a move toward process reliabilism.[8]

Williamson aside, there could be a safety theory of knowing that appeals to grounds without invoking processes or their reliability. Could such a safety theory be adequate? I argue to the contrary. Suppose S forms a belief in a true proposition *p* based on inference from a rich set of prior beliefs, beliefs that constitute knowledge (and hence, on Williamson's view, evidence). Further suppose that there are no beliefs in S's total corpus that (justificationally) undermine the premises from which S's belief in *p* is generated. Thus, the total set of grounds, or evidential beliefs, on which S bases his belief in *p* lends strong support to *p*, and no other evidence possessed by S defeats this support. Finally, suppose there is no close situation to the actual one in which *p* is false and S believes it on the same basis (that is, on the same grounds). In other words, S's belief in *p* passes the safety test. Would it follow from all this that S's belief in *p* is knowledge?

No. This is not implied, because there are not adequate constraints on *how* S bases his belief on *p*. The mere fact that the belief is based on the indicated grounds leaves it wide open how S's reasoning proceeds *from* the grounds *to* the belief in *p*. Not all such reasoning processes or methods would license a knowledge attribution for the conclusion. Roughly, a proper method of reasoning is one that properly exploits or reflects the pertinent (for example, logical, probabilistic, abductive) relationships between the evidence propositions.

---

[8] Also at one point Williamson seems to confuse process reliabilism with the safety brand of reliabilism. He writes: "If one believes *p* truly in a case *a*, in which other cases must one avoid false belief in order to count as reliable enough to know *p* in *a*? There is no obvious way to specify in independent terms which other cases are relevant. This is sometimes known as the *generality problem* for reliabilism" (p. 100). This is not exactly right. The generality problem is a problem for process reliabilism specifically, not safety theory. It is the question of which process (or method) *type* is the correct type to use when fixing the reliability of a belief's generating process. That Williamson gets this terminology wrong—and otherwise neglects process reliabilism—suggests that he has little interest in this theoretical angle.

Such a method would tend to have comparatively strong reliability properties.[9] A poor or improper method of reasoning would be one that fails to take due account of the pertinent relationships between the evidence propositions. It might proceed, for example, in a very random, haphazard, or arbitrary fashion. Such a method might occasionally coincide in its selected output belief with that of an ideal method. It might occasionally produce a belief that is indeed supported by the evidence. But that does not mean that it would be a good method in general. On the contrary, its global reliability score would be low. My claim, then, is that, if S uses a method of this inferior sort, the resulting belief (in *p*) would not merit the status of knowledge.[10]

Would a globally *un*reliable method of the sort just described automatically lead to violation of the safety condition? Equivalently, does safety imply global reliability? If so, then adding a global-reliability condition would be redundant. However, I do not think that a (local) safety condition does imply global reliability of the method used. Notice that in counterfactual cases covered by the safety condition—that is, in "close" counterfactual cases—the items of evidence S uses are assumed to be true (known). Since they are S's *basis* for belief in *p*, and the basis is held fixed in counterfactual cases, these evidence propositions are still true in these possible scenarios. So whatever the prospects for *p*'s falsity in such counterfactual situations, they are not affected by the *method* S uses to form a belief in *p* from that specified basis. If we assume in the present case that safety is satisfied—and that has been our assumption—it leaves open the question of whether the belief-forming method used is superior or inferior—that is, globally reliable or unreliable. I claim that, unless a superior, globally reliable, method is used, knowledge is not attributable. That is something Williamson's account neglects.

6. IS EVIDENCE CO-EXTENSIVE WITH KNOWLEDGE?

The rest of this chapter addresses Williamson's theory of evidence. Williamson contends that a person's body of evidence is all and only what she knows. In other words, E = K. Is this thesis correct? Does it provide the best way to think and talk about evidence? Section 9.6 of *Knowledge and its Limits* (pp. 200–3) offers a number of arguments why all propositional evidence should be knowledge. Let us review these arguments in detail. Since many of these arguments have the form "It is hard to see what rival construal of evidence could account for

[9] In particular, it would have strong *conditional reliability* properties. The conditional reliability of an inference procedure is the proportion of times its belief outputs are true given that all the inputs to it are true. See Goldman (1979).

[10] Of course, introducing a global reliability constraint poses the well-known generality problem. I have nothing new to offer here on that topic.

the intuitive plausibility of datum X as well as E = K does," let me tentatively propose a competing construal of evidence, to test it against the various intuitive phenomena, or "data," Williamson adduces.[11] The rival construal of evidence I propose is:

(NPJ) Proposition P is an item of evidence for S at time t = $_{df.}$ P is non-inferentially, propositionally justified for S at t.

Call this the *non-inferential propositional justification* (NPJ) interpretation of evidence. By 'propositional justification' I mean the sort of justification an agent has vis-à-vis a proposition when she is justified *in* believing it, whether or not she actually believes it. A standard illustration of non-inferential propositional justification is having an experience as of seeing a computer screen before you. Being in this visual state might make you (prima facie) justified in believing the proposition "There is a computer screen before me," whether or not you do believe it. On the present account, a person in this condition would have the indicated proposition as an item of evidence.[12]

Now let us examine the arguments for E = K that Williamson offers in section 9.6. The first argument runs as follows: "When we prefer an hypothesis *h* to an hypothesis *h** because *h* explains our evidence *e* better than *h** does, we are standardly assuming *e* to be known; if we do not know *e*, why should *h*'s capacity to explain *e* confirm *h* for us?" (p. 200).

Our rival thesis, E = NPJ, would account for this phenomenon as follows. When we are propositionally justified in believing a proposition, we commonly (though not inevitably) believe we are so justified. If we believe we are so justified, we will also tend to assume that the proposition is true. If *e* is true, and if *h* explains its truth better than *h** explains it, then *h*'s capacity to explain *e* confirms *h* for us. There is no need to postulate E = K to explain this phenomenon.

The next two arguments run as follows: "It is likewise hard to see why the probability of *h* on *e* should regulate our degree of belief in *h* unless we know *e*. Again, an incompatibility between *h* and *e* does not rule out *h* unless *e* is known" (p. 200).

First, if we believe *e* to be true (given that we are justified vis-à-vis *e*), it is natural to regulate our degree of belief in *h* as a function of the truth of *e*. Specifically, it is reasonable to regulate our degree of belief in *h* by the probability

---

[11] Of course, my competing construal of evidence does not mesh with Williamson's evidentialist project of using the notion of evidence in a theory of justification, because my competing construal runs in the opposite direction—it uses justification in the account of evidence. But, if Williamson is to persuade *us* of his evidentialist project, he needs arguments to support or rationalize it. A pivotal group of such arguments is given in section 9.6, where he offers a challenge to find any account of evidence that fits as well with the "data" adduced there as E = K does. My competing construal is intended to meet that challenge, thereby undercutting the argument(s) for E = K, and indirectly undercutting the evidentialist program.

[12] I set aside the question of how such an approach to evidence would deal with cases in which prima facie justifiedness is defeated.

of *h* on *e*. Second, *e* does not have to be *known* (with all the baggage knowledge entails) for an incompatibility between *h* and *e* to rule out *h*. It suffices for *e* to be true. If *e* entails the falsity of *h*, and *e* is a given (that is, it is a given that it is true), then *h* can be ruled out.

Next Williamson adduces an extended example from which he derives several arguments for E = K.

Suppose that balls are drawn from a bag, with replacement . . . assume that someone else has already made the draws; I watch them on film. For a suitable number *n*, the following situation can arise. I have seen draws 1 to *n*; each was red (produced a red ball). I have not yet seen draw *n* + 1. I reason probabilistically, and form a justified belief that draw *n* + 1 was red too. My belief is in fact true. But I do not know that draw *n* + 1 was red. Consider two false hypotheses:

h: Draws 1 to *n* were red; draw *n* + 1 was black.
h*: Draw 1 was black; draws 2 to *n* + 1 were red.

It is natural to say that *h* is consistent with my evidence and that *h** is not. In particular, it is consistent with my evidence that draw *n* + 1 was black; it is not consistent with my evidence that draw 1 was black. Thus my evidence does not include the proposition that draw *n* + 1 was red. Why not? After all, by hypothesis I have a justified true belief that it was red. The obvious answer is that I do not *know* that draw *n* + 1 was red; the unsatisfied necessary condition for evidence is knowledge.   (pp. 200–1)

An alternative explanation is readily offered by E = NPJ. My evidence does not include the proposition that draw *n* + 1 was red because, although that proposition is justified, it isn't *non-inferentially* justified. On the contrary, it is justified by inductive inference. So the unsatisfied necessary condition for evidence, according to E = NPJ, is that evidence confers non-inferential justification.

Williamson comes close to anticipating this kind of response, but restricts the alternative possible explanation to justification based on *observation*. This leads him to another case, which he apparently takes to refute the contemplated alternative: "If I observe the truth of *e* and then forget all about it, my evidence no longer includes *e*. It is hard to see how evidence could discriminate between hypotheses in the way we want it to if it did not have to be known" (p. 201).

The thinking here appears to be that since I *did* observe the truth of *e*, the alternative theory has no way to account for my evidence *not* including *e* at the present time. But our theory, E = NPJ, accounts for the case quite easily. If I have forgotten about *e* (and am not currently observing *e*), then I am no longer non-inferentially propositionally justified in believing *e*. Hence, at the present time, *e* is not evidence for me.

Williamson's next argument runs as follows:

If evidence required only justified true belief, or some other good cognitive status short of knowledge, then a critical mass of evidence could set off a kind of chain reaction. Our known evidence justifies belief in various true hypotheses; they would count as evidence too, so this larger evidence set would justify belief in still more true hypotheses, which would in turn count as further evidence... The result would be very different from our present conception of evidence.   (p. 201)

Although the threat of a chain reaction may apply to a JTB account of evidence, it does not apply to the more restrictive account of evidence I am offering, which says that evidence propositions are *non-inferentially* justified propositions. No chain reaction is plausible under the NPJ account, because the chain would require inferential justification, which is precluded from the start. Secondly, however, I am puzzled that Williamson presents this argument against the JTB approach to evidence, because the contemplated chain reaction seems *almost* as threatening under the E = K construal. Clearly, E = K does not restrict evidence to non-inferential knowledge. So if one's 'basic' evidence justifies belief in various true hypotheses that are also *known*, a very similar chain reaction looms. It would probably be a less extensive chain reaction, because some of the justified true beliefs might not satisfy the requirement of safety, and hence not amount to knowledge. But failure of the safety requirement might not trim the chain reaction very much. So a comparably worrisome scenario seems applicable to the E = K thesis.

Williamson next proceeds to defend the truth requirement on evidence:

That propositional evidence is knowledge entails that propositional evidence is true. That is intuitively plausible; if one's evidence included falsehoods, it would rule out some truths, by being inconsistent with them. One's evidence may make some truths improbable, but it should not exclude any outright. Although we may treat false propositions as evidence, it does not follow that they are evidence. No true proposition is inconsistent with my evidence, although I may think that it is.   (p. 201)

Is it correct that evidence should never exclude a truth? Everybody agrees that there can be misleading evidence. Why cannot some evidence be deductively, as contrasted with inductively, misleading? The anticipated response is that, since the probability of an item of evidence on the total evidence is 1, the negation of an item of evidence will have a probability of 0, and that probability will be unrevisable via conditionalization. But it will not be unrevisable *full stop* unless evidence stays fixed, and it is an open question whether a proposition that is evidence at one time must be evidence forever. Indeed, Williamson himself rejects the evidence permanence thesis, which he calls "monotonicity" (pp. 206, 218). If *e* is ostensibly observed at one time, it may qualify as evidence at that time. But, at a later time, it may cease to qualify as evidence (and not merely through conditionalization). So allowing falsehoods as evidence does not entail that some truths are permanently consigned to epistemic oblivion.

A further reason Williamson gives for the view that all evidence consists of true propositions is that this explains the point of adjusting our beliefs to the evidence: "adjusting our beliefs to the evidence... is a way of adjusting them to the truth. Although true evidence can still support false conclusions, it will tend to support truths" (p. 202).

But E = K is not the only construal of evidence that can make sense of adjusting our beliefs to the evidence. E = NPJ can make sense of it too. If we assume that justified propositions are *likely* to be true (an assumption that conforms with many theories of justification), then adjusting our beliefs to the evidence is a way of adjusting them to what is usually or mostly true. Evidence so construed will sometimes support false conclusions, but this holds equally under E = K, as the foregoing passage concedes.

Next Williamson considers the objection that perceptual appearances can provide evidence even without belief, which implies the falsity of E = K.

But, a critic may suggest . . . [in cases of perceptual evidence] my evidence includes *e* because it is perceptually apparent to me that things are that way, whether or not I believe that they are that way. Even if I do believe *e*, my evidence included *e* even before I came to believe it; according to the critic, I came to believe it because it was perceptually apparent . . . We can ask the critic whether, for my evidence to include *e*, I must at least be *in a position* to know *e*? If so, then the critic's view does not differ radically from E = K. Given E = K, the evidence in my actual possession consists of the propositions which I know, but there is also the evidence in my potential possession, consisting of the propositions which I am in a position to know. The critic takes my evidence to be the evidence in my potential possession, not just the evidence in my actual possession. (pp. 202–3)

The critic imagined here endorses an approach not dissimilar to the one I am proposing. However, neither this critic nor I need to accept Williamson's characterization of the approach. For example, it is not being in a position to know *e* that makes it evidence; nor is having perceptual evidence a matter of the evidence merely being in my *potential* possession. Having evidence is a matter of (non-inferential) justification rather than knowledge. And in the perceptual case one is *actually* propositionally justified in believing *e*, not merely *potentially* so.

But Williamson poses a problem for this kind of view.

[S]uppose that I am in a position to know any one of the propositions $p_1, \ldots, p_n$ without being in a position to know all of them; there is a limit to how many things I can attend to at once. Suppose that in fact I know p_1 and do not know $p_2, \ldots, p_n$. According to E = K, my evidence includes only p_1; according to the critic, it includes $p_1, \ldots, p_n$. Let q be a proposition which is highly probable given $p_1, \ldots, p_n$ together, but highly improbable given any proper subset of them; the rest of my evidence is irrelevant to q. According to E = K, q is highly improbable on my evidence. According to the critic, q is highly probable on my evidence. E = K gives the more plausible verdict, because the high probability of q depends on an evidence set to which as a whole I have no access. (p. 203)

This argument says that the critic's view is implausible because the probability it assigns is based on a putative evidence set to which, as a whole, I (the cognitive agent) lack *access*. This is a highly unexpected argument to come from

Williamson. It is a core part of his book to deny that either knowledge or evidence is transparent. As he writes in the chapter on skepticism: "Rational thinkers are not always in a position to know what their evidence is; they are not always in a position to know what rationality requires of them . . ." (p. 164). So how can he regard it as a deficiency in the critic's position—or the closely related E = NPJ position—that one might not have access to one's evidence as a whole? It could still *be* one's evidence even if one does not have access to all of it.

Let me offer an example of my own to defend the greater plausibility of E = NPJ as compared with E = K. Consider a person who is quite cautious in doxastic matters, someone I shall call a *diffident doxastic agent* (DDA). One such person would be someone who suspends judgment about everything. We need not make our case, however, by reference to such an atypical, psychologically unrealistic, individual. Consider instead a DDA who has only mild states of credence, none of which rises to the level of belief (wherever that level of credence is set). It follows from the E = K thesis that such a DDA has no evidence at all, because knowledge requires belief.

Is it plausible to hold of such a DDA that he totally lacks evidence? This DDA, we may assume, has a full panoply of perceptual experiences. These experiences, I submit, provide him with evidence for many propositions. It might be debated exactly *which* propositions they are evidence for—physical-object propositions, internal state propositions, and so on. But a resolution of this debate does not affect the present argument. If, in virtue of these perceptual experiences, he is non-inferentially justified in believing any propositions, then according to E = NPJ, these propositions are items of evidence for him. This is a much more plausible view of his evidential state than E = K provides.

I conclude that Williamson does not offer a compelling rationale for the E = K thesis. A preferable view, notably different from E = K, has been outlined, which accounts for all the intuitive "data" Williamson adduces for E = K. No doubt there are many other possible views as well, intermediate between E = K and E = NPJ. The main point, however, is that no convincing argument has been given for E = K.

7. EVIDENCE AND SKEPTICISM

One of the chief attractions of E = K in Williamson's eyes is the help it offers in dealing with skepticism. A standard form of skepticism contends that one cannot know things about the external world even in the Good Case because one's evidence in the Good Case is identical to one's evidence in the Bad Case, so how can one tell that one is in the Good Case rather than the Bad Case? The E = K thesis makes it easy to reject the alleged evidential symmetry of the Good Case and the Bad Case, thereby undercutting the skeptic's argument. The skeptic is not entitled to assume that we have no more evidence in ordinary cases than in their skeptical counterparts, because the anti-skeptic contends that we do have more knowledge—hence more evidence—in ordinary cases than in their skeptical counterparts.

If our critique of the reasons given for E = K stands, E = K no longer looks so promising, and that seems to offer comfort to the skeptic. Is that the stance I mean to encourage? First, I do not mean to take a firm stance here on the best way(s) to reply to skepticism. Secondly, the alternative construal of evidence I have placed on the table may *also* leave room for the same reply to the skeptic Williamson favors—namely, that one has more evidence in the Good Case than in the Bad Case. Let us see why this is so.

Given E = NPJ, the extent of one's evidence in the Good Case and the Bad Case depends on the chosen account of non-inferential propositional justification. On certain approaches to justification, one would expect there to be more non-inferential propositional justification in the Good Case than in the Bad Case.[13] In particular, this is likely to hold for certain forms of externalism about justification, especially a form of reliabilism in which reliability is fixed by truth-ratios of belief *in the world in question*. An ordinary-world agent is likely to have more non-inferential propositional justification vis-à-vis perceptual propositions (about physical objects) than an experientially similar envatted agent would have.[14] Thus, the asymmetry of evidence between the Good Case and the Bad Case is defensible under *some* elaborations of the E = NPJ interpretation of evidence. Williamson, of course, would not be entirely happy with this upshot. He likes the E = K thesis in part because it fits with his "knowledge-first" approach to epistemology in general. The E = NPJ interpretation of evidence does not fit with the "knowledge-first" credo. I do not find that a liability, because I am unpersuaded of the "knowledge-first" theme. But it is a major virtue of Williamson's approach that it puts all these interesting theses on the table, and offers highly intriguing arguments for them.[15]

---

[13] Silins (2005) points out that there are various weaker versions of evidential externalism than the one Williamson offers. For example, an evidential externalist might accept the thesis that one's propositional evidence is what one justifiedly and truly believes (Silins 2005: 378). What is crucial to evidential externalism is that what evidence one has is sensitive to the environment one is in. Obviously, this is not equivalent to the E = K thesis. Silins himself weakly favors evidential internalism.

[14] For a defense of a process reliabilist account of immediate (non-inferential) justification, see Goldman (2008). However, that defense does not address the question of how reliability should be fixed. So it is silent on, and has no unambiguous consequences for, the present issue of skepticism.

[15] Special thanks to Dennis Whitcomb and Karson Kovakovich for extensive and astute comments on one version of this chapter, and to Alex Jackson, Igal Kvart, Ernest Sosa, and other participants in the Spring 2006 Epistemology seminar at Rutgers University for valuable comments on an earlier draft.

6

Knowledge and Objective Chance

John Hawthorne and Maria Lasonen-Aarnio

1

We think we have lots of substantial knowledge about the future. But contemporary wisdom has it that indeterminism prevails in such a way that just about any proposition about the future has a non-zero objective chance of being false.[1, 2] What should one do about this? One, pessimistic, reaction is scepticism about knowledge of the future. We think this should be something of a last resort, especially since this scepticism is likely to infect alleged knowledge of the present and past. One anti-sceptical strategy is to pin our hopes on determinism, conceding that knowledge of the future is unavailable in an indeterministic world. This is not satisfying either: we would rather not be hostage to empirical fortune in the way that this strategy recommends. A final strategy, one that we shall explore in this chapter, is one of reconciliation: knowledge of a proposition is compatible with a subject's belief having a non-zero objective chance of error.[3] Following Williamson, we are interested in tying knowledge to the presence or absence of error in close cases, and so we shall explore the connections between knowledge and objective chance within such a framework.

We do not want to get tangled up here in complications involved in attempting to formulate a necessary and sufficient condition for knowledge in terms of safety.

---

[1] We are not concerned in this chapter to explore the connection between knowledge and epistemic notions of chance, of the sort encoded by epistemic uses of modals. Note that in seeking reconciliation between knowledge and objective chance of error, we are not claiming that ordinary utterances of the form 'I know P and it might be that P is false' would be true, since it is epistemic modals that figure in such claims. Even if knowledge of P is compatible with an objective chance of error, that does not mean it is compatible with an epistemic chance of error.

[2] Not all notions of objective chance require indeterminism. For example, the conception of chance that one finds in statistical mechanics makes no such requirement. We are interested in how such notions relate to knowledge. But in this chapter we pursue the more limited goal of exploring how to salvage knowledge of the future in the face of indeterminism. (For more on chance in statistical mechanics, see Albert 2000).

[3] For reasons that will become clear below, a non-zero objective chance of error is not quite the same as the proposition believed being such that there is a non-zero chance of its being false.

Instead, we will assume the following rough-and-ready necessary condition: a subject knows P only if she could not easily have falsely believed P.[4] Assuming that easiness is to be spelt out in terms of close possible worlds, a subject knows P only if there is no close possible world in which she falsely believes P.[5] (We shall call the set of close possible worlds the 'safety set of worlds'.)

2

If the safety theorist wants to avoid widespread scepticism about knowledge of the future, he must be careful to disambiguate modal locutions such as 'could easily have been the case that' and 'there is a close possible world in which it is the case that'. In particular, not every world in which the same or very similar conditions obtain at a relevant time can be close. The problem is most acute in indeterministic worlds. But first let us introduce some terminology.

Branching possibilities are possible worlds sharing their histories with the actual world up to and including some time t. More precisely, let $H_{w, t}$ be a proposition stating the entire history of a world w up to and including a time t, and entailing the laws of nature at w. $H_{w, t}$ is necessarily equivalent to the conjunction of propositions about w up to and including t together with the laws of nature.[6] A branching possibility at a time t and world w is any possible world in which $H_{w, t}$ is true.[7] Indeterminism can be stated in terms of the notion of a branching possibility: a world is indeterministic if and only if it has branching counterfactual possibilities. Obviously, a counterfactual possibility can be branching at a time t but no longer be branching at a later time t'. For instance, at a time t before a coin was tossed twice, there were branching possibilities in which the coin landed heads on both of these two tosses, but, once it has landed tails on the first toss, possibilities in which it lands heads on both tosses are no longer branching.

Close possibilities are just close, in whatever sense of close is relevant for knowledge. We will allow the closeness of a world to vary from one time to

---

[4] Safety theorists are aware that it is slightly more accurate to mention methods in formulating a safety requirement: one knows P only if one could not easily have believed P falsely by a relevantly similar method. Nothing we say turns on this, so, for the sake of exposition, we set aside this refinement. Further, safety principles gain more power if we extend the principle as follows: one knows P only if one could not easily have had a false belief using a relevantly similar method (where the false belief may be in a different proposition). We are inclined to endorse some such principle, but have no need for the extra explanatory power here.

[5] Williamson (2000: 126–7) uses a formulation along these lines, though he speaks of cases rather than worlds.

[6] We will assume that, at any time, the chance of the laws of nature changing is 0.

[7] If there were only finitely many branching possibilities at a time t, then we could say that branching possibilities at t are those possibilities that have a non-zero chance of being the case, and that a proposition is true in some branching possibility at t if and only if it has a non-zero chance of being true at t. However, if there are infinitely many branching possibilities, then either they cannot all be equally probable, or else they must be assigned infinitesimally small chances or chances of 0.

another, and speak of close possibilities at a world w and time t. Relativizing closeness to times allows for danger and safety to be time relative.[8]

So far nothing has been said about whether being a branching possibility at a time t entails being a close possibility at t. One might certainly be tempted to accept the entailment. Consider extremely unlikely and bizarre 'quantum' events such as the event that a marble I drop tunnels through the whole house and lands on the ground underneath, leaving the matter it penetrates intact. On natural interpretations according to which the wave function represents facts of objective chance, such events are not merely nomologically possible, but have a non-zero chance of occurring. When I drop a marble, the situation can be redescribed as a cosmic lottery with immensely many tickets. In this lottery, holding a winning ticket means having one's marble tunnel through the house. Redescribing the situation as a kind of lottery invites thinking of the actual world as being surrounded by a sphere of equally close worlds, among them worlds in which the marble does tunnel. One might thus be led to the following principle, where '$Ch_{w,\,t}(P)$' stands for 'the chance of P at t in w':

Chance–Close World Principle

For all worlds w, times t, and propositions P, if $Ch_{w,\,t}(P) > 0$, then at t in w there is a close possibility in which P.[9]

This principle is disastrous for knowledge of a chancy future. For assume that at t a subject believes P, the proposition that her marble will not tunnel through the house, but that $\sim P$ has a non-zero chance of being true. Then, the conjunction $(\sim P \,\&\, H_{@,\,t})$ has a non-zero chance of being true at t, since the chance of $H_{@,\,t}$ at t is 1. Because all worlds in which $H_{@,\,t}$ is true are branching possibilities at t, there is a non-zero chance of being in a branching possibility in which $\sim P$. By the above principle, some such branching possibility is close. But the subject believes P in all branching possibilities at t. And so there will be a close possible world in which the subject falsely believes P.

If the safety theorist wants to avoid scepticism about knowledge of the future, he is pressured to deny the *Chance–Close World Principle*.[10] Denying this principle entails denying that all branching possibilities at a time t are close at t.[11] For assume that there is a world w, time t, and proposition P such that $Ch_{w,\,t}(P) > 0$, but P is not true in any close world at t. This entails that the

---

[8] See Williamson (2000: 124) on the idea that safety is time relative. Following Williamson's own emphasis on cases, it may ultimately be best to articulate ideas about safety in terms of centred worlds. We shall return to this theme later.

[9] Let $Close_{w,\,t}$ be the proposition that is true in all and only close worlds at t in w. Then, the Chance—Close World Principle is equivalent to the claim that $Ch_{w,\,t}(Close_{w,\,t}) = 1$.

[10] Similar issues arise if one wishes to save the truth of ordinary counterfactuals in a chancy world. For discussion, see Hawthorne (2005b).

[11] Though note that the converse does not hold: one can deny that all branching possibilities at t are close at t without denying the Chance–Close World Principle.

conjunction $(H_{w,\,t}\ \&\ P)$ is not true in any close world at t. But the conjunction $(H_{w,\,t}\ \&\ P)$ is true in some branching worlds at t. So there are branching worlds that are not close and, generally, being a branching possibility at a time t does not entail being close at t (or, indeed, at any other time).

What about the other direction of the entailment, from being a close possibility at a time t to being a branching possibility at t? The safety theorist also has ample reasons to deny this entailment. Assume that a subject believes P at t, and P concerns events at t or at earlier times (that is, the present or the past). If the safety set of worlds for the subject's belief in P consists only of branching close possibilities at t, then the truth of P would seem to guarantee that her belief is safe—for, normally, holding everything fixed up to and including t will hold fixed both everything a subject believes at t, and the truth of all propositions concerning t and earlier times.[12] To make meeting the safety requirement non-trivial, the safety set of worlds for the subject's belief must contain worlds that are not close and branching at t. One might indeed want to allow for close worlds that are not branching at *any* time. Nevertheless, all close branching worlds at t belong to the safety set of worlds for a subject's belief in a proposition P at t, whatever else might be part of that set.

In this section we have considered a distinction the safety theorist needs to draw in order to accommodate knowledge of the future in indeterministic worlds. In particular, the safety theorist must allow for branching possible worlds that are not close. Our main argument will be to show that, given a plausible connection between chance and modal closeness, this move is not sufficient to avoid scepticism about knowledge of the future. However, before presenting our argument, we briefly discuss an alternative argument relying on a closure principle for knowledge.

3

The argument from Closure Under Conjunction makes use of the following closure principle:

> For any subject s, and any propositions P, Q, if s knows P and s knows Q and s comes to believe $(P\ \&\ Q)$ based on competent deduction from P, Q, while retaining knowledge of both P and Q throughout, then s knows $(P\ \&\ Q)$.

Assume that a subject Suzy knows each proposition in a set $S_P = \{P_1, P_2, \ldots, P_n\}$ of high-chance propositions. Assume, for instance, that S_P consists of all the propositions that Suzy knows about the future. Suzy retains knowledge of each

---

[12] But see below for knowledge of contingent a priori truths.

proposition, and competently deduces conjunctions of these, finally arriving at the conjunction $(P_1 \& P_2 \& \ldots \& P_n)$ at a time t. In so far as she satisfies the antecedent of Closure Under Conjunction at each step, Suzy now knows $(P_1 \& P_2 \& \ldots \& P_n)$. But assume also that the chance of $(P_1 \& P_2 \& \ldots \& P_n)$ at t is very low. There seems to be something seriously wrong with allowing subjects to know such low-chance propositions.[13]

Care must be taken in attempting to capture the intuitive epistemological principle that is violated by allowing subjects to know low-chance propositions such as $(P_1 \& P_2 \& \ldots \& P_n)$. On a somewhat tempting diagnosis, the problem is just that they are highly unlikely. And so:

> For all worlds w, times t, subjects s, and propositions P, if $\mathrm{Ch}_{w,\,t}(P)$ is low, then s does not know P at t in w.

But this principle has counter-examples created by knowledge of contingent a priori truths.

For instance, assume that a lottery draw is about to take place, and Suzy fixes the reference of 'Lucky' as 'the winner of the lottery'. Suzy knows that the lottery has 1,000,000 tickets, each owned by a different person, that it is fair, and that exactly one person will win. And assume that the winner is in fact John. Despite the fact that its reference was fixed by a description, 'Lucky' is a singular term, and the proposition expressed by 'Lucky will win the lottery' is not the necessarily true proposition that whoever will win the lottery will win the lottery but, rather, a contingent, singular proposition about John. In so far as Suzy can have this singular proposition as the content of her propositional attitudes in the situation described, and 'the winner of the lottery' picks out different people in different branching worlds at t, Suzy believes different singular propositions in different branching worlds. Moreover, at a time t prior to the draw she will be able to have a priori knowledge of the singular proposition expressed by 'Lucky will win the lottery', despite the fact that at t the chance that Lucky, that is, John, will win the lottery is very low.[14]

To avoid ruling out knowledge of low-chance contingent a priori truths, the epistemological principle that is violated by allowing subjects to know overwhelmingly unlikely conjunctions must be revised. This can be done by formulating a principle in terms of the chance of a belief-episode of a subject expressing a true proposition, rather than the chance of the proposition in fact expressed by the belief-episode:

Low Chance

For all worlds w, times t, subjects s, belief-episodes B, and propositions P, if at t s's belief-episode B expresses proposition P, at t the chance that B

---

[13] Hawthorne (2005a) gives this argument.
[14] Consider similarly known propositions of the form $\lceil P$ if and only if actually $P \rceil$.

expresses a true proposition is low, and at t s is not inadmissibly connected to the future, then s does not know P at t in w.[15]

The clause about inadmissible connections restricts the principle to cases in which there are no time-travellers from the future, clairvoyance by backwards causation, and so on. *Low Chance* is compatible with knowledge of low-chance, contingent a priori truths. For, though at t the chance that Lucky (that is, John) will win the lottery is low, Suzy's belief-episode does not have a low chance of expressing a truth. In different branching possibilities at t 'Lucky' will refer to different persons, in each world to whoever wins the race in *that* world. And in none of these branching worlds does Suzy's belief-episode express a false proposition.

It is also worth noting in passing that low-chance, contingent a priori truths create trouble for the so-called Principal Principle.[16] This principle entails that, if at a time t a subject is certain that the chance of a certain outcome is x, and is not inadmissibly connected to the future, then the credence she assigns to the outcome at t should likewise be x. Assume that in the case described Suzy is certain, and knows, that, for any one ticket in the lottery, the objective chance of that ticket winning is 0.000001. She is also certain that whoever 'Lucky' refers to, the objective chance of that person winning at t, prior to the draw, is 0.000001. By the Principal Principle, the credence Suzy should assign to the proposition that Lucky will win the lottery is 0.000001, since she is certain that that is the objective chance that Lucky will win. But this is not right, for, given that she is certain that the lottery has exactly one winner, and that 'Lucky' refers to this winner, the credence Suzy ought to assign to the proposition that Lucky will win is 1. To say the least, the Principal Principle needs to be revised in the light of contingent a priori knowledge.[17]

Setting such issues aside, there are various ways of responding to the argument from Closure Under Conjunction. One is to fault the argument's reliance on closure.[18] Another is to impose a constraint on what a subject can know at any one time that prevents problem-generating cases from arising. In particular, if $\{B_1, B_2, \ldots, B_n\}$ is the set of all belief-episodes giving rise to beliefs in propositions that a subject knows at a time t, then the chance at t that at least one of these belief-episodes expresses a false proposition cannot be high. This allows for knowledge of the future, but restricts how much a subject can know at any

---

[15] We speak of 'inadmissably connected' instead of the more usual 'inadmissable evidence', because we do not wish to deny either knowledge of the future or that knowledge is evidence.

[16] See Lewis (1986a).

[17] There is similarly no Principal Principle style connection between objective chance and evidential probability.

[18] Assume a threshold model of outright belief on which assigning a sufficiently high credence to a proposition entails believing it. Someone might try to deny that the antecedent of Closure Under Conjunction can ever be satisfied when a conjunction is low-chance, simply because rational subjects never believe such conjunctions. The problem with this response is that, though credences filter down across multi-premiss entailments, they might not do this quickly enough, since the credence a subject assigns to a proposition need not equal its chance.

one time. It thus prevents subjects from pooling together their knowledge, since the conjunction of everything various subjects know might have a low chance.

Neither of these responses will help with the argument we present below. Our argument does not rely in any way on closure. It is also compatible with the suggested restriction on what can be known by a subject at any one time, since it assumes only that one subject can know one proposition about the future. The argument does rely on the assumption that there should be no restriction on how many subjects can know things about the future at any time t. If there is knowledge of the future in the first place, then it should be possible for each subject in a very large set of subjects to know some high-chance proposition about the future, even if the conjunction of all the known propositions has a very low chance of being true. It also relies on a principle stating that high-chance propositions are true in some close worlds.

4

What we call the *High Chance–Close Possibility* argument rests on the following principle connecting high chance and modal closeness:

> *High Chance–Close Possibility Principle* (HCCP principle)
>
> For any world w, time t, and proposition P, if $\mathrm{Ch}_{w,\,t}(P)$ is high, then there is a close branching possibility at t in w in which P.

This principle states that high-chance propositions are true in some close worlds. Let CloseBranching$_{w,\,t}$ be the proposition that is true in all worlds that are close and branching at t in w. The High Chance–Close Possibility Principle is equivalent to a principle stating that for any world w and time t, it is not the case that $\sim$CloseBranching$_{w,\,t}$ has a high chance.[19]

Prima facie at least, it looks as though the safety theorist ought to subscribe to the HCCP principle. It is overwhelmingly natural to think that high-chance events could easily have occurred. If there is a high objective chance of a washing machine breaking down, it is hard to deny that it could easily break. If there is a high chance that I will die climbing a certain route, then it is not safe for me to embark on the climb. Similarly, *mutatis mutandis*, for belief and error. Assuming

---

[19] The HCCP principle entails that $\mathrm{Ch}_{w,\,t}(\sim$CloseBranching$_{w,\,t})$ is not high. For assume that $\mathrm{Ch}_{w,\,t}(\sim$CloseBranching$_{w,\,t})$ is high. Then, by the HCCP principle, there would have to be a close branching world at t in w in which $(\sim$CloseBranching$_w)$ is true, which is impossible. That $\mathrm{Ch}_{w,\,t}(\sim$CloseBranching$_{w,\,t})$ is not high entails the HCCP principle. Assume that $\mathrm{Ch}_{w,\,t}(\sim$CloseBranching$_{w,\,t})$ is not high, and that P is not true in any close branching possibility at t in w. Then, P entails $\sim$CloseBranching$_w$, and $\mathrm{Ch}_{w,\,t}(P) \cdot \mathrm{Ch}_{w,\,t}(\sim$CloseBranching$_{w,\,t})$. But because $\mathrm{Ch}_{w,\,t}(\sim$CloseBranching$_{w,\,t})$ is not high, $\mathrm{Ch}_{w,\,t}(P)$ likewise is not high. Hence, there can be no proposition that is not true in any close branching world at t in w and that has a high chance at t in w. (We are here assuming that the chance of any proposition is either high or not high.)

the modal analysis—which is part of the framework of safety theory—events that could easily occur, or events that are not safe from not occurring, will occur in some close worlds. This validates the HCCP principle.

The problem created by the HCCP principle is the following. Suppose that I have just dropped a marble. Assume, contra the sceptic, that I can know, while it is in midair, that it will land on the floor. Moreover, this piece of knowledge should not, it seems, depend on what else is going on in the world outside what we assume for all practical purposes to be a closed system consisting of me and my marble—in particular, it should not depend on how many other subjects hold beliefs about other falling marbles. The existence of such subjects should have no effect on my epistemic position. Then, it looks to be nomologically possible for there to be a very large set of propositions $S_P = \{P_1, P_2, \ldots, P_n\}$, a world w, a time t, and a set of subjects $s = \{s_1, s_2, \ldots, s_n\}$ such that

(i) at t in w, each proposition $P_i \in S_P$ is known by exactly one subject $s_i \in s$,

(ii) each proposition $P_i \in S_P$ is about a time t' after t,

(iii) at t the chance of the conjunction of all propositions in S_P (P_1 & P_2 & ... & P_n), is low.

(For example, consider a world where many subjects have just dropped a marble, each believing simultaneously that their recently dropped marble is floor-bound. Suppose that each marble has a non-zero chance of tunnelling through the floor and that there is probabilistic independence.[20] If the number of subject–marble pairs is large enough, the conjunction of all the propositions believed by the subjects about their marbles will be highly unlikely.)

By safety, if each of our subjects knows the relevant proposition in S_P, then none will falsely believe that proposition in any world that is close and branching at t. In the present case, this requires that, for any subject s_i, proposition P_i will be true in all close branching worlds at t. Here is why. For reasons given above and having to do with contingent a priori truths, it cannot be assumed that a subject holds exactly the same belief at t in all worlds that are branching possibilities at t: externalism about the contents of thoughts extends outside a subject's skin not only to the environment, but also to the future. But not all thoughts supervene on future facts. If I now believe that this marble is floor-bound, there is no reason to think that just which content I entertain depends on the future. If each subject in the case described above is to satisfy safety, then the relevant marble-belief of each subject must be true in all branching worlds at t. Hence, if (i) above is true, and each proposition in S_P is known by some subject at t, the conjunction (P_1 & P_2 & ... & P_n) must be true in all close branching worlds at t.

---

[20] The simplifying assumption of independence is not essential for our argument. Suppose, for example, that, instead of the tunnelling possibilities being probabilistically independent, there was 'entanglement' that disrupted independence. So long as the chance of any given marble tunnelling is low but the chance of at least one marble tunnelling is high, the argument in the text applies.

Because the conjunction (P_1 & P_2 & ... & P_n) has a low chance of being true at t, then by the HCCP principle its negation ($\sim P_1$ or $\sim P_2$ or ... or $\sim P_n$), will be true in some close branching world at t: at least one of the marbles tunnels in a close branching world at t. Then, by safety, not every subject can know of his or her marble that it will come to rest on the floor, and our assumption is false.

It is essential to the problem-generating case that each subject is in the same epistemic position. This is hard to challenge. It would be ad hoc to select a privileged set of knowing subjects. But denying all of the subjects knowledge would be equally implausible, for it would make knowledge depend on facts that it seems it ought not to depend on. In particular, how could facts such as how many other subjects hold beliefs about the future have any impact on whether one subject knows that her marble will not tunnel? Odd counterfactuals would come out as true: 'Had those other subjects held beliefs about their marbles, I would not have known that my marble would come to rest on the floor.' (There is, of course, the sceptical alternative of denying that subjects can ever know propositions with non-zero chances of being false. But we are currently in the anti-sceptical business.)

Despite this, someone might bite the bullet and allow that what a subject knows depends on how many other subjects there are in her world holding beliefs about the future, placing the following restriction on the set of propositions that are known by some subject or other at a time: the conjunction of all the propositions in the set must have a high chance at that time.[21] This would make knowledge much more sparse than it appears to be, vindicating at least partial scepticism. And the problem of choosing just which beliefs constitute knowledge is by no means minor. Do I know that my marble is floor-bound or that my pen is? That I am meeting John on Tuesday or that I am attending a seminar on Wednesday?

Similar problems arise for knowledge of the present and past, though in those cases trouble cannot be created *just* by appeal to the HCCP principle, for if a proposition P is true at a time t, then its chance at t is 1, and there is no branching world at t in which it is false. Rather, what would be needed is some principle connecting high chance at a time t with close possibilities at a slightly later time t'. Suffice it to say that in many cases such connections seem very plausible. For instance, if a lottery draw has recently taken place and I won, but the result has not been announced, and I believe all along that I am the winner, then there is still now a close world in which I falsely believe I won, given that I had a high chance of losing prior to the draw. In the light of this, the case discussed above could be altered in the following way: it is 12.01, and for each subject, a different marble was dropped at noon somewhere where it could not

---

[21] Applying the ingenious model in Williamson (2005e: 485–7) to reconcile widespread knowledge with widespread risk would mean imposing some such requirement.

be observed by anyone. At 12.01 each subject believes of his or her marble that it is on the floor.

5

We have been discussing cases in which each belief in a large set of beliefs is held simultaneously. But perhaps the lesson can be extended to diachronic cases. In particular, there are chains of knowledge acquisition, transmission, and preservation stretching across time that are globally risky despite consisting of locally excellent steps. Because it is highly likely that something goes wrong at some step in the chain, one might worry that some principle very much like the High Chance–Close Possibility Principle forces the safety theorist to fault some step in the chain. But, the worry is, this would mean giving up some plausible principle concerning knowledge, such as the principle that a belief in a proposition competently deduced from a known single proposition itself constitutes knowledge (single-premiss closure). Devotees of closure are pushed to transmit knowledge across chains that are, overall, highly risky.

Here are a few examples of the sorts of chains we have in mind. First, the *deduction chain*. Assume that at t_0 a subject knows a true proposition P_0, and deduces from it a proposition P_1. She is an excellent deducer, but, prior to the deduction, there is a 0.000001 chance that her deductive capacities will lead her astray. For, whenever she is about to perform a deduction, a random lottery occurs in her brain, and in the unlucky case she infers a falsehood without realizing her predicament. Now she goes on to perform 99,999 more successful deductions, reaching a true proposition P_n. At t_0 there is a high chance of going wrong at some step of a 1,000,000-step deduction. Further, let us assume that at t_0 there is a high chance of forming a false belief as the result of a 1,000,000-step deduction. If close branching worlds at t_0 are a subset of the safety set of worlds for the subject's belief in P_n, then the safety theorist will have to say that the subject does not know proposition P_n. Consequently, single-premiss closure will fail: there will be a step in the deduction at which the subject knows a proposition P_i, competently deduces from it a proposition P_{i+1}, but fails to know proposition P_{i+1}.

Similar cases are easy to construct for testimonial transmission of knowledge from one subject to another, and preservative memory. In the latter case, a subject knows a proposition P at a time t_0, and retains a belief in P over a long period of time, up to and including t_n. During each i-length interval of time beginning from t_0 there is a non-zero chance that the subject's preservative memory malfunctions in a way that leads her to form a false belief. Assume that at t_0 there is a high chance that some malfunction of memory will occur during the period $t_0 \ldots t_n$ and, further, that at t_0 there is a high chance that by t_n the subject's preservative memory will have produced in her a false belief. Call this the *memory chain*. Again, if branching worlds at t_0 are a subset of the safety class of worlds for the subject's belief in P at t_n, then she will fail to know P at t_n. If the safety theorist denies that the subject knows P at t_n, one might worry that some plausible principle along the following lines will be violated: if a subject knows a proposition P at t_i, and competently preserves P in memory between t_i and t_{i+1}, then at t_{i+1} the subject knows P.

However, in such diachronic cases it is more difficult to find a plausible principle connecting chance and modal closeness as a means to showing that some step in the chain fails to transmit or produce knowledge. Just like chance, closeness and safety are time relative. For instance, assume that yesterday there was a high chance that at noon today I am drugged and undergo a hallucination of a tree. Despite this, at noon today worlds in which I am drugged need not be part of the safety set of worlds. If the person who would have drugged me happened to die and at noon I veridically perceive a tree, then there will be no close world with relevantly similar initial conditions in which I form a false belief. Hence, it cannot be simply assumed that in the chain cases described close branching worlds at a time t_0 are a subset of the safety set of worlds for a belief a subject holds at a time t_n.

Whether or not knowledge is allowed to transmit across the sorts of chains described, there are puzzles to solve. In each chain case described, some knowledge transmission principle forces attributing knowledge across the chain. These principles state that knowledge is extended over competent deduction, competent preservation of belief in memory, or competent testimonial transmission. If knowledge does not transmit across the chains described, some seemingly very plausible principle about knowledge such as single-premiss closure has to give. If it does, various oddities will have to be dealt with. Among these are peculiar asymmetries of the following sort, created by the seemingly magical effect had by being appropriately linked to a knowledge-transmitting or knowledge-producing chain.

Take the deduction chain described above. Let us assume that Suzy underakes such a chain of deductions, and that she also knows the relevant facts about the chain. At t_0 she knows that there is a high chance that, if she attempts to carry out 1,000,000 deductions, she will end up believing a falsehood. For simplicity, assume also that it is certain that she will enter a chain involving 1,000,000 inferences. By single-premiss closure, as long as Suzy in fact deduces competently throughout, it looks as though at the end of the chain, at t_n, she knows proposition P_n.[22] Now consider an onlooker, John. At t_0 it is certain on John's evidence that Suzy will enter a 1,000,000-step inferential chain. John

---

[22] Those that are inclined to deploy the rhetoric of defeaters as an all-purpose fix to epistemological problems will surely be inclined to trot out that rhetoric here. We believe that the concept of a defeater is both woefully underdeveloped and woefully overdeployed, but here is not the place to pursue the matter.

knows the relevant facts about Suzy's deductive abilities, and at t_0 it is highly likely on John's evidence that the proposition at the end of Suzy's chain is false. Moreover, John has no intuitions about the truth of the propositions deduced by Suzy, is incapable of deducing, and could not spot possible mistakes made by Suzy. At t_n John learns that the chain has led Suzy to believe proposition P_n. It looks as though at t_n the probability on John's evidence that the proposition at the end of Suzy's chain is true is exactly the same as the probability on his evidence at t_0 that the proposition at the end of Suzy's chain is true, and equals the probability at t_n on John's evidence that P_n is true. John, unlike Suzy, is not in a position to know P_n.

Suppose that John is disposed to believe whatever Suzy comes up with at the end of long deductions by eavesdropping. Presumably this does not generate knowledge any more than John could get knowledge from a highly unreliable barometer (albeit one that sometimes delivers correct information thanks to myriad locally excellent steps). Safety does nothing to explain the asymmetry between John and Suzy. Given that the truth of both Suzy's and John's beliefs depends on Suzy's deductions, the truth of the relevant beliefs marches in step across close possible worlds. If Suzy's beliefs are safe, so are John's. So why does John not know P_n? The peculiarity of the situation is only sharpened by assuming a transmission principle for testimony stating that, if a subject s knows a proposition P, and another subject s^* comes to believe P solely based on s's competent testimonial transmission of P, then s^* knows P. For then John could come to know P_n based on Suzy's testimony, even if he could not know by eavesdropping! Further, prior to Suzy's testimony, John would not be in a position to know that, if Suzy testifies that P_n, then P_n. But, once the testimonial transmission has taken place, John is in a position to know P_n. Chain-related issues are indeed bewildering, but we shall not pursue them further here.

6

The High Chance–Close Possibility Principle combines with the following assumption to create sceptical trouble: knowledge of P entails that there is no close possible world in which the subject holds a relevant false belief.

There are three main non-sceptical options for the safety theorist. The first is to liberalize safety by conceding that knowledge is tolerant to holding a false belief at a small proportion of close worlds: it is enough that a subject avoids false belief in *most* close worlds. The second is to revise the modal account of safety by framing safety not in terms of possible worlds, but in terms of subject-centred worlds. The third is to deny the HCCP principle, thereby forsaking any systematic connection between objective chance and modal closeness. In the remainder of this chapter we briefly outline these options. (We leave it as an exercise to the reader to figure out why adding a dose of contextualism to safety does not help.)

(i)

Let 'most worlds safety' refer to the modified safety requirement on which knowledge is compatible with holding false beliefs in some close possible worlds. The most worlds safety theorist is much better equipped to accommodate knowledge of the future in indeterministic worlds. Within such a framework, there is no need to give up the *Chance–Close World Principle* in the first place.

Most worlds safety at least encourages one to think that one can know that a ticket in a lottery will lose (so long as it does lose). But perhaps this result is to be welcomed. After all, it is desperately difficult to explain why such propositions cannot be known even though much of our alleged knowledge is subject to similar risks.

A potentially more worrying entailment is that multi-premiss closure fails. For, even if P is true in most close worlds and Q is true in most close worlds, the conjunction (P & Q) might fail to be true in most close worlds. Though we cannot argue for the claim here, the most worlds safety theorist even has trouble with single-premiss closure, for the simple reason that even competent deduction from a single premiss can bring with it an element of risk or danger.[23]

If multi-premiss closure is false, then any reasoning from more than one premiss becomes problematic, no matter how infallible the deductive capacities of a subject are. And even the simplest practical reasoning typically proceeds from two premisses:

1. P.
2. If P, I should φ.

Therefore,

3. I should φ.

Most worlds safety allows situations to arise in which a subject knows P; knows that, if P, she should φ; competently deduces and comes to believe that she should φ from these premisses, but does not know that she should φ.

And there are further problems. A safety requirement for knowledge (and not some extra tacked-on requirement), we take it, is supposed to eliminate the problematic sort of epistemic luck involved in Gettier cases. But the revised safety requirement seems unable to rule out standard Gettier cases, for the reason that any belief-episode with a high chance of being true looks to be safe.[24] But beliefs in high-chance propositions can be Gettiered. Take the following example. A

---

[23] This is argued by Lasonen-Aarnio (forthcoming).
[24] Lasonen-Aarnio (2007).

pyromaniac is about to strike a match. At a time *t* prior to striking the match she infers, and thereby comes to believe, that it will light when struck from her knowledge that it is a dry match of a brand that has always lit for her when dry and struck. There is a small chance that the particular match she holds will not light by friction when struck. And, in fact, the match does not light by friction. But it lights nevertheless, because of a burst of rare *Q*-radiation.[25] This looks very similar to Russell's stopped-clock case in which a subject fails to have knowledge of the time based on having looked at a normally reliable clock that just happened to stop twelve hours before. The pyromaniac has a justified belief that is due to a bout of luck, but seems to lack knowledge. Nevertheless, her belief is actually true, and true in most close worlds, since in most close worlds the match lights in the normal way by friction.

<h2 style="text-align:center">(ii)</h2>

Upon closer inspection, the idea that knowledge requires avoiding false belief in close worlds seems implausible to begin with. When evaluating whether a subject could easily have held a false belief, we are ordinarily only interested in whether things could easily have been a certain way as regards *that subject*. The worry is that, even if closeness is relativized to times, global similarities elsewhere can outweigh radical, local dissimilarities regarding the situation of one subject. For instance, allowing one subject to be envatted, but keeping everything else fixed as far as possible, might make for a possible world that is, overall, close to the actual world.

In effect, Williamson gives modal truth-conditions for safe belief in terms of close cases rather than worlds. He states that a case is 'like a possible world, but with a distinguished subject and time', or what Lewis calls a 'centred world'.[26] Centring on times was already implicit in our discussion above, and now the idea is to centre further on subjects.

We will follow Lewis in thinking of centred words as pairs of worlds and space–time points in those worlds.[27] For instance, $<(l, t), w>$ is a centring of world w under the space–time point (l, t). Some space–time points are occupied by subjects. Let such occupied centred worlds be *subject-centred worlds*. Surrounding each subject-centred world is a possibility-space consisting of subject-centred worlds with relevantly similar centrings, occupied by the same subject. The new safety requirement is stated in terms of avoiding false belief in close subject-centred worlds. To get the right anti-sceptical results, the closeness relation for subject-centred worlds must assign special weight to propositions believed by the subject occupying the centre of a world. So, for instance, if Suzy is to know that her marble is floor-bound, there can be no close subject-centred

[25] The case is modified from Skyrms (1967: 383).   [26] Williamson (2000: 52).
[27] Lewis (1983: 149).

world in which her marble tunnels, though there might well be close worlds in which other subjects' marbles tunnel. Indeed, assuming some analogue of the High Chance–Close Possibility Principle, some tunnelling will have to take place in close subject-centred worlds.[28]

One problem with the resulting position is that, as long as it is assumed that high-chance propositions are true in some close subject-centred worlds, there is still a limit to how much any one subject can know at any one time. In particular, the chance of the conjunction of everything a subject knows at any one time cannot be low, whether or not the subject believes the conjunction. (As a result, different subjects cannot pool their knowledge together.) Allowing the epistemic status of a subject's belief to depend in this way on how many other beliefs the subject holds in propositions with non-zero chances of falsity is not as absurd as allowing the epistemic status of a subject's belief to depend on facts about how many *other* subjects hold beliefs in propositions about the future. But the sceptical worry remains that knowledge would become sparse. And is there any non ad hoc way of deciding just which propositions a subject knows at any one time?

Assume, for instance, that Suzy holds beliefs about very many marbles at one time t. At t each marble has exactly the same low chance of tunnelling, but the chance that at least one will tunnel is high. Moreover, each of Suzy's beliefs is based on the same sort of evidence. It would seem ad hoc to allow for some, but not all, of her beliefs to count as knowledge. But it would also be odd not to allow for her to know *any* of the propositions she believes about where marbles are headed. For then the following odd circumstance would obtain: had she formed beliefs only about n marbles, and not about $n + m$ marbles, she would have known of each of n marbles that it would come to rest on the floor.

A natural development of the subject-centred approach gives special weight to propositions that have special bearing on the life of the subject in the centre of the world. If I believe of many people that they will live through the night, and have the same kind of evidence for each, then it is the ones who are nearest and dearest that are known by me to be survivors. This protects much of the knowledge we care about, though at the cost of delivering very odd sounding truths: 'I know Bill, my friend, will live through the night, but not Fred, since I do not care about him.' 'I would have known that Fred would live through the night had I cared more about him.' Nor will such a move make the restriction problem go away entirely. After all, my friendships may be too plentiful.

The problems we have been considering might be escaped by some more centring. If the propositions believed by a subject must be assigned special weight

---

[28] Here is a rough-and-ready formulation of the principle applied to subject-centred worlds: for any time t, location l, world w, and proposition P, if $\mathrm{Ch}_{w,\,t}(P)$ is high, then there is a centred world close to $<(l, t),\ w>$ in which P.

in any case, why not also centre around belief-episodes? Let *super-centred* worlds be worlds that are centred not only around a subject and time, but also around a belief-episode of the subject. A subject's belief in a proposition P is safe if and only if there is no close super-centred world in which the relevant belief-episode gives rise to a false belief (or a mere illusion of content).[29]

One likely casualty of super-centring is multi-premiss closure. Even if a subject knows each of $P_1, \ldots P_n$, there is no guarantee that she is in a position to know their conjunction. For, when evaluating whether she knows the conjunction $(P_1 \& \ldots \& P_n)$, we centre around a belief-episode that is distinct from any of the belief-episodes giving rise to the subject's beliefs in $P_1, \ldots, P_n$. Moreover, if one adopts a suitable analogue of High Chance–Close Possibility while using super-centring to safeguard widespread knowledge, failures of multi-premiss close are bound to occur. This is far from devastating. Given the alternatives that precede and follow, an anti-sceptical solution grounded in super-centring is a serious option.

(iii)

A final option is simply to reject the High Chance–Close Possibility Principle. This would make safety powerless to prohibit knowledge that contravenes Low Chance. Allowing such knowledge risks disrupting intuitive connections between knowledge, ease of mistake, and danger. After all, as noted above, it is hard to deny that, if there is a high chance of an event of a certain type occurring, then an event of that type could easily have occurred. And it is similarly hard to deny that high-chance events are in danger of occurring.[30] Rejecting the HCCP principle threatens to sever the very connections between knowledge and objective danger that were seemingly integral to motivating a safety requirement on knowledge in the first place. (Note that such motivations were front and centre in Williamson's own discussions of safety.[31]) Of course, it is conceivable that one could reject the HCCP principle but still prohibit low-chance knowledge on grounds other than safety. Unless combined with a much more widespread scepticism, this would make multi-premiss closure untenable. Moreover, it would considerably dilute the explanatory work that safety was fit to perform in epistemological theorizing.

---

[29] Interestingly, once one has super-centring, it is rather less clear whether one needs the distinction between close worlds in which relevantly similar methods are deployed and those in which they are not. Why not just make methods a criterion of closeness of super-centred worlds?

[30] It is at least less clear that, in the ordinary sense of hope and danger, any non-zero chance event has a hope of/is in danger of occurring. (After all, I may say that there is no hope of you finding a ring that you dropped on a vast beach, and that there is no danger of dying from a simple medical procedure, owing to the fact that the relevant chances are so small they can be discounted.)

[31] See, e.g., Williamson (2000: 123–4).

CONCLUSION

The sceptical pressures posed by chance are not to be underestimated. It is very tempting to surrender to scepticism about knowledge of the future when faced with chance-based considerations, thereby initiating descent into a more widespread sceptical abyss. The epistemically brave of heart will have to super-centre, embrace knowledge in the face of danger, or take refuge in something like most worlds safety. Such choices cannot be made by casual head counting on judgements about cases. After all, it is clear that resisting scepticism will require giving up a range of highly intuitive judgements about knowledge, which in turn casts doubt on a simple case-driven methodology. The best we can do is to reflect on what is structurally important about knowledge to our cognitive lives.[32]

[32] This joint project was prompted by the discovery that we had independently come up with the 'High Chance–Close Possibility Argument' as well as the same taxonomy of possible solutions. The choice of formulation stays close to the version in Lasonen-Aarnio's D.Phil. thesis. We are most grateful to Timothy Williamson for extended discussion, which helped sharpen the central arguments and drew our attention to the broader significance of the contrast between global risk and local excellence.

7

Primeness, Internalism, Explanation

Frank Jackson

1.   We often explain what happens in terms of the possession of factive mental states. We explain Jones's turning up on time in terms of his *remembering* when the appointment was. Smith won the spelling bee because she *knew* how to spell 'antimacassar'. And the factive element is typically important to the explanation. Part of the reason Jones turned up on time is that his opinion about the time of the appointment was correct. Part of the reason Smith won is that her opinion about the spelling was correct. But being in a factive mental state places a requirement both on how one—the subject in the factive state—is, and on how one's environment is. A sufficient reason for stones' not remembering or knowing anything is that they are never the right way to remember or know anything; a sufficient condition for no one's remembering or knowing that the Battle of Hastings was fought in 1070 is that it was not. This raises the question of the relative contributions to the explanatory task of, on the one hand, the way the subject is, and, on the other, the way the environment is.

Many have held, for one reason or another, first, that the state of the subject plays a privileged role in the explanatory task, and, secondly, that, in any case, we do best to separate out the explanatory contributions of the two elements. When we appeal to Smith's knowledge of how to spell 'antimacassar' as the explanation of her winning the spelling bee, the explanation is, runs this line of thought, best thought of as proceeding in terms of something more particularly about her—say, her believing that 'antimacassar' is the right way to spell 'antimacassar'—together with the fact that 'antimacassar' is indeed the right way to spell 'antimacassar', perhaps combined with whatever it is about the belief that makes it count as knowledge and not mere true belief. The first will especially bear on her producing the word 'antimacassar' at the appropriate stage of the spelling bee; the second will especially bear on her receiving the tick for that answer that allowed her to draw ahead of the competition; and the third will especially bear on, as it might be, whether her winning was a fluke. *Mutatis mutandis* for the example of remembering, and for a variant on the spelling bee example where the explanation of her winning the spelling bee is her remembering how to spell 'antimacassar'.

This line of thought is generated by various combinations of views about causal explanations of behaviour and views about the nature of factive mental states that lead in one way or another to the idea that factive states, or any way the examples of memory and knowledge, are composite or conjunctive states. In *Knowledge and its Limits*[1] Timothy Williamson (2000) lays down an extended, important challenge to this line of thought and the idea that these states are composite. The issues are complex, involving the intersection of questions about the nature of mental states, the notion of causal efficacy and its relation to causal explanation, what kinds of states can be causally efficacious, and what it is for a state to be a conjunctive or composite state.

I seek to cast light on the issues by stating what I take to be the line of argument that starts from reflections on explanations in terms of mental states to the conclusion that remembering and knowing are conjunctive states. I end up, that is, opposing Williamson's view that such states are *prime*. It seems to me that a majority of philosophers of mind have taken it to be more or less obvious that remembering and knowing are not prime states. But when something is thought obvious—maybe, in some cases, thought to be too obvious to need argument—it can be salutary, and far from easy, to say why, exactly, we should hold that remembering and knowing are conjunctive. Williamson has laid down an important challenge to orthodoxy.

2.   What does the thesis that factive mental states like knowing and remembering are conjunctive or composite come to? One way to construe the question is as one about the possibility of reductive analyses of sentences ascribing states of knowing and remembering in terms of conjunctions of more fundamental notions. The analysis of knowing that *p* in terms of true justified belief that *p* would be an example; so would an analysis of remembering that *p* in terms of believing that *p* suitably caused by the fact that *p*, provided that 'suitably' was given a non-circular construal. We might think of this construal as the *de dicto* way of understanding our topic. Our concern, however, will be with our topic understood *de re*—as, that is, a thesis about the states themselves. There are interesting questions about the relation between our topic understood *de dicto* and our topic understood *de re*, but we will not address them here.

As a thesis about the states themselves, conjunctivism is a claim about the similarity patterns through logical space that obtain for knowing and for remembering. Squareness is that which unites all square things in logical space.[2] Remembering that *p* is that which unites all cases of remembering that *p* in

    [1] References to Williamson in this chapter are to this work.
    [2] Or the relevant similarity among square things in our world; phrasing matters in terms of that which unites square things across logical space allows us to sidestep the problem that the square things in the actual world will have indefinitely many similarities over and above their squareness.

logical space. The type, remembering that *p*, is the unifier of all the tokens of so remembering; the pattern they all fall under. The conjunctivist holds that the pattern is a conjunctive or composite pattern; as it might be, the tokens are alike in being tokens of believing that *p* and in their relation to a past in which *p* obtains. *Mutatis mutandis* for knowing that *p*. The *de dicto* version of conjunctivism can then be thought of as an expression of confidence in the ability of language to capture the conjunctive pattern in question in a certain way—but, as we said, that's a question for another time.

As we will see, construing conjunctivism as a thesis about the states themselves is not ducking a disagreement with Williamson, but more on this anon. For now, I want to lay out the argument path to conjunctivism.

3.   Some preliminaries

(i) I take it for granted that explanations in terms of mental states are causal explanations. If remembering the spelling of 'antimacassar' explains winning the spelling bee, this is a species of causal explanation, which in turn requires that remembering the spelling does the appropriate causing.

(ii) I take for granted the anti-Davidson position that the causing in question is a relation between states, where states are types. For example, in the spelling bee example, we have a good causal explanation if, inter alia, the state of remembering—that way the world is—caused the state of winning—that way the world is. When we offer causal explanations, we are offering accounts of the causal evolution over time of ways our world is, and ways our world is are types.[3] As far as I can see, both presumptions (i) and (ii) are common ground with Williamson.

(iii) The explanatory value of broad information and consequently of explanations framed in terms of broad states is not at issue. We saw its value when we noted what an explanation of Smith's winning the spelling bee in terms of her knowing how to spell 'antimacassar' can add to an explanation in terms of her belief about how to spell it. Likewise, an explanation in terms of her remembering how to spell 'antimacassar' (if she did in fact remember how to spell it) will also often be better and for the same reason: it will give additional relevant information.

The value of broadness in the appropriate circumstances is common ground with Williamson, and he has many examples that make very clear the explanatory value of attributions of broad states to subjects.[4]

---

[3] See Davidson (1993) for his position. Many have urged against him the position that causation relates types; for a version that employs the 'ways' way of putting things, see Jackson (1995).

[4] And I take it we agree in looking at causal explanations in terms of information about causal history, as in Lewis (1986b).

Of course some argue that the factive nature of knowing and remembering means that knowing and remembering are not strictly speaking mental states, and so explanations in terms of knowing and remembering are *ipso facto* not good (or bad) explanations in terms of mental states. But that is not because they think they are not good explanations. These theorists hold, or should hold, that explanations in terms of what people know and remember are often good explanations, and sometimes better than ones in terms of what people believe, but they are not, in their view, to be classified as being explanations in terms of mental states.

I see no reason not to count knowing and remembering as mental states,[5] but the classification question is peripheral to our concern with whether or not these states are conjunctive states, and how the nature of explanations in terms of them casts light on that question.

(iv) We will conduct our discussion mostly using the example of remembering, but, as far as I can see, the points apply equally to knowing.

Final preliminary. There is an issue over whether remembering entails believing, and over whether knowing entails believing. The obvious first-up position is that both entail believing. To remember is at least to believe; ditto for knowing. However, it seems possible to be in a state that we describe somewhat as follows. 'I have a memory of seeing Frank "Typhoon" Tyson taking 7 for 27 at the MCG, but I know that the number of people who confidently claim to have seen this greatly exceeds the ground's capacity and I half-fear that I am one of the deluded.' In such a case one is in a state that represents that one saw Tyson taking 7 for 27, but one may well withhold belief. But if one in fact saw him take 7 for 27, and if that seeing is responsible in the right way for one's representing that he did, there is at least some plausibility in the contention that one remembers him doing so, despite failing to believe that he did.

In my view, the right thing to say about such examples is that, although one has a memory *image* of seeing Tyson taking 7 for 27, one does not actually remember him doing so unless one believes that things are as one's memory image represents them to be (in the regard in question). But obviously the matter is contentious.

There is a somewhat similar debate in the knowledge case over whether one can know without believing. We will presume (with the majority I take it and in my view correctly) that both remembering and knowing entail believing, but what we have to say below could be expressed in terms of the relevant representational notion.[6]

---

[5] Williamson argues at length in chapter 1 that they should be counted as mental states.
[6] For the debate in the memory case, see, e.g., Martin and Deutscher (1966). For the debate in the knowledge case, see, e.g., Williamson (2000: 42) and the references given there.

4. I start our journey to conjunctivism with the important distinction between whether mental states are internal and whether they are narrow—or perhaps I should say, with the important distinction that we will mark by distinguishing being internal from being narrow.

Breaking the four-minute mile occurred on 6 May 1954 in Oxford. It was confined to that bit of space-time. But what made it the breaking of the four-minute mile depended on the history of running up to that point. Had Landy, for example, run under four minutes before 6 May 1954, the event that was the breaking of the four-minute mile (by Bannister) would not have been the breaking of the four-minute mile. There is a distinction between the breaking being located in a certain place (true), and its character as a breaking of the four-minute mile depending just on how things are at that place (false). In the case of mental states we need to distinguish internalism from narrowness. To say that mental states are internal is different from saying that they are narrow. To say that they are internal is to say something about where they are located—namely inside subjects; to say that they are narrow is to say that what it takes for them to be the mental states they are depends just on how the subjects that are in them are.

The same point can be made using the footprint example.[7] A footprint is located in, say, a certain part of a sandy beach, but what makes it count as a footprint depends on matters beyond that location. Being a footprint involves two properties or types: (*a*) a certain shape, and (*b*) its having a certain causal history. The certain shape is a narrow property and this is why the footprint is located where it is; it counts as a footprint because of its history and this is why being a footprint is wide (not narrow).

How does this play out for the case of remembering? We can all agree that remembering is wide. What it takes for S to remember that p requires in addition to a suitable way S is, a suitable past and a suitable connection between that past and the way S is. There is, of course, considerable controversy over any particular analysis of remembering that p, and indeed over whether an illuminating analysis is possible. (Williamson is in plenty of company in holding that it is not.) But there is substantial agreement that there are (at least) three things that need to be the case if S is to remember that p: one to do especially with S, one with the past, and one with the connection between the past and how S is. The potential controversy is over whether remembering is internal, where this question is the question of whether we should think of S's remembering that p as involving (*a*) S's being a certain narrow way (in the sense that, for each case, there is a narrow way, not in the sense that there is a narrow way that obtains for every case), and (b) that narrow way bearing such and such relations to matters outside S.

---

[7] See Stalnaker (1999: 171–2). He should not be held responsible for my use of the example. A similar point can be made with Davidson's sunburn example (1986).

If this is the right way to think of remembering, then remembering is wide and internal, as we are using those terms.

The same distinction can, of course, be made for knowledge, and, if it comes to that, for belief, with the difference that the claim that belief is wide is more controversial than the uncontroversial claim that remembering and knowing are wide. One issue is whether knowledge and belief are narrow or wide; another is whether they are internal or external.

5.   How might we adjudicate the question as to whether remembering is or is not an internal state? Let us start by clarifying one issue and setting aside another. Some time in the future we may discover a cure for Alzheimer's that involves wireless connections between brains of sufferers and file servers, where what is on the file servers plays a *big* role in storing and processing memory traces. Would this show that internalism about remembering was false for these subjects, that we need to think of remembering that *p* for them as distributed across the brain and the server? It depends on how we clarify the notion of an internal state. I will use the term in a way that counts the relevant part of the server in this kind of case as part of those who remember. In effect we think of these subjects as having central processors that extend outside the skin. These subjects are more widely distributed in space than we are.

The second issue relates to the debate over the individuation of states of rememberings. Some hold that, for every distinct proposition remembered, there is a distinct state of remembering. Others hold that this is an implausibly extravagant multiplication of states of remembering. We should hold instead that in many cases where *S* remembers that *p*, and *S* remembers that *q*, there is one state of remembering, a single state that has the content that *p&q*. There exist states of remembering with rich complex contents, aspects of which we report in individual sentences, but there does not exist a distinct state for each reporting sentence. Some who oppose the view that remembering is an internal state seem to be advocating something like the last position.[8] This is an interesting issue but not the one we are placing on the table.[9]

Our issue is whether states of remembering—be they many or few—are internal.[10]

6.   I think we should adjudicate our issue by setting it in the context of an existing debate over the explanatory role of intentional state attributions in general.

[8] See Thau (2002: ch. 2, §6). He is discussing the view that belief is an internal state, but the remarks would apply equally to memory.

[9] For the connection between this issue and the language of thought see, e.g., Lewis (1995: 422–3).

[10] Incidentally, it is pretty clear that Thau would be equally opposed to internalism on this reading. For a discussion of Thau see Jackson (2005).

This debate starts from the observation that explanations of behaviour in terms of intentional states are typically of object-directed behaviour. My belief that there is beer in the glass explains my reaching for the glass; it does not explain my straightening my elbow to such and such a degree. My desire to score a goal explains my kicking the football towards the goal; it does not explain my moving my leg at a certain rate, at such and such an angle to my body. Moreover, the object towards which my behaviour is directed is typically part of the content of the intentional state: the movement explained is towards the goal and the content of the desire is that the ball ends up in the goal, and so on. Or suppose I extend my arm because I believe this will relieve the stiffness in it, and suppose that, in so extending my arm, I point towards the moon. This is some sort of explanation of why I point towards the moon but it is not the kind typical of intentional action explanations; it is very different from an explanation of pointing towards the moon because I desire to indicate to my granddaughter where the moon is in the night sky.

Considerations of this kind led Christopher Peacocke to claim that the relational character of the behaviour explained requires explanation in terms of essentially external states, or, as he calls them, 'externalist states'.[11] His idea is *not* that we have internal states whose contents are, in one way or another, settled by, *inter alia*, relations to subjects' surroundings, including the objects that the intentionally explained behaviour is directed towards. The position is externalist in the sense we distinguished above from being wide.

Or consider the doubts about internalism recently aired by Michael Thau.

when we consider the nature of intentional behavior, the demand for a causal explanation in terms of internal states turns out to be somewhat puzzling. When you, for example, kick a ball, though your behavior is *constituted* by a movement of your leg, insofar as what you're doing is intentional you are *not* moving your leg at such and such velocity and in such and such direction; what you are doing is *kicking a ball*. And, while an internal state may be the prima facie more appropriate candidate for explaining the leg movement that constitutes your behavior, a relation to a proposition is the prima facie more appropriate candidate for explaining the behavior itself. Your believing that, for example, if you kick the ball it will go in the opposing team's goal might be one of the causes of your behavior. Now the proposition that if you kick the ball it will go in the opposing team's goal should turn out to bear some interesting relation to the ball it is intuitively about. So, in virtue of bearing a relation to this proposition you will bear some relation to the ball. But something that involves a relation *to the ball* would seem to be a better candidate for a cause of your *kicking the ball* than would some internal state of yours . . . much of our behavior is itself essentially relational, so it is strange to start by assuming that the causes of this behavior couldn't be relational.[12]

The challenge for externalist positions is a marked disconnect with what happens in the natural sciences in the explanations those sciences offer of how

---

[11] Peacocke (1993).   [12] Thau (2002: 63–4).

complex organisms interact and relate to their environments. Plant biologists seek explanations of why some plants orient themselves so as to obtain maximum benefit from the sun's radiation, and animal biologists seek explanations of the imprinting phenomenon in ducklings. The explanations plant and animal biologists seek of phenomena are one and all internalist in the following sense. They seek explanations that come in two stages. One stage concerns the internal, information-carrying effects the environment has on the plants or animals in question; the other concerns how those distinctive effects explain causally the movements of the plant or animal in relation to its environment up for explanation. For example, when plant biologists try and explain the way some plants track the sun's position (positive heliotropism), they look for effects the sun's position has on the plants that might, on the one hand, carry information about the sun's position, and, on the other, might affect the plants in ways that cause that the plants' orientations to be towards the sun. Plant biologists would not and should not take seriously the suggestion that the explanation might proceed in terms of the plants' relation to the sun as such. They look for the wide in the sense that they look for effects on the plants qua information carriers about the sun's position; they know that what they will find (and did find) is internal in the sense that the information-carrying effects on the plants that do the controlling of the plants' orientation are inside them.

Similar remarks apply to imprinting. This is a highly distinctive behaviour of ducklings that orients them in various ways towards the first moving thing they see. There is much that is controversial about the process (I understand), but it is taken for granted that there will be two parts to any satisfactory account of the process: the part about the way the first moving thing they see affects the ducklings in an information-bearing way, and the part about how that effect affects their subsequent behaviour.

7.   How much does a disconnect between intentional explanation of human behaviour with what happens in plant and animal biology matter? Do we have in the previous section a serious problem for externalism?

One of the issues here is the plausibility of a doctrine in the metaphysics of causation that Williamson discusses at a number of points.

Here is one passage from pp. 60–1.

One motive for internalism is the combination of the idea that genuine states are causally efficacious with the idea that mental states are causally efficacious only if narrow. No action at a distance: causation is local, involving only narrow mental states . . .

Much needs to be probed and questioned in these internalist ideas. We should not assume that the notion of causal efficacy is clear, or derived from fundamental science, or known to apply only to local connections.

I think our emphasis on the difference between being narrow and being internal helps separate out what is unclear and what is comparatively clear here.

There is a difficult issue as to whether only the narrow is causally efficacious and, if it comes to that, what being efficacious precisely comes to, as Williamson notes. Might it not be the case that being taller than the rest of the players caused Robinson's being the first selected for a basketball team? Do we have to say that the causing was really done by his being such and such a height, conjoined with the rest of the players' heights being various such and suchs that come to something less than so and so? Maybe, maybe not. And that is not even to dip our toe into the debate in fundamental physics.

The easier question is whether or not, when Smith's remembering how to spell 'antimaccassar' explains her production of the word 'antimacassar', the fact that, let us say, she learnt the spelling the previous week plays its causal role via the memory trace the learning process laid down in her. It seems clear that the answer to this question is yes. We know that the causal chain from learning process to production of word goes via how things are inside her. The relevant cause is internal, be it narrow or not.

8.   The second reason the disconnect matters is that what is taken for granted in animal and plant biology is not something special to either science. It is a product of a very plausible idea about the best strategy for explaining the environmentally directed behaviour of complex parcels of matter.

Here is how the strategy plays out for us, in the broad. We know that our behaviour is caused neurophysiologically. Now it is relatively (*relatively*) easy to see how a neurophysiological state might explain my pointing towards the moon in the sense of explaining pointing in direction D, where direction D *happens* to be where the moon is. But then the fact that the motion is directed towards the moon is a fluke. How could a neurophysiological state explain *non-accidental* movement by me towards something as distant as the moon?

The very plausible idea is that it is able to do so by virtue of the fact, if it is a fact, that the moon impacted on me sometime before the pointing towards it took place. The pointing towards the moon is causally downstream from a perceptual contact with the moon—seeing the moon or hearing someone who has seen the moon telling me where the moon is told me where the moon is or whatever—and the contact modifies my internal neurological state in a way that carries information about where the moon is, which in turn guides my arm moon-wards. Schematically, the very plausible idea runs thus. Complex parcels of matter orient themselves with respect to their environments in non-flukey ways by virtue of their capacity to be affected internally by their environments in information-carrying ways that then causally impact on their behaviour with respect to that environment.

9.   We now have a reason for holding that remembering is conjunctive or composite. If remembering is to play its causal explanatory role, it had better

involve something about the rememberer, something that is in fact an internal state that carries the putative information that affects the behaviour to be explained. Remembering is a conjunctive state and part of the conjunction is a state internal to those doing the remembering. That is to say, part of what unites all those who remember is their being in such an internal state. But why take the extra step of holding that the relevant internal state is belief? That is another question altogether and that is the orthodoxy we are seeking to defend: the orthodoxy that remembering is a conjunction of *believing* with other stuff.

In discussing how we might make the extra step, I am going to make a simplification, a harmless one as far as I can see. I will assume that, for each case of remembering that p, there is a state of remembering that p, and for each case of believing that p, there is a state of believing that p. We noted earlier the possibility that the relation between propositions remembered and states of remembering might be many–one, and that the same possibility exists for believing. But we also noted that this issue is orthogonal to the question about whether or not remembering is conjunctive and whether or not remembering is internal.

There seem to me to be two reasons for holding that the relevant internal state is belief. The first is the plausibility of the contention that 'S remembers that p' entails that S believes that p as a result of some suitable causal history involving that p.

Most agree about this (except for those who would replace belief by some broader representational notion). The controversies are over how to spell out the details and especially over the possibility of doing so in a way that delivers a reductive analysis of remembering.

Now the fact that remembering that p entails believing that p as a result of some suitable causal history involving p does not entail that remembering is some kind of conjunction involving believing that p. (Williamson would agree with this negative point; see the discussion in chapter 2.) However, if there is independent reason for holding that remembering is some kind of conjunctive state involving how the subject is and how the subject is related to the past, then it seems to me that there is a good prima facie case for holding that the part concerned with how the subject is is belief. That is to say, when S remembers that p, S's remembering that p is an internal state of S that is one and the same as S's belief that p. There are not two states but one state—believing that p—which counts as remembering that p as a result of some suitable causal history involving p.

10.   The second reason for holding the relevant internal state is belief is occamist. Suppose I remember we have run out of milk and this that explains why I stop at the shops to buy some milk. I also thereby believe that we have run out of milk. Do the belief and the memory overdetermine my stopping? Or do I stop a bit more quickly because I both remember and believe? Or is one state operative and the other a stand-by cause; in which case which

is which? And do they differ in how they combine with my desire that we should have milk in the house in causing my stopping? These questions seem misconceived, and, if that is right, there is no reason to distinguish two internal states: believing that p and remembering that p. Of course, there is the important, common ground point that ascribing remembering when I do in fact remember is often a better causal explanation of my stopping: it gives more relevant information about how I come to stop. But that is no reason to posit two distinct internal states doing the causing. It is a reason to favour one way over another of describing the one state. We can make the key point with the sunburn example. What sunburn causes does not differ from what the burn that is sunburn causes—and it would be misconceived to ask about, say, overdetermination—but an explanation that describes a burn as sunburn may be a better explanation.

If my remembering that p is an internal state that is one and the same as my believing that p, how come I remember rather than merely believe? The obvious answer is that what makes it true that I remember is that my believing that p has a suitable relation to the past fact that p. We know that a suitable relation to the past fact that p is required: I do not remember if p does not obtain, and I do not remember if p does not causally lead to my believing that p.[13] There seems no reason to hold that more than an extra of this kind is needed to bring belief up to memory. A second application of occam then gives us a version of conjunctivism about memory according to which the uniter of memory tokens in logical space in the conjunction of belief with suitable causal history.

We can see the appeal of this position independently of issues to do with the possibility or otherwise of reductive analyses of remembering. Take sunburn again. Occam strongly suggests that what unites cases of sunburn is that they are cases of burns with a certain causal history involving the sun. At the same time it is notoriously hard to give a reductive analysis of sunburn in terms of a burn caused by the sun. A burn caused by a poker made hot by the sun is not a case of sunburn. We have to specify that the burn is caused in the right way by the sun—the right way to count as sunburn, that is. It is no easy task to say what the right way is non-circularly.[14] I am not saying it is impossible but I am saying that there would be something misconceived about holding that our troubles in finding the right words gave us reason to believe that there was something extra to being sunburnt over and above having a burn with a certain causal history involving the sun. There is nothing more to add in *re* to the burn to get the

---

[13] See the arguments in Martin and Deutscher (1966), with the proviso that the causal link in their view is to a representational state more inclusive than belief. The idea that remembering requires such a causal link to what is remembered is close to common ground in debates over memory.

[14] The problems are akin to those discussed in Davidson (1980). I borrow 'in the right way' from that essay.

sunburn over and above the history involving the sun, and that remains plausible despite the troubles in finding the words that say exactly what needs to be added in a non-circular manner.

11.   I said above that we were agreeing with Williamson in seeing the issue as one about similarity patterns, and in chapter 3 Williamson sets up the issue about primeness explicitly in terms of similarity patterns. He does this as a precursor to offering an interesting argument against conjunctivism—or, as he puts it, the view that factive states are composite—and in favour of primeness. I will close by indicating why I am unconvinced. There are two stages to his argument. The first gives the methodology for addressing the question of whether or not some state is prime in terms of similarity patterns. The second applies the methodology to the case of knowledge.

Here is the methodology (from pp. 67–8).

How can we show that a condition C is prime? Suppose that C obtains in two cases α and β. Consider a case γ internally like α but externally like β . . . Now suppose that C is the conjunction of a narrow condition D with an environmental condition E. Then E obtains in γ. For since C entails D, D obtains in α; since D is narrow, D also obtains in γ, which is internally like α. Similarly, since C entails E, E obtains in β; since E is environmental, E also obtains in γ, which is externally like β. Since C obtains whenever both D and E obtain, and they both obtain in γ, C obtains in γ, as required. Thus we can show that C is prime simply by exhibiting three cases α, β, and γ, where γ is internally like α and externally like β, and C obtains in α and β but not in γ.

The issue of whether or not C is prime turns on the obtaining or otherwise of C across cases that stand in various similarity and difference relations. This is the sense in which Williamson's basic approach is like ours. However, there is a flaw in the test he proposes, or so I will shortly argue. But it helps to have a concrete example before us. Here is the example Williamson offers as showing that knowledge is prime, using the methodology given above.

Let α be a case in which one knows by testimony that the election was rigged; Smith tells one that the election was rigged, he is trustworthy, and one trusts him; Brown also tells one that the election was rigged, but he is not trustworthy, and one does not trust him. Let β be a case which differs from α by reversing the roles of Smith and Brown; in β, one knows by testimony that the election was rigged; Brown tells one that the election was rigged, he is trustworthy, and one trusts him; Smith also tells one that the election was rigged, but he is not trustworthy, and one does not trust him. Now consider a case γ internally like α and externally like β. In γ, one does not trust Brown, because one does not trust him in α, and γ is internally like α. Equally, in γ, Smith is not trustworthy, because he is not trustworthy in β, and γ is externally like β. Thus, in γ, neither Smith nor Brown is both trustworthy and trusted . . . Consequently, in γ, one does not know that the election was rigged. Yet, in α and β, one does know that the election was rigged. Thus the condition that one knows that the election was rigged is prime.

Two things are clear about this example. First, Williamson is right that in γ one does not know that the election is rigged. Secondly, we could construct a similar example for remembering. Here in outline is how case α might go warped across to memory. One remembers through having been told in the past that the Battle of Hastings was fought in 1066. Smith and Brown told one on separate occasions. You paid attention to Smith's utterance only because you (rightly) thought he alone remembered the date; Brown was simply producing the first date that came into his head and got it right by fluke. Case β for memory will reverse the roles of Smith and Brown, and we will get as case γ a case where that which leads one to accept that the date is 1066 has the wrong kind of connection to the fact that the date is 1066 to count as remembering that the date is 1066.

It follows that, if Williamson's test for primeness is correct, neither knowing nor remembering is composite. But there is a flaw in the test. Consider the difference between being the 100th person to have uttered the sentence 'Colorless green ideas sleep furiously' and being the 100th person to have uttered the sentence 'Colorless green ideas sleep furiously' at one end of an information-preserving causal chain that starts with Chomsky's original production of the sentence. Both are conjunctive states but only one is, as we might put it, purely conjunctive. What makes it the case that you are (if you are) the 100th person to have uttered the sentence 'Colorless green ideas sleep furiously' depends on one's uttering the sentence and there being ninety-nine who said it before you did. No connection between you and the other sayers of the sentence is needed. In the second case a connection is needed. Your *relation* to your environment is part of what makes it the case that you are (if you are) the 100th person to have uttered the sentence 'Colorless green ideas sleep furiously' at one end of an information-preserving causal chain that starts with Chomsky's original production of the sentence.

Equally a connection of the right kind between environment and subject is needed both for knowing and for remembering. That has been a recurring theme in the debate over knowing and remembering, and is something his example brings home. So when Williamson said 'Thus we can show that C is prime simply by exhibiting three cases α, β, and γ, where γ is internally like α and externally like β, and C obtains in α and β but not in γ' what he said was correct if 'prime' means not purely conjunctive. But the many who have thought that factive states like knowing and remembering were conjunctive meant by their view that such states were some kind of conjunction or composite of how the subject is and how the subject's environment is, where how the subject's environment is includes its relation to the subject.

8

Williamson's Casual Approach to Probabilism

Mark Kaplan

I

The Requirement of Total Evidence enjoins you to proportion your beliefs to the support they receive from your total evidence. How exactly are we to understand what it is asking you to do? In *Knowledge and its Limits*[1] Timothy Williamson offers the following proposal. Your total evidence is just the totality of what you know. The support p receives from your total evidence is just the conditional probability of *p* on your entire body of knowledge. The Principle of Total Evidence thus enjoins you to have a degree of belief in *p* equal to the conditional probability of *p* on your entire body of knowledge.

Now, there is an obvious problem with this proposal—a problem I have already raised elsewhere.[2] Consider any proposition p that you know. Since *p* is part of your body of knowledge, your body of knowledge logically entails *p*. It is a consequence of the axioms of probability that the conditional probability of a proposition, on a set of propositions by which it is logically entailed, is equal to 1. Thus the probability of *p* on your body of knowledge is equal to 1. Thus, on Williamson's proposal, you should invest the maximum degree of belief in *p*: you should invest as much belief in *p* as you do in an obvious tautology, say $(p \vee \sim p)$.

But this is an unhappy result. You are presumably certain, and entitled to be certain, of the truth of $(p \vee \sim p)$. So it would seem to follow, from the fact that you should invest as much belief in p as you do in $(p \vee \sim p)$, that you should likewise be certain, that you are likewise entitled to be certain, that *p*. But we do not want to say that the entitlement to be certain that *p* (as certain as you are that $(p \vee \sim p)$) is a requirement for knowledge that *p*, is required for *p* to count as part of your total evidence. Nor does Williamson. He means his proposal to be entirely compatible with the fact that "when we give evidence for our theories,

---

[1] Williamson (2000). All parenthetical page references in the text are to this work.
[2] Kaplan (2003: 113–15).

the propositions which we cite as evidence are themselves uncertain" (p. 209). The claim that knowing *p* entails the entitlement to be (in this sense) certain that *p* is one that Williamson consistently repudiates throughout his book.

Of course, this critique of Williamson's proposal turns on a crucial assumption: that to have the maximum degree of belief in *p* *is* to be certain that *p*. On the Bayesian way of thinking about things, this assumption is borne out: to have a degree of belief (a degree of confidence, a subjective probability) equal to 1 in *p* is indeed to be certain that *p*—it is to be willing (or, at least, it is to open one's position to criticism unless one is willing) to bet anything on p for even the most modest prize.

Williamson thinks, however, that there is a kind of belief that comes in degrees—he calls it "outright belief"—that are not to be identified with subjective probabilities. And it is degrees of outright belief that he means (p. 209) the Requirement of Total Evidence to constrain. He writes (p. 99) that "one's degree of outright belief in *p* is not in general to be equated with one's subjective probability that *p*; one's subjective probability can vary while one's degree of outright belief remains zero." So what *is* outright belief? Williamson's view is this: "one believes *p* outright when one is willing to use *p* as a premise in practical reasoning" (p. 99). And how can outright belief come in degrees? By virtue of the fact that "one may be willing to use *p* as a premise in practical reasoning only when the stakes are sufficiently low" (p. 99). Thus, he maintains: "Since using *p* as a premise in practical reasoning is relying on *p*, we can think of one's degree of outright belief in *p* as the degree to which one relies on *p*" (p. 99).

But this does not eliminate the difficulty. For, however independently they may operate in other regions of their respective scales, the two measures of belief under discussion would seem bound to agree on what they assign their respective maxima. Recall, to have the maximum degree of confidence in *p* (assign maximum subjective probability to *p*) is to be willing (or, at least, to open your position to criticism unless you are also willing) to bet anything on *p* for even the most modest prize. What Williamson appears to have told us is that to have the maximum degree of outright belief in *p* is to be willing to rely on *p*—to use it as a premise in practical reasoning—no matter how high the stakes. And these come to exactly the same thing: the very certainty that Williamson (rightly) wants to deny is a requirement for knowing (and for counting as evidence). As he puts it (p. 86), "I know many things without being prepared to bet my house on them." Thus, even if we interpret the Requirement of Total Evidence as constraining outright belief, the unhappy result remains: insofar as everything you know, everything that counts as part of your evidence, must receive probability 1 on Williamson's proposal, his is a proposal on which, unless you are entitled to be as certain that *p* as you are that (p v $\sim p$), you do not know that *p*, and *p* is no part of your evidence.

Of course, it is perfectly compatible with this that there is, in fact, some other way of construing outright belief—even some interesting way of construing outright belief—on which outright belief comes in degrees but a maximal degree of outright belief is *not* to be equated with certainty.[3] Nothing I have so far said suggests otherwise. That is, there is nothing in what I have so far said (and nothing I said in my earlier piece on this matter) that suggests that Williamson's proposal suffers from any problem that cannot be gotten round by coming up with a new construal of outright belief, on which maximal outright belief is compatible with uncertainty. In fact, however, I think Williamson's proposal is more deeply flawed than this. My purpose here is to explain why.

II

Let me begin with a confession: I am a probabilist. By this I mean that I hold that the probability calculus places a pervasive constraint on our opinions—that is to say, a constraint on our opinions to which there are no exceptions. In particular, I am a Bayesian probabilist: it is upon our confidence assignments to propositions that I hold the probability calculus to impose a pervasive constraint.[4] I see this constraint as a consistency constraint on a degree of confidence assignment,[5] and the charge that a person's degree of confidence assignment violates the constraint to have the same force as any other charge to the effect that the person's position is, in some respect, inconsistent. Finally, I hold (and this is another tenet of Bayesian probabilism) that there is another important consistency constraint, this one connecting confidence and preference: the constraint is, roughly, that you be more confident that *p* than you are that *q* if and only if you prefer the prospect of having a stake in *p*'s truth to the prospect of having the same stake in *q*'s truth.[6]

Now a second confession: I have not always been a Bayesian probabilist. By this I mean that there was a time—a time I remember quite vividly—at

---

[3] Unlike most Bayesians, I am not hostile to the idea that there is a sense of "believe" that cannot be defined in terms of degrees of confidence, yet in which what we ought to believe is important to our lives as inquirers. On the contrary, I have long argued that the Bayesian position is strengthened by the acknowledgment of such a sense of "believe". See Kaplan (1981a, 1981b, 1996, 2002).

[4] I break with Bayesian orthodoxy in not holding the constraint to require—indeed, I argue that it must not require—that a precise degree of confidence to be assigned to every proposition. But, since the break, and my reason for making it (see Kaplan 1996: 23–31; 2002: 434–43), have no role to play in what I have to say about Williamson's proposal, I will write as if I hold to the orthodoxy.

[5] By this I do not mean that the violation of this constraint somehow commits the violator to a set of claims that cannot all be true. Rather, I mean that the constraint is formal in the same way logical consistency is. Take a set of sentences in a formal language where the set is closed under truth-functional operations. Just as the consistency of any subset of that set can be determined without regard to the actual truth-values of the non-logical components of the sentences, so it can be determined whether a degree of confidence assignment to any subset of the set satisfies the probability calculus without regard to the actual truth-values of the non-logical components of the sentences.

[6] For a more careful statement, and a defense, of this constraint, see Kaplan (2002: 443–6).

which I did not see why I should suppose that the probability calculus imposes this pervasive a constraint on degrees of confidence. I do not mean, of course, that I thought the probability calculus *never* imposes a constraint on degrees of confidence. Suppose you had set before me an opaque urn containing 100 balls of equal weight and size, you had mixed them thoroughly, and you were about to draw one from the urn. Had you satisfied me that half the balls in the urn were black and half white, I would have been happy to admit that I should have a degree of confidence equal to 0.5 that the ball would be black, and a degree of confidence equal to 0.5 that the ball would not be black.

What I did not see is why I should suppose that what goes for this case goes for all. Suppose you had not satisfied me that half the balls in the urn were black and half were white. Suppose all I knew was that each ball in the urn was either black or white—I knew absolutely nothing about the proportion of black balls to white ones. I did not see what would be wrong with having a degree of confidence equal to, say, 0.4 that the ball would be black and a degree of confidence equal to 0.4 that the ball would not be black. I did not see why I should not think that the constraint the probability calculus imposed on my degrees of confidence in the first case simply did not apply to the second.

I recognized, of course, that this degree of confidence assignment violates the axioms of probability, which require that the two degrees of confidence sum to 1. I recognized, too, that the objective probability that the ball would be black, and the objective probability that it would not be black, must sum to 1. But, it seemed to me, since I did not know what those objective probabilities were, the fact that they must sum to 1 was of small moment. Indeed, it seemed to me, the fact that I did not know what the objective probabilities were—the fact that the evidence I could bring to bear on the matter was thus so much worse in quality than the evidence I possessed in the first case—ought to be registered in the degrees of confidence I adopted. And I did not see why the assignment I chose could not be thought to register the inferior quality of my evidence in the current case in just the right way.

Moreover, it struck me that cases of this latter sort—cases in which my evidence was inferior in quality to my evidence in the first case—were more the rule than the exception. It seemed to me that when it came to the matter of how to distribute my degrees of confidence between hypotheses like "Caesar kissed his wife on the morning of the day he died" and its negation, "John Dos Passos wore brown shoes on his tenth birthday" and its negation, "It will hit 80 degrees Fahrenheit in Bloomington Indiana on April 16, 2020" and its negation, the strategy I adopted for the second case above (a strategy that violates the axioms of probability) was no less appropriate.

I was not alone in this. There is an entire school of statistics devoted to the proposition that the probability calculus has purchase on our opinions only in cases in which objective probabilities are known or statistical evidence has been collected.[7] There are writers, within both the philosophical and the statistical communities, who have claimed that the laws governing the rational assignment of degrees of confidence demand the violation of the axioms of probability in precisely the sorts of cases in which I thought they deserved to be violated.[8] I was not alone in recognizing that there is (at the very least) a burden to be borne by the people who are on the other side—a burden to be borne by Bayesian probabilists, committed as they are to holding that the degrees of confidence I wanted to adopt are ones I ought *not* to adopt. That burden is to come up with a way of saying why what I wanted to do, what seemed entirely reasonable to me to do, what is entirely reasonable by the lights of the philosophers and statisticians to whom I referred a few sentences back, is nonetheless *wrong* to do.

It is a burden Bayesians have, from the very beginning, acknowledged. From the very beginning, in the work of Frank Ramsey and Bruno de Finetti, Bayesians have offered arguments as to why one ought not to arrange one's degrees of confidence so that they will violate the axioms of probability.[9] Variants of those early arguments have been honed, refined, and (above all) promulgated by Bayesians to this very day.[10] From the very beginning, Bayesians have recognized that probabilism isn't obviously correct. It needs to be argued for.

Williamson is, in his own way, no less a probabilist than any Bayesian: he too holds that the probability calculus imposes a pervasive constraint on our opinions. He holds (p. 211) that there is "an initial probability distribution P" that "measures something like the intrinsic plausibility of hypotheses prior to investigation." And he holds (p. 211) that P satisfies the axioms of the probability calculus. That is, he holds that, for any proposition p, there is a fact of the matter as to how intrinsically plausible p is; and he holds that it is a condition on the truth of a judgment as to the intrinsic plausibility of a set of propositions, that the plausiblities attributed to the propositions in the set satisfy the axioms of probability. That is, he holds that, no matter what set of propositions we choose, no matter what the circumstance, the probability calculus constrains our judgments as to the intrinsic plausibility of that set of propositions: any such judgment is false if it attributes, to the propositions in the set, intrinsic plausibilities that do not satisfy the axioms of probability.

Of course, it is no more obvious why (as Williamson maintains) we ought to think that intrinsic plausibility satisfies the axioms of probability than it is why (as Bayesians maintain) our degrees of confidence ought to satisfy the axioms of the

---

[7] For discussion, see Barnett (1999).

[8] L. Jonathan Cohen is a philosopher who fits this description, Glenn Shafer a statistician. See Cohen (1977); Shafer (1976).

[9] Ramsey (1990); de Finetti (1937).

[10] The most influential has been Savage (1954/1972). For a nice exposition and defense, see Maher (1993). I offer an argument designed to address exactly the violation of the axioms of probability described above (actually, a qualitative version of it) in Kaplan (1996: ch 1). Howard Raiffa does likewise (though, to my mind, without carrying conviction) in Raiffa (1968: 110–14).

probability.[11] That is to say, it is not obvious why, when, prior to investigation, the quality of the available evidence as to *p*'s truth is much poorer than it is in the first case I described above, it is a mistake to think that the intrinsic plausibility of *p* and the intrinsic plausibility of not-*p* do not sum to 1. It is not obvious why the intrinsic plausibility that the ball drawn will be black, and the intrinsic plausibility that ball will not be black, should sum to 1 when all that is known is that the ball will be drawn from an urn containing 100 balls, and nothing is known about how many of those balls are black.

So, naturally, one expects to find in Williamson's discussion some indication of how he thinks it can be argued that, even if it is not *obvious* why the intrinsic plausibility of hypotheses prior to investigation is something that the probability calculus can properly be thought to measure, it is nonetheless *true* that intrinsic plausibility is properly so measured. Just as one sees Bayesians taking on the task of arguing that, however it may initially appear, our degrees of confidence ought to satisfy the axioms of probability, one expects to see Williamson offer at least some idea of how he would argue that, however it may initially appear, an assignment of intrinsic plausibility to propositions will satisfy the axioms of probability.

But one finds nothing of the sort. Indeed, far from recognizing the burden Bayesians have acknowledged, Williamson is apparently oblivious to the existence of any such burden. He writes (p. 211) as if Bayesians' insistence on linking probability, confidence, and preference is a manifestation of nothing more than fussiness—a manifestation of their thinking that probability is somehow suspicious unless properly operationalized. This thought, he argues, is misguided. It is as misguided as the thought that we should abandon set theory until mathematicians have provided us with a precise definition of "set". "Consider an analogy," he writes (p. 211). "The concept of *possibility* is vague and cannot be defined syntactically. But that does not show it is spurious. In fact, it is indispensable. Moreover, we know some sharp structural constraints on it: for example, that a disjunction is possible if and only if at least one of its disjuncts is possible. The present suggestion is that probability is in the same boat as possibility, and not too much the worse for that."

---

[11] After all, it is not as if *every* mode via which we appraise propositions, and that admits of degrees, satisfies the axioms of probability. Take, for example, our assessments of how desirable we find the prospect of a proposition's being true. In at least a great many cases, insofar as you find the prospect of *p*'s being true more desirable than the prospect of *q*'s being true, you will also find the prospect of *p*'s being true more desirable than the prospect of (*p* v *q*)'s being true. Imagine, for example, *p* is "You win $100" and *q* is "You win $5." (See Jeffrey 1983: 146, where Jeffrey suggests that it is a general truth about desirability that, if the prospect of *p*'s being true is more desirable than the prospect of *q*'s being true, then the prospect of *p*'s being true is more desirable than the prospect of (*p* v *q*)'s being true.) But, if so, assessments of how desirable we find the prospect of propositions' being true are *not* things that the probability calculus can be thought to measure. For, while we can regard the prospect of *p*'s being true as more desirable than the prospect of (*p* v *q*)'s being true, we can under no circumstance regard p as more probable than (*p* v *q*): it is a consequence of the axioms of probability that no proposition is more probable than a proposition it entails.

Now, to be fair, the history of Bayesianism is not free from the very sort of fussiness that Williamson rightly decries. Bayesianism was born in the 1920s, during the heyday of logical empiricism. Many early Bayesians were motivated by revulsion toward what they saw as the metaphysical spookiness involved in positing objective probabilities. They sought refuge in an account that would construe talk of probability as merely expressing the speaker's degree of confidence.[12]

But this sort of fussiness has never been the only motivation for Bayesians' insistence on connecting probability, confidence, and preference. Indeed, I am not sure I know a contemporary Bayesian philosopher who is fussy in this way. All the ones I know embrace without qualification talk of objective probability. Why, then, do so many contemporary Bayesians want to connect—why do so many insist on connecting—probability, confidence, and preference? It is out of the recognition that, while *probability* is indeed in the same boat as possibility in the very way Williamson thinks it is, *probabilism* is not. They recognize that probabilism—the thesis that the probability calculus places a pervasive constraint on our opinions—is not obviously true: it needs to be argued for. And they see, in the connection between confidence and preference, materials sufficient—and, to those who are the most insistent on making that connection, the *only* materials sufficient—for constructing such an argument.[13]

III

Williamson will doubtless think that it is of small moment whether it is fussiness or something else that is motivating Bayesians to try to get a probabilistic constraint out of some connection between confidence and preference—and even of small moment whether their resulting efforts are successful. For Williamson is convinced that there is no way for them to get the probabilistic constraint *he* is interested in out of such materials. There is no way, he argues, to make sense of the probability of *h* on present evidence in terms of states of confidence or preference.

His argument (pp. 209–10) is this. First, one cannot make sense of it by reference to any actual person's states of confidence. After all, it is perfectly compatible, with an actual person's being certain that h on present evidence, that in fact the probability of h on that evidence is very low: simply suppose that the person's confidence in h on present evidence is quite irrational. Secondly,

---

[12] This motivation operates, for example, very strongly in de Finetti's case. See, e.g., de Finetti (1974: p. x).

[13] To get a rough idea of how the connection can furnish such materials, see Kaplan (2002: 443–6). For a full-fledged exploitation of these materials, consult one of the works cited in nn. 9 and 10.

one cannot make sense of the probability of h on present evidence by appeal to how much confidence an ideal rational being would have in h given our evidence. Such a being's evidence would inevitably be quite different from ours, and her states of confidence would reflect as much. "The hypothesis of a perfectly rational being with our evidence," writes Williamson (p. 210), "is impossible." Thirdly, the latter difficulty hobbles, in exactly the same way, any attempt to make sense of the probability of h on present evidence by appeal to what preferences an ideal rational being would have given our evidence.

Williamson appears to think that these three gambits exhaust the ways a Bayesian could seek to exploit states of confidence and preference by way of making sense of the probability of h on present evidence. It is on the strength of the argument just rehearsed that he feels free to dismiss (pp. 213–14) the worry that his proposal commits him to the view that it is a requirement for h to count as part of your evidence—for *h* to count as something you know—that you be certain that *h*. True enough, he concedes, the probability of *h* on your evidence must equal 1, on his proposal. "But," he writes (p. 214), "since evidential probabilities are not actual or counterfactual credences, why should evidential probability 1 entail absolute certainty?"

I do not see why Williamson thinks that the three gambits he criticizes are the only ones available to a Bayesian who wants to make sense of the probability of *h* on present evidence in terms of confidence and preference. It seems to me that the following gambit is every bit as available: a Bayesian can simply say that the probability of *h* on present evidence is just the degree of confidence it is reasonable to have in h on present evidence. The thought would be that satisfaction of the axioms of probability is a necessary, but insufficient, condition for a degree of confidence assignment to count as the degree of confidence it is reasonable to have in *h* on present evidence.

The thought is nothing new. Going all the way back to Ramsey, there have always been Bayesians who thought that the constraint on opinion imposed by the axioms of probability needs to be supplemented if one wants a constraint whose satisfaction will ensure a reasonable degree of confidence assignment.[14] To be sure, it is folly to imagine that the additional constraints, which need to be satisfied for a degree of confidence assignment to count as the one it is reasonable to have on present evidence, can be stated with the precision of the first. It is perhaps even folly to imagine that all the additional constraints can be stated in any helpful general way. Achieving the degree of confidence assignment it is reasonable to have on present evidence may well require a sensitivity to context that resists general characterization. All the same, we can and do say helpful things about what degree of confidence is the reasonable one to have in a

---

[14] See Ramsey (1990: 97–101). I am one of many Bayesians who are allied with Ramsey in this. See Kaplan (1996: 23–31, 85–8, 186; 2002: 440–2).

proposition h on present evidence, and identify (at least in some such situations) what degree of confidence *is* the reasonable one to have in *h*.

But if it thus turns out that there *is* (Williamson to the contrary) a Bayesian alternative to Williamson's way of making sense of the probability of *h* on present evidence, how does it compare to Williamson's own proposal?

I doubt that he would think it fares terribly well. I would not expect him to complain that the Bayesian alternative's appeal to reasonableness renders it excessively vague. That would be to engage in precisely the fussiness that, as we have seen, Williamson thinks is quite unjustified. Rather, I suspect that Williamson would complain that the appeal to reasonableness in the Bayesian alternative makes implicit appeal to his own proposal. "Successful Bayesian treatments of specific epistemological problems (for example, Hempel's paradox of the ravens)," he writes (p. 212), "assume that subjects have 'reasonable' prior distribution. We judge a prior distribution reasonable, if it complies with our intuitions about the intrinsic plausibility of hypotheses. This is the same sort of vagueness as infects the present approach, if slightly better hidden."

I do not see the merit of the complaint. First, the reasonableness to which Bayesians appeal (the reasonableness to which my Bayesian proposal appeals) is reasonableness all things considered. The intrinsic plausibility of hypotheses prior to investigation—the thing that Williamson's probability distribution P measures—would seem to amount to something quite different. "The probability distribution P," he writes (p. 187), "is informed by some but not all of [a subject] S's evidence."[15] So it is hard to see how intuitions about the intrinsic plausibility of propositions prior to investigation can be thought to inform the judgments of reasonableness to which Bayesians treatments (and the Bayesian proposal under discussion) appeal. Secondly, there is no reason (and Williamson gives us no reason) to suppose that we have any more purchase on—any more robust intuitions about, or insights into—the intrinsic plausibility of hypotheses prior to investigation than we have on how much confidence it is reasonable to have in hypotheses. Without such a reason, it seems presumptuous to suppose that our judgments about the latter are informed by our intuitions about the former.

Of course, there is another respect in which I expect that Williamson would think his proposal superior to the Bayesian alternative I have suggested. As we have already noted, it is a consequence of his proposal that, for each proposition that is included in your evidence—and that means, on his proposal, each proposition that you know—the probability of that proposition on your evidence must equal 1. This consequence, understood in the way our Bayesian

---

[15] And P must be so informed if adverting to P is going to help with the problem of old evidence, as Williamson thinks it will (pp. 189–90, 220–1). I am indebted to James Joyce for this point—and for reminding me that the thought that the satisfaction of the axioms of probability does not suffice to render a degree of confidence assignment reasonable is present in Ramsey.

proposal would have us understand it, would issue the following unpalatable result: only if the reasonable degree of confidence to have in a proposition on your evidence is absolute certainty can that proposition count as part of your evidence—only then can the proposition count as one you know. In contrast, if one thinks of probability as a measure of intrinsic plausibility and one does not identify the intrinsic plausibility of a proposition with the degree of confidence it is reasonable to have in that proposition on your evidence, the consequence issues no unhappy result at all: there is no reason to equate probability 1 with certainty.

But is this apparent reason for thinking that Williamson's way of making sense of the probability of a proposition on present evidence is better that the Bayesian one genuine? It surely is, if Williamson is right to suppose that the probability of a proposition on present evidence is to be understood as the conditional probability of that proposition on that evidence. But he is not right.

To see why, suppose that among the things you know is e: there is a fair 10-ticket lottery to be held tomorrow at noon. You were told by a reliable source: you have knowledge by testimony. And suppose that, like many of the things you know, e is a proposition whose truth is not (on anyone's view) maximally probable: the probability of e is 0.9. Let t be: ticket No. 1 in that lottery will lose. How probable is t on your evidence, e? By Williamson's lights, the answer is to be determined by looking at the conditional probability of t given e: the answer is 0.9.

But notice that, on this way of understanding things, the probability of t on your evidence e is exactly the same in the case at hand—a case in which the probability of e is 0.9—as it would be in a case in which the probability of e were 1. That is to say, this way of viewing things requires you to commit something akin to the base rate fallacy: it requires you not to take into account as you determine the probability of t on your evidence e (and so, insofar as you conform to the Requirement of Total Evidence, not to take into account as you determine the degree of confidence that you should have in t), the probability that your evidence is false.

The right way to determine the probability of t on your evidence e is by determining what probability t has, *given the probability e has*. You take the conditional probability of t given e and give that probability only 9/10th of its weight (this by way of reflecting that the probability of e is itself only 0.9); then you take the probability of t given *not-e* and give that probability 1/10th of its weight (this by way of reflecting the fact that the probability of *not-e* is 0.1); then you add the two. The result? The probability of t given your evidence e is $p(t|e)p(e) + p(t|{\sim}e)p({\sim}e) = 0.81$.

Of course, on this way of understanding matters, the fact that a proposition is included in your evidence does not require that proposition to receive probability 1 on your evidence. On the contrary. The probability of e on the present evidence in the case at hand is $p(e|e)p(e) + p(e|{\sim}e)p({\sim}e) = 0.9$. But then there is nothing to Williamson's complaint about views that would, as our Bayesian proposal does, understand the probability of a proposition on present evidence in terms of confidence: the complaint rests on mistake about how the probability of a proposition on a body of evidence is to be computed. The virtue Williamson sees in his own way of making sense of the probability of a proposition on present evidence—that this proposition can be included in present evidence yet it not be reasonable to be certain of the truth of the proposition on that evidence—is no virtue the Bayesian proposal cannot claim. The apparent reason for thinking that the Bayesian alternative must be rejected—that the Bayesian alternative makes it a condition on a proposition's being a part of our evidence (on its being known) that it be reasonable to be certain of its truth on our evidence—is, being false, no reason at all.

What, then, can we make of the Requirement of Total Evidence on the Bayesian proposal? My suggestion is this. The Requirement of Total Evidence enjoins you to satisfy the following two constraints: (*a*) that your degree of confidence in a proposition *h* be equal to the degree of confidence it is reasonable to have in *h*, on your total evidence *e*, where [supposing "$p(\cdot)$" is understood to represent the degree of confidence it is reasonable to have in ·] that is equal to $p(h|e)p(e) + p(h|\sim e)p(\sim e)$; and (*b*) that (so long as *h* is not part of your evidence) your degree of confidence assignment to the set of propositions that constitute your total evidence play a role in determining the degree of confidence you assign to *h*, but that the latter play no role in determining the former.[16]

And what exactly counts as your total evidence? Now that there is no worry that something can count as your evidence only if it is reasonable to be certain that it is true on that evidence, I see no compelling reason to resist Williamson's suggestion:[17] your total evidence consists in the set of propositions you know. Indeed, I see in the suggestion a virtue very much like the one Williamson means it to have: the suggestion provides a natural way of specifying what your evidence is, without having any implications whatsoever as to what degree of confidence it is reasonable to invest in the propositions that constitute your evidence.[18]

---

[16] The first clause may seem trivial: after all, it is a consequence of the axioms of probability that, for any *h* and *e*, $p(h) = p(h|e)p(e) + p(h|\sim e)p(\sim e)$. But it is not trivial, insofar as it requires that we advert to (instead of ignoring, as on Williamson's proposal) the degree of confidence it is reasonable to have in *e*, by way of determining the probability of *h* on your evidence. The second clause demands fidelity to the evidence in another way. Without the second clause, there would be nothing in this rendering of the Requirement of Total Evidence that even suggested why, if you found that your degree of confidence assignment to *h* (where *h* is not part of your evidence) was in conflict with your assignment to *e* (where *e* *is* part of your evidence), you should not revise your assignment to e.

[17] As I did in Kaplan (2003: 115).

[18] I argue for just such a conception of knowledge—and for its compatibility with Bayesian probabilism—in Kaplan (2006).

IV

It seems to me that Williamson worked up his proposal (as to how to understand the Requirement of Total Evidence) with a particular adversary in mind. The adversary he had in mind is a Bayesian probabilist: she holds that the probability calculus places a pervasive (that is to say, exception-free) constraint on our opinions, and she holds that it is upon our degree of confidence assignments to propositions that the probability calculus imposes this pervasive constraint. The adversary he has in mind is also a Bayesian *imperialist*. She is committed to understanding everything having to do with our opinions and their epistemic appraisal in terms of degree of confidence assignments, and to regarding as unintelligible any proposal that would seek to understand these matters in any other terms.

Williamson is a probabilist himself. He, too, holds that the probability calculus places a pervasive constraint on our opinions. (Of course, the probabilism he advocates is not of the Bayesian variety. On his view, the probability calculus imposes its pervasive constraint on our judgments as to the intrinsic plausibility of propositions.) So, having recognized the common ground between himself and his Bayesian adversary on the propriety of probabilism—the propriety of holding that the probability calculus places a pervasive constraint on our opinions—Williamson (it seems to me) decided to devote his attentions exclusively to an anti-imperialist struggle. He decided to devote his attention exclusively to disarming the charge that, because of the approach he takes to probability—he offers no definition of probability and does not understand probability in terms of confidence—his form of probabilism is insufficiently intelligible (and so any proposal in which it plays a role is insufficiently intelligible) to merit serious consideration.

I am not a Bayesian imperialist.[19] And I have not argued that, because Williamson does not understand probability in terms of degrees of confidence, his proposal is somehow unintelligible. The brief I have carried is a very different one. My brief has been that probabilism is an extremely powerful epistemological doctrine. It is a doctrine that is by no means obviously true. On the contrary, there are intuitive considerations that suggest it is *not* true. Thus it behooves an epistemologist who champions probabilism to offer us some reason to think that, despite these intuitive considerations to the contrary, probabilism *is* true. Bayesians, to their credit, have always recognized as much and have, from the very beginning, had arguments on offer designed to show why their particular form of probabilism is correct. My complaint has been that Williamson has not done likewise. He appears not even to recognize the obligation to provide some reason to suppose his brand of probabilism is true.

[19] See nn. 3 and 18.

I recognize that not everyone is going to be swayed by this line of criticism. Not everyone finds the arguments Bayesians offer, in support of their form of probabilism, convincing. And there will be some readers of this chapter who will doubtless be, in general, reluctant to place much weight on a priori arguments[20] for epistemological doctrines. They will be drawn to a different model of how to assess an epistemological doctrine—a model that takes its lead from how we assess hypotheses in the empirical sciences. Their thought will be that, just as we judge the adequacy of an empirical hypothesis by looking at how much it explains and how well it explains it, we should judge the adequacy of an epistemological hypothesis by looking at how much it explains (in, of course, the philosophical sense of "explain"), and how well it explains it. On this model, Williamson does not owe us any a priori argument in favor of his form of probabilism—no argument of the sort Bayesians have been so eager to offer for theirs. All he needs to do, to establish the propriety of his brand of probabilism, is to show that this brand of probabilism does a good job—and a better job than its rivals—of explaining what it can reasonably be expected to be able to explain.

I say all this because I see at least some evidence that Williamson is operating with just this model in mind. He writes (p. 213) that he does not expect that the few things he says about his way of thinking of the probability of a hypothesis on present evidence will "smother all doubts about the initial probability distribution. Their aim is to justify the procedure of tentatively postulating such a distribution, in order to see what use can be made of it in developing a theory of evidential probability." On one way of reading this, Williamson can be understood as saying that he is tentatively postulating the initial probability distribution with the idea of vindicating it by appeal to how much the theory it makes possible can explain, how well that theory explains it, and how well that theory compares, in these respects, to its rivals. I want to end this chapter by saying why I do not think Williamson's situation is in any way helped by viewing his contribution by the lights of this model.

We have not examined (there is not space to examine) every theoretical use to which Williamson puts (or could conceivably put) his assumption of an initial probability (qua intrinsic plausibility) distribution. But it is clear from the use to which we have seen him put it (to make sense of the Requirement of Total Evidence) that it does not in this use make possible a theory that explains, better than any rival, what one can reasonably expect such a theory to explain. As we have seen, the postulation of this intrinsic plausibility distribution does not enable Williamson to do anything that cannot be done by a Bayesian reasonable degree of confidence distribution. The alleged advantage the former has over any view that (like the latter) would associate probability with confidence is, as we

---

[20] Savage's argument, for example, derives the probabilistic constraint on confidence (he calls it "personal probability") from a small set of principles that purport to say how rational preferences behave.

saw, illusory. In contrast, however, the reasonable degree of confidence account of probability allows the explanation to be something that remains inexplicable on Williamson's view: the role that assessments of the probability of a hypothesis on the evidence play in decision making.

Suppose that you are suffering discomfort, and so go to the doctor. After the requisite examination and tests are completed, she tells you that your discomfort is not a sign of any dangerous condition. For all that, she continues, there is a procedure you can undergo that, if you have condition C, will completely alleviate the discomfort. If, however, you do not have condition C, your discomfort will remain as it is. The procedure is, however, quite expensive. The choice as to whether to undergo the procedure, she tells you, is up to you. Suppose further that, as far as you are concerned, the alleviation of your discomfort is more than worth the expense associated with undergoing the procedure.

Your doctor now asks, "Do you have any questions?" Is there any doubt that the answer is "Yes"? Is there any doubt that you will want to ask your doctor how probable it is on present evidence that you have condition C? Of course not. To undergo the procedure is to bet a lot of money that you have condition C. If you win the bet, you are better off: as we noted, you are happy to exchange the cost of the procedure for the alleviation of your discomfort. But if you lose the bet, you are worse off: your discomfort persists and you have spent the cost of the procedure. Before you make a bet like this, you will want to establish as best you can how probable it is on present evidence that the proposition, on whose truth your winning the bet depends—the proposition that you have condition C—is true. The natural thought is that, if it is probable enough, you will want to make the bet; if not, you will want to decline the bet.

And this is precisely what our Bayesian proposal, conjoined with Bayesian decision theory, tells you. It tells you that you should solve your decision problem in the following way. Decide what degree of confidence, r, you would have to have in the proposition that you have condition C for you to be indifferent between the status quo and undergoing the procedure. Then choose to undergo the procedure if the degree of confidence it is reasonable to have in the proposition that you have condition C is greater than r.[21]

---

[21] Here is a fuller story of how Bayesian decision theory would have you solve the problem. The problem takes the following form, where h stands for the proposition "You have condition C," x for "Your discomfort is alleviated at substantial expense," y for "You pay the substantial expense, but your discomfort remains," and z for "You suffer discomfort":

	h	$\sim h$
Undergo procedure	x	y
Status quo	z	z

Bayesian decision theory issues the following marching orders. Determine the subjective utility of (a relative measure of the intensity of your preference for) the three possible outcomes of the options before you: x, y and z. That is, assign the best outcome, x, a utility of 1, the worst, y, a utility of 0. So $u(x) = 1, u(y) = 0$. Then ask yourself how confident you would have to be that h for you to be

In contrast, Williamson's proposal cannot make any sense of why you would want to ask your doctor what, on present evidence, is the probability that you have condition C. On his proposal, the probability on present evidence that you have condition C has no consequence for whether you ought to undergo the procedure. On his proposal, your doctor might truthfully tell you that the probability on present evidence that you have condition C is 1—thus that the probability on present evidence that the procedure will succeed if undergone is 1—even though the reasonable thing, on present evidence, is to be uncertain that you have condition C, uncertain that the procedure will succeed if undertaken.[22]

---

indifferent between (on the one hand) z and (on the other hand) doing something that gives you the best outcome, x, if h and the worst, y, if $\sim h$. (As it happens, that is precisely what undergoing the procedure will do.) Assign the degree of confidence, r, upon which you settle by way of answering that question, to $u(z)$. (You thereby provide a relative measure of the intensity of your preference for z.) That much done, choose to undergo the procedure if and only if doing so has greater subjective expected utility than the status quo: i.e., if and only if (where "con(·)" is shorthand for "the degree of confidence it is reasonable for you to have in · on present evidence")

$$[\text{con}(h)u(x) + \text{con}(\sim h)u(y)] > [\text{con}(h)u(z) + \text{con}(\sim h)u(z)],$$

That is to say [since $u(x) = 1, u(y) = 0, u(z) = r$, and conformity to the axioms of probability requires that $\text{con}(h) + \text{con}(\sim h) = 1$], you ought to choose to undergo the procedure if and only if

$$\text{con}(h) > r.$$

All this, of course, assumes that both con(h) and r have precise values. You might reasonably find yourself unable to assign them precise values. But this is not a worry. The assumption is here only to shorten the tale. The Bayesian story as to how to solve your decision problem can be generalized so as to provide you marching orders even when neither con(h) nor r has precise values.

Of course, the mere fact that the Bayesian way of thinking thus arrives at a reasonable-sounding verdict in this case is not, of itself, sufficient reason to think that the Bayesian way of thinking is correct. All the same, I think that, properly generalized (so as not to assume unduly precise degrees of confidence or subjective utilities), it *is* correct—it has deep and compelling foundations. Again, see Savage (1954/1972) and the exposition and defense of Savage in Maher (1993). Maher provides much of the needed generalization. Kaplan (2002: sect II), provides yet more. See, too, Jeffrey (1983).

22 Williamson appears to see this as a virtue of his proposal. "We should question the association of evidential probability 1 and absolute certainty," Williamson writes (p. 213). "For subjective Bayesians, probability 1 is the highest degree of belief, which presumably is absolute certainty: If one's credence in p is 1, one should be willing to accept a bet on which one gains a penny if p is true and is tortured horribly to death if p is false. Few propositions pass this test. Surely complex logical truths do not, even though the probability axioms assign them probability 1." I am not sure what exactly is supposed to be the critical bite of the last sentence. If Williamson means to be saying here that one might reasonably be unwilling to accept the foregoing bet on a complex logical truth, then he is surely right. But it is no mark against the propriety of a rule (e.g., you should be willing to accept any bet on a logical truth) that a reasonable person will violate the rule in circumstances in which things are sufficiently complicated (as in the case in which one is confronted with a complex logical truth) that she is not able to *see* that she is violating the rule. Were it otherwise, the Requirement of Total Evidence would be similarly tarnished: a reasonable person can be expected to violate this rule when her evidence is sufficiently complicated that she does not see to what degree it supports a hypothesis. Indeed this point is one Williamson himself is at pains to make, arguing (p. 192) that our fallibility in applying rules is entirely compatible with the rules' expressing "a standard of correctness for action"—and, in that sense, a standard we ought to satisfy. In this case,

On his proposal, the probability on present evidence that you will win the bet you make if you choose to undergo the procedure may be as high as you like (or, for that matter, as low as you like), yet the question as to whether you should undergo the procedure remains quite unsettled. Indeed, his is a proposal that renders entirely mysterious why anyone would think that the probability of propositions on the evidence has any bearing on rational decision making.

Thus my first point. By the very lights of the model suggested—a model on which we do not need a priori arguments to vindicate an epistemological hypothesis, we need only to show that the hypothesis explains well what one would expect it to, and does so better than any of its rivals—Williamson's postulation of his degree of intrinsic plausibility distribution comes up short. Williamson's postulate has a Bayesian rival that explains everything Williamson can by use of his postulate, and also explains something important Williamson cannot.

My second point is that I do not see how the move to this model removes the burden that, I have complained, Williamson fails adequately to acknowledge. Among the things that one would expect a probabilist epistemology to be able to explain is why it is a mistake to credit the many intuitive considerations (of which I have discussed but one) that suggest that the probability calculus's constraint on our opinions is not pervasive. After all, these intuitive considerations constitute, at first blush, evidence that probabilism is false. And the Requirement of Total Evidence requires us to evaluate a hypothesis, not by paying attention only to the evidence in its favor (for example, what it explains and how well it explains it), but by evaluating the hypothesis on *all* the evidence. Thus a favorable evaluation of the probabilist hypothesis requires that we be able to say why these intuitive considerations ought *not* to be counted as evidence that the constraint the probability calculus places on our opinions is not pervasive.

I do not mean to suggest that none of the intuitive considerations that speak against the truth of probabilism can be neutralized without access to the sorts of argument from the connection between preference and confidence that Bayesians have been promulgating. I think that there are ways, compatible with the probability calculus's having a pervasive constraint on our opinions, both to weaken and to supplement probabilism so as to render it immune to some of the intuitive considerations that can be (and have been) raised against it. These ways of weakening and supplementing probabilism are no less available to a probabilist of Williamson's stripe than they are to a Bayesian probabilist. But I do not think that *all* of the intuitive considerations can be handled in this way. Some (including, in my opinion, the consideration I have raised here)

---

it is clear that, in refusing the bet on the complex logical truth, one *has* failed to meet a standard for correct action. Insofar as one wants to maximize one's fortune, one has acted (blamelessly, but all the same) in a manner that is inconsistent with one's own preferences: one has chosen an option that is guaranteed to leave one less well off.

require adverting to just the sort of arguments Bayesians have provided, and Williamson has not.[23] If this is right, then we cannot, by adverting to the model suggested, relieve Williamson of the burden of providing an argument as to why the intuitive considerations I have raised against probabilism are mistaken. And we cannot afford the distaste for such arguments that the move to the model is supposed to allow us to indulge. Some such argument is required.

But does it really have to be an argument that, like Savage's, makes essential appeal to the connection between confidence and preference? I am inclined to think it does. But I should note that not all Bayesian probabilists agree. Some have argued that Savage-style arguments are too pragmatic in character to be convincing. They have proposed other arguments—arguments that make no appeal to the connection between confidence and preference—that, they contend, do a better job.[24] In my view, they are mistaken on the first count. And (as I have already confessed) I am inclined to think them mistaken on the second as well.[25] But I do not mean to pursue this controversy here. I raise it only because it is of no small import to the proper evaluation of Williamson's probabilism. For, if it turns out that I am right—if it turns out that the only good arguments available for probabilism are of the Savage sort—then there is simply no way to defend a form of probabilism that (as Williamson's does) denies that there is a connection between preference and the opinions that the probability calculus constrains.[26]

And what if it turns out that *none* of us Bayesian probabilists is right? What if it turns out that there is *no* good argument, of the sort Bayesians have always thought is required, for the thesis that the probability calculus imposes (in *any* sense) a pervasive constraint on our opinions?

Then, it seems to me, probabilism is to be rejected. This does not, of course, require us to abandon the probability calculus. No one disputes that, in circumstances in which we have statistical evidence, or a chance set-up of known disposition,[27] the probability calculus constrains our opinions. There is no issue

---

[23] See Kaplan (1996, 2002), each of which has, as its explicit purpose, to show (the former in full detail) how Bayesian probabilism must be weakened, supplemented, and argued for if it is adequately to address the intuitive considerations that have been raised against it.

[24] See, e.g., Christensen (1996, 2001), and Joyce (1998).

[25] I explain why I am unmoved by Christensen's and Joyce's critique of Savage-style arguments in Kaplan (2002: 443–6). For a critique of the arguments Christensen and Joyce have offered in exchange, see Maher (1997, 2002). Christensen's latest statement of his position is to be found in Christensen (2004: 106–42).

[26] Recall that it is precisely because no such connection holds that Williamson can maintain that we can judge a proposition to have probability 1 (on his proposal as to how to understand probability) without judging it to be certain.

[27] A chance set-up (here I follow Hacking 1965: 13) is a device or part of the world on which there is a kind of trial that might be conducted and where, for each possible outcome of the trial (there must be a set of mutually exclusive and exhaustive possible outcomes of which the trial produces one), the chance set-up has a disposition, on the conduct of the trial, to produce that outcome with a particular probability. The drawing of an urn whose contents are balls of equal

as to whether the probability calculus places *any* constraint on our opinions. The issue is whether it places a *pervasive* constraint on our opinions—whether, even in cases in which we do not have statistical evidence or a chance set-up of known disposition, even in cases in which we have precious little evidence at all, the probability calculus constrains what opinions we should hold. Abandoning probabilism requires us to say that it does not. It requires us to deny that, as Williamson puts it (p. 209), "Given a scientific hypothesis *h*, we can intelligibly ask: how probable is *h* on present evidence?" Or, rather, it requires us to concede that, while we can intelligibly ask the question, we cannot demand that the question be in every case answered in terms congenial to the assumption under which it is asked: we cannot demand that the assessment of *h*'s probability, provided by way of response, satisfy the axioms of probability.

As a matter of fact, I think we have no call to abandon probabilism. That is because I think there are perfectly good Savage-style arguments for Bayesian probabilism. This, together with the explanatory virtues of which Bayesian probabilism can boast, leaves me feeling secure in my probabilism. What I do not see—and it has been the purpose of this chapter to explain *why* I do not see it—is how Williamson can feel secure in his.[28]

---

weight and size thus counts as a trial of a chance set-up. In the case in which I know that the urn contains 50 black balls and 50 white, it is a chance device of known disposition (at least to me). In the case in which I know nothing of the proportion of black balls to white, it is not.

[28] I want to thank Jim Joyce for helpful discussion, and Joan Weiner both for discussion of the issues that arose in the writing of the chapter, and for comments on the penultimate draft.

9

Assertion, Knowledge, and Lotteries

Jonathan Kvanvig

One of the central claims of Timothy Williamson's ground-breaking epistemology is the claim that knowledge is the norm of assertion. I believe this viewpoint is mistaken, and will argue that here. I will first explain Williamson's path to the conclusion he holds, identifying the two major arguments that he uses to support his claim that knowledge is the norm of assertion. I will then summarize the prima facie case for an alternative view,[1] following which I will address the tension between this prima facie case and Williamson's arguments. I will argue that a proper resolution of the conflict results in a denial of the idea that knowledge is the norm of assertion. Instead, I will maintain that, to the extent that appropriate assertion is subject to epistemic constraints, those constraints have to do with justification rather than knowledge.

One note before beginning. Williamson's discussion of the norm or norms of assertion assumes that such norms are indefeasible—that one always does something wrong when one asserts something one does not know. I see no reason for such a strong reading of the norm, though I do understand how one might get to this idea. If we think of sports games, such as baseball or basketball, we find rules or norms governing the game that must be interpreted as indefeasible. If the rules were defeasible, then we would expect that, for example, if one's life depended on getting away with a foul in the last seconds of a close game, the referee should overlook the infraction. In one sense, this can happen, for, in an emergency, the rules are violated by abandoning the game. But, if we are playing the game, the rules cannot be overridden by factors outside the rule book. Rules of a game of this sort are quite different from ordinary norms, such as norms of reasoning, social norms, norms of etiquette, aesthetic norms, or norms of polite discourse. Treating the norms of assertion as indefeasible requires an argument that, as Williamson puts it, there are constitutive norms for assertion akin to rules of a game. Williamson gives no argument that there are any such norms for assertion, but only suggests that we proceed on the assumption that there are such norms to see where it leads.[2]

---

[1] The view I defended in Kvanvig (2003).   [2] See, especially, pp. 238–40.

This assumption has two negative consequences for Williamson's view. The first consequence is that it makes the norm or norms of assertion quite different from the norms just mentioned that govern politeness, etiquette, art, reasoning, and the like. In general, the norms that govern human behavior are defeasible, so it would be surprising to find the norms governing assertion to be indefeasible.

The second consequence of Williamson's assumption is that it makes it more difficult to defend the view that knowledge is the norm of assertion. There are a variety of cases in which the norm is violated and yet we do not view the assertion as deserving of criticism. Skeptics claim not to know anything, and if we consider the possibility that they are correct, we need not demand that they speak no more. Eliminative materialists say that there are no beliefs, and they do not have to flout the norms of assertion to discuss this philosophical possibility, even if it should turn out that they are right. William James counsels nontheists who are convinced by his pragmatic argument to go to Mass and hope for the best. When they do, and engage in the practice of espousing theological claims that they do not (yet) believe, we may find humor in the situation, but there is nothing wrong with the attempt (barring some unforeseen argument that theistic belief and practice is always and everywhere irrational). Philosophers espouse positive views in all of its subfields that, on reflection, they agree that they do not know to be true; but they continue the practice unrepentant. Visualization techniques by sports psychologists often involve rehearsing a positive outcome regarding what is going to happen next in a competitive situation, and such rehearsal often involves thoroughly unwarranted assertions, such as "He's going to hang a curveball and I'm going to turn on it and drive it right down the left field line." Such techniques are often employed by aspiring academicians: "I'm going to send this paper to the best journal in my field and they'll accept it and hundreds, no, *thousands*, will read it; it will change the landscape of my discipline and I'll be famous!" (For those in this situation, do not be overly concerned about the example: just apply the other part of the technique, which is to ignore information that contributes to a defeatist mentality . . .)

In other cases, we assert things we do not believe because of a social role we inhabit. For example, a judge may give instructions to the jury that he does not believe are correct instructions. But his role requires that he give these instructions, and, in order to comply, he asserts them without believing them. In other cases, a teacher is required by law to teach certain material. Suppose, for example, that a teacher is required to teach certain sex education material to high-school students. One might do so to comply with the law even when one does not believe that what one is teaching is true. Note that, in some such cases, the material will be false, and yet teaching it will not be criticizable. In other cases, the material will be true, but will be disbelieved by a teacher with, let us say, "outlier" beliefs. Perhaps the teacher is a thoroughgoing fatalist who thinks that precautions are a waste of time, or perhaps has an unusual theory about reproduction and sexually transmitted diseases.

I have belabored this point in order to prevent the impression that stopgap measures might be useful in sustaining the view that the norms of assertion are indefeasible. For example, one might attempt to treat assertion not backed by belief as a kind of theater. In a play, actors vocalize sentences and do not believe what the sentences express, and perhaps apparent assertion not backed by belief could be modeled on this practice. I am not impressed by this treatment of the case. In the case of theatrics, we can pull the actors out of the context and ask whether they are asserting what their sentences express, and they'll say "no". That is an easy test to apply when a question arises about whether a person is asserting anything, and, applied to the above cases, the test will not turn out well for the view that assertions are not being made. Perhaps the speakers will also express some reservations if we remove them from the scripted situation, but the reservations will be about the truth of what they are asserting, not about whether they are asserting the claims in question. Regardless of the plausibility of specific stopgap measures, however, the examples above display how widespread are the examples in which assertions not backed by knowledge occur without deserving criticism. The simplest explanation of these data is that the norms of assertion are defeasible. This explanation has a further advantage as well over any collection of stopgap measures aimed at avoiding this explanation. This further advantage is that it construes the norms of assertion the same way that is appropriate for treating the other kinds of norms listed earlier: social norms, rules of etiquette, norms of politeness, aesthetics norms, and norms of reasoning, to name a few.

I raise this issue to put it aside in what follows. I will assume that the norms of assertion are defeasible in what follows, and making this assumption has the advantage that it makes it easier to defend Williamson's view from the above examples. If the norms of assertion are defeasible, then we have the option of explaining all of the above cases in terms of factors that defeat the claim that you should not say what you do not know to be true. The fundamental issues that separate Williamson and me on the relationship between assertion and epistemology are not here, however, so I will not require of the view that knowledge is the norm of assertion that it be an indefeasible norm.

1. THE KNOWLEDGE ACCOUNT

Williamson's discussion proceeds as follows. He begins with the working hypothesis that assertion has a constitutive rule. He grants that this hypothesis is by no means obvious, but suggests that pursuing the idea to see where it leads may prove fruitful. He then proposes two main accounts of a constitutive rule for assertion: the truth account and the knowledge account. According to the truth account, one has a warrant for asserting p only if p is true; according to the knowledge account, one has warrant for asserting p only if one knows p.

The notion of warrant here is stipulatively related to that of the idea of a constitutive rule: to have warrant for asserting a claim is simply to have satisfied the constitutive rule for assertion.

After proposing these two accounts, Williamson first argues against the truth account and in favor of the knowledge account. The remainder of his defense of the knowledge account consists in rebutting attempts to weaken the knowledge account so as allow there to be warrant for asserting something false. Perhaps, for example, one needs only to believe, or rationally to believe, that one knows in order to have such warrant.

The primary argument Williamson employs against the truth account involves lottery claims, such as the claim that a given ticket will lose. According to Williamson, there is something wrong with the assertion that one's ticket will lose, even given the truth of the claim. Williamson notes a natural response we have to such an assertion, which is to chastise the assertor by saying, "But you don't know that!"

This chastisement leads to the primary arguments Williamson offers on behalf of the knowledge account. Williamson first notes the conversational propriety of questions such as "How do you know that?" and "Do you know that?" Such questions presuppose the knowledge account, according to Williamson, for, if the knowledge account were false, the questions would appear to be irrelevant.

This line of argument may prove too much, however. It is also appropriate to ask, "Are you certain?", "Are you absolutely sure?" If the conversational propriety of various questions is an argument in favor of the knowledge account, the propriety of these questions is an argument in favor of a stronger account: that one must be absolutely certain in order for a claim to be assertible. Moreover, it is also appropriate to ask of an assertor, "Do you have any good reason to think that?" In fact, when asking "How do you know?", the answer we are looking for is one that cites the reasons that person has for thinking that the claim in question is true, and, when we get such an answer, we are satisfied. If conversational propriety of questions were our only data, we would have no good reason to single out the knowledge account as opposed to some weaker or stronger position.

It may be that, once we have a good argument for a position about the norm or norms of assertion, we will be in a position to return to this issue of appropriate questions and explain why one of the ways of questioning is primary and the others derivative. My point here is not to show that there is no way to explain away data not in accord with one's preferred theory. My point is only that the data about conversationally appropriate questions do not settle the matter as to the precise nature of the norm or norms of assertion.

Williamson's other major argument on behalf of the knowledge account is Moorean in character, appealing to the defective character of the assertion "p but I don't know that p." Williamson notes the viewpoint widely shared in recent epistemology that to assert p is to represent oneself as knowing p. Williamson cites as primary exponents of the view G. E. Moore, Michael Slote, Max Black, and Peter Unger; put in different order, we can honor these names by referring to the representational claim they all endorse as the BUMS view.[3] Williamson claims that a virtue of the knowledge account of assertion is that it offers a general explanation of the truth of the BUMS view: since the norms of a practice are presupposed by those involved in the practice, hearers expect speakers to know and speakers expect to be taken to know, thereby creating a situation in which an assertion represents the speaker as having knowledge.

Both the BUMS view and the knowledge account of assertion provide a basis for explaining the impropriety of asserting "p but I don't know p." On the BUMS view, the second conjunct contradicts the representation made by asserting the first conjunct, making incoherent the entire assertion. The knowledge account implies something stronger. It implies that there can be no propriety for the assertion, since the second conjunct directly contradicts the condition required for the propriety of asserting the first conjunct.

This argument relies on the intuitive impropriety of asserting "p and I don't know p," and this reliance raises a version of the problem noted earlier, for it is equally inappropriate to say "p but I am not certain whether p." Williamson's answer is to insist that the standards for knowledge and certainty in a context typically are the same, and, when they diverge, the knowledge account predicts the correct response. Thus, he holds, if one asserts "p and I lack Cartesian metaphysical certainty that p," no impropriety results.

2. THE JUSTIFICATION ACCOUNT

There are two other prominent alternatives to the knowledge account, one of which I will defend here. The two accounts are the belief account and the justification account. On the first approach, the only requirement on assertion is sincerity: say what you think.[4] This view will strike most everyone as excessively weak, but there is a way to make it a bit more plausible. We might say that belief is the fundamental norm of assertion, and that among the norms for belief are the other things that lead one to think that the sincerity requirement alone is too weak. So, for example, if one thinks that good reasons are required for assertion, that would be because it is a norm of belief that you should not believe things without good reasons. Assertion thereby inherits this derivative norm because of the sincerity requirement.

A full defense of the belief account of assertion would thus involve an account of the types of activity that are norm-governed and a relegation of

---

[3] Please do not interpret this light-hearted levity as a sign of disrespect. To get the right tone, one needs to imagine an accent from the Bronx and the phrase, "How aah ya, you's bums!"

[4] Kent Bach and Mike Harnish (1979) defend a version of this view.

each norm to its natural home or homes. I doubt that any such regimentation can be accomplished, however. More carefully, I am not sure that any one regimentation will be defensible as the best one, nor that it will be better than a view that refuses the project. Perhaps it can be done, but it is hard to see why it needs to be done, or what the value of it would be, except in service of the sincerity requirement itself. In what follows, then, I propose to ignore the issue of which norms are fundamental to a practice and which are derivative, and focus instead only on the norms of whatever level that govern the practice of assertion.

The other alternative to the knowledge and truth accounts is the justification account. According to this view, the propriety of an assertion is a function of one's justification for the content of the assertion rather than a function of whether one knows the content to be true. The primary argument for the justification view arises from two factors. The first factor is that there are four distinctive necessary conditions for knowledge, conditions described by the defeasibility theory of knowledge. According to this theory, where the notion of defeat is properly clarified, knowledge is (ultimately) undefeated justified true belief. This assumption may seem to conflict with Williamson's aversion to the idea that knowledge can be analyzed,[5] but in fact it does not. My assumption is only that the four distinctive conditions of the defeasibility theory are necessary conditions for knowledge, not that they constitute an analysis of knowledge. It may be that these four conditions are only some of the necessary conditions for knowledge, or it may be that these four conditions specify fully the nature of knowledge. Either view is compatible with a denial that knowledge can be analyzed. Like Williamson, I have little interest in the project of analysis, though I do have an interest in the nature of knowledge. If we give a suitable construal of each claim, it is correct to say that knowledge requires belief, truth, and a justification that is ultimately undefeated. The most controversial of these assumptions is the assumption that justification is required for knowledge, but the objections to this view generally begin by assuming that justification has some special character—that it is a deontological notion, that it requires voluntary control over belief, that it requires that one be able to construct an argument for each justified belief, and so on. In my view, justification is a function of the evidence one possesses, including mental states such as beliefs and experiences (though, of course, the assumption is not that all mental states are part of one's evidence). No account of knowledge can succeed without making justification, construed in this broad and general way, a necessary condition for knowledge.

The second central feature of the prima facie case for the justification view, beside the claim about these four necessary conditions for knowledge, concerns our attitudes when our assertions are corrected. In some cases of correction, we

---

[5] See, e.g., Williamson (2000: 130).

take back the content of our speech act, and in other cases *we apologize for, and regret, the very act itself.* For example, if we assert a claim and then are shown that the claim is false, we take back the content of our speech act, but we need not apologize for or regret the very act itself. Randy says, "I've studied music all my life; there's no piece of group music even moderately well known in the USA where part of the group is playing in 15/16 time and another part in 17/16 time," to which Michael responds, "That's certainly a reasonable judgment, except that you don't know enough about King Crimson. They are moderately well known, and they have just such a piece." Michael then shows Randy the piece (so, I am assuming that Michael is correct), to which Randy says, "I was wrong, I take it back." Now Randy may regret his assertion if he is the sort of person who strongly dislikes confronting his own fallibility. He may even vow to be much more careful not to say anything at all when he risks being wrong in order not to repeat this embarrassing moment, though such a response is surely overblown. Chagrin is normal, even mild embarrassment, but apologizing would be unctuous and overwrought. As I told the story, Randy responds appropriately. He does not apologize for making the assertion, but what he does instead is take back the content of the assertion. In fact, were he to apologize, the natural response would be dismissive: "Give it a rest, nobody's always right . . ."

In other cases, such remonstrance for apology would not be forthcoming. If we assert something that we do not in fact believe, we naturally apologize for the speech act itself when our assertion is challenged, and the apology is fully appropriate. Joe says, "I'm terrible at baseball, I can't hit a curve ball to save my life!", to which Jared responds, "Don't say that! You're just feeling bad because you're in a hitting slump." Joe's too down on himself to respond at the time, but by the next game, he is feeling better, and says, "Jared, you're right, I shouldn't have said that—I was just discouraged after striking out again." Here Joe is apologizing for and regretting the speech act itself, not just taking back its content. The apology is perfectly in order, unlike the case above, where the only fault concerns the content of the assertion.

This same distinction plays out with the other two conditions as well. Suppose you have been gettiered, and you assert, "Someone in this room owns a Ford." When it is pointed out that you have been duped by Nogot, you will take back the content of your assertion. You will also experience chagrin at being duped—it is not high on the usual lists of enjoyable experiences—but no apology for the speech act is in order. Practical jokes play off of this very fact. For those who find humor in such, the humor is in getting a person to respond in a fully appropriate way, even though the circumstances are not what the person reasonably judges them to be. In such a case, only a person suffering from a "private, preponderant horror at being duped"[6] would apologize for the action, and anyone who would

---

[6] This is the language of William James in describing those who say it is better to go without belief forever than risk being proven wrong.

so apologize deserves remonstrance for that action. The appropriate response is to take back the content of what is said, not apologize for the saying of it.

Things are different when you do not have justification for what you say. Suppose Billy Bob sees a headline on a tabloid in the checkout line at Walmart that reads "George Bush—A closet communist!" Billy Bob is a Texas Democrat and will believe almost anything negative about Bush, he despises him so much. So he believes that Bush is a communist, and upon seeing his best friend Bobbie Sue, says, "Hey, ja'hear Dubbya's a commie!" Bobbie Sue does not like Bush either, but she is skeptical: "Naw, yer jokin'," she says. "Naw I ain't—I saw't in da paper over at the Wawl-Mort!" "Billy Bob, them's *tabloids*! You don't trust *tabloids*!" Billy Bob, donning the accent of what those outside Texas take as a mark of intelligence, reflects and says, "Yes, you're right, I shouldn't have believed that paper and I shouldn't have said what I did. I take it back." Here he does the right thing; it is appropriate to regret and apologize for the speech act in question, even if by some bizarre twist in reality he turns out to be right.

The feature I am pointing out plays a central role in the prima facie case for the justification account of the norm of assertion. Only when the speech act itself is at fault, do we have reason to think that some norm of assertion is at work; when only the content of the assertion needs to be taken back, the assertion itself is not at fault. This point should be self-evident, but I emphasize it so that it is not overlooked: norms of assertion are norms governing a certain type of human activity, and thus relate to the speech act itself rather than the content of such an act. Notice that when we look at the four conditions for knowledge above, the only ones regarding which apology or regret for the speech act itself is appropriate are the belief and justification conditions. There is, therefore, a prima facie case that knowledge is not the norm of assertion, but rather justified belief is.

It is important as well to notice that the distinction here should not be accounted for in terms of a distinction between responsibility and blameworthiness. This distinction comes into play when our behavior is irresponsible though not blameworthy. For example, if Jim offends Billy Bob by making fun of Republican policies, not realizing that Billy Bob is a fan of these policies, Jim may be morally responsible for offending Billy Bob, but not blameworthy. After all, he might have had good reason to think that Billy Bob shared his disparaging attitudes toward Republican policies (I am assuming, of course, that such attitudes can be justified). Not knowing better, and not having been negligent in any way for not knowing better, Jim should not be blamed for offending Billy Bob, even though he is morally responsible for doing so. (Note that I am not implying here that he has done something that is, all things considered, morally wrong. The only point needed here is that he is morally responsible for offending Billy Bob, and that fact is a prima facie indicator of having done something morally wrong.)

Note, however, that in such cases, upon finding out the true nature of the situation, the proper thing for Jim to do is to apologize (assuming that he grants that he should not have offended Billy Bob). He cannot appeal to the inappropriateness of blame as a justification for not apologizing. The key here is that a correct understanding makes the apology appropriate. What we are called on to apologize for goes with responsibility, even when one is blameless for the action in question.

Applied to the topic at hand, this result shows that one cannot avoid the above prima facie case for the justification account by claiming that what one apologizes for tracks some secondary normative notion such as blameworthiness, and that a correct account of the norms of assertion should track a primary normative notion such as responsibility. The point of focusing on which speech acts one ought to apologize for, after learning the true nature of one's action, is to show that in the primary sense of responsibility, rather than the secondary sense of blameworthiness, there is strong evidence on behalf of the justification condition. Apologies are appropriate for being insincere and for speaking without adequate evidence. For the other necessary conditions for knowledge, the appropriate response is to take back the content of the assertion, but not to apologize for the speech act itself.

It is also important to note that one may need to apologize for the *consequences* of a speech act, even if the speech act itself does not call for one. If I tell you something false, but have very good reasons for what I think, and you are harmed in the future because you take my word on the matter, it would be appropriate and necessary for me to apologize for causing you harm. But it is one thing to apologize for the harm one's actions cause, and quite another to apologize for the speech act itself. In such cases, one feels in a special way the weight of responsibility, and one agonizes over the potential one has for causing unintended harm. There is a clear difference, however, between appropriate attitudes when one has caused harm by, say, driving while intoxicated and when one has caused harm when driving with an ordinary modicum of care. In both cases, one may regret driving because of the harm caused. In the first case, an apology for getting behind the wheel is certainly in order. In the second case, one may regret having gotten behind the wheel, thinking to oneself "if only . . .". One might even vow never to drive again, and, though such a decision may count as a rational one, it is certainly not morally required. Apologizing for harm caused is one thing, and apologizing for the actions that caused the harm is another.

I am assuming, in this example of driving with normal care and in the previous one of saying something false, that one has not done something negligent or careless in the course of performing the action in question that would make our assessment of the case more like the case of driving while intoxicated. That is precisely the right assumption to make, however, to compare with cases in which nature has conspired so as to deceive one regarding the truth. You have taken the ordinary modicum of care in the opinion in question, and such care is sufficient for justifying you in believing what you sincerely report. In such a case, just as in the ordinary driving case, there are grounds for regret and sorrow when one's actions cause harm. One may even apologize for ever getting in the car or opening one's mouth. To the extent that such an apology is fitting, however, to that extent we have reasons to doubt that there was enough evidence to justify the assertion in question. In the normal case, such an apology would count as an overreaction, albeit an understandable one. It is one thing to need to apologize for the harm caused, and it is quite another thing for the action itself to have been morally irresponsible.

So, two points are in order about this prima facie argument for the justification view. The proper approach to the topic of norms of assertion should focus on speech acts themselves. Hence, which acts of assertion demand apology is a good guide for determining where the norms of assertion lie. Moreover, by focusing on what demands apology, we have a criterion for distinguishing between blameworthiness and irresponsibility. Norms of assertion should concern what we are responsible for rather than what we are blameless for, and focusing on what demands apology places the focus on the concept of responsibility where it belongs.

This case for the justification account is prima facie only, and its implications cannot be endorsed without showing how the justification view fares once Williamson's arguments on behalf of the knowledge view are taken into account. As we have seen, the two primary arguments for that view involve the explanation of Moorean sentences and the related BUMS view, and considerations related to lottery sentences. I turn then to the question of how powerful these arguments are for the knowledge account, and whether they are powerful enough to undermine the prima facie case for the justification account.

3. MOOREAN SENTENCES AND THE BUMS VIEW

Williamson's Moorean argument arises from the claim that it is incoherent to say that p is true but that one does not know that p is true. This argument counts in favor of the knowledge account and against the justification account only if the justification account cannot explain the data in question. It can, if we employ the right kind of justification in the explanation. The kind of justification in question is the kind that puts one in a position to know—that is, that kind which, if ungettiered and combined with true belief, yields knowledge. I will term this kind of justification "epistemic justification." The crucial feature of such justification is that one cannot have it for believing p, but not enough for believing p to count as knowledge. That is not to say, of course, that such justification is sufficient for knowledge. Justified false beliefs are possible, as are justified true beliefs that are gettiered. What cannot happen though is that a true belief has an epistemic justification that is ungettiered, but where the level of justification falls below the threshold needed for knowledge.

In such a case, if one is justified in believing p, and one knows that one believes p, then one is justified in believing that one knows p. Showing that this claim is true will take some work, but, before taking on that task, it is worth seeing what the payoff will be. This fact, I will claim, is sufficient to explain the untoward character of a Moorean assertion. We ordinarily assume that speakers know whether they are being sincere, and, if the justification account is correct, they should not say anything without being justified in believing what they say. But, if they are justified in believing p, then they are justified in believing that they know p as well (given that they know whether they are being sincere). So, by whatever basis they have for asserting p, they also have a basis for asserting that they know p. From this point and a mundane principle about justification, it follows that, if they have a basis for asserting p, they lack a basis for asserting that they do not know p. So the Moorean sentence is out of order, and the justification account can explain this impropriety.

It can explain this impropriety, assuming that we can defend the principle used in this explanation, the principle that, if one is justified in believing p and knows that one believes p, then one is justified in believing that one knows p. The argument for this claim proceeds via the standard conditions for knowledge, showing that, if a person is justified in believing p, then they are justified in believing that each of the conditions for knowledge obtains. First, the principle stipulates knowledge that the belief-condition holds, and the truth-condition itself is trivial: if one is justified in believing p, one is justified in believing that p is true. The truth-condition would not be trivial if the consequent of this conditional required actual belief, but it does not. The phrase "justified in believing" can be interpreted in two ways, one of which requires belief and the other one not. Since the present topic concerns what the quality of evidence needed to put one in a position to know, we should not interpret the phrase as requiring actual belief. If we do not, the principle requires only that one's total evidence confirm the claim that p is true when that evidence confirms p, and, if anything in epistemology is an unremarkable truth, that is. Thus, one is justified in believing that the belief-condition and the truth-condition hold if one is justified.

Assume that we hold an internalist conception of justification. In one sense, a defender of the justification account is free to hold whatever conception of justification he wishes, so this assumption is not especially troubling. One implication of such a conception is usually put as follows: one's justification will be accessible to one on reflection. I will assume this point as well for now, though later I will show that it was an unnecessary assumption. An implication of the claim that one's justification is accessible by reflection is that one will be able to ascertain on reflection whether one's belief is justified, and, if one can so ascertain, then one's total evidence is sufficient for showing not only that *p* is true but also that one is justified in believing *p*.

One way to resist this argument is to question whether, in reflecting, one would be creating additional evidence so that the body of evidence apart from reflection need not itself be sufficient to justify believing that one has a justification for the claim in question. Here is the proper response, however. Take a person who is justified in the internalist sense, and then imagine an evil angel implanting the belief in this person that this person is justified in their belief. The proper thing to say about such a case is that the belief is one whose content is warranted, but where the believing itself is not warranted. It is not properly based, but it is simply false that the content of the belief has little going for it epistemically, as would be the case if the evil angel implanted the belief that there is an even number of grains of sand on a certain beach. No, the dark angel has done something to prevent doxastic justification (the kind of justification that attaches to a belief when its content is (propositionally) justified and the belief is properly based), but has also prompted a belief that could have been justified had it only been properly based. That is what suitable reflection provides. The role of the reflection is to bring it about that the belief formed is well founded or properly based, that it is suitably related to the evidence that is already present, so that the meta-belief that is formed is doxastically justified and not just propositionally justified. It is different if the metabelief is planted by an evil angel. In that case, the proper thing to say would be that the belief is propositionally justified though not doxastically justified because improperly based.

This argument assumes internalism about justification as well as a particular version of internalism, usually called access internalism. There are, of course, alternative conceptions of justification on which one can be justified and yet be in no advantaged position to tell that this is so. That need not bother us here, for, in the present context, we are free to specify whatever kind of justification we wish in giving an account of the norms of assertion. So the fact that there are other conceptions of justification or other kinds of justification is no objection to the claim that internalist justification has the property noted.

I do wish to point out, however, that the access aspect of the internalism used here is not necessary to the account. What really matters to the above argument is that the logic of justification honor the following principle:

(J) $Jsp \vdash JJsp$.

Talk of access to justificatory status is just an imaginative way of putting this point. Strictly speaking, however, (J) claims only that, if a body of information stands in the confirmational relationship to *p*, then that same body of information stands in that same relationship to the claim that *p* is justified. Talk of access will ordinarily mean something like principle (J), but it can also fail to do so in unusual cases. For example, suppose there is a demon who is devoted to keeping you from reaching any reflective conclusions. The demon is powerful and able to make good on his intentions. Then, if you were to reflect about anything, you would come to no conclusions at all. Such a result is a problem for access internalism, but not for principle (J). So the appeal to access internalism here should be viewed as simply an imaginative way of endorsing principle (J) in the sort of internalism being assumed. That principle is true in virtue of some capacity or disposition of a person who has evidence confirming *p*, but that ability or capacity or disposition need not be cashed out in terms of some subjunctive conditional concerning what would happen upon reflection. What matters for the internalism being assumed here is that evidence one possesses is a matter of which internal states one is in, and that the subject in question have the ability to detect these states in such a way that it can guide behavior, in terms of both belief and action. Given this limited internalism, we can still secure the result that if a body of information justifies a certain claim for a person, it also confirms for that person that the claim in question is justified by the relevant body of information.

One might wonder here whether it is possible to construct a sorites-like objection to this view, by constructing a sequence of bodies of evidence that are pairwise indistinguishable to an agent, but that begins with a body of evidence that definitely fails to confirm a given claim and ends with a body of evidence that definitely confirms that same claim. I do not think such an argument can be successful here, but a full defense of this claim depends on the argument I will give next concerning the gettier condition. For the present, I will merely assume the argument below in order to disarm this objection. The assumption is that, when you are epistemically justified in believing *p*, you are epistemically justified in believing that further inquiry into the truth of *p* is not needed. Given this principle, we can disarm this sorites-like counterargument. The central claim I wish to make in disarming this argument is this: if you cannot tell whether a given body of information confirms that further inquiry is not needed, it does not confirm that claim. So, if two bodies of evidence differ with respect to the degree of justification they provide for a given claim, either they both yield epistemic justification or neither yields it; there cannot be two bodies of evidence that as far as one can tell provide the same degree of confirmation for closing off inquiry regarding a claim and yet where one of the bodies of evidence legitimates closing off inquiry and the other one does not. That is not to say, of course, that one will be infallible in detecting the proper course of action to take given a particular body of evidence. It is only to say that there is a detectable difference between bodies of information that warrant abandoning further inquiry and those that do not.

Given this result, the only condition still to be considered is the gettier condition. What we have shown to this point is that, if you are justified in believing *p*, and know that you believe *p*, then you are justified in believing that your belief is true and justified. The consequent of the principle we are attempting to establish claims that you are justified in believing that you know *p*, and to finish the argument for this principle we need to show only that, if you are justified, your total body of evidence confirms that you have satisfied the gettier condition as well. In order to finish the argument, we need to take advantage of a special feature of knowledge. Knowing involves a justified attitude of closure to further inquiry, confirmed by the fact that it makes little sense to say, "I know that it is raining outside, but I think I should go check to make sure," or to say, "I know today is Thursday, but further inquiry regarding today's date is probably appropriate." Just imagine a news conference in which a scientist says: "We have investigated thoroughly the claim that there is some connection between electrical power lines and certain forms of cancer, and, as a result, we now know the answer: living close to electrical power lines simply does not cause these kinds of cancer. But we still need to investigate further . . ." Such a remark would be utterly bizarre, and the reason it would be bizarre is because knowledge involves a legitimate closure of investigation. In particular, it involves an inquiry that is of sufficient quality that it licenses the conclusion that any further learning could undermine one's present opinion only by presenting one with misleading information.

The point I am making should not be confused with a stronger point about the relationship between knowledge and further learning. One may be tempted here to say that inquiry adequate for knowledge licenses one to conclude that further learning could only confirm one's present opinion, but that claim is too strong. It is too strong because of the possibility of misleading pockets of information. A simple statistical case will suffice as an example of such. Suppose statistical knowledge is possible, and that one's investigation has given one knowledge that most tosses of a given die will not be sixes. It is consistent with such knowledge that, were one to investigate further, any finite string of sixes could occur on future tosses of the die. In some such cases, one's opinion would have to change in order to be rational (because the string that occurs is so long that it swamps the evidence obtained prior to that string). So the proper claim is not that no further learning could rationally undermine present opinion, but rather the weaker claim that any further learning that would rationally undermine present opinion would involve misleading information.

We need only tie this notion of misleading information to the defeasibility theory in order to complete our case that justification implies justification that one has not been gettiered. It is well known that knowledge is different from undefeated justified true belief, since some defeaters are misleading. I will not here present an account of the difference between misleading and non-misleading defeaters, but, even without a precise characterization of the difference, the following can be noted. If one's total evidence confirms that further investigation could undermine present opinion only by uncovering misleading information (as it must in order for the justification in question to be epistemic justification, the kind of justification that puts one in a position to know), then one's total evidence confirms that further learning could at worst reveal only misleading defeaters. Hence, if one is epistemically justified in believing *p*, one is justified in concluding that one's justification is ungettiered—that is, one's justification is defeated at most by misleading defeaters.

It is worth repeating here that these claims do not require any belief on the part of the epistemic agent regarding further learning. Nor do these claims require that the individual in question has the concept of justification or of further learning. The claims in question are claims about what total bodies of evidence confirm, not about what an individual believes or is capable of believing.

All the above to say this: the justification account of assertion can explain just as well as the knowledge account why the Moorean sentences are improper, and can explain the BUMS view as well. The reason the justification account can succeed here is that, to have the kind of justification in question, one must have a justification that also justifies the claim that one has knowledge, given that one knows what one believes. So, when a person makes an assertion, followed by a reflective judgment regarding a lack of knowledge, we justifiably suspect incoherence. The justification requirement on assertion implies that the person is in a position to assert that she knows the claim in question, so long as she reflects and notices that she believes the claim; and any reasonable account of first-person epistemic authority regarding our beliefs warrants the assumption that the speaker knows whether she is sincere in asserting the first conjunct of the Moorean sentence. So the justification view can explain the incoherence of Moorean assertions precisely because such remarks run counter to the kind of evidence needed to justify assertion and the reasonable assumptions we all make about the kind of access we have to our own beliefs.

The justification account can also explain the BUMS view, according to which we represent ourselves as knowing a claim when we assert it. The grounds needed for legitimate assertion constitute reasons accessible to the speaker for thinking that the speaker has met the nonpsychological conditions for knowing, and no one is entitled to assert a claim insincerely—that is, without believing it. So, in asserting, one is committed to the claim that the assertion is legitimate and sincere, and thus committed to the claim that one knows what one asserts (because that which legitimates the assertion also confirms that one has met the non-psychological conditions for knowledge). I take it that such commitments are sufficient for endorsing the claim that in asserting one *represents* oneself as knowing, but, if the notion of representation involves some further aspect, then I think the BUMS view is incautious and should be replaced by the commitment claim, that, in asserting, one commits oneself to the claim that one knows.

So the knowledge account cannot be judged superior to the justification account on the basis of Moorean considerations or the attitudes of BUMS. That leaves the primary stumbling block the issue of lottery propositions.

4. LOTTERY PROPOSITIONS

Regarding lottery propositions, Williamson's view seems to be straightforward. His view seems to be that the belief that my ticket will lose cannot be known to be true, but can be justified. It would appear, then, that on the justification account it is permissible to assert that my ticket will lose, but it is not permissible to so assert on the knowledge account. Since it is not permissible to assert that, the knowledge account wins.

There are several points at which this argument is questionable. The first point concerns the claim that we cannot know that a given ticket will lose. Though I share Williamson's viewpoint here, there is reason to question whether our opinions here are a holdover from the infallibilist epistemology we have all inherited from our ancestors. For much of the history of epistemology, it was assumed that one could not have knowledge if one's evidence failed to rule out every possible alternative to one's present viewpoint, and the continuing temptation of certain forms of skepticism witnesses to the present effects of this heritage. So perhaps Williamson and I are just wrong: we can know that a given ticket will lose.

This point becomes more plausible when one acknowledges the possibility of statistical knowledge. If we acknowledge this possibility and yet deny that we can know that a given ticket will lose, it is very difficult to explain the difference between statistical knowledge and lottery cases. We can, of course, find differences, but the question is whether the differences constitute an adequate explanation of the difference in epistemic status. The longer we search for such an explanation and fail to find one, the more plausible becomes the position that our refusal to grant the existence of knowledge in lottery cases is just a holdover from a bad epistemological heritage.

If we acquiesce and relinquish the view that knowledge is not possible in lottery situations, lottery cases no longer provide any sort of argument for the knowledge view over the justification view. That result I find comforting, but, unfortunately, I agree with Williamson that we do not know that a given ticket will lose. So I will proceed on the assumption that Williamson is correct in this matter, since I find that comforting too!

The second point at which the above argument is questionable, however, is more telling. One of the premises of that argument is that the justification account licenses the assertion of the claim that a given ticket will lose. Williamson holds a view of justification and rationality that supports such a claim. He writes,

It is plausible, nevertheless, that occurrently believing *p* stands to asserting *p* as the inner stands to the outer. If so, the knowledge rule for assertion corresponds to the norm that one should believe *p* only if one knows *p* . . . Given that norm, it is not reasonable to believe *p* when one knows that one does not know that *p*. If one knows that what one knows is only that p is very probable, then what is reasonable for one to believe is only that p is very probable. For example, I should not believe that my ticket will not win the lottery . . . On this analogy between assertion and belief, the knowledge rule for assertion does not correspond to an identification of reasonable belief with knowledge . . . The rule makes knowledge the condition for permissible assertion, not for reasonable assertion. One may reasonably do something impermissible because one reasonably but falsely believes it to be permissible. In particular, one may reasonably assert p, even though one does not know p, because it is very probable on one's evidence that one knows p. In the same circumstances, one may reasonably but impermissibly believe p without knowing p.[7]

In this passage, Williamson employs a notion of rationality on which it can be rational to assert that one's ticket will lose. Given the close connections between the concepts of justification and rationality, it is fair to conclude that Williamson could also have identified the concept in question as one of justification.

This notion to which Williamson appeals in this quote is not, however, the notion of justification in the view of the norm of assertion under discussion here. Recall the feature of internalistic epistemic justification noted above: such a justification for p is a justification for the claim that one knows p in the presence of knowledge of what one believes. Given that feature of justification, Williamson's concept of reasonability cannot be identified with the concept of epistemic justification.

The argument for this last claim is as follows. On the notion of justification being employed here, it is false that one can be epistemically justified in believing that a given ticket will lose (if it is false that one cannot know this). The kind of justification in question is the kind that puts one in a position to know—that is, is the kind that is sufficient for knowledge in the presence of ungettiered true belief. One has knowledge only when closure to further inquiry on the issue is legitimated, and such closure is a function of the quality of one's evidence. So, on the present view, one's total evidence must confirm that further inquiry would reveal only misleading information about the truth of what is believed. In ordinary lottery circumstances, however, one's evidence does not confirm that further inquiry would be a waste of time. In ordinary circumstances, those circumstances in which we are most inclined to deny knowledge that a given ticket is a loser, we take it to be worth checking the newspaper the next day to see if the improbable has occurred, and this attitude is itself justified. If so, however, our evidence confirms that the newspaper's word will be nonmisleading evidence about whether the ticket won. Because of this fact, whatever justification we have for holding that our ticket will lose, that justification is not the epistemic justification used here in the justification account of the norm of assertion.

---

[7] Williamson (2000: 255–6).

It is worth putting the argument that there is such a kind of justification in a different way. Imagine two cases of justified true belief, one of which counts as knowledge and the other of which involves a justification that is gettiered. In the case of knowledge, the closure aspect of knowledge is clearly present. Note, however, that it is not in virtue of the external conditions for knowledge that such closure is present. It is rather something about the character or quality of one's justification that licenses such closure. That is to say, the totality of one's evidence not only confirms the claim in question; it also confirms that further inquiry is not necessary in this case. By hypothesis, however, the totality of one's evidence is the same in the case that is not a case of knowledge: the relevant difference between the two cases is a difference not in the totality of one's evidence, but rather in the fact that one's justification is gettiered in one case but not in the other. Hence, given that the totality of evidence is the same in both cases, one is equally justified in holding that further inquiry is not necessary in the non-knowledge case as well. Put more simply, the closure aspect of knowledge is a feature of the kind of justification for knowledge, and is thus a function of the quality and character of one's total evidence. So, as advertised, there is a notion of justification—epistemic justification—on which closure to further inquiry is legitimated by the same evidence that confirms the truth of the claim in question.

This response to the lottery argument—that, in fact, the justification account has precisely the same implications about lottery sentences as does the knowledge account—may be harder to accept if one adopts Williamson's account of evidence, according to which one's body of evidence is simply one's knowledge. On this view of evidence, the account above claims that one's total body of knowledge can confirm that further investigation of a certain claim is not needed. That is obviously true when the claim in question is known, but it is less obvious when knowledge is not present. In such a case, we would need to ask what must be true of a body of knowledge in order for it to put one in a position to know that further investigation is not needed. If evidence is, and is only, what one knows, it might be plausible to answer that the only cases where one is in a position to know that further investigation is not needed will be cases in which one knows the truth-value of the claim in question.

If one refuses to identify evidence with knowledge, I think the temptation to this view is not nearly so strong. As argued above, whether one knows is a function of both the quality of one's total evidence and also the cooperativeness of the environment in which one finds oneself. Given this point, one should expect that the environment can function so as to undermine knowledge of the claim in question without impugning the quality of the evidence in question. If one believes that this claim about epistemic justification does not fit well with the view that evidence is knowledge, that strikes me as a reason to reject the knowledge view of evidence rather than reject the characterization of epistemic justification just given.

The reader might be left wondering, however, whether more can be done beyond merely giving my word on the matter. The answer, I think, is "yes," for there are independent reasons to be suspicious of the view that evidence is knowledge.

The implausibility arises when we consider Williamson's account of perceptual evidence in the case of illusions. In such a case, one clearly has perceptual evidence, but that evidence cannot be identified with a claim to the effect that, for example, there is water up ahead, since in fact there is not any water up ahead. Williamson's response is: "If perceptual evidence in the case of illusions consists of true propositions, what are they? The obvious answer is: the proposition that things appear to be that way."[8]

But why think that a person possesses that information or believes such a proposition? It is obviously true that one can suffer an illusion and never consider the question of how things appear to be. To this point, Williamson replies: "one may not consider the cautious proposition that things appear to be that way; one may consider only the unqualified proposition that they really are that way. But it does not follow that one does not know that things appear to be that way, for one knows many propositions without considering them."[9]

This response is true but insufficient to answer the objection. Even if there are cases in which we know propositions without ever having considered them, it would be a monstrous coincidence if in every case of unreflective illusion, the knowledge attribution were true. It is true that I knew that

$$11,111,111 + 1 = 11,111,112$$

prior to my just considering it now for the first time, but that gives us no reason as far as I can tell to think that, in every case of unreflective illusion, I know that I am being appeared to in a certain way. In the simple mathematical case above, it is plausible to hold that I dispositionally believed the claim in question prior to explicitly considering it. In other cases of simple addition, however, the proper thing to say is that I was disposed to believe, rather than dispositionally believed, the claim in question prior to explicitly considering it. Perhaps in some cases of illusion, I dispositionally believe the claim about how I am appeared to. But it is equally plausible to hold that, in other cases, I only have a disposition to believe the appearance claim, and thus do not know the way in which I am appeared to. One would expect in this regard that, the more salient the possibility of illusion, the better a case there is for holding that a dispositional belief is present. Correlatively, the more common and ordinary the case, when the possibility of illusion is the furthest thing from one's mind, the better the case for holding that there is only a disposition to believe that things appear to be a certain way.

---

[8] Williamson (2000: 198).   [9] Ibid. 198–9.

There is a deeper problem as well with Williamson's treatment of perceptual evidence. He views veridical experience as unproblematic, since, he holds, one can identify the propositional content of the experience and note that the person in question knows this content to be true. This knowledge, Williamson thinks, allows him to explain the evidence provided by veridical experience as a kind of knowledge.

This view strikes me as getting things backwards. When asked to defend the belief that there is a tree with yellowing leaves in the yard south of mine, I will appeal to experience. I do not appeal to my knowledge or to my beliefs. When I say, "I can see it," I am reporting an experience with propositional content that, in successful cases, is the same content as something I know, but my evidence is that content under a certain modality that is different from the modality of belief or knowledge. It is the modality of experience; my evidence is the content-as-experienced, not that content-as-believed nor that content-as-known. It may be that, in reporting one's evidence or in reflecting on one's evidence, the content in question gets transplanted into one's belief box or knowledge box; but that point should not obscure the fact that the evidence existed in the experience itself before the transplant. In reporting the experience, one is simultaneously reporting the existence of something believed and perhaps known to be true, but it is not the belief or the knowledge that is the evidence. The evidence is the experience itself.

The point of this digression was to block any argument against the account of epistemic justification that I am employing here that might arise from the knowledge account of evidence. If such an argument is forthcoming, it should be rejected, since there are good reasons to reject that account of evidence.

We can, therefore, return to the main thread of the discussion, which concerns the argument from lottery propositions against the justification account of assertion and in favor of the knowledge account of assertion. I argued above that the central claim of this argument—the claim that the justification account of assertion licenses the assertion that one's ticket will lose—is false when the kind of justification in question is epistemic justification. That is, for internalistic epistemic justification, it is false that one is justified in thinking that one's ticket will lose, and hence, if such justification is the norm of assertion, then the assertion that one's ticket will lose is inappropriate. Therefore, Williamson's lottery argument is ineffective at showing that the justification account of assertion is incorrect.

5. CONCLUSION

The proper conclusion to draw, then, is that the prima facie case for the justification view is an ultima facie case as well. The primary arguments that Williamson gives that can be used to try to undermine the justification view fail to do so. Their failure traces to a common flaw, the flaw of failing to notice that the ordinary notion of justification, on which one is justified in thinking that one's lottery ticket is a loser, is not suitable for use in an account of knowledge. The notion that is suitable has the following feature: when it obtains, one has reason for believing that all epistemic requirements for knowledge have been met. As a result, the justification account of assertion can explain the incoherence of Moorean assertions that a claim is true but unknown by the speaker as well as the BUMS view that in asserting we represent ourselves as knowing. In addition, this version of the justification account of assertion can explain why one should not say that one's lottery ticket is a loser. Even though there is an ordinary notion of justification on which one is justified in believing that one's ticket is a loser, in the appropriate epistemic sense of justification, one does not have such justification. One lacks such justification precisely because the character of one's evidence does not warrant the kind of closure experience with respect to further learning that is characteristic of knowledge. In short, one's justification for thinking that one's ticket is a loser is insufficient justification for knowledge. The failure of these objections to the justification account, combined with the positive defense of that account in terms of the distinction between taking back the content of an assertion versus taking back, regretting, and apologizing for the speech act itself, confirms that the justification account is the better account of the norm of assertion. Put succinctly, the proper counsel to give is not to quit saying what you do not know to be true, but to quit saying what you do not believe and what you do not have good epistemic reasons to believe.[10]

---

[10] I put the justification qualifier here in a weaker way than requiring that one justifiably believe the claim in question. The reason is that to say that one justifiably believes, in my terminology, implies that one's belief is properly based. I do not believe that proper basing is required for assertion, but arguing for this point goes beyond the scope of this chapter, so I merely note the point here without argument.

10

Defeating the Dogma of Defeasibility

Ram Neta

Ever since Edmund Gettier (1963) convinced English-speaking philosophers that justified true belief does not suffice for knowledge, many epistemologists have been searching for the elusive "fourth condition" of knowledge: the condition that must be added to justification, truth, and belief, in order to get a set of non-trivial conditions that are individually necessary and jointly sufficient for knowledge.[1] The problem of finding such conditions is generally known as the "Gettier problem." Many different fourth conditions have been proposed and subsequently counterexampled, and some philosophers have suggested that some of the other three conditions may need to be revised as well. But, recently, several philosophers have suggested that the Gettier problem is insoluble, and that the theory of knowledge should proceed in a more modest way: not by trying to specify a set of non-trivial conditions that are individually necessary and jointly sufficient for knowledge, but rather by trying to figure out whatever we can about knowledge, and in particular to figure out the role that knowledge, and knowledge ascription, play in our lives. Timothy Williamson (2000) has developed an epistemological view that falls within this latter, more modest approach to the theory of knowledge, and his work has been immediately and justly influential.

Now, it is all to the good to figure out whatever we can about knowledge, and to examine the role that knowledge, and knowledge ascription, play in our lives. But we should also try to understand what it is about knowledge and knowledge ascription that suit them to play those roles. Suppose that, as Williamson says, it is constitutive of the act of assertion that one is entitled to assert only what one knows to be true. Or suppose that, as John Hawthorne (2004) says, one can employ a premise in practical reasoning only if one knows the premise to be true. We might wonder what it is about knowledge that renders it suitable to

---

[1] Throughout this chapter I use the term "knowledge" to refer solely to factual knowledge, i.e., the kind of knowledge that is ascribed using assertions of the form "S knows that p," where "S" is a schematic variable that ranges over persons and "p" is a schematic variable that ranges over propositions. Factual knowledge is also, I believe, ascribed using assertions of the form "S knows wh– . . .".

play this constitutive role in assertion or in practical reasoning. What is it about knowing that makes it the case that one is entitled to assert only what one knows to be true, or one is entitled to reason practically from nothing other than what one knows to be true? What is so special about knowing that enables it to play these roles? These seem to be perfectly good questions, to which we should like answers.

Of course, if the nature of knowledge were exhausted by its role in assertion, or in practical reasoning, then the questions above could be answered trivially: what is special about knowing would be precisely that it has this role in assertion, or in practical reasoning, and there would be no further fact about knowing by virtue of which it has these roles—there would be nothing that *renders* knowledge suitable to play these roles, since knowledge would be *simply* whatever plays these roles. Now, in fact, this is not true of knowledge. Knowledge may be, as Williamson thinks, the constitutive norm of assertion, or it may be, as Hawthorne thinks, the norm for premises of practical reasoning. But that is not, on anyone's view, *all* that knowledge is. There is more to say about what knowledge is. And, it is fair to hope, some of what more we can say about what knowledge is can help us to understand what renders it suitable to play the role(s) it plays in our lives—for instance, if Williamson is right, to be the norm of assertion.

One way—of course not the only way—that we might try to answer questions about what renders knowledge suitable to play the role that it plays in our lives, and what makes it the case that knowledge has the various properties that it has, is by giving an informative account of *what knowledge is*, and then appealing to that account in order to explain various features of knowledge. Just as we can explain various features of water by appeal to an informative account of what water is, and we can explain various features of zebras by appeal to an informative account of what zebras are, and we can explain various features of inflation by appeal to an informative account of what inflation is, so too—one might hope—we might be able to explain various features of knowledge by appeal to an account of what knowledge is.

In order to offer a correct and informative account of what knowledge is, I claim that we will need to give up one of Williamson's main contentions—namely, that, for any epistemic agent S, S's evidence set (at a time t) comprises all and only those propositions that S knows (at t) to be true. If we give up this equation of evidence and knowledge, we will then be in a position to accept a particular account of knowledge as both true and informative—and, as we shall see, the account that I offer below helps to substantiate some other distinctive Williamsonian epistemological theses (for example, that, if S knows that p, then the conditional probability of p on S's evidence set is 1; and that the preceding point does not entail that S be rationally required to be completely confident that p is true). If we continue to accept Williamson's equation of evidence and knowledge, then the account of knowledge that I offer below may not seem to be informative, since that account explains what it is for S to know that p partly in terms of S's evidence.[2]

I accept a particular account of what knowledge is, and I propose to state some of its main features here. The account of knowledge that I accept implies that knowledge is indefeasible, and so it will strike virtually all epistemologists as suffering from obvious and devastating problems. For instance, Williamson offers an example to illustrate the defeasibility of knowledge, and his example will initially strike many philosophers as a clear counterexample to my account of knowledge. I devote Section 3 of this chapter to showing why this and other seemingly obvious counterexamples to the IJTB account of knowledge (specifically, to its indefeasibility) do not tell against that account.

But before proceeding to defend my account (which I call the IJTB account) against these various objections, I will devote Section 1 to laying out some competitor accounts, and presenting counterexamples to each of those accounts. Of course, my survey of competitor accounts in Section 1 will not aspire to historical completeness: such an aspiration could be realized only by a very lengthy book. Rather than identify all, or even most, of the actual competitors to the IJTB theory of knowledge, I will simply describe some simple competitor accounts that can be formed by adding to the JTB account various possible "fourth conditions," each of which has made its way into one or another prominent theory of knowledge. I have two reasons for doing this. First, I want to show that it is not at all unreasonable to despair of giving a correct and informative account of knowledge: the history of such attempts is not promising. Although I think we should not give up, it is easy to understand how someone might reasonably think otherwise. Secondly, I want to motivate the IJTB account by showing that it delivers the right verdicts about various cases described in Section 1, and that it identifies the kernel of truth in each of the competitor accounts described in Section 1.

In short, I hope to show that the traditional immodest program in the theory of knowledge can be brought to fruition, despite the bleak history of attempts to do so. We need not confine ourselves to finding out various features of knowledge and of knowledge ascription, but we can explain those various features of knowledge and of knowledge ascription by appeal to a true and informative answer to the question "what is knowledge?"

What we want from an account of knowledge, I take it, is this: the account should predict that, and explain why, clear cases of knowledge are indeed cases

---

[2] Of course, we could reject Williamson's equation E = K, but still accept the view that p is included in S's evidence at time t if and only if S knows that p at t. We could do this by saying (contra Williamson) that what it is to be in S's evidence is something other than simply to be known by S, but nonetheless, although it is not part of the very essence of being S's evidence that something is known by S, the biconditional is still metaphysically necessary. If Williamson were simply to hold that the biconditional is metaphysically necessary, without holding E = K, then he could still accept the account of knowledge that I offer below as informative. For reasons that I offer below and elsewhere, I do not even accept that the biconditional is true, let alone metaphysically necessary.

of knowledge; the account should predict that, and explain why, clear cases of non-knowledge are indeed cases of non-knowledge; the account should predict that, and explain why, unclear or disputable cases of knowledge are indeed unclear or disputable; and, finally, the account should help us to understand how it is that knowledge and knowledge ascription can play the role(s) that they play in our lives. I see no reason to demand that an account reduce knowledge to non-epistemic, let alone non-normative, phenomena. It is good enough if we can explain knowledge in terms of things other than knowledge, so long as we do not have to invent new primitives, or appeal to any notions that philosophers do not *already* need.

For the purposes of this chapter, I will start by assuming that a true account of knowledge is of the form:

S knows that p = S has a justified, true belief that p and . . .

where the dots are to be filled in by a specification of the fourth condition of knowledge, the anti-Gettier condition. It will eventually turn out that the satisfaction of the fourth condition will entail the satisfaction of two of the three standard conditions (justification and truth). Of course, there are plenty of questions that arise in connection with the three specified conditions on knowledge—that is, justification, truth, and belief. For instance, we might wonder what sorts of things can serve to confer justification (by which I here mean *doxastic justification*, not merely propositional justification) upon a belief (other beliefs? experiences? being caused or sustained by a reliable process? being sufficiently well supported by evidence given one's present purposes?) and we might wonder what sort of structure there is among such justifiers (foundationalist? coherentist? infinitist?). Again, we might wonder what relation there must be between a belief and the thing that confers justification upon it in order for the belief to be justified (that is, the nature of the "basing relation"). And, of course, there are any number of venerable questions about the nature of truth and the nature of belief. I will not address any of these important questions in this chapter. I confine myself to defending an account of knowledge that fills in the fourth condition above, and I will not say anything more in this chapter about the three standardly accepted conditions.

1. WHAT IS KNOWLEDGE? (IN SEARCH OF THE ELUSIVE FOURTH CONDITION)

Before Gettier's paper, one or another version of the following theory of knowledge was accepted by C. I. Lewis, A. J. Ayer, Roderick Chisholm, and others:[3]

---

[3] See, e.g., Ayer (1956) and Chisholm (1957).

JTB Theory

S knows that p = S has a true, justified belief that p.

But there are counterexamples to the JTB theory, such as the following:

> Smith's evidence clearly indicates that his coworker Nogot owns a Ford, and so Smith justifiably believes that Nogot owns a Ford. From this belief Smith infers that one of his coworkers owns a Ford. Unbeknownst to Smith, however, Nogot does not own a Ford, but another one of Smith's coworkers, Havit, does own a Ford. So Smith has a justified true belief that one of his coworkers owns a Ford, but he does not know that one of his coworkers owns a Ford.

The JTB theory is false. Since this was discovered,[4] many different accounts of knowledge have been proposed. In this section I briefly review a small sampling of those proposed accounts, and then give counterexamples to each of them. I make use of these counterexamples in the next section, when I show that my own IJTB account of knowledge delivers the right verdicts about all these examples.

Here, then, are some accounts of knowledge that have been offered in the wake of the demonstrated failure of the JTB theory.

No-False-Lemmas Theory

S knows that p = S has a justified true belief that p and S's belief that p is not based upon reasoning to p from any false premises.[5]

Counterexample: Latifa knows, on the basis of countless pieces of journalistic evidence, that US troops are in Iraq. But she bases her belief that US troops are in Iraq on many different inferences that she makes, from many different premises. Most of those inferences are sound, and the premises are known by her to be true, but not all of the inferences are like that. For instance, she infers that US troops are in Iraq from the false proposition that US troops have discovered

---

[4] Some people deny that this was discovered. For instance, Weinberg, Stich and Nichols (2001) claim that Gettier intuitions are culturally variable, and that this shows that they do not carry probative weight in epistemology. I am happy to grant that such intuitions are culturally variable, but I do not see why this suggests that they do not carry probative weight. The Mediterranean feels cold to Nigerians and hot to Eskimos—does this suggest that thermal sensation is not an epistemologically respectable guide to real thermal phenomena? It shows only that, when relying on thermal sensations, we need to discount the possible distorting influence of environment. If Gettier intuitions are the result of some such distorting influence, then of course we should discount them. But why should we think that they are the result of some such distorting influence? Simply because some people do not share them? Some people (e.g., non-English speakers) do not share our intuitions about the grammaticality of English sentences, and some people (e.g., xenophobes) do not share our intuitions about the irrelevance of race or ethnicity to moral status. But that has no tendency to show that our intuitions about the grammaticality of English sentences, or our intuitions about the irrelevance of race or ethnicity to moral status, are the result of distorting influence.

[5] Harman (1968, 1970, 1973).

weapons of mass destruction in Iraq. Her knowing that US troops are in Iraq is thus compatible with her basing her belief upon—inter alia—reasoning from a false premise.

Causal Theory

S knows that p = S has a justified true belief that p, and S is caused to believe that p (in the way that S believes it) by the fact that p.[6]

Counterexample: Henry is driving through the countryside, sees a barn, and thereby comes to believe that he sees a barn. He has a justified true belief that he sees a barn, and he is caused to believe that he sees a barn by the fact that he sees a barn. Nonetheless, he does not know that he sees a barn, since most of the apparent barns in this area are not barns at all, but only barn façades.

Explanation Theory

S knows that p = S has a justified true belief that p and the fact that p explains S's believing that p (in the way that S believes it).[7]

Counterexample: Rachel owns a Ford, but she does not want anyone to know that she owns a Ford. So she produces lots of evidence that the Ford belongs to Isaac. Rebecca thus forms a justified belief that Isaac owns a Ford, and infers from this the true conclusion that someone in her office owns a Ford. Rebecca thus comes to have a justified true belief that someone in her office owns a Ford, and the fact that someone in her office owns a Ford explains Rebecca's belief that someone in her office owns a Ford. Nonetheless, Rebecca does not know that someone in her office owns a Ford.

Sensitivity Theory

S knows that p = S has a justified true belief that p and S would not believe that p in the way that S does if p were not true.[8]

Counterexample: Bridget is driving through the countryside, sees a cow, and thereby comes to believe that that particular object (pointing to the object in question) is a cow. She thereby has a justified true belief that that particular object is a cow. But there is no possible world in which that same particular object (or its counterpart, if it has one) is not a cow. Thus, at least according to the standard Lewis–Stalnaker semantics for counterfactuals,[9] it is vacuously

---

[6] Goldman (1967) defends a causal theory of at least some kinds of empirical knowledge. The counterexample to it that is presented in the text was first published in Goldman (1976).

[7] See, e.g., Rieber (1999).

[8] Dretske (1971) propounds a version of the Sensitivity Theory, as does Goldman (1976). Nozick (1981) propounds a theory slightly stronger than the Sensitivity Theory: his theory adds a clause to the effect that, in all nearby p-worlds in which the believer forms a belief as to whether p, using the same method M, the believer continues to believe that p. But, though Nozick's version is stronger, it still does not handle the counterexample offered in the text.

[9] Lewis (1973); Stalnaker (1968).

true that she would not believe that that particular object is a cow if it were not a cow. Nonetheless, Bridget does not know that that particular object is a cow, since most of the apparent cows in this area are not cows at all, but rather cow façades.

One might worry that the counterexample depends upon a particular, contentious account of the semantics for counterfactuals. But, no matter what account we give of the semantics for counterfactuals, it is at least not clearly false that Bridget would not believe that that particular object is a cow if it were not a cow. But, according to the Sensitivity Theory, this would have to be clearly false in order for the case of Bridget to be (as it is) clearly such that Bridget does not know that that particular object is a cow. So, even if the Lewis–Stalnaker semantics for counterfactuals is wrong, the case still provides a counterexample to the Sensitivity Theory.

Safety Theory

S knows that p = S has a justified true belief that p and there is no nearby possible world in which S, forming her belief in the way that she does, falsely believes that p.[10]

Counterexample: in the course of being taught some rudimentary anatomy, Jacques seems to hear his teacher tell him that human beings have brains, and Jacques thereby comes to have a justified true belief that he, Jacques, has a brain. Furthermore, this belief is safe, because there is no possible world (a fortiori no nearby possible world) in which Jacques holds the belief but it is false. Nonetheless, Jacques fails to know that he has a brain, because his auditory experience as of his teacher telling him that he has a brain is illusory: in fact, his teacher was deceptively telling Jacques that human beings do not have brains, but Jacques simply misheard what the teacher said.

Indefeasibly Justified True Belief Theory

S knows that p = S has a justified true belief that p and there is no true proposition q which is such that, if S were to be justified in believing that q, then S would no longer be justified in believing that p.[11]

Counterexample: Siobahn believes that Elvis is still alive, and she knows that she believes that Elvis is alive. But, if Siobahn were to be justified in believing

---

[10] Though Sosa (1999a) and Williamson (2000) both defend a safety condition on knowledge, neither would accept what I am calling the Safety Theory. Pritchard (2005) argues that Safety is the anti-Gettier condition on knowledge. But if knowledge is justified, true unGettiered belief, and if Safety is the anti-Gettier condition, then knowledge is justified true safe belief. Since (I am assuming here) knowledge is justified true unGettiered belief, and since (I argue in the text) knowledge is not justified true safe belief, I conclude that Safety is not the anti-Gettier condition on knowledge.

[11] Lehrer and Paxson (1969) mention this theory but do not endorse it. I do not know of any philosophers who endorse it, but I mention it only in order to distinguish it from my IJTB theory, which is superficially similar.

that Elvis is dead, then she would not believe that Elvis is alive, and so she would then not be justified in believing that she believes that Elvis is alive. The counterexample here is induced by the use of the counterfactual conditional in the theory.[12]

No-Justified-Falsehoods Theory

S knows that p = S has a justified true belief that p and there is no true proposition e such that the total evidence set E′ (where E′ = the conjunction of e and S's actual evidence set E) does not constitute a justification for S to believe that p, and also does not constitute a justification for S to hold any false beliefs.[13]

Counterexample: I know lots of empirical facts, for example, that Barack Obama is the President of the United States. But take any proposition that is both true and extremely unlikely to be true—for instance, the proposition Z that states precisely the actual distribution of microphysical properties over points in space–time. Z is true, and therefore the following disjunction is true as well: Barack Obama is not the President of the United States, or Z is true. But my total evidence constitutes a justification for me to believe that this disjunction is false, and so the conjunction of my total evidence with the true proposition that, say, I am now thinking, constitutes a justification for me to believe a falsehood.

In general, whenever S has total evidence E, and S knows that p, there will be some extremely improbable truth that is such that S is justified in believing that it is false. (If we think that evidential justification is probabilistic, then we can put the point this way: there will in general be some true proposition q which is such that Prob (q/E) will be extremely low, and perhaps even lower than Prob (q).) And, if there is such a true proposition q, then E constitutes a justification for S to believe the falsehood that not-q. If that is correct, then, no matter what the value of E, it will constitute a justification for S to believe some falsehood.

Having briefly disposed of the accounts of knowledge given above, in the next section I will offer a first approximation to my own account of knowledge—the *Indefeasible* Justified True Belief account—and then show how it can handle cases that serve as counterexamples to other accounts.

2. KNOWLEDGE IS INDEFEASIBLE JUSTIFIED TRUE BELIEF

Here is a first approximation to the account of knowledge that I will defend in this chapter—what I call the IJTB account of knowledge. (I will provide a fully

---

[12] See Shope (1983) for an encyclopedic review of counterexamples of this form.
[13] Chisholm (1977).

accurate statement of the account, but only in Section 4. To start with, I will treat the following statement as accurate, and refine it only later.)

S knows that p = S has a justified, true belief that p, and there is no true proposition e such that the conjunction of e and S's actual evidence set E does not constitute a justification for S to believe that p.

Proposals similar to this one were considered early in the post-Gettier literature, but they were immediately dismissed on the allegedly obvious grounds that they are too strong. Knowledge, it is commonly thought, is at least sometimes defeasible by future evidence, and the IJTB account proposed above is incompatible with this obvious fact. Thus—it is inferred—the IJTB account is too strong. In the next section I will critically examine various putative counterexamples to the IJTB account of knowledge. Before proceeding to answer those alleged counterexamples to IJTB, I will devote the present section to showing how IJTB is strong enough to handle all the examples of non-knowledge that end up counting as knowledge according to the theories listed in the previous section.

The case of Havit's Ford. Though Smith has a justified true belief that someone in his office owns a Ford, the conjunction of his current evidence with the true proposition that Nogot does not own a Ford does not constitute a justification for Smith to believe that someone in his office owns a Ford. (A perfectly analogous treatment applies to the case of Rachel's Ford.)

The case of the barn façades. Though Henry has a justified true belief that he sees a barn, the conjunction of his current evidence with the true proposition that most of the apparent barns in this area are not barns does not constitute a justification for Henry to believe that he sees a barn. (A perfectly analogous treatment applies to the case of Bridget and the cow façades—and this is as it should be, given that the cases seem to be epistemically alike, even if metaphysically different.)

The case of Jacques's brain. Though Jacques has a justified true belief that he has a brain, the conjunction of his current evidence with the true proposition that he misheard his teacher's lecture does not constitute a justification for Jacques to believe that he has a brain.

The case of Siobahn's second-order belief. If Siobahn were to be justified in believing that Elvis is dead, then she would not believe that Elvis is alive, and so would not believe that she believes that Elvis is alive. But the conjunction of Siobahn's evidence set (including the fact that she believes that Elvis is alive) with the true proposition that Elvis is dead constitutes a justification for Siobahn to believe that she believes that Elvis is alive.

The IJTB account smoothly handles all of these examples. Furthermore, it specifies the kernel of truth in each of these other accounts. If it is true that you would believe that p even if p were false, then the conjunction of that truth with your total evidence will typically fail to justify you in believing that p. If it is true that your belief that p is based on your inferring p from a false premise, then the conjunction of that truth with your total evidence will typically fail to justify you in believing that p. If it is true that your belief that p is not caused by, or explained by, the fact that p, then the conjunction of these truths with your total evidence will typically fail to justify you in believing that p. And so on.

So the IJTB has something to be said for it. But is not the IJTB account subject to counterexamples of its own? In the next section, after considering some such examples, I argue for a negative answer to this question.

3. APPARENT COUNTEREXAMPLES TO THE IJTB THEORY OF KNOWLEDGE

Many philosophers would object that there are obvious and devastating counter-examples to the IJTB theory. In this section I critically examine those alleged counterexamples.

Williamson offers the following example to illustrate what he calls the "defeasibility" of knowledge:

I see one red and one black ball put into an otherwise empty bag [call this "e"] . . . Now suppose that on the first ten thousand draws a red ball is drawn each time, a contingency which my evidence does not rule out in advance, since its evidential probability is non-zero. But when I have seen it happen, I will rationally come to doubt e; I will falsely suspect that the ball only looked black by a trick of the light.   (Williamson 2000: 219)

Now, what does this example show? It shows that it is possible for the following sort of thing to occur: at a particular time, S knows that p on the basis of evidence e, and subsequently S gains additional evidence e' and thereby loses her knowledge that p. Knowledge is clearly, in this sense, defeasible.

But notice that S's gaining evidence e' might result in S's losing her belief that p is true, or it might result in S's losing some of her original evidence for p, or it might result in S's losing the ability *reasonably to form* her belief that p on the basis of her evidence (even if her total evidence continues to constitute a justification for her to believe that p). On any of these last three scenarios, S's gaining evidence e' will result in S's losing her knowledge that p. But all this is compatible with IJTB. IJTB says nothing about what *would* happen to our epistemic subject if she were to gain an additional bit of evidence. It says that, if S knows that p, then, for any true proposition e', the conjunction of our subject's actual evidence set with e' constitutes a justification for our subject to believe that p.

Now, Williamson himself might agree with the latter claim, since he thinks that E = K, and so, whenever S knows that p, p itself is included in S's evidence set. But, if p is in S's evidence set, then, for any true proposition q, the conjunction of q with S's evidence set will constitute a justification for S to believe that p, since p is implied by that conjunction. So, by Williamson's own lights, his example of the red ball would not serve as a counterexample to IJTB. Indeed, since Williamson accepts the claim that your evidence set includes all and only what you know to be the case, he might accept that the IJTB account (as presented so far) is true, but he might not regard it as informative.

But I reject Williamson's thesis that E = K. Indeed, I reject even the weaker thesis that your evidence set includes all and only what you know to be the case. The latter thesis is both too strong a condition on evidence, and also too weak a condition on evidence. It is too strong because sometimes p is in my evidence set even though I am not aware that p. For instance, at present I am visualizing a speckled hen, and my evidence set includes the fact that *the speckled hen image contains seven speckles*. (Seven is just a big enough number that I might *fail* to notice that there are that many speckles, but it is just a small enough number that I am able simply to *notice* that there are that many speckles—I do not need to employ any arithmetical procedures in arriving at the belief that there are that many speckles.) Whether I know it or not, I have evidence that gives me conclusive justification for believing that the image contains seven speckles—namely, the fact that the image does indeed contain seven speckles. That fact is in my evidence; it makes a difference to how I rationally ought to distribute my confidence over hypotheses. Some of the truths that are in my evidence set may be unknown by me, even if each one of those truths is knowable by me upon the right kind of reflection. And, of course, it is possible that each one of those truths is reflectively knowable by me even if all of them are not simultaneously knowable by me.

Williamson's account is too weak a condition on evidence because it allows that everything I know by deduction from my evidence is in my evidence set. But this is not true. Here is why: for any proposition q that is in my evidence set, if you ask me what evidence I have for q, I am entitled to reject your request for evidence, or else answer you simply by citing q itself. In other words, for it to be rational for me to believe q—if q is in my evidence set—I do not need to base my belief that q upon any evidence other than q. Now, suppose that I know that p, and I know it *solely* because I have competently deduced p from premises a, b, and c (each of which I know to be true), and then you ask me what evidence I have for p. In such a case, I typically cannot give you a true and complete answer without citing a, b, and c. But, if p itself were in my evidence set, then I could give you a true and complete answer to the question what evidence I have for p simply by citing p. Since there are at least some occasions on which I cannot do this, p is not (at least on those occasions not) in my evidence set, though I know it to be true. Thus, not everything that I know by deduction from my evidence is itself in my evidence set.

My evidence set at a particular time includes all and only those truths that I am entitled to take for granted in inquiry at that time.[14] Now, what is it for S to be entitled to take it for granted in inquiry that p? To be entitled to take it for granted that p, in the sense in which I am using that phrase here, involves at least this much: being entitled to appeal to p *without having to be able to defend p against challenges*. There are lots of things that I am now entitled to appeal to in the course of inquiring whether or not, say, it will rain tomorrow. But not all of these things that I am entitled to appeal to are things that I am entitled to *take for granted*; some of the things that I am entitled to appeal to are things my entitlement to appeal to which requires that I be able to defend them against reasonable challenges. For instance, in predicting whether or not it will rain tomorrow, I might be entitled to appeal to the claim that the warm front that is moving toward us from the west will probably reach here by tomorrow morning—but I would be entitled to appeal to this claim only if I could defend it against reasonable challenges, such as "how do you know that it will not slow down and not reach here until tomorrow night?" So, while I am entitled to appeal to the claim about the warm front in inquiring whether or not it will rain tomorrow, I am not entitled to *take it for granted*, in the relevant sense. So it is not in my evidence set, as I conceive of it. My evidence set will include only those truths that I am entitled to appeal to even if I cannot defend them against challenges. That might include statements like "I am now being appeared to redly," but it might also include statements about the physical world like "we are on the planet Earth." These are truths that I am entitled to appeal to, even if I cannot defend them against challenges. If someone challenges my claim that I am now being appeared to redly, or my claim that we are on the planet Earth, then I would probably have no idea how to defend my claims against those challenges, nor would I need to do so. I would simply dismiss the challenges as silly. Among the things that I am entitled to appeal to in judgment, the only ones that count as in my evidence set are those things that I am entitled to appeal to, *whether or not* I am able to defend them against challenges.[15]

This conception of evidence may seem more restrictive than our ordinary conception of evidence. If the weatherman tells me that there is a 70 percent chance of rain tomorrow, and then I ask him for his evidence, it may seem perfectly reasonable and correct for him to cite as his evidence the following fact:

[14] I defend this view in Neta (2008).

[15] Let E be my current evidence set. Can E provide me with conclusive evidence for any proposition? It can do so only if it provides me with maximal justification for believing that proposition. But cannot my justification for any proposition be improved? In fact, do I not improve my justification—however strong it may already be—by not merely relying upon my evidence, but also defending my evidence against challenges? I think the answer to this question is "no—not always." For instance, I do not improve my justification for believing, say, that I have hands, each time I get my eyes checked. Many epistemologists have views that commit them to disagreeing with me about this last claim. But on this issue, it seems to me, their views have a wildly implausible consequence.

the warm front that is moving toward us from the west will probably reach here by tomorrow morning. But if I challenge his belief that the warm front that is moving toward us from the west will probably reach here by tomorrow morning, does he not need to be able to defend this belief against this challenge? He can't simply dismiss my challenge as silly. Does he not need to be able to justify his belief, in order reasonably to appeal to it? If the answer to this question is "yes," then I do not count it as in his evidence that the warm front that is moving toward us from the west will probably reach here by tomorrow morning. What I count as his evidence in that case will then include the things to which he appeals in justifying his belief that the warm front that is moving toward us from the west will probably reach here by tomorrow morning—at least if those things are such that he can appeal to them without having to defend them against challenges. (These things might include the testimony of the meteorologist who feeds information to the weatherman, or they might include the readings of various measuring instruments that the weatherman consults, or they might include the weatherman's perceptual experiences.)

This suggests two tests that we might usefully employ in figuring out whether S is, at a certain time, entitled to take it for granted in inquiry that e. First: if S can, at time t, truthfully and relevantly answer a question of the form "how do you know that e?" by saying simply "e"—or, alternatively, if S is entitled to dismiss the question "how do you know that e?"—then this is one indication that S is entitled, at t, to take e for granted in inquiry. Secondly, if S can, at t, truthfully and relevantly answer other questions of the form "how do you know that p?" by saying "e, and e supports p," then this is a second indication that S is entitled, at t, to take e for granted in inquiry. These are all the general remarks that I will offer here about what it is for a proposition to be in one's evidence set.[16]

Let us consider how this account of evidence applies to cases. Consider the case of Henry driving through barn-façade country. What is Henry entitled to take for granted in inquiry? That depends on the details of the case, but the following would seem to be correct on any natural way of filling in the case. Henry is entitled to take it for granted that he sees something that looks like a barn. If asked how he knows that he sees something that looks like a barn, Henry could truthfully and relevantly answer by saying something like: "What a silly question! I just *do* see something that looks like a barn." And, if asked how he knows, say, that there are any objects that look like barns in this region, Henry could truthfully and relevantly answer by saying that he sees something that looks like a barn. But Henry is not entitled to take it for granted that he sees a barn. If asked how he knows that he sees a barn, Henry could not truthfully and relevantly answer by saying something like "what a silly question! I just do see a barn." It is, of course, *true* that Henry sees a barn, but, in the case envisaged, this is not a relevant answer to the question.

All of the above seems to me correct about the case of Henry driving through barn-façade country. But we can generate different verdicts about what Henry is or is not entitled to take for granted in inquiry by ringing changes on features of the case. For instance, if Henry is driving through a countryside in which there are hallucination-inducing drugs floating in the air, then Henry might not be entitled to take it for granted that he sees something that looks like a barn. In such a case, he might be entitled to take it for granted merely that *it looks to him as if* there is a barn before him. But in a case in which there are no such epistemic risks lurking—no barn façades, no hallucination-inducing drugs, nothing of the sort—Henry might be entitled to take it for granted that he sees a barn. I hope that these remarks about what someone is or is not entitled to take for granted in inquiry suffice for present purposes.

Given his own view that $E = K$, Williamson himself would not regard his own example of the black ball as a counterexample to the IJTB theory, but many other philosophers (those of us who reject Williamson's thesis that $E = K$) are likely to regard Williamson's example as a counterexample to the IJTB theory. Is it indeed a counterexample to IJTB? Before the ten thousand draws are made, but once I have seen the black ball in the bag, I know that

(p) there is a black ball inside the bag,

and I know that p on the basis of some visual evidence V—never mind precisely how to specify the propositional content of V (perhaps it is *that there is a black ball in the bag*, or it is *that I see a black ball in the bag*, or it is *that it looks to me as if there is a black ball in the bag*, and so on). Now after the ten thousand drawings are made, I have gained some additional evidence concerning the track record produced by the series of draws—call this track-record evidence T. Now, would I be justified in believing that p on the basis of the conjunction of V and T? Well, imagine that, at a particular moment, I have both pieces of evidence in my evidence set: I have visual evidence V *and* I have the track-record evidence T. (We can imagine what it would be like to have this conjunction in our evidence set all at once by imagining that the bag is transparent.) This conjunction of V and T justifies me in believing that p. In that case, why is it that, in Williamson's example, once I have made the ten thousand drawings, then I am no longer justified in believing that p (that is, there is a black ball in the bag)? It is because my memory of V is not as good evidence for p as is V itself. Indeed, it normally tends to happen that, as the time at which I have evidence V recedes farther and farther into the past, the strength of my evidence for p grows weaker and weaker. Williamson's example is not a counterexample to the IJTB theory.[17]

---

[17] For that matter, it is also not a good reason to reject Jeffrey's rule of conditionalization. It is a consequence of Jeffrey's rule that, if Prob $(p/e) = 1$, then new evidence cannot, *by itself*, reduce the degree of credence one should lend p. But it is not a consequence of Jeffrey's rule that new evidence cannot cause one to lose one's old evidence, and thereby reduce the degree of credence one should lend p.

Harman (1968) and Klein (1971) each describe other cases that might be thought to be counterexamples to the IJTB theory. I will now describe these cases along with a further apparent counterexample, and then describe a recipe for generating further such apparent counterexamples to IJTB. Finally, I will argue, on grounds that are independent of IJTB, that these cases cannot serve as counterexamples to IJTB.

The case of the retracted newspaper story. A famous official has just been assassinated, and you read about the assassination on the front page of a major newspaper. You thereby acquire knowledge that the official has been assassinated. The next day, the government decides to cover up the assassination, and forces all the newspapers to run a retraction of the earlier story, claiming that the official is doing fine, and the assassination attempt was not successful. You hear nothing about the retractions, and continue to have a true belief that the official was assassinated, but your knowledge has (allegedly) been defeated. (Harman 1968: 172, with slight modifications)

The case of the library thief and his lying mother. You have just seen Tom Grabit steal a book from the library. You know Tom Grabit reasonably well, and are therefore justified in believing that it is Grabit whom you saw. You now know that Grabit stole a book from the library. Once she finds out about the episode, though, Tom's mother tells the authorities that Tom has an identical twin brother, John, and it was John who stole the book from the library. In fact, Tom has no brother, and his mother made up the whole story in order to protect Tom from prosecution. But your knowledge has (allegedly) been defeated. (Klein 1971: 474, with several modifications)

The case of the A's that are mostly B's. Suppose that almost all of the 1,000,000 A's are B's, and I have seen 100 A's, and all of those A's have been B's. It may seem that this suffices, at least under certain conditions, for me to know that most A's are B's. But what if, among the 1,000,000 A's, there are 1,000 A's that are not B's. Does the conjunction of the true proposition that there are 1,000 A's that are not B's, along with my current evidence, still justify me in believing that most A's are B's? It may seem clear that it does not, for I have observed only 100 A's so far—and so this case seems to be a counterexample to the IJTB theory.

All of the three examples above share a common profile, and we can appeal to this profile in order to construct a general recipe for generating putative counterexamples to IJTB, a recipe adapted from Harman (1973). Suppose that S knows that p, and knows it on the basis of her evidence e, which is such that Prob $(p/e) < 1$. Let Z be a true proposition that is very unlikely to be true, given S's total evidence e: for instance, let Z be a true proposition specifying precisely the distribution of microphysical states over all points in space–time. The disjunction (Z or not-p) is true, since the first disjunct is true. Now does the conjunction of that disjunction (Z or not-p) with e constitute a justification for S to believe that p? It may seem that it cannot do so, since Prob $(p/e$ & (Z or not-p)) is very low. (In a chancy world in which some quantities vary continuously, we can pick a true Z which is as unlikely as you please.) But then the IJTB theory rules against the possibility of knowing p on the basis of evidence e if Prob (p/e) < 1. Is that not a reductio of the IJTB theory?

We can state the argument above more precisely: if we let q = the disjunction (Z or not-p), and if we let N be an arbitrarily large finite number such that Prob (Z) < 1/N, and if we suppose that, for S, Prob (p) > 0, Prob (p/e) < 1, and 0 < Prob (q) < [Prob (p) x Prob (e & not-p)], then:

(1) Prob(q) < Prob(p)Prob(e&not−p) (follows from the stipulations)
(2) Prob(p/e&q) = Prob(p&e&q)/Prob(e&q) (definition of Prob)
(3) (p&e&q) is logically equivalent to (p&e&Z)
(4) Prob(p/e&q) = Prob(p&e&Z)/Prob(e&q) (from 2, 3)
(5) (p&e&Z) logically entails Z
(6) Prob(p&e&Z) < or = Prob(Z) = 1/N (from 5)
(7) (e&not−p) logically entails (e&q) (from definition of q)
(8) Prob(e&not−p) < or = Prob(e&q) (from 7)
(9) Prob(p/e&q) < or = (1/N)/Prob(e&q) (from 4, 6)
(10) (1/N)/Prob(e&q) < or = (1/N)/Prob(e&not−p) (from 8)
(11) (1/N)/Prob(e&not−p) < Prob(p)Prob(e&not−p)/Prob(e&not−p) (from 1)
(12) Prob(p)Prob(e&not−p)/Prob(e&not−p) = Prob(p)
(13) Prob(p/e&q) < Prob(p) (from 9−12)

So what we can conclude from this is that, if S knows that p on the basis of evidence e, where Prob (p/e) < 1, and then—given that there are many truths that are very unlikely to be true, given our total evidence—there will be a true proposition Z such that Prob (p/e&Z) is very low, and much lower than Prob (p). And so there will be a true proposition Z such that e&Z does not constitute a justification to believe that p. This seems decisively to refute the IJTB theory of knowledge, at least if S can know that p on the basis of evidence e such that Prob (p/e) < 1.

But this is the crucial question: is it possible for S to know that p on the basis of evidence e if Prob (p/e) < 1? In the next section, I will argue that it is not.

4. KNOWLEDGE REQUIRES BELIEF BASED ON INFALLIBLE EVIDENCE

In this section I will argue that, if S knows that p on the basis of evidence e, then, for S, Prob (p/e) = 1. Indeed, I will argue for an even stronger conclusion than this—namely, that S cannot know that p on the basis of evidence e unless there is no *possible* situation in which S has e and yet p is not true.

My argument will employ the following premises:

Two-premise closure. If S knows that p, and S knows that q, and S competently deduces r from p and q, while retaining her knowledge that p and her knowledge that q, then S knows that r.

Transmission of empirical evidential basis. If S knows that p solely on the basis of S's empirical evidence e, and if S knows that q solely by deducing q from the conjunction of p and e, then S knows that q on the basis of empirical evidence e.

Now, I will argue that, if S knows that e, and S knows that p on the basis of e, then e is infallible evidence for p—that is, e is such that S cannot have e unless p is true.

Consider the following facts:

I cannot know that the paper I am reading is not in error, solely on the basis of the evidence that the paper says that a famous official was assassinated.

I cannot know that the 100 A's I have observed are representative of A's with respect to their B-hood solely on the basis of the evidence that A1 is a B, A2 is a B, . . ., A100 is a B.

I cannot know that my visual experience as of Tom stealing the library book is accurate solely on the basis of the visual experience as of Tom stealing the library book.

There are, as a matter of empirically obvious fact, countless more facts of the kind above, in which e is fallible evidence for some proposition p, but S cannot know, on the basis of e alone, that e is not misleading with respect to p. A survey of such cases inductively justifies the following conclusion: if e is fallible evidence for p, then one cannot know, on the basis of e alone, that e is not misleading with respect to p.

Now consider the following additional facts:

I cannot know a priori that the paper that I am reading is not in error in saying that the famous official was assassinated.

I cannot know a priori that the 100 A's that I have observed are typical of A's with respect to their B-hood.

I cannot know a priori that my visual experience of Tom stealing the book is veridical.

Again, there are, as a matter of empirically obvious fact, countless more facts of the kind above, in which e is fallible evidence for some proposition p, and S cannot know a priori that e is not misleading with respect to p. A survey of such cases inductively justifies the following conclusion: if e is fallible evidence for p, then one cannot know a priori that e is not misleading with respect to p.

Now, by two-premise closure, if S knows that p on the basis of empirical evidence e, and if S deduces from e and p that e is not misleading with respect to p, then S has knowledge that e is not misleading with respect to p. If S has this knowledge *by* deducing it from e and p, then, by the transmission of empirical evidential basis, S has this knowledge on the basis of evidence e alone. But our first survey of cases above showed that, if e is fallible evidence for p, then S cannot know that e is not misleading with respect to p solely on the basis of e. And our second survey of cases above showed that, if e is fallible evidence for p, then S cannot know a priori that e is not misleading with respect to p. So, if S knows that e is not misleading with respect to p, then either S knows this on the basis of some evidence e′ that is distinct from e, or else e is not fallible evidence for p.

Let us consider the first disjunct. If S knows, on the basis of e′, that e is not misleading with respect to p, then how might S know that the conjunction e and e′ is not misleading with respect to p? Does S know this on the basis of some further evidence e″? The appeal to further evidence e′ simply sets us on a regress. I conclude that the second disjunct is true: if S knows that e is not misleading with respect to p, then e is not fallible evidence for p. And so, if S knows that p on the basis of evidence e, then e is not fallible evidence for p. For e to give me knowledge that p, e must be the kind of evidence that is such that, on the basis of that evidence alone, I can know that it is not misleading with respect to p. The survey of cases above inductively confirms the hypothesis that no fallible evidence satisfies this latter description. We have thus shown, by means of this inductive argument, that fallible evidence cannot give one knowledge.[18]

This last argument provides all the resources necessary to handle proposed counterexamples to the IJTB theory. If it is a necessary condition of S's knowing that p that S's evidence e for p be infallible—that is, such that there is no possible situation in which S has e but p is not true—then the conjunction of e with anything constitutes a justification for S to believe that p. This guarantees that we will not be able to find cases of knowledge that fail to satisfy the controversial fourth condition of the IJTB theory.

Of course, if Williamson is right that E = K, then of course knowledge requires infallible evidence. But we can reject the thesis that E = K, as we have done above, even while holding that knowledge requires infallible evidence.[19] Perceptual knowledge that x is F may require that one *perceive* x to be F—and this is something one can do even if one does not know that Fx. (There is a difference here between perceiving that x is F and perceiving x to be F. Both are sufficient for x to be F, but only the former is sufficient for *knowing* x to be F.) Testimonial knowledge that x is F may require that one be *informed* of x's being F—and this is something that can happen to one even if one refuses to believe that Fx, and so even if one fails to know that Fx. (Again, there is a difference here between being informed of x's being F and learning that x is F. I take it

---

[18] If fallible evidence cannot give us knowledge, then can the inductive argument have given us knowledge that its conclusion is true? Yes. Inductive arguments can give us infallible evidence for their conclusion, as I argue below in the text.

[19] Duncan Pritchard and I interpret John McDowell as holding this view. See Neta and Pritchard (2007).

that both suffice for x to be F,[20] but only the latter suffices for knowing x to be F.) Inductive knowledge that A's are B's may require that one be *informed* of A's being B's—and this is something that can happen to one even if one refuses to believe that A's are B's, and so even if one fails to know that A's are B's. It is possible for one to perceive x to be F, or to be informed of x's being F, or of A's being B's, without knowing that Fx, or that A's are B's. But it is not possible for one to perceive x to be F, or to be informed of x's being F, unless x is in fact F. And it is impossible to be informed of A's being B's without A's in fact being B's.

Some philosophers may worry that such truths as that one is informed of x's being F, or of A's being B's, cannot be in one's evidence set, for one's evidence set includes only those truths that one can know to be true solely by reflection (either reflection on the contents of one's own mind, or a priori reflection). Now it is true that sometimes such truths are not in one's evidence. For instance, when Henry, in barn-façade country, sees a barn to be in front of him, the fact that he sees a barn to be in front of him is not in his evidence set. When you read a newspaper story that informs you of the assassination of a famous official, the fact that you have been so informed is not in your evidence set if, say, later newspapers retract that story. To be informed of x's being F is one thing—to have the fact that one is so informed in one's evidence set is a further thing. Only if one is entitled to take it for granted in inquiry that one has been so informed does the fact of one's having been so informed make its way into one's evidence set.

But, according to the objection voiced above, such facts as one's having been informed of x's being F never make their way into one's evidence set, and this is because one cannot know such facts by reflection alone. Now, even supposing it is true that one's evidence set can include only those truths that one can know to be true by reflection alone (and I would need to hear why we should accept it), why cannot the present view accommodate this constraint on what can be in one's evidence set? Why cannot one know, by reflection alone, that one sees the table to be red? I have elsewhere argued that, pending further illumination concerning what it is to know something by reflection alone, there is no good answer to this question.[21]

Knowledge, on the present view, is belief that is properly based on infallible evidence (indeed, on evidence that can be known—perhaps upon reflection alone—to be infallible). So it follows that knowledge is *also*, as the IJTB theory says, justified true belief that is indefeasible by any further evidence: if S knows that p on the basis of evidence e, then e is infallible evidence for p, and so the conjunction of e with any other true proposition is also infallible evidence for

---

[20] Bill Lycan reports hearing a use of "inform" on which being informed that x is F is compatible with x's not being F. I confess that I do not hear such a use of "inform," but perhaps I am being deaf. If so, then I should find a better word to denote the factive relation at issue here. Perhaps English does not supply such a word. If such a word does not exist, epistemology will have to invent it.

[21] I discuss this complicated issue more fully in my "Refutation of Internalist Fallibilism".

p, and therefore constitutes a justification for S to believe that p. Of course, there may be examples in which S is *justified* in believing that p on the basis of evidence that can be expanded into something that is not a justification for S to believe that p—justification itself may be defeasible. But knowledge is not defeasible, according to the IJTB theory. The theory that I have been calling the IJTB theory—the theory that says that knowledge is indefeasible justified true belief—is just a first approximation to the theory that I would like, in the end, to defend: the *infallibly* justified true belief theory of knowledge. For convenience, I will henceforth use the expression "IJTB theory" to refer to the latter theory of knowledge, the theory that expresses precisely what I hold, rather than the earlier approximation to it.

If I want to defend a theory according to which knowledge is infallibly justified true belief, then why did I make a detour through indefeasibility? Indefeasibility is an important feature of knowledge, because it is the indefeasibility of knowledge that explains why knowledge, and knowledge ascription, is important to us. Recall that we wanted a theory of knowledge to tell us what knowledge is, and we wanted to know what knowledge is in order to be able to explain how it is that knowledge, and knowledge ascriptions, can play the role that they play in our lives. We are now in a position to provide at least some of the latter explanatory story.

5. WHY IT MATTERS WHAT YOU KNOW

Knowledge and knowledge ascription play many different roles in our lives. A complete account of knowledge would help us to understand how they manage to play these various roles. But a complete account of knowledge would have to say something about the nature of the justification required for knowledge, the nature of the basing relation required for knowledge, and the nature of belief and truth. In this chapter I have said almost nothing about these complicated issues, and I will not say anything more about them in this section. I have focused exclusively on the anti-Gettier condition on knowledge, the indefeasibility condition. Can our discussion of this indefeasibility condition help us to understand what roles knowledge and knowledge ascription play in our lives, and how it is that they play those roles?

I believe it can, and, in order to substantiate this, I will focus on just one example in this chapter. According to the IJTB theory, knowledge is indefeasible, in the following sense: so long as the agent who knows that p retains all her current evidence, her acquisition of new evidence will never render her justified in disbelieving that p. But then, *so long as she retains her current evidence*, she will never be justified in disbelieving that p. Now suppose that such an agent adopts a dogmatic attitude toward p: she treats p as a fixed or settled point in inquiry, and so, when she is confronted with recalcitrant evidence that might be thought to tell against p, she revises some belief other than p. What epistemic cost would such an agent incur? Of course, if the agent does not know that p, but only thinks that she knows that p, then she may end up incurring the epistemic cost of never finding out that she was wrong about p, or at least of holding beliefs that she is not justified in holding. But, by hypothesis, our agent knows that p, and retains all her evidence for p, so, at least according to the IJTB theory, these are not costs that she could incur. Indeed, I cannot think of any cost that such an agent might incur by being dogmatic about p. If there is indeed no such cost, then knowing that p entitles one to be dogmatic about p, at least so long as one retains one's evidence for p.

To be dogmatic about p is not the same as being highly confident of p, or even rationally highly confident of p. Dogmatism need not involve a high degree of confidence or of rational confidence. One may be dogmatic about p but not about q, even if one is actually and/or rationally more confident of q than of p. Rather, dogmatism about p is a disposition to treat further evidence as not calling p into question. If I believe that p, and I am disposed to treat all further evidence as not calling p into question, then I am dogmatic about p. So long as I know that p, and I retain the evidence on the basis of which I possess this knowledge, rationality entitles me to be dogmatic about p, because there is no epistemic cost that I might incur by continuing to believe that p no matter what new evidence may come my way.

Many philosophers think that it is generally unreasonable to be dogmatic, even about those propositions that we know to be true. Witness the popular reaction to the dogmatism paradox that was formulated by Kripke, and first presented in print by Harman. Harman states the argument for the allegedly paradoxical conclusion as follows:

If I know that h is true, I know that any evidence against h is evidence against something that is true; so I know that such evidence is misleading. But I should disregard evidence that I know is misleading. So, once I know that h is true, I am in a position to disregard any future evidence that seems to tell against h. (Harman 1973: 148)[22]

---

[22] Ginet (1980) notes that Harman's argument, as stated, is enthymematic, he reformulates it thus (this quote is slighty adapted):

For any propositions h and f:
(Premise 1) If (a) I know that h is true, then (b) I know that, if in the future I come to know f to be true, my then counting f as evidence against h would be to count f as evidence against a truth;
(Premise 2) If (b) I know that if in the future I come to know f to be true then my counting f as evidence against h would be to count f as evidence against a truth, and I do not forget this knowledge, then if in the future I come to know that f is true then at that time I know that my counting f as evidence against h would be to count f as evidence against a truth;
(Premise 3) If (d) I know that f is true and that my counting f as evidence against h would be to count f as evidence against a truth, then I am entitled not to count f as evidence against h;
(Conclusion) Therefore, if (a) I know that he is true, and I do not forget this knowledge, then (e) if in the future I come to know that f is true, then at that time I am entitled not to count f as evidence against h.
Ginet rejects Premise 2 of the argument, so formulated, and he plausibly takes Harman to be best understood as implicitly rejecting Premise 2 as well.

After stating this argument for dogmatism, Harman (and several other philosophers following Harman) criticize the argument by claiming that gaining
new evidence can make one lose one's knowledge. Now, the proponent of IJTB
can agree that gaining new evidence can make one lose one's knowledge—if
this connection is understood as a causal connection. Gaining new evidence can
cause one to lose one's old evidence for p, or can cause one to lose one's belief
that p, and either way it can cause one to lose one's knowledge that p. But,
according to IJTB, gaining new evidence cannot, all by itself and apart from any
effects it may have, cause one to lose one's knowledge or one's justification for
believing that p. So, while Harman and other anti-dogmatist philosophers are
right to say that gaining new evidence can make one lose one's knowledge, this
is compatible with the thesis of the indefeasibility of knowledge that is being
advanced here. If it is generally unreasonable to retain one's beliefs in the face
of apparently contrary evidence, that is because gaining such evidence can shake
one's confidence, or cause one to lose some of one's old evidence, and either
way it can rob one of knowledge. But it cannot rob one of knowledge simply by
tipping the evidentiary scales, without depriving one of any old evidence.

So what role does knowledge, and knowledge ascription, play in our lives? The
proponent of IJTB is in a position to answer this question as follows. Knowledge
is important to us because it entitles us to hold certain points fixed in inquiry.
Knowledge ascription is important to us because it records those points that we
are entitled to *hold fixed* in inquiry. (What we are entitled to hold fixed in inquiry
is not the same as what we are entitled to take for granted in inquiry, even though
there is overlap in the extension of the two categories. For instance, some of what
I am entitled to hold fixed I am not entitled to take for granted, because I must
be able to defend it against challenges.) If we did not have knowledge, then we
really would be in a predicament no better than the one that Neurath described:
having to rebuild the raft of our opinions while we are afloat on it. Those of us
who prefer to stay safely on dry land while rebuilding our raft should be grateful
therefore that we do actually know a lot, and we do not have to settle for merely
justified true beliefs.[23]

[23] For comments and discussion I am grateful to Bill Lycan, John Roberts, Dylan Sabo, and
other members of an audience at the University of North Carolina, Chapel Hill. I am also grateful,
as always, to Duncan Pritchard and to Jonathan Schaffer.

11

Evidence = Knowledge: Williamson's Solution to Skepticism

Stephen Schiffer

A single argument template—the *EPH template*—can be used to generate versions of the best-known and most challenging skeptical problems. In his brilliantly groundbreaking book *Knowledge and its Limits* Timothy Williamson presents a theory of knowledge and evidence which he clearly intends to provide a response to skepticism in its most important forms. After laying out EPH skepticism and reviewing possible ways of responding to it, I show how elements of Williamson's theory motivate a hitherto unexplored way of responding to EPH-generated skeptical arguments. Then I offer reasons to doubt the correctness of Williamson's response.

1. EPH SKEPTICISM

The EPH argument template has as its ingredients an uncontentious fact E, a run-of-the-mill proposition P, and a skeptical hypothesis H such that:

- common sense supposes that one would know and be justified in believing P on the basis of E;
- H entails both E and not P; and
- it appears that if E cannot justify one in believing not H, then there is nothing else available to justify one in believing not H.

Using these ingredients, the skeptic argues as follows, where by stipulation the subject "I" is a rational thinker who is fully and actively aware that P and H are incompatible and that H entails E:

1. I am not justified in believing P unless I am justified in believing not H.
2. I am not justified in believing not H unless something other than E justifies me in believing not H.
3. There is nothing other than E to justify me in believing not H.
4. ∴ I am not justified in believing P.

5. If I am not justified in believing P, then I do not know P.
6. ∴ I do not know P.

When we take E to be the proposition that I am having such-and-such sensory experiences as of a red cube, P the proposition that there is a red cube before me, and H the hypothesis—call it BIV—that I am a brain floating in a cubeless vat of nutrients and attached to a device that is causing me to have the such-and-such sensory experiences as of a red cube which I am now having, then we get:

External World

1. I am not justified in believing that there is a red cube before me unless I am justified in believing not BIV.
2. I am not justified in believing not BIV unless something other than the fact that I am currently having such-and-such sensory experiences as of a red cube justifies me in believing not BIV.
3. There is nothing else to justify me in believing not BIV.
4. I am not justified in believing that there is a red cube before me.
5. If I am not justified in believing that there is a red cube before me, then I do not know that there is a red cube before me.
6. ∴ I do not know that there is a red cube before me.

By a straightforward extrapolation and generalization, the argument may be continued to show that no facts about my sensory experiences can justify me in believing anything about the external world, and that therefore my sensory experience cannot give me knowledge of the external world. And if "I"—that is, a rational thinker in epistemically optimal conditions—cannot have knowledge or justified belief of the kind in question, then no one can have such knowledge or justified belief.

When we take E to be the fact that I have egg on my shirt and seem to remember eating eggs for breakfast, P the proposition that I had eggs for breakfast, and H the hypothesis—call it NEW—that the universe just this moment came into existence, completely as is, with the fact that I have egg on my shirt and seem to remember eating eggs for breakfast, then we get:

Past

1. I am not justified in believing that I had eggs for breakfast unless I am justified in believing not NEW.
2. I am not justified in believing not NEW unless something other than the fact that I have egg on my shirt and seem to remember eating eggs for breakfast justifies me in believing not NEW.
3. There is nothing else to justify me in believing not NEW.

4. ∴ I am not justified in believing that I had eggs for breakfast.

5. If I am not justified in believing that I had eggs for breakfast, then I do not know that I had eggs for breakfast.

6. ∴ I do not know that I had eggs for breakfast.

By a straightforward extrapolation and generalization, the argument may be continued to show that no facts about the present can justify me in believing anything about the past, and that therefore such facts cannot give me knowledge of the past. And if I—a rational thinker who is actively aware of relevant entailments—cannot have knowledge or justified belief of the kind in question, then no one can have such knowledge or justified belief.

When we take E to be the fact that Al broke his toe by stubbing it against a rock and is screaming and writhing on the ground, P the proposition that Al is in pain, and H the hypothesis—call it ZOMBIE—that Al is a zombie who has no sentient mental states, even though he broke his toe by stubbing it against a rock and is screaming and writhing on the ground and in general behaves in ways I expect sentient humans to behave, then we get:

Other Minds

1. I am not justified in believing that Al is in pain unless I am justified in believing not ZOMBIE.

2. I am not justified in believing not ZOMBIE unless something other than the fact that Al broke his toe and is screaming and writhing on the ground justifies me in believing not ZOMBIE.

3. There is nothing else to justify me in believing not ZOMBIE.

4. ∴ I am not justified in believing that Al is in pain.

5. If I am not justified in believing that Al is in pain, then I do not know that Al is in pain.

6. ∴ I do not know that Al is in pain.

By a straightforward extrapolation and generalization, the argument may be continued to show that no facts about the behavior of, or causes acting on, another body can justify me in believing anything about the sentient mental states of others, not even that others have such states, and that therefore such facts cannot give me knowledge of other minds, not even that there are other minds. And if "I" cannot have knowledge or justified belief of the kind in question, then no one can have such knowledge or justified belief.

When we take E to be the fact that all observed ravens have been black, P the proposition that the next observed raven will be black, and H the hypothesis—call it NONUNIFORMITY—that, while all observed ravens have been black, no observed ravens after now will be black, then we can even get:

Induction

1. I am not justified in believing that the next observed raven will be black unless I am justified in believing not NONUNIFORMITY.

2. I am not justified in believing not NONUNIFORMITY unless something other than the fact that all observed ravens have been black justifies me in believing not NONUNIFORMITY.

3. There is nothing else to justify me in believing not NONUNIFORMITY.

4. ∴. I am not justified in believing that the next observed raven will be black.

5. If I am not justified in believing that the next observed raven will be black, then I do not know that the next observed raven will be black.

6. ∴. I do not know that the next observed raven will be black.

By a straightforward extrapolation and generalization, the argument may be continued to show that no facts about past regularities can justify me in believing that any past regularities will continue to hold, and that therefore such facts can give me no knowledge of the future. And if "I" cannot have knowledge or justified belief of the kind in question, then no one can have such knowledge or justified belief.

It is important to appreciate that the different skeptical paradoxes are instances of the same argument form, because that motivates a defeasible expectation that, if any one of the four skeptical arguments goes wrong in a particular way, then they all go wrong in that way. In other words, we should not expect there to be one solution to the problem of the external world and a different solution to, say, the problem of other minds.

Skeptical arguments may take other forms, but it is reasonable to suppose that a resolution of the problems raised by EPH arguments will have application to the skeptical arguments that take those other forms, and that any fully adequate response to those other arguments will have application to the EPH arguments.

For the rest of this chapter I shall focus just on the EPH argument template as it concerns justified belief—that is, on the template:

EPH

1. I am not justified in believing P unless I am justified in believing not H.
2. I am not justified in believing not H unless something other than E justifies me in believing not H.
3. There is nothing other than E to justify me in believing not H.
4. ∴. I am not justified in believing P.

It is not that no one has thought to challenge premise (5) (if I am not justified in believing P, then I do not know P). Some have challenged the claim that knowing P entails believing P, while others have conceded that knowing P entails believing P but have challenged the claim that knowing P entails being *justified* in believing P. I am not sure why no one has thought to challenge the claim that knowing P entails that P is true, since we sometimes say such things as "I *knew* she would say yes" when we know that she did not say yes, and that sort of use of "know" is pretty much on all fours with the examples that are supposed to loosen the ties between knowledge and belief or justification. In any case, I am not aware of any good reasons to deny (5); Williamson evidently would not deny it; and, even if (5) were false, an argument that concludes that we cannot be justified in believing the things we are certain we are justified in believing is itself, needless to say, a skeptical paradox worth grappling with.

EPH is a valid argument form, and we come to the skeptical arguments already believing that their conclusions are false. The plausibility of the premises, however, must be earned. We will be in a better position to appreciate the nature of Williamson's innovative response to EPH skepticism if I first briefly review enough of what might be said in support of each of the three EPH premises to justify treating the EPH arguments as *paradoxes*—valid arguments with apparently true premises and apparently false conclusions (thereby showing, once again, that you cannot always go by appearances).

Premise (1) (I am not justified in believing P unless I am justified in believing not H). Recall that the "I" of the argument is by stipulation a rational thinker who is actively aware that P entails not H. Given that, the plausibility of (1) is entailed by the plausibility of the closure principle:

JBC For any propositions P, Q, one who is actively aware that P entails Q is justified in believing P only if she is also justified in believing Q.

It is easy to see why JBC is plausible. If one may be justified in believing P but not Q when one is actively aware that P entails Q, then it need not be irrational for one to believe that P is true and to doubt whether Q is true even while being fully and actively aware that it is impossible for P to be true unless Q is true. But it is doubtful that such a combination of attitudes is possible, let alone can be rationally held.

I do need to say something about the intended meaning of "is justified in believing" as it occurs in EPH, and thus in JBC. Three justification relations need to be distinguished:

IS E *is* a justification for S to believe P.

HAS E is a justification that S *has* to believe P.

IN E justifies S *in* believing P.

On the intended reading of IS, E can be a justification for S to believe P even though S is not aware of E and does not believe P. For example, a certain symptom may be conclusive evidence that I have a certain disease, even though I am unaware of the symptom, unaware that I have the disease, and would be unaware that the symptom was evidence of the disease even if I were aware of it.

On the intended reading of HAS, in order for E to be a justification that S *has* to believe P, S must know, or at least believe, E—or at least simply have E, if E is an experience or sensation. (If we assume Williamson's theory, wherein only evidence can justify and a proposition belongs to S's total evidence just in case S knows it,[1] then E is a justification that S *has* for believing P if and only if E is a justification for S to believe P and S knows E.)

On the intended reading of IN, E can be a justification that S has for believing P and yet not be what justifies S *in* believing P, even though S is justified in believing P. For example, S may know a certain fact about a DNA fingerprint found in a hair sample at the scene of a murder; this fact may be virtually conclusive evidence that the chauffeur was the murderer; and S may not know that the DNA fingerprint implicates the chauffeur yet still be justified in believing that the chauffeur committed the murder on the basis of knowing that two independent and uninvolved witnesses say they saw the chauffeur commit the murder. To be *justified in* believing P is to believe P and to be justified in doing so, and for E to be what justifies S in believing P it must be that S believes P on the basis of S's having, knowing, or at least believing E, in a sense of "on the basis of" that awaits explication but can be used to sort cases. Assuming Williamson's theory of evidence (see below), we may say that evidence E justifies S in believing P only if S's knowing E accounts for the fact that S is justified in believing P. This in turn implies that, all other things being equal, if E justifies S in believing P, then S would not be so justified if S did not know E.

---

[1] Williamson's equating a person's evidence with her knowledge—an equation he calls $E = K$ (p. 185)—is a cornerstone of his theory of evidence (unless otherwise noted, all page references for Williamson are to *Knowledge and its Limits*). The doctrine that only evidence can justify belief occurs in a few places (e.g., p. 208), and is evidently also pretty central to Williamson's theory. It has, however, a weak and a strong reading. The weak reading is that if E justifies one's believing P, then E is known, and thus, by $E = K$, belongs to one's total evidence. The stronger reading is that, if E justifies one's believing P, then E is evidence for P for one. Williamson sometimes gives the impression that he accepts the stronger reading, as when he says that "evidence for a mathematical conjecture may consist of mathematical knowledge" (p. 207), but here he is probably using "evidence" in a loose vernacular way, since on his account of evidence, nothing can be evidence for a mathematical proposition, and no mathematical proposition can be evidence for any proposition. This is because E is evidence for P only if it raises the probability of P, in the sense that $\text{Prob}(P/E) > \text{Prob } P$, and for Williamson every mathematical proposition has probability 1 or 0. The fact that nothing can be evidence for a mathematical proposition may be taken to be a problem for Williamson's theory of evidence, since we may well want to say such things as that my evidence for P's being a theorem of number theory is that the brilliant number theorist Jones told me that it was. We needn't, however, bother about any of this, since all the issues in this chapter about what a person is justified in believing pertain only to contingent propositions.

Premise (2) (I am not justified in believing not H unless something other than E justifies me in believing not H). The argument for premise (2) is this:

(i) We may take it as given that (*a*) I know for certain that H entails E; (*b*) I come to know E at a certain time t*[2]; and (*c*) prior to t*, both E and H were uncertain to me.

(ii) If (i), then E is evidence *for* H for me at t*.

(iii) E cannot be part of what justifies me in believing *not* H at t* if E is evidence *for* H for me at t*.

(iv) ∴ I am not justified in believing not H at t* unless something other than E justifies me in believing not H at t*.

Only (ii) and (iii) need justification. Let t* continue to be the time alluded to in the argument, and let

$Prob_{old}$ = probability on all the evidence acquired up to the time just before t*, the time at which Prob(E) becomes 1.

Now, it is a theorem of probability theory that

$$[(Prob_{old}(E/H) = 1)\ \&\ (0 < Prob_{old}(E) < 1)\ \&\ (0 < Prob_{old}(H) > 1)] \rightarrow Prob_{old}(H/E) > Prob_{old}(H),$$

and it is transparently plausible that

E is evidence for H for S at t* if (*a*) S knows E at t* and (*b*) $Prob_{old}(H/E) > Prob_{old}(H)$,

and from those two things (ii) follows. Two points also secure (iii). First, E is evidence *against* not H for me if E is evidence *for* H for me (this is reflected in probabilistic terms by the theorem that Prob(H) + Prob(¬H) = 1). And, secondly, E cannot be part of what justifies me in believing not H if E is evidence *against* not H for me—after all, if E is evidence against not H for me, then E should *lower* my confidence in not H, and something that lowers my confidence in a hypothesis cannot be part of what justifies me in believing it.

Premise (3) (There is nothing other than E to justify me in believing not H). One cannot provide a prima facie justification for the instances of premise (3) in question without regard to the particular values of H and E. But in each case there is the same pattern of argument: there is nothing other than E to justify me in believing not H because (*a*), if there is to be evidence against H, it will ultimately

---

[2] I hope my use of "a certain time t*" is clear enough. To do the quantification over times properly would make for a less neat statement of the argument. I shall omit temporal references when doing so is harmless.

come down to evidence of the kind to which E belongs for propositions of the kind to which P belongs; but (*b*), as the instance of EPH shows, no E-type fact can justify one in believing a P-type proposition unless there is a justification for disbelieving an H-type hypothesis that is independent of that E-type fact. Here is how this plays out with respect to External World:

1. Since BIV is a contingent empirical hypothesis, I would be justified in disbelieving it only if I have empirical evidence against it.

2. But any such evidence would itself have to consist in propositions belief in which was directly or indirectly justified by my sensory experience.

3. Since any such experience will encounter its own BIV hypothesis, if any sensory experience could justify me in believing not BIV, my such-and-such sensory experiences as of Cube could, too.

4. But, as we have seen, my such-and-such sensory experiences as of Cube cannot justify me in believing not BIV.

5. So, there is nothing other than my such-and-such sensory experiences as of Cube to justify me in believing not BIV.

2. RESPONSES TO EPH SKEPTICISM

EPH skeptical arguments presuppose that whatever justifies you in believing P if you really do know P will also justify you in believing P if the skeptical hypothesis H is true, and vice versa. Let us call this the *same-justification assumption* (SJA). It will be helpful to restate SJA in the following Williamson-inspired way. In order to make my discussion more concrete, I will be concerned with SJA only with respect to External World. The EPH skeptic launches External World against the presupposed background of a *best-case scenario* (BCS): a scenario that is consistent with BIV but is otherwise optimal for my having perceptual knowledge that there is a red cube before me, if there is a red cube before me (so, if there is a red cube before me and I cannot know it there, then I cannot know it anywhere). The skeptic then envisages two incompatible further descriptions of BCS. Let us adopt Williamson's untendentious labels and call one of these further descriptions Good and the other Bad:

> *Good*: BIV is false and I perceive, and thus know, that there is a red cube before me (Cube, for short).
>
> *Bad*: BIV is true (and therefore I do not know Cube), but otherwise my situation is as much like Good as it's possible for it to be.

Then SJA, applied to BCS, has it that, if anything justifies me in believing Cube in either realization of BCS—that is, either in Good or in Bad—then it also justifies me in believing Cube in the other, and that that one thing is the fact that I am having such-and-such sensory experiences as of Cube.[3]

Most responses to External World accept SJA.

This is true of the contextualist response, which finds indexicality in External World and holds that it expresses a sound argument in certain "high-standards" contexts, such as a context in which skepticism is being discussed (like there is another context in which you would find External World?).

It is true of the only way of denying premise (1)—namely, denying the closure of justified belief under known entailment—which I think is advocated only by Fred Dretske.[4]

It is true of the only way of denying premise (2), the "dogmatism" whose proponents include John Pollock, Jim Pryor, Tyler Burge, and Christopher Peacocke.[5]

It is true of the inference-to-the-best-explanation response to premise (3), which claims that, while the evidence is the same in Good and Bad, we are justified in believing not BIV because the commonsense explanation of the fact that I am having my sensory experiences as of Cube, according to which my experience is a veridical perception, can be said to be a better explanation than BIV of that fact just on the basis of an invidious comparison of BIV with the commonsense explanation with respect to theoretical virtues and vices.[6]

And it is true of the response to premise (3)—flirted with by Crispin Wright and accepted by others[7]—which holds that by default we are *a priori* justified in disbelieving BIV simply by virtue of the presuppositional status the commonsense material world hypothesis enjoys in our belief system.

For the record, I do not find any of these responses plausible.

There are, however, in principle two different ways to deny SJA, and either would enable one to challenge premise (3). One way is to claim that I have *no* justification for believing Cube in Good which I also have in Bad, even on the assumption that the fact that I am having such-and-such sensory experiences as of Cube justifies me in believing Cube in Bad. This is the so-called *disjunctivism* of John McDowell and others, according to which I may be justified in believing Cube, and thus in disbelieving BIV, in both Good and Bad, but that what justifies me is different in the two cases, a perception of a red cube in the one case, and a hallucination of a red cube in the other, these not being states that share a qualitative sensory state that would itself provide justification for believing

---

[3] It seems clear that, if one can be justified in believing Cube in Good, then one can also be justified in believing Cube in Bad, *if* one can *entertain* Cube in Bad. A person who only recently became disembodied and envatted can entertain Cube, but it may be arguable that a creature who has been envatted its entire life would not have the concepts required to entertain Cube. This issue matters with respect to a possible problem for Williamson that I discuss below, but otherwise we should understand BIV in a way that allows for me to entertain Cube in Bad.

[4] Dretske (1970). Robert Nozick (1981) denies closure for knowledge but not for justified belief.

[5] Pollock (1986), Pryor (2000), Burge (2003a), and Peacocke (2004).

[6] See, e.g., Vogel (1990).   [7] Wright (2004); see also, e.g., White (2006).

Cube.[8] I think that disjunctivism is an implausible response to skepticism for several reasons, two of them being that it yields no response to Induction and an extremely strained response to Other Minds.

The second way of denying SJA holds (i) that, even in Bad I am justified in believing Cube, (ii) that what justifies me in believing Cube in Bad is the fact that I am having such-and-such sensory experiences as of Cube, (iii) that that justification is also a justification for believing Cube that I have in Good, but (iv) that in Good there is another, knowledge-securing justification for believing Cube, which I do not have in Bad, that justifies me in believing Cube. No one to my knowledge has ever responded to EPH skepticism in this way—*unless* this is the response to which Timothy Williamson is committed by the theory of evidence and the reply to skepticism he advances in *Knowledge and its Limits*.

3. E = K AND WILLIAMSON'S IMPLIED RESPONSE TO EPH SKEPTICISM

With respect to the skeptical argument External World, the *same-justification assumption* (SJA) holds that whatever *justifies me in believing* Cube if I really do know Cube will also justify me in believing Cube if the skeptical hypothesis H is true, and vice versa.

Williamson does not consider skepticism in its EPH form, nor does he explicitly consider SJA. He does, however, consider a version of external-world skepticism that accepts what we may call the *same-evidence assumption* (SEA)—namely, that the *evidence* one has in Good is exactly the same as the evidence one has in Bad. Applied to External World, SEA holds that whatever is evidence for Cube for me in Good is also evidence for Cube for me in Bad, and vice versa.

In responding to the version of skepticism he considers, Williamson argues that the skeptic goes wrong in accepting SEA. The falsity of SEA follows from two tenets of Williamson's theory of evidence:

> **EV** E is evidence for P for S if and only if (i) S's evidence includes E and (ii) $\text{Prob}_{old}(P/E) > \text{Prob}_{old}(P)$.

E = K S's evidence includes E if and only if S knows E.

For suppose I know Cube (and am thus in Good and not in Bad). Then, by E = K, my evidence includes Cube. And, since it is clear that $\text{Prob}_{old}(\text{Cube/Cube}) > \text{Prob}_{old}(\text{Cube})$, it follows from EV that Cube is evidence for Cube for me. Indeed, I can have no better evidence for Cube than Cube: since $\text{Prob}_{new}(\text{Cube}) = \text{Prob}_{old}(\text{Cube/Cube}) = 1$, Cube is conclusive evidence for me that Cube. Thus, I have conclusive evidence for Cube in Good that I

---

[8] McDowell (1982); see also Martin (2004).

do not have in Bad—namely, Cube. And, since Prob($\neg$BIV/Cube) = 1, I also have conclusive evidence for not BIV in Good that I do not have in Bad.

We are concerned with the External World instance of EPH—that is to say, with:

1. I am not justified in believing Cube unless I am justified in believing not BIV.
2. I am not justified in believing not BIV unless something other than the fact that I am currently having such-and-such sensory experiences as of Cube justifies me in believing not BIV.
3. There is nothing else to justify me in believing not BIV.
4. ∴ I am not justified in believing Cube.

It is clear that Williamson would deny the conclusion of this valid argument. But which of its premises would he deny? Given what he says about "intuitive closure" (p. 119), we may infer that Williamson would accept (1). What about (2)? I am not sure whether Williamson would accept or reject this premise. It presents one problem for him if he accepts it, and another if he rejects it. To see why, we need first to appreciate that, as already intimated, the crux of his reply to the argument will be his denial of premise (3). Here, I believe, he would claim that there is something other than the fact that I am having such-and-such sensory experiences as of Cube to justify me in believing Cube, because in Good my justification for believing Cube includes evidence that I do not have in Bad—namely, that there is in fact a red cube before me. I will elaborate on this presently. In the meantime, let us return to the problem (2) presents.

I said that (2) presents one problem for Williamson if he accepts it, and another if he rejects it. The problem in both cases turns on how Williamson can account for my being justified in believing Cube in Bad. (It is clear that it is possible for there to be a token of Bad in which I believe Cube—for example, one in which I am only recently envatted—and that when I do I will be justified in believing Cube, unless skepticism is correct and it is impossible for anyone to have a justified perceptual belief about the external world. And, of course, if I am justified in believing Cube in Bad, then, by the closure principle JCB, I am also justified in believing not BIV in Bad.) Now, the crux of Williamson's response to the version of skepticism he considers is that one has evidence in good cases that one does not have in bad cases precisely by virtue of having perceptual knowledge in good cases. The implication is that this is what is *required* to respond to the skeptic—and presumably to the skeptic about justified belief, as well as to the skeptic about knowledge. If, therefore, Williamson can account for my being justified in believing Cube in Bad in a way that does not entail the evidential difference he finds between good and bad cases of perceptual belief, then he will have shown that the response he gives to skepticism in his book is not *required* to account for how perception can justify us in believing propositions about the external world. That is the problem Williamson would encounter if he denies premise (2), thereby endorsing a claim that entails that no evidence provided by my *knowing* external-world propositions is required for me to be justified in believing not BIV. So it would seem that Williamson is constrained to accept premise (2) on the grounds that I can be justified in believing not BIV only by evidence provided by my knowing external-world propositions—in other words, on the grounds that one cannot have justified beliefs in bad cases unless one has knowledge in good cases. He has a plausible way of making that case, but only if it is plausible for him to claim that it is impossible for me to believe Cube if I have been a brain in a vat my whole life. We know the twin-earth case to be made for that impossibility; the trouble is that there is some doubt about how good it is when applied to propositions like Cube or BIV. On the other hand, if it is possible only for the recently envatted to believe propositions like Cube, then Williamson might reasonably argue, say, that it is precisely by virtue of knowledge gained in good cases that one can be justified in believing that one is not a brain in a vat.[9] In any case, I propose that this issue be bracketed for the rest of this chapter and that we proceed on the assumption that Williamson can justify his accepting (2) provided he can justify his not accepting (3).

So how, specifically, might Williamson argue against premise (3) of External World? It would not be eristically effective to argue against (3) in a way that presupposed that I was justified in believing Cube, but, if Williamson is justified in doubting (3), then he should have at hand an argument to show that the EPH skeptic has not shown herself to be warranted in asserting (3). He would have such an argument if he could argue that the EPH skeptic failed to see that there was something other than the mere fact that I am having sensory experiences as of Cube that would be available to justify me in believing Cube if I was in Good and thus knew Cube. And it is apt to seem that Williamson has such an argument if his theory of evidence is correct, an argument that in effect showed that his case against SEA also provided the wherewithal for a case against SJA. The argument to which I allude is as follows:

1*. If I am in Good and thus know Cube, then Cube is conclusive evidence for me that Cube.

2*. If Cube is conclusive evidence for me that Cube, then Cube is available to justify me in believing Cube and thus, via JCB, in believing not BIV.

3*. ∴ That part of SJA is false that claims that whatever can justify me in believing Cube if I am in Good and thus really do know Cube will also be available to justify me in believing Cube if I am in Bad and BIV is true.

4*. The EPH skeptic's case for premise (3) of External World presupposes that false part of SJA.

---

[9] Nico Silins (2005) exaggerates the extent to which having to account for justified beliefs in bad cases is a problem for Williamson.

5*. ∴ The skeptic is unwarranted in asserting premise (3) (since her case for it relies on an unwarranted false assumption).

Let us call this argument W. Might the EPH skeptic have a way to question W?

I think she may; I think she might well have doubts about W's premise (2*). Given that E is conclusive evidence for P for me if my evidence includes E and Prob(P/E) = 1, then it does follow from Williamson's theory that Cube is conclusive evidence for Cube for me. And it does seem right that, if E is conclusive evidence for P for me, then E is a conclusive justification that I have for believing P. But in distinguishing the three justification relations IS, HAS, and IN, we saw that E can be a justification that one has for believing P but yet not be what justifies one *in* believing P, even when one is justified in believing P. So, while Williamson's theory of evidence might entitle him to claim that Cube is a conclusive justification that I *have* for believing Cube, given that I know Cube, he has not *thereby* shown that Cube is available to justify me *in* believing P, given that I know Cube. Even when we grant his theory of evidence, we may still question whether Williamson is in a position to claim that Cube is something that may justify me *in* believing Cube, given that I know Cube.

But is it not *analytic* that, if E is conclusive evidence for P for me, then E at least stands *available*, as things are, to justify me *in* believing P? Actually, it is not true, let alone analytic, that E stands available to justify me in believing P if E is conclusive evidence for P for me. For suppose I see that my patio is wet and on the basis of that evidence come to know, and thus to be justified in believing, that my patio is wet because it rained during the night. If Williamson's EV and E − K are correct, then the fact that my patio is wet because it rained during the night is *conclusive evidence* that my patio is wet; in fact, evidence does not get any better than that. But the fact that my patio is wet because it rained during the night is not—and cannot be, given the facts of the story—what *justifies me in believing* that my patio is wet. What justifies me in believing that my patio is wet, and all that is available in the circumstances to justify me in believing that my patio is wet, is that I saw that it was.

In fact, Williamson himself implicitly acknowledges that E's being conclusive evidence for x for P does not secure that E stands available to justify x in believing P. The following passage leaves little doubt that Williamson would agree that the awkward symmetry noted in the patio example presents a counterexample to the claim that, if E is conclusive evidence for P for me, then E is available to justify me in believing P:

If all knowledge is evidence, then EV . . . [has] the effect of making evidential interconnections within one's knowledge symmetric. For Prob(P/Q) > Prob(P) if and only if Prob(P & Q) > Prob(P)Prob(Q); since the latter condition is symmetric in P and Q, Prob(P/Q) > Prob(P) if and only if Prob(Q/P) > Prob(Q). Thus, given that S's evidence includes both P and Q, P is evidence for Q for S if and only if Q is evidence for P for S by EV. Consequently, given that one knows P and Q and that all knowledge is evidence,

EV implies that if P is evidence for Q for one then Q is evidence for P for one. We could avoid this result by modifying EV. For example, we could stipulate that E is evidence for H for S only if S's belief in E does not essentially depend on inference from H. But it might be neater to retain EV unmodified and say that E is *independent* evidence for H for S only if S's belief in E does not essentially depend on inference from H. (p. 204)

If we accept Williamson's theory of evidence, then in Good Cube is conclusive evidence for Cube for me. But we have just seen that even Williamson must admit that something can be conclusive evidence for P for me yet incapable of justifying me in believing P. So, given that we accept Williamson's theory of evidence and given that E is conclusive evidence for P for me, *what else* must be true of E in order for it to be able to justify me in believing P?

Williamson's "independent-evidence" fix suggests that he would say:

E justifies S in believing P *only if* E is *independent* evidence for P for S,

from which it follows that

Even if E is extremely strong or conclusive evidence for P for S, E is incapable of justifying S in believing P if E is not independent evidence for P for S.

(E is *independent evidence* for P for S if and only if (i) E is evidence for P for S and (ii) S does not believe E on the basis of P ("S's belief in E does not essentially depend on inference from" P).)

Can we also say that

E is capable of justifying S in believing P *if* E is extremely strong or conclusive *independent* evidence for P for S,

or are there still further necessary conditions that extremely strong or conclusive independent evidence must satisfy if it is to be capable of justifying S in believing P? I believe that the following three examples show that the displayed condition is false and that, therefore, some further condition is required.

Raven example. Suppose I know that the next observed raven will be black on the basis of knowing that all observed ravens have been black. It is surely preposterous to say that even part of what justifies me in believing that the next observed raven will be black is that the next observed raven will be black (what justifies me in believing that the next observed raven will be black is that all observed ravens have been black). But the fact that the next observed raven will be black is for me conclusive independent evidence that the next observed raven will be black.

Smithers example. I know (because his instructor told me) that Smithers failed his logic final and on that basis know, and am justified in believing, that a D is the best grade he can receive in the course (D, for short). I also independently know that Smithers did not study for the final, and that is pretty good evidence for me that D. But there is this asymmetry between the two evidence facts. The fact that Smithers failed the final has its evidential status for me regardless of whether or not Smithers studied for the final: I can infer D from that whether or not I even believe that he did not study, but I could not infer D from the fact that he did not study unless my reason for believing that he failed the final was just that he did not study for it. Here the fact that Smithers did not study may be strong enough independent evidence for D for me—independent because I did not infer that he did not study from D—but, nevertheless, incapable in the circumstances of justifying me in believing D because of the way it is screened off from the only thing in the circumstances that could justify me in believing D—namely, the fact that Smithers failed the final.

Coke example. I infer, and thereby come to know, that the Coke machine is sold out from the fact that the machine's "Sold Out" sign is lit. I would be justified in inferring that the machine is sold out from the fact that it says it is sold out whether or not the machine is sold out; but, as I have no other way in the circumstances of inferring that the machine is sold out, I justifiably would not believe that the machine was sold out unless I inferred that from the fact that the machine says it is sold out. Now, in the circumstances, the fact that the Coke machine is sold out is conclusive independent evidence for me that the Coke machine is sold out, but that is not what justifies me in believing that the machine is sold out. What justifies me in believing that is that the machine says it is sold out. So, once again, we see that E can be conclusive independent evidence for P for S yet incapable of justifying S in believing P.

Let me suggest then the following criterion, which assumes that Williamson's theory of evidence is correct (and which uses "infer" in Williamson's sense, a sense some might think is better expressed by "on the basis of," especially as regards the way in which sensory experiences function to justify the beliefs they induce[10]):

$E \neq J$ Even if E is very strong or conclusive independent evidence for P for S in circumstances C, E is incapable of justifying S in believing P in C if in C there is evidence E' such that (i) S can become justified in believing P in C only by inferring P from E', and (ii) S's becoming justified in believing P in C by inferring P from E' doesn't depend on E's being true.

Thus, in the raven example, E = P = the fact that the next observed raven will be black, and E' = the fact that all observed ravens have been black; in the Smithers example, E = the fact that Smithers did not study for the final, E' = the fact that Smithers failed the final; and P = the proposition that a D is the best grade Smithers can receive in the course; and, in the Coke example,

---

[10] Many philosophers think that, e.g., a creature's having a visual experience as of P can justify it in believing P even though it does not know, or even believe, that it is having that visual experience. Williamson must deny this, since he holds that E = K and that only evidence can justify a belief. He argues against the claim that perceptual experience is a kind of non-propositional evidence on pp. 197–200.

E = P = the proposition that the Coke machine is sold out, and E′ = the fact that the machine says that it is sold out.

Now, by definition of Good, I know Cube (= that there is a red cube before me) in Good and do not infer Cube from Cube, and therefore, given Williamson's theory of evidence, Cube is conclusive independent evidence for Cube for me in Good. But if E ≠ J is correct, Cube is not available in Good to justify me in believing Cube. For (i) in Good I come to be justified in believing Cube by inferring it from the fact that I am having such-and-such sensory experiences as of Cube, and I cannot become justified in believing Cube in Good other than by inferring it from that evidence; and (ii) my becoming justified in believing Cube by inferring it from the fact that I am having those sensory experiences does not depend on Cube's being true—I would become justified in believing Cube by that inference even if all else were the same except that Cube was false.

So I provisionally conclude that, while Williamson may have given us reason to disbelieve *SEA*—the assumption that I have the same *evidence* for Cube in Good and in Bad—he has not given us good reason to disbelieve *SJA*—the assumption that what *justifies me in believing* Cube in Good is the same as what justifies me in believing Cube in Bad. Applied to the argument W—the argument one might think one discerns in Williamson—we see that Williamson has not entitled us to think that W is sound, because, even if we concede his theory of evidence and allow that in Good Cube is conclusive evidence for Cube for me, he still has not entitled us believe that premise (2*) is true. Further, since it is plausible that one knows a proposition only if one is justified in believing it, Williamson also has not shown that it is even possible for me to be in Good.

4. SOME POSSIBLE REPLIES

I reckon the probability that Tim Williamson will accept my argument to show that he has not provided a solution to EPH skepticism to be, say, ≤ 0.000013. But *how* will he respond to it? If I have correctly represented how he would respond to EPH skepticism, he must either deny that the application of E ≠ J to Good shows that Cube is incapable of justifying me in believing Cube in Good, or else he must deny the criterion E ≠ J.

There are in principle two ways to deny my claim about the application of E ≠ J to Good. One might deny that condition (i) is satisfied by arguing that I can become justified in believing Cube in Good in some way other than by inferring it from Experience (= the fact that I am having such-and-such sensory experiences as of Cube), or one might deny that condition (ii) is satisfied by arguing that Cube does have to be true in order for me to become justified in believing Cube in Good by inferring it from Experience. Both ways seem unpromising to me.

The first way requires my becoming justified in believing Cube in some way other than by inference from Experience. What could such a way possibly be? It cannot be that one becomes justified in believing Cube in Good by *inferring* it from Cube. If one did infer Cube from itself, then Cube would not be *independent* evidence for itself, and thus, evidently, ruled out on that account as being that which justifies me in believing it. There are cases where it is perhaps not unreasonable to suppose that the fact that P justifies believing P. One might hold that what justifies one in believing that one is in pain is just the fact that one is in pain. But, in the first place, perceptual beliefs do not seem at all like that, and, in the second place, Williamson seems not to be in a position felicitously to hold even that the fact that Sally is in pain justifies her in believing that she is in pain. For what is not altogether implausible is that what justifies Sally in believing that she is in pain is just the fact that she is in pain; but it does not seem at all plausible that what justifies Sally in believing that she is in pain is that she knows that she is in pain and infers that she is in pain from the fact that she is in pain. One can hardly become justified in believing a proposition by inferring it from itself. I suppose Williamson would have to say that Sally has underived knowledge that she is in pain and that that is what makes her justified in believing that she is in pain. To reconcile this with his doctrine that only evidence can justify, he could say that the fact that she is in pain justifies her in believing that she is in pain somehow by virtue of its being conclusive evidence that she is in pain, but not by virtue of her *inferring* that she is in pain from that evidence. One wants to hear more, but in any case the model does not fit my knowing Cube by perception.

The second way to deny my claim about the application of E ≠ J to Good—denying that condition (ii) is satisfied—strikes me as even more unpromising. If I am not justified in believing Cube in Bad, it will be because the EPH skeptical argument is sound. If it is possible for me to be justified in believing Cube at all, then I am surely justified in believing it in Bad. Should I learn that BIV was true, I certainly would not conclude that I was not justified in believing Cube. But if I am justified in believing Cube in Bad, then it is surely by inference (given Williamson's theory of evidence, which I am taking as given). So, as Cube is false in Bad, Cube's being true cannot be a necessary condition of my becoming justified in believing Cube by inferring it from Experience. And, if it is not a necessary condition in that way in Bad, then it is very implausible that something about Good makes it a necessary condition in Good.

So much for denying the application of E ≠ J to Good. Perhaps denying the criterion E ≠ J will yield a more promising response. There are, after all, prima facie counterexamples to E ≠ J. For example, when asked what justifies him in thinking that Alice kissed Ben, it might be appropriate for Harold to reply that Alice informed him that she kissed Ben. Harold would not have come to believe that Alice kissed Ben by inferring that Alice kissed Ben from the proposition that

Alice informed him that she kissed Ben, since in order for him to believe that Alice *informed* him that she kissed Ben he would already have to believe that Alice kissed Ben. This is apt to appear to be a counterexample to E ≠ J because the fact that Alice informed Harold that she kissed Ben is conclusive evidence that she kissed Ben (x informed y that P entails P), but in the circumstances Harold could become justified in believing that Alice kissed Ben only by inferring that she did from the evidence that she *told* him that she kissed Ben, and Harold's becoming justified in that way in believing that Alice kissed Ben does not depend on its being true that Alice kissed Ben.[11]

It is unclear whether the example provides a counterexample because being asked what justifies someone in believing a proposition is a request for an explanation, and we often appropriately respond to such questions in ways that do not actually give the correct explanation or give the explanation embedded in information that is not essential to the explanation, as when we explain that the car will not start because something is wrong with the ignition, or that the window broke because your niece Wilma kicked her new orange soccer ball into the window. Still, a more systematic way of challenging E ≠ J might proceed in the following way:

> We need to distinguish *the way in which* x becomes justified in believing P from *that which* justifies x in believing P. The idea is that while I become justified in believing Cube in the same way both in Good and in Bad—namely, by inferring Good from Experience—the justification I acquire in that way in Good differs crucially from that which I acquire in Bad. Roughly speaking, the justification I acquire in Good includes the justification I acquire in Bad, but has as an additional component the fact that Cube. I gain one justification for believing Cube when I infer it from Experience, but I gain an even better one when the fact that I had such-and-such sensory experiences as of Cube was caused by the fact that there was a red cube before me. Both in Good and in Bad I become justified in believing Cube by inferring it from Experience, but in Bad the justification I have for believing Cube consists just in the fact that I had such-and-such sensory experiences as of a red cube, whereas in Good it also contains the additional evidence for Cube that is owed to the fact that my having such-and-such sensory experiences as of a red cube was caused by the fact that there was a red cube before me.

There may be more than one thing wrong with this response, but the main thing wrong with it is that (*a*) I would not be justified in being more confident of Cube in Good than I am in Bad, but (*b*) I would be so justified if I had a better justification, one based on better evidence, for believing Cube in Good than I

---

[11] This sort of example was pressed on me by Anna-Sara Malmgren and Nico Silins.

have for believing it in Bad.[12] Let me motivate (*a*) by starting with a change of example.

I wake up one February morning and look out the window. I see that Washington Square Park and the surrounding streets are covered in snow, and I infer that it snowed during the night. I have no positive reason, skepticism aside, to suspect that it did not snow, but of course I am aware of the *possibility* of various ways in which, compatible with what I seem to see, it did not snow during the night, and thus the degree of confidence that I am justified in having is less than complete confidence, though still pretty high. Let us pretend that degrees of confidence can be measured by real numbers in the interval [0, 1] and suppose I am justified in being confident to degree 0.93 that it snowed during the night. Now, my description of the scenario is compatible with two more complete descriptions of it. In one, it did snow during the night, and that is why I see the snow. In this completion, I count as knowing that it snowed during the night. In the other completion, though I had no reason at all to suspect it, the snow did not fall from the sky but was artificially manufactured and placed on the ground by a film crew that was not visible when I saw the snow. By construction of the example, I remain confident to degree 0.93 that it snowed in both completions. I submit that my being justified in having that degree, but no greater degree, of confidence is unaffected by which completion obtains. The parallel with the ongoing Cube example should be obvious. I seem to see a red cube before me and I have no reason (skepticism aside) to doubt that my experience is veridical other than my knowledge of the possible ways in which it might not be. So I am not justified in being absolutely confident that there is a red cube before me, but I am justified in being pretty confident. Let us say I am confident to degree 0.93. I submit that I remain justified in having that degree, but no greater degree, of confidence in Cube, whether the completing description of my situation places me in Good or in Bad.

So much for (*a*). Might (*b*) be denied? If my justification for believing Cube in Good is better than my justification for believing it in Bad, then I am more justified in believing Cube in Good than I am in Bad. By construction of the example, my degree of confidence in Cube is the same in both Good and Bad. If I am more justified in believing Cube in Good than I am in Bad, then I *should* be more confident of Cube in Good. If I am less confident than I should be, then I am not justified in having the degree of confidence I have. As Silins makes clear,[13] it would be rather bizarre to hold that my degree of confidence in Cube is justified in Bad but not in Good. I see no reason to suppose I am doing anything epistemically wrong in Good. On the contrary, what would be epistemically wrong would be for me to be more confident of Cube in Good than I am.

---

[12] This objection derives from the "equal-justification" problem Nico Silins (2005) raises for Williamson's theory of evidence.

[13] Silins (2005).

I suppose Williamson must disagree. After all, he says that, for any proposition P, if you know P, then P has evidential probability 1 for you, and he also says that "rationality requires one to conform one's beliefs to one's evidence" (p. 12), where by this he means that "the norm of credence is to proportion one's degree of belief to the evidence."[14] This, I take it, means that rationality requires me to believe Cube to degree 1 in Good. Still, Williamson is explicit about our needing "a conception of rationality on which we are not always in a position to know what it demands" (p. 15). So perhaps he would say that, while I am being perfectly reasonable in believing Cube only to degree 0.93 in Good, this is because I am not in a position to know what rationality requires of me. But it is not clear that he can say that. When Williamson acknowledges that we are not always in a position to know what rationality requires of us, in requiring us to respect our evidence, it is because we are not always in a position to know what our evidence is. Now, for Williamson, who holds that E = K, if I do not know what my evidence is, this can only be because I do not know what I know. But, in a normal case of Good, I would not only know Cube, but would also know that I know Cube, and therefore I *would* know what my evidence is, and thus, presumably, *would* be in position to know what rationality requires of me. Could he argue that I might know what my evidence is but still not know what rationality requires of me, either because I do not know that the probability of Cube on my evidence is 1 or that I do not know that "the norm of credence is to proportion one's degree of belief to the evidence"? I doubt it. I doubt that Williamson would want to say that the only people who are in a position to know what rationality requires of them are those who accept his theory of evidence and rationality. In believing Cube to degree 0.93 in Good, I seem neither to be acting irrationally nor failing to know what rationality requires of me. I see no reason to doubt that appearance.[15]

[14] Williamson (2005b: 432).

[15] Earlier versions of this chapter were given as talks at Rutgers University and the University of St Andrews, and presented in a seminar I gave at NYU, all in fall 2005. The final version benefited from the discussions at those events, and from written communications or comments from Adam Elga, John Hawthorne, Anna-Sara Malmgren, Nico Silins, and Dean Zimmerman.

12

Timothy Williamson's *Knowledge and its Limits*

Ernest Sosa

Timothy Williamson's *Knowledge and its Limits* brilliantly interweaves themes
from epistemology and philosophy of mind, for a radically new position that
brings together two disciplines somewhat distanced in recent decades.[1] As part
of that effort, Williamson argues that knowledge is a mental state, powerfully
challenging the widespread assumption that knowledge is mental only by courtesy
of the contained belief. The *natural* view, we are told, is that knowledge is a
mental state as fully as any propositional attitude.

> If the content of a mental state can depend on the external world, so can the attitude to
> that content. Knowledge is one such attitude. One's knowledge that it is raining depends
> on the weather; it does not follow that knowing that it is raining is not a mental state.
> The natural assumption is that sentences of the form 'S knows *p*' attribute mental states
> just as sentences of the forms 'S believes *p*' and 'S desires p' do.   (p. 6)[2]

Believing truly, on the other hand, is not a mental state, and hence not an
attitude (except by courtesy of the contained believing). This becomes important
for the book's later attempt to characterize knowledge as the most general factive,
stative attitude, the most general stative attitude that one can have only to true
propositions. If believing truly were a stative attitude, then believing truly would
be a more general factive stative attitude than knowledge, which would falsify
the account of knowledge.

Ideally, a claim that knowledge is a mental state would rest on a well-founded
account of what makes a state mental, and as usual Williamson does not
disappoint. He gives an account of the mentality of states, by way of a theory of
the mentality of concepts, one founded on a distinction between those that are
intuitively mental and those that are not.

---

[1] As compared with the time of, say, Sellars's "Empiricism and the Philosophy of Mind" (1956),
though the work of Davidson, Dretske, Goldman, McDowell, Pollock, and Stich, among others,
has sustained the connection all along.
[2] Parenthetical references in the text are to Williamson (2000).

This chapter has four parts. The first lays out Williamson's account of mental concepts and mental states, and his characterization of knowledge as the most general factive stative attitude. The second problematizes the account of mental states and the characterization of knowledge, and offers an alternative account of when a state is *purely* mental; according to this account, knowledge really is mental only by courtesy of the contained belief (an internalist intuition opposed to the externalism featured in the book). The third part reflects on possible sources and support for such a conception of the purely mental. The fourth and last part takes up the KK principle, Williamson's reductio of it, and the consequences of that for the possibility of reflective knowledge.

1. WILLIAMSON'S ACCOUNT

a. Mental Concepts and Mental States

The concept *mental state* can at least roughly be defined in terms of the concept *mental concept of a state*: a state is mental if and only if there could be a mental concept of that state.   (p. 28)

If the concept C is the conjunction of the concepts $C_1, \ldots, C_n$, then C is mental if and only if each C_i is mental.   (p. 29)

[The] metaphysical contrast [between kinds of mental states] does not immediately entail the conceptual contrast. Nevertheless, it is hard to see why someone should accept one contrast without accepting the other. If the concept *believes truly* is non-mental, its imagined necessary coextensiveness with a mental concept would be a bizarre metaphysical coincidence. If the concept *know* were a non-mental concept of a mental state, its necessary coextensiveness with a mental concept would be an equally bizarre metaphysical coincidence.   (p. 29)

On this basis an important contrast is drawn between knowing and believing truly. Knowing that snow is white qualifies as a mental state or attitude while believing truly that snow is white does not. We can factor believing truly into the belief part and the truth part, but we cannot factor knowing similarly. *S believes truly that snow is white* is tantamount to the conjunction *S believes that snow is white and it is true that snow is white*, the second conjunct of which is non-mental. Accordingly, the *concept* of believing truly that snow is white fails to be mental. As for the *state* of believing truly that snow is white, that will be mental only if some other concept of that state, other than that of believing truly, is mental. But there is no apparent reason to think that there is any such concept.

b. A Characterization of Propositional Knowledge

Factive attitudes are ones we can have only to truths: for example, perceiving that such and such, and remembering that such and such. Some such attitudes are states, 'stative' attitudes. Knowing, we are told, is the most general factive stative attitude, the one you must bear to a truth if you bear to that truth any of the others.

So much for what a factive stative attitude is, and for the place of knowledge among such attitudes. Now, a factive stative attitude is characteristically expressed in language by means of a *factive mental state operator* (an FMSO). Syntactically these function like verbs, semantically they are unanalysable: that is to say, no such operator is "synonymous with any complex expression whose meaning is composed of the meanings of its parts" (p. 34). Any such operator Ø must also meet three further conditions:

First, Ø typically takes as subject a term for something animate and as object a term consisting of 'that' followed by a sentence. Second, Ø is factive, in the sense that the form of inference from 'S Øs that A' to 'A' is deductively valid . . . Third, 'S Øs that A' attributes a propositional attitude to S.   (pp. 34–5)

The ensuing discussion of FMSOs may be summarized as follows (as it is by Williamson on p. 39): *'Know' is an FMSO, and if Ø is an FMSO, then from 'S Øs that A' one may infer both 'A' and 'S knows that A.'* "In the material mode, the claim is that knowing is the most general stative propositional attitude such that, for all propositions p, necessarily if one has it to p then p is true" (p. 39).

It is crucial that 'believes truly' *not* count as an FMSO. From 'knows' one may infer 'believes truly' but the converse inference is invalid. If 'believes truly' were an FMSO, therefore, believing truly would be a more general stative propositional attitude than knowing, so knowledge would not be the most general such attitude, and the account would be refuted. Williamson recognizes this threat and blocks it by requiring that FMSOs be semantically unanalysable, a condition that 'believes truly' does not meet.

So I begin by focusing on two main ideas in the book. First is the idea that knowledge is a mental state as fully as belief or any other propositional attitude. Second is the characterization of knowledge as the most general factive stative attitude.

2. A CRITIC'S CRITICAL COMMENTS

a. Safe Belief and The Account of Knowledge as The Most General Factive Stative Attitude

Consider first how to understand *safe* belief, which is a kind of reliable belief. As we are reminded later in the book, the "argument of Chapters 4 and 5 connected knowledge and safety. If one knows, one could not easily have been wrong in a similar case" (p. 147). According to Chapter 5, "one avoids false belief reliably in [a given case alpha] if and only if one avoids false belief in every case similar enough to [alpha]" (p. 124). Compare with this the following two conditions:

(i) One would believe p only if it were true (or, alternatively, one would not believe p without its being true).
(ii) Not easily would one believe p without being right.

A belief safe in sense (ii) can still be false, so long as it is of a relevant sort enough instances (or a sufficient proportion) of which would be true. But Williamson's notion of safe belief requires (i), not just (ii). It requires that one avoid false belief in *every* case similar enough to the actual case of belief. And there is no case more similar to the actual case than the actual case. So if a belief is *safe* then it must be true.

That being so, safe belief is itself a factive stative attitude if a stative attitude at all. Williamson hence could not consistently allow that knowing implies safe believing without insisting also that safe believing implies knowing. Once it is allowed that knowing implies safe believing, then only if *safely believes* is another concept of the state of knowledge will the theory stand firm in all its main components. For, if safe believing, the state, is entailed by knowing without entailing it, then it is a more general factive stative attitude than knowledge. So knowledge could not then be the most general such attitude.[3]

Based on a requirement of safety, Williamson attacks the luminosity of our mental states, and the myth of the given. Simple safety is dubious as a general requirement for propositional knowledge, however, and Williamson's attack has

---

[3] It might be replied that 'safely believes that p' is not an FMSO, since it is semantically analysable. In considering this reply, let us first recall that semantic analysability is distinguished in the book from syntactical complexity. Thus, we are told that 'She could feel that the bone was broken' is (roughly) synonymous with 'She knew by the sense of touch that the bone was broken'. Compare 'She could hear that the volcano was erupting' which is said to be synonymous with 'She knew by the sense of hearing that the volcano was erupting'. These are said nevertheless to be semantically fused, unanalysable. In what respect, however, is 'safely believes that p' different from 'knows by the sense of touch that p' so that the former is semantically analysable though the latter is not?

It is open to doubt that 'safely believes that p' is semantically analysable and fails for that reason to be an FMSO. But, if it is an FMSO, then safe belief bids fair to be a factive stative attitude, in which case the account of knowledge as the most general such attitude will stand only if the concept *safely believes* is necessarily equivalent to the concept *knows*. Once committed to the necessary equivalence of *knows* with *safely believes*, one might well claim a solution to the Gettier problem, an analysis of knowledge. Not an analysis in any sense that would require analysans and analysandum to be synonyms (or at least the corresponding expressions in the expression of the analysis to be such), but this has not been the objective since the early days of the Gettier project. Rather it would be an analysis through being an interesting necessary biconditional, especially a non-circular one. It would be tempting now to say that knowledge is just equivalent to safe belief, which would save the account of knowledge as the most general factive stative attitude. Unfortunately, safe belief is clearly not equivalent to knowledge, since belief in any necessary truth would seem safe no matter how ill-formed, as is belief in contingent propositions such as the one that you affirm in thinking you have a brain.

been rebutted through rejection of simple safety.[4] Nevertheless, the attack can be mounted through a more defensible requirement of aptness, according to which, in order to know that p, one must believe aptly that p—that is to say, the correctness of one's belief that p must be attributable to an epistemic competence exercised through that belief.[5] A deep problem for the attack on the given remains nonetheless—namely, that the concept of luminosity invoked by Williamson is unfairly and implausibly strong. By his lights what is required to make a condition luminous is that one could not possibly be in it without being in a position thereby to know that one is in it. However, a much more reasonable requirement is weaker—namely, that a condition is quasi-luminous only if there is a degree to which one can be in it, such that, if one is in it at least to that degree, then one is in a position to know that one is in it (NB: 'that one is in it,' *not*: 'that one is in it to that degree'). Of course, 'luminous' is a technical term with a stipulated meaning. Why then is it 'much more reasonable' to invoke the broader quasi-luminosity? Because this seems so much the more charitable way of understanding the doctrines of cognitive home and the given that are put in question by reference to luminosity.[6]

That is an initial sketch of the position. We might then approach the question whether knowledge is a mental state as follows:

(a) X is a mental state only if *consciously X'ing* is quasi-luminous.
(b) Consciously knowing is not quasi luminous.
(c) So, knowing is not a mental state.

Consciously knowing is not a quasi-luminous mental state either because it does not have degrees, or because, although it does have at least one degree, it does not meet the other requirements specified above.

b. The Purely Mental

Closely related to our present discussion is a further question also taken up by Williamson: namely, whether there is some core of purely mental states that excludes knowledge. Here now is my text for the discussion to follow:

What is at stake is much more than whether we apply the word 'mental' to knowing. If we could isolate a core of states which constituted pure mind by being mental in some more thoroughgoing way than knowing is, then the term 'mental' might be extended to knowing as a mere courtesy title. On the conception defended here, there is no such core of mental states exclusive of knowing. If we want to illustrate the nature of mentality, knowing is as good an example as believing . . . For similar reasons, other truth-entailing

---

    [4] See Neta and Rohrbaugh (2004).
    [5] I argue extensively for the substitution in Sosa (2007), the 2005 Locke Lectures.
    [6] Of course, it remains to be seen whether one's states of knowing qualify as quasi-luminous so as to give us an access to them no less privileged than the access we enjoy to our mental states generally.

attitudes such as perceiving and remembering that something is the case may also be classified as mental states. Knowing can be understood as the most general of such truth-entailing mental states.   (p. 6)

Williamson thinks it impossible to isolate any such core of purely mental states. His strategy is to view the mentality of a state as requiring that there could be a mental concept of that state. But a concept is mental only if it is *not* a conjunction of concepts at least one of which is non-mental. Using this basic strategy for conceiving of pure mentality, it is argued persuasively that there is no notion of the purely mental that excludes knowing from that inner core.

However, there is an alternative way of understanding degrees of purity. Token cases of knowing are token cases of believing that satisfy some further conditions.[7] For example, I argue elsewhere that a belief—that is, a token believing—qualifies as an instance of animal knowledge only if it is a believing that gets it right because of how it manifests a competence of the believer's. (But the point to follow could be made equally well if we preferred to require truth + justification, or having been reliably formed, and so on.) Still, the very token believing that is knowledge might have failed to be knowledge, since it might have been false, for one thing, or might not have been right attributably to any competence of the believer's. The state in question would then seem plausibly to be mental because of its being a believing, in such a way that it would have been mental whether it had been a knowing or not, so long as it had been a believing. That token believing could not possibly have been mental in virtue of being a knowing, however, without being mental in virtue of being a believing. Besides, the mental-making power of its property of being a knowing is plausibly inherited from the mental-making power of its property of being a believing. The token state is, after all, both a believing and a knowing, and it is guaranteed to be a mental state by each of those properties. But it could not have been mental in virtue of being a knowing without being mental in virtue of being a believing, whereas it would have been mental in virtue of being a believing whether it had been a knowing or not. Moreover, it would have been mental whether it had been safe or not, so long as it had been a believing.[8] So its mentality would seem to derive from its being a believing. Its being a believing

---

[7] Although the argument to follow is put in terms of token states, I believe that to be inessential. It could be made in terms of mental states directly, where some states, such as belief, are entailed by other states, such as knowing, with the same content.

[8] Or, to detach from tokens, when one knows one would have mentalized (would have been in a mental state) by being in the entailed belief state, whether one had been in a state of knowing or not, but one would not have been in a mental state of knowing except by being in a mental state of believing with the same content. So one mentalizes by virtue of believing and by virtue of knowing, but one would have mentalized by virtue of so believing whether one had so known or not, whereas one could not have mentalized by virtue of so knowing without mentalizing by virtue of so believing.

that is safe and amounts to knowledge seems inconsequential vis-à-vis whether it is mental or not.[9]

That at least is how on the surface it would *seem*, but there is some subtlety beneath that surface. For convenience we are coining the term 'mentalizing' for being in a mental state or engaging in some mental activity. Our question then is whether knowing is subserved by a more thoroughgoing way of mentalizing, in such a way that to know is to mentalize only by courtesy.

Compare ways of being coloured (*chromatically* coloured). A surface can be coloured by being red, for example, or, alternatively, by being blue. Of course, it can in turn be red by being, more specifically, scarlet. Plausibly, being scarlet is a way, a more specific way, of being coloured. And this is so even in the case of something that is both red and scarlet. Despite the fact that this surface would still have been coloured even if it had not been scarlet but only red, nevertheless it is coloured by being scarlet, and in virtue of being scarlet; and being scarlet is a specific way of being coloured.

Compare, further, ways of being shaped. Something can be 'shapely' (*regularly* shaped) by being spherical, or, alternatively, by being cubical. Of course, it can also be *surprisingly* spherical. And, necessarily, if surprisingly spherical, then it is spherical. Moreover, it might be spherical without being surprisingly spherical. In some sense, however, being surprisingly spherical is not a more determinate shape property, nor a species of shapeliness. And this remains so even if the property of being surprisingly spherical cannot be factored into a pure shape component, and, as a separate (conjunctive) factor, some non-shape component involving surprise.

I submit that knowing is to mentalizing as being surprisingly spherical is to being shaped, and not as being scarlet is to being coloured. Knowing is not a more specific way of mentalizing, just as being surprisingly spherical is not a species of shapeliness. *Knowing* is mental by courtesy of the involved believing

---

[9] An entity's mentality might be viewed as a fundamental, intrinsic, and even essential category of it, as it was by Descartes. Alternatively, the entity might be viewed as fundamentally only physical, and mental in virtue of some contingent, perhaps relational properties of it, as it is by physicalists. If we take the second view, then a state's mentality is not a fundamental property of the state. Mentality, the purity thereof, and the lack thereof, may even concern in the first instance only our concepts. Williamson shows signs of *perhaps* viewing things this way in defining mentality directly for concepts and indirectly for states. A state is said to be mental if there could be a mental concept of it. Now this will in any case depend on what it means for a concept to be *of* a state. One thing it cannot mean is simply that it refers to the state. For the state of the earth of its now quaking is not made mental by being the one that the victims are now thinking about as such a state. What then is it that makes a state one of which a concept is a concept? Perhaps the realizer of a functional concept is a state of which the functional concept is a concept? But then it is hard to set limits on what could possibly be a mental concept. Who knows what possible superphysical entities might realize mental concepts through earthly quaking? And, besides, a single physical state could realize several non-equivalent functional concepts, whereas for Williamson concepts are of the same state only if necessarily coextensive. So I confess to some unclarity on what sort of framework of states and their concepts is used in the book, and in particular on what makes a concept a concept of a certain state.

analogously to how *surprising sphericity* is a shape state by courtesy of the involved sphericity.

Even someone who shares that intuition might well wonder, however, what more generally lies behind it. What accounts for it? What is it that distinguishes the relation between surprising sphericity and sphericity from the relation between being scarlet and being coloured? One relevant difference is that the surprisingness of the sphericity of a sphere is somehow extrinsic to its sphericity, while the scarletness of the scarlet chromaticity of a surface is not similarly extrinsic to its chromaticity, but is simply a more specific form of the chromaticity.

The proposal is then that knowings can be such *in part* by virtue of being believings that satisfy such further conditions as safety and truth, even if there is no factorization of knowledge into some set of such conditions, where the believing is isolated from all other components. This is similar to how something can be surprisingly spherical in part by virtue of the fact that its sphericity is or would be surprising, even if there is no relevant factorization of being surprisingly spherical into some set of such conditions, one that isolates the sphericity from all other components.

We are thus free to insist that, just as being surprisingly spherical is not a more specific form of being shapely (regularly shaped) by comparison with being spherical, so knowing is not a more specific way of being mental, by comparison with believing. This lends plausibility to the notion that knowing is mental if at all then only by courtesy of the involved believing, just as being surprisingly spherical is a regular-shape state if at all then only by courtesy of the involved sphericity.

3. FURTHER REFLECTIONS

I confess that it is not yet clear to me how much turns on this issue of taxonomy. Why does it matter just where we draw the boundaries of the purely mental? How does the concept of the mental connect with human concerns so as to sustain our intuitive drawing of the boundaries where we do draw them? What connections with what concerns speak in favour of so drawing them?

Williamson adduces much subtle and persuasive reasoning for the view that factive states are explanatorily relevant beyond any contained non-factive states, and for the view that knowledge in particular is a prime example. But why should that tend to show that knowledge is mental, and mental not just by courtesy of the contained belief? It is not as though only seriously mental states can have explanatory efficacy. If he were right, that would, of course, tend to show that our concepts of factive mental states do connect with important human concerns, those involved in the prediction and explanation of human conduct. What remains unclear is why this should be thought to imply that knowledge, along with other factive stative attitudes, must be mental in the most serious and underivative way. Even less is it clear why, compatibly with its explanatory importance, knowledge cannot be mental only by courtesy of the contained belief.

In addition, other human concerns, besides our interest in the explanation of human conduct, may lead us to distinguish those mental states that are purely mental. Are there such concerns?

Before we go into that question, it bears notice that the distinction between states that are purely mental and those that are not is arguably built into common sense and ordinary language. This would help explain why individuals draw the distinction as they do, but not why the community does so. What wants explaining is why we join together in making the distinction between the mental and the non-mental as we do, and, more specifically, why our relevant intuitions permit a delimitation of the purely mental as above. Assuming we do have such a conception of the purely mental, one may well wonder about its sources. That it is part of common sense and reflected in ordinary language is not the sort of answer sought, since what we want to understand is why we make the distinction as we do intuitively enough that it counts as part of common sense and ordinary language.

Here I would like to sketch one possible source of our interest in the purely mental: namely, its connection with issues of basic normative responsibility, of proper praise or blame, or at least of proper admiration and contempt. Plausibly it is to the purely mental that we look for basic determinants of such responsibility. This is a possible source of our distinction, or at least a correlative stance. Consider, for example, the victim of Descartes's evil demon, and focus not just on her beliefs and their epistemic standing, but also on her choices, intentions, policies, and character. Detached from physical surroundings, her mental states and episodes, practical and theoretical, could not have their normal consequences, and may be entirely ineffectual physically. Nevertheless, is it not powerfully intuitive that such a victim may be no less admirable or contemptible, no less worthy of praise or blame, than a twin so plugged into its surroundings that its mental goings-on do have their normal physical effects?

This sort of general human concern has a more specific epistemic form, involving our interest in epistemic responsibility, in proper epistemic praise or blame, admiration or contempt. Compatibly with this, our distinction might, of course, also derive from some less direct important sources. For our interest in the assessment of ourselves and our fellows does itself have proper sources of its own, including the desire for self-improvement and the need for proper allocation of trust. In conclusion, I would like to sketch how the more direct sources specified (and their own sources in turn) comport with our account of the purely mental. Consider then our interest in epistemic responsibility, credit and blame, admiration and contempt. How does this interest bear on the richness of our epistemic conceptual repertoire, and specifically on how this repertoire goes beyond the concepts of truth and reliability?

A belief that constitutes knowledge must be appropriately derived. But it is not enough that the process whence it derives be a reliable process. It must also be a process appropriately related to the subject, by manifesting a competence or intellectual virtue seated in that subject. Our epistemic conceptual repertoire permits the assessment of a belief as true, of course, and also as 'reliable'. But these two concepts would yield only an impoverished epistemology. Unless we go beyond them, we would be unable to do justice to the intuitions engaged, for example, by the following two cases.

> *New Evil Demon.* If things appear the same to two subjects from the inside, and if this is so throughout their lives, and if all along they are the same in how they manifest their relevant dispositions to be in purely mental states, then they cannot differ in their respective degrees of justification for any present belief. At least there does seem to be some such internal, or subjective, justification that a belief might have independently of being true or reliable.[10]

> *Clairvoyance.* A belief might be true and even safe despite the subject's lack of justification for hosting it. Because Claire has been blessed with a special faculty that puts her reliably in touch with facts that normal humans so situated could not discern, she finds herself believing things quite reliably and correctly, things that she evidently could not be remembering (by construction of the example). So here would be a sort of case where the reliable (and, of course, correct) believing would come detached from justification (in some appropriate, internal sense).

Various proposals are on offer as to how we might best understand such cases. Here are three examples, each of which profiles a kind of justification allowed to the Demon's victim while denied to Claire the clairvoyant. Each specifies a condition that any belief of yours would have to satisfy in order to be justified.

> *Foley-rationality:* that your belief comport on appropriate reflection with your deepest epistemic standards.

> *Classical foundationalism* (BonJour, Fumerton, Conee, Feldman, Lewis): that your belief relate properly to your evidence, conceived of as your basic experiences (and memories). On one way of developing this approach, the belief must result from appropriately taking the given, either through introspection or through perception, and reasoning properly from there, with the strategic aid of memory all along the way.

> *Virtue contextualism and perspectivism* (disclosure: this is an approach that I myself favour): that your belief derive from the good performance of cognitive virtues seated in the subject (features whose operation would generally deliver relevant epistemic goods, such as truth, in the actual world, for beings of

---

[10] This might be thought incompatible with proper externalist restrictions on concept possession, but similar thought-experiments escape this objection.

your kind in your normal habitat), a fact that does not escape your reflective awareness.[11]

Obviously, these are barely sketches. Still they indicate further epistemic desiderata to which epistemologists have been sensitive. And they all plausibly cater to our interest in self- and fellow-assessment in world-independent respects. Even more than the formalized law, with its multiple practical constraints, common sense is interested not only in successful murders but also in botched attempts, no matter how remotely they may have failed. We are also interested in how well an astronaut performs in simulated flight tests and not just in real-life performance. Or take a thermostat in a display room, which may perform well or ill, even when it is controlling the temperature of no space. Similarly, we can perform epistemically well or ill even if detached from any environment in which that performance would have its characteristic, desired outcome: namely, reasonable, safe, and apt belief—that is, knowledge.

In assessing the performance of the thermostat, in judging it to perform well or ill, we attribute what it does to the device itself as *its* doing. In such assessments of a device, we go by the extent to which the outcome performance derives from its relevant character, from its combination of stable mechanisms (input, processing, and output) whose combined good performance would enable it to work well in securing its proper objectives. ("How are the relevant objectives set, and properly set?" An interesting question, increasingly so as we move from artefacts to animals, humans, groups, and back again.) We *credit* (*blame*) the device for its good (bad) performance under simulation, and on a certain dimension it is no less to its credit (blame) than if it had been a real-life performance.

The concept of the purely mental jibes with this dimension of our self- and fellow-assessment, of what we care about even in a simulational performance. But wherein lies the value of that kind of assessment of one's own actions or states, or those of one's fellows? What is the point of engaging in such assessments? Our interest in them plausibly derives at least in part from our interest in rating ourselves and others as performers in various dimensions. This interest in turn seems plausibly enough to have a variety of sources. It is worth knowing how good we already are if we wish to improve. It is good to know our flaws if we aim to remove them, our strengths if we aim to preserve them. We want to know how reliable our fellows are, especially those we join in common endeavours. It is hard to set limits on our need for such knowledge, moreover, or on the practical potential for such need. So, again, we are interested in our flaws, and in our strengths, along various dimensions of potential accomplishment. That way we can better tell whom to trust in what circumstances. On the present account, assessing offline performance is of interest because it bears on assessment

---

[11] For a discussion of whether and how Alvin Goldman also falls under this approach, see Goldman (2001) and Sosa (2001).

of the performer, who is properly credited or blamed through such assessment. And assessment of the performer is of interest for the reasons specified, among others.

If that is roughly right, does it mean we are treating each other as little better than thermostats? Not at all. The proper dictum is *not* that one must never treat others as means. This would be impossible for social beings to obey. Others must not be treated *only* as means, true enough: one's interactions must be sensitive to the proper intrinsic respect that our rational fellows deserve. But this is not in the least endangered by the analogy between our dimensions of assessment of thermostats, and our dimensions of self- and fellow-assessment in epistemic respects. Whether something is a mere tool and is properly so treated is independent of whether its performances can be evaluated under simulation in ways that matter enough to earn it credit and trust.

4. THE KK THESIS AND THE STATUS OF REFLECTIVE KNOWLEDGE

Internalists tend to like the KK thesis, while externalists tend to reject it. For externalists, knowledge is belief that satisfies external conditions of causation, tracking, or reliability. You do need to *be* awake, of course, in order to know by perception, but you need not know that you are awake. By contrast, internalists require for perceptual knowledge that one know oneself to be awake and not dreaming. Some internalists back up their intuitions with a general principle: *that really knowing requires you to know that you know*, the KK thesis.

As it stands, the KK thesis leads immediately to vicious regress, but a better version avoids the regress:

KK If one knows that p, and considers whether one does, then one knows that one does.

Williamson argues that this still reduces to absurdity if accepted in its full generality. It reduces to absurdity for magnitudes M such that:

W One knows that: if one knows that x does *not* have M to degree i, then x does not have M to degree $i + 1$.[12]

Many magnitudes and measures plausibly fit this bill. Indeed it is difficult to find a magnitude that does not admit a measure under which it plausibly fits our bill.

---

[12] This is not exactly Williamson's formulation, but it is a close relative, and seems plausible enough for present purposes.

So it seems far from generally true that one knows something only if one knows that one knows it.

Williamson's reductio highlights the following form of reasoning:

1. One knows x not to have M to degree 0. (Assumption)
2. One knows 1. (By KK)
3. One knows that if one knows 1, then x does *not* have M to degree 1. (From principle W, above)
4. One deduces from one's knowledge in 2 and 3 that x does *not* have M to degree 1. (Assumption)
5. One knows x not to have M to degree 1. (By intuitive closure)

By iterating such reasoning *mutatis mutandis* one can derive that one knows x not to have M to degree n, for any particular n no matter how high.

That would reduce to absurdity the KK principle, granted just 1 plus an assumption about our limited powers of discrimination and how that affects our reliability and hence our ability to know, an assumption that underlies the truth of 3 and its like. Again, the assumption takes in general the form of principle W above.

The reductio is compelling, which sets a problem for anyone who believes in a bi-level epistemology, with a lower level where only conditions of reliable and rational belief are required, and a higher level that also requires rational awareness of one's reliability. Such reflective knowledge and animal knowledge would seem to differ precisely in that the former requires a KK principle like the following, whereas the latter does not.

KK If one knows that p, and considers whether one does, then one knows that one does.

But this is just what Williamson's reductio would reduce to absurdity, which may seem to render incoherent the very idea of reflective, perspectival knowledge, or at least to gut it of all interest. Would not the internalist be committed to the view that, if one reflectively knows that p, then one reflectively knows that one so knows that p?

In assessing this it helps to focus on the distinction between (rational) animal knowledge, which we may symbolize with the simple K, and reflective knowledge, which we may symbolize as K+.

Both of the following principles would run afoul of the reductio (where we implicitly assume in the antecedent of each that the subject considers whether he knows):

KK Kp only if KKp

K + K+ K + p only if K + K + p

Some "KK principles" still escape the reductio, however, and the one involved in a bi-level epistemology of animal versus reflective knowledge is among those that are safe. Here is a formulation:

K + K K + p only if KKp

The reductio leaves it open that we may have lots and lots of knowledge that we know. It even leaves it open that the cases where we *are* in a position to know that we know vastly outnumber the cases where we are *not*. Accordingly, it is open to us to introduce a level of knowledge, reflective knowledge, that, either definitionally or by trivial implication from its definition, requires that in order *reflectively* to know something you must have animal-level knowledge *that* you know it at that same animal level. In part through animal knowledge that one animal-knows that p, one may thus bootstrap up to *reflective* knowledge that p. And the K + K principle would thus be perfectly safe.

Such a bi-level epistemology, with its animal/reflective distinction, offers a defensible way to meet the severally plausible requirements that seem to clash in the internalism/externalism and the foundationalism/coherentism debates. So it is reassuring to find that its distinctive K + K principle is safe from the otherwise damaging reductio.

Also reassuring, with some irony, is the fact that traditional sceptical reasonings can be revived with unreduced plausibility and remain about as initially threatening against a kind of reflective knowledge thus conceived. For example, it will still be a problem to see how one can avoid vicious circularity in ascending from animal knowledge that p to rationally defensible knowledge that one enjoys such knowledge through one's actual complement of faculties or virtues.[13, 14]

---

[13] "Animal" knowledge is understood here to require rationality or reasonableness in its constitutive belief; it is this that makes bootstrapping seem vicious, not rationally acceptable, and hence no source of knowledge, not even of the animal grade. That the viciousness is an illusion, both in the Cartesian Circle and in more recent versions of bi-level epistemology is argued in Sosa (1997).

[14] This chapter derives from an APA symposium on Williamson (2000). It has been helpful to discuss these issues with John Hawthorne, Brian McLaughlin, David Sosa, and Tim Williamson.

13

Are Mental States Luminous?

Matthias Steup

1. AGAINST LUMINOSITY

In *Knowledge and its Limits* Timothy Williamson gives a fascinating argument against the claim that mental states or conditions are luminous. He defines luminosity as follows: 'A condition C is luminous iff for every case α, if in α C obtains, then in α one is in a position to know that C obtains' (Williamson 2000: 95).

Suppose headaches are luminous. If so, then whenever one has a headache 'no obstacle blocks the path to knowing' that one has a headache (Williamson 2000: 95). To acquire knowledge of one's headache, one merely needs to consider whether one has a headache. Obviously, non-mental conditions are not luminous. Consider the presence of milk in my refrigerator. My refrigerator's having milk in it is not a luminous condition, since I am not *always* in a position to know whether it obtains. For example, right now I have forgotten whether there is milk in the fridge. Hence I am not, right now, in a position to know whether there is milk in the fridge. I would have to go and look.

To show that mental conditions are not luminous, Williamson considers a particular example of a mental condition, that of *feeling cold*, and argues that it is not luminous. From this he generalizes: a parallel argument can be made for any other mental condition. Hence we get the result that no mental conditions are luminous.

For the purpose of deriving the conclusion that feeling cold is not luminous, Williamson describes a case, subsequently referred to as case α, in which 'one feels cold at dawn, very slowly warms up, and feels hot by noon' (Williamson 2000: 94). The case is divided into a series of times t_0, t_1, ..., t_n leading in one-millisecond intervals from dawn to noon. So α_0 is the case at dawn, α_n is the case at noon, and α_i is the case at a time t_i where $0 \leq i \leq n$. The noteworthy features of the case are the following:

(i) In α_0 one feels cold.

(ii) In α_n one does not feel cold.

(iii) One's feelings of heat and cold change so slowly during this process that one is not aware of any change in them over one millisecond. (NAC, for no awareness of change.[1])

(iv) Throughout the process one thoroughly considers how cold or hot one feels.

Features (i) through (iv) are meant to describe an ordinary case in which nothing controversial is going on. The argument based on this case is of the reductio type. Williamson asks us to assume that feeling cold is a luminous condition. Given assumption (iv), if feeling cold is luminous, then at any given time during the dawn–noon interval at which one feels cold, one knows one feels cold. Thus we have:

(L) If (cold) in a_i, then K(cold) in a_i.[2]

In addition to (L), Williamson assumes a second key premiss—namely

(R) If K(cold) in a_i, then (cold) in a_{i+1}.

Given (L) and (R), we can derive that one feels cold in a_n. This contradicts assumption (ii). Hence we must conclude that either (L) or (R) is false. Williamson claims that we must select (L) as the culprit since (R) is backed up by solid reasons. Let us first see how the conjunction of (L) and (R) produces the contradictory outcome that one believes one is cold in a_n. Then we will have a look at Williamson's argument for (R).

The contradiction results as follows: Given assumption (i) and (L), we have:

(1) K(cold) in a_0.

Given (1) and (R), we have:

(2) (cold) in a_1.

Given (2) and (L), we have:

(3) K(cold) in a_1.

Given (3) and (R), we have

(4) (cold) in a_2,

and so forth. Eventually, continued applications of (L) and (R) yield the unbecoming outcome:

   (cold) in a_n.

---

[1] Here I am following Ramachandran (2005).
[2] Let '(cold)' stand for 'one feels cold' and 'K(cold)' for 'one knows one feels cold'.

As already mentioned, the unbecoming outcome gives us a reason to reject (L) only if (R) is well defended. What, then, is Williamson's defence of (R)?

Williamson motivates (R) by appeal to the plausible thought that knowledge requires reliability. According to Williamson, this requirement is to be understood as follows:

(P_R1) If one knows that p in a given case, then p is true in every similar case in which one believes that p.

Now suppose we have:

(*a*) K(cold) in a_i.

Since knowledge requires belief, we also have:

(*b*) B(cold) in a_i.[3]

What is going on one millisecond later in a_{i+1}? NAC tells us that, even though in a_{i+1} one feels slightly less cold, one is not aware of this change. Hence, for any interval a_i-a_{i+1} such that B(cold) in a_i, one will in a_{i+1} believe one is cold. So we have:

(*c*) B(cold) in a_{i+1}.

The step from (*a*) to (*c*) supplies Williamson with another premiss:

(P_R2) If K(cold) in a_i then B(cold) in a_{i+1}.

Since cases a_i and a_{i+1} are only one millisecond apart, and since one only feels only slightly less cold in a_{i+1} than one did in a_i, cases a_i and a_{i+1} are very similar. Given that the two cases are similar, (P_R1) and (P_R2) yield (R).

2. NAC: THE NO-AWARENESS-OF-CHANGE ASSUMPTION

How can the luminosity of the mental be defended against Williamson's argument? Since the only substantive premises are (L) and (R), a defence of (L) would have to aim at finding a flaw in Williamson's defence of (R). Some have argued that, in defending (R), Williamson has made questionable assumptions about the nature of knowledge.[4] I will argue that Williamson's defence of

---

[3] Williamson thinks of knowledge requiring confidence rising to the level of belief. In the present context, this terminological difference is irrelevant.

[4] See Brueckner and Fiocco (2002) and Neta and Rohrbaugh (2004).

(R) rests on something else there is good reason to view as problematic—namely, NAC: the assumption that, in case α, there are one-millisecond changes of feeling less cold than before of which one is not aware. Williamson articulates this assumption as follows:

NAC Suppose that one's feelings of heat and cold change so slowly during this process that one is not aware of any change in them over one millisecond. (Williamson 2000: 94)

During the dawn–noon interval, one continuously undergoes changes of feeling less cold than a moment before. Williamson assumes that, for one-millisecond intervals, one is not aware of these changes. There is a weak and a strong sense in which one can fail to be aware of something. I can fail to be aware of something that is right before my eyes simply because, owing to inattention, I did not notice it. For example, there might be an empty coffee cup on my desk without my being aware of it. Although I am not aware of it, I am nevertheless in a position to know that there is an empty cup on my desk. All I need to do is notice it. This example illustrates the weak sense in which I might not be aware of something. In the strong sense, one fails to be aware of something because cognitive access to it is impossible.

When Williamson assumes that in case α there are unnoticed episodes of feeling less cold, he has the stronger sense in mind: in case α, one is not aware of one-millisecond changes because, since they are so short, they are *not noticeable at all*. Lasting only one millisecond, these changes of feeling less cold than before are so tiny that it does not seem to one that one feels less cold than before. In general terms, the point is that, as Williamson himself puts it, 'it is metaphysically possible for experience to appear other than it really is' (Williamson 2000: 474). So according to Williamson, each time in case α a one-millisecond change of feeling less cold than before occurs, one experiences reality other than it really is: it appears to one that no change of feeling less cold has occurred when such a change has in fact occurred.

3. INDISCERNIBLE EPISODES OF FEELING LESS ϕ

Figure 13.1 illustrates, for a mental condition of feeling ϕ, the conception of experience that Williamson assumes.

Consider first one's feeling ϕ. The degree to which one feels ϕ is represented by the distance between the two converging lines. At t_2 the distance between the lines is less than at t_1; so at t_2 one feels less ϕ than one did at t_1. Towards t_4, the lines continually converge; approaching t_4 one feels continually less and less cold. Finally, at t_4, the lines meet; one feels ϕ no longer. Next, consider one's awareness of feeling ϕ. The three intervals t_1-t_2, t_2-t_3, t_3-t_4 represent the smallest possible intervals of noticing a difference in the degree of one's

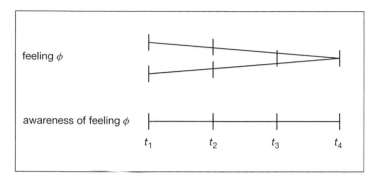

feeling ϕ

awareness of feeling ϕ

t_1 t_2 t_3 t_4

Figure 13.1.

feeling ϕ. Let us call such intervals *minimally discernible* changes, as opposed to *indiscernible* changes. Even though during the t_1-t_2 interval one continues to feel less ϕ, one is not aware of feeling less ϕ until one is at t_2; only then is one aware of feeling less ϕ than one did before. Likewise, one will be aware of feeling less ϕ again only at t_3 and t_4, even though, throughout the t_2-t_4 interval, one has *continuously* felt less ϕ.

So in between each minimally discernible change of feeling ϕ, one undergoes a multitude of *indiscernible* changes of feeling ϕ. That is how we must understand Williamson's key assumption about case a. In case a, we have many intervals of the following kind: in a_{i+1} one feels less cold than one did in a_i, but this change is indiscernible. Therefore, one remains unaware of it. If we assume that a minimally *discernible* change takes at least one second, then we have within that second many *indiscernible* occurrences of feeling less cold than before.

4. LUCY THE LUMINOSITY FRIEND

Next meet Lucy, an advocate of the luminosity of feeling cold in particular and mental states in general. Lucy holds that, according to her conception of what it is to *feel* ϕ, there is no such thing as feeling ϕ without being aware of it. If you are not aware of feeling an itch, then you do not feel an itch. If you are not aware of feeling pain, then you do not feel pain. And if you are not aware of feeling cold, then you do not feel cold. The entailment, according to Lucy, also holds in the opposite direction. If you are aware of feeling pain, then you feel pain, and if you are aware of feeling cold, then you feel cold. In general terms, Lucy holds that there is no feeling ϕ without being aware of feeling ϕ, and no being aware of feeling ϕ without feeling ϕ. In short, feeling ϕ ↔ being aware of feeling ϕ, or $F\phi \leftrightarrow A(F\phi)$.

Matthias Steup

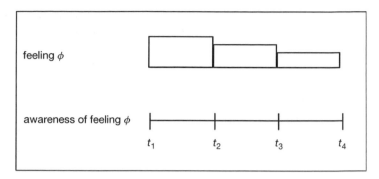

Figure 13.2.

What holds for feeling ϕ, Lucy will say, also holds for *feeling less ϕ than a moment before.*[5] If you are not aware of feeling less cold than a moment before, then you do not feel less cold than a moment before. And if you are aware of feeling less cold than before, then you feel less cold than before. The same applies to other mental changes such as feeling less tired than before, feeling less pain than before, or feeling less hungry than before. In general, feeling less ϕ $\leftrightarrow$ being aware of feeling less ϕ, or $F_L\phi \leftrightarrow A(F_L\phi)$.

Given that Lucy holds $F_L\phi \leftrightarrow A(F_L\phi)$, she will say that the phenomenology of feeling less cold, as illustrated by Figure 13.1, gets things wrong. If in between the times t_1 and t_2 there are no further times at which one is aware of feeling less cold than before, then after t_1 and before t_2 one's feelings of cold and heat remain unchanged between t_1 and t_2. So according to Lucy, the correct phenomenology of feeling less cold is illustrated by Figure 13.2.

Figure 13.2 differs from Figure 13.1 in the following respect: it does not show any indiscernible occurrences of feeling less ϕ. Assume that, at t_1, one feels ϕ to a clearly discernible degree. At t_4 one has stopped feeling ϕ. During the t_1-t_4 interval one's awareness of feeling ϕ changes twice: at t_2 and t_3. One's feeling ϕ also changes twice, namely at the very same times. In between these times, one's awareness of feeling ϕ does not change. Neither does one's feeling ϕ. So one's feeling ϕ and one's awareness of feeling ϕ change concurrently. A change in one does not occur without a change in the other. So, according to Figure 13.2, the smallest changes of feeling ϕ coincide with the minimally discernible changes of feeling ϕ. According to Lucy, that these changes so coincide is a matter of metaphysical necessity. Feeling cold works like that, and so does any other phenomenal mental condition, such as feeling tired, feeling hungry, or feeling pain. So, according to Lucy, when it comes to mental conditions of the feeling ϕ kind, there is no such thing as an indiscernible change. If one feels cold at t_1, and

---

[5] I will use 'feeling less ϕ' as a short for 'feeling less ϕ than a moment before'.

one does not notice any difference in the degree to which one feels cold between t_1 and t_2, then in between t_1 and t_2 the degree to which one feels cold remains unchanged.

Given that Lucy holds $F\phi \leftrightarrow A(F\phi)$ and $F_L\phi \leftrightarrow A(F_L\phi)$, what will she say in response to Williamson's anti-luminosity argument? Obviously, Lucy will say that case a, since it involves episodes of feeling less cold in which one is not aware of feeling less cold, is metaphysically impossible. Lucy will not think, therefore, that Williamson has supplied her with a successful argument against the luminosity of feeling cold in particular and the luminosity of phenomenal mental states in general.

5. TWO READINGS OF NAC

Let us again have a look at the exact wording of the passage in which Williamson articulates NAC: 'Suppose that one's feelings of heat and cold change so slowly during this process that one is not aware of any change in them over one millisecond.' There are two things about this passage that I find problematic. First, the passage is not ideally explicit regarding the assumption Williamson actually employs. Secondly, the appeal to milliseconds does not quite fit the case as described. In this section I will be concerned with the first of these problems. In the next section I will discuss the second.

There are two ways of reading NAC: one utterly innocuous, the other highly controversial. Suppose the following is true:

(1) I am not aware of any change.

The explanation of why (1) is true might simply be that no change has taken place. No such explanation is possible for:

(2) There has been a change of which I am not aware.

If (2) is true, then a change has taken place, and it is a change of which I am not aware. Likewise, if we consider:

NAC* In case a, there are no one-millisecond intervals of feeling less cold of which one is aware,

there is the possibility that NAC* is true for the following reason: one is not aware of any one-millisecond intervals of feeling less cold because no such intervals have occurred. Lucy would find this possibility utterly unobjectionable. On the other hand, we might read NAC this way:

NAC** In case a, there are many one-millisecond changes of feeling less cold than before such that one is not aware of them due to their being indiscernible.

While a luminosity friend like Lucy need not reject NAC*, she will of course reject NAC**. Now, the premiss on which Williamson's argument depends is not NAC* but NAC**. Without the assumption that indiscernible one-millisecond changes of feeling less cold than before actually occur, Williamson will not be able to justify

(P$_R$2) If K(cold) in a_i then B(cold) in a_{i+1}.[6]

But Williamson needs (P$_R$2) for his defence of (R). We must, therefore, interpret NAC as NAC**.

It is important to notice the difference between NAC* and NAC**, because, when reading Williamson's anti-luminosity argument, one might easily interpret NAC as the innocuous NAC*. Not noting that the premiss actually at work in Williamson's argument is NAC**, one might overlook that NAC** is a controversial metaphysical claim. As a result, one might ascribe more strength to the anti-luminosity argument than it really possesses.

6. WARMING UP SLOWLY AND WARMING UP QUICKLY

Let us continue with the second problematic feature of NAC: the choice of milliseconds. For a fast-moving thing such as light, we use a short unit of measurement: the speed of light is 299,792,458 metres per *second*. For comparatively slow-moving objects like cars, cyclists, or pedestrians, we measure their speed in miles or kilometres per *hour*. Suppose a car crashes into a building, coming to an almost instant stop. Since its slowdown is so *fast*, we probably want to measure deceleration in milliseconds. In contrast, suppose a 100-car freight train loses power and slows down very *slowly*, taking about an hour to come to a complete stop. Since it decelerated so slowly, there is no need to measure its deceleration in milliseconds. Minutes will do just fine. Now, in Williamson's example, one warms up very *slowly*. Since one warms up only slowly, it is just not plausible to assume that in case a there are any one-second, let alone any *one-millisecond*, changes of feeling less cold than before. Indeed, since one's warming up is stretched out over several hours, it is not even plausible to assume that there are one-minute changes of feeling less cold than before.

---

[6] Why, if case a will not involve indiscernible one-millisecond changes of feeling less cold, will Williamson not be able to justify (P$_R$2)? Case a is a case in which one gradually warms up; it must be viewed as a long series of changes of feeling less cold than before. Now, if we think of an a_i–a_{i+1} interval as possibly encompassing a change of feeling less cold than before such that one is *aware* of this change, then we get the possibility of K(cold) in a_i and ~B(cold) in a_{i+1}. To block this possibility, Williamson must assume that the change of feeling less cold occurring during an a_i–a_{i+1} interval is such that one cannot be aware of it. Hence Williamson needs NAC**.

The assumption that one undergoes one-millisecond changes of feeling less cold is more plausible when we consider a case of a short duration in which one warms up very *quickly*. If I go to my mailbox on a cold winter day in Minnesota when it's $-10°F$, I get very cold even though I am outside for just a couple of minutes. When I step back inside the well-heated house, warming up again also takes just a couple of minutes. Since, once back in the house, I warm up quickly, it might be that I feel less cold in such rapid increments that my awareness of the process lags behind. So, while I am aware of one one-second changes of feeling less cold, perhaps there are many one-millisecond changes of feeling less cold of which I am unaware.

The use of milliseconds is essential for Williamson. Why think that an episode of feeling less cold than before might not be noticeable to one? Answer: it will not be noticeable when it lasts for only one millisecond. So let us focus on the plausibility of one-millisecond changes of feeling less cold than before.

7. FEELING LESS COLD IN ONE MILLISECOND

Williamson, I take it, considers NAC an uncontroversial premiss, a mere stipulation that even a luminosity friend such as Lucy should accept. Let us examine whether this is so. Lucy would say that the issue is not empirical but a conceptual or metaphysical. Metaphysically, feeling less ϕ and being aware of feeling less ϕ cannot come apart, just like one's feeling ϕ and one's *being alive*, or one's feeling ϕ and one's *being conscious* cannot come apart. These things cannot come apart whether we consider minutes, seconds, or milliseconds. What matters is not the duration of the interval but the metaphysical nature of the episodes in question: episodes of feeling less ϕ than before not accompanied by any awareness. According to Lucy, episodes of that nature are metaphysically impossible. Choosing an extremely short interval does not change that. If an episode of feeling less ϕ without awareness is metaphysically impossible, it is still metaphysically impossible if it is supposed to last for only one millisecond. Lucy will deny, therefore, that the choice of milliseconds supplies her with a reason to consider NAC** plausible.

I must confess I find Lucy's position more plausible than Williamson's. When I put a pot of water on my stove, there might be one-millisecond increases in the water's temperature. When I put the pot of boiling water on my porch when it is $-20°F$, there might be one-millisecond decreases in the water's temperature. But *temperature* increases and decreases are one thing; a person's *feeling* more or less hot, or more or less cold, than a moment before is another. So the possibility of one-millisecond temperature changes provides no support for the claim that one can feel less cold than before within the span of one millisecond.

Let us switch to other mental states. Are there indiscernible episodes of feeling less pain, indiscernible episodes of feeling less tired, or indiscernible episodes of feeling less happy? I would have to agree with Lucy's view. *Feeling* less pain, less tired, or less happy is, by its very nature, not the sort of thing that can take place without awareness of it. I see no reason to suppose that this is different for feeling less cold.

Suppose we grant the metaphysical possibility of feeling less ϕ without being aware of feeling less ϕ. Will we then have to attribute plausibility to the claim that it is possible for one to undergo *one-millisecond* episodes of feeling less cold? Here is a reason to think not. Consider the Minnesota Winter case. Having stepped back inside the well-heated house, I warm up very quickly. Since I warm up very quickly, it is perhaps plausible to say that each *minute* constitutes a change of feeling less cold than before. Perhaps we should even allow for *twenty-second* changes of feeling less cold than before. But do I also undergo *millisecond* changes of feeling less cold? What reason is there to think I do? There is only one candidate: my *warming up rapidly*. But my warming up rapidly is not a compelling reason for thinking that I undergo millisecond changes of feeling less cold.

Let us compare two propositions:

(T) In the Minnesota Winter case, I undergo *twenty-second* changes of feeling less cold.

(M) In the Minnesota Winter case, I undergo *one-millisecond* changes of feeling less cold.

My warming up rapidly is an important feature of the Minnesota Winter case. I think it is a reason to accept (T). But I do not think it is also a reason to accept (M). In granting (T), we are already taking into account that the Minnesota Winter case is one in which one warms up rapidly. Why grant (M) as well? If we are to view (M) as plausible, we need to be supplied with an *additional* reason. I do not find it easy to imagine what that reason might be.

What about *micro*seconds? Would Williamson want to say that there are also one-microsecond episodes of feeling less cold, or would he want to draw the line at milliseconds? If he does *not* hold that there are one-microsecond episodes of feeling less cold, then his position will be this: 'It is possible to undergo episodes of feeling less cold within the span of one one-thousandth of a second, but it is not possible to undergo episodes of feeling less cold within the span of one one-millionth of a second.' This position strikes me as a bit arbitrary. Is there any principled reason, other than the limits of one's own awareness, for marking a threshold beyond which an experience like feeling less cold than before can no longer occur? If there is such a reason, what might it be? Suppose there is a good reason for saying that microseconds of feeling less cold do not exist. If so, why would not that reason also be a good reason for saying that milliseconds of feeling less cold do not exist?

8. TAKING ON LUCY

Lucy holds the equivalence $F_L\phi \leftrightarrow A(F_L\phi)$. Therefore, she has no reason to accept NAC: the assumption that, in case α, there are episodes of feeling less cold than before of which one is not aware. As a result, Williamson's argument is not dialectically effective against Lucy. Lucy might say that the argument begs the question against her.

We can also look at the dialectical situation this way. Williamson's aim is to show that no mental conditions are luminous. To this end, he employs a reductio-type argument resting on the premiss that a mental condition such as feeling cold is luminous. But, in order to derive the contradiction the reductio requires, he presupposes a specific kind of non-luminosity: namely, the non-luminosity of feeling less cold than a moment before, where the moment in question is one millisecond. For two reasons, this assumption is problematic. First, it is unclear whether it is psychologically possible to feel less cold than before within the span of one millisecond. Secondly, Lucy will see no reason to grant that, whereas as feeling cold is luminous, feeling less cold than a moment before is not luminous. Consequently, Lucy will not think that Williamson's argument supplies her with a reason to abandon luminosity.

For Williamson's argument to be effective against a luminosity friend like Lucy, he would have to establish some common ground between Lucy and himself. The appeal to milliseconds, I take it, is intended to find such common ground. So, starting with the assumption that one-millisecond changes of feeling less cold than before are indiscernible, Williamson attempts to give luminosity friends a reason to abandon luminosity. However, since Lucy accepts the equivalence $F_L\phi \leftrightarrow A(F_L\phi)$, she has no reason to believe that one-millisecond changes of the kind in question are metaphysically possible. Her argument goes as follows: 'If one-millisecond changes of feeling less cold are psychologically possible, they would have to be discernible. If, on the other hand, the human mind is such that one-millisecond changes are not discernible, then there cannot be one-millisecond changes of feeling less cold.' The appeal to milliseconds does not, therefore, establish the common ground needed for supplying Lucy with a good reason to abandon the luminosity of feeling cold.

9. A DILEMMA

Consider again the following premiss, which Williamson needs for his defence of (R):

(P_R2) If K(cold) in α_i then B(cold) in α_{i+1}.

Why believe that, in case a, there will not be two times such that K(cold) in a_i and $\sim$B(cold) in a_{i+1}? Williamson's answer, I take it, is that a_i and a_{i+1} are just one millisecond apart, and within the span of one-millisecond one is not going to be aware of feeling less cold than a moment before. Suppose we allow for the a_i–a_{i+1} interval to be long enough to notice that one feels less cold than before. Then surely there will be a pair of times such that K(cold) in a_i and $\sim$B(cold) in a_{i+1}: in a_i one still feels cold and knows that one does, but in a_{i+1} one's feeling cold has passed and so one no longer believes one feels cold. Indeed, given that in case a one moves from feeling cold to eventually feeling hot, and given that one constantly monitors how one feels, there will have to be such a pair. So, if we permit the a_i–a_{i+1} interval to be long enough for there to be awareness of feeling less cold, then (P$_R$2) is false and (R) cannot be derived. That is why letting the a–a_{i+1} interval be no longer than one millisecond is essential to Williamson's argument.

However, as I have argued above, Williamson assumes that, in case a, one warms up very *slowly*. Suppose we disagree with Lucy and allow for the metaphysical possibility of indiscernible episodes of feeling less cold than before. Rejecting Lucy's view is not enough to render plausible the assumption that, in case a, there are one-millisecond intervals of warming up. For, in case a as described by Williamson, one warms up *slowly*. That is an excellent reason to think that in case a there are no one-millisecond warm-up episodes. What might be psychologically realistic? Considering that the warming-up process takes several hours, perhaps it is plausible to assume that one feels less cold every minute. But, if we think of the a_i–a_{i+1} interval as lasting one minute, then surely there is no reason to think that one's coming to feeling less cold during this interval is indiscernible. So, if we think of case a in terms of one-minute increments of warming up, nothing blocks the possibility of K(cold) in a_i and $\sim$B(cold) in a_{i+1}. That is the first horn of the dilemma.

Here is the second horn. To block the possibility of K(cold) in a_i and $\sim$B(cold) in a_{i+1}, Williamson needs to make the a_i–a_{i+1} interval as short as it realistically might be. Now, to make it plausible that one undergoes very short episodes of feeling less cold than before, we need a case in which one warms up rapidly. But, even in the Minnesota Winter case, one still does not warm up quickly enough for it to be plausible to think that the case is going to involve one-millisecond episodes of feeling less cold than before. Let us be charitable and allow for one-second episodes of feeling less cold than before. But a one-second episode of warming up still seems long enough to go from K(cold) to $\sim$B(cold).

Let us consider what might be the fastest possible case of warming up. Having been outside during a brutally cold Minnesota winter night, I come back home, immediately undress and get into my bathtub, which is filled with pleasantly warm water. Let us suppose that, upon immersing myself in the warm water, I do indeed feel less cold from one millisecond to the next.[7] Compared with the original case Williamson considers in which one warms up slowly, we are now looking at the other end of the spectrum. But why should we assume that, while luxuriating in my bathtub, the one-millisecond warm-up episodes I enjoy are not accompanied by awareness? If they are, we get the pair K(cold) in a_i and $\sim$B(cold) in a_{i+1} even though the a_i–a_{i+1} interval lasts only one millisecond.

Suppose you are in a pitch-dark room. Someone turns on the light. It seems plausible to me that here we have K(dark) at t_i and $\sim$B(dark) at t_{i+1} where t_i and t_{i+1} are only one millisecond apart. Or suppose it is pleasantly quiet now but then a screeching smoke alarm goes off. Again, I do not see why we should not think that you can pass within one millisecond from K(quiet) to $\sim$B(quiet). Likewise, if we assume maximum warm-up speed and make the contrast between feeling cold and feeling less cold maximally extreme, why should we not assume that a one-millisecond change of feeling less cold than before is accompanied by awareness?

So what is the dilemma? The two horns of the dilemma are (i) cases in which one warms up very slowly and gradually and (b) cases in which one warms up very quickly and suddenly. If the warming-up process is gradual, there is no reason to believe that the individual increments of warming up are very short. If they are not very short, it is not plausible to assume they are indiscernible. If, on the other hand, the warm-up speed is fast enough to render one-millisecond changes plausible, there is then again no reason to think that the warming-up increments are indiscernible. It is now the very speed of the warm-up process that gives us a reason to think that even one-millisecond changes might be discernible. So, no matter whether we consider a slow and gradual warm-up case or a fast and sudden warm-up case, it would seem we get the possibility of K(cold) in a_i and $\sim$B(cold) in a_{i+1}. As a result, even if we do not agree with Lucy's metaphysics, we may wonder why we should accept Williamson's reasoning in support of (R).

10. BEING APPEARED TO ϕ-LY

Let us be done with mental states such as feeling less ϕ. Instead, let us consider mental states such as *being appeared* to ϕ-ly. Williamson holds that the following is metaphysically possible: it appears to one that one is in the state of being

---

[7] Getting into the tub will take longer than one millisecond. So let us suppose the series of one-millisecond changes of warming up begins once I am fully immersed in the warm water.

appeared to ϕ-ly while one is actually in the state of being appeared to ϕ^*-ly. Williamson describes the following case:

Suppose that Jones has a clear and distinct experience E as of seeing 29 stars. On the basis of having E, Jones forms the belief that he is having an experience as of seeing 29 stars . . . However, for any natural number n between 20 and 40, when Jones has an experience as of seeing n stars, he usually forms a belief that he is having an experience as of seeing 29 stars. In most cases, this belief is false. The underlying psychological mechanism is the same for all those values of n. He makes no attempt to count but simply estimates the number from his general impression; forgotten events in his childhood caused a strong bias in favour of the number 29.   (Williamson 2000: 471)

So according to Williamson, it is possible for Jones to believe himself to have an experience as of 29 stars when in fact he as an experience of, say, 30 stars. But is this really possible?

   Let us distinguish between type-one deception and type-two deception. Type-one deceptions occur when one's perceptual faculties represent one's *physical environment* other than it really is. Type-two deceptions occur when one's introspective faculties represent one's own *mental states* other than they really are. Modelled after Williamson's example, here is an illustration of a type-one deception: it seems to me that I am seeing 29 stars, but I am actually seeing 30 stars. The number of stars in my visual field is one thing; my experience of them is another. There is no necessary connection between them. Therefore, the possibility of a type-one deception like that is entirely unproblematic. When a type-two deception occurs, we have again an experience that represents an external reality other than it really is. But, in this case, the external reality is one's own mind, and the misleading experience is of the introspective kind. Using Williamson's example involving the perception of stars in the sky, we might want to think of the two types of deception as follows:

Type-One Deception

Reality	There are 30 stars in the sky.
Visual Appearance	It visually seems to me that there are 29 stars in the sky.

Type-Two Deception

Reality	It visually seems to me that there are 30 stars in the sky.
Introspective Appearance	It introspectively seems to me that it visually seems to me that there are 29 stars in the sky.

According to Williamson, introspective deception about how the external world appears to one in one's perceptual experiences is just as possible as perceptual deception about what the external world outside of one's mind is really like.

But why should we assume that type-two deceptions are possible? Well, Williamson has described an example that enjoys at least some initial plausibility. I will argue, however, that neither Williamson's example nor any other example of that kind is likely to give us a compelling reason for the metaphysical possibility of type-two deceptions.

Consider an assertion of the form: 'It's possible for one to believe one is appeared to ϕ-ly when in fact one is appeared to ϕ^*-ly.' To acquire a reason to believe that what this assertion alleges to be possible is actually possible, we need to be given *details* that help us understand exactly *how* such a deception about one's own mental states can come about. Williamson supplies us with details meant to accomplish this task. They are as follows (switching from Jones to myself as the subject):

The Details (D)

Forgotten events in my childhood have caused in me a strong bias in favour of the number 29. This bias kicks in whenever I perceive *n* objects, where *n* is a natural number between 20 and 40.

But (D) does not force us to interpret Williamson's example as involving type-two deception. Note that, when it comes to interpreting what is going on in Williamson's example, we have two options. We could say that, given (D), the example is plausibly viewed as one involving type-two deception. However, (D) allows equally well for interpreting the example as involving type-one deception. The example will give us a reason to believe in the metaphysical possibility of type-two deception only if (D) is incompatible with type-one deception, thus forcing us to interpret the example as an illustration of type-two deception.

I can detect no such incompatibility. Given (D), we might say that, even though there are 30 stars visible in the sky, it seems to me that there are 29 stars in the sky, not because I have counted but because of my bias in favour of the number 29. Of course, the example *could* also be interpreted as involving a type-two deception. But, to a luminosity friend such as Lucy, such an interpretation is bizarre, conflicting with the following intuition: necessarily, if it introspectively appears to one that one is appeared to ϕ-ly, then one *is* appeared to ϕ-ly. Thus, if it seems to me (introspectively) that it seems to me (visually) that there are 29 stars in the sky, then it (visually) seems to me that there 29 stars in the sky. If one shares this intuition with Lucy, then one will not easily agree that Williamson's example represents a genuine metaphysical possibility. One will agree that the example is metaphysically possible only if one is given details that mandate interpreting the example as involving a type-two deception. However, (D) does not require us to adopt such an interpretation. I do not think, therefore, that Williamson's star example gives us a reason to doubt the luminosity of being appeared to ϕ-ly.

11. LUMINOSITY AND EVIDENTIAL DEFEAT

In a symposium on Williamson's *Knowledge and its Limits* Earl Conee has proposed an argument against the luminosity of mental states that is based on the possibility of evidential defeat. Conee assumes the following premiss:

D1 If someone has evidence against *p* that is strong enough to defeat whatever grounds the person has for believing that S is true, then the person is insufficiently justified to know that *p* is true. (Conee 2005: 448)

Suppose I believe I feel cold. What justifies this belief? There are no uncontroversial answers to this question. For the sake of discussion, let us settle on the following answer, which will work well for discussing Conee's argument: what justifies my belief is that it (introspectively) appears to me that I feel cold: Ap(cold) justifies B(cold). According to Conee (2005: 448), Ap(cold) is vulnerable to defeating evidence, even if we 'reject a decidedly dubious distinction between how things seem to be experienced by someone, and how they really are experienced'. It would appear Conee is sympathetic to Lucy's view, which includes as well the following equivalence: one's feeling ϕ always goes together with it appearing to one that one feels ϕ. One cannot occur without the other. So: Fϕ ↔ Ap(Fϕ). Conee's argument appears to be that, even granting this equation, it is still possible for one to feel Fϕ while having evidence for believing one does not feel ϕ. Conee says:

For instance, a defeating argument can appeal abstractly to experts who are alleged to have discovered a very subtle difference here. Or it can be alleged that introspection gives us access to our phenomenal qualities via modes of representation of those qualities, and it has been discovered how to stimulate a brain so as to duplicate such modes in the absence of the quality.

In fact, no explanation of the possibility is required. Sheer testimony can be strong enough. For instance, one who is known by Smith to be an expert can quite credibly assert to Smith that merely apparent phenomenal qualities are possible, without explaining how this can be . . .

Suppose Smith is given some . . . reason to doubt that she is experiencing a certain chilly feeling, and she has nothing available to her to refute it. The reason then defeats the evidence provided by her experience of the chilly feeling. With her evidence defeated, we can infer by D1 that she does not know herself to experience that quality. (Conee 2005: 448)

Of course, if a mental condition C is luminous, it need not be the case that, whenever C obtains, one knows that C obtains. Rather, if C is indeed luminous, it would have to be the case that, whenever C obtains, one is in a position to know that C obtains. Hence Conee continues:

Is [Smith] still in a position to know that she is in the condition [of experiencing a certain chilly feeling]? We began with Tim's characterization of the things that one is in a position to know as facts that are open to one's view, unhidden, and without any obstacle to one's knowing them. We now have reason to separate the first two features from the third. The fact of Smith's experiencing the feeling remains open to her view and unhidden. But her justification for believing herself to experience the feeling has been defeated. This is an obstacle to her knowing the fact of her experiencing the feeling and, absent new evidence, it is an obstacle that she cannot surmount.   (Conee 2005: 448)

Williamson responds to Conee's reasoning noting that he has 'considerable sympathy for Conee's anti-luminosity argument'. Williamson anticipates a friend of luminosity to reply that, 'despite the defeaters, the agent is still in a position to know, and perhaps would know if she ignored the defeaters'. However, Williamson (2000: 473) adds: 'I do not endorse such a reply.'

Well, let us have a look at what we might call the *indefeasibility view*. Suppose Ingrid, a friend of Lucy's, endorses that view. What might Ingrid say in response to Conee's argument? She might reason as follows:

Ingrid's Indefeasibility View

Suppose you have a splitting headache. Can an 'expert' really defeat your evidence for believing you have a headache, thus preventing you from knowing you have a headache? Not really. You are aware of your headache. Your headache hurts. Such evidence defeats all defeaters. The 'expert' might tell you a story about the latest research in cognitive psychology. He might show you a faculty ID from one of the most prestigious universities in the country. But no matter what he says, he cannot succeed in defeating your awareness of your headache as evidence for believing that you have a headache. Since you are aware of your headache, you have an excellent reason to believe that, on this occasion, the seemingly renowned 'expert' is mistaken. You remain, in spite of what the expert says, in a position to know that you have a headache. Analogous reasoning applies to believing that you feel cold. If you feel cold, then you are aware of feeling cold. Such awareness defeats all defeaters. Whenever you have such evidence, you are in a position to know that you feel cold, no matter what an 'expert' is going to tell you about your feeling cold.

Ingrid does not recommend that you *ignore* the expert's testimony. There is no need to ignore it, since you have a defeater for it: your awareness of your mental state. What Ingrid recommends is to conclude, on the basis of your awareness, that the person who appears to be an expert got it wrong.

Is Ingrid obviously mistaken? Perhaps she is mistaken, but not obviously so. As for myself, I would have to say I find her view more plausible than the view

Conee and Williamson endorse. Expertise has its limits. When an expert attempts to convince me that, while I am aware of feeling cold, I am or might be mistaken in believing I feel cold, the limits of expertise have been reached. I am still in a position to know I feel cold. Or so it seems to me. I do not think, therefore, that Conee's argument succeeds in undermining the luminosity of feeling cold.

12. LUMINOSITY AND EXPERIENTIAL FOUNDATIONALISM

In addition to the truth of the matter, what is at stake in the debate over the luminosity of mental states? Consider experiential foundationalism, a theory placed well within the internalist framework that Williamson's *Knowledge and its Limits* systematically and thoroughly rejects.[8] We might wonder whether experiential foundationalism somehow depends on the luminosity of experiences.

Suppose I have a perceptual experience as of p; Ep. According to experiential foundationalism, Ep can, without the aid of any further beliefs, justify me in believing that p. From an internalist point of view, Ep qualifies as a justifier because, if one has an experience as of p, one can tell that one does. That is why such an experience gives one a reason to believe that p. If experiences are luminous, then, whenever Ep occurs, one is in a position to know that Ep occurs. Suppose, then, experiences are not luminous. If so, there are occasions when Ep occurs, but one is not in a position to know that Ep occurs. If there were such occasions, would that be a problem for experiential foundationalism?

Internalist foundationalism has been accused of breeding scepticism. The basic charge is that, if justification is to meet internalist accessibility constraints, justification becomes too difficult to come by.[9] Experiential foundationalism is not vulnerable to this objection. The view asserts that an ordinary experience as of p can justify a person in believing that p. Neither beliefs about one's experience, nor metabeliefs about one's belief that p, nor any appeal to any epistemic principles are required. The experience as of p by itself, if undefeated, is sufficient for justifying a person in believing that p. Moreover, the view qualifies as internalist because experiences are mental states, and as such differ from external reality in being . . . well, *luminous*. So, if Williamson is right about the non-luminosity of mental states, then we might think that experiential foundationalism no longer qualifies as an internalist theory. This, however, does not follow.

---

[8] See Feldman (2003: 70–8, 145 ff.); also Pryor (2000), Huemer (2001), and Steup (2004).
[9] See Goldman (1999).

Suppose Williamson is right: mental states are not luminous. If they are not luminous, then they are *not always* recognizable. But they will still be recognizable *a lot of the time*. Experiential foundationalism can easily accommodate this result. Let us distinguish between restricted and unrestricted experiential foundationalism:

Unrestricted Experiential Foundationalism (UEF)

Whenever one has an experience as of *p*, one has internalist justification for believing that *p*.

Restricted Experiential Foundationalism (REF)

Whenever one has a discernible experience as of *p*, one has internalist justification for believing that *p*.

According to UEF, all experiences are justifiers; according to REF, only those that are discernible, that is, only those one is in a position to know one has them. UEF requires luminosity, for internalists would not want to view an indiscernible experience as of *p* as something that can justify a subject in believing *p*. REF, on the other hand, does not. By restricting justifying experiences to discernible experiences, REF accommodates the existence of indiscernible experiences. The latter, experiential foundationalists would say, are not a source of justification precisely because they are indiscernible.

So, if we assume, hypothetically, that mental states are not luminous, then experiential foundationalists can retreat from UEF to REF. This would not be much of a loss. After all, Williamson's attack on luminosity does not suggest that a huge percentage of our experiences is indiscernible. Attacking luminosity is not the same as making a case for universal scepticism about knowledge of one's own experiences. After all, indiscernible experiences occur only, if they occur at all, in the close vicinity of the transition point when one gradually changes from feeling ϕ to not feeling ϕ. Moreover, indiscernible experiences do not prompt beliefs whose justification needs to be accounted for. Suppose it appears to me that I feel ϕ, but actually I feel ϕ^* because my experience changes in a subtle and unnoticeable way from feeling ϕ to feeling ϕ^*. So my feeling ϕ^* is indiscernible to me. Well, if so, I will not believe I feel ϕ^*. Rather, I will still believe I feel ϕ. This belief, though mistaken, is justified. What justifies it is that it *appears to me* that I feel ϕ, which is a discernible experience. Of course, this experience is misleading. It justifies me in believing something false. But the fallibility of experiential justification is just one more feature of experiential foundationalism, to be viewed as one of the theory's virtues. It is difficult to see, then, why we should think that abandoning indiscernible experiences as a source of justification should be a problem for experiential foundationalism.

However, the need for the retreat from UEF to REF arises only if it is true that mental states are not luminous. Of the three anti-luminosity arguments discussed here, each turned out to be problematic. I do not think, therefore, that they supply experiential foundationalists with any compelling reason to retreat to the restricted position.[10]

[10] I wish to thank Mylan Engel, Allen Habib, Omar Mirza, Duncan Pritchard, Casey Swank, and Kenneth Williford for helpful discussion and comments.

14

Cognitive Phenomenology, Semantic Qualia, and Luminous Knowledge

Neil Tennant

1. INTRODUCTION

For Timothy Williamson (2000: 93), a *cognitive home* is a region of logical space in which 'everything lies open to our view':

in our cognitive home . . . mistakes are always rectifiable . . . we are not omniscient about our cognitive home. We may not know the answer to a question simply because the question has never occurred to us. Even if something is open to view, we may not have glanced in that direction . . . the point is that such ignorance is always removable.   (p. 94)

The anti-realist, for whom all truths are knowable, would here contemplate, for each knower, the rosy prospect of a spacious and well-furnished home, with creature comforts reflecting the tastes, interests, and sensibilities of its owner. But, it turns out, the *bourgeoisie* are to be dispossessed. Epistemically, we are all street persons. It is not clear whether Williamson laments our condition, or points it out with grim satisfaction:

. . . we are cognitively homeless. Although much is in fact accessible to our knowledge, almost nothing is inherently accessible to it. (p. 94)

The eviction order applies even to the occupancy of our own mental states. For Williamson, 'there is no central core of mental states', central in the special sense that 'if S belongs to that core, then whenever one attends to the question one is in a position to know whether one is in S' (p. 93). Such a state S (or the occupancy thereof) would be a case of a *luminous* condition holding. A condition C is luminous just in case (p. 95) 'for every case α, if in α C obtains, then in α one is in a position to know that C obtains', where 'if one is in a position to know p, and one has done what one is in a position to do to decide whether p is true, then one does know p . . . if one is in a position to know p, then p is true'. Williamson maintains that ('with rather trivial exceptions' (p. 13)) no proposition can be the content of luminous knowledge. That is, even though an agent A might know that *p*, it would not follow from that fact alone that *A* would be in a position to know that *A* knows that *p*. This claim is of course no threat to the knowability principle of the anti-realist, who would maintain only, concerning the assumed truth '*A* knows that *p*', that it is knowable—that is, that it could be known at some time by *some* agent, even if not by the agent *A* himself.

This chapter ventures to offer a modest doss house to Williamson's epistemic hobo. It will be argued that thinkers have cognitive homes with the following minimal chattels: when they are in a state of understanding, with respect to any sentence, that it is meaningful for them (as a representation of how things are), then they indeed know (or at least are in a position to know) that they are in that state. That is to say, the condition of *having a given declarative sentence be meaningful for one* is luminous.[1] The case to be made here will not be taking issue with Williamson on anti-realist grounds. Rather, it will take issue with him by adducing a kind of knowledge on the part of any agent that, simply by virtue of his having it, must be knowledge that he knows he has. The knowledge in question is therefore luminous, in Williamson's sense. And it is not subject to any kind of Sorites-based scepticism at higher order. It is knowledge to the effect that one grasps a given sentence as meaningful—as making a declarative statement. In order to pick up the trail to such knowledge, we have to turn to 'the other place'.

2. MOORE'S COGNITIVE PHENOMENOLOGY

G. E. Moore, in his essay 'Propositions' (in Moore 1953: 52–71; at pp. 57–9) wrote of 'some act of consciousness which may be called the understanding of [words'] meaning'. For Moore, it was 'plain that the apprehension of the meaning of one sentence with one meaning, differs in some respect from the apprehension of another sentence with a different meaning'.

This meaning-apprehension was a form of *cognitive phenomenology*. It was likened, by Moore, to the phenomenology of sensory qualities. He could not, however, say whether the two kinds of phenomenology were the same, or distinct (pp. 67–8). For Moore, the claim of cognitive phenomenology was not a conclusion based on philosophical argument. It played the role, rather, of an intuitive *given*, from which he would proceed, later in his essay, to make certain other points about propositions. Apprehensions of meanings were simply members of 'a new class of facts which I want to call your attention to' (p. 56). They were 'quite plain' (p. 58).

Moorean propositions are in one regard, at least, different from Fregean thoughts. For Frege, thoughts are senses of sentences. A thought 'gets clothed in

---

[1] Note that this is a different claim of luminosity than the one that Williamson finds implicit in Dummett's claim (1978: 131), that 'it is an undeniable feature of the notion of meaning—obscure as that notion is—that meaning is *transparent* in the sense that, if someone attaches a meaning to each of two words, he must know whether these meanings are the same'.

the perceptible garb of of a sentence, *and thereby we are enabled to grasp it'* (Frege 1918/1977: 4–5; emphasis added) whereas for Moore (1958: 61)

We may . . . apprehend a proposition, which we desire to express, before we are able to think of any sentence which would express it . . . we . . . often apprehend [propositions], when we neither see nor hear any words which express them, and probably often without even having before our minds any *images* of words which would express them.

Moorean propositions, however, like Fregean thoughts, are public and objective. On p. 63 Moore tells his reader

What we . . . mean . . . when we say that [two] persons have the same belief, is that *what* is believed in both of the two different acts is the same: we mean by a belief, in fact, *not* the act of belief, but *what* is believed; and what is believed is just nothing else than what I mean by a proposition.

So: the propositions are public and objective, while our apprehendings of them may be private. But, it may be emphasized, so it is too with colours: colours may well be public and objective, while the *colour-qualia* in any individual mind are nevertheless private.

In the course of naturalizing philosophy since Moore wrote on these matters, and under the influence of linguistic behaviourism in particular, many philosophers of language were inclined to dispense altogether with propositions as theoretical entities. For some peculiar reason, hardly any attention was paid to the plain facts of cognitive phenomenology to which Moore drew our attention. Yet a mistaken impression of something is no less real, as a mental phenomenon, for its turning out to be an impression of a non-existent. To the extent that we are reminded, today, of the 'hard' problem of consciousness, it is a problem generated almost exclusively by the recalcitrant nature of sensory qualia, which, some believe, still elude any kind of physical, behavioural-dispositional, or functional reduction.

There is a historical irony here. Philosophers working within a broadly Quinean tradition seem to be in the grip of an unarticulated dogma. This time the dogma does not involve the analytic/synthetic distinction, but is based on another important Kantian dichotomy—that between the operation of our sensibility and the operation of our understanding. The dogma in question holds that recalcitrant qualia—the ones that make the problem of consciousness hard—are confined to the side of *sensibility*. This is the 'phenomenal' or 'subjective' side of mind. For one who holds the dogma, it is as though the operation of a Kantian understanding could be 'functionalized away' to general satisfaction. (The operations of Kantian understanding are, today, subsumed under what is variously called 'intentional' or 'psychological'; while the word 'phenomenal' covers what has to do, by and large, with Kantian sensibility.)

By reminding oneself of Moore's simple insight, one hopes to bring post-Quinean philosophers of mind to the realization that they might have been, all along, in the grip of yet another unexamined dogma—the dogma to the effect that *what it is like* for a knowing subject is a matter only of *sensibility*, with the *understanding* contributing nothing at all to the phenomenology involved. (This dogma is to be distinguished from the so-called third dogma of empiricism, to the effect that there is a scheme/content distinction.)

There are a few contemporary philosophers who have revived the Moorean insight. Galen Strawson (1986, 1994) and Charles Siewert (1998) are significant examples. With the orthodox opposition well on the way to Quining even sensory qualia, however, the burden of proof, even concerning what ought to be matters of simple intuition, seems to have shifted. (Here 'intuition' is used in the sense of 'reflective datum', a relative 'given' for the pursuit of a theoretical enquiry, rather than in the Kantian sense.) Today it is no longer enough to appeal to intuition the way Moore did; instead, a new kind of argument is needed.

An argument is offered below, whose purpose is to establish that there is such a thing as what it is like to apprehend a declarative proposition. It will establish this conclusion by means of a suitable thought-experiment. The thought-experiment is intended to reveal how apprehension of a proposition can be lamentably, but understandably, *absent*. It can be absent even when there are well-formed forms of words being exchanged by agents who happen to be unaware of their expressing propositions, *given the very use that the agents are making of them.*

3. SENSORY QUALIA

The sensory qualia so beloved of phenomenologically minded philosophers are sometimes described as 'raw feels', but without any specifically haptic connotation. Examples are: a red patch in one's visual field; a brief musical note heard; a bitter after-taste on the back of one's tongue; an acrid whiff; a sharp stabbing pain on the tip of an index finger; a sudden wave of queasiness as one is lurched around. Across all sensory modalities, a Kantian would reckon these qualia to the manifold of sensory intuition. They are the primary mental stuff from which knowledge of one's own body and of the external world are to be forged. It is only with the application of concepts that raw feels are synthesized into experience in Kant's sense—that is, cognition. When we descry objects, events, and causal interactions, we are cognizing. But this requires the use of various concepts of the understanding: sortal or classificatory concepts, and the relational concept of cause itself.

But there is a 'pre-conceptual' sense in which we still want to say, departing from Kant, that we *experience* qualia. Formless or uncategorized though this kind of experience might be, there is nevertheless something that it is like to undergo it. It is perhaps our most peripheral but also most acute form of awareness. It is the outermost surface of our sentience, where the impacts of the world are at their most vivid. Cognition, said Kant, needs this vivid raw material; for concepts without intuitions (here, qualia)—are *empty* (B75).

Even though, correlatively and metaphorically, intuitions without concepts are *blind*, there is still *something it is like* for *the subject* to experience a motley sum of simultaneous raw feels, even short of appending the famous 'I think' of B137. And that something that it is like is *pre-conceptual*. The quality of one's experience is grounded in qualia that are antecedent to experience in Kant's sense. And those qualia are experienced in the ordinary sense.

Against this, some might say that even the rawest kinds of experience need a little conceptual massaging. We do not see little red patches; rather, we get glimpses of a tomato. We do not have any awareness of, say, the sound of a major fifth; it will be more definite than that, something more like major-fifth-on-a-piano. We do not have bitter after-tastes except with the awareness of their being after, and because of, our chewing those mouldy nuts (say). We do not have, as it were, unsourced acrid whiffs; rather, such whiffs present themselves as of over-roasted coffee beans. One does not have just that sharp stabbing pain on the tip of one's index finger; rather, one feels it as caused by some pointed object pressing against it. This is an argument for at least some 'conceptual infusion' of even the most primitive phenomenological materials.

But all that is needed, as the departure point for our current reflections, is the something-that-it-is-like to be a subject enjoying qualia-informed-by-concepts. Consider just the sight of a tomato, short of any perceptual judgement concerning the tomato. There is something that it is like to see that red tomato, short of being drawn into any of a myriad possible states of judgement, such as that the tomato in question is round and ripe, or that it is within reach, or whatever. The awareness that is involved in cognition is still, basically, *sensory* awareness.

The familiar kinds of qualia just considered are the simplest phenomenal constituents in the something-that-it-is-like to have sensory awareness.

4. SEMANTIC QUALIA

The goal now is this: to show how one can say, with Moore, that sensory qualia (with or without conceptual infusion) are not the only qualia. There are also *semantic* qualia. That is what the rest of this chapter seeks to establish. Just as a visual percept might be broken down into its component colour-qualia, so too the cognitive-phenomenological grasp (or conscious, Moorean understanding) of a proposition can be broken down into its component semantic qualia. The semantic correlate of one's sensory awareness of a red patch in one's visual field is one's cognitive awareness that the word 'and' (say) means *and*. And the semantic correlate of one's conscious visual perception of a scene is one's conscious, Moorean understanding of the proposition expressed by a declarative sentence.

There is something-that-it-is-like to make logically structured judgements about the external world. There is something-that-it-is-like to represent the world (in private thought, or in communicative utterances) as being thus-and-so. If this was what Kant was onto in saying that it must be possible for an 'I think' to accompany any representation, then it cannot be claimed that the view was original with Moore; *especially* if Kant meant to allow also that there could be subjects whose representations happen *not* to be so accompanied. The sentential semantic quale φ is the content that one is aware of judging to hold—what one takes oneself, consciously, to be *thinking*—when offering a representation of the world as making φ true. Sentential semantic qualia are internally complex, on the one hand, but possessed also of an integrative unity, on the other. Their logical structure does not, however, detract from their experiential unity or immediacy.

The something-that-it-is-like in question here has nothing to do with one's sensory manifold (except only indirectly, in certain cases). Instead, it is a kind of reflective awareness of the content and point of any given exercise of one's conceptual and representational capacities, when one makes an assertion or assumes a proposition hypothetically, for the sake of argument. The propositional contents may be empirical; but they could also be mathematical. And the mere fact that sensory imagery is not *necessary* for abstract mathematical thought shows that conscious grasp of mathematical contents cannot presuppose the having of phenomenal qualia. One wants to say that there is something that it is like to judge that φ and to be aware of what, exactly, so doing amounts to; and that this something-that-it-is-like is in principle distinct from phenomenal experience.

It is very difficult to put this higher-order intuition into words. With qualia of any kind, there is the threat of ineffability. The colour spectrum, for example, *seems* continuous, so in some sense has to be beyond the fumbling, discrete combinatorics of words. (Diana Raffman (1995) has made this point convincingly.) Words fail qualia, even though (if Frege was right) words have to be adequate unto any judgement based on qualia. To have the sorts of raw feels in question is to know what it is that perhaps cannot be put into words. One has to let the subject find out for herself. One cannot say to her 'Look, I will clue you in as to what sort of quale I am talking about, and which you, lamentably, have never enjoyed. It is like this, you see . . .', whereupon one tells her a long story that does not *induce* her to *have* any such qualia (such as the qualia of boredom at your holding forth), but instead lamely attempts to make her aware, by proxy as it were, of what she might have been missing. There can be no substitute for the real thing; she is going to have to find out, directly, for herself. 'Cerise? It's like *this*!'—whereupon one flashes a card in front of her, of the precise colour with which she has never been acquainted. Then, and only then, does she know.

This is the method of the missed-out, but now made-up-for, kind of experience. Different subjects can get some idea of each other's type-experiential lacunae; and they can visit upon one another the awareness of what, precisely, it is that they have been missing out on. It works, however, only for sensory qualia. It does not work for semantic qualia.

The method that works for semantic qualia is somewhat different. Recall the ancient Greeks' story about the music of the spheres. We cannot hear those celestial strains, because they are (supposedly) always there. But, if the music of the spheres were to stop, we would be acutely conscious of its cessation. A more mundane analogy would be the noise of cicadas in the tropics. One becomes so used to their near-incessant chirping that one ceases to be aware of it. Awareness of the background din returns only when they all stop—which they will do, in concert, whenever they are disturbed.

Our foreshadowed thought-experiment is designed to make one appreciate the fact that there is something that it is habitually like to make judgements that represent the world as being thus and so. But, because it has always been like that for each of us for as long as we can remember, the reader has to be made aware of what this special kind of 'it' is like. The reader has to be enabled to imagine what it would be like—or how it would not be like anything at all—if it were not at all like that any more.

To exploit another analogy: consider the curious phenomenon of blindsight. Subjects with lesions in their brains can apparently process visual information, but without any visual awareness of the objects in their environment. Phenomenologically, as it were, they are blind; but, given how they move around and avoid obstacles in their way, they appear not to be. The thought is that, in the blindsighted subject, visual information is somehow being processed in the usual way—so that the brain mediates between visual perception and motor action—but that the subject, for some reason to do with the lesions, does not enjoy the usually concomitant visual *awareness*.

I shall seek to make the following analogy with blindsight. There could be subjects whose effectively communicative use of declarative language is, for all that natural selection might 'see', as good as our own, but for whom there is nothing that it is like to be making representational judgements about the world. (They are, if you like, 'judgemental zombies'.) The only difference is that, with the victim of blindsight, the blindness is attributed on the basis of his own sincere claims to be visually unaware. In the case of semantic qualia, one cannot have a 'semantically snuff' subject making similar claims while in the grip of an attack of not-enjoying-semantic-qualia. Instead, the task here is to convince the reader, by means of a thought-experiment, that these imagined subjects are indeed (or, at least, could very well be) semantically snuff, but that they could be made to acquire a nose for what they have been missing. They can become aware of what they have been missing, thereby making what has been missed a reality. But the reader, who has never missed it, needs this thought-experiment in order to appreciate that one will be aware of having semantic qualia only by being made aware of what it would be like *not* to have them. This is like the ancient Greeks appreciating the very presence of the music of the spheres only when it ceases.

Or, rather, it is like their appreciating the possibility of the presence of the music by being asked to imagine what it might be like if, should the music really be there, constantly, in the background, it were suddenly to cease.

Before the promised thought-experiment can be described, the reader needs an explanation and description of a certain kind of game.

5. THE GAME, DESCRIBED ASEMANTICALLY

Let there be two players, α and β. There are also two 'role hats', labelled, respectively, 1 and 2. At any stage of the game, each player will have exactly one of these hats on her head. Let the $1-1$ assignment of hats to players be called R. Thus if $R(1) = \alpha$ (whence $R(2) = \beta$), player α has hat 1 on her head, while player β has hat 2 on hers. If the players were to exchange their hats, the new hat-assignment would be $\overline{R}$. Hence $\overline{\overline{R}} = R$.

The players play the game with respect to 'play-charts' and a 'playing-field'. A playing-field is a collection of individuals, each with various 'properties' and perhaps also standing in various 'relations'. These properties and relations will be represented by predicate-letters (or simply, predicates). If one wanted to make a 'playing-field' for the purposes of having friends over to play the game, one might use a collection of solid shapes of different colours and sizes. One-place predicates could then represent shapes and colours, and two-place predicates such relations as 'is bigger than', 'is darker than', and so on. If P is an n-place predicate, and $x_1, \ldots, x_n$ are individuals in the playing-field M, then we shall write $\underline{P}(x_1, \ldots, x_n)$ when those individuals stand in the relation represented by P in the playing-field M. The statement $\underline{P}(x_1, \ldots, x_n)$ belongs to the formalized language in which the game theory is given. Note that this formalized language has not yet been called a metalanguage!—for there is, as yet, no 'object language' under consideration.

The play-charts to be used alongside the playing-field are constructed by an inductive process. The basic materials from which one constructs play-charts are tags $x, y, z \ldots$; predicate-letters; and the three numerals 0, 1, and 2. All these primitive constituents (and those to be introduced below) are assumed to be distinct. That is, there is no overlap among any pairs of categories of primitive constituents. This is a standard condition to impose upon inductively defined entities, in order to secure the uniqueness of their method of composition. It is not peculiar to the study of semantically interpretable syntactic complexes.

Note that tags, predicate letters, and numerals are abstract types, and that one has to be able, in general, to distinguish different *occurrences* of some same tag, predicate letter, or numeral. Our rules of formation for play-charts are accordingly very abstract. But actual realizations of play-charts, for use by players, will be made out of concrete inscriptions, on pieces of paper, or board. Thus what is referred to abstractly as a play-chart of type $n\psi\xi$ ($n = 1$ or 2), where ψ and ξ are themselves play-charts, might well be inscribed as nested rectangles, say:

Since there are only two values for n, one might adopt a convention whereby for $n = 1$ we have the diagram

and for $n = 2$ we have the diagram

The graphical possibilities are endless; assume only that some convention for play-chart inscription is settled upon, and adhered to. One can then proceed with the abstract inductive definition of play-charts, however they might be inscribed for use in actual play.

First there are the *basic* play-charts. These are formed by concatenating one predicate letter and an appropriate number of tags (among which repetitions may be permitted). Thus, with the two-place predicate L, one could form such basic play-charts as Lxy, Lxx, and so on. The tags in a basic play-chart are said to be *untied*.

Secondly there are the 'composite' play-charts. If φ and ψ are any two play-charts, the following will also be play-charts:

- 0φ (whose untied occurrences of tags will be those of φ);
- $1\varphi\psi$ and $2\varphi\psi$ (whose untied occurrences of tags will be those that are untied in φ and those that are untied in ψ).

Thirdly, there are the 'tying' play-charts. Let φ be a play-chart with an untied occurrence of x. Then $1x\varphi$ will be a play-chart, whose untied occurrences of tags will be those of φ, except for the untied occurrences of the tag x in φ, all of which occurrences are now said to be *tied* by the prefix $1x$. Similarly for 2 in place of 1.

A play-chart with no tags untied is called a *starting play-chart*.

A play of the game involves a starting play-chart φ and a playing-field M. The two players start by tossing a coin. The winner of the toss chooses which hat

(1 or 2) to wear at the outset. That choice of course determines the initial hat-assignment R for the play of the game. Play consists of finitely many successive stages. Each stage is characterized by

  (i) the play-chart ψ currently attended to;
  (ii) the current hat-assignment; and
  (iii) which individuals in M have thus far been labelled by which tags untied in ψ (see the rules below).

Thus a stage (or state of play) against the background of M can be represented as

$$[\psi, R, f],$$

where f is a finite mapping of the untied tags of ψ to individuals in M. The notation $f(x/\mathbf{x})$ will represent the assignment that results from f by extending it or modifying it so that the tag x is assigned the individual $\mathbf{x}$.

  With a starting play-chart φ (which has no untied tags) the initial state of play will be of the form

$$[\varphi, R, \varnothing].$$

where $\varnothing$ is the empty assignment. The rules of the game are as follows:

1. If the current state of play is of the form $[0\psi, R, f]$ then the players must advance to the state of play $[\psi, \overline{R}, f]$. They have no choice in the matter. (The effect of the prefix 0 is thus to make the players *swap hats* as player 1 and player 2.)

2. If the current state of play is of the form $[n\psi\theta, R, f]$ ($n = 1$ or 2), then $R(n)$ chooses which of the following states of play will indeed be the next one: $[\psi, R, f]$; or $[\theta, R, f]$.

3. If the current state of play is of the form $[nx\psi, R, f]$ ($n = 1$ or 2), then $R(n)$ chooses an individual $\mathbf{x}$ from the playing-field M, and the next state of play will be $[\psi, R, f(x/\mathbf{x})]$.

4. If the current state of play is of the form $[P(x_1, \ldots, x_n), R, f]$, then play stops. If $\underline{P}(f(x_1), \ldots, f(x_n))$, then $R(1)$ has won; otherwise, $R(2)$ has won.

Given these constitutive rules for this two-person, zero-sum game, it is easy to define the notion

$$\mathcal{P}_M[\psi, R, f]$$

(the player who can win, in state of play $[\psi, R, f]$, against the background of playing-field M). Consider first the two cases of states of play in which the players do not exercise any choices. The degenerate case where play ends (in a state of play involving a basic play-chart) is easy: the player who *can* win is simply the player who *does* win. Thus

$$\mathcal{P}_M[P(x_1, \ldots, x_n), R, f] = R(1) \text{ if } \underline{P}(f(x_1), \ldots, f(x_n));$$

and

$$\mathcal{P}_M[P(x_1, \ldots, x_n), R, f] = R(2) \text{ if not-}\underline{P}(f(x_1), \ldots, f(x_n)).$$

Another easy case is where the state of play is of the form $[0\psi, R, f]$. Since the players advance to the next state of play without exercising any choices, the *person* who can win immediately before the hat-swap is the one who can win immediately after the hat-swap. Thus

$$\mathcal{P}_M[0\psi, R, f] = \mathcal{P}_M[\psi, \overline{R}, f].$$

Or, put another way,

$$\mathcal{P}_M[0\psi, R, f] = R(1) \text{ iff } \mathcal{P}_M[\psi, \overline{R}, f] = \overline{R}(2)$$

—whence also

$$\mathcal{P}_M[0\psi, R, f] = R(2) \text{ iff } \mathcal{P}_M[\psi, \overline{R}, f] = \overline{R}(1).$$

Next consider states of play in which the players do exercise choices. First look at such states of play that involve composite play-charts. What happens in a state of play of the form $[n\psi\theta, R, f]$ ($n = 1$ or 2)? The player $R(n)$ gets to choose which of ψ or θ to have in the next state of play. That is, $R(n)$ gets to determine whether the next state of play is $[\psi, R, f]$ or $[\theta, R, f]$. Now here is a simple conceptual point about being in a winning position: *when it is your turn to make a choice, you are in a winning position before your choice if and only if there is a choice open to you that puts you in a winning position after it. Moreover, if (and only if) at any stage all your choices would put your opponent in a winning position, then at that stage your opponent is in a winning position.* Thus

$$\mathcal{P}_M[1\psi\theta, R, f] = R(1) \text{ iff either } \mathcal{P}_M[\psi, R, f] = R(1) \text{ or } \mathcal{P}_M[\theta, R, f] = R(1);$$

and

$$\mathcal{P}_M[1\psi\theta, R, f] = R(2) \text{ iff } \mathcal{P}_M[\psi, R, f] = R(2) \text{ and } \mathcal{P}_M[\theta, R, f] = R(2).$$

Likewise

$$\mathcal{P}_M[2\psi\theta, R, f] = R(2) \text{ iff either } \mathcal{P}_M[\psi, R, f] = R(2) \text{ or } \mathcal{P}_M[\theta, R, f] = R(2);$$

and

$$\mathcal{P}_M[2\psi\theta, R, f] = R(1) \text{ iff } \mathcal{P}_M[\psi, R, f] = R(1) \text{ and } \mathcal{P}_M[\theta, R, f] = R(1).$$

Finally, look at states of play involving tying play-charts. What happens in a state of play of the form $[nx\psi, R, f]$ ($n = 1$ or 2)? The player $R(n)$ gets to choose an individual $\mathbf{x}$ from the playing-field, and to tag it as x. Thus $R(n)$ gets to determine the next state of play, which has to be of the form $[\psi, R, f(\mathbf{x}/x)]$. The simple conceptual point reasserts itself: *when it is your turn to make a choice, you are in a winning position before your choice if and only if there is a choice open to you that puts you in a winning position after it. Moreover, if (and only if) at any stage all your choices would put your opponent in a winning position, then at that stage your opponent is in a winning position.* Thus

$$\mathcal{P}_M[1x\psi, R, f] = R(1) \text{ iff for some } \mathbf{x} \text{ in } M \ \mathcal{P}_M[\psi, R, f(x/\mathbf{x})] = R(1);$$

and

$$\mathcal{P}_M[1x\psi, R, f] = R(2) \text{ iff for every } \mathbf{x} \text{ in } M \ \mathcal{P}_M[\psi, R, f(x/\mathbf{x})] = R(2).$$

Likewise,

$$\mathcal{P}_M[2x\psi, R, f] = R(2) \text{ iff for some } \mathbf{x} \text{ in } M \ \mathcal{P}_M[\psi, R, f(x/\mathbf{x})] = R(2);$$

and

$$\mathcal{P}_M[2x\psi, R, f] = R(1) \text{ iff for every } \mathbf{x} \text{ in } M \ \mathcal{P}_M[\psi, R, f(x/\mathbf{x})] = R(1).$$

6. AT EVERY STATE OF PLAY, EXACTLY ONE PLAYER IS IN A WINNING POSITION

Lemma. For all distinct a, β and for all $1-1$ functions $R : \{1, 2\} \to \{a, \beta\}$ the inductively defined function $\mathcal{P}$ from states of play to $\{a, \beta\}$ ($= \{R(1), R(2)\}$) is total.

Proof. By induction on the structure of play-charts.

Basis. On states of play involving basic play-charts, it is determinate whether or not the state of affairs $\underline{P}(f(x_1), \ldots, f(x_n))$ obtains. So $\mathcal{P}$ is total on these states of play.

Inductive Hypothesis. Assume that $\mathcal{P}$ is total on all states of play involving simpler play-charts than the play-chart φ under consideration. We consider φ by cases, according to whether it is of the form (i) 0ψ, (ii) $1\psi\theta$, (iii) $2\psi\theta$, (iv) $1x\psi$, or (v) $2x\psi$ (where ψ and θ are, of course, simpler than φ).

Case (i): φ is 0ψ. By definition,

$$\mathcal{P}_M[0\psi, R, f] = \mathcal{P}_M[\psi, \overline{R}, f].$$

By Inductive Hypothesis, the right-hand side exists; whence the left-hand side $\mathcal{P}_M[0\psi, R, f]$ is well defined.

Case (ii): φ is $1\psi\theta$. The definition of $\mathcal{P}$ specifies that

$$\mathcal{P}_M[1\psi\theta, R, f] = R(1) \text{ iff either } \mathcal{P}_M[\psi, R, f] = R(1) \text{ or } \mathcal{P}_M[\theta, R, f] = R(1).$$

By Inductive Hypothesis,

$$\text{either } \mathcal{P}_M[\psi, R, f] = R(1) \text{ or } \mathcal{P}_M[\psi, R, f] = R(2);$$

and

$$\text{either } \mathcal{P}_M[\theta, R, f] = R(1) \text{ or } \mathcal{P}_M[\theta, R, f] = R(2).$$

This yields the following four cases to consider:

$$\mathcal{P}_M[\psi, R, f] = R(1) \text{ and } \mathcal{P}_M[\theta, R, f] = R(1);$$
$$\mathcal{P}_M[\psi, R, f] = R(1) \text{ and } \mathcal{P}_M[\theta, R, f] = R(2);$$
$$\mathcal{P}_M[\psi, R, f] = R(2) \text{ and } \mathcal{P}_M[\theta, R, f] = R(1);$$
$$\mathcal{P}_M[\psi, R, f] = R(2) \text{ and } \mathcal{P}_M[\theta, R, f] = R(2).$$

In the first three of these cases, it follows by definition that

$$\mathcal{P}_M[1\psi\theta, R, f] = R(1).$$

In the fourth case, it follows by definition that

$$\mathcal{P}_M[1\psi\theta, R, f] = R(2).$$

Hence $\mathcal{P}_M[1\psi\theta, R, f]$ is well defined.
Case (iii) is similar to case (ii).
Case (iv): φ is $1x\psi$. The definition of $\mathcal{P}$ specifies that

$$\mathcal{P}_M[1x\psi, R, f] = R(1) \text{ iff for some } \mathbf{x} \text{ in } M \ \mathcal{P}_M[\psi, R, f(x/\mathbf{x})] = R(1);$$

and

$$\mathcal{P}_M[1x\psi, R, f] = R(2) \text{ iff for every } \mathbf{x} \text{ in } M \ \mathcal{P}_M[\psi, R, f(x/\mathbf{x})] = R(2).$$

Unlike Case (ii), one cannot give a finite proof by cases here, for there might be infinitely many individuals $\mathbf{x}$. Note, however, that by Inductive Hypothesis we have

for every $\mathbf{x}$ in M either $\mathcal{P}[\psi, R, f(x/\mathbf{x})] = R(1)$ or $\mathcal{P}[\psi, R, f(x/\mathbf{x})] = R(2)$.

This is of the form $\forall x(Ax \lor Bx)$. From this it follows by classical logic that $\exists xAx \lor \forall xBx$. But the first disjunct is the condition for

$$\mathcal{P}_M[1x\psi, R, f] = R(1)$$

to hold; while the second disjunct is the condition for

$$\mathcal{P}_M[1x\psi, R, f] = R(2)$$

to hold. It follows that $\mathcal{P}_M[1x\psi, R, f]$ is well defined.
Case (v) is similar to case (iv). $\qquad\qquad QED$

7. THE THOUGHT-EXPERIMENT

Imagine a society in which there evolves a battle of wits among people of leisure. They came to play the foregoing game, and with great ceremony. That their elaborate rituals count as playing *this* game, under the abstract description given above, is the product of both anthropological and mathematical insight; for the matter is not at all that clear to the contestants involved.

Their playing-field is, literally, a playing-field. Figurines and other familiar objects can be displayed and relocated on the arena. There is a stock of monadic and dyadic predicates that determinately apply, or fail to apply, by universal agreement, to any object, or pair of objects, within the arena.

A coin-toss determines which player begins as Player 1, and which as Player 2. (The winner of the toss chooses.)

The player whose move it is makes a choice: either of a sub-chart, ψ or θ; or of an individual on the arena to be labelled with the untied tag x. In the former case, the rest of the chart is covered, and only the chosen sub-chart remains exposed to view. In the latter case, where an individual has to be chosen, the chooser places against it a placard inscribed with the appropriate tag. Recall that on a play-chart of the form $nx\psi$, (he who at that stage is) Player n will choose some individual and tag it with x. The most able players will also *remove* tags from the objects in the tableau, as and when their presence would no longer be required, given the course of play that has transpired.

The professional circuit is dominated by the most agile minds. These are the geniuses who, after brief inspection of a fresh play-chart and a newly arranged playing-field, can elect to be Player 1 or Player 2 at the outset, and display amazing resourcefulness in subsequently winning play after play of the game.

Small children are reared on the game in parlour form. Famous play-charts of yore can be purchased in miniature form at the local shops. For those who cannot afford the ersatz playing-fields with plastic figurines, there are booklets containing diagrammatic representations of famous playing-fields, indicating the layouts of the actual figurines and other objects to which they bore observable and determinate relationships.

In due course, in response to the needs of post-game analysis, someone develops a linear notation for describing play-charts. It is some peripatetic Pole who first thinks up the new notation. He writes $1\psi\xi$ for the two-dimensional play-chart and similarly writes $2\psi\xi$ for the play-chart

Indeed, the Pole hits on exactly the notation that was used above for the inductive definition of play-charts! With a little practice, his interlocutors catch on to what these linear notations *denote*. They *stand for* the two-dimensional play-charts with which players would actually play at the big meets.

The Pole also realizes that the playing-fields need shorthand designations, but cannot devise a succinct naming system in general. He adopts, instead, the local nomenclature, involving short descriptive terms, such as 'The Sicilian', for playing-fields that are really quite complex. Fortunately, his interlocutors are such avid followers of the game that they can recall every structural detail about playing-fields thus described. In due course they come to say things like 'So-and-so would have loved to be Player 1 on The Sicilian with $1x2y010LxyLyx$'.

Travelling home from work, colleagues might look at the local playing-field (on which the figurines were always left in their final arrangement at the end of any big meet), and venture terse comments like '$2x1y2z02Lxy0Lzy$'. These were understood as meaning that the champion they had just been discussing would have been unbeatable as Player 1 on that playing-field, with the play-chart just designated. Such 'comments' would never be understood as assertions. If any 'speech-act' had to be read into such an utterance, it would be something like a performative: an expression of preparedness to bet that (whoever started as) Player 1 would win on the play-chart in question, on the playing-field in question.

But such opinions about how the great might wish to play are understood only as that: opinions about how the great might wish to play. The play-charts are *mentioned*, not used, by devotees of the game. And even the great players who really do use them (by playing on them) do not use them in the sense relevant to the use-mention distinction in semantics. They use them, rather, as a chess-player uses the chessboard and the chess pieces on it: that is, as non-semantic items by means of which one plays a game. When one looks at a board position near the end-game, and says 'White should win', one does not take the board position to be *saying* anything. For no p does it bear the content that p. In the same way, it would never occur to the devotees of our game that a play-chart *said* anything about the playing-field—that it bore a semantic content, determined by its structure, and was accordingly *true* or *false* as a representation of the playing-field. In relation to the play-charts, the gamers are without what Moore called 'some act of consciouness which may be called the understanding of their meaning'.

8. THE MOST IMPORTANT BICONDITIONALS; AND A HOMOMORPHISM

We leave our thought-experiment for the time being, and return to some game theory. It has a lesson for us about semantic qualia, and about how light can dawn suddenly over the whole.

Equipped with the Lemma proved in Section 6, one can now deduce certain consequences of the definitional clauses specifying the notion $\mathcal{P}_M[\psi, R, f]$ above.

Making the classical assumption that it is determinate whether or not any basic fact obtains, one can infer:

$$\mathcal{P}_M[P(x_1, \ldots, x_n), R, f] = R(1) \text{ if and only if } \underline{P}(f(x_1), \ldots, f(x_n))$$

Because $\mathcal{P}$ is total, the clause for hat-swaps implies:

$$\mathcal{P}_M[0\psi, R, f] = R(1) \text{ iff not-}[\mathcal{P}_M[\psi, \overline{R}, f] = \overline{R}(1)]$$

Recall also that we already have the following:

$$\mathcal{P}_M[1\psi\theta, R, f] = R(1) \text{ iff either } \mathcal{P}_M[\psi, R, f] = R(1) \text{ or } \mathcal{P}_M[\theta, R, f] = R(1)$$

$$\mathcal{P}_M[2\psi\theta, R, f] = R(1) \text{ iff } \mathcal{P}_M[\psi, R, f] = R(1) \text{ and } \mathcal{P}_M[\theta, R, f] = R(1)$$

$$\mathcal{P}_M[1x\psi, R, f] = R(1) \text{ iff for some } \mathbf{x} \text{ in } M \ \mathcal{P}_M[\psi, R, f(\mathbf{x}/x)] = R(1)$$

$$\mathcal{P}_M[2x\psi, R, f] = R(1) \text{ iff for every } \mathbf{x} \text{ in } M \ \mathcal{P}_M[\psi, R, f(\mathbf{x}/x)] = R(1)$$

Thus far no attempt has been made to interpret play-charts as making statements about the playing-field. Let φ be a play-chart and let f assign to each tag untied in φ either an individual (from M) or a variable in our formalized language for game theory. No two distinct tags may be assigned the same such variable by f.[2] Suppose f is an assignment dealing with exactly the untied tags

---

[2] Strictly speaking, since this discussion of f and τ^f_M is taking place in a language one level up from the language of our game theory, one should use, as the mapping referred to by this superscript,

in φ, and suppose further that ψ is a subformula of φ. Then f^ψ will be the restriction of f to tags that are free in ψ. Now define a homomorphic mapping τ_M^f from play-charts φ, and relative to such assignments f, to sentences of our formalized language of game theory.

$$\tau_M^f(P(x_1,\ldots,x_n)) =_{df} \underline{P}(\tau_M^f(x_1),\ldots,\tau_M^f(x_n));$$

$$\tau_M^f(0\psi) =_{df} \neg\tau_M^f(\psi);$$

$$\tau_M^f(1\psi\theta) =_{df} (\tau_M^{f^\psi}(\psi) \vee \tau_M^{f^\theta}(\theta));$$

$$\tau_M^f(2\psi\theta) =_{df} (\tau_M^{f^\psi}(\psi) \wedge \tau_M^{f^\theta}(\theta));$$

$$\tau_M^f(1x\psi) =_{df} \exists x\tau_M^{f(x/x)}(\psi);$$

$$\tau_M^f(2x\psi) =_{df} \forall x\tau_M^{f(x/x)}(\psi).$$

Note that nothing more than a syntactic mapping has been defined here, from play-charts to sentences of the formalized language in which the game theory is being presented.

Here is an example to illustrate the action of τ_M^f as just defined. Consider the play-chart

$$2y10Ayx1xBx.$$

Note that the tag x has both tied and untied occurrences therein. The leftmost occurrence of x is untied. No other tag has an untied occurrence. So suppose f maps x to the individual γ in M. Then f is simply $\{< x, \gamma >\}$. We can now calculate $\tau_M^{\{<x,\gamma>\}}(2y10Ayx1xBx)$ as follows:

$$\tau_M^{\{<x,\gamma>\}}(2y10Ayx1xBx)$$

$$= \forall y\tau_M^{\{<x,\gamma> <y,y>\}}(10Ayx1xBx)$$

$$= \forall y(\tau_M^{\{<x,\gamma> <y,y>\}}(0Ayx) \vee \tau_M^\emptyset(1xBx))$$

$$= \forall y(\neg\tau_M^{\{<x,\gamma> <y,y>\}}(Ayx) \vee \exists x\tau_M^{\{<x,x>\}}(Bx))$$

$$= \forall y(\neg\underline{A}(\tau_M^{\{<x,\gamma> <y,y>\}}(y), \tau_M^{\{<x,\gamma> <y,y>\}}(x)) \vee \exists x\underline{B}(\tau_M^{\{<x,x>\}}(x))$$

$$= \forall y(\neg\underline{A}(y, \gamma) \vee \exists x\underline{B}(x)).$$

not f itself, but a mapping f^* closely related to f. Where f assigned to any tag an individual from M, f^* would assign to that tag some name (in the language of our game theory) for the individual. This would ensure that $\tau_M^{f^*}(\varphi)$ would always be a sentence of the language of our game theory. Here, however, one simplifies slightly by avoiding such niceties. Alternatively, one could just stipulate that the language of our game theory simply contained all the relevant expressions of its own metalanguage.

9. TOWARDS CONVENTION T

Theorem. Suppose f deals with all the untied tags of φ. Then for all R,
$\mathcal{P}_M[\varphi, R, f] = R(1)$ is interdeducible with $\tau^f_M(\varphi)$.

Proof. By induction on the complexity of the play-chart φ.

Basis. Immediate from the basis clause in the definition of τ^f_M and the first boxed
biconditional above.

Inductive Hypothesis. Suppose the result holds for all play-charts simpler than φ.

Inductive Step. Consider φ by cases. We shall deal here only with the case where
φ is of the form 0ψ. We have

$$\mathcal{P}_M[0\psi, R, f] = R(1) \text{ iff not-}[\mathcal{P}_M[\psi, \overline{R}, f] = \overline{R}(1)].$$

By Inductive Hypothesis, we obtain

$$\mathcal{P}_M[0\psi, R, f] = R(1) \text{ iff not-}[\tau^f_M(\psi)].$$

By definition of τ^f_M, it follows that

$$\mathcal{P}_M[0\psi, R, f] = R(1) \text{ iff } \tau^f_M(0\psi).$$

The remaining cases are similar.

Corollary. If φ is a starting play-chart, then for all R, $\mathcal{P}_M[\varphi, R, \varnothing] = R(1)$ is
interdeducible with $\tau^f_M(\varphi, \varnothing)$.

Note that $\tau^f_M(\varphi)$ does not involve R. It follows that if any

$$R : \{1, 2\} \xrightarrow{\text{1-1}} \{\alpha, \beta\}$$

makes it the case that $\mathcal{P}[\varphi, R, f] = R(1)$, then every such R makes it so. Our
theorem above therefore essentially correlates a relational property—call it $\mathcal{S}$—of
φ, M, and f with the condition $\tau^f_M(\varphi)$. And, in the special case where φ is
a starting play-chart (with all tags tied), this relational property $\mathcal{S}$ of φ, M,
and the null assignment is being correlated with the condition $\tau^f_M(\varphi, \varnothing)$. The
latter is simply a statement about the model M. One can further ignore the
null assignment, and write $\mathcal{T}(\varphi, M)$ instead of $\mathcal{S}(\varphi, M, \varnothing)$; and write $\tau_M(\varphi)$
for $\tau^\varnothing_M(\varphi)$.

One has, therefore, fulfilled a model-relative form of Tarski's material adequacy
condition on definitions of would-be truth-predicates (see Tarski 1956):

for every play-chart φ with no tags tied, and for every playing-field M, $\mathcal{T}(\varphi, M)$ is
interdeducible with $\tau_M(\varphi)$.

Now Tarski took the view that if τ_M was a *translation mapping* relative to M from *what were regarded as* object-language sentences into (what would accordingly be regarded as) the *meta*language, then fulfilment of his material adequacy condition ensured that $T(\varphi, M)$ would capture the truth of φ in M.

No claim has yet been entered to the effect that these 'play-charts' are sentences—that is, interpretable as statements about the 'playing-field' M. The charts have been treated as non-semantic, albeit quasi-syntactic structures.

It is time now to take a leap. Let the play-charts be *interpreted* in the obvious way given by τ above: basic play-charts are atomic predications; 0 is negation; 1 is disjunction; 2 is conjunction; $1x$ is the existential quantifier; and $2x$ is the universal quantifier. The reader will be quick to realize that play-charts, as they were presented above, are in Polish notation. Tags are variables; the tied and untied ones are bound and free, respectively. Everything now falls into place. Courtesy of Tarski's adequacy condition on theories of truth, one can now regard the game-theoretical property

$$\mathcal{P}_M[\varphi, R, \varnothing] = R(1)$$

as that of *the truth of φ in M*.

A mathematically sophisticated member of the culture in our thought-experiment could be brought, by the foregoing considerations, to realize that *play-charts are propositional representations*, and that *they represent the ways things are on the playing-field in question*. They will be able to 'flash-grasp' that

1. Player 1 is *asserting* the proposition expressed by the playing-chart;
2. Player 2 is *denying* it;
3. Player 1 can win, regardless of what Player 2 might do, provided that the playing-chart *is true of* the playing-field;
4. Player 2 can win, regardless of what Player 1 might do, provided that the playing-chart *is false of* the playing-field;
5. 0 means negation;
6. 1 means inclusive disjunction;
7. 2 means conjunction;
8. $1x$ means 'for some x';
9. $2x$ means 'for every x';
10. play-chart construction is in accordance with grammatical rules;
11. truth and falsity are objective;
12. a winning strategy for Player 1 on a (finite) playing-field takes the form of an 'evaluation proof' of the play-chart with respect to the field;
13. a winning strategy for Player 2 on a (finite) playing-field takes the form of an 'evaluation disproof' of the play-chart with respect to the field;

14. the play-chart's truth-conditions can be expressed by a sentence (in a logician's version)[3] of one's ordinary language (assuming that it contains equivalents of the aforementioned logical operators, along with the necessary extralogical predicates).

The point is, all these insights can dawn in one sudden revelation, enlightening the gamer as to the true nature of what he is up to. Coming to see any given play-chart as truth-evaluable (on any given playing-field) is a matter of seeing that it is true if and only if . . . (where the dots are filled in by some translation of the play-chart into the expressively adequate language, or logician's version thereof, that the formerly naive gamer has already mastered).

Before such enlightenment, the gamer has no semantic qualia in connection with the play-charts, against the background of a playing-field. After his enlightenment, the gamer *cannot help but* experience the play-chart as semantically contentful, as making a *truth-evaluable* claim about the playing-field, a claim that is *translatable* into (a slightly formalized extension of) one's ordinary language. The gamer formerly used *descriptions* of play-charts (descriptions constructed in what he took to be an extension of his ordinary language), and he uttered them in contexts in which his speech-act was at best intended as a performative. He now realizes that these erstwhile descriptions can be reinterpreted as *declarative sentences* in their own right. They form a new language. He realizes that he is, in effect, using these sentences to make *assertions* about the playing-field. He is now capable of that Moorean 'act of consciousness which may be called the understanding of their meaning'. A certain intellectual light has dawned on the whole. The sentences in question now afford the understander *semantic qualia*. He knows that the sentences are meaningful representations; and, by virtue of that fact alone, he knows that he knows it. Semantic knowledge is luminous.[4]

---

[3] What is meant here is a language that, like so-called logician's English, allows one to render bound variables explicitly in surface form, rather than attempt to deal with them only by means of anaphoric pronouns.

[4] I would like to thank Adam Podlaskowski, Galen Strawson, and Michael Type for helpful correspondence.

15

Aristotle's Condition

Charles Travis

Tim Williamson is the best sort of provocative philosopher. What he provokes is thought. He has made *me* think long and hard about what I am most convinced of. I would like to provoke someone else as much. I would settle for less.

I have a point to make here about truth, and then several others about meaning. For the point about truth I need not invoke my own views on that second topic. It is a point on which I disagree with Williamson. Specifically, I will suggest that bivalence does not hold *as he conceives it*. As for bivalence as one should conceive it, I do not understand what it would be for that not to hold. Bivalence, on Williamson's conception, seems essential to (the motivation for) his own account of vagueness. Perhaps, then, my point threatens that. If so, this is not because of any qualms on my part about there being facts one could not know.

As for meaning, the problem is to locate Williamson's view of that. In fact, he has suggested two views, which move in opposing directions. My own view rules out either of these. But the present project is not to adjudicate. It is rather to see where the crucial issues lie. One of Williamson's suggested views severs the link one finds, for example, in Donald Davidson (e.g., 1967) between what words mean and the conditions under which they would be true (of something). Thus far, Williamson and I are on the same side. The other view has the same shape as a later view of Davidson's (1983), and, for the same reasons, will not (in my view) do. Knockdown arguments to that effect, though, are not here in the offing.

1. ARISTOTLE

Williamson, following Tarski, begins a discussion of truth by quoting Aristotle (*Metaphysics* Γ 7.27): "To say of what is that it is not, or of what is not that it is, is false, while to say of what is that it is, or of what is not that it is not, is true" (as quoted in Andjelković and Williamson 2000: 214, and in Williamson 1994: 188). So someone who says of what is that it is, or of what is not that it is not, speaks truth. And, presumably, conversely (since Aristotle means this as a definition). If *words*, or an utterance, or anything else, say(s) of what is that it is, or of what is not that it is not, then they are (it is) true. And presumably conversely. *Mutatis mutandis* for falsity. Something is either true or false (someone speaks either truth or falsity) on condition that it (he) satisfies either the stated condition for truth or the stated condition for falsity. I will call that disjunction of conditions *Aristotle's condition*. It might be expressed this way: to say of what is either that it is or that it is not; or to say of what is not either that it is not or that it is. If the pig is eating turnips, then saying it to be eating them satisfies Aristotle's condition, as does saying it not to be. If the pig is not eating turnips, Aristotle's condition is satisfiable in just the same ways.

One might find substance in Aristotle's condition if one thinks this way. To represent things as a certain way is to impose, or deploy, a particular scheme for categorizing things being as they are: their being that way places them in the one category, their not in the other. It is open to the world to oblige such representing by articulating into things being the way in question, or things not; or, again, to fail so to oblige. If the world obliges, Aristotle's condition is satisfied. If not, not.

So far, I think, Aristotle has an important insight. He continues: "so that he who says of anything that it is, or that it is not, will say either what is true or what is false." Williamson endorses the remark. To my mind, the insight just got lost.

There are things to do besides satisfying Aristotle's condition. Everything a drop of water does is something else. So, usually, is lighting a cigar, or going for a walk. Uttering some words need not satisfy that condition either if, for example, they are arbitrarily chosen. Williamson thinks, though, that there is something else that guarantees satisfaction of that condition. It is saying something (to be so). To say that P, on his view, is *always* to satisfy that condition. So it is always either to say what is true or to say what is false. Informally, this is what Williamson means by bivalence. But what is so special about saying that P? What allows it to provide such guarantees? Why is it thus different from, for example, saying 'P'? I am about to sketch a case that there is nothing thus special about saying that. To do this I will employ 'say that' in one natural way. I think we could, in fact, carve out another way of speaking of saying that on which saying that P *would* entail satisfying Aristotle's condition. That would make it harder (in general) to establish that one *had* said something to be so. And it would make problems erupt for Williamson in a different place. But it is best to stick to just one use of 'say that' for a start. We can turn to alternative formulations of the core point once *some* formulation of it is in hand.

Whatever the reasons for thinking that saying that *is* special in the above way, there are reasons for thinking it is not. For a start, there are cases where, intuitively, it seems not to be. I will sketch a few. They will tend to be farfetched—of course, since we are prepared for the expected, and (normally) take measures accordingly so that Aristotle's condition will be satisfied.

1.   Consider being a bachelor. To win its campaign against premarital sex, the State of Oklahoma passes a law marrying everyone born in the state at birth. (Some random method is used to pair up—of course—babies of opposite sexes.) These marriages are not recognized in any state west of the Rockies, or east of Dubuque and north of the Ohio, and in few others. Roy was born and raised in Oklahoma. So, in that state, he is married to one Laverne, whom he has never seen. Looking to better his prospects, he arrives, at age 30, in Providence, Rhode Island, where he proceeds to cut a fine figure. Is Roy a bachelor? (A pressing question for several of the female persuasion.) Well, yes and no. He is in a way, and he is not in a way. You cannot just say that he is, or that he is not. Neither is exactly true. We are accustomed to categorize people as bachelors or not. But, thanks to the State of Oklahoma, the world is not cooperating with our efforts in that direction.

Case Ia.   Forget Oklahoma. Roy, a native of Providence, is unqualifiedly single, and eligible in nearly every relevant sense. It is just that there are these little pills. With them, one can change gender overnight. Roy avails himself of these rather indiscriminately. So one day it is Roy, the next day Royine; one never knows quite what to expect. The English 'bachelor' is meant to speak of *males*. So is Roy a bachelor? Again, yes and no. Thanks to science, this time (better things for better living through chemistry), the world refuses to cooperate in this classifying project.

2.   Sid has once again lost an expensive leather wallet. For the last time, he swears. Rather than replacing it with another, he constructs 'wallets' out of heavy paper envelopes—a few small ones, for credit cards, business cards, and the like, pasted to the inside of a larger one, where Sid keeps banknotes. Such is what he now uses for a wallet. The new policy, though, does not improve his attention to what he is about. Last night, he left his 'wallet' in a taxi. Overhearing Sid once again engaged in cancelling his credit cards, Pia reports, 'Sid has lost a wallet again.' Is this true or false? Well, he did lose a wallet, and he did not. He did if we accept his improvisations as wallets. He did not if, on his new policy, he does not use a wallet. There is no one right ruling as to how we must describe him in this respect. So it is not quite true to say that he lost a wallet (*sans phrase*); but also, equally, not quite true to say that he did not. To say he had lost a wallet (at least in the way Pia did) is not unqualifiedly to say things to be as they are, but nor, equally, is it to say things to be otherwise.

3.   Sid slams the door shut. Except that he slams it so hard that it shatters into a thousand shards. There is no door at all left in the doorway. Did Sid shut the door? As in the above, he did and he did not. He did something that normally would count as shutting the door. (The door reached the shut position;

otherwise it would not have shattered.) In this case, though, there is reason not to count what he did as shutting the door. Normally, if one shut the door, then (until further notice) it *is* shut. Not this time. So there is good, normally conclusive, reason for counting what he did as shutting the door; but equally compelling reason for refusing to. (The door is not shut.) If that 'equally' is right, then neither policy can be correct as such. So neither that Sid did shut the door, nor that he did not, can count as true *tout court*.

4. Finally, a very simple, and very hypothetical, scientific case. Since we are discussing Aristotle, I will set it in a fictitious Aristotelian time. In this time, people (or scientists) thought in terms of an undifferentiated notion of quantity of matter. They thought they had developed two equally good methods of measuring this quantity: spring scales and balance scales. In their environment, the two methods always yielded the same result (within reasonable margins of accuracy). Later, though, it came to be noticed that in certain other environments, for example, at great heights, the two methods diverged. The balance scales continued to deliver the same results. But the spring scales delivered different results at heights from what they did at sea level. It thus became apparent (I am supposing) that there are really two different quantities: one measurable by spring scales (and relative to a height), and the other measured by balance scales (and had *tout court*).

The original scientists took themselves to be thinking of a quantity, had by an object in a given degree full stop, and measurable in two ways. They might, in fact, have been thinking of the one of the above two quantities, or of the other. But there *might* be no fact of the matter as to which they were thinking of. Suppose that an original scientist would have used the words 'O peseert n livros' to say object O to have the quantity he had (or took himself to have) in mind to degree *n* (measured in *livros*). Suppose that the scientist was, determinately, speaking of the quantity measured by balance scales. Then all is well. Suppose he was, determinately, speaking of the quantity measured by spring scales. Nothing has *that* quantity to any degree outright. An object can have that quantity (in degree *n*) only relative to a height. If the scientist said O to have that property (in degree *n*) outright, then he did not speak truth. One cannot speak truth in saying any object to have that property outright. But suppose there is no fact of the matter as to which property it is he spoke of. You could take him to have spoken of the first one, or you could take him to have spoken of the second. Then there is no fact of the matter as to whether things are as he said, or not. So he cannot count as having spoken truth. But, equally, he cannot count as having spoken falsehood.

If you could call Roy a bachelor, and you could say he was not, each thing one would say equally consistent with things being as they are, then, so far, neither course could be (as such) saying what is so. For if it were, the opposite course would be saying what is not so. But each, as well as the other, might have either status. Nothing chooses which should have which. So neither course could be saying of what is either that it is, or that it is not. Neither could satisfy Aristotle's condition. *Mutatis mutandis* for the other cases. So Aristotle's condition *may* be failed by what says (asserts) something—that P; and if, in a given case, it is not failed, then *substantial* thanks are due to the world for permitting itself to be spoken of, truly, or falsely, in that particular way. Or so the intuition goes.

There is, as noted, another way of speaking of saying that. One could so deploy this notion that in all these cases nothing was said to be so. In that case it is not decided whether something was said to be so in any given case unless it is decided independently that Aristotle's condition is satisfied. If things here are what they seem, then the world may upset satisfaction of that condition. Nothing is said (on this alternate way of speaking) if the world has done so. So saying that will be a highly world-involving affair. This alternate way of talking does nothing to diminish the importance of Aristotle's condition (if these cases are what they seem).

Accepting appearances, Aristotle's condition may be failed even where, on our initial way of speaking, something was said to be so. Pia called Sid a bachelor. So she said that he was one. That is saying something so. As fate has it, though, the condition is failed. And so on. How must we then think of (something) being true? For the moment, suppose truth to be a property of sayables—that is, of something one might say in saying something so. If to be a sayable is *ipso facto* to satisfy Aristotle's condition, then satisfying that condition cannot be part of what separates *true* sayables from others. It is not something demanded of a sayable if that sayable is to be, moreover, true. In that sense it is not *truth* that requires this. Things are otherwise if Aristotle's condition can be failed in the ways just indicated. In that case we can decompose truth, and falsity, into two independent and substantial elements. The first is satisfying Aristotle's condition. On our present notion of saying that, not all sayables do that. The second, in the case of truth, is a condition I will call *merit*; and, in the case of falsity, one I will call *demerit*. Think of merit as not saying things to be other than they are. Think of demerit as saying things to be not only what they are. Failing Aristotle's condition, one may still not have said things to be other than they are; so satisfied the condition on merit. Satisfying Aristotle's condition, what one said may still lack merit. *Mutatis mutandis* for demerit. Writing 'A(ξ)' for *satisfies Aristotle's condition*, 'M(ξ)' for *satisfies merit*, 'D(ξ)' for *satisfies demerit*, 'T(ξ)' for *is true*, and 'F(ξ)' for *is false*, we now have:

(T1) T(P) $\leftrightarrow$ A(P) & M(P)

(F1) F(P) $\leftrightarrow$ A(P) & D(P)

So something may fail to be true either because it fails Aristotle's condition, or because it satisfies Aristotle's condition but says things to be other than they are; and it may fail to be false either because it fails Aristotle's condition, or because it satisfies that condition, but says things to be no other than they are. Now writing 'S(ξ, ζ)' for *utterance ξ says that ζ*, we have:

(T2) T(u) $\leftrightarrow$ S(u,P) & A(P) & M(P)

(F2) F(u) $\leftrightarrow$ S(u,P) & A(P) & D(P)

So, if P does not satisfy Aristotle's condition, then P is not true, and P is not false. Similarly for utterances that say something to be so but fail Aristotle's condition. On our present way of thinking, some values of P may fail that condition. They may be expressed by some utterances that say something to be so.

In assigning such substance to truth, how far do we stray from bivalence? One version of bivalence would be: any P is either true or false. Schematically,

(B1) For any P, T(P) or F(P).

Williamson defines bivalence for utterances. He says (1994: 187): "If u says that P, then either u is true or u is false." Schematically,

(B2) For any u, S(u,P) $\rightarrow$ T(u) or F(u).

If Aristotle's condition has the substance presently envisioned for it, then neither of these versions of bivalence can be correct. But, as we will see, that result puts classical logic in no real jeopardy.

2. CLASSICISM

There are cases, I have suggested, where, if asked 'P?', we would reply, 'Well, yes and no.' These are cases where we would not be prepared to assert that P, nor, again, that not-P. Neither assertion seems to fit the case. So, equally, we would not be prepared to assert that P is true, nor that it is false. On the view that I am suggesting, that is because it is not so, in those cases, that P is true, nor that P is false. Aristotle's condition is not satisfied for P; both its truth and its falsity require that. Satisfying that condition is thus a substantive part of what being true is. What stands in the way of taking that idea seriously?

Here, I think, is the main thing. Assume P. If we have that much, what more could we want for T(P)? I confess I cannot think of anything. So T(P) follows. Now assume T(P). Assuming that much, how could it possibly fail to be that P? I do not know. If that did fail, then how could it be that T(P)? So P follows. By conditional-introduction we thus have P $\rightarrow$ T(P) and T(P) $\rightarrow$ P. Combining these by classical logic, we get:

Pseudodisquote   P $\leftrightarrow$ T(P)

('Pseudodisquote' because P is not made up of words; it is a sayable.) Given classical logic, this gives us: not-T(P) $\rightarrow$ not P. But not-P, like P, entails A(P). On my suggested view of truth, for some value of P, perhaps not-A(P); which would entail not-T(P). But, by the above reasoning, that entails, in turn, A(P). So not-A(P) entails a contradiction. So, where P is a sayable, it is contradictory to suppose not-A(P), just as Williamson suggests. (If some substitution for P were not a sayable, then, presumably, pseudodisquote would not hold of it, which would block the present untoward result.)

What might block this unwanted result? Tinkering with classical logic *might* do that. In the above reasoning, for example, trouble started with contraposing one side of pseudodisquote. To do that we need negation introduction. And this seems to have a feature we do not want. Suppose that from P we can derive a contradiction. Then we had better not assert P. But there are two ways for P to be defective. If a statement that P fails Aristotle's condition, then we had better not assert P if we aim to say things to be as they are. Again, asserting P may satisfy Aristotle's condition, but then, not-P. Negation introduction moves us directly to this last case. From the contradiction we may infer not-P. But how did that other sort of failure get ruled out? Perhaps we should not be so quick to conclude what negation introduction says we may.

But such local tinkering seems to lack the required generality. Negation introduction is one route to unwanted results. Are other inference rules more sensitive than it to the possibility that Aristotle's condition is failed? I think not. In our informal argument for pseudodisquote we saw that to assume P is already, in effect, to assume that P is true. No gap remains between what we have assumed already and what would need to be so for P to be true. Similarly, in assuming P, in some proof, we already assume that Aristotle's condition has not been failed. If it were, it would not be right to assume P. I cannot coherently suppose that P, but not A(P). And similarly, again, wherever we assume some complex an element of which consists in speaking of P as so (for example, where we assume that if not P, then Q).

And that points to what is needed here. When we are reasoning about Aristotle's condition, or, again, about truth, what needs revising is the rule of assumption (or premiss-introduction). We need to insist that it be made explicit, in a proof, just how, or where, satisfaction of Aristotle's condition has been tacitly assumed. So the new rule of assumption should be (at first approximation): wherever there is an assumption, there must be, for each atomic formula in that assumption, the further assumption that that atomic formula satisfies Aristotle's condition. If P occurs in some assumption, then we must operate under the further assumption, A(P). More exactly, and to prevent regresses of required assumptions, the new rule of assumption should insist that a rule of inference can be applied to an assumption only under the further assumptions that that assumption's atomic constituents each satisfy Aristotle's condition.

Has classical logic been revised? Yes and no. (Another example of Aristotle's condition doing work.) One might say that the rule of assumption is integral to classical logic. We have certainly revised that. So, on that way of looking at things, yes. On the other hand, one might look at what we did as simply revising the way classical logic applies to given specific sayables. In fact, perhaps not even that. Perhaps we have merely made explicit something that was always implicit in the correct uses made of classical logic. In any event, in an important respect the revision is not radical. Suppose that Φ is a classical theorem containing propositional variables $P_1, \ldots, P_n$. Then our revision leaves us with $A(P_1, \ldots, P_n) \vdash \Phi$. Suppose that $\Gamma \vdash \Delta$ is a classically valid deduction involving atomic formulae $P_1, \ldots, P_n$. Then $A(P_1, \ldots, P_n), \Gamma \vdash \Delta$ remains valid. So, in particular, $A(P) \vdash P \vee \text{not-}P$.

As for truth and Aristotle's condition, we have $A(P) \vdash T(P) \vee F(P)$; and $A(A(P)) \vdash \text{not-}T(P) \to (A(P) \to \text{not-}P)$, as per the substance I have assigned Aristotle's condition. Also, $P \to A(P)$ and $\text{not-}P \to A(P)$. We can also now see that my intuitive argument for pseudodisquote should have led to this conclusion: $A(P) \vdash P \leftrightarrow T(P)$. None of these things is a theorem, or law, of *logic*. Logic does not unfold the laws of truth in that way. Unfolding the content of Aristotle's condition in mentioning it, as in the above, is the task of a specialized bit of conceptual analysis. Similarly for *so* unfolding the content of truth. (Frege would have insisted: logic does not *mention* truth, nor Aristotle's condition, or it could not be the *most general* science. Rather, it *reflects*, in the structure of its laws, some of truth's structure.) Logic is none the worse for such division of labour.

In the normal course of events we are concerned with applying classical logic in cases where satisfaction of Aristotle's condition is not in question. In those cases, we can simply ignore the modified rule and follow the standard one. Satisfaction of Aristotle's condition goes without saying. It is another matter where truth, and Aristotle's condition, are some of what we want to talk about. Where it does not matter, we can apply classical logic unrevised.

One might object here that logic is concerned with the most general inferential structure of systems of sayables—a structure that would be there whether these sayables satisfied Aristotle's condition or not. But that structure is just the structure there would be if all relevant sayables satisfied Aristotle's condition. With the revised rule of assumption, logic continues to speak to that. Even if Roy is not quite a bachelor, but equally not quite not one, it *may* remain so that, if he were one, he would be unmarried. (Though if I knew that Aristotle's condition were failed by the proposition that Roy is a bachelor, I might well lose some of my faith in that entailment.)

When we see something not to satisfy Aristotle's condition, we will no longer hold to it in guiding thought and conduct. We will find other, more adequate, ways of capturing the relevant aspects of things being as they are. Moreover, so long as atomic formulae stand for what speaks of things being thus and so, the first concern of logic will be, not with representations (though, perhaps, facts about representations can be derived from what it says), but, rather, with ways things are and ways things are not—with the sorts of things a successful representation would represent as so. The fact is that the roast is burnt; *that*, and not some representation of it, is what means that we shall dine out. There is something for logic to get a grip on, in the way things are, just where, in representing it as so, Aristotle's condition would be satisfied.

What is at stake here is how we apply logic, not logic itself. In applying classical logic to some given set of statements, we assume things as to their satisfying Aristotle's condition. We have seen how that idea is built into classical logic itself. Where such things as satisfying that condition are not subjects of discussion, we need no revised premiss–introduction rule. In the cases at issue here, what we want to do is apply logic to a discussion of the satisfaction (or not) of Aristotle's condition (or of other successes, such as truth, that entail such satisfaction) by some given set of statements. For those purposes, we (of course) do not want to build it into the very application itself that these statements just do satisfy that condition. What we might take as unproblematic are *statements* that these statements do (or do not) satisfy that condition. In fact, we had better do so if we are to get anywhere. Where (as may be) their satisfying the condition *is* unproblematic, we *may* do so. So far, we have envisioned a case in which there are some statements, P, Q, and so on, under discussion. Their satisfaction of Aristotle's condition is part of what is under discussion. But whether that they satisfy Aristotle's condition satisfies Aristotle's condition is not. If we change the case, so that the satisfaction of Aristotle's condition by these further sayables is also under discussion, then they, too, should fall into the class of statements that require our revised premiss introduction rule.

We are now arrived in this position. On the one hand, bivalence as Williamson states it does not hold. That is because he has assigned the wrong significance to saying that P. On the other, classical logic remains intact so far as its theorems, and rules for drawing inferences are concerned. What has changed if anything, or at least what is now explicit in the logic itself, is a view as to how logic applies to thoughts (in present terms, to sayables). Logic remains in the same business as always. At most we have revised slightly our conception of what that business is.

3. PARADOX

It would be rash to claim to have a way of blocking all semantical paradoxes. But many start from a premiss meant to capture a way in which a certain proposition, occurring in that premiss, is about truth, or some related property. To assume that premiss is, as always, to suppose that its atomic parts satisfy Aristotle's condition. So it is interesting to see what happens when that supposition is made explicit according to our revised rule of assumption. (Of course, if there simply is no proposition satisfying the condition that the premiss states, then the relevant argument cannot get started and there is no paradox. That would be an alternative account of what is happening in any given case.)

I begin with the most familiar paradox. Let *ik* be the proposition that ik is not true. So we have:

ik ↔ not-T(ik).

By pseudodisquote, we also have:

ik ↔ T(ik).

Which gives us T(ik) ↔ not-T(ik), from which contradiction follows by the usual route. With our new rules, though, all of this happens under a further assumption, A(ik). (And A(T(ik)), a consequence of A(ik).) So we do not have a contradiction on no assumptions, as in the usual presentation of the paradox. So we do not yet have, officially, a paradox.

One move left open here is denying A(ik). Applying standard logic, we could derive its negation from the contradiction derived already. Which would cancel that assumption. (Of course, to do that derivation we would need to assume A(A(ik)).) Now, though, we may seem to be in new trouble. For not-A(ik) → not-T(ik). But, as we have seen already, not-T(ik) entails a contradiction. So we arrive at a contradiction on no assumptions. But, on second thought, no we do not. To get to that contradiction we need to reinstate A(ik) (since ik occurs in both of our initial conflicting premises). So what we actually derive is a contradiction from not-A(ik) on the assumption A(ik). As one might write this, A(ik) ⊢ not-A(ik) → (T(ik) & not-T(ik)) (if that is the contradiction we choose to derive). But this is not paradox. It is just an expected result. So we may rest with our conclusion, not-A(ik). (We *could* also refuse that conclusion by denying A(A(ik)). *Logic* does not force a choice between these tactics.)

A different threat of paradox might appear in the following way. Let ik be the proposition that not-A(ik). So we have:

ik ↔ not-A(ik).

We also have, by the nature of Aristotle's condition,

ik → A(ik).

From these we can derive not-A(ik) → A(ik), from which it follows that not-A(ik) entails a contradiction. From which we can derive not-not-A(ik), or, since our inference rules remain classical, simply A(ik). From A(ik) nothing particularly untoward follows. So, it seems, we have proved A(ik).

It may well seem, on reflection, that we have not proved very much here. For the derivation from the premises to not-A(ik) → A(ik) must proceed on the assumption A(ik). So our conclusion, A(ik), also rests on that assumption. An argument for A(ik) proceeding under the assumption that A(ik) might plausibly be taken to leave the question whether A(ik) open. So let us ask whether A(ik). Nothing may seem to dictate the one answer or the other. But then, since ik is supposed to say (in some sense) not-A(ik), and since nothing settles the question whether things are that way, that might lead one to conclude, plausibly, that ik does not satisfy Aristotle's condition, so not-A(ik). I do not present this argument as decisive. Suppose, though, that you feel moved by it. Trouble very obviously brews. For, since not-A(ik) is what ik was meant to say, it would seem that ik does thus satisfy Aristotle's condition after all. So we are stuck with both A(ik) and not-A(ik). Our plausible conclusion thus seems to entail a contradiction.

If this informal argument were made rigorous, under present constraints on derivations, it would be seen to depend on the assumption A(ik). In that form, it cannot quite count, as it stands, as paradox. Still, neither that ik satisfies Aristotle's condition, nor that it does not, seems a satisfactory thing to say. If I try to say that it does not, I presuppose that what I am saying satisfies Aristotle's condition. But, since that seems to be what ik is saying, it would seem that I am supposing that ik satisfies that condition too. I do not want to suppose such things. So I must not say that ik does not satisfy Aristotle's condition. But to say that I must not say it not to is to say that what I would thus say—that ik does not satisfy Aristotle's condition—does not satisfy Aristotle's condition. Equally, then, for the thought that it does. So we have not-A(A(ik)). We might see ik itself as trying to say something near enough to this to be true if what we say is, namely, not-A(not-A(ik)). But we need not agree that it succeeds in saying this. Not so far, at least. So we might plausibly see this last suggestion as a result.

4. SEMANTICS

So far I have expressed no view about meaning. I have cited intuitions in favour of the role I have assigned Aristotle's condition. That role may rule out *some* views of (linguistic) meaning. For example, it would rule out a view on which the meaning of an open English sentence, in each case, is, or fixes, a function that assigns every object a truth-value. But I have not derived my view of Aristotle's condition from any specific characterization of what meaning does, or of the properties an expression has in, or by, meaning what it does. I do have a view on that matter, though, which I think there would be no room for if Aristotle's condition did not work as I said. As noted, Williamson sketches two different views of meaning, each of which is at odds with mine, though each for a different reason. The rest of this chapter aims to identify these points of conflict, and thus the issues on which adjudication rests. It is not meant as a refutation of either of Williamson's views, though if all goes well it may have some persuasive power. I begin with my own view in five points.

1.   The English 'is blue' speaks of (an item's) being (coloured) blue. The English 'wrote a novel' speaks of (someone's) having written a novel. The English

'grunts' speaks of (a creature's) being a grunter. The English 'weighs one kilo' speaks of (an item's) weighing one kilo. And so on. These are the sorts of properties a *language's* expressions, or at least its open sentences, have in and by meaning what they do. At the very least, they are properties such expressions *have*.

2.   English expressions (or open sentences) thus speak of what admits of understandings. Being blue, for example, admits of understandings. It is a particular way for an item to be (coloured). But take Lac Leman on a sunny day. Is *it* blue? It is if you understand (a lake's) being blue in one way, but not if you understand this in another. On one understanding, the reflected sky makes it blue. On another, since the sky does nothing to change the composition of the water (it looks the same when bottled), the lake is not blue. These are both understandings being blue admits of; things it would not be wrong (*tout court*) to take a lake's being blue to be. Similarly for having written a novel. Our modern authors try to stretch the boundaries, but, in my view, sometimes cross them. Must a novel have narrative structure? Must it be a connected story, or even a story at all? Or may it be (à la Pynchon) rambling ruminations, akin to the bar bore's 'And another thing I don't like'? Are de Beauvoir's memoirs, names changed, a few fantasy scenes intentionally added, fictional enough to be a novel? How must novels be distinguished from history or travelogue? As to the writing, may that be ghosted, and to what extent? Or, if Burroughs writes a text, cuts the pages in half, shuffles them, pastes them back together into pages, and we all agree that the result *is* a novel, did he *write* it? There is an understanding of writing a novel on which this is writing one, and an understanding on which it is not. Some of the problems here have to do with borderlines (how much ghostwriting?). But some, like the last, do not. Similarly for the other examples. And similarly throughout the things spoken of by a language's open sentences.

3.   Where an open sentence speaks of (precisely) A, and A admits of understandings, the open sentence, as such, speaks of A on none of these understandings in particular. For, if it did, what it would speak of, in meaning what it does, would be, not A, but rather A on such-and-such special understanding of it; which, by hypothesis, it does not. So, for example, the English 'is blue' does not, in or by meaning what it does, speak of a lake's being blue on an understanding on which reflected sky would make a lake that; nor on one on which reflected sky, so far as that went, would fail to do the job. It speaks of being blue in a way that is neutral between these options. Otherwise it would not, full stop, speak of being blue. Which it does. Corollary: What 'is blue' means does not yet determine whether it is true of Lac Leman on a sunny day, or when it would be true of Lac Leman, or of anything else. Meaning does not connect with truth like that. Meaning might supply some materials for truth; but some materials must come from elsewhere.

4.   If, on an occasion, you use 'is blue' to say something of a lake, using it to mean what it does mean in English, you will thus have called it blue, or described it as blue, or said it to be blue. If you use it of a lake non-assertively (for example, 'If Lac Leman is blue, I shall take fish for lunch'), then you speak of the lake as being blue. That is, if, on the occasion, you want to do what it would then be to call a lake blue, or speak of it as blue, and if speaking English will do the trick, then, more specifically, 'The lake is blue' will do the trick. In the circumstances of your so speaking, there *may* (though need not) be something that would, naturally, reasonably, be understood by a lake's being blue. Sid and Pia, walking along the shores of Lac Leman, exult at their escape from grey North Sea skies. Sid exclaims to Pia, 'How blue the lake is!' It would surely be churlish for Pia to scoop a cupful of water out of Lac Leman, show it to Sid, and say, 'No it's not.' Churlish is an understatement. If she is not joking, then she failed to grasp what it is that Sid said. Insofar as there is such a thing as an understanding there would be of what one would be speaking of in speaking, on an occasion, of (a lake's) being blue, in speaking of its being blue, on that occasion, you speak of its being blue on that understanding. (That is, whether things are as you said turns on whether the lake is blue on that understanding.) So for any understanding (a lake's) being blue bears, if you find the right occasion, you may use the words 'is blue' to mean what they do and thereby speak of a lake's being blue on that understanding. Meaning constrains what is said no more than that. I hope it is clear how the example generalizes to other cases.

5.   Therefore, where there is an item that may be sensibly, understandably, called blue, it is, in general, both possible to speak truth, and possible to speak falsehood, of that item, at a given time, in using 'is blue' of it, and as meaning what 'is blue' does. There are truths to be expressed, but also falsehoods to be expressed, in using 'Lac Leman is blue' to say something about Lac Leman-at-a-moment. In any event, what 'is blue' means does not determine when it would be true of what. Again the example generalizes.

That, in brief, is how I see meaning. I note a corollary about the notion of saying that. On the above view, the words 'Lac Leman is blue' are for doing a certain sort of thing. An apt title for that sort of thing is: *saying that Lac Leman is blue*. If you use those words, on an occasion, to speak of Lac Leman, and you say something (to be said in speaking English), then you produce an instance of that thing there is to do. So what you do merits the title *saying that Lac Leman is blue*. This fixes *one* reading of the expression 'say that Lac Leman is blue'. To credit you with doing that, on this reading, is not to credit you with speaking on any particular understanding of a lake's being blue. So it is not to say what fixes when what you thus said would be true. But 'say that Lac Leman is blue' also admits of another reading. This is a reading those words are likely to bear if I tell Pia, 'Lac Leman is dull grey today', and she protests, disappointed: 'But Sid said that it is blue.' I speak on a particular understanding of a lake's being dull grey. Pia is to be understood as speaking on an understanding on which what she credits Sid with saying is inconsistent with what I thus did. To credit Sid with such a thing is to credit him with speaking on a particular understanding of a lake's being blue. Context here provides that understanding. It is one that matches up, in the intended way, with the understanding my words 'is dull grey' bore. So there is also this reading of 'say that'. On it, to say that a lake is blue *is* to say this on a particular understanding. The occasion of that use of 'say that' must determine what understanding this is.

Using 'is blue' as meaning what it does, speaking English, speaking of a given object, is not doing enough to ensure satisfying Aristotle's condition. In fact, if one is speaking of a typical lake, and one does no more than this, one will not satisfy that condition, since a typical lake is blue on some understandings of so being, not on others. So what the words thus used *mean* does not do enough to make either for saying things to be as they are, or for saying things to be as they are not. One could do that only in speaking on some particular understanding of an object's being blue, thus an understanding that went beyond what is fixed by what the English words 'is blue' mean, or speak of, as such. Perhaps using 'is blue' of an object, speaking English, so that 'is blue' so spoken meant what it does mean, is enough to make for saying that that object is blue, on our first reading of saying that. If so, then saying that P, on this reading of 'saying that', is not enough to ensure satisfying Aristotle's condition. What of the second reading? Suppose you say the object to be blue, speaking on a particular understanding of an object's being blue. If there is not enough in what words *mean* to guarantee satisfying the condition, then neither is there enough in this more specific accomplishment to *guarantee* that. For it may turn out that there are understandings of being blue on the understanding on which you spoke of this, on some of which the object would be blue, on others not, and that nothing in what you did makes it so that you spoke on an understanding of the first sort rather than one of the second sort, or vice-versa. Which would place *your* words 'It's blue' in exactly the same position as the English words 'It's blue.' For the same reason that *they* neither say a given object to be as it is, nor say it to be as it is not, as fate would have it, neither do your words, given the understanding they in fact bore.

In the event, Williamson thinks my view of meaning rests on a mistake (or several). He says (1998: 10n.):

According to Travis, meaning and reference underdetermine what is said . . . However, his account of what underdetermines what is said seems to conflate use and mention. He assumes that someone who says 'That is round' of a ball, using the words with their usual meanings, describes the ball as round, and argues that, given the way the ball is, whether it is true to describe it as round depends on the context of utterance. This commits Travis to rejecting the plausible principle that it is true to describe the ball as round if and only if it is round. But once we accept that 'round' is context dependent, we should reject Travis' assumption, just as we should reject the assumption that if you say 'That is mine' of something, you describe it as mine . . . 'Mine', with its usual meaning, does not always refer to the property of being mine; why should 'round', with its usual meaning always refer to the property of being round? With this correction, Travis' argument can be reconstructed as leading to the less radical conclusion that meaning alone ubiquitously underdetermines what is said. However, he simply takes the sameness in meaning of the words in his examples as obvious, and does not discuss the possibility of slight meaning changes, as postulated below.

There are here two different views of meaning. I will consider each in turn.

The first view combines two thoughts. First, the English predicate 'is round' does not always speak of being round. (That is, not always of the property I just mentioned in those words, assuming that I did just mention one.) Secondly, it speaks of (refers to) different properties on different occasions of its use—just as 'mine' speaks of different people on different occasions of its use. I take it that what goes for 'is round' here goes for 'is blue', and so on (more or less) systematically throughout English.

First, then, Williamson speaks of 'round' as referring (or, in the event, not) to "the property of being round". He thus presupposes that *he* referred to some property or other in *his* speaking of those words. So, sometimes, in speaking English, we do, in his view, refer to, or speak of, properties. Whatever property he did speak of on this occasion, he suggests that the English word 'round' (or predicate 'is round') does not "always" refer to that one. Well, if it does not *always* refer to that property, then *it* (that bit of English) does not refer to, or speak of, that property, full stop. We can delete the 'always'. The property of speaking of that property is not one that *it* has. If I have the property of being fat, I do not merely have it when speaking to you, but not when speaking to Jones. (Bizarre images come to mind when one tries to imagine that. They are not ones of my being fat.) Nor do I have it merely on some uses of me (citing me in the *TLS*, say), but not on others (citing me in the *Crimson*). Having the property of being fat, when that feat is accomplished, calls for no relativization. Similarly for the property of speaking of being round. Moreover, in the only aspect of 'speak' on which it makes sense to think of a bit of English as speaking of something (roughly habitual, or functional, as in 'Persil gets clothes really white'), for the English word 'round' to speak of some property would be for that to be what you speak of in using it, provided you are speaking English, using its words to mean what they do. 'Round' speaks of that property, as Persil does its thing, *when used* (properly).

So the English 'round' does not speak of the property Williamson mentioned in his words "the property of being round". If I am right about properties, or ways for things to be, then, if it does not do this for the reasons Williamson has in mind here, it does not speak of any property (or, in my terms, way for a thing to be). For if I am right, just mention a property (as Williamson did), and, as soon as we are clear on what property that is, I will show you how it admits of understandings. In which case, if the English 'round' spoke of that one, then, in so using it, you would sometimes speak of *that* property on *this* understanding of it, sometimes on *that* one. And we would be driven back to Williamson's suggestion that 'round' does not always speak of the property you mentioned.

I think that the English 'is round' speaks, as such, of being round. So I think it speaks of that on every use of it that is (a case of) speaking proper English. I am not dissuaded from this view by the fact that, on different such speakings of it, it will make different contributions to the truth conditions of wholes of which it may, then, be part. There is a fact about that bit of English that I hope I can capture in that way. It is that the meanings of those words constrain, in a particular way, what you can say on an occasion in using them—even if they do not narrow things down to just one thing. I can, occasion permitting, call the squash ball round and speak truth of it even as it begins its rebound off the wall. But I cannot so easily call it round and speak truth of it just in case it barks, or is made of lead, or is on fire. My idea is: I can use 'is round', on an occasion, of a ball, to say what I would say on that occasion in *calling it round*; and (*ceteris paribus*, perhaps) that is all I can use those words to say of it. And, further, to say what I just did is to say how the meanings of those words constrain their use. I cannot use those words of the ball (speaking English, so that they mean what they do) and thereby say the ball to be on fire, unless there is an understanding of being round on which to be round is to be on fire. (Which, so far as I can see, there is not.) I do think this is a pretty stringent constraint on what you can use 'is round' to say in speaking English. If Williamson does not want to capture it as I do, if he does not want to say that 'is round' speaks of (refers to) being round, then I am curious as to just how he would capture it.

I turn now to the second component in Williamson's first view. Williamson suggests that 'is round', in, say, 'The ball is round', refers to different properties on different uses of it. So, on different such uses, it makes different contributions to the truth-conditions of the resultant whole. In one case, that whole is true just in case the ball has one property; in another the whole is true just in case the ball has a certain different property. And so on. This is to say that, as to the English 'is round', there is no one contribution to truth-conditions that is *the* one that it makes. So, in constructing a semantic theory, we can seize on no such supposed contribution in order to identify what it is that that expression means.

Suppose we aimed for a semantic theory in Tarski style, as Davidson (1967) conceives this. Then we would want to assign a certain bit of English, 'is round', a 'satisfaction condition'. This amounts to adopting (or trying to adopt) an 'axiom' of our theory that would be written like this: 'The English predicate "is round" is true of something just in case that thing is round.' (I adjust terminology slightly here.) The words of the axiom, to the right of the 'just in case', purport to identify those conditions under whose obtaining the predicate would be true of a given thing. More perspicuously (I think), they purport to identify that condition (*Zustand*) of a thing in which it would be such that the predicate was true of it. Varying terminology once again, it purports to identify that property the having of which would make the predicate 'is round' true of a thing. And now, Williamson's idea, if correct, provides a very perspicuous way of saying why this project is doomed to failure. Suppose those words to the right do mention (speak of) a property. That will be one the words 'is round' do not refer to as such. As Williamson puts it, they do not always refer to it. But then the proposed axiom states a generalization that is false. Now suppose that those words to the right do not mention *any* property. Then no condition for the truth of that predicate of something has been stated at all.

If things work as Williamson suggests, then, so far as bits of English are concerned, there is no satisfaction to be had. Thus far Williamson and I are entirely on the same side. Is there anywhere we differ? Williamson speaks of different speakings of 'is round' as referring to different properties. I speak of them as speaking of being round on different understandings of being round. If there is any difference here, it lies in our conceptions of, respectively, an understanding and a property. On my view, to speak of being round on a particular understanding is to speak such that there are particular things to be understood as to when something would count as being round, where these things are not built into the notion of being round itself. That they are not is visible in the fact that they need not always be understood wherever one speaks of being round. For example, it may be to be understood that the squash ball's momentary geometry, as it rebounds, is irrelevant to whether it is as said *here* in calling it round. In a happy case enough is to be understood of this for it to be clear, given the way the ball is, whether one ought to call what was said true, or false. In an unhappy case this will not be so. (The point of Aristotle's condition.) But for there to be enough to decide what needs deciding in the case at hand need not be for there to be enough to decide everything that ever might need deciding.

I suspect that Williamson builds a bit more into his notion of a property. In fact, he must do so if he is to deny Aristotle's condition substance. If we think of our (shared) environment as inhabited by some determinate collection of objects, and we ignore issues about categories, should there be such, then, on Williamson's conception, a property, as such, partitions this set exhaustively into two disjoint ones: the set of all those objects that have the property, and the set of all those that lack it. In fact, a property (if it really is that) is guaranteed to do this, no matter how things happen to be. This conception of a property underwrites Williamson's conception of bivalence. A statement is true if the objects it speaks of have the properties it ascribes them, and false if some of them lack some of those properties. It is in the nature of a property, so conceived, always to make either the one thing or the other the case. My own view, though, is that this conception of a property is inconsistent with Williamson's supposition that we sometimes speak of them. I do not believe that we know how to identify anything for us to speak of (any way for a thing to be, that is) that does not admit of competing understandings (in ways we are entirely equipped to recognize). I have given here no knockdown argument for that. This, though, is the key point on which Williamson and I differ about meaning.

Williamson's second view of meaning is contained in the last sentence of the above quote. It is that the meanings of words change, sometimes subtly, over time. If there is such a thing as English, and things *its* words mean, then time can be the only relevant variable here. If we want to think of different speakers at a time (both speaking English, if we speak loosely enough about doing so) speaking slightly different idiolects in which words have slightly different meanings, then we might try to relativize meaning to that too. I am sure that words do change meaning over time, and that that is why, for example, the Dutch *typies* and Portuguese *esquisito* do not mean, respectively, 'typical' and 'exquisite'. But I think the meaning changes Williamson has in mind here are meant to support a certain idea about what meaning does. In the case of a predicate, such as 'is round', that idea would be that, for a *fixed* meaning (its meaning at a moment), there is a unique, invariant, contribution it would make to the truth-condition of any whole it was a part of while meaning that. Though the meaning of 'is round' may change over time, freeze it at a time, and it does have a satisfaction condition of just the sort Davidson envisaged. *Mutatis mutandis* for relativization to idiolects. As meaning changes, so do conditions on satisfaction. This view *preserves* Davidson's conception of what the meaning of an open sentence does—that it fixes an effective condition on satisfaction—whereas, by contrast, Williamson's first view of meaning abandons that connection.

But for currently irrelevant details as to how an idiolect is fixed, and the importance of speaker intentions (or understandings) in fixing what was, in fact, said on an occasion in given words, this idea about meaning is essentially the later view of Davidson (1983) on that topic. It blocks the following kind or argument: 'Jones said something true of that ball in saying of it, "The ball is round"; Smith said something false of that same ball (in that same condition) in saying of it, "The ball is round"; hence what "is round" means is compatible both with saying something true, and with saying something false, of a ball in that condition.' For now, all the premises give us for sure is that 'is round', when Jones used it, meant what was compatible with saying one thing; and, when Smith used it, meant what was compatible with saying another. Which is not yet the result we wanted. For we do not yet have that it meant the *same* on both uses.

Still, the idea here fails to do the work required. For the mainspring of the opposing view was this. Choose any way for a thing to be. Specify it any way that you are able. Then we can recognize various competing understandings of being that way—various competing things it might be for a thing to be that way. That is not, as it stands, a thesis about words. So freeze an idiolect at a time. Pick a predicate in it. Now tell me what that predicate speaks of in *that* idiolect at *that* time. Then I will show you various understandings of something being that way. Which says something about what predicates are for: *not* imposing some given condition on satisfaction, but rather for speaking, on whatever occasion, of whatever it is that might count on that occasion as being thus and so.

One can put this point in terms of something we all share as thinkers, across any variation in our idiolects. My understanding 'is round' as I do, in my perhaps highly idiosyncratic idiolect of the moment, makes me prepared to use it in any of indefinitely different ways, as need arises. My understanding of it (in my idiolect) shows me that it *has* all those different ways of being used, given what it speaks of there and then. In assigning it the meaning I do, I am prepared to recognize all those different things as ways it, so meaning, may be used. What matters here is not the specifics of any particular idiolect, but rather what it is, in general, to say something to be a given way. I do not know the fine details of your idiolect. But I am sure you share with me this general conception of how words work—if not explicitly, then at least in what you are prepared to recognize. If I only *think* I have the understanding of predication that I do (and not just of this or that predicate), what I need is some considerations showing (or making probable) that this is so. The present idea, common to Williamson and Davidson, even if accepted, would not militate in that direction.

5. BOUNDARIES

Frege (1903: §56) writes:

A definition of a concept . . . must unambiguously determine, as regards any object, whether or not it falls under the concept . . . Thus there must not be any objects as regards which the definition leaves in doubt whether it falls under the concept; though for us men, with our defective knowledge, the question may not be decidable. We may express this metaphorically as follows: the concept must have a sharp boundary . . . A concept that is not sharply defined is wrongly termed a concept. Such quasi-conceptual constructions cannot be recognized as concepts by logic; it is impossible to lay down precise laws for them. The law of excluded middle is really just another form of the requirement that the concept should have a sharp boundary . . . Would the sentence 'Any square root of 9 is odd' have a comprehensible sense at all if *square root of 9* were not a concept with a sharp boundary? Has the question 'Are we still Christians?' really got a sense if it is indeterminate whom the predicate 'Christian' can truly be asserted of, and who must be refused it?

Logic, Frege tells us, does not describe the behaviour of concepts without precise boundaries. It would not apply to such concepts mechanically. It would apply to such "quasi-concepts" only insofar as they are harmlessly idealized in taking them for (Fregean) concepts. It takes a sensitive eye to see just when this would be so. (Compare the way mechanics applies to actual bodies.) He may further *suggest* that without this precision words have no definite sense, which is to say, express no determinate thought, say nothing in particular to be so. I endorse Frege's claim about logic, read as I just have. If you want to apply laws of what has precise (enough) boundaries to what does, or may, not, then you must be careful to mark, or note, the discrepancies between what those laws are designed to hold of, and what you are, in fact, applying them to. Explicitly assuming satisfaction of Aristotle's condition where its satisfaction is in question in an argument is one way to take such care. I dissent from the further suggestion, if there is one. Saying something to be so (saying that P) does not *per se* require deploying concepts with sharp boundaries in Frege's sense. In discussing semantics I have suggested that our concepts do not in fact have such sharp boundaries, so that it is open to the world to decide, in being as it is, whether a given deployment of them satisfied Aristotle's condition or not. Further, I have argued, in the first part of my discussion, that nothing in logic should dissuade us from such a view. As Frege emphasizes, logic is not aimed at *such* questions at all.

Williamson's account of vagueness requires, not just Frege's view of what laws of logic are about, but Frege's further suggestion as to the connection between precision and making sense: that wherever something is said to be so, there will always, of necessity, be a sharp boundary between that which is things being as thus said to be, and that which is not. So, where something is said to be thus and so, there will always be a sharp boundary between that which is as that thing was said to be, and that which is not. It is thus this suggestion that divides us.

The suggestion applies to vagueness through cases like these. We arrange paint chips in a series so that they are pairwise indistinguishable by sight in colour, but so that the first member of the series is clearly red, the last clearly orange. Now pick a chip somewhere in the middle. Then Williamson's idea is: of necessity, either it is red, or it is not. That is so even if, as will be if the chip is well chosen, we do not, and cannot, know which.

It has struck many as absurd to suppose that a chip is red, or, equally, that it is not, if no matter how much else we knew about it, no matter how full our access to its being as it is, nothing available to us would so much as give us reason to think it red, or, as the case may be, not. The operative principle here would be: if thought that things are such-and-such is to be a *truth-evaluable* stance towards the world—a stance suitably correct, or not, by virtue of things being as they are—then the world's being as it is must be able to bear on the question what we are to think *in re* things being such and such—whether that is the thing for us to think, or not. So that the chip is red is not truth evaluable, so not a genuine thought at all, if the world *could* not bear on the question whether we are to think the chip that way. Against this line of thought Williamson has argued, if

I understand him, that an epistemologically sound economy of thought would have to make for truths we could not know. I will not approach that argument here. But two brief remarks.

First, we are now in a position to see that a case against the idea that the chip is red, or not, but unknowably so, need not begin from premises about our ignorance. There are things we *do* know about the sort of chip at issue here. We know that there are truths to tell in saying it to be red, and also truths to tell in saying it not to be. For we may say it to be red on any of many understandings of its being so. Our apparent helplessness in the face of the philosopher's chosen chip is (thus) an artefact of the circumstances of the choosing (namely, doing philosophy). In the circumstances in which we are asked to say whether the chip is red, there is insufficient (or no) point in saying the one thing or the other; no consequences of our so saying, no expectations thus aroused, which might arrange for our speaking (in, say, calling the chip red) either on an understanding on which one of those truths would be told, or on one on which one of those falsehoods would.

Suppose that you say O to be F. Suppose that whether O is F depends, substantively, on what one understands being F to be: there *is* an understanding of being F on which O is F, but also one on which O is not. Suppose there is no more reason to understand you to have said O to be F on the one sort of understanding than there is to understand you to have said this on the other sort. So neither way of understanding what you said is better than the other. So neither is *right*. Then there is nothing in (or about) what you said that determines, at a place where determination happens to be needed, how the world should be to make what you said true. In such a circumstance the world is powerless to be, in being as it is, either as you said it is, or not. Such is the nature of the gaps that may arise between saying something to be so and, satisfying Aristotle's condition, thereby saying something true or false. When it comes to answering the philosopher's question what colour the chip is, we are discernibly, determinately, in that position.

Secondly, *perhaps* the idea of saying, or thinking, something either true or false does come apart, in the odd case, at least, from the idea of the world, in being as it is, being capable of bearing on the question whether we are to think that thing—that is, of the world being capable of providing us with reasons we could see to bear on the question whether that thing is so; reasons that actually militated in favour of its being so, or (as the case may be) not. The world's being as it discoverably is may show that there are cases where these two ideas cannot be held together. There is room for discovery (by physics, say) that truth-evaluability is not what one would, at first, have thought it. I am sceptical as to philosophy, or logic, one day showing such a thing. In the present instance, logic (and philosophy) are meant to have paved the way to the parting of these two ideas in this way: logic shows that there is no room for failure of bivalence in Williamson's sense—for something to be said to be so that, for all that, fails Aristotle's condition; to call the paint chip red is to say something to be so (it would be poor philosophical methodology to suppose otherwise); hence, to call the paint chip red is to say something either true or false. But, I hope to have shown, logic shows no such thing as the first step in this line of thought.

REPLIES TO CRITICS

Timothy Williamson

Acknowledgements

Philosophy thrives on disagreement. Most of us enjoy disagreeing more than we enjoy being disagreed with, but the two are hard to separate. When I published *Knowledge and its Limits*, I knew that if it did not provoke disagreement it would have failed. In that respect the present volume is very reassuring. As with my other books, my short run aim was to persuade readers to take certain ideas seriously. In the long run, once the ideas are properly out there they can look after themselves, standing or falling on their merits. This volume will contribute significantly to that process.

I am conscious of a great debt of gratitude to each of the sixteen authors and friends who have contributed essays: Tony Brueckner, Quassim Cassam, Lizzie Fricker, Sanford Goldberg, Alvin Goldman, John Hawthorne, Frank Jackson, Mark Kaplan, Jon Kvanvig, Maria Lasonen-Aarnio, Ram Neta, Stephen Schiffer, Ernie Sosa, Matthias Steup, Neil Tennant, and Charles Travis. It is an honour to have such a distinguished group of philosophers engage so vigorously, so cleverly, and in so much detail with one's work. If I have repaid their disagreement with my own, that is probably what they expected. In conformity with the conventions of analytic philosophy, large areas of agreement have been passed over in silence by both sides.

I also owe a huge debt of gratitude to the two editors, Duncan Pritchard and Patrick Greenough, for suggesting the project in the first place (in February 2004) and for carrying it through to publication with so much patience, efficiency, and good judgement. Theirs has been a selfless task, if not an entirely thankless one—in virtue of these acknowledgements. They provided me with fast and helpful comments on my replies, on both philosophical and editorial matters. Like the authors, they had to put up with long delays in the writing of my replies, when my other commitments intervened. Gallingly for them, the promptest authors will have had to wait the longest.

Writing my replies has given me a valuable incentive to revisit and clarify many of the ideas in *Knowledge and its Limits*. In some cases I have used the opportunity to develop the ideas further—for instance, on evidential probability and safety in the reply to John Hawthorne and Maria Lasonen-Aarnio. In other cases I have brought what I said in *Knowledge and its Limits* into line with my more recent thinking—for instance, on conditions for concept possession in the reply to Quassim Cassam. In no case have I used the opportunity to water down the original conception.

Reply to Anthony Brueckner

In 'E = K and Perceptual Knowledge', Anthony Brueckner fails to make sense of my view because his discussion is imbued throughout with the traditional assumptions that I am denying.

In Brueckner's main example, he comes to know C (that his cup is red) in the ordinary way, by looking. He writes: 'what is the evidence that *generated* my knowledge of C, enabling that knowledge to serve as the evidential justifier for my belief of C? . . . C must have gotten into my total evidence *as a result of* my coming to justifiably believe it *on the basis of* some evidence' (emphasis added). This presupposes that he had some crucial evidence *before* he knew C, evidence nevertheless gained by looking at his cup. Of course, he may have had such evidence, if his knowledge of C happened to be inferential. But that is not the critical case; it does not pose so much as an apparent difficulty for my view. Assume for the sake of argument that Brueckner's knowledge of C was not derived from prior knowledge. Then no knowledge *generated* his knowledge of C; if evidence is knowledge, no evidence *generated* his knowledge of C. Rather, when he came to know C, C *ipso facto* became part of his total evidence. Similarly, if Brueckner's 'on the basis of' implies some temporal order, then he did not come justifiably to believe C *on the basis of* evidence. Rather, when he came to know C, and C simultaneously became part of his total evidence, he *ipso facto* came justifiably to believe C. Likewise, C did not get into his total evidence *as a result of* his coming justifiably to believe it; both things happened simultaneously in his coming to know C. When you recognize someone in the street, you are typically not justified in believing that it is her before you perceptually recognize her: but perceptually recognizing her *is* coming to know that it is her. Similarly, Brueckner was not justified in believing that his cup was red before he recognized any of its colour properties. Perceptual knowledge that preceded its perceptual evidence would indeed be blind: but perceptual knowledge coeval with its perceptual evidence is as sighted as it needs to be.[1]

We should not allow ourselves to be distracted by the presence of corroborating evidence with other contents. For instance, Brueckner probably also knows that his cup *looks* red. Thus his total evidence includes the proposition that his cup looks red as well as the proposition that it is red, and in many cases of uncertainty the former proposition would be evidence for the latter. But that does not imply

---

[1] The interpretation of the quoted passage as presupposing exactly what I deny is confirmed by Brueckner's later description of it as raising 'questions about how my belief of C becomes justified and how C then is able to enter into my body of total evidence'.

that in cases of no special uncertainty Brueckner's knowledge that his cup is red is in any way derivative from his knowledge that it looks red. For present purposes, the crucial element of his total evidence is C itself.

Curiously, Brueckner writes as though I hold that his total evidence includes the proposition that the cup looks red only in the bad case in which he does not know that it is red, and on that basis describes me as a 'disjunctivist' about evidence, despite my explicit disavowal of disjunctivism (pp. 44–8).[2] On the contrary, since one can know in a good case both that the cup is red and that it looks red, my view obviously implies that his total evidence can include both propositions simultaneously. It is just that the proposition about appearances does more work in the bad case than in the good one, where it is nearly redundant.

Presumably, the propositions that the cup is and looks red do not exhaust the richness of Brueckner's visual evidence on the occasion. He can see far more detail than that, including the more specific shade of red that the cup is. But this extra detail only complicates the picture without changing the epistemological fundamentals.

Brueckner thinks that I am committed to the claim that

I [AB] am justified in believing that my cup is red in virtue of, or because of, my belief that my cup is red.

On my view, he is justified in believing that his cup is red because he knows that his cup is red. How does he manage to replace knowledge by belief as the justifier on my view? He does so by importing another assumption about justification and evidence utterly at variance with my view. He explains it by example:

Suppose that I am justified in believing that Miles is sad and that my evidence is that he is crying in a characteristic way. Then I am justified in believing that Miles is sad in virtue, or because of, my belief of my evidential justifier—namely, the proposition that Miles is crying in a characteristic way.

The first sentence does not imply the second. Suppose that Brueckner is justified in believing that Miles is sad because his total evidence includes the proposition that Miles is crying in the characteristic way. Given E = K, it follows that Brueckner is justified in believing that Miles is sad because he knows that Miles is crying in the characteristic way. It does not follow that Brueckner is justified in believing that Miles is sad because he believes that Miles is crying in the characteristic way. Merely having the belief does not justify one in believing anything. If one believes on silly grounds that Miles is crying in that way, and infers that he is sad, one lacks knowledge and is not justified in believing on that basis that Miles is sad or anything else. Thus Brueckner is not justified in believing that Miles is sad in virtue or because of his belief that Miles is crying in the characteristic way.

---

[2] All page references in my replies are, unless otherwise specified, to *Knowledge and its Limits*.

One might try reading the definite description 'his belief that Miles is crying in the characteristic way' in the context of 'in virtue or because of' *de re*, as denoting what is in this case his *knowledge* that Miles is crying in that way. However, Brueckner later assumes that biting the bullet of the claim 'I am justified in believing that my cup is red in virtue of, or because of, my belief that my cup is red' would involve treating the belief as self-justifying in a way that would 'seem to imply that that every true belief about one's immediate environment is justified since justified by itself'. Since the *de re* reading has no such apparent consequence, applicable even to true beliefs that fall short of knowledge, it is presumably not what Brueckner intends. It would in any case not serve him dialectically, since it would remove the appearance of absurdity from the view he is ascribing to me in his attempted *reductio ad absurdum*.

Brueckner's chapter demonstrates the psychological power of an old-fashioned epistemological theory over those in its grip, rendering them unable to grasp plainly stated alternatives. That does not make the theory in less urgent need of replacement.

Reply to Quassim Cassam

1. In his searching contribution 'Can the Concept of Knowledge be Analysed?', Quassim Cassam suggests that my practice in *Knowledge and its Limits* is much closer than my overall theory allows to reductive conceptual analysis. For I characterize the verb 'know' as, up to synonymy, the most general factive mental state operator—the most general FMSO—and take myself to have explained the concept of an FMSO without using the concept of knowledge (pp. 37–9). What is this but an attempt at non-circular, reductive analysis of the concept of knowledge?

As I point out in the book, the account entails that it is not a decomposition of the concept of knowledge in any sense that implies that 'know' is semantically analysable, since semantic unanalysability is built into the definition of 'FMSO' as a necessary condition (pp. 36, 40). The concept of knowledge is not being identified with the concept of the most general factive mental state.[1] However, it may still seem that what I am proposing is, in Cassam's words, 'a non-decompositional but nevertheless reductive account of the concept of knowledge'.

In the end, Cassam detects an inconsistency between two lines of thought that he takes to be at work in my discussion, one reductive and one non-reductive. Both characterize the concept of knowledge in terms of the concept of an FMSO, and so involve some sort of conceptual analysis. The reductive line of thought insists that the concept of an FMSO can itself be explained without using the concept of knowledge. It makes the conceptual analysis reductive. By contrast, on the non-reductive line of thought, 'we will not have understood the notion of an FMSO unless we regard factive mental states as states of *knowledge*' (Cassam's words and emphasis). That makes the conceptual analysis non-reductive, in a more relaxed Strawsonian spirit: one traces conceptual connections between concepts at the same level, where ultimate circularity is only to be expected. His basis for ascribing the latter line of thought to me is one of the logical principles that I propose for FMSOs (p. 39):

(1) If Φ is an FMSO, from 'S Φs that A' one may infer 'S knows that A'.

---

[1] The individuation of concepts is notoriously problematic. For present purposes, we can think of them as types of linguistic or mental representation, typed by their meanings. Since different meanings may determine the same reference, different concepts may refer to X, for example when X = knowledge; thus 'the concept of X' is to be read as referring to the concept type of 'X'. When 'X' is a complex expression, the concept of X is a complex concept.

However, in the book I propose that being disposed to reason in accordance with a principle like (1) is necessary for possession of the concept of knowledge, not that it is necessary for possession of the concept of an FMSO (p. 40). Thus Cassam's explicit basis for ascribing the non-reductive line of thought to me fails to justify the ascription. This avoids the immediate inconsistency. Still, what about the alleged commitment to 'a non-decompositional but nevertheless reductive account of the concept of knowledge'?

Cassam reasonably stipulates that 'A concept C is more explanatorily basic than another concept D if and only if C can be explained without using D but D cannot be explained without using C'. On the reductive line of thought that he ascribes to me, the concept of an FMSO is explained without using the concept of knowledge, but the concept of knowledge cannot be explained without using the concept of an FMSO. So that line of thought treats the concept of an FMSO as explanatorily more basic than the concept of knowledge. According to Cassam: 'The distinguishing feature of reductive approaches to the concept of knowledge is precisely that they attempt to analyse this concept in terms of concepts that are more basic in the explanatory sense.' Therefore, on his view, my characterization of the concept of knowledge in terms of the concept of an FMSO counts as reductive.

We can distinguish more than one sense of 'explanation'. By giving examples or a rough verbal definition, one can often say enough to enable someone to become linguistically competent for the first time with an expression for some concept; call that a *working explanation* of the concept. A very different task is to give a theory about the underlying nature of a concept or its role in a wider setting, a theory that may come as a surprise to those who already have the concept and may not enable those who do not to acquire it; call that a *theorizing explanation* of the concept. To lump working explanations and theorizing explanations together will only obscure matters. We had better treat Cassam's definition of 'explanatorily more basic' for concepts as ambiguous, since 'explained' in it can be taken in either the working or the theorizing sense.

In the sense in which I explained the concept of an FMSO without using the concept of knowledge, I was giving a working explanation of the concept of an FMSO. I said enough to enable my readers to become linguistically competent for the first time with the expression 'FMSO'. But in that sense the concept of knowledge can certainly be explained without using the concept of an FMSO. By giving ordinary examples, one can say enough to enable someone to become linguistically competent for the first time with the word 'know'. Except in bizarre hypothetical cases, giving a working explanation of the concept of knowledge does not involve using the concept of an FMSO. One can have the concept of knowledge without having the sophisticated theoretical concept of an FMSO, for a disposition to reason in accordance with (1) requires only some causal sensitivity to the property of being an FMSO, not possession of the concept of an FMSO: on pain of an infinite regress, possessing a concept does not require possessing all the metaconceptual concepts used to characterize what it takes to possess the original concept (p. 40). Thus, in the working sense, neither the concept of knowledge nor the concept of an FMSO is explanatorily more basic than the other, because one can give a sufficiently good working explanation of either concept without using the other.

If the account in the book is correct, one cannot give a sufficiently good *theorizing* explanation of the concept of knowledge without using the concept of an FMSO, since one needs the latter concept in fully characterizing the logical role of the former, by rules such as (1). Equally, however, one cannot give a good theorizing explanation of the concept of an FMSO without using the concept of knowledge, since we shall not have acquired a good *theoretical* understanding of the concept of an FMSO unless we appreciate that the mental states to which operators that fall under the concept of an FMSO apply are states of knowledge, again in view of (1). Thus, in the theorizing sense, neither the concept of knowledge nor the concept of an FMSO is explanatorily more basic than the other, because one cannot give a sufficiently good theorizing explanation of either concept without using the other.

Consequently, the appearance of a reductive account of the concept of knowledge was a mere artefact of conflating different senses of 'explanation'. In no single sense is the concept of an FMSO explanatorily more basic than the concept of knowledge. However, that reopens the possibility that my account is a non-reductive conceptual analysis, in the relaxed Strawsonian sense that Cassam proposes. For knowing is indeed uniquely characterized (up to logical equivalence) in terms of FMSOs by two principles in the book, (1) and (2):

(2) 'Know' is an FMSO.

The book assimilates the unique characterization of knowledge by the principles (1) and (2) in status to the unique characterization of identity by the principles of reflexivity and Leibniz's Law (p. 40). Just as the metalogical concepts used in formulating Leibniz's Law are far more sophisticated than the simple concept of identity, so the metalinguistic concept of an FMSO is far more sophisticated than the simple concept of knowledge. It would be strange to call the unique characterization of identity by reflexivity and Leibniz's Law an 'analysis' of the concept of identity; it would be equally strange to call the unique characterization of knowledge by (1) and (2) an 'analysis' of the concept of knowledge.

In *Knowledge and its Limits* I do insist that in order to have the concept of knowledge one must be disposed to reason in accordance with (1) and (2), just as in order to have the concept of identity one must be disposed to reason in accordance with reflexivity and Leibniz's Law, although I allow that one can have the concepts while consciously rejecting the corresponding logical rules (pp. 40–1). The picture there is that one retains the underlying inferential disposition needed for possession of the concept even when it is inhibited by conscious thought processes. Such a putative constraint on concept possession supports the description of the account as an account of the *concept* of knowledge, not just of knowledge itself, and of the corresponding account as an account of the *concept* of identity, not just of identity itself.

In more recent work (Williamson 2007a: 99–133) I have come to reject the idea that being disposed to reason in accordance with associated canonical principles is necessary for having logical and other concepts. Even when theoretical unorthodoxy filters all the way down into speakers' underlying dispositions, they can retain linguistic competence, as their overall use of the language makes clear. For example, a native speaker of English, a philosopher confused by reading too much Hegel, may deny the reflexivity of identity and acquire a settled disposition to reject any statement of the form '*a* is *a*', as inconsistent with the dialectical nature of reality. When that disposition becomes second nature to him, he may lose any primitive disposition he once had to accept such statements. Nevertheless, his not unusual willingness to adopt ad hoc measures allows him to remain otherwise largely orthodox in his use of 'is'. He still accepts many statements of the form '*a* is *b*' and uses various other everyday patterns of reasoning whose derivation in standard logical systems involves the reflexivity of identity, although he rejects derivations by which instances of '*a* is *a*' could be recovered given his other commitments. He accepts 'Hesperus is Phosphorus' but not the reasoning from that premiss and the symmetry and transitivity of identity to the conclusion 'Hesperus is Hesperus'. His problem is that he is not very good at logic and philosophy (despite having a tenured university position teaching them), not that he lacks competence as a speaker of English. He retains linguistic understanding of the word 'is'; it would miss the point to send him off to language school for a refresher course. Correspondingly, he still possesses the concept of identity; he just has silly beliefs about identity. The overall shared practice of using 'is' by speakers of English so determines its reference that it in fact applies to every ordered pair of the form $<a, a>$, given the comparative unnaturalness of the alternatives (Williamson 2007a: 268), and our dissenter participates sufficiently in that practice for 'is' to retain its public semantics in his mouth.

Similar considerations apply to the concept of knowledge. Indeed, (1) is not uncontroversial, as I made clear in the book (pp. 37–8). For example, some philosophers treat 'remember' as a counter-example to (1). They hold that, given misleading evidence that one's memory is malfunctioning, one may remember that A without knowing that A, even though 'remember' is an FMSO (Steup 1992). If I am right, those philosophers are wrong; but obviously their error does not amount to linguistic, conceptual, or even philosophical incompetence. It is simply a misjudgement of a tricky case. That is quite compatible with the validity of (1) as an exceptionless generalization. On the view in *Knowledge and its Limits*, those philosophers presumably must have had an underlying overridden disposition to make the correct judgement. I now see no need to postulate such a disposition in them. Underlying errors about tricky hypothetical cases are well within the bounds of linguistic and conceptual competence. If I am right, the overall shared practice of using 'know' by speakers of English so determines its reference that (1) is in fact universally truth-preserving, given the comparative unnaturalness of the alternatives, and those philosophers participate sufficiently in that practice for 'know' to retain its public semantics in their mouths.

Once a disposition to reason in accordance with principles like (1) and (2) is no longer required as a necessary condition for possessing the concept of knowledge, it becomes even less tempting to regard the account as an analysis of the *concept* of knowledge. Even in its non-reductive Strawsonian form, conceptual analysis is still supposed to be an enquiry into our conceptual scheme. The conceptual connections that it aims to trace are presumably supposed to have some sort of analytic status. For example, if, as I am suggesting, the connection between 'remember' and 'know' has no such analytic status, why regard it as reflecting a connection between the *concept* of factual memory and the *concept* of knowledge, rather than simply a connection between factual memory and knowledge themselves?

Of course, (1) and (2) are formulated in explicitly metalinguistic terms. They mention the word 'know' rather than using it. That may seem to undermine the claim that their primary concern is with knowledge itself. However, in formulating a rule of inference, one is typically forced into semantic ascent, in order to state exactly what counts as an instance of it: imagine, for instance, explaining Leibniz's Law for a particular language to a novice. It does not follow that the subject matter of the rule is in any sense metalinguistic or metaconceptual. Its instances comprise sentences of the object-language, which are no more about words or concepts than other sentences of the object-language are. If Leibniz's Law is about anything, it is about identity, not the concept of identity. Similarly, (1) and (2) are metalinguistic formulations of rules that are about knowledge and other factive mental states, not the concepts of those states, if they are about anything.

If principles like (1) and (2) are not analytic, how can we know them? They are not immediately obvious. If we know them at all, we know them by a methodology in which the evaluation of actual and counterfactual examples plays a central role. To evaluate such examples, we must answer questions of forms like these: Does S remember that A? Does S know that A? If such-and-such were the case, would S remember that A? If such-and-such were the case, would S know that A? Those are simply questions about factual memory and knowledge in actual and counterfactual cases. Of course, one is ill placed to answer them if one does not understand the words 'remember' and 'know', but that is just an application of the obvious general point that one is ill placed to answer any question that one does not understand; it has no special connection with analyticity. One answers the questions by deploying concepts of factual memory and knowledge, but again there is nothing special in that. Typically, one answers the questions about actual cases by deploying those concepts online, and one answers the questions about counterfactual cases by deploying the same concepts offline. 'Conceptual connections' are no more needed in the latter case than they are in the former.[2]

To characterize knowledge as the most general factive state is not to engage in conceptual analysis, however relaxed and circular. It is simply to theorize about knowledge.

2.   Much of Cassam's chapter is a critical examination of my reasons for denying that the concept of knowledge can be analysed into more basic concepts. He takes my best argument to be what he calls the Inductive Argument, from the long history of failures in that enterprise, and he seems to allow it significant weight. I agree that the Inductive Argument gives the clearest independent evidence for the unanalysability of the concept of knowledge into more basic concepts. Cassam reasonably complains that the brevity of its presentation—one paragraph (p. 30)—could easily mislead the reader into underestimating its dialectical importance in the book. The reason for the brevity was simply that I had no appetite for writing, and conjectured that few readers had much appetite for reading, yet another account of the failure of all attempts so far. I lazily referred readers to Robert Shope (1983) for the history up to his time of writing, and commented that an equally complex book could be written on later developments. I also widened the basis of the induction by citing the long histories of failures to analyse other philosophically interesting concepts, such as the concepts of meaning and of causation, into more basic concepts (p. 31).

As a supporting consideration, I argued that there is no positive reason to expect the concept of knowledge to be analysable into more basic concepts. Cassam calls that the False Expectations Argument. In particular, the fact that truth and belief are necessary for knowledge does not entitle one to expect that those necessary conditions can be expanded to some (non-circular) conditions that are jointly sufficient and individually necessary for knowledge, just as the fact that being coloured is necessary for being red does not entitle one to expect that that necessary condition can be expanded to some (non-circular) conditions that are jointly sufficient and individually necessary for being red. Cassam objects that this analogy does not show that the concept of knowledge cannot be analysed into more basic concepts, since it has not been ruled out that the concept of knowledge is complex while the concept of being red is simple. But the analogy was not supposed to show that the concept of knowledge cannot be analysed into more basic concepts. It was only supposed to show that the fact that truth and belief are necessary for knowledge does not by itself entitle one to expect

---

[2] The epistemology of the method of cases and the critique of analyticity gestured at here are developed at much greater length and breadth in Williamson (2007a).

that the concept of knowledge can be analysed into more basic concepts. In that more modest task, the analogy succeeds. That truth and belief are necessary for knowledge does not by itself entitle one to expect that the concept of knowledge *is* complex in the relevant sense.

Some grand philosophical theories entail that an ambitious programme of conceptual analysis can in principle succeed (pp. 31–2). For instance, some strong versions of empiricism do so. I noted that many analytic philosophers have continued to pursue the programme even after giving up the rationale for expecting it to succeed. Cassam suggests that a general desire to understand the nature of knowledge provides a more plausible rationale for contemporary epistemologists' attempts to analyse the concept of knowledge, where the standard for success is something like non-trivial a priori necessary equivalence rather than concept identity. It is doubtful that a general desire to understand the nature of knowledge provides a good rationale for the highly specific way in which the post-Gettier tradition developed. Indeed, many of the proposed analyses made knowledge look so gerrymandered that its nature was not worth understanding, and our caring about it a puzzle (p. 31). Moreover, given the picture of concept possession sketched in the previous section, this looser sort of 'conceptual analysis' has no special connection with concepts. But I agree with Cassam that the most effective way to demonstrate the limitations of the post-Gettier tradition is by developing a better alternative. That was my main concern in *Knowledge and its Limits*, as it is Cassam's in *The Possibility of Knowledge* (2007).

Cassam devotes much of his attention to what he calls the Distinct Concepts Argument. This is the argument that the concept of knowledge is distinct from the complex concept of the analysans in a traditional analysis, because the former concept is purely mental while the latter is not, since the analysans includes truth as a separate condition. To the premiss that the concept of knowledge is purely mental, Cassam objects that it is too contentious to carry the required dialectical weight. In particular, he denies that there is a pre-theoretic presumption in its favour:

As Williamson's own discussion illustrates, it takes a good deal of sophisticated argument to weaken the prejudice that a factive attitude can't be merely a state of mind, and this is difficult to reconcile with the suggestion that we have a pre-theoretical commitment to the idea that knowing is merely mental.

One issue here is whether 'the prejudice that a factive attitude can't be merely a state of mind' comes from common sense or from background philosophical theory. I suspect that Cassam might agree, for instance, that sceptical arguments often rely on prejudices that come from background philosophical theory and run contrary to common sense, even though it takes a good deal of sophisticated argument to weaken them. There may still be a pre-theoretic presumption in favour of the common sense alternatives to those prejudices. But the Distinct

Concepts Argument was in any case never intended to persuade readers that the concept of knowledge cannot be analysed in the traditional way. The intended direction of support was rather the opposite. The hypothesis that the concept of knowledge is purely mental predicts that it is distinct from the complex concept of the analysans in a traditional analysis; experience inductively confirms this prediction, and thereby supports the hypothesis that the concept of knowledge is purely mental by inference to the best explanation (p. 30).

Cassam concludes that my account of knowing 'is the beginning rather than the end of the story in epistemology'. It never occurred to me to think of anything in *Knowledge and its Limits* as even close to the end of the story. I am no enemy of positive theorizing in philosophy. I am not convinced by Cassam's specific Kantian framework for theorizing about knowledge by explaining how different kinds of knowledge are possible, since I take those explanatory tasks to be primarily reactive, clearly defined only in the presence of pre-existing theoretical arguments against the possibility of those kinds of knowledge, but that may not be a very deep difference between us. It often strikes me that in epistemology we are still scratching at the surface of the phenomena. But I take the nature of knowledge to be our best indication of the way to go deeper; perhaps Cassam would agree.

Reply to Elizabeth Fricker

In 'Is Knowing a State of Mind? The Case Against', Elizabeth Fricker defends a combination of internalism about the propositional attitudes with externalism about the contents of those attitudes. However, the arguments in the book already contain the resources to undermine her defence.

1. Fricker denies that any purely mental state is sufficient for knowing. She does not go so far as to claim that some particular conjunction of a mental with a non-mental condition is necessary and sufficient for the condition that one knows. Rather, she defends a claim about individual instances of knowing:

> *CI (Compound Instances)*: Every instance of someone's knowing that P consists in her being in some mental condition short of knowing, plus some non-mental condition obtaining.

Fricker treats defending CI as tantamount to arguing against the thesis that knowing is a purely mental state.

According to Fricker, if CI were true, so would be this supervenience claim:

> *Supervenience of Knowing*: In every situation Si in which someone NN knows that P, there is a weakest compound (mental and non-mental) condition CC(Si) that holds of NN, specifiable without predicating 'knows' of NN, such that any other situation in which CC(Si) obtained would be one in which she knows that P.

She glosses 'weakest' thus:

> For all conditions CC(Si)-minus, which include some but not all components of CC(Si), there are possible situations in which CC(Si)-minus holds of NN, but NN fails to know that P.

The non-mental component of CC(Si) is to be understood as irredundant.

CI may appear to permit the mental component to vary in type from one instance to another. But Fricker holds that the fatal failure of internalism about content was to specify in mental terms the postulated narrow, purely mental fillets of broad content ascriptions in natural languages. She accepts that 'the burden of proof is on the denier of KMS [the thesis that knowing is a purely mental state] to show that non-factive mental fillets of knowing exist'. Moreover, she is willing to meet the challenge by specifying in mental terms a quite general non-factive purely mental fillet of knowing (although, of course, this purely mental fillet will be subject to content externalism, and in that respect broad rather than narrow). Indeed, she says: 'Whether such a general condition exhausting the mental component in knowing can be formulated is thus an absolutely crucial question in the case for KMS.' Her candidate is justified belief. More specifically, she holds that knowing adds nothing mental to justified belief, in this sense:

(J) For any possible situation $S(JB - K)$ of justified belief that is not an instance of knowing, there is a possible situation $S(JB + K)$ that is an instance of knowing, where $S(JB - K)$ and $S(JB + K)$ differ only in non-mental factors.

Presumably, therefore, the mental condition in CI and the Supervenience of Knowing is always justified belief with the relevant content.

The Supervenience of Knowing as formulated by Fricker may also exert some pressure in the direction of the sort of generality that (J) exhibits. For assume the Supervenience of Knowing and let Si and Sj be any two situations in which someone knows that P. Since $CC(Si)$ and $CC(Sj)$ hold in Si and Sj respectively, the disjunctive condition $CC(Si) \vee CC(Sj)$ holds in both Si and Sj. Since $CC(Si)$ and $CC(Sj)$ are both specifiable without predicating 'know' of the subject, so is $CC(Si) \vee CC(Sj)$. Since the subject knows that P in any situation in which $CC(Si)$ holds and in any situation in which $CC(Sj)$ holds, the subject knows that P in any situation in which $CC(Si) \vee CC(Sj)$ holds. Does $CC(Si) \vee CC(Sj)$ count as a 'compound (mental and non-mental) condition'? It has not been shown to be a *conjunction* of mental and non-mental condition. However, Fricker insists that those who conceive knowing as a metaphysical hybrid of the mental and the non-mental need not conceive it as the conjunction of something purely mental with something purely non-mental, since it may also include relations between the purely mental and the purely non-mental.[1] Apparently, therefore, $CC(Si) \vee CC(Sj)$ counts as a 'compound (mental and non-mental) condition' in the sense that Fricker herself regards as most relevant. Since $CC(Si)$ is supposed to be the weakest condition meeting the given constraints, and $CC(Si) \vee CC(Sj)$ meets those constraints and is at least as weak as $CC(Si)$, $CC(Si) \vee CC(Sj)$ must entail $CC(Si)$, otherwise it would be a weaker condition than $CC(Si)$ meeting those constraints, contrary to hypothesis. But then $CC(Sj)$ also entails $CC(Si)$, since it entails $CC(Si) \vee CC(Sj)$ and entailment is transitive. Conversely, $CC(Si)$ entails $CC(Sj)$, by an exactly analogous argument. Thus $CC(Si)$ and $CC(Sj)$ are equivalent to each other. Since Si and Sj were any two situations in which someone knows that P, the apparent scope in the Supervenience of Knowing for

---

[1] Contrary to Fricker's claim that the book neglects this possibility of non-conjunctive compounds (in her terminology, three-component hybrids), a whole section is devoted to it (pp. 89–92). She claims that the possibility undermines my argument against the analysability of knowing, at both the conceptual and the metaphysical level. She seems to be confusing this argument with the argument that knowing is prime. But the inductive argument against analysability (pp. 30–1) is quite separate, and in no way restricted to conjunctive analyses.

the compound condition to vary from one instance to another of knowing that P is illusory.[2]

In view of some obscurities in the details of Fricker's formulation of the Supervenience of Knowing, the foregoing argument is not quite decisive. Nevertheless, the cost of resisting it in ad hoc manœuvring is likely to be high.

Let us examine critically Fricker's overall position, as summed up in CI, the Supervenience of Knowing and (J).

2.   In the book, knowing is a *general* mental state. Different people at different times may all be in the state of knowing **p**. The idea of a token state is explicitly abjured (p. 40). As noted there, Helen Steward's work (1997: 105–34) has shown how problematic it is. The thesis that knowing is a mental state says what kind of general state knowing is. It does not say what the metaphysics of instances of that general state is, because it is does not even employ the idea of an instance of a general state. According to Fricker, however, the thesis says nothing surprising or metaphysically radical unless it has significant consequences for the metaphysics of instances of knowing—if not, she does not dispute the thesis. As CI illustrates, Fricker opposes the thesis that an instance of knowing cannot be analysed into a mental condition short of knowing and a non-mental condition. She is not concerned to oppose the thesis that the general state of knowing has no such analysis.

Fricker maintains that at various points in the book I commit myself to 'this idea of realizing instances and what constitutes them making sense'. In support, she quotes a passage in which I say 'No doubt the particular circumstances that in some sense realize the state [of knowing] in a given case can be described in many different ways' (p. 63). But the circumstances in question are simply a supervenience base for knowing in the given case. The supervenience base may be describable in purely physical terms. This is not the level at which the question whether knowing is a mental state arises.

By analogy, consider the thesis that being evil is a physical state. It is surely contentious. But what is most contentious about it is not the thought that in any given case the supervenience base for being evil consists of physical circumstances, which many who oppose the thesis might accept. Rather, the thesis is contentious as a claim about what kind of state being evil is. The thesis that knowing is a mental state is contentious in a similar way.

Perhaps by an 'instance' of a general state Fricker does not mean a supervenience base. But then it is not clear what she does mean. Her claim CI requires that an instance of a general state 'consists in' a condition 'plus' another condition 'obtaining'. Her conditions are general, like mine, her engagement with the

---

[2] CI seems to lack this powerful consequence of the Supervenience of Knowing. If so, the Supervenience of Knowing does not follow from CI.

discussion in the book suggests that she intends to be using the term with the same sense as there, and she offers no alternative explanation. One might, therefore, expect the instance to inherit some generality from the conditions in which it consists. But she gives no account of any such generality for instances. Again, her gloss on 'weakest' in the Supervenience of Knowing speaks of the 'components' of the condition CC(Si). But conditions in my sense do not have components. Their individuation is coarse-grained: conditions are identical if and only if they obtain in the same cases (pp. 52, 94). A condition has no privileged decomposition into components, just as a set has no privileged decomposition into the supersets of which it is the intersection.[3]

The book's focus on general conditions is not merely in order to avoid metaphysical obscurity. Its primary motivation is positive. Only by focusing on general conditions can we identify the crucial causal-explanatory factors in a given case. This is argued at length (pp. 80–9). The book uses correlation coefficients to measure a combination of how nearly sufficient and how nearly necessary a candidate explaining condition S1 is for the condition S2 to be explained. The component that measures how nearly necessary S1 is for S2 is what rewards the relevant generality of S1. Fricker significantly mischaracterizes this idea by glossing 'correlation coefficient' as 'more or less equivalently, the conditional probability of S2 on S1'; that probability concerns only how nearly *sufficient* S1 is for S2. Thus her gloss omits exactly what is now at issue, the value of generality.

Despite Fricker's unwillingness to dispute the thesis that knowing is a mental state in its intended sense, her view is incompatible with the position developed in the book. More specifically, her claim (J) that knowledge adds nothing mental to justified belief is directly disputed in the book with reference to an earlier version of her critique (pp. 57–9). The discussion is phrased in terms of 'rational belief', but it is noted that 'justified belief' would have done as well. We therefore turn to the assessment of (J).

3.   Fricker herself unintentionally raises a problem for (J) by claiming, as a criticism of the book's account of belief, that belief is compatible with a lower level of confidence than knowledge requires. Thus knowing entails a higher level of confidence than believing does. Suppose that knowing entails having a confidence level greater than c, while believing does not. Presumably, therefore, there is a possible situation S(JB − K) of justified belief with confidence level no greater than c. Thus S(JB − K) is not an instance of knowing. Consequently, according to (J), there is a possible situation S(JB + K) that is an instance of knowing, where S(JB − K) and S(JB + K) differ only in non-mental factors.

---

[3] This is one complication with the argument for the invariance of CC(Si) at the end of the previous section. However, that argument uses the most charitable reconstruction of 'weakest' that makes sense for conditions.

Since S(JB + K) is an instance of knowing, the confidence level in S(JB + K) is greater than c. Thus S(JB − K) and S(JB + K) differ in confidence level. But one's level of confidence is uncontentiously a mental factor. So S(JB − K) and S(JB + K) differ in a mental factor after all. Therefore (J) is false.

Can a revised version of (J) meet this problem by specifying a confidence level? The trouble is that what is to be specified is the minimum confidence level necessary for *knowledge*. Fricker writes: 'Crucially, I do not accept Williamson's own view that what it is for a belief to be justified itself has to be explained in terms of knowledge . . . I think one can give an independent, mentalistic . . . account of justifiedness of belief.' She does not address the problem of giving an account, without reference to knowledge, of what level of confidence is required for knowledge or of what justifies belief with that level of confidence.

I will not press this particular objection to (J), because it depends on Fricker's unsupported claim that knowledge requires more confidence than belief, which I do not accept. Modest people know many things without being especially confident of them. Instead, I will sketch the objections to (J) in the book.

Fricker concedes that (J) fails for beliefs in necessarily false propositions and for false beliefs about one's own mental state, two cases mentioned in the book (p. 56). In fact, they are used there against the analogue of (J) without 'justified' but not against (J) itself, since some internalists may say that such false beliefs are unjustified, but we can take Fricker's word for it that they are exceptions to (J) as she intends it. She says that 'we surely need not worry about [them], since they are clearly special'. She does not explain why it is legitimate to dismiss counter-examples to one's view as 'clearly special' here but not everywhere else. Presumably, her intention is to modify (J), replacing 'any possible situation' by 'most possible situations'. Of course, if for even one possible situation S(JB − K) of justified belief that is not an instance of knowing there is a possible situation S(JB + K) that is an instance of knowing, where S(JB − K) and S(JB + K) differ only in non-mental factors, then knowing is not a mental state, for otherwise S(JB − K) and S(JB + K) would differ in the mental factor of knowing. Thus even a drastically watered-down version of (J) would be incompatible with the thesis that knowing is a mental state. Dialectically, however, the purpose for which Fricker proposed (J) was not simply to be incompatible with that thesis but to meet the challenge to specify the supposed 'mental fillet' of knowing short of knowing itself. The more exceptions (J) has, the less it does to meet that challenge.

Fricker says that, apart from the examples above, my case against (J) 'is confined to the claim that there are "notorious difficulties in stating a correct justification condition on knowledge"' (p. 57). That is indeed where the relevant discussion ended in the original article (Williamson 1995), which did not explicitly consider (J). She has failed to notice the extended discussion of (J) that follows in the book (pp. 57–9), presumably because it did not appear in the 1995 article.

One point in the book is that (J) creates a problem of motivation for those, like Fricker, who accept externalism about the contents of propositional attitudes but reject externalism about the attitudes themselves. Consider a possible case in which you endorse an argument of the form 'A is F, therefore something is F', and on that basis comes to believe that something is F. Everything is fine, except that the singular term 'A' suffers undetectable reference failure—it may be a perceptual demonstrative in a case of illusion—in such a way that, by the relevant sort of content externalism, 'A is F' fails to express a proposition, and you have no belief from which you reached the belief that something is F by existential generalization. Clearly, you do not know that something is F. Call that situation S(JB − K). Suppose that in S(JB − K) your belief that something is F is nevertheless justified. Therefore, (J) implies, there is a possible situation S(JB + K) that is an instance of knowing, where S(JB − K) and S(JB + K) differ only in non-mental factors. But whether one's belief in an existential conclusion derives by existential generalization from one's belief in a corresponding premiss is a mental factor. Therefore, in S(JB + K) too the subject's belief in the existential conclusion does not derive by existential generalization from their belief in a corresponding premiss, and so in the circumstances is not adequately based. Thus in S(JB + K) too the subject does not know, contrary to hypothesis. Hence in S(JB − K) your belief that something is F is not justified after all. This is a sort of externalism about the attitude of justified belief, induced by the combination of (J) and content externalism. Whether your existential belief is justified is sensitive to whether you are the victim of an undetectable illusion, even though you have the existential belief in both the good and bad cases. For Fricker, justified belief is a purely mental state. But, if a purely mental state can be subject to this degree of externalism, not just with respect to its content but with respect to the attitude to that content, what is the objection to the claim that knowing is a purely mental state? The combination of (J) and content externalism makes the denial that knowing is a mental state ill motivated.

A further problem for (J) raised in the book is similar to the one about confidence levels, without depending on Fricker's controversial assumption that knowledge requires more confidence than belief. Suppose that someone believes on strong probabilistic grounds that her ticket will not win the lottery. If this belief is justified, then by (J) there is a corresponding possible situation in which the subject knows on probabilistic grounds that her ticket will not win. But that belief would not constitute knowledge: one cannot know on merely probabilistic grounds whether a ticket will win the lottery. Therefore in the original situation the belief is not justified after all. Yet there does not appear to be anything wrong with the belief, by non-sceptical standards, until one asks whether it could constitute knowledge. How can one specify an appropriate standard of justification that excludes the original belief, without reference to knowledge?

The objections in the book to Fricker's position, and specifically to (J), stand. She has not responded to them. Consequently, she has not shown how to specify the supposed 'mental fillet' of knowing short of knowing itself. As she acknowledges, without such a specification her denial that knowing is a mental state is implausible in the same way as is the denial of content externalism.

4.   Fricker has another style of argument for her account and against the thesis that knowing is a mental state. She presents two alternative accounts of the semantics of 'knows' on which it lacks an analysis of the standard kind. According to her, both accounts 'sit naturally with the view that instances of knowing are hybrid' (CI), and are better than the bare account in the book at explaining the entailments of 'knows'. One of her semantic accounts says that 'knows' is a family resemblance term. The other says that 'knows' is an evaluative term.

Why should such accounts be conducive to CI? The considerations that Fricker adduces are quite generic. They show at best that her semantic accounts sit naturally with the view that in any given case knowing supervenes on an independently specifiable basis. That supervenience claim is entirely compatible with the thesis that knowing is a mental state, as the book makes clear.

The generic family resemblance account of 'knows' can easily be developed in the direction of the book. Just as something is a case of knowing if and only if it is a case of one of an open-ended list of specific ways of knowing, such as seeing (p. 34), so something is a case of a game if and only if it is a case of one of an open-ended list of specific types of game, such as board games.[4] The generic family resemblance account does not favour CI. Nor would one expect a family resemblance account to yield anything as definite as (J), on which the mental consequences of knowing can be neatly circumscribed.

The generic evaluative account of 'knows' too can easily be developed in the direction of the book. I suggested that 'Knowing is . . . the best kind of believing' (p. 47). 'Knows' might pick out the mental state towards which all believing aspires. The generic evaluative account does not favour CI. One might initially expect an evaluative account to be more conducive to (J), since 'justified' is itself an evaluative term. However, Fricker requires 'justified belief' to import a *different* standard of evaluation from 'knowledge', for otherwise the purely mental fillet of knowing in (J) would be tantamount to knowing itself. If the standards of evaluation differ, one still has to explain why the purely mental fillet of believing that counts as good by one standard should be believing that counts as good by another standard.

---

[4] I avoided the notion of a family resemblance term in the book because it is too slippery and unhelpful.

Although I do not endorse either semantic account, even as developed in the direction of the book, the ease of such developments shows how little the generic semantic accounts support Fricker's argument.

The book acknowledges several consequences of knowledge: truth, belief, safety, justification, the absence of false lemmas. According to Fricker, both the family resemblance account and the evaluative account do better than the account in the book in terms of factive mental state operators (FMSOs) at explaining these entailments. Unfortunately, she gives almost no details as to *how* her semantic accounts explain them. The best we get is this:

The default hypothesis is that these conditions are knowable by us to be necessary for knowing just through reflection, because our tacit grasp of them mediates our everyday applications of the concept—either as elements in a family resemblance concept, or as deeply entrenched folk theory about what is necessary for 'the right to be sure'.

Neither of these suggestions advances her case. Knowledge of necessary conditions is exactly the sort of thing that mastery of a family resemblance concept is supposed *not* to deliver. Wittgenstein's paradigmatic discussion of 'game' as a family resemblance term famously does not issue in a set of necessary conditions for being a game (1958: §§66–71). Indeed, on a standard conception of a family resemblance term, one would expect that the absence of any one of the associated features could be compensated for by the sufficiently marked presence of several others. As for the suggestion that, on the evaluative account, one can explain knowledge of the necessary conditions for knowing as deeply entrenched folk theory about what is necessary for the right to be sure, it could just as well be explained as deeply entrenched folk theory about what is necessary for knowing, without the digression through the evaluative account. Neither of Fricker's semantic accounts provides a good explanation of the phenomena at issue.

In the book, I briefly suggest that one can sometimes know by reflection that one thing is necessary for another without relying on any semantic complexity in the relevant terms: in that way one may know that being red is necessary for being crimson and that believing is necessary for knowing (pp. 43–4). I did not conceive the logical principles for 'knows' in terms of FMSOs as implying any semantic structure in 'knows', any more than the logical principles for '=' imply any semantic structure in '=' (p. 40).[5] However, I did say that, although possession of the relevant concepts is consistent with conscious rejection of the logical rules governing them, it does require at least a disposition to reason according to those rules (pp. 40–1). That last concession I now regard as unwarranted. When enough else remains in place, someone can lose even the disposition and still retain possession of the concept and linguistic competence with the word (Williamson 2007a: 99–133). What explains reflective knowledge

---

[5] In this sense Fricker is incorrect to say that the FMSO account attributes semantic complexity to 'knows'.

of necessary conditions formulated in terms of simple concepts is not their possession conditions but one's skill in applying them (compare ibid.: 165–9). Two people can both understand the word 'knows' in its same everyday sense, and possess the corresponding concept, while disagreeing, even at the level of their dispositions, about its necessary conditions. The level of skill required for knowledgeably assessing necessary conditions is much higher than the level required for mere linguistic competence and possession of the concept.

Moving from epistemological to metaphysical phenomena, Fricker says: 'I do not believe there is a coherent account of the source of these supposed essential features of states other than explaining them as conceptual in origin.' But it is unclear how essential features of the states in question could be conceptual in origin. States are not themselves conceptual in nature. Different concepts can pick out the same state: the state of having a part made of gold *is* the state of having a part made of the element with atomic number 79. To try to explain why whales are mammals by talking about the word 'mammal' is a use–mention confusion; whales would be mammals however we used the word 'mammal'. To try to explain essential features of states by talking about how we conceptualize those states looks like the analogue for concepts of a use–mention confusion; the states have those essential features however we conceptualize them. If there is a good explanation, it is at the metaphysical not the conceptual level.

Semantics will not give Fricker what she wants. There is no evidence that 'knows' has any kind of semantic complexity that would constitute a threat to the view that it picks out a purely mental state.

Reply to Sanford Goldberg

1. In 'The Knowledge Account of Assertion and the Nature of Testimonial Knowledge', Sanford Goldberg proposes an indirect empirical test of the knowledge account of assertion, by comparison of its predictions with those of rival accounts of assertion concerning hearers' reactions to testimony. I have no quarrel with the general nature of his enterprise. On the knowledge account, 'Assert only if you know' is the constitutive rule of assertion. Arguably, the knowledge account, if true, is necessarily true, like other accounts of the essential nature of kinds (p. 239). In that case it does not by itself entail any contingent claims about hearers' behaviour. But that does not stop us testing it by observing contingencies, just as we can test 'Gold is the element with atomic number 79' by observing contingencies. For, if we conjoin a non-contingent hypothesis with independently well-confirmed contingent auxiliary hypotheses, we can derive further contingent predictions that we can independently verify or falsify by observation, thereby testing the non-contingent hypothesis. The knowledge account of assertion is as susceptible to this methodology as any other non-contingent hypothesis.

Goldberg goes further, claiming that we are not in a position to accept the knowledge account until we have carried out the empirical tests (with positive results). This claim is uncomfortably close to a fallacy that is in the offing with much 'experimental philosophy': that, if we *can* test a proposition empirically in a certain way, then we are not justified in accepting it until we *have* tested it in that way. By that standard, we are justified in accepting virtually nothing. For example, we could in principle test the claim that there is a bridge over the Thames in London by making observations of Earth from Mars with fantastically powerful instruments, and we have not done so. Nevertheless, we are already justified in accepting that there is a bridge over the Thames in London. Similarly, we could in principle test the claim that there is no largest prime number empirically, by emailing 10,000 professors of mathematics to ask whether it is true (plausible auxiliary hypothesis: for fairly simple mathematical propositions, acceptance by professors of mathematics is highly correlated with truth). Despite not having done so, we are already justified by the standard proof that there is no largest prime. Although the knowledge account is nothing like as well established as the two claims just mentioned, the question remains whether the particular tests that Goldberg recommends would in practice be of much use in helping one decide between it and its rivals.

2.   The task is not unlike that of trying to work out the rules of a game from watching it being played, without access to a rule book. Too crude a use of statistical correlations will lead us astray. For example, suppose that we have already managed to identify the umpire and a particular penalty. From our large data set, we calculate that receiving the penalty is more highly correlated with appearing to the umpire to have one's foot over a certain line than with really having one's foot over that line. Should we conclude that what the rule forbids is appearing to the umpire to have one's foot over the line, not having one's foot over the line? Surely not. After all, on the hypothesis that what the rule forbids is really having one's foot over the line, we still expect receiving the penalty to be more highly correlated with appearing to the umpire to have one's foot over the line than with really having one's foot over the line, because we expect it to be more highly correlated with appearing to the umpire to have broken the rule than with really having broken the rule, since it is the umpire there and then who imposes the penalty. The genuine differences in predictions between the two hypotheses are subtler than that. Once we make a more fine-grained analysis of the data, we realize that they support the hypothesis that what the rule forbids is really having one's foot over the line against the alternative hypothesis. For example, we can observe the anger of the disadvantaged players when the umpire imposes the penalty but they can see that the foot was not over the line, or the umpire imposes no penalty but they can see that the foot was over the line.

The obvious worry is that Goldberg's proposed empirical tests depend on similar methodological errors. For example, he supposes that whether hearers' accept a stranger's assertion on a matter concerning which they lack prior information is highly correlated with how much apparent confidence the assertion was made with, which is in turn more highly correlated with whether the speaker is justified in believing that she knows than with whether she really does know.[1] He seems to think that such results would (defeasibly) support the hypothesis that the rule of assertion is 'Assert only if you are justified in believing that you know' against the hypothesis that it is 'Assert only if you know'. That is analogous to the mistake above of thinking that the data support the hypothesis that the rule is 'Don't appear to the umpire to put your foot over the line' against the hypothesis that it is 'Don't put your foot over the line'. For, on the hypothesis

---

[1] A further problem with Goldberg's argument is that it does not adequately distinguish between accepting an assertion of **p** in the sense of accepting **p** on the basis of that assertion and accepting that the assertion conformed to the relevant norm (the difference is relevant to whether the hearer is willing to go on and assert **p** herself). The difference in extension is comparatively small on the knowledge account: if one accepts that the speaker knew **p** then one presumably accepts **p** itself, given the factiveness of knowledge, and, conversely, it would be unusual (although not impossible) to accept **p** on the basis of an assertion of it without accepting that the speaker knew **p**. The difference is larger on the rival accounts that Goldberg considers, on which the epistemic norm for assertion is a non-factive justification condition. For then one can consistently accept that the speaker met the justification condition for asserting **p** without accepting **p** oneself.

that the rule is 'Assert only if you know', we still expect the hearer's belief as to whether the speaker violated the rule to be more highly correlated with whether the speaker appeared to the hearer to be violating the rule than with whether the speaker really was violating the rule. In the absence of other sources of evidence (which Goldberg stipulates), the appearance of knowing may sometimes boil down to little more than the appearance of confidence. The genuine differences in predictions between the two hypotheses are subtler. We need to make a more fine-grained analysis of the data in order to realize that the data support the hypothesis that the rule is 'Assert only if you know', not 'Assert only if you are justified in believing that you know'. *Knowledge and its Limits* supplies just such a fine-grained analysis of the conversational data (pp. 252–63).

Naturally, any further means of squeezing testably different predictions out of rival accounts of the norms of assertion are to be welcomed. Data about the transmission of testimony may turn out to be a good source for such tests. But the crude comparisons that Goldberg proposes do not work, because they do not properly consider what predictions the rival hypotheses actually make. At one stage in writing on assertion I had hoped to give a further argument for the knowledge account based on the epistemology of testimony, but the relevant considerations depended on so many uncertain auxiliary assumptions that they did not offer a reliable way of discriminating between the rival hypotheses. A good explanation of the transmission of knowledge by testimony must assume some account of assertion, and the knowledge account of assertion is the obvious candidate. However, no account of assertion can solve all problems in the epistemology of testimony, and the complexities of the epistemology of testimony give any account of assertion much room for manœuvre. In *Knowledge and its Limits* I contented myself with a few inconclusive remarks on the matter (pp. 267–8). It should be possible to integrate the epistemology of testimony with an account of the knowledge norm of assertion more systematically. I leave the challenge open.

Reply to Alvin Goldman

Alvin Goldman's 'Williamson on Knowledge and Evidence' divides naturally into two parts, one on my account of knowledge (the first five sections) and one on my account of evidence (the final two sections). I deal with each in turn.

1. Goldman argues that my account of knowledge in terms of safety is no advance on other reliability accounts of knowledge. However, two misconceptions about my account pervade his discussion.

The first misunderstanding is methodological. Goldman says of me that 'he regards [a safety condition] as a non-circular necessary condition [for knowledge]'. I do not, now or in the book. On my view, one knows in a given case only if one avoids error in cases similar to that one, but we cannot specify in a non-circular way how similar a case must be to fall under that condition, or what relative weights should be given to different respects of similarity. On the contrary, with the 'knowledge-first' methodology of *Knowledge and its Limits*, we should expect to have to use our understanding of knowledge to determine whether the similarity to a case of error is great enough in a given case to exclude knowledge. As I put it in the book (pp. 100–1):

> The vagueness in 'sufficiently similar' matches the vagueness in 'reliable', and in 'know'. Since the account of knowledge developed in Chapter 1 implies that the reliability condition will not be a conjunct in a non-circular analysis of the concept *knows*, we need not even assume that we can specify the relevant degree and kind of similarity without using the concept *knows*. . . We cannot expect always to apply a vague concept by appeal to rigorous rules. We need good judgement of particular cases. Indeed, even when we can appeal to rigorous rules, they only postpone the moment at which we must apply concepts in particular cases on the basis of good judgement. We cannot put it off indefinitely, on pain of never getting started.

In many cases, someone with no idea of what knowledge is would be unable to determine whether safety obtained. Although they could use the principle that safety entails truth to exclude some cases, those are not the interesting ones. Thus Goldman will be disappointed when he asks what the safety account predicts about various examples in which conflicting considerations pull in different directions. One may have to decide whether safety obtains by first deciding whether knowledge obtains, rather than vice versa.

The obvious worry about such a circular account is that it is uninformative. But circularity does not entail uninformativeness, as Nelson Goodman pointed out long ago. When David Lewis gave the semantics of counterfactual conditionals in terms of similarity relations between possible worlds, his methodology was to work out what respects of similarity carry most weight from which counterfactuals are true. He readily conceded that his statement of the truth-conditions for counterfactuals is vague, but insisted that what matters is that its vagueness matches the vagueness of the original (Lewis 1986a: 91–5). In many tricky examples, Lewis's account does not deliver a clear independent prediction as to the truth-value of a counterfactual conditional. Nevertheless, his account is highly informative, especially about structural matters such as the logic of counterfactuals. Likewise, the role of the safety account in *Knowledge and its Limits* is not to deliver clear independent predictions as to the truth-values of knowledge claims in particular tricky examples. Nevertheless, it is highly informative, especially about structural matters such as the (in)validity of the KK principle. In the anti-luminosity argument—which Goldman does not challenge—what is in effect the safety condition plays an essential role. That does not require us to determine exactly how much similarity is relevant or exactly what relative weights are to be given to different respects of similarity. Since successive members of the sorites-like series can be taken arbitrarily close together, it is clear that they can be taken close enough together for the purposes of safety, even though it is not clear how close that is. One point on which the safety account may be more informative than the relevant alternatives account to which Goldman unfavourably compares it is in generating these verdicts on the KK principle and on luminosity.

An analogy is drawn in *Knowledge and its Limits* between general principles about knowledge and general principles about identity (pp. 40–1). It is apt here too. General principles about identity (such as Leibniz's Law) need not deliver clear verdicts on grounds independent of identity in particular tricky examples. Their role is to give information about structural matters, such as the logic of identity. General principles about knowledge such as safety play a parallel role.

More generally, Goldman wonders what there is for an account of knowledge to do, if not to seek non-circular necessary or sufficient conditions for knowledge. The foregoing comments indicate at least part of the answer: to investigate structural features of knowledge. To ask what conditions are luminous or whether the KK principle holds is to enquire into fundamental features of knowledge, but not into its non-circular necessary or sufficient conditions. Although one *can* do philosophy of science by seeking non-circular necessary or sufficient conditions for being science, and one *can* do philosophy of art by seeking non-circular necessary or sufficient conditions for being art, that looks unlikely to be the most fruitful way of pursuing those branches of philosophy. In this respect, why should the philosophy of knowledge be any different?

Goldman's second misunderstanding concerns the nature of the similarity relation in my version of safety. For two cases to be relevantly similar, I require the beliefs in question in them to have similar *bases* (pp. 97, 99, 128). But what are bases here? Goldman writes:

Let us distinguish between two ontological types that could bear causal relations to (resultant) beliefs. The first ontological type is a *ground* for belief, where prime examples of grounds are mental *states* such as perceptual experiences or (other) beliefs. The second ontological type is a cognitive or computational *process* or *operation*, which might take one or more grounds as inputs and produce a belief as an output . . . The term 'basis' is most naturally applied to grounds, not to processes or operations.

Goldman therefore interprets my bases as grounds, not as processes. He argues that only processes or operations, not grounds, have global reliability properties, and therefore interprets my view as quite unlike process reliabilism.

Whether or not the terminology was misleading, by 'bases', I did not mean *grounds*; I meant something more like *processes* than Goldman appreciates. I had in mind a very liberal conception, on which the basis of a belief includes the specific causal process leading to it and the relevant causal background. The internalist conception of grounds that Goldman sketches is obviously alien to the spirit of *Knowledge and its Limits*; but I should have been more explicit. Although my view is not process reliabilism in Goldman's sense, it is not quite as distant from process reliabilism as he thinks. This makes a significant difference to the treatment of his examples.

In Goldman's dachshund-wolf example (1976), the external and internal differences between seeing a dachshund and seeing a wolf turn out to constitute a large enough dissimilarity between the bases of one's belief that one is seeing a dog to allow one to know: the cases are not similar enough to exclude safety. The examples offered by Ram Neta and Guy Rohrbaugh (2004) that Goldman quotes likewise involve large external differences between the processes that actually generate the beliefs in question in the good cases and the processes that generate errors in the corresponding bad cases. Again, these differences turn out to constitute large enough dissimilarities between the bases of one's beliefs to allow one to know: the cases are not similar enough to exclude safety.

As should be expected given what was said above, these judgements of sufficient dissimilarity and safety are made post hoc; they draw on the judgement that the cases involve knowledge. But any other reasonable account of knowledge is likely to be in the same boat. For in many examples one can reverse the verdict as to whether there is knowledge by varying some physical parameter along a continuous dimension. For example, whether fake barns prevent one from knowing that one is seeing a real barn depends on how many miles away the fake barns are. Nevertheless, it would be quite unreasonable to require any account of knowledge to specify in advance exactly how many miles away the fake barns must be for one to know that one is seeing a real barn. Again, if (unbeknownst to you) many nearby wolves are so misshapen by disease as to look exactly like dachshunds, although not exactly like this particular dachshund in front of you, then you do not know that you are seeing a dog when you look at it. Nevertheless, it would be quite unreasonable to require any account of knowledge to specify in advance exactly where the line comes between the cases where one can know that one is seeing a dog and the cases where one cannot know.

Goldman complains that my safety account neglects the importance of the method used to form the belief. As just noted, this complaint is unwarranted, given the role of bases in my sense in the account. Equally unwarranted is Goldman's charge that in raising the generality problem about the appropriate typing of processes (or methods) for my safety account (p. 100) I confused safety reliabilism with process reliabilism. The generality problem arises for my safety account because, like process reliabilism, it faces the question 'How similar must counterfactual processes [bases] be to count towards reliability/safety?' Indeed, my raising and answering the problem for my account might have alerted Goldman to the incorrectness of his interpretation of my account as one for which the generality problem does not arise.

Once Goldman's two misconceptions about the safety account have been cleared up, his critique of it dissolves. Of course, the account is not a *complete* account of knowledge—it leaves many significant questions about knowledge unanswered—and I never claimed otherwise. But a complete (and correct) account of knowledge is too much to ask of any epistemologist. Even an account with the traditional form of a claim that a given non-circular condition is necessary and sufficient for knowledge will be incomplete as well as incorrect, since it will not thereby answer structural questions about knowledge of the kind discussed above, such as whether the KK principle holds or what conditions are luminous. Although answers to some such questions may be comparatively easy to derive from an analysis of this sort, there is no reason to expect that answers to all will be. A principle is a universal generalization, which may be just as hard to prove or refute concerning the analysans as it is concerning the analysandum (knowledge) directly. We are not even close to the end of epistemology.

2.   The last third of Goldman's chapter criticizes my equation $E = K$ of one's total evidence at a time with the totality of what one then knows, and the arguments I provide for it.

According to Goldman, the data that I take to support $E = K$ are equally well explained by the equation $E = NPJ$ of one's total evidence at a time with the totality of what one is then non-inferentially propositionally justified in believing (whether or not one actually believes it).

The most striking difference between the two equations is that on $E = K$ all evidence is true, since knowledge is factive, while presumably on $E = NPJ$ some evidence is false. For Goldman:

A standard illustration of non-inferential propositional justification is having an experience as of seeing a computer screen before you. Being in this visual state might make you (prima facie) justified in believing the proposition 'There is a computer screen before me,' whether or not you do believe it. On the present account, a person in this condition would have the indicated proposition as an item of evidence.

I can have an experience as of seeing a computer screen before me, with nothing to alert me to the fact that something is wrong, even though no computer screen is before me. Presumably I can then be non-inferentially propositionally justified in Goldman's sense in believing that there is a computer screen before me. Therefore, given $E = NPJ$, the proposition that there is a computer screen before me is then part of my evidence, even though it is false.

Goldman does explicitly 'set aside the question of how such an approach to evidence would deal with cases in which prima facie justifiedness is defeated', but there is no indication that he has such cases of purely external defeat in mind. The contrast between $E = K$ and $E = NPJ$ would be much less marked if he had. Moreover, when he considers my arguments against the possibility of false evidence, he does not suggest that $E = NPJ$ may not imply that possibility or that in such cases justification may be defeated. Rather, he simply argues that 'allowing falsehoods as evidence' does not have bad consequences. We may, therefore, interpret Goldman's equation $E = NPJ$ as implying the possibility of false evidence.

The obvious argument against the possibility of false evidence is given in the book (p. 201):

if one's evidence included falsehoods, it would rule out some truths, by being inconsistent with them. One's evidence may make some truths improbable, but it should not exclude any outright. Although we may treat false propositions as evidence, it does not follow that they are evidence. No true proposition is inconsistent with my evidence, although I may think that it is.

Goldman responds to this passage by asking why there cannot be false, deductively misleading evidence. But an earlier passage in his chapter contains apparent hints of a different attitude to what it takes for evidence e to rule out a hypothesis h: 'e does not have to be *known* (with all the baggage knowledge entails) for an incompatibility between h and e to rule out h. It suffices for e to be true.' This suggests that the truth of evidence is crucial to its role in ruling out hypotheses. However, Goldman continues: 'If e entails the falsity of h, and e is a given (that is, it is a given that it is true), then h can be ruled out.' This suggests that what is crucial to the role of evidence in ruling out hypotheses is *not* mere truth after all, but givenness, whatever that is. After all, the occurrence of 'true' in 'it is a given that it is true' is redundant, since the propositional content of what is true will suffice: saying that it is a given that it is true that grass is green adds nothing useful to saying that it is a given that grass is green.

If being a given is equated simply with being taken for granted, then Goldman's claim is that, if e entails the falsity of h, and e is taken for granted, then h can be ruled out. This is not a normative claim, since e may be taken for granted quite inappropriately: one need not be propositionally justified, inferentially or non-inferentially, in believing it, and it need not be part of one's evidence. One cannot make one's evidence rule out h just by taking the falsity of h for granted. It may be wrong but is not impossible to take for granted the falsity of something that is compatible with one's evidence. Thus the 'taken-for-granted' sense of 'given' does not yield a pertinent reading of Goldman's claim.

By contrast, if 'given' is interpreted in a more epistemologically loaded sense, then the given may entail at least as much baggage as knowledge does. Moreover, if the given can be false, then incompatibility with the given does not rule out a hypothesis: it may still be true. On the other hand, if the given must be true, then it sounds much more like knowledge than Goldman suggests. His attitude to the truth-value of evidence in the ruling out of hypotheses is unclear, and perhaps ambivalent.

On Goldman's account, it is not even clear that one's evidence must be *consistent*, let alone *true*. For some perceptual illusions involve unobvious inconsistencies in the perceptual appearances. For example, one may see a twisted closed loop of stairs $S_0, S_1, S_2, \ldots, S_n$ such that S_0 looks below S_1, S_1 looks below $S_2, \ldots, S_{n-1}$ looks below S_n and S_n looks below S_0. Since the stairs may not be especially salient, and there may be no special reason to trace this particular series round, spotting the inconsistency may take considerable ingenuity. Perhaps in these circumstances one is non-inferentially propositionally justified in believing that S_0 is below S_1, non-inferentially propositionally justified in believing that S_1 is below $S_2, \ldots$, non-inferentially propositionally justified in believing that S_{n-1} is below S_n and non-inferentially propositionally justified in believing that S_n is below S_0 (even if one is not propositionally justified in believing the conjunction of those propositions). If so, on Goldman's equation $E = NPJ$, one's evidence contains the proposition that S_0 is below S_1, the proposition that S_1 is below $S_2, \ldots$, the proposition that S_{n-1} is below S_n and the proposition that S_n is below S_0, in which case one's evidence is inconsistent, given that it is part of the logic of being below to be a transitive irreflexive relation. But there are grave difficulties in making sense of evidential probabilities on inconsistent evidence, since conditional probabilities are usually taken to be undefined when conditioned on something inconsistent. In particular, any proposition has probability 1 conditional on itself, and any contradiction has probability 0 conditional on anything (since conditional probabilities are probabilities): but these constraints cannot both be met for probabilities conditional on a contradiction (the conjunction of the inconsistent evidence propositions). Goldman does not say enough to enable us to tell how he would handle this case. Obviously it presents no difficulty to a view such as $E = K$ on which all evidence is true, since then one's total evidence is automatically consistent. For a view on which not all evidence is true, the possibility of inconsistent evidence presents a significant threat.

We could consider a variant of $E = NPJ$, $E = TNPJ$, on which one's evidence consists of those *true* propositions that one is non-inferentially propositionally justified in believing. However, such a view is a rather unnatural hybrid; the truth condition is an ad hoc afterthought, not an organic consequence.

Another challenge to E = NPJ implicit in the book (p. 203) is that E = NPJ allows cases in which one has no access to one's evidence set, even if it is consistent: for example, coming to believe one of the propositions that I am non-inferentially propositionally justified in believing might prevent me from coming to believe one of the other propositions that I am non-inferentially propositionally justified in believing. Goldman's response is that I am in no position to give such an argument since, on my view, one is not always in a position to know just what one's evidence is (p. 164). However, on E = K, one *does* have access to one's evidence itself, in the most straightforward way: by knowing it. Without any sort of access constraint at all, evidence cannot play its distinctive role. What one may not be in a position to know, on my view, is something else: whether a given proposition is part of one's evidence—a higher-order truth *about* one's evidence. The difficulty for E = NPJ is that it may exclude access to one's evidence set itself in some cases, rather than just excluding access to truths about one's evidence set. There is no inconsistency in mounting this objection to E = NPJ from my standpoint.

The arguments for E = K that Goldman quotes were intended only as the first phase of support for that equation. The second phase of support in the book comes from the incorporation of E = K into a working theory of evidence, including, for example, a theory of evidential probability (pp. 209–37). Goldman does not attempt to incorporate his equation E = NPJ into a working theory of evidence. For example, he does not say whether one's evidential probabilities result from conditionalization on one's evidence, so that whatever one is non-inferentially justified in believing has probability 1. He has not done enough to make E = NPJ into a serious competitor to E = K.

Goldman presents one example that is intended to favour E = NPJ directly over E = K. It concerns a *diffident doxastic agent* (DDA) who 'has only mild states of credence, none of which rise to the level of belief' but 'a full panoply of perceptual experiences'. Since the DDA has no beliefs, he has no knowledge, and therefore no evidence according to E = K. But, Goldman contends, it is more plausible that the DDA has plenty of evidence, given his perceptual experiences, which is what E = NPJ permits, since one can be non-inferentially propositionally justified in believing something even if one does not in fact believe it.

It is not easy to imagine the DDA correctly. For instance, when the DDA has a perceptual experience as of seeing a red patch, it is tempting to imagine him as at least knowing that he seems to see a red patch, or that there seems to be a red patch ahead, but Goldman's DDA has no such knowledge. By hypothesis, he knows nothing whatsoever about the perceptual experiences he is having, or about how things appear to him. Once we appreciate the radical nature of his predicament, and its distance from normal human experience, the verdict of Goldman's equation E = NPJ, that the DDA has plenty of evidence, looks much less plausible. The verdict of E = K becomes more attractive: the DDA has wilfully deprived himself of evidence (although he is still in a position to recover it). At any rate, this far-fetched case provides no good reason to abandon the equation E = K. Thus Goldman's case against my account of evidence fails.

Reply to John Hawthorne and Maria Lasonen-Aarnio

1.   As John Hawthorne and Maria Lasonen-Aarnio appreciate, some of the central issues raised in their 'Knowledge and Objective Chance' arise for all but the most extreme theories of knowledge. In a wide range of cases, according to very plausible everyday judgements, we know something about the future, even though, according to quantum mechanics, our belief has a small but non-zero chance (objective probability) of being untrue. In easily constructed examples, we are in that position simultaneously with respect to many different propositions about the future that are equiprobable and probabilistically independent of each other, at least to a reasonable approximation. Taking the contents of all these pieces of knowledge as premises, we can competently deduce their conjunction, and believe it on that basis. By a very plausible multi-premiss closure principle for knowledge, we thereby come to know the conjunction. Since the chance that our belief in the conjunction is true is the product of the chances that the separate conjuncts are true, given independence, it can be made arbitrarily close to zero by choosing an example with enough conjuncts. But this contradicts the very plausible-sounding principle that a belief constitutes knowledge only if it has a reasonable chance—at any rate over $1/2$—of being true. Thus if we follow our inclination to accept each of these very plausible claims about knowledge, we are led into inconsistency.

Extreme sceptics happily deny that we know the conjuncts. Eccentrics who regard true belief as sufficient for knowledge happily assert that we know the conjunction. For the rest of us, the problem is more serious.[1] Of course, the argument needs clarification and qualification in various respects, but they can be provided; Hawthorne and Lasonen-Aarnio supply many of the details.

Those who deny the principle of bivalence for future contingents may think that an objective chance is the closest a future contingent can now come to a truth-value. On that view there is no knowledge of chancy future contingents, since knowledge requires truth, and therefore no knowledge of the improbable

---

[1] In the book I endorse an example of Michael Slote's that requires that I do not know that I shall not be run over by a bus tomorrow (p. 255). This has been interpreted, not unreasonably, as an endorsement of the general view that we cannot know future contingents. I did not intend anything quite so general. It would have been better to have emphasized philosophers' absent-mindedness when crossing roads. In any case, as noted below, the problem that Hawthorne and Lasonen-Aarnio raise can be generalized far beyond future contingents.

conjunction. But, by the same reasoning, there is no knowledge of the probable conjuncts, so Hawthorne and Lasonen-Aarnio's challenge is a non-starter. Like them, I happily assume bivalence for future contingents.

The problem is in any case robust. It does not really depend on any contentious metaphysics of the future, for it arises even for knowledge after the critical events have occurred but before the outcomes have been observed or reported. An analogous problem arises in a version of the preface paradox. A meticulous historian writes a long book full of separate factual claims. Given human fallibility, it is almost inevitable that the book will contain errors somewhere or other, for any of which she apologizes in the preface. Nevertheless, she competently deduces the conjunction of all the separate claims in the book (excluding the preface) from its conjuncts and believes it on that basis. As it happens, she does in fact know each conjunct. Therefore, by closure, she knows the conjunction. But how can she know it when it is almost certain to be false? These analogues may not involve chance in the strict sense, since they concern knowledge of the past, not of the future. Despite the consequent loss of drama, they provoke a very similar epistemological unease: how can the closure principle for knowledge be reconciled with the combination of small probabilities of error for each premiss into a large probability of error for the conclusion?

I have just posed the problem without mentioning the epistemological framework distinctive of *Knowledge and its Limits*. Thus the question naturally arises, how far Hawthorne and Lasonen-Aarnio's discussion really concerns a special problem for the theory in *Knowledge and its Limits*, as opposed to the special form that a problem for almost everyone takes when translated into the language of the book. Section 2 explores the general problem of closure in terms of evidential probability, as characterized in the book. Section 3 discusses the divergence between evidential and objective probability. Section 4 considers whether the upshot undermines what the book says about safety and danger.

2.   Let c_1 & . . . & c_n be the conjunction of n equiprobable, mutually probabilistically independent conjuncts $c_1, . . ., c_n$. Suppose that, for each i, I know c_i without knowing that I know c_i (this sort of possibility is defended at pp. 114–23). More specifically, suppose that, for each i, although I know c_i, the probability on my evidence that I know c_i is high but less than 1. On the theory of evidential probability the book defends, with the equation $E = K$ of one's total evidence with one's total knowledge, that I know c_i entails that the probability of c_i on my evidence is 1, for c_i is then part of my evidence, and so part of what my evidential probabilities are conditionalized on. That the probability on my evidence that I know c_i is less than 1 entails that I do not know that I know c_i, for otherwise the proposition that I know c_i would be part of my evidence, and so would have probability 1 on my evidence. Conversely, given the regularity assumption that all possibilities consistent with my evidence have non-zero probability on my evidence (p. 225), that it is consistent with what I

know that I do not know c_i entails that the probability on my evidence that I know c_i is less than 1. Suppose, furthermore, that the propositions that I know c_i ($1 \leq i \leq n$) are also equiprobable and mutually probabilistically independent on my evidence. That evidence does not favour some of them over others, and does not treat patterns of knowledge and ignorance in some cases as positively or negatively correlated with patterns of knowledge and ignorance in others, but simply as dependent on independent contingencies of the subject matter (this is a simplifying idealization; a version of the argument below still holds on the more realistic assumption that, conditional on knowledge of some c_i, knowledge of others is slightly more probable). Then, although the probability on my evidence of $c_1 \& \ldots \& c_n$ is 1, the probability on my evidence that I know every c_i separately is the probability that I know a given c_i raised to the power of n, and so becomes arbitrarily small as n becomes arbitrarily large. Suppose that it is quite clear on my evidence that I believe $c_1 \& \ldots \& c_n$ by competent deduction from its conjuncts, and that I do not know $c_1 \& \ldots \& c_n$ in any other way, so that I know $c_1 \& \ldots \& c_n$ only if I know every c_i separately. Then the probability on my evidence that I know $c_1 \& \ldots \& c_n$ is no greater than the probability on my evidence that I know every c_i separately. Thus the probability on my evidence that I know $c_1 \& \ldots \& c_n$ becomes arbitrarily small as n becomes arbitrarily large. Nevertheless, I do in fact know $c_1 \& \ldots \& c_n$, by the closure principle, because I do in fact know each of its conjuncts and believe the conjunction by competent deduction from its conjuncts. Hence, even though closure holds, if my judgements of whether I know go with whether it is probable or improbable on my evidence that I know, then I shall judge truly of each conjunct that I know it while also judging falsely that I do not know the conjunction. This suggests that we may be able to explain why such cases appear to be counter-examples to closure, even though really they are not.

We can construct a toy model of epistemic logic to check the coherence of the foregoing account. For worlds we use n-tuples of numbers drawn from the set $\{0, 1, \ldots, 2k\}$, where k is a large natural number. Thus there are $(2k + 1)^n$ worlds in the model. Think of the n components of a world as its positions on n independent dimensions of a state space; the ith dimension is the one relevant to c_i. Some notation will be convenient: the ith component of the n-tuple w is w_i; the world just like w except that its ith component is m is $w[i|m]$, so $w[i|m]_i = m$ and $w[i|m]_j = w_j$ if $i \neq j$. Let c_i be true at w if and only if $w_i > 0$. To evaluate knowledge ascriptions in the model, we need an accessibility relation between worlds: as usual, $\mathbf{Kp}$ ('one knows p') is true at a world w if and only if $\mathbf{p}$ is true at every world accessible from w. This semantic clause validates the strongest form of closure, on which one automatically knows every conclusion that follows from premises that one knows, and a fortiori validates more realistic closure principles; for present purposes, logical omniscience is a harmless idealization. Let x be accessible from w (wRx) if and only if for all i, $|w_i - x_i| \leq k$, that is, w and x do not differ by 'too much' in any of their respective components. In effect, a 'safety' condition is applied to each of the n dimensions separately. This accessibility relation is obviously reflexive and symmetric. We can easily check that, for any world w, c_i is known (Kc_i is true) at w if and only if $w_i > k$. For if $w_i > k$ and wRx then $|w_i - x_i| \leq k$, so $x_i > 0$, so c_i is true at x; thus Kc_i is true at w. Conversely, if $w_i \leq k$ then $wRw[i|0]$, because $|w_i - w[i|0]_i| = |w_i - 0| = w_i \leq k$ and if $i \neq j$ then $|w_j - w[i|m]_j| = 0$; but c_i is false at $w[i|0]$ because $w[i|0]_i = 0$, so Kc_i is false at w. By a similar argument, for any world w, c_i is known to be known (KKc_i is true) at w if and only if $w_i > 2k$; in other words, c_i is not known to be known (KKc_i is not true) at any world in this model. In particular, at the world $<2k, \ldots, 2k>$, each c_i is known and none is known to be known.

When evaluating probabilities over the model, it is convenient to assign them to propositions regarded as sets of worlds. In accordance with the approach of *Knowledge and its Limits*, we start with a prior probability distribution Pr. We treat all worlds as initially equiprobable; thus $\Pr(\{w\}) = 1/(2k+1)^n$. The evidence at w is equated with what is known at w, which consists of exactly the set of accessible worlds, $\{x: wRx\}$, since that proposition and nothing stronger is known at w. The probability at w of a proposition $\mathbf{p}$ on the evidence is $\Pr_w(\mathbf{p})$. It results from conditionalizing the prior probability on the evidence at w:

$$\Pr_w(\mathbf{p}) = \Pr(\mathbf{p}|\{x: wRx\}) = \Pr(\mathbf{p} \wedge \{x: wRx\})/\Pr(\{x: wRx\})$$

The ratio is well defined because R is reflexive, so $\{x: wRx\}$ is non-empty, so $\Pr(\{x: wRx\}) > 0$.

We must check that the model verifies the required probabilistic independence of the n dimensions. To be more precise, for any given i, a proposition $\mathbf{p}$ is *i-based* if and only if for all worlds x and y, if $x_i = y_i$ then $\mathbf{p}$ is true at x if and only if $\mathbf{p}$ is true at y ($1 \leq i \leq n$). That is, whether an *i*-based proposition is true at a world depends only on the ith component of that world. In particular, c_i is an *i*-based proposition. Obviously, the negation of any *i*-based proposition is also *i*-based, as is any conjunction of *i*-based propositions. We can also prove that, whenever $\mathbf{p}$ is an *i*-based proposition, so is $\mathbf{Kp}$.[2] Thus Kc_i and KKc_i are also *i*-based propositions. Then we can prove that, whenever for each i $\mathbf{p}_i$ is an *i*-based proposition, $\mathbf{p}_1, \ldots, \mathbf{p}_n$ are mutually probabilistically independent on the evidence in any world, in the usual sense that the probability

---

[2] Proof: Suppose that $\mathbf{p}$ is *i*-based and $x_i = y_i$. Suppose also that $\mathbf{Kp}$ is false at x. Then for some z, xRz and $\mathbf{p}$ is false at z. But then $yRy[i|z_i]$, for $|y_i - y[i|z_i]_i| = |y_i - z_i| = |x_i - z_i|$ (because $x_i = y_i$) $\leq k$ (because xRz), and if $i \neq j$ then $|y_j - y[i|z_i]_j| = 0$. Moreover, $\mathbf{p}$ is false at $y[i|z_i]$ because $\mathbf{p}$ is false at z and *i*-based and $y[i|z_i]_i = z_i$. Hence $\mathbf{Kp}$ is false at y. Thus if $\mathbf{Kp}$ is true at y then $\mathbf{Kp}$ is true at x. The converse follows by parity of reasoning.

(on the evidence at that world) of their conjunction is the product of the probabilities (on the evidence at that world) of the conjuncts.[3] Although a model could have been constructed in which the evidence at some worlds establishes epistemic interdependences between the different dimensions, for present purposes we can do without such complications. In particular, $c_1, \ldots,$ c_n are mutually probabilistically independent on the evidence in any world. Thus the epistemic propositions $Kc_1, \ldots, Kc_n$ are also mutually probabilistically independent on the evidence in any world. But, on the evidence in the world $<2k, \ldots, 2k>$, for any given i, the probability that c_i is known is $k/(k+1)$.[4] By probabilistic independence, the probability of the conjunction $Kc_1 \& \ldots \& Kc_n$ is $(k/(k+1))^n$. That is the probability that each conjunct is known. But, by the closure principle built into the model, knowing a conjunction $(K(c_1 \& \ldots \& c_n))$ is equivalent to knowing all the conjuncts $(Kc_1 \& \ldots \& Kc_n)$. Thus the probability on the evidence in $<2k, \ldots, 2k>$ that the conjunction $c_1 \& \ldots \& c_n$ is known is also $(k/(k+1))^n$. For fixed k, this probability becomes arbitrarily close to 0 as n becomes arbitrarily large. Thus, for suitable k and n, the world $<2k, \ldots, 2k>$ exemplifies just the situation informally sketched: for each conjunct one knows it without knowing that one knows it, and it is almost but not quite certain on one's evidence that one knows the conjunct; one also knows the conjunction without knowing that one knows it, and it is almost but not quite certain on one's evidence that one does *not* know the conjunction.

---

[3] For any world w, proposition q and $1 \leq i \leq n$, set:

$$\#(i, q, w) = \{j : 0 \leq j \leq 2k, q \text{ is true at } w[i|j] \text{ and } w, \quad j| \leq k\}.$$

For each i, let p_i be i-based. Note that for any worlds w and x, the following conditions are equivalent:

(i) wRx and $p_1 \& \ldots \& p_n$ is true at x
(ii) for all $i, x_i \in \#(i, p_i, w)$

The proof is trivial: for each i, p_i is true at x if and only if it is true at $w[i|x_i]$ since p_i is i-based. Now let $|X|$ be the cardinality of the set X. Since Pr makes all worlds equiprobable, $Pr_w(p_1 \& \ldots \& p_n) = |\{x: wRx \text{ and } p_1 \& \ldots \& p_n \text{ is true at } x\}|/|\{x: wRx\}|$ for a given world w. By the equivalence of (i) and (ii): $|\{x: wRx \text{ and } p_1 \& \ldots \& p_n \text{ is true at } x\}| = |\{x: \text{ for all } i, x_i \in \#(i, p_i, w)\}| = |\#(1, p_1, w)| \ldots |\#(n, p_n, w)|$. By the special case of this equation in which each p_i is replaced by the tautology t (which is trivially i-based for any i), $|\{x: wRx\}| = |\#(1, t, w)| \ldots |\#(n, t, w)|$. Consequently:

$$Pr_w(p_1 \& \ldots \& p_n) = (|\#(1, p_1, w)| \ldots |\#(n, p_n, w)|)/(|\#(1, t, w)| \ldots |\#(n, t, w)|)$$

For any given i, consider another special case in which p_j is replaced by t whenever $i \neq j$. Since $n - 1$ of the ratios cancel out, $Pr_w(p_i) = |\#(i, p_i, w)|/|\#(i, t, w)|$. Therefore $Pr_w(p_1 \& \ldots \& p_n) = Pr_w(p_1) \ldots Pr_w(p_n)$, as required.

[4] Proof: We have already established that Kc_i is true at a world x if and only if $x_i > k$. Thus, in the notation of n. 3, $\#(i, Kc_i, <2k, \ldots, 2k>) = \{j : k < j \leq 2k\}$, so $|\#(i, Kc_i, <2k, \ldots, 2k>)| = k$, while $\#(i, t, <2k, \ldots, 2k>) = \{j : k \leq j \leq 2k\}$, so $|\#(i, t, <2k, \ldots, 2k>)| = k + 1$. By the formula for $Pr_w(p_i)$ in n. 3, $Pr_{<2k, \ldots, 2k>}(Kc_i) = k/(k+1)$.

   In some examples, one's epistemic position with respect to each conjunct is better: one not only knows it but knows that one knows it. If one also knows the relevant closure principle, and knows that one satisfies the conditions for its application, one may even know that one knows the conjunction. Consequently, the probability on one's evidence that one knows the conjunction is 1. However, the previous pattern may still be repeated at a higher level of iterations of knowledge. For example, for each conjunct one knows that one knows it without knowing that one knows that one knows it, and it is almost but not quite certain on one's evidence that one knows that one knows the conjunct; one also knows that one knows the conjunction without knowing that one knows that one knows it, and it is almost but not quite certain on one's evidence that one does *not* know that one knows the conjunction. To adapt the previous model to this case, we can simply expand the set of worlds by using n-tuples of numbers from the set $\{0, 1, \ldots, 3k\}$ rather than $\{0, 1, \ldots, 2k\}$, leaving the definitions of accessibility and the truth-conditions of the c_i unchanged (so c_i is true at w if and only if $w_i > 0$); then $<3k, \ldots, 3k>$ is a world of the required type. More generally, if one uses as worlds n-tuples of numbers from the set $\{0, 1, \ldots, hk\}$, leaving the other features of the model unchanged, then $<hk, \ldots, hk>$ will be a world at which one has $h - 1$ but not h iterations of knowledge of each conjunct, and it is almost but not quite certain on one's evidence that one has $h - 1$ iterations of knowledge of the conjunct; one also has $h - 1$ but not h iterations of knowledge of the conjunction, and it is almost but not quite certain on one's evidence that one does *not* have $h - 1$ iterations of knowledge of the conjunction.

   Many other variations can be played on the same theme. The general idea is this. One attains a given epistemic status E with respect to each conjunct, without knowing that one does (this is possible by the anti-luminosity argument). By a principle of multi-premiss closure for E, one also attains status E with respect to the conjunction (supposing E to be an epistemic status of a type to which multi-premiss closure considerations apply), without knowing that one does. Then for each conjunct it may be almost certain on one's evidence that one attains E with respect to it, even though it is almost certain on one's evidence that one does *not* attain E with respect to the conjunction. Hence multi-premiss closure may appear to fail for E even though it really holds, for if one's judgement of whether one attains E with respect to a given proposition goes with whether it is probable or improbable on one's evidence that one attains E with respect to that proposition, then one will judge that one attains E with respect to each conjunct but not with respect to the conjunction.[5]

   [5] See Williamson (forthcoming) for more on knowing when it is almost certain on one's evidence that one does not know (and iterations thereof), and Williamson (2008) for some related semantic issues. The phenomenon discussed in the text involves the apparent loss of only one iteration of knowledge between premises and conclusion. However, the apparent absence of a given

General principles similar to closure are often more secure than apparent counter-examples to them. Consider a loose analogy. Suppose that my way of judging tallness perceptually has the effect that I am more likely to judge a thin person tall than a fat person of the same or slightly greater height. Fat y is slightly taller than thin x. In a given context in which I am looking at neither x nor y, I may simultaneously have both these dispositions:

(a) on looking at x alone, to judge that he is tall;
(b) on looking at y alone, to judge that he is not tall.

In the same context I may well also have the disposition on looking at x and y together, to judge that y is taller than x. This would not be plausible as a counter-example to the general monotonicity principle that if x is tall and y is at least as tall as x then y is tall. Rather, we should hold onto the general principle and conclude that my dispositions to judge in particular cases whether people are tall are not wholly accurate. Similarly, concerning knowledge, we should hold onto the general principle of closure and conclude that our dispositions to judge in preface-like cases whether people know are not wholly accurate.

We cannot plausibly resolve these problem cases by postulating contextual variation in the reference of 'know' or 'tall'. It does not help to say that the reference of 'tall' varies between the context in which I am looking at x alone and the context in which I am looking at y alone (with 'tall' as used in the former context applying to both x and y and as used in the latter applying to neither), for the problem concerns the extension of 'tall' as used in the single *original* context in which I have both (a) and (b) as unmanifested dispositions. If that extension is closed under the monotonicity principle, it does not perfectly match those dispositions. Similarly, concerning knowledge, the problem concerns the extension of 'know' as used in a single everyday context in which we have both (a^*) and (b^*) as unmanifested dispositions, with respect to a preface-like case in which the subject clearly satisfies the conditions for a suitable version of the principle that knowledge is closed under competent deduction to apply:

(a^*) on considering any conjunct, to judge that the subject knows it;
(b^*) on considering the conjunction, to judge that the subject does not know it.

If that extension is closed under the deductive closure principle, it does not perfectly match those dispositions. We have seen in this section how such mismatches can arise, without denying closure or falling into scepticism.

3.   Hawthorne and Lasonen-Aarnio formulate their challenge in terms of objective chance, not evidential probability. Much of its force will be felt by any

number of iterations of knowledge can cause doubts about all lower numbers of iterations, by a domino effect, since lack of knowledge that one has $n + 1$ iterations implies lack of warrant to assert that one has n iterations (Williamson 2005c: 233–4).

view that endorses a plausible closure principle for knowledge and is robustly anti-sceptical about knowledge of the future. For the view will imply that one can know a long conjunction about the future, even though there is a high objective chance that one's belief is false. Even when it is luckily true, will not that be a Gettier case rather than a case of knowledge? Similar problems arise for knowledge not of future contingents, as in the preface paradox. Although Hawthorne and Lasonen-Aarnio show that this challenge requires various refinements, as in their Low Chance principle, the underlying problem remains.

On the account defended here and in the book, knowledge corresponds to the highest evidential probability. Before considering the relation between knowledge and chance, it is therefore worth asking a more general question: what is the relation between evidential probability and chance? The answer is: very little. In particular, zero chance is compatible with any level of probability on one's evidence. For example, suppose that you know that a given fair coin was tossed n times in the past, and that the tosses were independent, but have no further information about the outcomes. On any reasonable view, the probability on your evidence that not every toss came up heads is $(2^n - 1)/2^n$, and so becomes arbitrarily close to 1 as n becomes arbitrarily large. Indeed, if n is countably infinite, the probability is 1 (by the argument of Williamson 2007c, with the order of the tosses reversed). But if by chance every toss did come up heads, then the chance that not every toss came up heads is now 0. Thus not even chance 0 for a proposition puts a non-trivial upper bound on its evidential probability. The same point applies to the future. Suppose that we know only that a coin has already been selected for a future toss, and that with probability x on our evidence a two-headed coin was selected, otherwise a two-tailed coin was selected. Then the probability on our evidence that the selected coin, whichever it is, will come up heads is x. But if in fact the two-tailed coin was selected, the chance that the selected coin will come up heads is 0. Thus, if low chance puts a non-trivial bound on knowledge, that is a very specific feature of knowledge; it does not reflect a more general correlation between chance and evidential probability.

Of course, if one knows something about chances, that knowledge will contribute to one's evidence, and thereby to probabilities on one's evidence. In examples of Hawthorne and Lasonen-Aarnio's kind, such knowledge is often available. One can know that the long conjunction is objectively improbable, and that each of its conjuncts is objectively probable. Indeed, for simplicity, we may even pretend that the exact chances of the long conjunction and of each of its conjuncts are known.

A salient proposal about the impact of evidence about chances comes from David Lewis's Principal Principle:

Let C be any reasonable initial credence function. Let t be any time. Let x be any real number in the unit interval. Let **ch** be the proposition that the chance, at time t, of p's holding equals *x*. Let **e** be any proposition compatible with **ch** that is admissible at *t*. Then $C(p \mid ch \& e) = x$.[6]

For suppose that one's evidential probabilities at *t* result from conditionalizing some reasonable initial credence function on one's knowledge of the chances at *t* and other evidence admissible at *t*. Then by the Principal Principle one's evidential probabilities at *t* for the long conjunction and for each of its conjuncts will have the same value as the respective chances.

As Hawthorne and Lasonen-Aarnio point out, examples of contingent a priori knowledge will force some revision of the Principal Principle. However, since those examples turn on the use of special rigidifying devices such as an 'actually' operator that are not directly germane here, it is not obvious that the required qualifications will make any difference for present purposes.

Of more immediate concern is that the Principal Principle itself poses a challenge to knowledge of the future, given the closure of knowledge under competent deduction. For suppose that I know each conjunct about the future and believe their conjunction on the basis of competent deduction; by closure, I know the conjunction. However, I also know their respective chances. Suppose that my credences at *t* result from conditionalizing some reasonable initial credence function on the known chances at *t* and other evidence admissible at *t*. Then by the Principal Principle my credences at *t* for the conjunction and for each of its conjuncts have the same value as the respective chances. Thus my credence in each conjunct is very high, while my credence in the conjunction is very low. But this seems to violate the principle that knowledge entails belief. How can I know the conjunction if my credence in it is very low? Indeed, given the Principal Principle, any adjustment of my credences to assign high credence to the conjunction looks irrational.

Lewis himself denies that knowledge entails belief. Following Woozley and Radford, he allows knowledge without belief 'in the case of the timid student who knows the answer but has no confidence that he has it right, and so does not believe what he knows' (1999: 429; see also 1996). But merely postulating knowledge without belief does not solve the problem. For the problematic cases are not simply ones in which I do not in fact believe the chancy conjunction; they are cases in which I *ought not* to believe the conjunction. How can one know **p** if one is right not to believe **p**?

For Lewis, the solution is not to reject closure. On his account, one knows **p** if and only if **p** holds in every [contextually relevant] possibility left uneliminated by one's evidence, where evidence consists of perceptual experiences and memories and eliminates just those possibilities in which one's perceptual experience and memories have a different content (Lewis 1999: 422–5; see also 1996). As Lewis realized, this implies a form of logical omniscience, with respect to any

6 Lewis (1980, 1986a: 87) (with trivial differences of notation); for refinements see Lewis (1994).

fixed context: one's knowledge is closed under necessary consequence, whether or not one carries out the appropriate deductions, for if q holds in every possibility in which $p_1, \ldots, p_n$ all hold, and each of $p_1, \ldots, p_n$ holds in every possibility relevant in a given context, then q holds in every possibility relevant in that context (1999: 440–2; see also 1996).[7] Nor is it consonant with Lewis's methodology to become a sceptic about the future. A relaxed conversational context can make a bizarre future possibility irrelevant in his sense, so that one knows a chancy future contingent. Given a context lax enough to make most such possibilities irrelevant, one may know a future contingent even though it has a very low chance of holding, and one's credence in it—rationally obtained by updating a reasonable initial credence function on known chances and other admissible evidence—is equally low. This uneasy situation arises because possibilities ignored in determining knowledge are not ignored in determining chance and therefore, by the Principal Principle, in determining rational credence.

Lewis has a Rule of Belief, according to which 'A possibility that the subject believes to obtain is not properly ignored, whether or not he is right to so believe'. A possibility that is not properly ignored is contextually relevant for the purposes of Lewis's account of 'know'. He amplifies the rule to take account of degrees of belief and degrees of specificity in possibilities (1999: 428; see also 1996): 'A possibility may not be properly ignored if the subject gives it, or ought to give it, a degree of belief that is sufficiently high, and high not just because the possibility in question is unspecific.'

Thus, if the subject, in obedience to the Principal Principle, gives the possibility that the chancy conjunction is false a very high degree of belief, then the Rule of Belief seems to imply that the possibility that the conjunction is false is not properly ignored after all. Of course, in a possibility in which the conjunction is false, one of the conjuncts is false too—say, c_i. But Lewis also has a Rule of Resemblance, according to which, if one possibility saliently resembles another, and the former possibility may not properly be ignored (in virtue of rules other than this one), then the latter possibility also may not properly be ignored (1999: 429; see also 1996). Given the nature of Hawthorne and Lasonen-Aarnio's examples, for each j the possibility in which c_i is false saliently resembles a possibility in which c_j is false ($1 \leq j \leq n$). Since the possibility in which c_i is false may not properly be ignored (in virtue of the Rule of Belief), the possibility in which c_j is false may not properly be ignored (in virtue of the Rule of Resemblance). Moreover, all the possibilities in question are uneliminated by the subject's evidence, as Lewis understands it. Therefore, on Lewis's account, none of the conjuncts is known after all: a highly sceptical result. Invoking the Rule of Belief in an attempt to reconcile Lewis's contextualism about knowledge with the

---

[7] The postulated closure of knowledge under logical consequence seems to imply that knowledge without belief is a far more widespread phenomenon than Lewis's exemplification of it with the timid student suggests—unless the closure of belief under logical consequence is also postulated.

Principal Principle merely undoes the anti-sceptical work that the contextualism was designed to do.

An alternative is to permit updating on evidence that is inadmissible in the sense of the Principal Principle. For example, I may update by conditionalizing on some contingent truth that I know about the future. Then I may have credence 1 in that truth, even though I know that its chance is less than 1. That is consistent with the Principal Principle, which is logically neutral as to the results of conditionalizing on inadmissible evidence, despite the forbidding connotations of the word 'inadmissible'. For Lewis, however, future contingents do not constitute evidence, in the sense in which he holds that one knows something if and only if it holds in every relevant possibility left uneliminated by one's evidence. Rather, as already noted, he equates one's evidence with the fact about the present that 'one's entire perceptual experience and memory are just as they actually are' (Lewis 1999: 424; see also 1996), which is admissible. In discussing the Principal Principle, Lewis works with a more liberal notion of evidence, envisaging any proposition strictly about the past as admissible evidence; but propositions strictly about the future remain the paradigms of inadmissibility.[8] In contrast, by equating one's total evidence with one's total knowledge, including one's knowledge of the future, my approach permits one to update by conditionalizing on inadmissible evidence in Lewis's sense. In particular, if I know each of the conjuncts, then their conjunction automatically receives probability 1 on my evidence, because each of its conjuncts does, whether or not I carry out the deduction. This is not to reject the Principal Principle but to move outside its conditions of application. The equation E = K enables one to avoid the combination of knowledge with very low rational credence that threatens to arise on Lewis's view.

Once we have granted that there is some knowledge of future outcomes in addition to knowledge of their present chances, we are not entitled to assume that the latter always screens out the former evidentially. Strange though it may sound, we cannot take for granted that there is no knowledge of future outcomes whose chances are known to be low. A fortiori, we cannot take for granted that there is no knowledge of future outcomes whose chances *are* low. Indeed, as Hawthorne and Lasonen-Aarnio show, there can be such knowledge, in cases of the contingent a priori. If there is a defensible principle in the vicinity, it is something like their *Low Chance*:

> For all worlds *w*, times *t*, subjects *s*, belief-episodes *B*, and propositions **p**, if at *t* in *w s*'s belief-episode *B* expresses proposition **p**, at *t* in *w* the chance that *B* expresses a true proposition is low, and at *t* in *w s* is not inadmissibly connected to the future, then *s* does not know **p** at *t* in *w*.[9]

---

[8] Otherwise one could put **e** = **p** in the Principle and derive a contradiction whenever $x \neq 1$, for $C(\mathbf{p} \mid ch \ \& \ \mathbf{p}) = 1$.

[9] I have changed the wording in unimportant ways. Hawthorne and Lasonen-Aarnio intend knowing future contingents not *ipso facto* to count as being inadmissibly connected to the future.

But not even Low Chance is satisfactory as it stands. For example, if s at t in w has two belief-episodes B and B^*, both of which express **p**, where at t in w the chance that B expresses a true proposition is low but the chance that B^* expresses a true proposition is high, then presumably s may still know **p** at t in w. To register this point, we may expand the consequent of Low Chance to 's does not know **p** at t in w as far as B goes'. Once all such required qualifications have been added to Low Chance, the result hardly looks self-evident.

4.   The question remains whether I am committed to something similar enough to Low Chance to make trouble given considerations in the book, such as the conception of knowledge as safely true belief. In effect, Hawthorne and Lasonen-Aarnio suggest such an argument. One premiss is their *High Chance–Close Possibility* principle HCCP.

HCCP

For any world w, time t, and proposition **p**, if the chance at t in w of **p** is high, then there is a close branching possibility at t in w in which **p** holds.

One might take the conception of knowledge as safely true belief to be committed to SAFETY*:

SAFETY*

For all worlds w, times t, subjects s, belief-episodes B, and propositions **p**, s knows **p** at t in w as far as B goes only if B expresses a true proposition in every possibility that is close at t in w.

From HCCP and SAFETY* we can derive a principle similar to Low Chance:

LC*

For all worlds w, times t, subjects s, belief-episodes B, and propositions **p**, if the chance at t in w that B expresses a true proposition is low then s does not know **p** at t in w as far as B goes.

For suppose that the chance at t in w that B expresses a true proposition is low. Then the chance at t in w that B does not express a true proposition is high (something has a low chance if and only if its contradictory has a high chance). Therefore, by HCCP, at t in w there is a close possibility in which B does not express a true proposition. Therefore, by SAFETY*, s does not know **p** at t in w as far as B goes. Thus HCCP and SAFETY* together entail LC*. In the cases at issue, LC* excludes knowledge of the long conjunction of future contingents.[10]

The cases the qualification is intended to exclude are those 'in which there are no time-travellers from the future, clairvoyance by backwards causation etc.'.

[10] LC* even lacks the restriction in Low Chance to subjects not inadmissibly connected to the future.

Hawthorne and Lasonen-Aarnio suggest that I am prima facie committed to HCCP by the discussion of close possibility in terms of ease and difficulty, safety and danger in the book (pp. 123–4): could not a given high chance event easily occur? There is no straightforward connection. As emphasized in the book, determinism does not trivialize safety; safety and danger are not defined in terms of chances (p. 123). Although the deterministic laws could not easily be broken, a ball precariously balanced on the tip of a cone is not safe from falling, for the initial conditions could easily have been slightly different.[11] This point does not refute HCCP, for presumably in a deterministic world the chance at t in w of p is high only if p holds in w, which is therefore itself a close branching possibility at t in w in which p holds. Nevertheless, a gap between closeness and branching remains to be bridged: 'branching' and 'close' are not equivalent. Even in a non-deterministic world, not all close possibilities are branching possibilities. But why should not most or all branching possibilities be close possibilities? In that case, SAFETY* will still have sceptical consequences.

As Hawthorne and Lasonen-Aarnio note, the discussion in the book is conducted in terms of close subject-centred cases rather than close worlds. It also adverts to one's basis for a belief, conceived not specifically as one's warrant or evidence for it but more generally as the epistemically relevant features of the belief. Here is a pertinent formulation of safety (compare p. 102):

SAFETY

If in a case a one knows p on a basis b, then in any case close to a in which one believes a proposition p^* close to p on a basis close to b, p^* is true.[12],[13]

Hawthorne and Lasonen-Aarnio suggest that multi-premiss closure may fail under such a subject-centred conception of safety. Let us first see how SAFETY is compatible with multi-premiss closure.

Say that one *safely believes* p on a basis b in a case a if and only if one believes p on basis b in a and in any case close to a in which one believes a proposition p^* close to p on a basis close to b, p^* is true. Thus SAFETY says that knowledge entails safe belief. Is safe belief closed under competent deduction? More specifically, if one safely believes some premisses and believes a conclusion

[11] Sainsbury (1997, 2002: 117–18) and Peacocke (1999: 310) make this point.

[12] A further relativization may be needed to levels of confidence of belief or near-belief, as discussed in the book (pp. 98–9). Since this relativization can be treated in formal parallel with the relativization to bases, it is omitted here.

[13] Suppose that in case a I know that Mary is married, on the basis of seeing that she is wearing a ring (on the appropriate finger), while in a case a^* that could very easily have occurred instead of a I believe falsely that Mary is unmarried, on the basis of seeing that she is not wearing a ring—she hardly ever wears her wedding ring, but on this occasion forgot to take it off (this is a variant of an example in Sainsbury (1997, 2002: 114)). Is this a counter-example to SAFETY? No. To a first approximation, I really do know in a that Mary is married only if wearing a ring is a far more reliable indicator of being married than not wearing one is of being unmarried, in which case the bases are not sufficiently close.

on the basis of competent deduction from those premises as believed on the relevant bases, does it follow that one safely believes the conclusion on that basis?

A positive answer requires some link between closeness with respect to the conclusion and the closeness with respect to the premises. This will do:

DEDUCTION

If in case α one believes a conclusion $\mathbf{q}$ on a basis b, which consists of competent deduction from $\mathbf{p}_1, \ldots, \mathbf{p}_n$ as believed on bases $b_1, \ldots, b_n$ respectively, then in any case close to α in which one believes a conclusion $\mathbf{q}^*$ close to $\mathbf{q}$ on a basis b^* close to b, b^* consists of a truth-preserving deduction from propositions $\mathbf{p}^*_1, \ldots, \mathbf{p}^*_n$ close to $\mathbf{p}_1, \ldots, \mathbf{p}_n$ respectively as believed on bases $b^*_1, \ldots, b^*_n$ close to $b_1, \ldots, b_n$ respectively.

On the natural conception of bases underlying DEDUCTION, the basis of an inferential belief incorporates the bases of the beliefs from which it was inferred; the basis is not merely the inference itself. This cumulative conception of bases will be crucial for multi-premiss closure. As for 'truth-preserving deduction' in DEDUCTION, it replaces 'competent deduction' in SAFETY because cases just above the threshold for competence may be close to cases just below the threshold. 'Truth-preserving' stands to 'competent' for deduction as 'true' stands to 'known' for propositions; thus DEDUCTION embodies a safety conception of deductive competence. That is legitimate, for our concern is precisely with the implications of safety for multi-premiss closure. Although DEDUCTION may require some further fine-tuning, it will do for present purposes.

To see that DEDUCTION implies that safe belief is closed under competent deduction, suppose that in a case α one safely believes premisses $\mathbf{p}_1, \ldots, \mathbf{p}_n$ on bases $b_1, \ldots, b_n$ respectively and believes a conclusion $\mathbf{q}$ on basis b, which consists of a competent deduction from $\mathbf{p}_1, \ldots, \mathbf{p}_n$ as believed on bases $b_1, \ldots, b_n$ respectively. Consider any case β close to α in which one believes a conclusion $\mathbf{q}^*$ close to $\mathbf{q}$ on a basis b^* close to b. Therefore, by DEDUCTION, in β one believes $\mathbf{q}^*$ on the basis of truth-preserving deduction from propositions $\mathbf{p}^*_1, \ldots, \mathbf{p}^*_n$ close to $\mathbf{p}_1, \ldots, \mathbf{p}_n$ respectively as believed on bases $b^*_1, \ldots, b^*_n$ close to $b_1, \ldots, b_n$ respectively. By definition of safety, since β is close to α and in β one believes $\mathbf{p}^*_1, \ldots, \mathbf{p}^*_n$ on bases close to $b_1, \ldots, b_n$ respectively, $\mathbf{p}^*_1, \ldots, \mathbf{p}^*_n$ are true in β. By DEDUCTION the deduction of $\mathbf{q}^*$ from $\mathbf{p}^*_1, \ldots, \mathbf{p}^*_n$ is truth-preserving in β, so $\mathbf{q}^*$ is true in β. This is just what was needed to show that in α one safely believes $\mathbf{q}$. Thus safe belief is closed under competent deduction. SAFETY, formulated in terms of close cases, is quite compatible with multi-premiss closure.

The pooling of knowledge from many individuals by testimony can be similarly explained. When the hearer knows something on the basis of testimony from a knowledgeable speaker, the basis of the hearer's belief incorporates the basis of the speaker's belief, even if the hearer is largely ignorant of the latter basis. Bases need not be introspectively available. Again, in memory-based knowledge, the basis of one's present belief incorporates the basis of one's earlier belief, even if one has forgotten the latter basis.

Does chance create counter-examples to SAFETY? Let α be the actual case in which I drop my marble and know that it will land on the floor. Still, there is a small non-zero chance that it will not land on the floor. Let β be a case just like α up to now in which I drop my marble but, by a quantum-mechanical blip, it does not land on the floor; since the laws of nature are indeterministic, the same ones can hold in β as in α. In β, I still believe that my marble will land on the floor, but my false belief does not constitute knowledge. Why is not β a case close to α in which I believe on exactly the same basis that my marble will land on the floor? If so, this is a counter-example to SAFETY. But the occurrence of an event in β that bucks a relevant trend in α may be a relevant lack of closeness between α and β, even though the trend falls well short of being a strict law. Thus β is not close to α after all; perhaps the belief's basis in β is also not close to its basis in α. The accumulation of such cases may then yield violations of HCCP, as formulated in terms of cases rather than possibilities.

This does not mean that safety is totally unconstrained by chance. For example, the pattern of chances may determine whether a general type of causal process by which beliefs are acquired counts as a form of perception, and so as a basic source of knowledge of the environment: if the chances of error are too great, it does not count as perception. That is, chance constrains safety globally, not locally case by case.

The structural divergence between knowledge and high chance that Hawthorne and Lasonen-Aarnio exploit in trying to separate knowledge from safety (as ordinarily conceived) is analogous to a structural divergence between safety (as ordinarily conceived) and high chance. Suppose that I am not safe from being shot. On the ordinary conception, it follows that there is someone x such that I am not safe from being shot by x (assume that if I am shot, I am shot by someone). On the high-chance conception of safety, that is a non sequitur. For each individual x, the chance of my being shot by x may be low enough for me to count as safe from being shot by x, even though the chance of my being shot by someone or other may be too high for me to count as safe from being shot. Again, on the ordinary conception of danger, if for each individual x I am in no danger of being shot by x then I am in no danger of being shot. On a chancy conception of danger, even if for each individual x I am in no danger of being shot by x, I may still be in danger of being shot. The ordinary conception posits just the sort of closure principle for safety that the high-chance conception undermines. If $\mathbf{p}_1, \ldots, \mathbf{p}_n$ entail $\mathbf{q}$ then '$\mathbf{p}_1$ is safe from falsity', ..., '$\mathbf{p}_n$ is safe from falsity' entail '$\mathbf{q}$ is safe from falsity'.

The ordinary conception of safety can look like a primitive refusal to acknowledge the potential for many small risks to add up to a big one. But that is already to misconstrue the ordinary conception. It is a 'no-risk' conception of safety, not a 'small-risk' conception. This is achieved not by a confused equation of little with nothing but by a tight restriction to close cases, where closeness is determined by considerations of similarity (to the actual case) as much as of chance. To be safe from a danger is to avoid it in *all* close cases.

Unlike the high-chance conception of safety, the ordinary conception of safety at least delivers the elementary but crucial consequence that, if one is safe from undergoing something, then one does not undergo it: high-chance events do not always occur, but the actual case is close to itself. If someone was shot, he was not safe from being shot. This factiveness of safety complements its closure under logical consequence. Together they combine to make the logic of safety at least as strong as the modal logic T ($=$ KT), the weakest normal modal logic with the axiom $\Box p \to p$; it serves as an idealized but non-luminous epistemic logic in *Knowledge and its Limits* (p. 305).

The closeness conception of safety might be thought to be of less practical use than the high-chance conception. But in many situations it is the opposite. Often we have so little idea of the objective chances that it is infeasible to reason in terms of them. Rather, we think in terms of making ourselves safe from a disjunction of dangers by making ourselves safe from each disjunct separately. That way of thinking assumes a closure principle for safety that the closeness conception can deliver and the high-chance conception cannot. The chance of the disjunction is much higher than the chance of any disjunct, but if each disjunct is avoided in all close cases, so is their disjunction. For that to be achievable in practice, many branching possibilities will have to count as not close. Hawthorne and Lasonen-Aarnio show in effect how far the closeness and high-chance conceptions of safety can diverge in some cases, but that is no fault in the closeness conception. Similarly, the wide divergence between them in deterministic worlds enables the closeness conception to do much better there than the high-chance conception, which disallows unrealized dangers in those cases.

Of course, in many situations the best way of handling risk does involve reasoning about chances, where their numerical values can be reasonably estimated. Even there, a closeness conception may still be needed in the background, since we can never take account of all the bizarre outcomes that have a slight chance of occurring through quantum-mechanical blips, just as known evidence is in the background of reasoning about probabilities on one's evidence. No concept is a panacea. Sometimes thinking with probabilistic concepts is more useful than thinking with the concept of safety. When we are too much in the dark about the probabilities, thinking with the concept of safety is often more feasible than thinking with probabilistic concepts.

Once we understand the distinctive structural virtues of the closeness conception of safety, we can more easily understand the corresponding virtues of the ordinary conception of knowledge. They depend on the same features, such as closure and factiveness. It is not perverse to focus on a property that is cumulative (closure) and success-oriented (factiveness). Since high chance lacks both those features, the failure of closeness to map neatly onto the probabilistic structure of chances becomes an advantage.

What still requires much more detailed investigation is the nature of closeness, and its relation to past and future similarities. We cannot expect it to be a perfectly natural relation; given the anti-reductionism about knowledge for which *Knowledge and its Limits* argues, we cannot expect to identify just what degree and kind of safety is required for knowledge in non-epistemological terms. Still, we do not want closeness to be *too* unnatural.[14] On the ordinary conception, safety is firmly enough rooted in the actual structure of the world, irrespective of its appearance to the agent (Hawthorne and Lasonen-Aarnio call safety 'objective'). Knowledge also has such roots. Its divergence from high chance does not prevent it from being as natural and objective as one can reasonably demand of any epistemic matter. The divergence is a price well worth paying for the structural virtues of knowledge.[15]

[14] In Williamson (2005b: 484–7) I show formally how to limit the divergence by ensuring that only high-chance propositions are true in all close worlds, but I agree with Hawthorne and Lasonen-Aarnio that in many cases of interest that model would avoid sceptical consequences only if it used a very unnatural measure of closeness.

[15] Thanks to audiences at the University of Texas at Austin and the University of Santiago de Compostela for comments on versions of this material.

Reply to Frank Jackson

In 'Primeness, Internalism, Explanation', Frank Jackson repeatedly describes himself as opposing my view that knowing and remembering are prime. At the end he effectively concedes the correctness of my claim, on the definition of 'prime' in the book, but maintains its compatibility with my intended opponents' view.

Jackson goes to some trouble to identify common ground between us. However, the framework of his discussion is far more alien to mine than he seems to realize. The upshot is that he misses the point of my discussion of primeness and explanation.

In the book, it is conditions that are prime or composite. For present purposes, we can think of conditions as sets of cases or of centred worlds. A condition C is *narrow* if and only if whether a case belongs to C is determined by the internal physical state of the agent in that case. C is *wide* if and only if it is not narrow. C is *environmental* if and only if whether a case belongs to C is determined by the physical state of the environment external to the agent in that case. C is *composite* if and only if it is the conjunction (intersection) of a narrow condition with an environmental condition. C is *prime* if and only if it is not composite (p. 66). Conditions are not states if, as Jackson assumes, states imply similarity patterns in what they are states of, for conditions are closed under truth-functions such as negation and disjunction (p. 52) while similarity-implying states are not. It is not even clear what the conjunction of a state of the agent with a state of the external environment would be a state *of*. Nevertheless, Jackson applies the term 'prime' to states rather than to conditions throughout his chapter.

A more important divergence concerns the nature of states. In the book, states are universals. Different people can be in the same state at different times (pp. 40, 63). Knowing p is a general state S such that a necessary and sufficient condition for being in S is knowing p (p. 21). More generally, φing is a state a necessary and sufficient condition for being in which is φing. Thus *de re* claims about states themselves are easy to derive from corresponding *de dicto* claims. Jackson appears to share some of this conception when he writes of states themselves in terms of similarity patterns: 'Remembering that p is that which unites all cases of remembering that p in logical space' (presumably, it is also that which divides all such cases from those that are not cases of remembering p). However, he adds: 'The type, remembering that p, is the unifier of all the tokens of so remembering; the pattern they all fall under.' By contrast, in the book I reject the idea of a token state as of doubtful coherence (p. 40) and refer to perceptive work to that effect by Helen Steward (1997: 105–34). Given Jackson's appeals to Ockham's Razor later in his argument, it is surprising that he helps himself without comment to an obscure and contentious ontology of token states.

Even if there are token states, focusing on whether *they* are prime misses the point of the chapter on primeness (pp. 65–92). The most token-like conditions are the maximally specific ones. That maximally specific conditions are composite is easily conceded (pp. 80–1). Primeness is a special kind of generality, one that turns out to be central to many intentional explanations of action (pp. 81–9). Since token states lack generality, looking for primeness in them is a waste of time. Unfortunately, Jackson's chapter provides considerable evidence that he is doing just that.

Jackson's main example of the sort of mental state at issue is remembering. He distinguishes two questions: whether remembering is *narrow*, and whether it is *internal*. His definition of 'narrow' is unhelpful: 'to say that [mental states] are narrow is to say that what it takes for them to be the mental states depends just on how the subjects that are in them are.' Remembering *p* might seem to be a way that a subject can be, making it a narrow sense in Jackson's sense, but that is not what he intends. He classifies it as uncontentiously a wide (non-narrow) state, because it entails 'a suitable past and a suitable connection between that past and the way [the subject] is'. Thus his use of 'wide' and 'narrow' is similar to that in the book, with conditions replaced by states, once the latter are understood as state types. For Jackson the significant question, to which he devotes much of his chapter, is not whether remembering is narrow but whether it is internal, where: 'To say that [mental states] are internal is to say something about where they are located, namely inside subjects.' To ask where a state type is located makes little sense. Subjects are in mental states, not vice versa. Jackson seems to be asking for the location of mental state *tokens*.

The impression is confirmed by Jackson's later claim: 'when *S* remembers that *p*, *S*'s remembering that *p* is an internal state of *S* which is one and the same as *S*'s belief that *p*. There are not two states but one state—believing that *p*—which counts as remembering that *p* as a result of some suitable causal history involving *p*.' In this passage Jackson is presumably thinking of state tokens. For, since it is possible to believe *p* without remembering *p*, the state type of believing *p* is obviously distinct from the state type of remembering *p*. Jackson's idea seems to be that a single token state may be a token both of the state type of believing *p* and of the distinct state type of remembering *p*. Another token state may be a token of the state type of believing *p* but not of the state type of remembering *p*.

Naturally, none of this makes very much sense without some clarification of what token states are supposed to be, which Jackson does not provide. Still, it is the only apparent way of making at least potential sense of his argument. Alas, so interpreted, his argument misses the point of my discussion of primeness and explanation, which is not concerned with token states. In particular, it does not address my account of externalist causal–psychological explanations as fitting good explanatory practice in the natural sciences by identifying significant generalizations.[1] Once knowing and remembering are treated as general states, the arguments for their primeness go through as usual.

In a final sentence, Jackson suggests that even a prime state may be the conjunction of a narrow state with an environmental state in a more liberal sense of 'environmental' that includes relations to the subject. This possibility is addressed in the book (pp. 91–2). A relation of the environment to the subject is just the converse of a relation of the subject to the environment. Since it would be ad hoc to exclude cognitive relations of the subject to the environment, knowing and remembering may in effect count as environmental in that sense. Being remembered by the subject to contain an oasis one day's march to the north may be part of how the environment is. Such cognitive environmental states have no need to be conjoined with any further narrow state of the subject in order to fulfil their causal–explanatory function. They already embed the required state of the subject. Jackson's suggestion casts no doubt on the ineliminable and unfactorizable role of knowing and remembering in scientifically illuminating causal explanations of action.

---

[1] Jackson's account of explanations in plant biology fudges exactly the issues about generality whose centrality my analysis highlights.

Reply to Mark Kaplan

1.   'Williamson's casual approach to probabilism', according to Mark Kaplan, involves assuming without argument that there are evidential probabilities satisfying the standard axioms of probability. Less casual probabilists give arguments to show that those axioms are or should be satisfied. They typically rely on assumptions about the preferences of a rational agent. Kaplan cites an argument in this vein from his earlier book (1996: ch. 1).

I agree with Kaplan that the assumption that there are evidential probabilities satisfying the standard axioms of probability is far from trivial. I did not pretend otherwise in *Knowledge and its Limits*. I wrote:

> the axioms of probability theory [when applied to evidential probability] embody substantive claims, as the axioms of set theory do. For example, the restriction of probabilities to real numbers limits the number of gradations in probability to the cardinality of the continuum. Just as the axioms of set theory refine our understanding of sets without reducing to implicit definitions of 'set', so the axioms of probability theory refine our understanding of evidential probability without reducing to implicit definitions of 'evidential probability'.   (p. 213)

I described my procedure as 'tentatively postulating' an initial distribution of evidential probabilities 'in order to see what use can be made of it in developing a theory of evidential probability' (p. 213). I took the probability axioms to be plausible for evidential probability but not self-evident. I did not attempt to derive them from 'more basic' premises, because I could and can see no good candidates for such premises, just as I am sceptical about attempts to derive the axioms of set theory from 'more basic' premises. In particular, I see only very limited value in the project of arguing for the simple, plausible axioms of probability from more complex and no more plausible assumptions about the preferences of rational agents, for example, between dollar bets—money is not that basic (the premises of the argument that Kaplan cites from his own book are too complex to lay out here). An abductive methodology holds more promise: judge theories by their fruits.

To a first approximation, postulating evidential probabilities is just postulating that how well off a proposition is on the evidence can be measured. To be a little more precise, consider (coarse-grained) propositions as subsets of a set of worlds ω. *Knowledge and its Limits* argues that evidence consists of propositions, so that one's total evidence is tantamount to a single proposition, the conjunction of all those propositions that are part of one's evidence (pp. 194–200). The best off a

hypothesis **h** can be on evidence **e** is to be entailed by **e**: that is, *all* **e** worlds are
h worlds. The worst off **h** can be on **e** is to be inconsistent with **e**: that is, *no* **e**
worlds are **h** worlds. The aim is to find intermediate gradations in the relation of
e to **h** between entailment and inconsistency (p. 212). Suppose that the 'size' of
every relevant set **p** of worlds is measured by a non-negative real number $M(\mathbf{p})$,
where M is a *measure* in the mathematical sense, so $M(\{\}) = 0$ (the null set has
zero 'size') and M is countably additive, that is, $M(\cup_i \mathbf{p}_i) = \Sigma_i\, M(\mathbf{p}_i)$, where the
index i ranges over the natural numbers and the $\mathbf{p_i}$ are pairwise disjoint (the 'size'
of a set is the sum of the 'sizes' of its disjoint parts). Of course, the set of all
world should have some positive 'size': $M(\omega) > 0$. Then we can measure how
well off **h** is on **e** by the proportion of **e** worlds that are **h** worlds, that is, by the
ratio $M(\mathbf{e} \cap \mathbf{h})/M(\mathbf{e})$ of **e** worlds that are **h** worlds to **e** worlds, whenever **e** has
positive 'size' ($M(\mathbf{e}) > 0$). We can now define an initial probability measure Prob
by setting $Prob(\mathbf{p}) = M(\mathbf{p})/M(\omega)$; that Prob satisfies all the usual probability
axioms follows trivially from the assumptions already made.[1] Moreover, the ratio
$M(\mathbf{e} \cap \mathbf{h})/M(\mathbf{e})$, which measures how well off the hypothesis **h** is on evidence **e**,
in other words, the probability of **h** on the evidence, is equal to the conditional
probability of **h** on **e**, $Prob(\mathbf{h} \mid \mathbf{e})$, defined as $Prob(\mathbf{e} \cap \mathbf{h})/Prob(\mathbf{e})$, whenever **e**
has positive 'size', exactly as claimed in *Knowledge and its Limits* (p. 212). Of
course, none of this proves beyond doubt that there are evidential probabilities;
a sceptic can still doubt that there is a suitable measure M of the 'size' of sets of
worlds. But it does make the postulation of evidential probabilities attractively
natural.

Various liberalizations are possible. We could weaken countable additivity to
finite additivity (where the index i ranges only over finite sets). We could allow
M to take infinitesimal values in a non-standard model of analysis. But these are
technical variations on an underlying theme.

In *Knowledge and its Limits* I argued that the subjective Bayesian tradition
of trying to ground probability theory in decision theory is inappropriate to
evidential probability, and more generally that pragmatist attempts to operation-
alize epistemology rest on false assumptions about rationality and evidence (see
further Williamson 2008). Although Kaplan's ambitions are more modest, it is
unclear what alternative motivation he has for insisting that strong assumptions
in epistemology should be derived from equally strong assumptions in decision
theory (or elsewhere).

Kaplan complains that my approach leaves 'inexplicable' 'the role assessments
of the probability of a hypothesis on the evidence play in decision making'. But
it is a fallacy to suppose that epistemology can be relevant to decision theory

---

[1] Kaplan misinterprets a description of a probability distribution as informed by some but not
all of the subject's evidence (p. 187) as describing the initial probability distribution. The point of
that passage is rather to handle the problem of old evidence by distinguishing background evidence
from the target evidence whose probability-raising effect on a hypothesis is at issue.

only by being built on decision theory. An agent's knowledge that water will satisfy her thirst plays a role in her decision making. To try to explain that simple fact by giving a decision-theoretic analysis of knowledge is to engage in a deeply unpromising project.[2] Similarly, an agent's knowledge that it is very probable on her evidence that there is water by that clump of trees can play a role in her decision making because it approximates to knowledge that in most possibilities consistent with her evidence there is water by that clump of trees. To understand that fact, we do not need a decision-theoretic analysis of knowledge or evidence. Rather, epistemological notions are implicit or explicit in the posing of the central questions of decision theory: how should agents act, given limited knowledge of the consequences of their actions?[3]

2.   Much of Kaplan's critique is directed at a more specific point, the interpret-ation of evidential probability 1. On the account in *Knowledge and its Limits*, all of one's evidence automatically has evidential probability 1; if **e** entails **e*** then Prob(**e***|**e**) = 1. Moreover, one's evidence consists of whatever one knows (pp. 184–207). Thus whatever one knows automatically has evidential prob-ability 1. But the standard for knowledge is not set sceptically high. We know many ordinary truths about the external world that are not 'absolutely certain'; they are not immune to doubts even of quite everyday kinds. Thus many truths that are uncertain in that sense have probability 1 on our evidence. But we are recommended to proportion our belief to our evidence (p. 189). Since evidential probabilities measure how well off propositions are on our evidence, we are apparently recommended to give the maximum degree of belief to whatever we know, even though it is uncertain. Is not that a bad recommendation?

Unfortunately, Kaplan's presentation of the problem is marred by misinter-pretation. He takes the recommendation to be to proportion one's degree of outright belief in **p** to the probability of **p** on one's evidence.[4] Roughly, one's degree of outright belief in **p** is the degree to which one is willing to use **p** as a premiss in one's practical reasoning (p. 99). But *Knowledge and its Limits* does not connect degrees of outright belief and evidential probabilities in the way Kaplan imagines. For example, suppose that a fair coin is about to be tossed. Let **h** be the hypothesis that the coin comes up heads. The probability of **h** on my evidence is ¹⁄₂. Nevertheless, I am and should be completely unwilling to use **h**

---

[2] The role of knowledge in decision making is, of course, not explained merely by its factiveness, for the mere fact that P does not play the same role in decision theory as the agent's knowledge that P.

[3] The first sentence of the first section ('A Decision Problem') of Kaplan's book is 'You know precious little about the election' (1996: 1). Knowledge first!

[4] In the passage Kaplan cites for the connection (p. 209), I distinguish probabilities on the evidence from credences (degrees of belief in something like the Bayesian sense) and credences from degrees of outright belief, but that of course is not to equate probabilities on the evidence with degrees of outright belief, or to recommend proportioning the latter to the former.

as a premiss in my practical reasoning, so my degree of outright belief in **h** is 0, and I am and should be equally unwilling to use ¬**h** as a premiss in my practical reasoning, so my degree of outright belief in ¬**h** is also 0. The degrees of outright belief even of a perfectly rational agent are not required to satisfy the probability axioms. In the sense in which I should have degree of belief ½ in **h**, degrees of belief are more like Bayesian credences than like degrees of outright belief. Of course, my credences can still fail to coincide with probabilities on my evidence; perhaps my credences are not what they should be.

Nevertheless, even when Kaplan's misinterpretation is cleared up, a problem remains. For why should I give maximum credence to uncertain propositions? Should I bet everything I hold most dear for trivial gain on every item of casual knowledge I happen to have?

The first point to note is that versions of this problem arise for all theories of epistemic probability. In particular, as I emphasized in the book (p. 213), the standard probability axioms require every logical truth, no matter how complex and unproved, to have probability 1. Should I bet everything I hold most dear for trivial gain on every logical truth—that is, if we are still treating propositions as sets of worlds, on the set ω of all worlds as presented by every logically true sentence I happen to encounter, no matter how complex and unproved? Kaplan gives a simple instance of the law of excluded middle as an example of an obvious tautology of whose truth one is 'presumably certain, and entitled to be certain'. But even in that case, although it is in fact a logical truth, is it prudent to bet everything I hold most dear for trivial gain on something that has been rejected by many able proponents of deviant logics (intuitionistic logic, Kleene's three-valued logics, fuzzy logic, . . .)?

Kaplan proposes equating the probability of **h** on present evidence with the degree of confidence it is reasonable to have in **h** on the present evidence. In an ordinary sense of 'reasonable', it is *not* reasonable to have the greatest possible degree of confidence in a complex unproved logical truth on present evidence. We should rightly regard someone who bet everything he held most dear for trivial gain on such a logical truth as far more deserving of criticism than someone who refused the bet. The former manifests hubris in foolishly dismissing the possibility that he might make a logical slip. Even on the counterfactual supposition that someone is in fact perfectly rational, it does not follow that it is wise for her to be perfectly confident that she is perfectly rational—for example, when she is presented with misleading evidence that appears to show that she was often irrational in the past. Thus, given the standard axioms of probability, Kaplan's equation fails on a normal sense of 'reasonable'.

The problem is not confined to logical truths. In probability theory, we are often compelled to use probability distributions that are *non-regular*, in the sense that they assign probability 0 to some non-empty sets of worlds. Suppose that there will be infinitely many independent tosses of a fair coin. Let **h** be the hypothesis that it comes up heads on every toss. For each natural number n, the probability (on my present evidence) that it comes up heads on each of the first n tosses is $\frac{1}{2}^n$, so for each n the probability of **h** is at most $\frac{1}{2}^n$. Thus the probability of **h** can only be 0; hence the probability of ¬**h** is 1. But how can one be completely confident that the outcome will not be **h**? For **h** is as well off on my evidence as any other specific outcome, in particular as well off as the true outcome—for all I know, it is the true outcome.

Some philosophers have tried to escape this problem by dropping the requirement that probabilities be real-valued and assigning **h** a probability infinitesimally greater than 0. However, an argument that **h** must have probability 0 can be given that goes through even if infinitesimal probabilities are allowed; it depends only on the nature of the example and very broad structural features of probability (Williamson 2007c). Thus, whether or not infinitesimal probabilities are allowed, the probability on my evidence of ¬**h** is 1: an obvious tautology is no more probable on my evidence than the straightforwardly empirical claim ¬**h**. Indeed, if **x** describes what is in fact (unbeknownst to me) the true outcome, then the probability on my evidence of **x** is also 0, by parity of reasoning, so the probability on my evidence of ¬**x** is 1: the obvious tautology is no more probable on my evidence than the straightforwardly empirical falsehood ¬**x**. These results in no way depend on the theory of evidential probability in *Knowledge and its Limits*.

On just about any view, the structure of probability sometimes imposes the same probability on propositions that are not equally open to doubt. It is a crude measure of how well off propositions are on our evidence. It is essentially coarse-grained, not just in the sense of logical omniscience; it cannot always distinguish even between propositions with different truth-values. We cannot rely on probabilities for all the distinctions we need in epistemology. Even the requirement to proportion one's belief to the evidence can only be cashed out in probabilistic terms to a first approximation. Nevertheless, a first approximation is better than nothing.

Non-regular probabilities have repercussions in decision theory. Suppose, for simplicity, that the only relevant value is money. Then it is very plausible that you should want to conform to the following principle (Kaplan 1996: 8):

CONFIDENCE For any hypotheses **p** and **q**, you are more confident in **p** than in **q** if and only if you prefer a ticket that gives $1 in case **p** and $0 in case ¬**p** to a ticket that gives $1 in case **q** and $0 in case ¬**q**.

But let **p** be the hypothesis that the coin comes up heads on each of the infinitely many tosses, and **q** an obvious logical contradiction. By the previously mentioned argument, you should give probability 0 both to **p** and to **q**. If so, and your degrees of confidence are ordered by those probabilities, you are *not* more confident in **p** than in **q**. Therefore, if you satisfy CONFIDENCE, you do *not* prefer a ticket that gives $1 in case **p** and $0 in case ¬**p** to a ticket that gives $1 in case q and \$0 in case $\neg q$. But, given what you know, surely you should prefer the ticket that gives \$1 in case p and \$0 in case $\neg p$ to the ticket that gives \$1 in case q and \$0 in case $\neg q$, for you know that the former has a chance of giving you \$1 and no chance of losing you anything while the latter has no chance of gaining you anything. In such cases, CONFIDENCE is hard to reconcile with a probabilistic treatment of confidence.

Again, consider this equally plausible analogue of CONFIDENCE:

CONFIDENCE*   For any hypotheses p and q, you are equally confident in p and q if and only if you are indifferent between a ticket that loses \$1 in case p and \$0 in case $\neg p$ and a ticket that loses \$1 in case q and \$0 in case $\neg q$.

For each possible outcome o of the infinite sequence of tosses, let T_o be a ticket that loses \$1 in case o occurs and \$0 otherwise, and S_o a ticket that loses \$1 in case a given contradiction is true and \$0 otherwise. By the same argument as before, you should give probability 0 to both the occurrence of o and the truth of the contradiction. If so, and your degrees of confidence are ordered by those probabilities, you are equally confident in the occurrence of o and the truth of the contradiction. Therefore, if you satisfy CONFIDENCE*, you are indifferent between T_o and S_o. Suppose that you start with a distinct ticket S_o for each possible outcome o. This infinite collection of tickets is logically guaranteed to lose you nothing. Now you simultaneously swap each S_o for T_o. By hypothesis, each swap is a matter of indifference to you, and in each case your total loss is just the sum of your losses on each ticket.[5] But as a result you end up with a set of tickets that constitute a Dutch book: you will lose \$1 no matter which outcome occurs.

Obviously, the example is fanciful. But the point is this. Consider a set of plausible decision-theoretic constraints $C_1, \ldots, C_n$ on a rational agent from which it is provable that the agent's degrees of confidence can be represented as probabilities. Then, in some logically possible situations, such as the one above, any agent (even if logically omniscient) is bound to violate at least one plausible decision-theoretic constraint: for example, either one of $C_1, \ldots, C_n$, or CONFIDENCE, or the principle that if one knows that option X has a chance of doing better than option Y and no chance of doing worse then one should prefer X to Y.[6]

The moral, of course, is not that anarchy reigns in decision theory. Rather, it is that decision theory has to be pursued in something like the abductive spirit that I advocated for probabilistic epistemology, in which we tentatively postulate strong, plausible principles in order to explore their consequences and

---

[5] The sum is well defined, since at most one ticket yields a non-zero loss.

[6] Another alternative is that the agent violates one of the principles that, in the circumstances, exclude assigning a non-zero probability to any one outcome of the sequence of tosses.

limitations. Although much is to be learned from investigating the relations between principles of epistemology and principles of decision theory, the latter plays no foundational role whatsoever with respect to the former. In particular, the best defence of evidential probability in situations like the one above may be by loosening its ties to decision theory.

3. In *Knowledge and its Limits* I argued that, whatever evidence is, we are not always in a position to know how much we have of it. Something can be part of our evidence even though we are not in a position to know that it is part of our evidence, and it can fail to be part of our evidence even though we are not in a position to know that it is not part of our evidence. By the same token, whatever evidential probability is, we are not always in a position to know what values our evidential probabilities take. Thus the sense in which evidential probabilities can guide our actions is not a fully 'operational' one. In fact, the idea of a fully 'operational' guide to action is an illusion—it is not as though probabilities of some other kind were the real guide to action.

Once we have given up the hopeless aspiration to make evidential probabilities transparent to the agent, we can accept the natural understanding of evidential probability as probability on the evidence, in the sense of probability conditionalized on the evidence. Trivially, therefore, every part of the evidence has probability 1 on the evidence, even though instances of this may not be obvious even to the logically omniscient agent. Some parts of one's evidence may have other epistemic advantages over others: for instance, one may know of some parts of one's evidence that they are part of one's evidence while not knowing (or even being in a position to know) of other parts of one's evidence that they are part of one's evidence. Thus some propositions with evidential probability 1 will have epistemic advantages over other propositions with evidential probability 1. But that will hold for *any* useful notion of evidential probability: one will know (or at least be in a position to know) of some propositions with evidential probability 1 for one that they have evidential probability 1 for one while not knowing (or even being in a position to know) of other propositions with evidential probability 1 for one that they have evidential probability 1 for one. Since such epistemic differences between propositions that share evidential probability 1 are inevitable, I am unmoved by their emergence on my account of evidential probability. One's knowledge is not all on a par in all epistemic respects, even though all of it has probability 1 on one's evidence. No single probability distribution can capture all those epistemic differences.

Kaplan accuses me of committing 'something akin to the base rate fallacy' by not multiplying the probability of a hypothesis **h** conditional on the evidence **e** by the unconditional probability of **e** in calculating the probability of **h** on the evidence. This criticism completely misses the mark, since on my view once **e** becomes evidence its probability in the relevant sense is 1, so multiplying by it makes no difference. More precisely, let Prob be the initial probability distribution and Prob_e be the probability distribution on one's evidence once one's evidence is e. On my view, $\text{Prob}_e(\mathbf{h}) = \text{Prob}(\mathbf{h} \mid e)$. Thus, in particular, $\text{Prob}_e(e) = 1$. By contrast, Kaplan claims that the probability of $\mathbf{h}$ on evidence e is $p(\mathbf{h} \mid e)p(e) + p(\mathbf{h} \mid \neg e)p(\neg e)$—which is, of course, just $p(\mathbf{h})$. Thus, for Kaplan, the probability of any given hypothesis on evidence e_1 is the same as its probability on any other evidence e_2. This pointlessly trivializes the notion of the probability of a hypothesis on evidence.

Kaplan's real quarrel is with my claim that e always acquires probability 1 when it becomes evidence, because he thinks that in that case it may be unreasonable to have the highest possible degree of confidence in e. But, as already argued on independent grounds, there is no simple link of the kind that Kaplan's argument requires between probability 1 and the reasonableness in a normal sense of the highest possible degree of confidence. Indeed, Kaplan himself insists in the case of complex logical truths that the propriety of a rule is compatible with its violation by reasonable agents when they cannot see what it requires. They may fail to assign the highest level of confidence to a logical truth when it is not perfectly clear to them that it is a logical truth. Similarly, on my view, reasonable agents may excusably fail to assign the highest level of confidence to part of their evidence when it is not perfectly clear to them that it is part of their evidence. Kaplan fails to identify any decisive normative difference between the two cases.

Probabilistic epistemology needs a less reductionist treatment, in which we do not attempt to define evidential probabilities in other terms. The trick is to do that without leaving it insufficiently constrained by the rest of epistemology.

Reply to Jonathan Kvanvig

1.   In 'Assertion, Knowledge, and Lotteries', Jonathan Kvanvig argues that the epistemic norms of assertion concern justification rather than, as I argued, knowledge. I will dispute his argument at just about every point. I see no reason to modify my account of assertion, on which it is governed by a single characteristic norm: 'Assert only if you know.' This norm is a constitutive rule, like a rule of a game.

Kvanvig begins by claiming that my account makes the knowledge rule implausibly indefeasible, unlike most ordinary norms: 'if we are playing the game, the rules cannot be overridden by factors outside the rule book.' The content of the knowledge rule indeed contains no fudging qualification 'other things being equal'. However good one's reasons for asserting **p** when one does not know **p**, in doing so one violates the norm of assertion, and in that sense subjects oneself to a criticism internal to the practice of assertion. Nevertheless, as I made clear in the book (pp. 240, 256), in the overall moral or practical assessment of one's action, the violation of the norm of assertion can easily be overridden by more important considerations. In nasty circumstances, you may have to make a lying assertion or cheat at cards in order to save an innocent person's life, and act well; although you thereby break a constitutive rule of a speech act, that infraction is trivial by comparison with what is at stake. Similarly, in rushing to save a life you may have to push a bystander rudely aside: you act well, despite violating a rule of etiquette. Kvanvig is mistaken in claiming a contrast between constitutive rules and rules of etiquette on this point.

Kvanvig lists various cases in which, according to him, an assertion violates the knowledge rule without being viewed as deserving of criticism. It is worth going through his cases to get a feel for the robustness of the knowledge account.

(*a*)   Kvanvig says: 'Skeptics claim not to know anything, and if we consider the possibility that they are correct, we need not demand that they speak no more.'[1] Of course, assertion is not the only speech act; sceptics who only ask awkward questions do not violate the knowledge rule, however little they know, because they do not assert anything. But there is nothing new about the idea that a sceptic who *asserts* 'I know nothing' undermines his own assertion. What entitles

---

[1] Even granted the falsity of sceptics' claim to know nothing, one still cannot know that one knows nothing: for, since knowledge is factive, if one knows that one knows nothing then one knows nothing, but equally if one knows that one knows nothing then one knows something.

him to make it? Is he also willing to make the Moore-paradoxical assertion to which it commits him, 'I know nothing and I don't know that I know nothing'? Although we may learn something of philosophical interest by thinking about his assertion, it is defective nonetheless.

(*b*)   We are told: 'Eliminative materialists say that there are no beliefs, and they do not have to flout the norms of assertion to discuss this philosophical possibility, even if it should turn out that they are right.' Let us grant what Kvanvig is assuming, that if there are no beliefs then nobody believes anything, so nobody knows anything (because knowledge entails belief). But he is also assuming that, according to a coherent version of eliminative materialism, speech acts still have propositional content, so that one can '*say that* there are no beliefs [emphasis added], and. . . discuss this philosophical possibility', which is far more dubious. *If* eliminative materialism is true, then most of *Knowledge and its Limits* is false, as is most of Kvanvig's chapter, and all bets are off: but that does not show that most of *Knowledge and its Limits* actually is false. Of course, if anybody knows that eliminative materialism is true, then eliminative materialism is true, by the factivity of knowledge, in which case nobody knows anything, so nobody knows that eliminative materialism is true; thus it is impossible to know that eliminative materialism is true. Consequently, anybody who asserts that eliminative materialism is true thereby violates the knowledge rule. Are they also willing to make the Moore-paradoxical assertion to which they are committed, 'Eliminative materialism is true and I don't know that eliminative materialism is true'? Indeed, few philosophers think that eliminative materialists' arguments even *justify* belief that eliminative materialism is true; the assertion that it is true arguably violates Kvanvig's weaker norm of assertion too. Nevertheless, we need not wish to silence eliminative materialists, because we can hope to learn something from discussion with them, although not the truth of eliminative materialism itself. In that discussion, *we* need not violate the knowledge rule.

(*c*)   Kvanvig says that 'there is nothing wrong with the attempt' of non-theists who take William James's pragmatist advice and espouse theological claims that they do not (yet) believe. For myself, I find such behaviour utterly contemptible, an abject evasion of epistemic responsibility unworthy of any human adult, although that is more than the present argument requires. In any case, the example is underdescribed. Are these non-theistic pragmatists willing to make the Moore-paradoxical assertion 'This bread is the body of Christ and I don't believe that this bread is the body of Christ'? Or do they pretend to believe that this bread is the body of Christ? Either way, their position is deeply problematic. Their assertion violates norms of sincerity and (epistemic) justification, not only of knowledge.

(*d*)   According to Kvanvig: 'Philosophers espouse positive views . . . that, on reflection, they agree they do not know to be true; but they continue the practice unrepentant.' But this is too crude a description of the typical case. When philosophers take a detached, third-personal view of their own philosophical interventions, they often disavow knowledge, just as people often do when sceptical scenarios become salient, but in that mood they are reluctant to make the original assertions without qualifiers like 'It seems to me plausible that'. When they resume the more engaged, first-personal stance towards their philosophical interventions, they often revert to speaking as if they had knowledge, just as people often do when sceptical scenarios drop back out of sight. This oscillation should not be misinterpreted as a stable intermediate option on which asserting does not require knowing. Some evidence of this is that most philosophers are unwilling to combine the two stances by making Moore-paradoxical assertions of the form 'X and I don't know that X'.

(*e*)   Kvanvig mentions the power of positive thinking, unwarranted assertions of positive outcomes made, for instance, on the advice of sports psychologists. Such cases prove nothing, since one's only interest in making such assertions is to manipulate oneself into playing well. Whatever the norms of assertion, sports psychologists will advise violating them if that is the way to better performance.

(*f*)   According to Kvanvig: 'a judge may give instructions to the jury that he does not believe are correct instructions. But his role requires that he give these instructions, and, in order to comply, he asserts them without believing them.' The case is poorly described, since instructions are more naturally taken to be conveyed by imperatives than by indicatives. If the judge has to tell the jury that they are required to proceed in a certain way, when privately he believes that they ought not to be required to proceed in that way, he may still know that they *are* required to proceed in that way, in which case the knowledge rule is not violated. If the judge's role really does require him to make an insincere assertion, then he is in an unhappy position. Even if we judge that, all things considered, he acted for the best in making the assertion, we do not find his assertion straightforwardly felicitous.

(*g*)   Teachers may be required by law to teach material that they do not believe. In some such cases, according to Kvanvig, compliance is not 'criticizable'. But the most obvious point to make about such cases is that the teacher has been put in a difficult position. The difficulty arises because the education law *conflicts* with the norm of assertion. If the content of the norm were consistent with insincere assertion in these circumstances, or the circumstances somehow rendered the norm inoperative, there would be no conflict, and the teacher's position would not be as difficult as it actually is. Naturally, when norms conflict, we do not criticize someone for choosing what we consider to be the weightier norm: but our attitude does not involve assigning zero weight to the violated norm.

None of Kvanvig's examples (*a*)–(*g*) is at all surprising on the assumption that the knowledge rule is constitutive of assertion, just as I argued in *Knowledge and its Limits*. This is some evidence for the robustness of the knowledge account.

2. Kvanvig objects to the argument for the knowledge account from conversational patterns (pp. 252–4), on the grounds that it proves too much. If the propriety of the questions 'How do you know that?' and 'Do you know that?' shows that asserting requires knowing, he asks, why does not the propriety of the questions 'Are you certain?' and 'Are you absolutely sure?' show that asserting requires being absolutely certain? But this is to miss the fine distinctions necessary for a proper understanding of the argument from conversational patterns.

Questions typically presuppose that they have an answer; that is, the speaker treats it as part of the common ground of the conversation that the question has an answer. For example, since an answer to the question 'How does X F?' is of the general form 'X Fs in way W', which entails 'X Fs', the question presupposes that X Fs. In particular, 'How do you know that?' presupposes that you do know that. This presupposition is well explained by the hypothesis that knowledge is a norm for assertion. Without any such norm, the question would be inappropriate, through presupposition failure (p. 252).

By contrast, the question 'Do you know that?' does not presuppose that you do know that, since 'No' is a potential answer. My argument for the knowledge rule using the latter question appealed not to its *propriety* but to its *aggressiveness*. If knowledge were not required for assertion, why should it be aggressive to treat whether the speaker knows as an open question? The questions 'Are you certain?' and 'Are you absolutely sure?' sound much less aggressive and abrupt than 'Do you know that?' The natural explanation of this difference is that the latter constitutes a much more direct challenge to the speaker's authority to make the assertion than the former do. Of course, even 'Are you certain?' and 'Are you absolutely sure?' are unsettling, as one would expect on the knowledge account, since any uncertainty as to the truth of the assertion is in effect uncertainty as to its compliance with the knowledge rule.

The proper analogue of 'How do you know that?' is a question that presupposes that the speaker is certain—for instance, 'Why are you certain?' or 'Why are you absolutely sure?' But such questions are not generally appropriate responses to an assertion, unless the asserter's manner of making it evinced unusual confidence. More natural are the questions 'How can you be certain?' and 'How can you be absolutely sure?'[2] They presuppose not that the addressee *is* certain or absolutely sure but only that she *can be* certain or absolutely sure. Still, one might worry that being in a position to be certain places a more demanding constraint than knowing on the asserter's epistemic standing. However, as pointed out in *Knowledge and its Limits* (p. 254), the relevant standard of certainty need not

---

[2] The questions 'How are you certain?' and 'How are you absolutely sure?' are awkward in the same way as 'How do you believe?'; 'Why can you be certain?' and 'Why can you be absolutely sure?' are awkward in the same way as 'Why do you know?'

be higher than knowing already requires. For, once we make a high standard of certainty explicit, by asking 'How can you be utterly certain?' or 'How can you attain Cartesian certainty of that?', the question ceases to be generally appropriate. It is naturally regarded as introducing an irrelevantly high epistemic standard into the conversation.[3]

The conversational phenomena are considerably more discriminating than Kvanvig implies. They discriminate in favour of the knowledge account.

3. In making a prima facie case that justification rather than knowledge is the epistemic norm of assertion, Kvanvig claims that, if we assert **p** on the basis of a justified false belief in **p**, when we discover our mistake we take back the content of the assertion but do not apologize for making it: 'Chagrin is normal, even mild embarrassment, but apologizing would be unctuous and overwrought.' This seems wrong. I doubt that it even correctly describes Kvanvig's own behaviour; he has always struck me as rather courteous. Misrecognizing someone, I may say: 'That's Sasha—no, sorry, it's not—it's just someone who looks very like him.' If I plead at length with you to forgive me, *that* would be unctuous and overwrought, but saying 'sorry' is perfectly normal polite behavior. Nor is it strange for a newspaper to apologize to its readers for an error in a previous edition, or for the author of a book to apologize in the preface for any remaining errors, even though every effort has been made to ensure that the contents are correct.[4]

Falsity is a defect in an assertion. It is not merely a defect in the asserter's belief system, revealed by the assertion. By contrast, if a sincere creationist is asked whether he genuinely believes that creationism is true, the proper answer for him to give is 'Yes, I do', for he knows that he genuinely believes that creationism is true. His true assertion that he genuinely believes that creationism is true is not itself defective, even though it reveals a defect in his belief system—that he has the false creationist belief. We make a clear distinction between defects in an assertion and defects in the asserter revealed by the assertion, and falsity comes on the former side. The justification account, unlike the knowledge account, fails to predict this (p. 262).

4. The knowledge account explains another conversational pattern: the impropriety of Moore-paradoxical assertions of the form 'X and I don't know that

---

[3] See also Stanley (2008).

[4] Kvanvig quotes a passage in which I say that one may reasonably but falsely and impermissibly assert **p** because one reasonably but falsely believes that one knows **p**; it is very probable on one's evidence that one knows **p** (pp. 255–6). He equates reasonableness in my sense with having enough justification to know in his, and claims in effect that on this notion of justification one may be justified ('rational') in asserting that one's lottery ticket will lose. But I deny that it is reasonable to believe that one knows that one's ticket will lose. Although it is very probable on one's evidence that one's ticket will lose, it is not at all probable on one's evidence that *one knows that* one's ticket will lose.

X', for by a familiar argument one cannot know: X and I do not know that X (p. 253). Kvanvig argues that the justification account too can explain this datum, provided that justification is understood as 'the kind that puts one in a position to know'. We can call it 'enough justification to know'.

A crucial premiss of Kvanvig's attempted explanation of the impropriety of the Moore-paradoxical assertions is his principle (J), that if one has enough justification to know **p** then one has enough justification to know that one has enough justification to know **p**. This JJ principle is suspiciously similar to the notorious KK principle, that if one knows then one knows that one knows, against which I argued at length (pp. 114–19). Indeed, the argument in *Knowledge and its Limits* against the KK principle also refutes the principle that if one is in a position to know **p** then one is in a position to know that one is in a position to know **p**, which is even closer to (J). Kvanvig neither attempts to rebut those arguments nor acknowledges their relevance to (J). Indeed, the point of those arguments is that KK-like principles lead one into sorites paradoxes, and Kvanvig asserts the major premiss of a sorites paradox in his defence of (J). For he says: 'there cannot be two bodies of evidence that as far as one can tell provide the same degree of confirmation for closing off inquiry regarding a claim and yet where one of the bodies of evidence legitimates closing off inquiry regarding a claim and the other one does not.' Call that 'Kvanvig's tolerance principle'.

To see that Kvanvig's tolerance principle generates a sorites paradox, imagine watching a plant grow from a seed until it is 2 feet tall. Let $t_0, \ldots, t_n$ be a sequence of times at one second intervals from a time t_0 at which it was a seed to a time t_n at which it is 2 feet tall. Consider any time t_i before the last in the series. As far as you can tell, your body of evidence at t_i and your body of evidence at t_{i+1} provide the same degree of confirmation for closing off enquiry regarding the claim that the plant will eventually grow to a height of more than 1 foot; as far as you can tell, the plant has not grown at all in that one-second interval. Hence, by Kvanvig's tolerance principle, if your body of evidence at t_{i+1} legitimates closing off enquiry regarding the claim that it will eventually grow to a height of more than 1 foot, then your body of evidence at t_i legitimates closing off enquiry regarding the same claim. This holds for any i from 0 to $n - 1$. Thus, by transitivity, if your body of evidence at t_n legitimates closing off enquiry regarding the claim, then your body of evidence at t_0 legitimates closing off enquiry regarding the claim. Your body of evidence at t_n clearly legitimates closing off enquiry regarding the claim, because you see plainly that the plant is much more than a foot tall. But your body of evidence at t_0 clearly did not legitimate closing off enquiry regarding the claim, since it was then a very realistic possibility that the plant would not grow properly at all. By *reductio ad absurdum*, Kvanvig's tolerance principle is false. With it falls his defence of (J), and therefore his explanation of the impropriety of the Moore-paradoxical assertions.

A variant of the justification account that explains the impropriety of those assertions without generating sorites paradoxes is the view that the required epistemic standard for asserting **p** is being justified in believing that one knows **p**. For, if an obvious argument shows that one cannot know the conjunction that X and one does not know X, then presumably one is not justified in believing the conjunction that one knows that X and one does not know X. However, I argued against just such a view in *Knowledge and its Limits* (pp. 261–3). In particular, unless justification entails truth, the view does not explain why falsity is a defect in an assertion, not just in the asserter. It is unnecessary to go into the arguments again here.

5.   In the last part of his chapter, Kvanvig argues against my equation E = K of one's total evidence with one's total knowledge and in favour of a more experiential view of evidence.

Kvanvig's initial objection to E = K is that it can deprive the subject of too much evidence in cases of perceptual illusion. If it looks to me as though there is water up ahead, when there is no water up ahead, my belief that there is water up ahead does not constitute knowledge, so the proposition that there is water up ahead is not part of my evidence. What relevant truth is part of my evidence? There is the truth that it looks to me as though there is water up ahead, which I am at least in a position to know. However, Kvanvig objects that, if I have no reason to suspect an illusion, it may not occur to me to form the cautious belief that it looks to me as though there is water up ahead, even though I have a disposition to form it if the question arises; but the question does not arise, and I simply form the less cautious belief that there is water up ahead. Since knowledge entails belief, I do not know that it looks to me as though there is water up ahead. Thus not even the truth that it looks to me as though there is water up ahead is part of my evidence.

I am willing to grant that much of Kvanvig's description of the case. My actual evidence, consisting of the truths that I actually know, is radically impoverished. But there is also my potential evidence, consisting of the truths that I am in a position to know, to make part of my evidence. That it looks to me as though there is water up ahead is still part of my potential evidence, since I am in a position to know that it looks to me as though there is water up ahead. In that sense, I still have ready access to that piece of evidence. Moreover, the factors that give me this ready access to the rich evidence also play a large and direct role in causing my belief that there is water up ahead. In cases like these, we are willing to overlook the poverty of the subject's actual evidence.

Kvanvig accuses E = K of getting things backwards even in genuine cases of perceptual knowledge, because it does not acknowledge the priority of experience:

When asked to defend the belief that there is a tree with yellowing leaves in the yard south of mine, I will appeal to experience. I do not appeal to my knowledge or to my beliefs. When I say, 'I can see it', I am reporting an experience with propositional content that, in successful cases, is the same content as something I know, but my evidence is that content under a certain modality that is different from the modality of belief or knowledge. It is the modality of experience . . .

This description of the case is problematic in several ways. For instance, what we say when asked to defend a belief depends on dialectical considerations that do not simply reflect the epistemic basis of the belief. We aim for common ground with the challenger; its location depends on the challenger's beliefs as well as on our own.

Moreover, 'I can see it' reports an experience only in the anodyne sense in which 'I met John Boorman' reports an experience. It does not, for example, describe what it was like to have the experience. Rather, the speaker explains how he knows that there is a tree with yellowing leaves in the yard south of his: by sight. In fact, it is natural to interpret the pronoun 'it' in 'I can see it' as referring to the tree. In that case, the statement reports an instance of object perception; it does not specify the propositional content of a perceptual state. But let us suppose that the speaker means 'I can see that there is a tree with yellowing leaves in the yard south of mine', and has some kind of perceptual state with the content that there is a tree with yellowing leaves in the yard south of his. Still, I have argued that 'I can see that X' entails 'I know that X' (pp. 37–8); Kvanvig does not challenge that argument. Consequently, what the speaker is reporting is not an experience somehow prior to knowledge, but simply a particular kind of knowledge: visual knowledge. Thus Kvanvig's description of his example undermines the argument that he wants it to illustrate.

Kvanvig does not explain just what he means by saying that one's evidence is a propositional content under the modality of experience, although he does make it clear that the propositional content is the content of an experience. He seems to hold that both veridical perceptions and perceptual illusions have evidence-constituting contents. Thus, when I am under an illusion, my experience may have the false propositional content that there is water up ahead, and that content is evidence. Consequently, the hypothesis that there is no water up ahead is inconsistent with my evidence. But it is quite implausible to suppose that, if on independent grounds I override the visual appearances and form the true belief that there is no water up ahead, I thereby believe something inconsistent with my evidence. Nor is it at all clear how such a view could make sense of updating by conditionalizing on one's evidence, or of inference to the best explanation, where the content of the evidence is the content of the explanandum (pp. 194–6). Kvanvig cannot say that the content of the evidence is that it looks to me as though there is water up ahead, for that complex appearance proposition is not itself the content of my visual experience. His claim 'The evidence is the experience itself' suggests a non-propositional conception of evidence, since experiences themselves are not propositions; they are more like events. But then the view runs into trouble with the arguments for the conclusion that evidence must be propositional (pp. 194–200), which Kvanvig does not challenge. He has not provided a coherent alternative to $E = K$. The knowledge-centred conception of assertion and evidence stands.

Reply to Ram Neta

In 'Defeating the Dogma of Defeasibility' Ram Neta makes two main criticisms of my epistemology. First, he argues against the equation E = K between the contents of one's total evidence and one's total knowledge. Secondly, he presents a putative analysis of knowledge, which, if correct, would falsify the thesis that knowledge is unanalysable. I deal with these criticisms in respective sections.

1.   E = K is equivalent to the thesis that, necessarily, something is included in one's total evidence if and only if it is included in one's total knowledge. Neta presents alleged counter-examples to both directions of the biconditional.

Here is Neta's candidate for a fact included in one's evidence but not in one's knowledge. He is visualizing a speckled hen. The speckled-hen image contains seven speckles. He does not notice that it contains seven speckles, but he could have simply noticed that it contained seven speckles, without counting. He does not know that the speckled-hen image contains seven speckles. Nevertheless, according to Neta, the fact that it contains seven speckles is in his evidence.

I deny that the fact that the image contains seven speckles is in Neta's evidence. Consider his own characterization of evidence: 'My evidence set at a particular time includes all and only those truths that I am entitled to take for granted in inquiry at that time.' Suppose that, still without noticing or knowing that the image contains seven speckles, Neta at that time takes for granted in his enquiries that the image contains seven speckles. Perhaps he is in the habit of taking for granted that speckled-hen images contain seven speckles. The obvious objection to his doing so is that, in the circumstances, he is *not entitled* to take for granted that the image contains seven speckles if he has not even noticed that it contains seven speckles. To put the point in a way that does not depend on Neta's gloss on evidence, he is not entitled to treat the fact as part of his evidence, and the simplest explanation why not is that it is not part of his evidence. Of course, Neta could easily have noticed that the image contains seven speckles, in which case he *would have* known the fact and doubtless been entitled to take it for granted in his enquiry at that time. But an easily available counterfactual entitlement is not the same as an actual entitlement.

Neta further explains being entitled to take **p** for granted in his sense as being entitled to appeal to **p** without having to be able to defend **p** against challenges. This does not help him. If Neta has not even noticed that the image contains seven speckles, he is not entitled to appeal to the proposition that it contains seven speckles without having to be able to defend it against challenges.

One can envisage the example in such a way that Neta has knowledge that entails that the image contains seven speckles. For let $s_1, \ldots, s_7$ be the seven speckles. For each i, Neta may have noticed s_i, and thereby come to know that the image contains speckle s_i, and for each j distinct from i he may have noticed and thereby come to know that s_j is distinct from s_i ($1 \leq i, j \leq 7$). These facts entail that the image contains *at least* seven speckles. If by 'contains seven speckles' Neta means 'contains *exactly* seven speckles', then the fact that the image contains no speckles other than $s_1, \ldots, s_7$ is also needed, but it is quite consistent with the example that Neta noticed and thereby came to know that fact too. On this way of envisaging the example, what Neta knows straightforwardly entails that the image contains seven speckles, which may help to explain any temptation to judge that his evidence includes the fact that the image contains seven speckles. Of course, one can also envisage the example in such a way that Neta does not know all those premises. For instance, he may have failed to notice speckle s_7, and so may fail to know that the image contains s_7. But then the claim that he is entitled to take for granted in enquiry at that time that the image contains seven speckles looks even less plausible. Thus Neta has not provided a convincing example of a fact that is included in one's evidence but not in one's knowledge.[1]

Here is Neta's candidate for the converse, a fact included in one's knowledge but not in one's evidence. He knows **p** solely because he has competently deduced **p** from premises **a**, **b**, and **c**, each of which he knows. According to Neta, **p** is not included in his evidence. His argument for that claim concerns what happens when you ask him what evidence he has for **p**:

In such a case, I typically cannot give you a true and complete answer without citing **a**, **b**, and **c**. But, if **p** itself were in my evidence set, then I could give you a true and complete answer to the question what evidence I have for **p** simply by citing **p**.[2]

A *complete* answer to the question what evidence he has for **p** must cite *all* his evidence for **p**. Thus Neta's premiss in the second sentence implies that if **p** is in one's evidence set then one has *no* evidence for **p** other than **p** itself. But

---

[1] In a later phase of his discussion, Neta may intend to give further examples of evidence that is not knowledge. He writes: 'Perceptual knowledge that x is F may require that one *perceive* x to be F—and this is something one can do even if one does not know that Fx. (There is a difference here between perceiving that x is F and perceiving x to be F. Both are sufficient for x to be F, but only the former is sufficient for *knowing* x to be F.)' Perhaps he means that if I perceive x to be F then my evidence includes the fact that x is F, even if I do not know that x is F. But the idea of perceiving something to be F without perceiving that it is F is a figment—although one can perceive something *as* F without perceiving that it is F, because one can perceive it as F even if it is not F, and one can perceive something *being* F without perceiving that it is F, because one can perceive it being F without even formulating the proposition that it is F (related issues are discussed in the book at p. 38). Neta also speaks of being informed by someone of x's being F without knowing that x is F; perhaps he means that my evidence then includes the fact that x is F. When someone tells me **p**, I may fail to take in **p**; but then **p** is a poor candidate for being part of my evidence. Since Neta does not argue these cases in detail, I focus on his main discussion of E = K.

[2] Here and in other quotations I have made some trivial changes to Neta's notation.

that is far too strong. For example, when you see a cow in completely normal circumstances, you both know and are entitled to take for granted that you see a cow. On both my view and Neta's, your evidence includes the fact that you see a cow.[3] But it does not follow that you could give a true and complete answer to the question what evidence you have for the proposition that you see a cow simply by citing that very proposition. For example, your total evidence may also include the fact that you can hear the animal that you are looking at mooing or the fact that it visually appears to you that you see a cow, and both those facts are further evidence that you have for the proposition that you see a cow. If you do not cite them in saying what evidence you have for the proposition that you see a cow, you have not given a complete answer to the question. Thus Neta's stated argument for denying that the evidence includes **p** depends on a false premiss.

To be more charitable to Neta, we might reinterpret 'complete' as 'near enough complete for the purposes of the conversational exchange'. However, normally someone who asks you what evidence you have for **p** wants to be given more than just **p** itself. Sometimes the demand is so unreasonable that simply citing **p** is enough. But we usually prefer to give a more cooperative response: you may patiently cite the fact that you can hear the animal that you are looking at mooing. When one can easily cite more evidence for **p**, merely citing **p** is often not giving an answer near enough complete for the purposes of the conversational exchange.[4] These Gricean observations do not show that one's evidence fails to include **p**. Merely being asked what evidence you have for **p** does not remove **p** from your evidence, or create a context in which **p** no longer falls in the extension of the word 'evidence'. By no reasonable standard does your total evidence include the fact that you can hear the animal that you are looking at mooing but not the fact that you see a cow.

Neta's example concerns inferential knowledge. Clearly, if I am aware of believing **p** on the basis of deduction from **a**, **b**, and **c**, I am being conversationally uncooperative if I do not cite them when asked what evidence I have for **p**. But that applies to any case in which I can easily give relevant new information about how I know **p**. Suppose, for example, that in completely normal circumstances I have non-inferential visual knowledge that Ana is in the garden and say to you by mobile phone 'Ana is in the garden'. Not knowing what my assertion is based on, you ask me what evidence I have for it. If I merely reply 'What a silly question! Ana *is* in the garden', without citing the fact that I can see her there,

---

[3] Neta allows that in favourable circumstances one's evidence includes facts about the external world: 'But in a case in which there are no such epistemic risks lurking—no barn façades, no hallucination-inducing drugs, nothing of the sort—Henry might be entitled to take it for granted that he sees a barn.'

[4] This point is anticipated in the book (pp. 187–8).

I am not being conversationally cooperative. But that does not show that my evidence excludes the fact that Ana is in the garden or that I am not entitled to take that fact for granted in enquiry.

For Neta, to be entitled to take something for granted is to be entitled to appeal to it without having to be able to defend it against challenges. In the inferential and non-inferential examples just considered, one is entitled to appeal to the proposition and one is in fact able to defend it against challenges.[5] But, of course, that does not show that the ability to defend the proposition against challenges was a condition of the entitlement. One can be entitled to appeal to **p** without *having* to be able to defend **p** against challenges and yet *be* able to defend **p** against challenges.

One may know **p** solely because one has competently deduced **p** from **a**, **b**, and **c** without knowing that that is how one knows **p**. One may forget the deduction, or it may have been unconscious. Consequently, one may be unable to defend **p** against challenges. Nevertheless, in appropriate circumstances one may still be entitled to take **p** for granted in enquiry. Philosophers have a professional temptation to exaggerate the significance of their own speciality, dialectical prowess, for the epistemic status of beliefs, but we must learn to resist this bias. Inarticulate, unreflective people may retain much inferential knowledge without being able to reconstruct the premises from which it was derived. They are entitled to appeal to what they know, even though they lack the ability to defend it against challenges.[6] Thus they are entitled to appeal to it without having to be able to defend it against challenges. Therefore they are entitled to take it for granted in Neta's sense, so on his view it is part of their evidence. It is also part of their evidence on my view, since it is part of their knowledge.

Thus Neta has also failed to provide a convincing example of a fact included in one's knowledge but not in one's evidence. His critique of the equation E = K fails in both directions.

2. Neta argues for a specific analysis of knowledge. If correct, it falsifies the claim in the book that knowledge is unanalysable.

As a first approximation to his view, Neta states what we may call the *indefeasibility analysis* of knowledge. It adds an indefeasibility constraint as the fourth condition for knowledge to the old justified true belief analysis; in a formulation logically equivalent to Neta's: 'To know **p** is to have a justified true belief in **p** such that, for every true proposition **e**, the conjunction of **e** and one's actual evidence set constitutes a justification for one to believe **p**.' Neta defends the

---

[5] Against *some* challenges, that is: but in practice we are never able to defend a proposition against *all* challenges. None of us is dialectically perfect.

[6] The book makes this point in relation to Brandom (p. 258 n.).

indefeasibility analysis against the usual objection that ordinary knowledge does not require indefeasible evidence by arguing that one can know p on the basis of evidence e only if, necessarily, if one has e, then p is true. In Neta's terminology, that is to say that one can know p only on the basis of infallible evidence for p. That argument inspires his preferred view, which we may call the *infallibility analysis* of knowledge. Unfortunately, in the chapter he states it only informally: 'Knowledge . . . is belief that is properly based on infallible evidence (indeed, on evidence that can be known—perhaps upon reflection alone—to be infallible).'

Since both the indefeasibility analysis and the infallibility analysis employ the concept of evidence, both are circular if the concept of evidence is explained in terms of the concept of knowledge, as in the book. Neta, of course, rejects that explanation, as noted in the previous section, but we saw his reasons for doing so fail. Thus his analyses face the threat of circularity. However, let us concentrate on problems for them that are independent of E = K.

As already noted, Neta's defence of the analyses against a common style of objection depends on his argument that if one knows p on evidence e then e is infallible evidence for p. This argument appears to contain a fallacy. From the supposition that S knows p on the basis of e, Neta argues that S can know by deduction that e is not misleading with respect to p, and that if so a disjunction holds: either S knows that e is not misleading with respect to p on the basis of evidence e′ distinct from e, or e is not fallible evidence for p. Neta claims that the first disjunct leads to an infinite regress, since S can then know that the conjunction e & e′ is not misleading with respect to p, and if so a further disjunction holds: either S knows that e & e′ is not misleading with respect to p on the basis of evidence e″ distinct from e & e′, or e & e′ is not fallible evidence for p. But at best this regress refutes the assumption that in *all* cases the first disjunct is true. It does not refute the assumption that in *some* cases the first disjunct is true; that assumption does not generate an infinite regress. Thus we can only conclude that the second disjunct is true in *some* cases (those in which the first disjunct is false), not that it is true in all. In particular, the argument as Neta gives it does not eliminate the following possibility: S knows that e is not misleading with respect to p on the basis of evidence e′ distinct from e; e is fallible evidence for p; S does not know that e & e′ is not misleading with respect to p on the basis of evidence e″ distinct from e & e′; e & e′ is infallible evidence for p. Consequently, Neta has not shown what he set out to show, that if S knows p on the basis of evidence e then e is infallible evidence for p. At best he has shown that some of S's knowledge is based on infallible evidence, not that all of it is. I will not attempt to determine whether there is some way of repairing Neta's argument on this point.

Another puzzling gap in Neta's discussion concerns his assumption that infallibility entails indefeasibility. He claims:

If it is a necessary condition of S's knowing p that S's evidence e for p be infallible—that is, such that there is no possible situation in which S has e but p is not true—then the conjunction of e with anything constitutes a justification for S to believe p.

But even if S's evidence is infallible, S may not know that it is. Furthermore, even if S does know that her evidence is infallible—that necessarily if S has e then p is true—on both Neta's view and mine S can have evidence e without knowing that she has e; nor has Neta tried to argue that if S's evidence includes e then it also includes the fact that S has e. Thus S may be in no position to reason to the truth of p. It is, therefore, far from obvious why, even if S knows that e is infallible evidence for p in Neta's sense, the conjunction of e with anything should constitute a justification for S to believe p. Consequently, Neta has not provided adequate support for his claim that infallibility entails indefeasibility.

Rather than dwell on obscurities in Neta's arguments, we can turn to the analyses themselves. A Gettier problem arises for the indefeasibility analysis. Neta explicitly allows that some justification is defeasible, even though knowledge is not: 'Of course there may be examples in which S is *justified* in believing p on the basis of evidence which can be expanded into something that is not a justification for S to believe p.' For otherwise the fourth condition in the indefeasibility analysis would be redundant, and the analysis would be equivalent to the old justified true belief analysis, which Neta does not want to defend, even as a close approximation. Presumably, therefore, S's evidence e can provide defeasible justification for a proposition p but indefeasible justification for another proposition q. If so, e also provides indefeasible justification for the disjunction p ∨ q, which is an obvious consequence of q. Suppose that S believes p on the basis of e, and believes p ∨ q solely by competent deduction from p; S's belief in p ∨ q in no way derives from q. In these circumstances, S knows p ∨ q only if S knows the premiss p. But on the indefeasibility analysis S does not know p, because S believes p on the basis of evidence e, which provides only defeasible justification for p. Thus S does not know p ∨ q. But then the indefeasibility analysis falsely predicts that S does know p ∨ q. For S believes p ∨ q, that belief is justified, since S is justified in believing p, from which she competently deduced the disjunction, and it is true, because the second disjunct of the disjunction is true. Thus S has a justified true belief in the disjunction, and the disjunction is indefeasibly justified by her evidence.

We can adapt the counter-example for use against Neta's preferred infallibility analysis by substituting 'fallible' and 'infallible' for 'defeasible' and 'indefeasible' throughout. The only concern is what Neta means by 'properly based' in 'properly based on infallible evidence'. But there is nothing obviously improper in the way S bases her belief in $p \vee q$ on her evidence e, which is in fact infallible evidence for $p \vee q$, since S has a justified belief in p on the basis of e, and she believes $p \vee q$ by competent deduction from p.[7] Since S has a justified belief in $p \vee q$ on the basis of evidence e, S's belief in $p \vee q$ is properly based on e for the purposes of justification. The demand that the belief be properly based on the evidence for the purposes of *knowledge* cannot as such enter a non-circular analysis. Nor could Neta demand that the evidence e be infallible in the stronger sense that, necessarily, if S has e then S has a true belief in p, for on his view S can have e without even noticing e, and without believing anything on the basis of e. The stronger demand would exclude many legitimate cases of knowledge, in which on Neta's view S knows p on the basis of infallible evidence e, even though S *could have* failed to notice e, and so failed to believe p on the basis of e. Of course, having a justified belief in p properly based on infallible evidence would be sufficient for knowing p if the sense of 'justified' were so strong that having a justified belief in p entailed knowing p, but that is not at all what Neta intends: it makes the key aspect of his analysis—the basis in infallible evidence—redundant. Moreover, it is unclear how justified belief can be sufficient for knowledge unless knowledge is what sets the standard for justification, in which case knowledge is being analysed in terms of itself.

As Neta states his infallibility analysis of knowledge in the chapter, it falls to fundamentally the same counter-example that refutes the indefeasibility analysis. Consequently, Neta's chapter constitutes more inductive evidence for the unanalysability of knowledge.

---

[7] S might even be in a position to know that e is infallible evidence for $p \vee q$, without actually knowing it.

Reply to Stephen Schiffer

1.   There is no silver bullet against scepticism. It is robust, in part because sceptical arguments form a complex terrain across which sceptics show great facility in subtly shifting their ground as they come under pressure at point after point.[1] An effective anti-sceptical strategy must be equally robust and flexible. Likewise, proofs of theism are fallacious in many different ways: despite their complex family resemblances, no single diagnosis will serve for all.

Knowledge and its Limits focuses on sceptical arguments of a specific form, articulated with the concept of evidence, because they bring out particularly clearly the sceptic's uncritical reliance on epistemological preconceptions to which knowledge-first epistemology offers an alternative. In particular, such arguments depend on the premiss that one has the same evidence in the bad case (the sceptical scenario) as in the good case (in which one non-sceptically takes oneself to be). On the equation advocated in *Knowledge and its Limits* of one's total evidence with one's total knowledge, that premiss is tantamount to the sceptic's conclusion.

In 'Evidence = Knowledge: Williamson's Solution to Skepticism', Stephen Schiffer challenges my response to scepticism by reformulating the sceptic's argument with the concept of justification rather than of evidence. According to Schiffer, my response fails to generalize properly to the reformulated argument. Such a generalization would involve some difference in what justifies one in believing Cube (the common-sense proposition in Schiffer's example) between Good (his good case) and Bad (his bad case). Apparently: one is justified in believing Cube in Bad, so something justifies one in believing Cube in Bad; whatever justifies one in believing Cube in Bad also justifies one in believing Cube in Good, so the same thing justifies one in believing Cube in both Good and Bad; one is thereby justified in believing Cube in both cases. Consequently, even if something else additionally justifies one in believing Cube in Good but not in Bad, it is redundant. Indeed, Schiffer claims, the degree to which one is justified in believing Cube in Bad is exactly the degree to which one is justified in believing Cube in Good. Thus the required asymmetry in justification between Good and Bad does not obtain.

---

[1] See *Knowledge and its Limits* (pp. 164–5): 'For simplicity, we can treat the sceptic as a generic figure, without attempting to track the protean variety of sceptical argument. Scepticism is a disease individuated by its symptoms . . . we should therefore not assume that it can be caused in only one way. The present aim is to identify one main such way, not to eliminate the disease entirely.' Williamson (2005a) has more on the diversity of sceptical arguments.

Much of Schiffer's detailed discussion is aimed at showing that my theory of evidence provides no answer to his challenge. In what follows, I will first respond to his challenge in its own terms, by speaking of justification rather than evidence, but in a way that is recognizably of a piece with the arguments of *Knowledge and its Limits*. I will then relate what I have said about justification to the book's theory of evidence.

2.   In speaking of 'justified belief', it is vital to distinguish two sorts of question. One concerns what further arguments, if any, the subject might have for the belief. Call that the *inferential* sense. The other concerns whether it is somehow OK for the subject to have the belief. Call that the *normative* sense. There is no presumption that beliefs are normatively justified only if they are inferentially justified. By non-sceptical standards, it is perfectly OK to have non-inferential beliefs. Scepticism about justification denies normative justification. Schiffer's further question '*What* justifies this belief?' is tolerably clear in the context of inferential justification. It seeks arguments of some kind with the belief as their conclusion (the premises of those arguments may do). The question '*What* justifies this belief?' is much less clear in the context of normative justification. Presumably it seeks some kind of information about why it is OK to have the belief, but for all that has been said the relevant story may be holistic, not localized, as in the inferential case.

The notion of what justifies someone in believing something is central to Schiffer's argument. He explains: 'for E to be what justifies S in believing P it must be that S believes P on the basis of S's having, knowing, or at least believing, E, in a sense of "on the basis of" that awaits explication but can be used to sort cases.' Unfortunately, even in sorting cases the phrase 'on the basis of' hovers uncertainly between inferential and normative senses of 'justification'. It is presumably intended to cover more than the premises of fully fledged arguments: for example, non-propositional experiences are candidate bases. Nevertheless, 'on the basis of' suggests a relation at least somewhat analogous to that between the conclusion and the premises of an argument. This unclarity is particularly awkward because Schiffer's running example concerns the ordinary perceptual belief that there is a red cube before me (the proposition Cube). Such cases are excellent candidates for non-inferential beliefs. Surprisingly, Schiffer asserts: 'in Good I come to be justified in believing Cube by inferring it from the fact that I am having such-and-such sensory experiences as of Cube, and I cannot become justified in believing Cube in Good other than by inferring it from that evidence.' This is a quite implausible account of the genesis of ordinary perceptual beliefs, which surely involve no such inference from the results of phenomenological self-examination. At any rate, Schiffer provides no support for an inferentialist theory of ordinary perceptual beliefs. Nor would it help him to stipulate that his example concerns an unusual case in which the subject *does* come to believe Cube by the phenomenological route, for a sceptical argument about an extraordinary route to believing Cube would not support scepticism about ordinary routes to believing Cube. I will, therefore, assume that Schiffer does not really intend to rely on an inferentialist theory of perceptual belief, since that would give me too easy a response. Instead, I will work on the assumption that one believes Cube non-inferentially, and that questions about what justifies one in believing Cube concern how one's belief has its normative status.

On the account in *Knowledge and its Limits*, justification is to be explained in terms of knowledge rather than *vice versa*. Belief that falls short of knowledge is to that extent defective. If we conceive belief as the mental analogue of assertion, then just as the rule for assertion is 'Assert **p** only if you know **p**', so the norm for belief is 'Believe **p** only if you know **p**'.[2] In this sense, a belief is fully normatively justified if and only if it constitutes knowledge. Given that one knows Cube in Good and not in Bad, one is fully normatively justified in believing Cube in Good and not in Bad. Presumably one does not believe Cube *on the basis* of knowing Cube, even in Good, since knowing already involves believing. Nevertheless, in Good one is (fully normatively) justified in believing Cube *because* one knows Cube. Similarly, in Bad one is not (fully normatively) justified in believing Cube *because* one does not know Cube. On a more informative account of Good, one is (fully normatively) justified in believing that there is a red cube before one because one *sees* that there is a red cube before one, where seeing that something is so is one form of knowing that it is so. If required, a much fuller account could be given of how one sees that there is a red cube before one in this particular case, although it will not go via an analysis of seeing or knowing into necessary and sufficient conditions (it may provide a sufficient but highly unnecessary condition).

Unless more is said, that account will look unacceptably harsh on the belief in Bad. For all agree that in Bad one's case is indistinguishable from Good, in the sense that if one is in Bad then one is not in a position to know that one is not in Good. By anti-sceptical standards, it is clear even to one in Bad that if one is in Good then one is fully normatively justified in believing Cube.[3] Therefore, if one is in Bad then one is not in a position to know that one is not fully normatively justified in believing Cube. So the normative status of believing Cube in Bad cannot be too low. For example, it is not as low as the normative status of believing in Bad that there is a green sphere before one (which there does not even appear to be). But that does not imply that one *is* fully normatively justified

---

[2] That belief is a state while assertion is an act is not a relevant disanalogy for present purposes. Note also that what 'Believe **p** only if you know **p**' forbids is believing **p** at a time t without knowing **p** at t; it does not forbid believing **p** at a later time $t + \delta$ without knowing **p** at t; likewise for the rule of assertion. Thus there is no need to replace 'know' by 'in a position to know' in the rule governing belief in order to explain how belief can legitimately get started (given that knowing entails believing).

[3] For simplicity, I assume that Bad is a sceptical scenario is one in which one can still entertain Cube (e.g., one is a recently envatted brain).

in believing Cube in Bad. Rather, it just shows that one has a cast-iron *excuse* in Bad for believing Cube: a cast-iron excuse is not a full justification. Although both have normative force, a full justification has more of it than a cast-iron excuse has. Similarly, one may fail to know **p** without being in a position to know that one fails to know **p**. In such cases, if one asserts **p**, one lacks the required warrant for the assertion, but one has a cast-iron excuse for it, because one is not in a position to know that one lacks the required warrant.

Whatever the standard for full justification, one can lack it without being in a position to know that one lacks it. This is simply the conclusion of the anti-luminosity argument in *Knowledge and its Limits* applied to the condition that one is not fully justified in believing Cube. One can move through a gradual process from being fully justified in believing Cube to not being fully justified in believing Cube. The argument shows that in some cases one is not fully justified in believing Cube without being in a position to know that one is not fully justified in believing Cube. Shifting the standard for full justification from knowledge to something else (short of scepticism) would not prevent that predicament from arising. Its possibility does not suggest that the standard for full justification is anything other than knowledge.

3.   Towards the end of his chapter, Schiffer switches his focus to justified degrees of confidence. Following Nico Silins (2005), he suggests that exactly the same degree of confidence in Cube is justified in Bad as in Good. The only apparent ground for insisting that exactly the same degrees of confidence are justified in Good and Bad is that Bad is indistinguishable from the inside from Good.[4] But that form of argument leads to a sorites paradox, for there are chains of cases, each indistinguishable from the inside from the next, where by any reasonable standard quite different degrees of confidence are justified in the last case from the first (pp. 174–8).

Schiffer says little about what degrees of confidence are, or how they can be justified. Whatever the answers, the anti-luminosity argument shows that in some cases one is justified in having a degree of confidence x in Cube, although one is not in a position to know that one is justified in having a degree of confidence x in Cube. Indeed, if degrees of confidence come in a continuum, like probabilities, then it will very often be hard to know exactly what degrees of confidence one is justified in having. Thus some unease will very often be liable to attend the claim that one is justified in having a specified degree of confidence in a proposition. For if one is justified in having a degree of confidence x but one is not in a position to know that one is justified in having a degree of confidence

---

[4] Internalists may argue that justified degrees of confidence are the same in Good and Bad because they supervene on phenomenal properties, which are supposedly the same in Good and Bad. As I read him, Schiffer does not intend to appeal to a contentious, undefended internalist premiss. Williamson (2007b) is a critique of an internalist theory of justification.

x, then one seems after all not totally justified in having a degree of confidence *x*. In principle we can preserve consistency by distinguishing senses of 'justified': given a sense S there is a stronger sense S+, where one is justified in sense S+ if and only if one is in a position to know that one is justified in sense S. But our pre-theoretic applications of the term 'justified degree of confidence' cannot be expected to track the differences between all the senses in this hierarchy.

Similarly, the anti-luminosity argument shows that in other cases one is not justified in having a degree of confidence *x* although one is not in a position to know that one is not justified in having a degree of confidence *x*, in which case one seems after all not totally unjustified in having a degree of confidence *x*. We can again preserve consistency by distinguishing senses of 'justified': given a sense S there is a weaker sense S−, where one is justified in sense S− if and only if one is not in a position to know that one is not justified in sense S. Thus if in Good one is justified in sense S in having a given degree of confidence, then in Bad one is justified in sense S− in having that degree of confidence. Since 'justified' is vague, it will naturally be unclear that one is justified in Good but not Bad in having a given degree of confidence in Cube.[5]

4. Schiffer spends much of his chapter making trouble for various putative connections between what justifies believing a proposition and what is evidence for it according to my account of evidence. Most are not connections that I have proposed. To a first approximation, how confident it is OK to be in a proposition supervenes on its probability on one's total evidence. That global issue cannot be straightforwardly localized to questions about which particular bits of one's evidence are evidence *for* it—that is, raise its probability with respect to a prior distribution. Some evidence for a hypothesis raises its probability only slightly, or still leaves it low.

In Good, it is OK to believe Cube simply because one knows Cube; it is unnecessary to discuss evidence as such. It is in Bad that evidential probability comes into its own. The equation of one's total evidence with one's total knowledge does not deprive one of all evidence in Bad, for one can still know e, that one's experience is as of Cube. If one does know e in Bad, e is evidence for Cube, because it raises the probability of Cube. In part for this reason, Cube is moderately probable on one's evidence in Bad. In that sense, moderate confidence in Cube is normatively justified in Bad. In Good too, e is part of one's evidence and is evidence for Cube. But in Good e is upstaged by a stronger part of one's evidence, Cube itself.

The matter is not straightforward. In both Good and Bad, one's primary interest is in Cube, the proposition about the external scene, not in e, the

<hr>

[5] Schiffer's final argument about degrees of confidence targets the specific issue of degree of confidence 1. This issue is discussed at length in my reply to Mark Kaplan.

proposition about appearances. Cube is in no sense inferred from e. One need
not even formulate e. But, presumably, if one fails to formulate e then one fails
to know e. In that case, e is not part of one's evidence; the same applies to other
propositions similar to e. Thus Cube need not be even moderately probable on
one's evidence in Bad after all. In such cases, there is a dearth of actual evidence,
a wealth of potential evidence. However, it is so easy for the subject to actualize
the potential evidence—just by taking thought—that in thinking about such
cases we tend sloppily to treat the potential evidence as though it were actual.

A related point is that, even if one does entertain and know e, doing so
plays no direct role in non-inferentially believing Cube. It might therefore be
objected that in Bad the probability of Cube is insufficiently related to one's
confidence in Cube to justify that confidence. Quite generally, no matching of
degrees of confidence to probabilities on the evidence guarantees that the latter
explain the former. Still, probabilities on one's evidence are what one's degrees
of confidence must match if one is to satisfy the norm of proportioning one's
belief to the evidence. In Bad, if one knows e and falsely believes Cube, one
deviates from that norm with respect to Cube by only a little, even if that result
is partly the outcome of one's blunder in misconstruing the extent of one's
evidence. But how one reaches one's degrees of confidence is a matter for further
norms.

In another respect too, evidential probabilities provide only very coarse-grained
information about the facts relevant to the normative standing of one's degrees
of confidence. If p and q are mathematically equivalent, they have exactly the
same probability. Yet, if the equivalence is unobvious, why should exactly the
same degree of confidence be normatively justified for p as for q? Nevertheless,
this is not a good reason to abandon the insights and rigour provided by the
probabilistic framework. It is simply a reminder that the framework must be
supplemented by other epistemic distinctions in a full account.

Schiffer points out that, since a mathematical theorem always has probability
1, nothing is evidence for or against it in the probabilistic sense. This will apply
to *any* reasonable account of evidence in terms of classical probability theory,
not just mine. Yet, as he suggests, it is often natural to speak of evidence 'for'
or 'against' a mathematical theorem (perhaps before it was proved), and I did
so myself in *Knowledge and its Limits*. Schiffer adds: 'We need not, however,
bother about any of this, since all the issues in this chapter about what a person
is justified in believing pertain only to contingent propositions.' However, the
problem arises just as much for contingent propositions. For example, let m be
a complex mathematical theorem (a necessary truth) and c a contingent claim
irrelevant to m; thus ¬c and ¬(c & m) are also contingent. Since ¬(c & m)
is mathematically equivalent to ¬c, any evidence e will have exactly the same
probabilistic relations to ¬c as to ¬(c & m). But if e is the known fact that
twenty eminent professors of mathematics all testified that m has been refuted,
it is natural to say that e is evidence for ¬(c & m) without being evidence

for ¬c.[6] Again, the proper response is not to abandon the probabilistic notions of evidence for and against a hypothesis, since their formal content gives them distinctive advantages, but rather to supplement them with less formal notions that allow us to make further distinctions.[7]

5.   Like other conditions, normative conditions are not luminous. One can satisfy a norm without being in a position to know that one has satisfied it, and one can fail to satisfy the norm without being in a position to know that one has failed to satisfy it. The result is a multiplication of norms. For every norm N, there is both the stronger norm of being in a position to know that one has satisfied N and the weaker norm of not being in a position to know that one has not satisfied N. No two of these norms are equivalent. Inevitably, when one satisfies some of these norms one fails to satisfy others, even with respect to the very same state or act. Complex, nuanced descriptions of the epistemic status even of a single belief are typically needed. The concept of justification is too crude an instrument to capture all these differences. This complexity does not depend on any distinctive feature of the account of evidence in *Knowledge and its Limits*. Rather, it is just the working-out of anti-luminosity in the normative domain.

---

[6] Similar problems arise even when the contingent claim cannot be easily factored into necessary and contingent components.

[7] Schiffer himself says 'it is transparently plausible that E is evidence for H for S at t^* if (*a*) S knows E at t^* and (*b*) $\text{Prob}_{old}(H/E) > \text{Prob}_{old}(H)$'. Suppose that (*a*) and (*b*) in fact hold but S at t^* has been assured by many experts that E is inconsistent with H, and has no inkling of (*b*). Then one might be reluctant to say, informally, that E is evidence for H for S at t^*.

Reply to Ernest Sosa

Ernest Sosa's chapter 'Timothy Williamson's *Knowledge and its Limits*' briefly criticizes various externalist theses in the book and briefly sketches some motivation for internalism. I will deal with these two phases in turn.

1. Sosa's first criticism is that safe belief is a counter-example to my account of knowledge as the most general factive mental state, the factive mental state implied by all factive mental states. According to Sosa, safe belief is a factive mental state that does not imply knowledge. In his sense, one safely believes **p** just in case one believes **p** and would believe **p** only if **p** were true. The two conjuncts together imply that **p** is true by *modus ponens* for the counterfactual conditional, so safe belief is indeed factive. Furthermore, as Sosa notes, it does not imply knowledge, since whoever believes a necessary truth does so safely, however bad their reasons. But is safe belief in Sosa's sense a mental state?

The full account in the book is formulated in terms of factive mental state operators (FMSOs). The question is then whether 'safely believes' is an FMSO, given that by definition FMSOs are semantically unanalysable. Sosa notes that the syntactic complexity of the phrase by itself does not entail semantic complexity. The relevant meaning of 'safely believes' is not obviously composed from the usual meanings of 'safely' and 'believes'. That is hardly surprising, since Sosa in effect stipulates that 'safely believes **p**' is to be synonymous with 'believes **p** and would believe **p** only if **p** were true'. But then 'safely believes **p**' is semantically analysable in just that way, and is therefore not an FMSO.[1] Correspondingly, safe belief is not a factive mental state, and the counter-example fails.

Sosa calls safety as just defined 'simple safety'. He claims that the anti-luminosity argument assumes that simple safety is necessary for knowledge and that Ram Neta and Guy Rohrbaugh (2004) have shown that it is not. However, the safety condition on which the anti-luminosity argument relies is subtler than simple safety in various ways. The most relevant is that **p** is required to be true

---

[1] Sosa misunderstands the discussion of semantic analysability in the book. For example, where I give 'She knew by the sense of touch that the bone was broken' as 'a rough paraphrase' of 'She could feel that the bone was broken', Sosa misreports me as claiming synonymy (p. 36). If they were synonymous, 'could feel' would be semantically analysable and therefore not an FMSO, contrary to the claim in the book. But they are not synonyms. The meaning of 'know' is a component of the meaning of the former sentence but not of the latter, even though she could feel that the bone was broken only if she knew by the sense of touch that it was broken. This misunderstanding confuses Sosa's discussion of analysability.

only in similar cases in which it is believed on a similar basis (pp. 97–102).[2] The basis of one's belief in this sense does not comprise only one's reasons for the belief; it also includes the relevant causal background. Although one could give special weight to similarity in respect of the basis of belief when assessing the overall similarity of cases, that is not implicit in Sosa's account of simple safety. Moreover, in all Neta and Rohrbaugh's examples of knowledge without safety, saliently different mechanisms operate in the false-belief case from those that operate in the knowledge case; that constitutes a relevantly large difference in the basis of the belief, in its causal background. Once construed as examples of knowledge, they are also examples of safe belief in the sense relevant to the anti-luminosity argument.[3] Of course, given the unanalysability of knowledge, one cannot hope to specify exactly how much similarity is required without reference to knowledge, but the anti-luminosity argument allows for that by permitting the successive members of the sorites-like series to be chosen arbitrarily close together.

Sosa's next criticism is that, even if the anti-luminosity argument is sound, it refutes only a strong form of luminosity. He suggests falling back on quasi-luminosity, where a condition C is quasi-luminous just in case for some degree d, in every case in which C obtains to at least degree d, one is in a position to know that C obtains (although perhaps not to know that C obtains to degree d). Since being in apposition to know is factive (p. 95), it follows from quasi-luminosity that C obtains in every case in which it obtains to at least degree d. Sosa offers no explanation of the requisite notion of a degree to which a condition obtains. Do all conditions come in degrees? He contemplates the possibility that consciously knowing does not. For any condition that does not come in degrees, quasi-luminosity reduces to luminosity and Sosa's revision gives no help. The anti-luminosity argument for a condition C does not require C to come in degrees; it merely requires the possibility of a gradual transition from cases in which C obtains to cases in which C does not obtain. For instance, a particle can slowly move from being inside a sharply defined region to not being inside the region, even though its being inside the region does not come in degrees. In some intermediate cases, C neither clearly obtains nor clearly fails to obtain, but 'clearly' here is an epistemic qualification: it does not imply that C obtains to some intermediate degree. If degrees merely concerned epistemic status, quasi-luminosity would merely imply that for some epistemic status, in every case in which C has at least that epistemic status, one is in a position to

---

[2] Other differences are that the safety requirement in the anti-luminosity argument concerns degrees of confidence rather than flat belief and that it extends to similar belief contents beyond the original one. Sosa's examples of simple safety without knowledge are not examples of safety in the sense directly relevant to the anti-luminosity argument.

[3] In Neta and Rohrbaugh's examples, at a slightly earlier time there was a high probability that the deceptive mechanism would be activated. For reasons explained in my reply to John Hawthorne and Maria Lasonen-Aarnio in this volume, this fact about probability is not directly relevant to safety.

know that C obtains: but that is trivial, for being such that one is in a position to know that it obtains is itself such an epistemic status.

A further problem for Sosa's revision of luminosity is that it is inadequately motivated. He says that quasi-luminosity gives 'a more charitable way of understanding the doctrines of cognitive home and the given'. It may be more charitable in the sense that it yields a claim easier to get away with: for conditions that do come in degrees, quasi-luminosity is harder than luminosity to refute. But the question is whether the underlying philosophical outlook that can be taken to motivate claims of luminosity can equally well be taken to motivate claims only of quasi-luminosity, for otherwise the latter will be ad hoc and improperly motivated. The picture of a cognitive home is not simply a picture of some facts that are more easily known than others. It is a picture of facts whose nature shortcuts substantive enquiry on the part of the subject, by contrast with the nature of ordinary physical facts. But, if a condition can obtain when one is not in a position to know that it obtains, as a quasi-luminous condition can, then its nature does not shortcut substantive enquiry on the part of the subject. Thus the underlying philosophical outlook motivates claims of luminosity, not just of quasi-luminosity. If the claims of luminosity fail, something was wrong with the original philosophical outlook. Quasi-luminosity is a pointless compromise.[4]

Sosa's final criticisms target the thesis that knowing is a mental state. He proposes that, 'just as being surprisingly spherical is not a more specific form of being shaped (regularly shaped) by comparison with being spherical, so knowing is not a more specific way of being mental, by comparison with believing'. Just as being surprisingly spherical adds nothing geometrical to being spherical, so knowing allegedly adds nothing mental to believing. But that claim is already refuted on multiple independent grounds in the book (pp. 56–7). For instance, knowing **p** adds to believing **p** the clearly mental condition that one does not believe **p** only for (internally) irrational reasons. Thus Sosa's comparison fails. Knowing has more specific mental consequences than believing has.[5]

Sosa complains about the arguments in the book for the role of knowing in the causal explanation of action: 'What remains unclear is why this should be thought to imply that knowledge . . . must be mental only in the most serious and underivative way.' But those arguments were not intended to show by themselves that knowing is a mental state. Rather, they were intended to rebut one common objection to the thesis that knowing is a mental state: the objection that mental states play an essential role in the causal explanation of action while knowing

---

[4] See also Williamson (2005b: 476–8) for discussion of John Hawthorne's notion of coziness, which in some respects resembles quasi-luminosity.

[5] Sosa's linked footnote discussion of the relation between mental states and mental concepts goes wrong when he assumes that the concept of being uniquely thought about by the earthquake victims is mental. A concept is not made mental in the relevant sense merely by having a mental component if it also has non-mental components, such as the concept of the earthquake victims (p. 29).

does not. Refuting the objection knocks one support from under the denial that knowing is a mental state but does not unaided cause it to collapse altogether.

Thus Sosa's criticisms of the book all fail. We now turn to his positive motivating remarks about internalism.

2. Sosa presents his positive case in a short but wide-ranging discussion that refers to a variety of dimensions: subjectivity and appearance; responsibility and liability to praise or blame; character and dispositions, strengths and weaknesses; internal constitution and world independence. None of these dimensions is equivalent to any of the others, and it is not entirely clear what relations between them Sosa is claiming.

The emphasis on subjectivity occurs mainly in Sosa's presentation of a case he calls 'New Evil Demon':

If things appear the same to two subjects from the inside, and if this is so throughout their lives, and if all along they are the same in how they manifest their relevant dispositions to be in purely mental states, then they cannot differ in their respective degrees of justification for any present belief. At least there does seem to be some such internal, or subjective, justification that a belief might have independently of being true or reliable.

He contrasts New Evil Demon with Clairvoyance, a case of brutely reliable belief formation from which, he says, justification 'in some appropriate, internal sense' is missing. Sosa discloses that the approach he favours to understanding such cases is 'Virtue contextualism and perspectivism', which delivers this condition for justification:

that your belief derive from the good performance of cognitive virtues seated in the subject (features whose operation would generally deliver relevant epistemic goods, such as truth, in the actual world, for beings of your kind in your normal habitat), a fact that does not escape your reflective awareness.

Whether this condition for justification obtains is, of course, not a purely subjective matter; it does not supervene on how things appear (and have appeared) to be to the subject. For, given a good case in which the condition obtains, there is a corresponding bad case in which how things appear (and have appeared) to be to the subject is the same, but the condition does not obtain, because the belief has a different, merely lucky causal origin and does not derive from the good performance of cognitive virtues seated in the subject. Thus Sosa is not really offering a type of justification that supervenes on appearances.

Of course, if present appearances to the subject are exactly the same between two cases, then, *whatever* justification is, the belief will appear to the subject of one case to be justified to a given degree if and only if it appears to the subject of the other case to be justified to that degree. If subjective justification is no more than the appearance to the subject of non-subjective justification, then we can all agree that it supervenes on appearances. But Sosa's addition to sameness in present appearances of sameness in past appearances too and of the further clause 'all along they are the same in how they manifest their relevant dispositions to be in purely mental states' suggests that he has more in mind. At any rate, his mention of subjectivity is too undeveloped to warrant further discussion here.[6]

Much of what Sosa says about the other dimensions of justification is uncontentious. For instance: 'common sense is interested not only in successful murders but also in botched attempts, no matter how remotely they may have failed. We are also interested in how well an astronaut performs in simulated flight tests and not just in real life performance.' Presumably, we are interested in the astronaut's performance in simulated flight tests because it manifests many of the same dispositions as his or her real-life performance, and so is a good predictor of the latter. No serious form of internalism is needed to explain that. Simulating the first flight to the moon does not earn the same medal as actually achieving it. Common sense is interested in botched attempts at murder because they can reveal the same evil intentions as successful performance. Past intentions are properly praised or blamed and cast light on future actions. But common sense does not say that botched attempts at murder, no matter how remotely they failed, should be blamed or punished as severely as successful performances. Nor does common sense say that there is no such thing as moral luck. No serious form of internalism is needed to explain our interest in attempted murder. Although Sosa speaks of 'assessment in world-independent respects' with reference to these examples, that gloss is not warranted by the nature of our interest in them.

Sosa continues: 'In assessing the performance of the thermostat, in judging it to perform well or ill, we attribute what it does to the device itself as *its* doing' (emphasis in original). But italicizing the possessive does not deliver an internalist concept of performance. In assessing the performance of the murderer, we attribute what he did to the man himself as *his* doing, even though murder is not a world-independent act. Although some features by which we judge artefacts are internal ones, not all are. For instance, whether a house with a given internal structure is a good house depends on the climate at its location. Whether a thermostat is performing well or ill depends on whether the numbers on its dial are supposed to represent degrees Fahrenheit or Celsius.

Sosa explains our interest in performance under simulation thus:

It is worth knowing how good we already are if we wish to improve. It is good to know our flaws if we aim to remove them, our strengths if we aim to preserve them. We want to know how reliable our fellows are, especially those we join in common endeavours. It is hard to set limits on our need for such knowledge, moreover, or on the practical potential for such need. So again, we are interested in our flaws, and in our strengths, along various dimensions of potential accomplishment. That way we can better tell whom to trust in what circumstances.

---

[6] See Williamson (2007b) for more discussion of such an internalist conception of justification.

All this is quite plausible, but it does not imply that any of our strengths or weaknesses supervene purely on internal factors. We may learn about whether someone behaves politely by their behaviour in a society simulator, however constitutively dependent polite behaviour is on social circumstances. Nothing in Sosa's discussion warrants assigning any special role to the internal in epistemology or the philosophy of mind

Sosa's final section concerns the KK principle that if one knows then one knows (or is in a position to know) that one knows. He describes the book's reductio of this principle as 'compelling'. Sosa wishes to distinguish reflective knowledge from mere animal knowledge, but, since the reductio applies to each level of knowledge separately, he cannot distinguish them by holding that reflective knowledge satisfies such an iteration principle while animal knowledge does not. Instead, he proposes that having reflective knowledge of **p** implies having animal knowledge that one has animal knowledge of **p**. As he says, this claim is untouched by the reductio of the KK principle, and it remains open that we have masses of reflective knowledge. Of course, if reflective knowledge of **p** just is animal knowledge that one has animal knowledge of **p**, then reflective knowledge is just a special case of animal knowledge, albeit with respect to a different content. Further iterations of animal knowledge will yield an infinite hierarchy of still more special cases.

Reply to Matthias Steup

Matthias Steup's paper 'Are Mental States Luminous?' is, of course, a critique of the anti-luminosity argument. As presented in the book, the argument uses an example in which one gradually feels less cold. Steup's main objections concern the conditions under which one can feel less φ than before, where 'cold' is a typical substitution for 'φ'.[1]

Steup overlooks a scope ambiguity in the phrase 'feel less φ than before'. It can mean either a feeling of change or a change of feeling.

On the feeling of change reading, the words 'less φ than before' are all within the scope of 'feel'; they give the content of the feeling. A rough paraphrase of 'one feels less φ than before' in this sense is 'one has the feeling that one is less φ than before'. Since feelings need not be veridical, that one has a feeling of change does not entail that one has had or is having a change of any kind. For example, today I may have the feeling that I am less cold than I was yesterday, even if in fact I am exactly as cold as I was yesterday and today's feeling of cold is exactly the same in all relevant respects as yesterday's. I may simply misremember how cold I was and felt yesterday. Similarly, I may now have the feeling that I am less cold than I was a moment ago, even if in fact I am exactly as cold as I was then and this moment's feeling of cold is exactly the same in all relevant respects as the last moment's feeling of cold.

By contrast, on the change of feeling reading, only 'φ' is within the scope of 'feel', and 'feel φ' is within the scope of 'less than before'. A rough paraphrase of 'one feels less φ than before' in this sense is 'the degree to which one feels φ is less than the degree to which before one felt φ'. That one has had a change of feeling does not entail that one has or had a feeling of change. For example, the degree to which today I feel cold may in fact be less than the degree to which yesterday I felt cold, even if I have no feeling of change whatsoever. I may simply forget or misremember how cold I was and felt yesterday. Similarly, the degree to which

---

[1] Steup's initial presentation of the argument is flawed. His replacement of the degrees of confidence used in the book by ungraded belief is not the mere 'terminological difference' he claims, for it involves the argument in a quite unnecessary sorites paradox for belief. That is, he attributes to my argument the assumption that, if one believes that one feels cold (B(cold)) in a case a_i, then one believes that one feels cold in the next case a_{i+1}, which of course implies by transitivity the obviously false conclusion that if one believes that one feels cold in the initial case a_0 then one believes that one feels cold in the final case a_n. The argument in the book works with degrees of confidence in order to avoid this problem.

now I feel cold may in fact be less than the degree to which a moment ago I felt cold, even if I have no feeling of change.[2]

Let us trace how both of Steup's main objections to the anti-luminosity argument essentially depend on equivocation between the two readings.

Steup's first main objection involves a defender of luminosity, Lucy, who maintains that, as a matter of metaphysical necessity, one feels φ if and only if one is aware of feeling φ, and that one feels less φ than a moment before if and only if one is aware of feeling less φ than a moment before. Steup complains that the initial description of the central example in the anti-luminosity argument begs the question against Lucy, since it assumes that one can undergo a process during which one's feelings of heat and cold change so slowly during this process that one is not aware of any change in them over one millisecond. More specifically, he complains that the description implies that one sometimes feels less cold than a moment before without being aware that one feels less cold than a moment before, contrary to Lucy's principles. This is surprising, since most defenders of luminosity have taken the initial description of the example in the spirit in which it was intended, as simply concerning an extended example of a general type of process familiar from everyday experience. But let us try Steup's objection on each of the two readings of 'feels less φ than a moment before'.

Initially, the feeling of change reading looks to be the intended one, since Steup appears to treat 'feel less φ than a moment before' as a special case of 'feel φ', presumably with the substitution of 'less φ than before' for 'φ' in the scope of 'feel', which gives the relevant logical form.[3] However, a moment's reflection makes it clear that this reading is dialectically irrelevant, since it is fully within both the letter and the spirit of the original example that during the gradual process one *never* feels less cold than a moment before (in the feeling of change sense) and is correspondingly never aware of feeling less cold than a moment before (in that sense). On this reading, the biconditional on which the objection turns holds vacuously throughout the process, so Steup would have trivially failed to show that the initial description of the example begged the question against Lucy.

On the change of feeling reading, Lucy is claiming that, as a matter of metaphysical necessity, one has a change of feeling over a brief period if and only if one is aware of having a change of feeling over that period. This claim is obviously false and I am aware of no defender of luminosity (with the possible exception of Steup) who makes it. On any reasonable view, it is metaphysically

---

[2] Steup does not turn the difference between a day and a moment into a matter of metaphysical principle.

[3] Steup says 'What holds for feeling φ, Lucy will say, also holds for *feeling less φ than a moment before*' without further comment. That would be to ignore a vital issue if the change of feeling reading were intended.

possible to forget or misremember exactly how one was feeling a moment before, and so to undergo a slight change of feeling without being aware that one has done so. On this reading, the initial description of the example has no need to respect Lucy's silly view.

On neither reading has Steup provided any reason to doubt the metaphysical possibility of the example as initially described. Thus his first objection fails.

Steup's second objection is that, even if we ignore Lucy, there is no reason to believe that for a sufficiently slow process there are sufficiently short episodes of feeling less cold than before, for the purposes of the anti-luminosity argument. Let us try this objection too on the two readings.

On the feeling of change reading, there may well be no episodes of feeling less cold than a moment before. Since this is entirely within the letter and spirit of the original example, it is no objection to the anti-luminosity argument.

On the change of feeling reading, there is a quite straightforward reason to believe that, however slow the process and however short the episodes, some of them involve feeling less cold than before. Let C be the relation that holds between times t and t^* if and only the degree to which at t^* one feels cold is as great as the degree to which at t one feels cold. C is transitive, since being as great as is a transitive relation between degrees. Now let $t_0, t_1, \ldots, t_n$ be the times in the anti-luminosity argument. If t_i has C to t_{i+1} for each i from 0 to $n-1$ then by transitivity t_0 has C to t_n. But t_0 certainly does not have C to t_n, since at t_0 one feels very cold and at t_n one feels very warm. Thus, for some i, t_i does not have C to t_{i+1}: the degree to which at t_{i+1} one feels cold is less than the degree to which at t_i one feels cold, as required. Of course, one can fuss with some details of this argument as stated (Steup does not, since he does not consider it). The argument assumes that degrees of feeling cold are linearly ordered, so that if degree d^* is not as great as degree d then d^* is less than d. It assumes that at any given time in one's conscious life there is a unique degree to which one feels cold. It assumes classical logic. But these assumptions are not essential to the anti-luminosity argument. Let C′ be the relation that holds between times t and t^* if and only if at t^* one has qualitatively exactly the same feelings of heat and cold as one has at t. Then C′ is a transitive relation, and by a version of the preceding argument on much weaker assumptions than before one can show that it is not always the case in the slow process that one has qualitatively exactly the same feelings of heat and cold at successive moments of the relevant time series. This refutes the claim that there is no change in those feelings over any of the short periods.

Thus Steup's second objection to the anti-luminosity argument also fails on both readings.

In defence of luminosity, Steup also disputes my claim that one can have an experience as of seeing (at least) 30 stars while believing oneself to be having an experience as of seeing (at most) 29 stars—for example because one has a bias in favour of the number 29 (Williamson 2005b: 471). This claim is less controversial than the anti-luminosity argument, and not part of it. Perhaps most friends of luminosity will be inclined to grant it; but Steup does not. He demands more details of the case. They are easily supplied. Jones looks at the night sky and sees each of 30 stars clearly, without counting them. His bias in favour of the number 29 does not render any of the stars less visible to him. There is nothing unusual or specially misleading about his experience. For each of 30 visibly different directions, a star is visible in that direction and his experience is as of there being a star in that direction. This seems to be a central case of having an experience as of seeing (at least) 30 stars. However, without bothering properly to count, Jones dogmatically judges that (at most) 29 stars are visible and concludes that he is having a visual experience as of (at most) 29 stars. We could flesh out even more details of the case if necessary, but perhaps these are enough to be getting on with. Resistance to the possibility (indeed, actuality) of commonplace examples of this sort can only discredit the philosophical position from which it issues.

Finally, Steup asks, if mental states are indeed not luminous, what philosophical consequences follow? He concedes that this would refute the following internalist theory:

Unrestricted Experiential Foundationalism (UEF)

Whenever one has an experience as of p, one has internalist justification for believing that p.

However, he maintains that this would be only a minor blow to internalism, since this nearby fallback position would still be available:

Restricted Experiential Foundationalism (REF)

Whenever one has a discernible experience as of p, one has internalist justification for believing that p.

Steup explains 'discernible experiences' as 'those one is in a position to know one has'; presumably, a discernible experience as of **p** is an experience such that one is in a position to know that it is an experience as of **p**. As he notes, the conclusion of the anti-luminosity argument is compatible with *most* of our experiences as of **p** being discernible experiences as of **p**. Thus the antecedent of REF may apply almost as widely as the antecedent of UEF.

Nevertheless, the retreat from UEF to REF is dangerous for internalism, because it concedes that an experience as of **p** contributes to justification not simply as such, but only through the subject's being in a position to know that it is an experience as of **p**. Consequently, what matters for justification is not whether one is experiencing something but whether one is in a position to know that one is experiencing it. If so, why do not other things one is in a position to know contribute in a similar way to justification? Once the access to justification comes through being in a position to know rather than through mere experiencing, the restriction of the content of the potential knowledge to propositions about experience looks ad hoc. The danger for internalists is that they will not find a well-motivated way to prevent the slide from UEF to REF taking them all the way to the view that one's total evidence is the total content of what one is in a position to know. That view, discussed in the book (pp. 202–3), is already highly externalist; it is a close cousin of the equation $E = K$ of one's total evidence with the total content of what one knows defended there. Indeed, it is doubtful that what one potentially knows but does not actually know should contribute to one's actual rather than potential justification. If I am in a position to know that I am having an experience as of **p**, but do not in fact know that I am having an experience as of **p**, am I already justified in believing **p**? Thus the slide may go all the way to the equation $E = K$. In retreating from UEF to REF, Steup has opened a gap for the thin end of the externalist wedge. Nothing he says in the chapter stabilizes his position.

Reply to Neil Tennant

In 'Cognitive Phenomenology, Semantic Qualia, and Luminous Knowledge', Neil Tennant insists that 'there is something that it is like to understand a sentence as expressing a thought'. Taken modestly, this strikes me as harmless and even salutary. One can be conscious that 'Dogs bark' means *dogs bark*—although one is not conscious of it *all* the time one understands the sentence. But Tennant claims that semantic consciousness is a counter-example to the anti-luminosity argument.

Sometimes Tennant identifies the allegedly luminous condition as the condition that a given linguistic expression is meaningful for one, sometimes as the condition that *one knows that* the expression is meaningful for one; sometimes his focus is on the condition that the expression has a given meaning for one. Probably he thinks that all these conditions are luminous. Unfortunately, he gives no argument for their luminosity. He argues at great length that whether one understands a sentence makes a difference to consciousness, but that is not the point at issue. Whether one feels cold makes a difference to consciousness, but it does not follow that whenever one feels cold one is in a position to know that one feels cold, as luminosity requires. Even the condition that one is conscious of being cold is subject to the anti-luminosity argument. Similarly, Tennant has not shown that, whenever a sentence is meaningful for one, one is in a position to know that it is meaningful for one, or that, whenever it has a given meaning for one, one is in a position to know that it has that meaning for one, or that, whenever one knows that it is meaningful for one, one is in a position to know that one knows that it is meaningful for one. Thus he has not shown that the application of the anti-luminosity argument to these conditions leads to false conclusions.

Tennant does not say whether he considers his semantic examples to be *better* candidates for luminosity than the prototypically phenomenological conditions, such as the condition that one feels cold, on which the presentation of the anti-luminosity argument was originally focused. If they are supposed to be better candidates, he does not say why. He does not raise the question *where* the anti-luminosity argument might go wrong, as directed against his semantic examples. Nothing in his discussion points to any specific way in which they would be better equipped to resist the argument than are the original phenomenological conditions. If his semantic examples are not supposed to be better candidates, then he has merely restated a claim of the sort against which I was arguing.

Perhaps Tennant thinks that his presentation of his main example makes its luminosity obvious. Instead, it nicely sets the stage for the relevant application of the anti-luminosity argument. He sketches the evolution of a non-semantic game into the meaningful use of a language. His account leaves it realistically unclear at exactly what point the meaningful use emerges.[1] Some of his phrasing suggests that the activity involved meaningful use even when this fact was still hidden from the players:

> A mathematically sophisticated member of the culture in our thought-experiment could be brought, by the foregoing considerations, to realize that *play-charts are propositional representations*, and that *they represent the ways things are on the playing-field in question* . . . The point is, all these insights can dawn in one sudden revelation, enlightening the gamer as to the true nature of what he is up to. (emphasis in original)

This realization that the play-charts have propositional meanings is presented as a significant cognitive achievement. If they had such meanings from the very start of the game-playing, that is clear neither to the members of Tennant's imagined community nor to his readers; it is a contentious philosophical claim for which heavy-duty argument would be needed. More plausibly, the play-charts acquired propositional meanings only in the course of the evolution Tennant describes—just when, it is hard to know. Thus he has described a promising counter-example to the claim that the condition that the play-charts have propositional meanings for one is luminous, of just the kind on which the anti-luminosity argument turns. They can have such meanings even when the players are not in a position to know that they do.

Tennant's talk of 'sudden revelation' suggests that he may be thinking of the condition that *one knows that* the play-chart has propositional meaning for one as the luminous condition, since that epistemological development is not gradual in the way that the anti-luminosity argument requires. However, the anti-luminosity argument does not require the process underlying the switch from absence to presence of the condition *always* to be gradual. It requires only one possible *example* of such a gradual process. Dawn does not always break suddenly. Indeed, Tennant comments 'A certain intellectual light has dawned on the whole', presumably alluding to Wittgenstein's apt metaphor for the slow, holistic growth of understanding: 'Light dawns gradually over the whole' (1969: §141). In such cases, it is hard even for the enlightened subject to know exactly when light has dawned: one may properly doubt whether a play-chart has propositional meaning for one, and a gradual process underlies the switch from ignorance to knowledge that it has propositional meaning for one. Thus Tennant has put in place just what is needed to apply the anti-luminosity argument to the condition that one knows that a play-chart has propositional meaning for one. He has done my work for me.

---

[1] Another laudable feature of Tennant's account is that it uses classically valid but intuitionistically invalid reasoning.

Reply to Charles Travis

1. In 'Aristotle's Condition' Charles Travis challenges my defence of the principle of bivalence. That defence is mounted primarily in *Vagueness* (Williamson 1994), and elaborated elsewhere (Andjelković and Williamson 2000). It is not a theme of *Knowledge and its Limits*. However, the latter work does occasionally use the more fundamental principles about truth and falsity that underlie the defence of bivalence—for example, when it takes for granted that the belief that there are tigers is true if and only if there are tigers (2000: 53). Furthermore, Travis's arguments are far more subversive of ordinary deductive reasoning than he appears to realize. Since *Knowledge and its Limits* contains several deductive arguments, it is at least in the area of potential collateral damage for Travis's arguments—as are most works of philosophy. Thus a response to Travis is relevant in this volume.

2. In order to articulate most perspicuously what is at stake between Travis and me, I will apply the words 'true' and 'false' to sentences in contexts of utterance. If 's' refers to a sentence and 'c' to a context, read '**True**(s, c)' and '**False**(s, c)' as 's is true [as potentially uttered] in c' and 's is false [as potentially uttered] in c' respectively. In his chapter, Travis applies 'true' and 'false' to utterances and sayables rather than sentences in contexts, but the present terminology is used in one of the pieces he cites (Andjelković and Williamson 2000) and his discussion can easily be transposed without prejudice to this setting. Read '**Say**(s, c, P)' as 's [as potentially uttered] in c says [is used to say] that P', where 'P' is to be replaced by a declarative sentence (unlike 's', which is to be replaced by a singular term that refers to a declarative sentence). Then the key principles about truth and falsity are that, if a sentence in a context says that something is so, then the sentence is true in that context if and only if that thing is so and the sentence is false in the context if and only if that thing is not so.[1] In symbols we can eliminate the apparent reference to things:

(T) $\mathbf{Say}(s, c, P) \supset [\mathbf{True}(s, c) \equiv P]$

(F) $\mathbf{Say}(s, c, P) \supset [\mathbf{False}(s, c) \equiv \neg P]$

---

[1] The worry that a given sentence in a given context might be used to say several non-equivalent things is discussed in Andjelković and Williamson (2000).

Correspondingly, the principle of bivalence says that, if a sentence in a context says that something is so, then the sentence is either true or false in that context:

(B) **Say(s, c, P) ⊃ [True(s, c) ∨ False(s, c)]**

The argument from (T) and (F) to (B) in classical logic is quite straightforward. It can be formulated using an instance of the classical law of excluded middle (something is either so or not so):

(LEM) **P ∨ ¬P**

The rest of the argument is equally elementary. The underlying insight goes back to Aristotle, and was made more explicit by Tarski.

According to Travis, (B) fails in some instances. His proposed counter-examples have the following structure, as articulated in the present framework. In some contexts, the sentence 'P' is so understood that it is true.[2] In other contexts, 'P' is so understood that it is false. In both sorts of context, 'P' says that **P**. In a third sort of context, not enough has been done to commit us either to understanding 'P' in the first way or to understanding 'P' in the second way. In the third sort of context too, 'P' says that **P**. According to Travis, in a context **c** of the third sort, there is no fact of the matter (whatever that means) as to whether things accord with the first disjunct of (LEM) or the second: although we have that **Say** ('P', c, P), we have neither that **True**('P', c) nor that **False**('P', c). Thus (B) fails.[3]

Travis does not argue against an epistemicist interpretation of his examples, on which 'P' is either true or false in **c** but we have no way of finding out which. Thus, as an attempt to refute the positive epistemicist theory in *Vagueness*, on which bivalence holds, his chapter hardly gets off the ground. Let us therefore read him more charitably as trying to undermine my arguments *for* that theory by providing an attractive theoretical alternative on which bivalence fails and flaws can be located in my arguments for it. Consequently, the focus in what follows will not be on epistemicism, which I have discussed sufficiently elsewhere, but on the unattractive features of the alternative that Travis is offering, insofar as one can work out what it is.

3. A first observation is that, although Travis's examples look like cases in which the reference of a key expression depends on context, he insists on reporting homophonically what speakers have said using that expression. For instance, suppose that in my context the word 'round' is so understood that it is correct to apply it to a normal rubber ball even when its shape is momentarily distorted

---

[2] Treat quotation marks as corner quotes.
[3] The inference from failure of the disjuncts to failure of the disjunction may not appeal to supervaluationists, but it is valid by my classical lights.

on impact with a wall, while in Mary's context 'round' is so understood that it is incorrect to apply it to the ball in those circumstances. Travis plausibly asserts that Mary and I may nevertheless both be using the word with its usual linguistic meaning in English. 'It is round', used of the ball, is true as uttered in my context and false as uttered in Mary's context. On the usual contextualist account of such a case, the word 'round' varies its reference across contexts; in my context it refers to a property that the ball has, in Mary's context it refers to a different property that the ball lacks. The properties themselves are non-linguistic, and the ball has or lacks them independently of the context of utterance (although not independently of what time it is and which possible world obtains).[4] Thus I can truly say 'It is round' while Mary truly says 'It is not round', speaking of the same ball at the same time, without ambiguity in the word 'round'.

Travis has a different account. On his view, Mary and I both speak truly, but the word 'round' refers context-independently to the single property of being round. I truly say that the ball has that property, while at the same time Mary truly says that the same ball lacks the same property. How is that possible? Travis's explanation is that different 'understandings' are operative in the two contexts of what it is to have that property. This leads to surprising results. For instance, I say:

(1) This ball is round and Mary says truly that it is not round.

By ordinary standards, (1) is pretty much a contradiction. But on Travis's account I spoke truly in uttering (1), for the first conjunct is true on the relevant understanding of 'round' (mine), while the second conjunct is true because the variation in the understanding of what is said does not make for variation in what is said. For analogous reasons, Travis must reject both directions of the biconditionals in both (T) and (F) in many cases even when the condition '**Say(s, c, P)**' holds. These purported failures of standard principles about truth and falsity need not even involve borderline cases, since the different assignments of truth-value may each be clearly correct with respect to the relevant context.

In effect, Travis treats constancy of linguistic meaning as sufficient for homophonic reporting across contexts, at least in the examples under discussion. But such a policy is well known to yield incorrect results in paradigm cases of indexicality. For example, Mary and I use the word 'mine' with the same linguistic meaning, its normal one in English, on which (to a first approximation) 'mine' as uttered in a context applies to all and only the things that belong to the speaker of that context.[5] Looking at my watch, Mary says truly 'It is not mine'. But I cannot truly say:

(2) This watch is mine and Mary says truly that it is not mine.

---

[4] The parenthetical time and world parameters concern the circumstance of evaluation rather than the context of utterance, in the terminology of Kaplan (1989).

[5] Strictly speaking, since 'mine' is a possessive, there is also contextual variation in the relevant possession relation. This only reinforces the point in the text.

For when Mary says 'It is not mine', she does not say that it is not *mine*; she says that it is not *hers*. The word 'mine' does not express the property of being mine whenever it is uttered with its normal English meaning. It is quite unclear why Travis assumes that the word 'round' expresses the property of being round whenever it is used with its normal English meaning. Obvious contextual variation in reference yields obvious failures of homophonic reporting in indirect speech; why should the contextual variation to which Travis points not be conceived as unobvious contextual variation in reference that yields unobvious failures of homophonic reporting in indirect speech? The bizarre failures of standard principles about truth and falsity to which Travis is committed even in non-borderline cases constitute a strong reason for preferring a more orthodox contextualist account to his, since the orthodox account is perfectly consistent with (T) and (F).

What is missing in Travis's discussion at this point is any recognition of the relevance of something like David Kaplan's distinction between character and content (1989). Roughly speaking, the content of an expression in a given context is its contribution to what is said by sentences containing it in that context; the character of the expression is the function that takes each context to the content of the expression in that context. To a first approximation, sameness of linguistic meaning is sameness of character, not sameness of content, whereas homophonic reporting in indirect speech requires sameness of content, not sameness of character. Travis tends to write as though variation across contexts in the content of an expression automatically undermines the project of truth-conditional semantics, because the linguistic meaning of the expression fails to determine its contribution to truth-conditions. But that is quite premature, as Kaplan's semantics for indexicals makes clear. The linguistic meaning of the expression determines its character, which determines its contribution to what is said and therefore to truth-conditions with respect to each given context.

A sign of Travis's confusion is his claim that, if the word 'round' does not always (that is, in all contexts) refer to a given property, then it (the word type) does not refer to that property, 'full stop'. For the word type 'round' can still have the relational characteristic of referring to that property in (with respect to) a given context of utterance, and such relational characteristics may constitute its linguistic meaning (its character).

Travis also claims that my classical view that everything either has or lacks a given property is 'inconsistent' with my view that we sometimes use an expression to refer to a property such as being round. There is, of course, no inconsistency. The epistemicist theory in *Vagueness* reconciles the two views; referring to a property is a far less transparent matter than is usually assumed.

Travis appears to have been misled by another paper of mine (1998), in which I argued that the semantic and set-theoretic paradoxes may trigger slight unnoticed shifts of linguistic meaning (character), rather than slight unnoticed shifts of context and content with an unchanging non-constant character. In the footnote from which he quotes, I point out that earlier work of his neglects this possibility of slight unnoticed shifts of linguistic meaning. Naturally, to make that point is in no way to repudiate the distinction between character and content. The latter distinction is needed for a proper treatment of indexicals like 'mine'. Specific reasons are needed for attributing a change in the truth-value of what by ordinary standards is the same sentence to a shift in linguistic meaning rather than a shift in context and content with an unchanging non-constant character (of course, both options undermine Travis's reliance on homophonic reporting in indirect speech). In 'Aristotle's Condition', Travis takes the sentences in his examples not to be shifting their linguistic meaning. I happily accept that assumption, and therefore attribute the change in truth-value to a shift in context and content with an unchanging non-constant character.[6] The supposed tension between two movements in my thinking is an artefact of Travis's misreading.

One might suppose Travis's mistaken reliance on homophonic reporting in indirect speech to be marginal to his argument. For, even if, in his examples, what is said in the cases of clear truth differs from what is said in the cases of clear falsity, and neither need be the same as what is said in the borderline cases, why cannot Travis simply concentrate on the borderline cases alone, and argue that bivalence fails in them? Unfortunately for this line, the concession that what is said by an unambiguous sentence can vary across contexts undermines Travis's assumption that something is said in the borderline cases, for it cannot rest on the mere fact that the sentence is being used with its normal linguistic meaning. If one rejects the standard epistemicist treatment of borderline cases, one must take very seriously the alternative that in the relevant sense nothing is said. But, if nothing is said in borderline cases, they are not counter-examples to bivalence, as formalized in (B), which then holds vacuously.

4.   Travis claims that on his rejection of bivalence 'classical logic remains intact so far as its theorems, and rules for drawing inferences are concerned'. What he has modified is only our conception of 'how logic applies to thoughts'. These comments grossly underestimate the consequences of his unorthodoxy.

On Travis's view, classical reasoning involves the tacit assumption that the relevant sentences satisfy what he calls 'Aristotle's condition', that either things are as they say them to be or things are not as they say them to be. He proposes to make this explicit by requiring that 'a rule of inference can be applied to an assumption only under the further assumptions that that assumption's atomic constituents each satisfy Aristotle's condition'. Travis writes Aristotle's condition

---

[6] Another alternative to Travis's treatment would be an error theory, on which the apparent change in truth-value is an illusion.

for a formula **P** as **A(P)**. For example, instead of the rule of *modus ponens* in the form **P**, **P** ⊃ **Q** ⊢ **Q** (where **P** and **Q** are atomic) we have only

A(P), **A(Q)**, **P**, **P** ⊃ **Q** ⊢ **Q**

Instead of (LEM) we have only

A(P) ⊢ **P** ∨ ¬**P**

Travis must intend that, when an assumption is discharged in a natural deduction rule such as *reductio ad absurdum*, conditional proof or argument by cases, the corresponding assumptions of the form **A(P)** are not discharged, otherwise they would be discharged in a natural deduction proof of (LEM), contrary to his intentions.

As it stands, Travis's proposal does not work for axiomatic formulations of classical logic, since they allow proofs of (LEM) in which no assumptions are used at any point. A more general restriction in a similar spirit would be that any line in a proof depends on the assumption **A(P)** for each atomic formula **P** that has occurred in the proof up to and including that line.

Travis's claim that his proposal preserves the theorems and rules of inference of classical logic is false. Since every formula contains at least one atomic formula, a Travis system has no theorems whatsoever: every conclusion depends on at least one assumption of the form **A(P)**.[7] Similarly, it has no derivable sequents at all of the form Γ ⊢ C in which Γ is a set of formulas of a standard propositional language and C is a formula, since the standard propositional language does not contain formulas of the form **A(P)**. In this sense, virtually all of classical logic has been ditched. We can keep the extra premises in the background when their truth is taken for granted, but it is sophistry to talk as though they were not there.

Another non-standard feature of a Travis system is that it does not satisfy the principle of uniform substitution. For example,

A(P) ⊢ **P** ∨ ¬**P**

is derivable but its substitution instance

A(Q & R) ⊢ (**Q & R**) ∨ ¬(**Q & R**)

is not; we have only

A(Q), **A(R)** ⊢ (**Q & R**) ∨ ¬(**Q & R**)

(where **P**, **Q** and **R** are all atomic).

The extent of Travis's logical deviance becomes clearer once we consider more expressive languages. For example, in first-order logic we have quantified versions

---

[7] One could make some minor exceptions, for instance for languages with a falsity constant (⊥).

of the law of excluded middle, such as ⊢ ∀ x (Fx ∨ ¬Fx). On Travis's view, this must be replaced by something like

∀ x A(Fx) ⊢ ∀ x (Fx ∨ ¬Fx)

just as

⊢ (Fa ∨ ¬Fa) & (Fb ∨ ¬Fb) & (Fc ∨ ¬Fc)

(where **F** is an atomic monadic predicate) must be replaced by

A(Fa), A(Fb), A(Fc) ⊢ (Fa ∨ ¬Fa) & (Fb ∨ ¬Fb) & (Fc ∨ ¬Fc)

In other words, we must assume that every member of the domain satisfies Aristotle's condition: ∀ x A(Fx). But for most ordinary atomic predicates **F** in most ordinary contexts, Travis's view makes that an implausibly strong, indeed almost certainly false, assumption. For most such predicates, borderline cases are not only possible but actual in domains of ordinary size. For example, Aristotle's condition fails with respect to 'round' over a domain that includes balls on impact with walls. Thus the background assumptions that we must make in order to simulate classical first-order logic in the way Travis describes are, on his view, usually false. That is no small revision of classical logic.

A related problem arises for propositional modal logic. In any normal modal logic we have ⊢ □(P ∨ ¬P), by applying the rule of necessitation to (LEM). The only atomic formula here is P, so Travis's restriction appears to yield

A(P) ⊢ □(P ∨ ¬P)

But that sequent does not fit the rationale for Travis's restriction. Let **P** be 'It is round', said of a lump of clay in circumstances in which it is definitely false (the speaker had his back turned and did not realize that the lump had just been flattened). Thus **P** straightforwardly satisfies Aristotle's condition. But of course the lump *could have been* a borderline case for 'round', in counterfactual circumstances in which, according to Travis, it would not have satisfied Aristotle's condition. With respect to those circumstances, Travis will presumably not want to assert that the ball would have been either round or not round. Thus he is committed to accepting A(P) and rejecting □(P ∨ ¬P). The natural move is to replace A(P) ⊢ □(P ∨ ¬P) by

□ A(P) ⊢ □(P ∨ ¬P)

(compare ∀ x A(Fx) ⊢ ∀ x (Fx ∨ ¬Fx)). But on his view assumptions of the form □A(P) will usually be false, as in this example. Things that are not borderline usually could have been borderline. Thus the background assumptions that we must make in order to simulate classical modal logic in the spirit of his proposal are, on his view, usually false too.

Travis gives no account at all of what reasoning we should use when we recognize, as we often should on his view, that the relevant versions of Aristotle's condition are not satisfied. His chapter evades recognizing the drastic repercussions for logic of implementing his proposal seriously. Consequently, even if the chapter is read as a merely defensive attempt to explain a workable alternative to bivalence, the attempt fails.

References

Adler, J. (1996). 'Transmitting Knowledge', *Noûs*, 30: 99–111.

Albert, D. Z. (2000). *Time and Chance*. Cambridge, MA: Harvard University Press.

Andjelković, M., and Williamson, T. (2000). 'Truth, Falsity, and Borderline Cases', *Philosophical Topics*, 28: 211–44.

Austin, J. L. (1979). 'Other Minds', in his *Philosophical Papers*. Oxford: Oxford University Press, 76–117.

Ayer, A. J. (1956). *The Problem of Knowledge*. New York: St Martin's Press.

Bach, K., and Harnish, M. (1979). *Linguistic Communication and Speech Acts*. Cambridge, MA: MIT Press.

Barnett, V. (1999). *Comparative Statistical Inference*. 3rd edn. Chichester: John Wiley and Sons. First edition published in 1973.

Brewer, W. (1999). *Perception and Reason*. New York: Oxford University Press.

Brueckner, A. (2005). 'Knowledge, Evidence, and Skepticism According to Williamson', *Philosophy and Phenomenological Research*, 70: 436–43.

Brueckner, A., and Fiocco, O. (2002). 'Williamson's Anti-Luminosity Argument', *Philosophical Studies*, 110: 285–93.

Burge, T. (1979). 'Individualism and the Mental', *Midwest Studies in Philosophy*, 4: 73–121.

—— (1986). 'Individualism and Psychology', *Philosophical Review*, 95: 3–45.

—— (2003a). 'Perceptual Entitlement', *Philosophy and Phenomenological Research*, 67: 503–48.

—— (2003b). 'Concepts, Conceptions, Reflective Understanding: Reply to Peacocke', in M. Hahn and B. Ramberg (eds.), *Essays on the Philosophy of Tyler Burge*. Cambridge, MA: MIT Press.

Cassam, Q. (2007). *The Possibility of Knowledge*. Oxford: Clarendon Press.

Chisholm, R. (1957). *Perceiving*. Ithaca, NY: Cornell University Press.

—— (1977). *Theory of Knowledge*. 2nd edn. Englewood Cliffs, NJ: Prentice-Hall.

Christensen, D. (1996). 'Dutch Book Arguments Depragmatized: Epistemic Consistency for Partial Believers', *Journal of Philosophy*, 93: 450–79.

—— (2001). 'Preference-Based Arguments for Probabilism', *Philosophy of Science*, 68: 356–76.

—— (2004). *Putting Logic in its Place: Formal Constraints on Rational Belief*. Oxford: Oxford University Press.

Cohen, L. J. (1977). *The Probable and the Provable*. Oxford: Clarendon Press.

Conee, E. (2001). 'Preference-Based Arguments for Probabilism', *Philosophy of Science*, 68: 356–76.

—— (2005). 'The Comforts of Home', *Philosophy and Phenomenological Research*, 70: 444–51.

Davidson, D. (1967). 'Truth and Meaning', *Synthese*, 17: 304–23.

—— (1980). 'Intending', repr. in his *Actions and Events*. Oxford: Clarendon Press, 83–102.

Davidson, D. (1983). 'A Coherence Theory of Truth and Knowledge', in D. Henrich, (ed.), *Kant oder Hegel?* Stuttgart: Klett-Cotta.

——(1986). 'Knowing One's Own Mind', *Proceedings of the American Philosophical Society*, 60: 441–58.

——(1993). 'Thinking Causes', in John Heil and Alfred Mele (eds.), *Mental Causation*. Oxford: Clarendon Press, 3–17.

Dretske, F. (1969). *Seeing and Knowing*. Chicago: University of Chicago Press.

——(1970). 'Epistemic Operators', *Journal of Philosophy*, 67: 1007–23.

——(1971). 'Conclusive Reasons', *Australasian Journal of Philosophy*, 49: 1–22.

——(1981). *Knowledge and the Flow of Information*. Cambridge, MA: MIT Press.

Dummett, M. (1978). *Truth and Other Enigmas*. London: Duckworth.

Feldman, R. (2003). *Epistemology*. Upper Saddle River, NJ: Prentice Hall.

Finetti, B. de (1937). 'La Prevision: Ses lois logiques, ses sources subjectives', *Annales de l'Institut Henri Poincaré*, 7: 1–68.

——(1974). *Theory of Probability*, vol. i. London: John Wiley and Sons.

Fodor, J. A. (1981). 'Methodological Solipsism Considered as a Research Strategy in Cognitive Psychology', in his *RePresentations*. Brighton: Harvester Press, 225–53.

——(1998a). 'Review of Peacocke's *A Study of Concepts*', in his *In Critical Condition*. Cambridge, MA: MIT Press.

——(1998b). *Concepts: Where Cognitive Science Went Wrong*. Oxford: Clarendon Press.

Frege, G. (1903). *Grundgesetze der Arithmetik*. vol. ii. Jena: Verlag Hermann Pohle.

——(1918/1977) 'Der Gedanke. Eine logische Untersuching', *Beiträge zur Philosophie des deutschen Idealismus*, 1: 58–77; trans. as 'Thoughts', in P. T. Geach (ed.), *Logical Investigations*. Oxford: Blackwell, 1–30.

Fricker, E. (1987), 'The Epistemology of Testimony', *Proceedings of the Aristotelian Society*, supp. vol., 61: 57–106.

——(1994). 'Against Gullibility', in B. K. Matilal and A. Chakrabarti (eds.), *Knowing from Words*. Amsterdam: Kluwer, 125–61.

——(1998). 'Self-Knowledge: Special Access Versus Artefact of Grammar—A Dichotomy Rejected', in C. Wright, B. Smith, and C. MacDonald (eds.), *Knowing our own Minds*. Oxford: Clarendon Press, 155–206.

Gettier, E. (1963). 'Is Justified True Belief Knowledge?' *Analysis*, 23: 121–3.

Gilbert, D. T. (1991). 'How Mental Systems Believe', *American Psychologist*, 46: 107–19.

——(1992). 'Assent of Man: Mental Representation and the Control of Belief', in D. M. Wegner and J. Pennebaker (eds.), *The Handbook of Mental Control*. New York: Prentice-Hall.

Gilbert, D. T., Krull, D. S., and Malone, P. S. (1990). 'Understanding the Unbelievable: Some Problems in the Rejection of False Information', *Journal of Personality and Social Psychology*, 59: 601–13.

Gilbert, D. T., Tafarodi, R. W., and Malone, P. S. (1993). 'You Can't Not Believe Everything You Read', *Journal of Personality and Social Psychology*, 65: 221–33.

Ginet, Carl (1980). 'Knowing Less by Knowing More', in P. French, T. Uehling, and H. Wettstein (eds.), *Midwest Studies in Philosophy*, v. *Studies in Epistemology*. Minneapolis, MN: University of Minnesota Press.

Goldberg, S. (2007). 'How Lucky Can You Get?', *Synthese*, 158: 315–27.

Goldberg, S., and Henderson, D. (2006). 'Monitoring and Anti-Reductionism in the Epistemology of Testimony', *Philosophy and Phenomenological Research*, 72: 600–17.

Goldman, A. (1967). 'A Causal Theory of Knowing', *Journal of Philosophy*, 64: 355–72.

—— (1976). 'Discrimination and Perceptual Knowledge', *Journal of Philosophy*, 73: 771–91.

—— (1979). 'What Is Justified Belief?', in G. Pappas (ed.), *Justification and Knowledge*. Dordrecht: Kluwer.

—— (1986). *Epistemology and Cognition*. Cambridge, MA: Harvard University Press.

—— (1992a). 'A Causal Theory of Knowing', in his *Liaisons: Philosophy Meets the Cognitive and Social Sciences*. Cambridge, MA: MIT Press.

—— (1992b). *Liaisons: Philosophy Meets the Cognitive and Social Sciences*. Cambridge, MA: MIT Press.

—— (1999). 'Internalism Exposed', *Journal of Philosophy*, 96: 271–93.

—— (2001). 'Replies to Contributors', *Philosophical Topics*, 29: 461–511.

—— (2008). 'Immediate Justification and Process Reliabilism', in Q. Smith (ed.), *Epistemology: New Essays*. New York: Oxford University Press, 63–82.

Grice, H. P. (1989). 'Postwar Oxford Philosophy', in his *Studies in the Ways of Words*. Cambridge, MA: Harvard University Press, 171–80

Hacking, I. (1965). *Logic of Statistical Inference*. Cambridge: Cambridge University Press.

Harman, G. (1968). 'Knowledge, Inference, and Explanation', *American Philosophical Quarterly*, 5: 164–73.

—— (1970). 'Knowledge, Reasons, and Causes', *Journal of Philosophy*, 67: 841–55.

—— (1973). *Thought*. Princeton: Princeton University Press.

Hawthorne, J. (2004). *Knowledge and Lotteries*. Oxford: Oxford University Press.

—— (2005a). 'Knowledge and Evidence', *Philosophy and Phenomenological Research*, 70: 452–8.

—— (2005b). 'Chance and Counterfactuals', *Philosophy and Phenomenological Research*, 70: 396–405.

Hinton, J. M. (1973). *Experiences*. Oxford: Oxford University Press.

Huemer, M. (2001). *Skepticism and the Veil of Perception*. New York: Rowman and Littlefield.

Jackson, F. (1995), 'Mental Properties, Essentialism and Causation', *Proceedings of the Aristotelian Society*, 95: 253–68.

—— (2005). 'Is Belief an Internal State?', *Philosophical Studies*, 132/3: 571–80.

Jeffrey, R. C. (1983). *The Logic of Decision*, 2nd edn. Chicago: University of Chicago Press. First edition published in 1965.

Joyce, J. (1998). 'A Nonpragmatic Vindication of Probabilism', *Philosophy of Science*, 65: 337–42.

Kant, I. (1932). *Critique of Pure Reason*, trans. N. Kemp Smith. London: Macmillan.

Kaplan, D. (1989). 'Demonstratives: An Essay on the Semantics, Logic, Metaphysics, and Epistemology of Demonstratives and Other Indexicals', in J. Almog, J. Perry, and H. Wettstein (eds.), *Themes from Kaplan*. New York: Oxford University Press, 481–563.

Kaplan, M. (1981a). 'A Bayesian Theory of Rational Acceptance,' *Journal of Philosophy*, 78: 305–30.

—— (1981b). 'Rational Acceptance', *Philosophical Studies*, 40: 129–45.

Kaplan, M. (1996). *Decision Theory as Philosophy*. Cambridge: Cambridge University Press.

—— (2002). 'Decision Theory and Epistemology', in P. Moser (ed.), *The Oxford Handbook of Epistemology*. Oxford: Oxford University Press, 434–62.

—— (2003). 'Who Cares What You Know? Critical Study of Timothy Williamson's *Knowledge and its Limits*', *Philosophical Quarterly*, 53: 105–16.

—— (2006). 'Deciding What You Know,' in E. J. Olsson (ed.), *Knowledge and Inquiry: Essays on the Pragmatism of Isaac Levi*. Cambridge: Cambridge University Press, 225–40.

Klein, P. (1971). 'A Proposed Definition of Propositional Knowledge', *Journal of Philosophy*, 68: 471–82.

Kornblith, H. (2002). *Knowledge and its Place in Nature*. Oxford: Oxford University Press.

Kvanvig, J. (2003). *The Value of Knowledge and the Pursuit of Understanding*. New York: Cambridge University Press.

Lackey, J. (2007). 'Learning from Words', *Philosophy and Phenomenological Research*, 73: 77–101.

Lasonen-Aarnio, M. (2007). 'Review of Duncan Pritchard's *Epistemic Luck*', *European Journal of Analytic Philosophy*, 3/1: 67–79.

—— (forthcoming). 'Single Premise Deduction and Risk', *Philosophical Studies*.

Lehrer, K., and Paxson, T. (1969). 'Knowledge: Undefeated Justified True Belief', *Journal of Philosophy*, 66: 225–37.

Lewis, D. (1973). *Counterfactuals*. Oxford: Blackwell.

—— (1980). 'A Subjectivist's Guide to Objective Chance', in R. Jeffrey (ed.), *Studies in Inductive Logic and Probability*, vol. ii. Berkeley and Los Angeles: University of California Press.

—— (1983). 'Attitudes *De Dicto* and *De Se*' (and postscript), in his *Philosophical Papers*. Oxford: Oxford University Press, i. 133–56.

—— (1986a). 'A Subjectivist's Guide to Objective Chance', in his *Philosophical Papers*. Oxford: Oxford University Press, ii. 83–113.

—— (1986b). 'Causal Explanation', in his *Philosophical Papers*. Oxford: Oxford University Press, ii. 214–40.

—— (1986c). *Philosophical Papers*, vol. ii. Oxford: Oxford University Press.

—— (1994). 'Humean Supervenience Debugged', *Mind*, 103: 473–90.

—— (1995). 'Reduction of Mind', in *A Companion to the Philosophy of Mind*. Oxford: Basil Blackwell, pp. 412–31.

—— (1996). 'Elusive Knowledge', *Australasian Journal of Philosophy*, 74: 549–67.

—— (1999). *Papers in Metaphysics and Epistemology*. Cambridge: Cambridge University Press.

McDowell, J. H. (1982). 'Criteria, Defeasibility and Knowledge,' *Proceedings of the British Academy*, 68: 455–79.

—— (1986/1998). 'Singular Thought and the Extent of Inner Space', in P. Petit and J. H. McDowell (eds.), *Subject, Thought, and Context*. Oxford: Clarendon Press, 137–68 in his *Meaning, Knowledge and Reality*. Cambridge, MA: Harvard University Press (Reprinted, 1998).

Maher, P. (1993). *Betting on Theories*. Cambridge: Cambridge University Press.

—— (1997). 'Depragmatized Dutch Book Arguments', *Philosophy of Science*, 64: 291–305.

—— (2002). 'Joyce's Argument for Probabilism', *Philosophy of Science*, 69: 73–81.

Martin, C. B., and Deutscher, M. (1966). 'Remembering', *Philosophical Review*, 75: 161–96.

Martin, M. (2004). 'The Limits of Self-Awareness', *Philosophical Studies*, 120: 37–89.

Moore, G. E. (1953). *Some Main Problems of Philosophy*. London: Allen and Unwin.

Neta, R. (2004). 'Skepticism, Abductivism, and the Explanatory Gap', *Philosophical Issues*, 10: 296–325.

—— (2008). 'What Evidence Do You Have?', *British Journal for Philosophy of Science*, 59: 89–119.

Neta, R., and Pritchard, D. H. (2007). 'McDowell and the New Evil Genius', *Philosophy and Phenomenological Research*, 74: 381–96.

Neta, R., and Rohrbaugh, G. (2004). 'Luminosity and the Safety of Knowledge', *Pacific Philosophical Quarterly*, 85: 396–406.

Nozick, R. (1981). *Philosophical Explanations*. Cambridge, MA: Harvard University Press.

Peacocke, C. A. B. (1992). *A Study of Concepts*. Cambridge, MA: MIT Press.

—— (1993). 'Externalism and Explanation', *Proceedings of the Aristotelian Society*, 92: 203–30.

—— (1999). *Being Known*. Oxford: Clarendon Press.

—— (2004). *The Realm of Reason*. Oxford: Oxford University Press.

Pettit. P., and McDowell J. H. (1986) (eds.). *Subject, Thought, and Context*. Oxford: Clarendon Press.

Pollock, J. (1986). *Contemporary Theories of Knowledge*. Totowa, NJ: Rowman and Littlefield.

Pritchard, D. (2005). *Epistemic Luck*. Oxford: Oxford University Press.

Pryor, J. (2000). 'The Skeptic and the Dogmatist', *Noûs*, 34: 517–49.

Putnam, H. (1975). 'The Meaning of "Meaning"', in his *Mind, Language and Reality*. Cambridge: Cambridge University Press, 215–71.

Raffman, D. (1995). 'On the Persistence of Phenomenology', in T. Metzinger (ed.), *Conscious Experience*. Paderborn: Schöningh, 293–308.

Raiffa, H. (1968). *Decision Analysis: Introductory Lectures on Choice under Uncertainty*. Reading, MA: Addison-Wesley.

Ramachandran, M. (2005). 'Anti-Luminosity', MS. Available at <http://www.sussex. ac.uk/Users/muralir/pubs/>.

Ramsey, F. P. (1990). 'Truth and Probability', in D. H. Mellor (ed.), *Philosophical Papers*. Cambridge: Cambridge University Press, 52–109. Written in 1926 and first published (in a form slightly different from the 1990 version) in 1931.

Rieber, S. (1999). 'Knowledge and Contrastive Explanation', *Noûs*, 32: 189–204.

Roush, S. (2005). *Tracking Truth*. Oxford: Oxford University Press.

Sainsbury, R. M. (1997). 'Easy Possibilities', *Philosophy and Phenomenological Research*, 57: 907–19.

—— (2002). *Departing from Frege*. London: Routledge.

Savage, L. J. (1972). *The Foundations of Statistics*, 2nd edn. New York: Dover. First edition published in 1954.

Sellars, W. (1956). 'Empiricism and the Philosophy of Mind', in H. Feigl and M. Scriven (eds.), *Minnesota Studies in the Philosophy of Science*, Vol. 1: *The Foundations of Science and the Concepts of Psychology and Psychoanalysis*. Minneapolis, MN: University of Minnesota Press, 253–329.

Shafer, G. (1976). *A Mathematical Theory of Evidence*. Princeton: Princeton University Press.

Shope, R. (1983). *The Analysis of Knowing: A Decade of Research*. Princeton: Princeton University Press.

Siewert, C. (1998). *The Significance of Consciousness*. Princeton: Princeton University Press.

Silins, N. (2005). 'Deception and Evidence', *Philosophical Perspectives*, 19: 375–404.

Skyrms, F. B. (1967). 'The Explication of "*X* Knows that *p*" ', *Journal of Philosophy*, 64: 373–89.

Snowdon, P. (1980). 'Perception, Vision and Causation', *Proceedings of the Aristotelian Society*, 80: 175–92.

Sosa, E. (1997). 'Reflective Knowledge in the Best Circles', *Journal of Philosophy*, 94: 410–30.

—— (1999a). 'How to Defeat Opposition to Moore', in J. Tomberlin (ed.), *Philosophical Perspectives*, 13: 141–53.

—— (1999b). 'How Must Knowledge Be Modally Related to What Is Known?', *Philosophical Topics*, 26: 373–84.

—— (2001). 'Goldman's Reliabilism and Virtue Epistemology', *Philosophical Topics*, 29: 383–401.

—— (2004). 'Relevant Alternatives, Contextualism Included', *Philosophical Studies*, 119: 35–65.

—— (2007). *A Virtue Epistemology: Apt Belief and Reflective Knowledge*. Oxford: Oxford University Press.

Stalnaker, R. (1968). 'A Theory of Conditionals', in N. Rescher (ed.), *Studies in Logical Theory*. Oxford: Blackwell, 98–112.

Stalanker, R. C. (1999). 'On What's in the Head', in his *Context and Content*. New York: Oxford University Press, 169–93.

Stanley, J. (2008). 'Knowledge and Certainty', *Philosophical Issues*, 18: 33–55.

Steup, M. (1992). 'Memory', in J. Dancy and E. Sosa (eds.), *A Companion to Epistemology*. Oxford: Blackwell.

—— (2004). 'Internalist Reliabilism', *Philosophical Issues*, 14: 401–25.

Steward, H. (1997). *The Ontology of Mind: Events, Processes and States*. Oxford: Clarendon Press.

Strawson, G. (1986). *Freedom and Belief*. Oxford: Oxford University Press.

—— (1994). *Mental Reality*. Cambridge, MA: MIT Press.

Strawson, P. F. (1992). *Analysis and Metaphysics: An Introduction to Philosophy*. Oxford: Oxford University Press.

Stroud, B. (2000). 'Scepticism and the Possibility of Knowledge', in his *Understanding Human Knowledge*. Oxford: Oxford University Press, 1–8.

Sutton, J. (2007). 'Earn their Trust', MS. Available at <http://faculty.smu.edu/jsutton/earnit.pdf>.

Tarski, A. (1956). 'The Concept of Truth in Formalized Lnaguages', in J. H. Woodger (ed.), *Logic, Semantics, Metamathematics*. Oxford: Clarendon Press, 152–278.

Thau, M. (2002). *Consciousness and Cognition*. Oxford: Oxford University Press.

Unger, P. (1975). *Ignorance*. Oxford: Clarendon Press.

Vogel, J. (1990). 'Cartesian Scepticism and Inference to the Best Explanation', *Journal of Philosophy*, 87: 658–64.

Weinberg, H., Stich, S., and Nichols, S. (2001). 'Normativity and Epistemic Intuitions', *Philosophical Topics*, 29: 429–60.

Whitcomb, D. (2005). 'Factivity without Safety', MS. Rutgers University Department of Philosophy.

White, R. (2006). 'Problems for Dogmatism', *Philosophical Studies*, 131/3 (Dec.): 525–57.

Williamson, T. (1994). *Vagueness*. London: Routledge.

—— (1995). 'Is Knowing a State of Mind?', *Mind*, 104: 533–65.

—— (1996). 'Knowing and Asserting', *Philosophical Review*, 105: 489–523.

—— (1998). 'Indefinite Extensibility', *Grazer Philosophische Studien*, 55: 1–24.

—— (2000). *Knowledge and its Limits*. Oxford: Oxford University Press.

—— (2005a). 'Knowledge and Scepticism', in F. Jackson and M. Smith (eds.), *The Oxford Handbook of Contemporary Philosophy*. Oxford: Oxford University Press.

—— (2005b). 'Précis of *Knowledge and its Limits*', *Philosophy and Phenomenological Research*, 70: 431–35.

—— (2005c). 'Contextualism, Subject-Sensitive Invariantism and Knowledge of Knowledge', *Philosophical Quarterly*, 55: 213–35.

—— (2005d). 'Replies to Commentators', *Philosophy and Phenomenological Research*, 70: 468–91.

—— (2005e). 'Reply to Hawthorne', *Philosophy and Phenomenological Research*, 70: 476–87.

—— (2007a). *The Philosophy of Philosophy*. Oxford: Blackwell.

—— (2007b). 'On Being Justified in One's Head', in M. Timmons, J. Greco, and A. Mele (eds.), *Rationality and the Good: Critical Essays on the Ethics and Epistemology of Robert Audi*. Oxford: Oxford University Press, 106–23.

—— (2007c). 'How Probable Is an Infinite Sequence of Heads?', *Analysis*, 67: 173–80.

—— (2008). 'Why Epistemology Can't Be Operationalized', in Q. Smith (ed.), *Epistemology: New Philosophical Essays*. Oxford: Oxford University Press, 277–300.

—— (forthcoming). 'Improbable Knowing', in T. Dougherty (ed.), *Evidentialism and its Discontents*.

Wittgenstein, L. (1958). *Philosophical Investigations*, 2nd edn, trans. G. E. M. Anscombe. Oxford: Blackwell.

—— (1969). *On Certainty*, ed. G. E. M. Anscombe and G. H. von Wright, trans. D. Paul and G. E. M. Anscombe. Oxford: Blackwell.

Woodfield, A. (1982) (ed.). *Thought and Object*. Oxford: Clarendon Press.

Wright, C. (2004). 'Warrant for Nothing (And Foundations for Free)?' *Supplement to the Proceedings of the Aristotelian Society*, 78 (2004): 167–75.

Index